KILLING HITLER'S REICH

The Battle for Austria 1945

William Alan Webb

Helion & Company

Helion & Company Limited
Unit 8 Amherst Business Centre
Budbrooke Road
Warwick
CV34 5WE
England
Tel. 01926 499 619
Email: info@helion.co.uk
Website: www.helion.co.uk
Twitter: @helionbooks
Visit our blog http://blog.helion.co.uk/

Published by Helion & Company 2019
Designed and typeset by Mach 3 Solutions (www.mach3solutions.co.uk)
Cover designed by Paul Hewitt, Battlefield Design (www.battlefield-design.co.uk)
Printed by Gutenberg Press Limited, Tarxien, Malta

Text © William Alan Webb 2019
Maps drawn by George Anderson © Helion & Company 2019

ISBN 978-1-911628-84-2

British Library Cataloguing-in-Publication Data.
A catalogue record for this book is available from the British Library.

For details of other military history titles published by Helion & Company Limited contact
the above address, or visit our website: http://www.helion.co.uk.

We always welcome receiving book proposals from prospective authors.

To Kathy, without whose love and support none of this would have been possible.

Contents

List of Maps

A	Army
Armd.	Armoured
Ausb.	Training
Baon.	Battalion
C.	Corps
Cav.	Cavalry
Div.	Division
Ers.	Replacement
Gesch.	Wing
Gd.	Guard
Geb.	Mountain
Gren.	Grenadier
Hun.	Hungarian
H.Gr.	Army Group
Inf.	Infantry
Jg.	Jäger
K.	Korps
Kav.	Cavalry
Kdo.	Command
K.Gr.	Kampfgruppe
Kpf.	Kampf
Mech.	Mechanised
Mtn.	Mountain
Pz.	Tank
R.	Rifle
Rgt.	Regiment
Stv.	Acting/Deputy
T.	Tank
Vbd.	Unit/Formation/Group
W.	Waffen
z.B.V.	For Special-Purposes

Map Key

Introduction

In 2006 my family and I visited Austria. It was a whirlwind trip that didn't allow for extensive exploration, so I wanted to fill in the holes in our itinerary by reading a good account of the combat in Austria during the Second World War, my favorite era of history and the one I've devoted my life to writing about and studying. Much to my surprise I couldn't find such a work.

Plenty of books mentioned the battle for Vienna in passing. A few devoted a chapter to it, but only one specialized work covered it in detail, Georg Maier's splendid *Drama Between Budapest and Vienna, The Final Battle of the 6. Panzer-Armee in the East, 1945*. And while Maier's work gives the best account we have in English of this combat, it remains flawed in several ways. For my purposes, not the least drawback is that it only covers one of *Heeresgruppe Süd*'s four armies.

Books in German did exist but had not been translated into English, the most definitive being Manfred Rauchesteiner's *Krieg in Österreich*. Friedrich Brettner wrote extensively on this topic, also in German, but again the strategic narrative was incomplete. Once I realized there was a major gap in the historiography of the war, I decided that since such a book didn't exist, I would write one. Little did I understand the vast scope of the project I'd undertaken.

Work on this book started in late 2006. Writing it took longer than the Third Reich existed. The idea for my book was to write a comprehensive history of *Heeresgruppe Süd* starting on 1 January, 1945. To that end, during the next eight years I wrote something over 100,000 words. In September 2014, completely without warning, everything changed when I sat down and wrote two novels back to back, *Standing The Final Watch* and *Standing In The Storm*. They were meant to be fun diversion, but both became major hits and I had a brand new career on my hands as a fiction writer. Even as I type these words I am getting messages on social media wanting to know when the next book will be out. It was only in spring of 2017 that I once again began work on this book.

However, rather than spend another decade bringing the concept for the original book to life, I decided to complete the last part of it first, the Battle for Austria. This was, after all, the part that didn't already have a good history written about it, and the reason I had been inspired to tackle this project in the first place. Time permitting, and if the market demands it, I'll get back to the rest of it later. There's some good stuff already there.

I knew from the start I didn't want my history to be just dry facts. This or that battalion moved here and attacked there, and then moved 22 miles to attack so and so at such and such village. There would have to be a lot of that, of course, because that's what writing military history entails, but I wanted the book to encompass more. What was the geography of the region, who were the people, what did they produce? When one day your home is within the Third Reich and the next day the Russians are your overlords, then your life has undergone a major change. I wanted the reader to feel part of this massive campaign, at least as much as such a thing is possible.

But this is a military history, not a social history, and I also knew that I wanted to weave the story of lesser known formations, such as *37. SS-Freiwilligen-Kavallerie-Division Lützow*, *SS-Kampfgruppe-Division Böhmen und Mähren* and *14. Waffen-Grenadier-Division-der-SS Galizien (Ukrainische Nr. 1)* into the narrative, using whatever information is available. The death struggle of *III Panzerkorps* in the mountains of East-Central Austria is virtually unknown in the west, particularly the incredible defensive work of *1. Volks-Gebirgs-Division*, or the remarkable coun-terattack of *117. Jäger-Division*. Some books written in German do exist with personal histories of many such units, but these are mostly unavailable from either primary or secondary avenues of acquisition, and costly. In other words, they're hard to find, expensive, and written in German.

There are too many obscure *Wehrmacht* units to count, and surely more whose existence have passed without notice into history. Sometimes only a name exists, with no information. Rather than cataloguing every short-lived formation I chose those who either had a significant impact on the fighting, or for which reliable information could be found. The reader should imagine many unnamed others who are represented by those I write about.

Scattered throughout this narrative are intense but localized battles for small towns and villages, and again these should be considered representative of all the other towns and villages whose story could not be told for lack of time and space. The experiences of a division like *118. Jäger-Division* may not be covered in detail, but those of its fellow divisions that are shared should be considered similar. But I do see this book as being something alive, something shared by the larger community of those who continue to be fascinated by the Second World War, and therefore something subject to expansion. By putting out the name of some unknown unit it might bring forward information known only to a few. Perhaps someone, somewhere, has a diary kept by a member of the formation, or anecdotes passed down through the family. In such a case I could use this evidence to expand the narrative for future editions or bonus online content.

The book centers mostly on the German defense, but I did want to cover the major Russian personalities and formations to give the reader a picture of the other side. Including a comprehensive look at the Red Army experience would stretch the book I envisioned past a reasonable length. Long-term plans include such a book from the Russian viewpoint.

War crimes that may, or may not, have been committed by the various Nazi agencies and organizations is beyond the scope of this book, except as it might enter the narrative concerning the defense of Austria. For example, in 2009 a former member of *5. SS-Panzer-Division Wiking* was accused of murdering 58 Jews in the Hungarian border town of Deustsche Schütze on 29 March 1945, after first forcing them to dig a defensive trench. The accused man died before trial, so whatever evidence had been collected was never presented in court. Had this incident fallen within the time frame of this book it would have been included in the main text, as it was allegedly a direct result of the fighting.

Likewise, the massacre of Jews at Rechnitz when the Russian Twenty-Sixth Army was closing in occurred as a consequence of the fighting, but not during the period of the book. Nor did it have direct impact on the military situation. It happened, and I'm aware of it, but it falls outside the parameters of this work.

Nor is the ongoing debate about possible war crimes of the *14. Waffen-Grenadier-Division der SS Galizien* covered. That topic could be the issue of an entire book by itself, and in trying to cover as much ground as I am with this work it would make the task I have set myself impossible to achieve, instead of merely difficult. I try to dismiss the notion of impossibility, but some things really are impossible. The same could be said for *2. SS-Panzer-Division Das Reich*, or *3. SS-Panzer-Division Totenkopf.* When dealing with Nazi Germany in general and SS formations in particular, these questions must either be the topic at hand, or compartmentalized lest they take over the narrative. Perhaps another writer could manage all of this simultaneously, but this one cannot.

The same caveats apply to both alleged American and Russian war crimes since the same rules apply: except where it affects the narrative these fall outside the scope of this work. One such example is the allegation that hundreds of members of *Das Reich* were simply gunned down by US soldiers after surrendering in Czechoslovakia, but that nobody cares because they were SS men. The men of *Totenkopf* make the same claim. There also seems no point in dwelling on the mass rapes that accompanied the Red Army across Europe. Some two million women were said to have been victimized, but except where combat troops came across evidence this is for a different book than mine. Indeed, it has already been covered in many other worthy works. There are a few incidents mentioned about what happened in Austria, because hard numbers are available in many towns, but it may safely be assumed this was the norm in newly conquered areas.

The most difficult part has been disentangling contradictory references and details, which happened on every single page on this book. Every…single…page. Misidentified units, unknown units, conflicting dates, missing reports…literally hundreds, if not thousands, of hours were spent trying to determine where the weight of evidence lay in those countless contradictions. In the end I made the decisions that made the most sense to me, but I anticipate friendly debate on some of these subjects. After all, we learn best by defending our beliefs to others. To that end I have a place for errata on my website, www.thelastbrigade.com.

I also made considerable effort to determine unit strengths at any given moment during the course of the battle. I have always appreciated this when reading military history, so that unit names aren't simply ambiguous titles but have numbers to flesh them out in the reader's mind. Of course, German unit strength returns after March 1945 are few and far between. In some places I've made estimates to give the narrative flavor, but these aren't wild guesses. I'm confident these numbers are very close to accurate.

Lastly, anyone writing about the *Wehrmacht* has to decide what nomenclature they'll use to list the dizzying array of units, sub-units, alarm units, *Kampfgruppe*, etc., used by the Germans in the Second World War. For a variety of reasons the book sticks with the exact German designation.

So there you have it. This book exists in its current form because it's what I would want to read. I hope you enjoy reading it as much as I did writing it, but make no mistake; if this work has merit, it's because I stand on the shoulders of the giants who came before me.

Preface

Winston Churchill had no illusions about Joseph Stalin's plans for postwar Austria. He wrote letters to both President Franklin Roosevelt and then to Harry Truman expressing concerns about a Soviet bloc in Eastern Europe, including all or part of Austria. The Americans didn't share his worries and trusted Stalin more than Churchill ever did. Events proved Churchill correct. The Russians did try to set up a pro-Soviet government in Vienna, which only failed in the long term because the American and British Armies overran much of southern and western Austria, including the most mountainous regions. Eastern Austria, the region area held by the Russians, was far less easily defended.

But what if the Russians had captured most or all of Austria? Would Stalin have allowed free elections, as promised? Or would he have installed a puppet Communist regime as he did in Poland, Czechoslovakia, Hungary and all the other Warsaw Pact nations? After all, he tried to do it anyway, but what if the Red Army had occupied the whole country? If we assume the war-weary western powers would have turned a blind eye as they did in the case of those other hapless nations, then the answer seems to be a profound yes. Austria would have voluntarily voted to join the Warsaw Pact because Stalin would only have tolerated a government that would do so. The question would then arise whether America and Britain would have gone back to war to free Austria from the Soviet grip, and it seems safe to answer that with a firm no. Clement Attlee's government was far more pro-Soviet than Churchill's, and without the British on board the Americans would not have had the ability to successfully wage war on the Russians, even if they'd had the will. Austria would have been lost and with it, perhaps, the Cold War.

Because even if Britain came back to the fight, Austria's central position in Europe would have driven a wedge into the NATO alliance nations, completely severing the direct land bridge between Germany and Italy. In a shooting war between the Western Nations and Russia, Germany would have been completely outflanked on the south, rendering its defense difficult, if not impossible. This didn't happen because Adolf Hitler poured scarce German resources into a theater most of his advisers considered secondary.

When Budapest was surrounded on Christmas Eve, 1944, trapping some 33,000 German troops inside the city, against the impassioned pleas of his advisers, he ordered *IV SS-Panzerkorps* from its positions around Warsaw to Hungary. His intention was to attack and relieve Budapest quickly, then transfer the SS Corps back north to Warsaw, where it served as the only armored reserve against the massive Russian winter offensive that loomed in Poland.

Like all German formations of the period, *IV SS-Panzerkorps* was badly under-strength. Its armored regiments had a mere 20 percent of their authorized strength. This amounted to roughly 40 panzers of all types in each regiment.[1] Neither of its organic divisions, *3. SS-Panzer-Division Totenkopf* or *5. SS-Panzer-Division Wiking*, was rated as even marginally ready to attack.[2] Both had a *III* rating, which in German nomenclature of the day meant suitable only for mobile defense.

---

1   In theory, SS Panzer Divisions had one panzer regiment of two battalions, a *panzerjäger* (anti-tank) battalion and a *Sturmgeschütz* (assault gun) battalion. This added up to some 200 or so armored fighting vehicles.

2   The *Wehrmacht* had four ratings for a division. Condition I meant fully ready for all offensive operations. II was ready for limited offensive operations, III meant ready for mobile defensive operations and IV meant static defense only.

Other German armored formations were already in Hungary, but this is misleading; all of the divisions were shells of their former selves. Nevertheless, by luck, surprise and the expertise of the few remaining veteran commanders, *Unternehmen Konrad I*, Operation Konrad I, launched on 1 January 1945[3] made excellent progress for several days, eventually stalling out as the Russians shifted troops from the siege of Budapest to stopping this German offensive.

Unternehmen Konrad II was a continuation of the attack on a more northerly axis and through a mountainous area. Again it caught the Russians off guard and by 12 January[4] the leading SS men had gotten close enough to pick up radio broadcasts from their trapped comrades in Budapest. Trucks and ambulances assembled near the front lines to evacuate the wounded, while gathered food supplies would immediately be shipped into the city. *SS-Obergruppenführer und General der Waffen-SS* Herbert Otto Gille, commander of *IV SS-Panzerkorps*, believed no more Russian units stood in his way and the road to Budapest was open. The leading spearheads were less than eighteen miles from the Hungarian capital's defensive perimeter.

But as he had done so many times before, Hitler intervened to snatch defeat from the jaws of victory. *Der Gröfaz*, the great general, a derogatory term used by German officers to describe the *Führer*, had never believed in an armored attack through the mountains. Even as the SS men eliminated the last Russians in the town of Pilisszentkereszt, and opened the way to Budapest, Hitler ordered the attack suspended. No protestations could change his mind.

A week later the rested and reorganized Germans gathered for yet another relief attempt, *Unternehmen Konrad III*. In a sign of things to come, Hitler reinforced the attack by adding a powerful formation, *Schwere Panzer-Abeteilung 509*, equipped with 45 brand new Tiger II panzers. It is no exaggeration to say this might have been the strongest armored formation in the entire *Wehrmacht* at that time. With the Russians then raging through Poland and Silesia, those Tigers IIs, fighting from defensive positions, could have inflicted serious losses on the attackers. Instead they were in Hungary.

Given the relative weakness of the attacking Germans, *Unternehmen Konrad III* succeeded beyond anyone's wildest dreams. Once again the Russians were surprised, and within a few days German panzers had regained the western bank of the Danube River, south of Budapest. The key city of Stuhlweissenberg, Sekezsfehervar to the Hungarians, fell to the German advance. Their spearheads came within a few miles of the Budapest perimeter, even closer than during *Unternehmen Konrad II*, but the advance couldn't be sustained. Long flanks had to be protected and a fierce tank battle east of Lake Velence ultimately halted the advance. Hitler ordered the retaken ground to be held, but that wasn't possible. The area was huge and the Germans few. By the end of January they were back at their start lines, having paid a heavy price and achieved nothing.

After the three Konrad offensives *IV SS-Panzerkorps* was nearly bereft of working armored vehicles. *Wiking* suffered more than *Totenkopf* but neither division would ever again be used for a major attack. There was simply nothing left for the SS men to attack with, aside from *Panzergrenadiers*.[5] As for *Schwere Panzer-Abteilung 509*, only five of its 45 Tigers remained operational, with 10 having been completely destroyed. The Russians had also suffered heavily, however, and even they couldn't replace all of their losses, so in that respect the attacks had accomplished something. Those casualties would be significant to the Russians in Austria.

---

3   There is some disagreement on the precise date of the offensive, but most sources agree on January 1.

4   As with so many other details of German operations from this period, the exact date is debatable.

5   Theoretically *panzergrenadiers* were infantrymen who rode into battle in armored half-tracks, called *schützenpanzerwagens*, and who were trained to fight in cooperation with panzers. But in practical terms, by 1945 it had become synonymous with infantry.

The Army divisions suffered a similar fate during the Konrad attacks, including *1. Panzer-Division*, *3. Panzer-Division* and *6. Panzer-Division*. Their authorized strengths were smaller than their *Waffen-SS* counterparts to begin with.

Meanwhile, January had been a disastrous month for the Germans everywhere else. The Ardennes Offensive, better known in the west as the Battle of the Bulge, ended in ruinous defeat. Losses had been catastrophic, especially in panzers and *Schützenpanzerwagen*, SPWs, which Americans called half-tracks, and which couldn't be replaced. The two armies that participated in the attack, *5. Panzerarmee* and *6. SS-Panzerarmee*,[6] lost most of their offensive power in the month-long battle, and yet *6. SS-Panzerarmee* still represented the most powerful formation Germany had left, even after the battle. So the pressing question of the moment was what to do with it?

Against all advice and logic, Hitler decided to send it to Hungary. To the generals this made no sense, but Hitler wasn't interested in defending Berlin or anywhere else. He still thought in terms of winning the war, and victory could only be achieved through attacks. This was true as far as it went, but the real truth was that Germany had irretrievably lost the war no matter what they did. Nevertheless, Hitler was determined to go down fighting.

Like all twentieth-century militaries the *Wehrmacht* ran on oil-based fuels, and two of the last sources of natural oil in German hands were the Hungarian fields around Nagykanitzsa and the Austrian fields at Zistersdorf.[7] Keeping these was vital to the war effort, even though their production was small compared to the needs. However, the German synthetic oil industry had been bombed into oblivion by the B-17s of the US Eighth Air Force and the Halifaxes and Lancasters of Britain's Bomber Command. Fuel shortages already crippled the *Wehrmacht* but at least with these fields there was some production.

Another reason for sending *6. SS-Panzerarmee* south was that once pumped out of the ground, oil had to be refined before it could be used, and most of Germany's remaining refineries were in Austria, particularly near Vienna. Once the oil was refined it then had to be transported by rail before the panzers, aircraft and ships of the *Wehrmacht* could use it, and by this point in the war the German rail system was in a shambles. What was simpler than bringing the fuel to the panzers and SPWs of *6. SS-Panzerarmee* was to bring the panzers to the fuel.

A third excuse for this redeployment was that when Hitler made the decision to transfer *SS-Oberstgruppenführer* Sepp Dietrich's command to Hungary, the Budapest garrison was fighting hard against the Russian siege. It seemed possible to use the panzer army to relieve the city. By the time Budapest fell on 13 February it was too late to reroute the army back to the north.

The fourth reason has to do with Hitler's understanding of history and his interpretation of the life of Frederick the Great. The Prussian king never gave up, never stopped being aggressive and was finally rewarded by the dissolution of the alliance facing him. Hitler saw himself as being in a similar situation, but his relentless focus on attacking makes it clear that he didn't believe a nation could win a war by remaining on the defensive. A decisive defeat could only be inflicted on the enemy by attacking.

Understanding this critical point is the key to understanding Hitler's motives for both disastrous offensives late in the war, *Unternehmen Wacht am Rhein*, the Ardennes Offensive, later renamed *Unternehmen Herbstnebel*, and *Unternehmen Frühlingserwachen*, Operation Spring Awakening. Conventional wisdom, both at the time and in hindsight, is that saving those precious forces for counter-offensives and reserves was their proper usage. The General Staff remembered devastating

---

6   *6. Panzerarmee* did not have the SS designation until much later in the war. However, in the intervening years it has become widely known as *6. SS-Panzerarmee*, and that designation is used here to avoid confusion.

7   In a January military conference Hitler mentioned having the Zistersdorf fields shut down to deny their use to the Russians.

counter-blows earlier in the war, such as Manstein's backhand blow to retake Kharkov in early 1943. The Red Army forces facing him were crushed by the attack, stopping the momentum of the post-Stalingrad westward movement. But Manstein had achieved this against Hitler's direct orders and his relief in 1944 could be traced back to this disobedience as a key moment when Hitler turned on him. Most people would rather be rich than right, but Hitler would have rather been right.

In 1945 Hitler was still fighting to win the war. We'll never know if he truly believed it was still militarily possible, wanted to prolong the fight in hopes of a miracle similar to Frederick the Great's salvation, or simply wanted to extend his own life as long as possible, regardless of the cost. Did he truly believe himself to be the savior of Europe and so his own life was more valuable than millions of others? Or was he a pathological narcissist who had no empathy for the misery he caused? Again, we can never truly know for sure.

Finally, Hitler made a curious remark when justifying moving *6. SS-Panzerarmee* to Hungary and, by extension, Austria. *General der Artillerie* Walter Warlimont quotes *Generalfeldmarschall* Wilhelm Keitel as saying that Hitler declared Vienna more important than Berlin.[8] This altogether bizarre remark interjects the possibility of sentimental reasons for Hitler's decision. He was, after all, Austrian, and despite repeated declarations of how much he hated Vienna, he always looked back on those years of struggle with nostalgia.

Was he a sentimental monster? Based on a variety of factors, there was definitely a hint of this in his decision to protect Austria above Berlin. But whatever the reason or reasons, whether this theory holds water or not, there's no doubt that *6. SS-Panzerarmee* found itself secretly transported to Hungary.

* * *

Meanwhile, February saw sporadic heavy fighting all along the front lines of *Heeresgruppe Süd*, Army Group South, especially at Székesfehérvár, as the Russians probed for weak spots. Both sides knew that city was the key to Western Hungary, but the Red Army had long since perfected its tactics for capturing heavily defended cities. Beginning in November of 1942, with attacks at both Velikiye Luki and Stalingrad, they first launched direct attacks on those cities to keep the defenders tied down, followed by attacks on the weaker flanks where the Germans typically deployed the less reliable elements of their allies, or German forces that were stretched too thin. In Western Hungary that allied formation was the Hungarian Third Army north of Székesfehérvár.

During the night of 11-12 February the surviving members of the Budapest garrison launched a desperate breakout to reach German lines. Between 17,000 and 28,000 Germans and Hungarians[9] attacked to the northwest out of their last positions in Buda's Castle District. But the Russians learned of their plans and zeroed in a massive amount of firepower on the escape route. The resulting slaughter left thousands of dead men strewn in heaps along streets clogged with shattered vehicles and ruined buildings. Fewer than seven hundred Germans made their way back to friendly lines. Budapest officially surrendered on 13 February.

* * *

Regardless of this loss, Hitler still insisted on attacking in Hungary. The name given to the offensive was *Unternehmen Frühlingserwachen,* Operation Spring Awakening. The concept was to clear the Soviets entirely from Western Hungary and to re-establish the Danube River as a defensive

---

8   Warlimont, General Walter, *Inside Hitler's Headquarters 1939-1945* (Novato: Presidio Press, 1990), p.499.

9   Sources differ on the exact number.

barrier, thereby guaranteeing the safety of the Hungarian oil fields. Then the armored forces could be transferred north to the Berlin front.

As a pre-condition for the offensive it was deemed critical to regain the defensive line of the Gran River, north of the Danube, where the Russians had a strong western bank bridgehead. To this end, on 17 February, 1945, elements of *I SS-Panzerkorps* participated in an attack to clear up the enemy intrusion. Within a week the Germans had won a significant victory by destroying the bridgehead and inflicting terrible losses on the Russians. But the cost was high. Aside from heavy losses in men and machines, the greatest casualty was the carefully constructed secrecy surrounding the *6. SS-Panzerarmee* transfer to the south. Once the Russians knew the SS was on hand, it was easy to figure out why.

On 6 March, 1945, against all advice and despite the protests of the commanders on the spot, Hitler ordered *Unternehmen Frühlingserwachen* to go forward. It was the most poorly conceived German offensive of the entire war.

The weather was atrocious. Sticky fields of mud lay under deep water from rain and melting snow. Conditions were so poor that German armor was restricted to the few passable roads, which made them easy targets for the fortified Russian *PAKfronts*.[10] A photo from the first day shows a Panther sunk to the turret in mud. Only days later could the panzers participate in the attack, putting all the pressure on the *Panzergrenadiers* who waded through waist-deep water, under fire, to capture the Russian positions.

By sheer skill and bravery the attack dragged forward in the area of *I SS-Panzerkorps*, but elsewhere it bogged dangerously. *II SS-Panzerkorps*, on the left flank of the attack, got stuck before Sarosd and went nowhere. Because of this *I SS-Panzerkorps* was left with an open flank and had to weaken the spearhead to protect it. After a week the offensive was virtually stopped, having accomplished nothing more than squandering resources and putting three German Corps into a critical position.

On 16 March, Second and Third Ukrainian Fronts launched their long-awaited Vienna Offensive. On the Germans' northern flank a strong Soviet attack penetrated the weak Hungarian 3rd Army and sped for the eastern tip of Lake Balaton. Once they got there, any German units south and east would be trapped. That included all of *6. SS-Panzerarmee* and much of *6. Armee*.

What followed was a fortnight of stand and retreat, stand and retreat. The retreat never became a rout, but the danger of the broken Germans being surrounded was constant. The only reason any of them survived was the professionalism and bravery of the veterans. *5. SS-Panzer-Division Wiking* stood against insurmountable odds at Sékesfehérvár to allow their SS comrades to escape. In turn *9. SS-Panzer-Division Hohenstaufen* was crushed while holding open a narrow escape corridor east of Lake Balaton.

The bloody roads west were lined with abandoned vehicles, wounded and surrendering *Landser*[11] and abandoned equipment. Combat, mechanical breakdowns and lack of fuel all combined to leave the panzer divisions without a meaningful number of operational panzers.[12] Heavy infantry casualties stripped the divisions of their combat efficiency. After two weeks of retreat the shattered formations reached the border of the Reich, with the Russians hot on their heels.

---

10   *PAK* is the generic German term for an anti-tank gun. In the case of the Russians this almost always meant the deadly ZiS-3 76.2mm wheeled artillery gun. The Russians became adept at field fortifying these ubiquitous guns in stout *paknests*, and a string of *PAK* nests became known as a *pakfront*. Attacking such a position without air support and heavy artillery support was dangerous in the extreme.

11   A common German word for soldiers.

12   The official German records for lost vehicles, and those remaining on hand, isn't reliable, so figures quoted should be looked upon with skepticism. Vehicles listed under short-term repair might need eight weeks or more of work. Complicating this was a shortage of skilled technicians and a critical scarcity of spare parts of all kinds.

Although on paper *Heeresgruppe Süd* was the most powerful formation in the *Wehrmacht*, it would be misleading to speak of it as having a main line of resistance on 1 April. The situation was that the Army Group's four armies were islands of resistance in the Red Army flood. Only *8. Armee*, north of the Danube, had anything approaching a cohesive defensive line. Beginning in March, the local populace had been put to work reinforcing the *Reichsschutzstellung* from the Thaya River, the border with old Czechoslovakia, to the Marchfeld, the flat area adjacent to the Danube River on the north. *6. SS-Panzerarmee*, *6. Armee* and *2. Panzerarmee* all had open flanks, with great gaps between them and the neighboring army.

On 1 April the Germans desperately fought to keep touch with the western end of Lake Balaton, where *2. Panzerarmee* and some retreating elements of the shattered *6. Armee* tried to shield the Nagykanisza oil field. It was hopeless. By then, Russian spearheads had reached the Austrian frontier south-west of Steinamanger. Following a breakthrough the weak German border fortifications of the so-called *Reichsschutzstellung*,[13] in the area between Guns and Odenburg, the Soviets had pressed forward to points south and south-west of Weiner Neustadt. Here they were held by an Army Cadet school after heavy fighting. Having turned the southern corner of the Neusiedlersee, Russian spearheads cleared the western bank as far as Rust. North of the Danube, Second Ukrainian Front fought its way closer to the Slovakian capital, Bratislava. Meanwhile, further south the Russians had broken through and drove on Graz.

Throughout April the German units kept fighting a war they all knew was lost. They fought hard and died in huge numbers, and a hard question to answer is why? What motivated them to risk their own lives for a lost cause? Dr Nordewin von Diest-Koerber, commanding officer of *Schwere Panzer-Abteilung Feldherrnhalle*, gives one answer in his diary entry for 30 March 1945: "This [continued resistance] allows as many German units as possible to get away to the west and also holds the way open for the...civilian population..."[14] Some might still have believed in the promised *wunderwaffe*, wonder weapons, or fought on to stop Bolshevism, or because of a diehard loyalty to the Nazi state. But most men probably kept fighting for the simple reason they didn't want to abandon the man next to them in the trench.

The Cuff Title Order

Few incidents have spawned more legends than the infamous Cuff Title Order. In response to criticism of his handling of *6. Armee* during the Soviet offensive then rampaging across Western Hungary, *General der Panzertruppe* Hermann Balck reportedly made the comment that if the *1. SS-Panzer-Division Leibstandarte Adolf Hitler* (*LAH*) couldn't hold the line, how was he expected to? This remark found fertile ground in the poisoned soil of Hitler's underground headquarters in Berlin, the so-called *Führerbunker*. The barely suppressed enmity between the *Waffen-SS* and the Army that had bubbled just below the surface for years leaned heavily in favor of the Army in the claustrophobic underground world of Hitler's last headquarters. Given the chance to blame disaster on their hated rivals, the Army generals were quick to back up Balck's version of events, and embellished it. Hitler, never slow to spot a scapegoat, latched onto this supposed failure of the *Waffen-SS* as the reason for the failure of *Unternehmen Frühlingserwachen*. Coming on top of

---

13   Reich protected positions. This was the so-called Southeast Wall, which was supposed to be a counterpart of the West Wall.

14   Dr Franz Wilhelm, *The Combat History of German Tiger Tank Battalion 503 in World War II* (Mechanicsburg: Stackpole, 2000), p.364.

Himmler's abject failure as commander of *Heeresgruppe Vistula*, Hitler didn't hesitate to single out the *Waffen-SS* for rebuke.

On 27 March Hitler ordered the SS divisions of *6. SS-Panzerarmee* to remove the honorific cuff title from the sleeves of their uniforms. In essence, this was like ordering men to disassociate themselves from their families. There was no greater insult and Hitler knew it.

If the *Führer* had any real friends, Sepp Dietrich could be counted as one of the few. But as happened with Ernst Röhm, the rare man with whom Hitler used the German familiar term *du*, the *Führer* had no compunction against punishing his friends. When the order came into the headquarters of *6. SS-Panzerarmee* Dietrich's anger at this betrayal was obvious. He ordered it suppressed but it leaked out anyway, some say by Hermann Balck himself. One persistent legend is that the fury of the SS men supposedly led Dietrich and his officers to throw their medals into a spittoon or cook pot and send them to Hitler, but this never happened. Nor were any remaining cuff title ordered removed. Dietrich wouldn't allow it, even though most cuff title had been removed for security reasons during the transfer to Hungary, and had never been sewn back on.

Hitler said the SS men had not fought hard enough in Hungary. In particular, he accused Dietrich of disobeying orders by leaving 30,000 men behind in Germany, anticipating a transfer to the Berlin front. This was pure fantasy, fueled by Balck's incessant negativity, Otto Wöhler's[15] backing of the *6. Armee* commander and the Army generals who had Hitler's ear, and the unending rivalry between the regular Army and the SS. However, there is one kernel of truth that could have been the inspiration for exaggeration into a major issue. When the *LAH* shipped out to Austria, it left behind a battalion's worth of men from *SS-Panzer-Regiment 1* at Osnabrück, in Northwest Germany. These men didn't have panzers and would soon be formed into infantry companies and shipped to Austria. The number involved was probably 300-400 men.

What seems likely to have happened is that someone at *Führer* Headquarters heard about these men and saw a chance to elevate the Army at the expense of the *Waffen-SS*. We can never be certain, of course, but we do know that even in the dying days of the Reich Hitler's paladins fought each other harder than ever for their position at his court. In his increasing paranoia, Hitler would blame anybody except himself for failure, and now it was Dietrich's turn.

Himmler was ordered to personally reprimand Dietrich. In late March he traveled to Vienna, ostensibly for this purpose. While there he reportedly spoke with Von Schirach about evacuating the last Jews in Vienna to Mauthausen, but to treat them well and keep them safe, apparently in a last-minute attempt to mitigate all that came before. But he and Von Schirach were never friendly, and Von Schirach ignored his wishes. Moreover, his influence with the *Waffen-SS* itself had waned.

No men had sacrificed more to advance the regime through military means than the *Waffen-SS*, who were often shot on sight even after surrendering. Once news of the cuff title order got out to *6. SS-Panzerarmee* the SS men's personal loyalty to Adolf Hitler was severely damaged and many looked on Himmler with contempt for not defending them. They would continue to obey orders as well as they could, but standing fast in suicidal situations just because Hitler told them to would never happen again. On his word they had fought their way across Europe, bled and died on a thousand battlefields and incurred the undying enmity of their foes, only to be betrayed in the final weeks. The SS men would still fight for each other, and to protect civilians, but not for the higher leadership.

The long-simmering rivalry between the Army and the *Waffen-SS* permeated all levels of the *Wehrmacht*, not just the high command. One example from *Heeresgruppe Süd* in 1945 is the case of *SS-Obersturmbannführer* Walter Klein from *16. SS-Panzergrenadier-Division Reichsführer SS*. Put in charge of an alarm company in southwest Hungary, on 29 March Klein was accused

---

15   Commander of *Heeresgruppe Süd*.

of retreating without orders by an Army court-martial. Three days later he was executed by the Army.[16] The staff of *16. SS-Panzergrenadier-Division Reichsführer SS* would certainly have been enraged by this incident as the *Waffen-SS* prided themselves on disciplining their own men.

Stavka[17] Directive for April 1945

The Soviet High Command issued new orders for Second and Third Ukrainian Fronts on 1 April, along with a new boundary between the two army groups. Third Ukrainian Front contained First Bulgarian Army and the Twenty-Sixth, Twenty-Seventh and Fifty-Seventh Soviet Armies on its left wing, with orders to advance toward Graz and Gloggnitz by 12 April at the latest. Its right wing comprised the Fourth, Sixth and Sixth Guards Armies, and was given the task of capturing Vienna. By 15 April it was supposed to hold a line 15 miles south of Sankt Pölten, up to Sankt Pölten and then north to Tulln.

Stalin frequently pitted one commander against another in a competition for honors and stature, and so, just as happened with Berlin, Stavka also gave Second Ukrainian Front the mission of taking Vienna. The Front contained Forty-Sixth Army, reinforced by II Guards Mechanized Corps and XXIII Tank Corps. South of the Danube it was ordered to advance through the Bruck Gap, at the city of Bruck an der Leitha, and from there to drive on and take Vienna. North of the Danube, it was to capture Bratislava and then drive west toward Stockerau, Znaim and Brno.[18]

Notes on names and numbers

The term *Wehrmacht* refers to all German armed forces, the *Kriegsmarine*, *Luftwaffe*, and *Heer*. The German *Heer*, the German Army, on the Eastern Front on Easter Day, 1945, consisted of *Heeresgruppe Vistula* in Poland, followed by *Heeresgruppe Mitte* in what was previously called Czechoslovakia, *Heeresgruppe Süd* in Western Hungary and Eastern Austria, and *Heeresgruppe E* in the Balkans. *Heeresgruppe F* had been recently dissolved and absorbed by *Heeresgruppe E*. *Heeresgruppe C* held northern Italy and will crop up late in this narrative.

The Germans had two words for 'army,' *heer* and *armee*. *Heer* generally refers to the larger organization while *armee* means the individual field armies, such as *6. SS-Panzerarmee*. *Heeresgruppen*, Army Groups, were precisely what the name implies, a collection of two or more armies, *Heeresgruppe Süd* had four armies, but it could just as easily have had three, or five. In theory a *Heeresgruppe* could have no less than eight divisions. In practice they often had more than or, as in 1945, less. Manpower in a *heeresgruppe* could be anything from 100,000-500,000 or more, counting supply, medical, veterinary and other miscellaneous components.

Although the Germans and Russians shared unit nomenclature, there was a difference in the authorized strengths represented by those designations. For example, a German battalion equaled a Russian regiment, a German regiment equaled a Russian brigade, and so on. A Soviet tank corps might have 150-170 tanks and self-propelled guns, which is roughly the same authorized strength as a *Waffen-SS* Panzer Division. A German corps could contain two such divisions, doubling its strength, while a similarly upgraded Russian unit would be called an army.

---

16   Landwehr, Richard, 'Waffen-SS Miscellany' *Siegrunen 55* (January 1994), p.85.

17   The Soviet High Command.

18   Maier, Georg, *Drama Between Budapest and Vienna, The Final Battles of the 6. Panzer-Armee in the East-1945* (Winnipeg: J.J. Federowicz, 2004), pp.342-343.

During 1945 authorized unit strengths were largely irrelevant. The few *Wehrmacht* units up to strength are labeled as such in the narrative, but most were in the same position as *5. SS-Panzer-Division Wiking*. Despite being authorized to have close to 190 armored fighting vehicles, it had so few that it disbanded its panzer regiment. Nor did Orders of Battle matter anymore, or replacement and supply channels, which were violated with regularity as units began to look after their own needs. Examples abound of combat troops appropriating what they needed outside the hitherto rigid logistical channels.

Perhaps the most misleading figures of them all are those for available combat strength. Some units showed they were actually over-strength in manpower, yet those new replacements generally had no basic training and quickly became casualties once committed to battle. The name *1. SS-Panzer-Division Leibstandarte Adolf Hitler* might seem impressive, but if the division had no panzers and half its men were untrained for combat, then its combat value would be much lower than its reputation might imply.

The Russian term for a collection of armies was 'Front'. Like the German term *Heeresgruppe*, Army Group, a Front had more than one army. Also like the German, it was an amorphous concept. A Front might have two or three armies, or it might have six. The Russian Fronts involved in the assault on Austria were the Second and Third Ukrainian Fronts. Second Ukrainian Front, fighting mostly on the north side of the Danube, was commanded by the young, energetic and very skilled Marshal Rodion Malinovsky, while Third Ukrainian Front's leader was Marshal Tolbukhin. Tolbukhin was unusual in the Red Army because he was not overly ambitious and did everything he could to keep casualties low while achieving his objectives, unlike men such as Georgi Zhukov who were indifferent to losses as long as the mission was accomplished. Both Russian commanders were first-rate military leaders and Tolbukhin is generally considered one of the best Soviet officers of the Second World War.

Units of Second and Third Ukrainian Front were lower on the supply chain than other Fronts, such as Zhukov's First Belorussian Front facing Berlin. Consequently, their equipment tended to be more of a hodge-podge than higher-priority units. For example, a large number of the tanks used in the Austrian campaign were either American Shermans, affectionately nicknamed *Emcha* by their Russian crews,[19] or British Valentines.[20] One Rumanian unit even drove old French Renault R-35s, a pre-war light tank, and First Bulgarian Army drove German Mark IV panzers and other *Wehrmacht* vehicles. Russian crews tended to like the western-made tanks for their greater comfort levels and radios, but overall combat capabilities lagged behind newer Soviet tanks such as the T-34/85.

Heeresgruppe Süd

Heeresgruppe Süd was the headquarters responsible for defending Austria. On its northern flank stood *Heeresgruppe Mitte* and to the south was *Heeresgruppe E*. On 1 April the *Heeresgruppe Süd* area of responsibility ran from near Zlin, in what is now the far eastern region of the Czech Republic, through Slovakia to the eastern suburbs of Bratislava, then across the Danube to the area of the Neuseidlersee and along the Austrian border until arcing southeast to near Nagikanizsa, Hungary. On its southern border it connected with *Heeresgruppe E* in extreme southwestern Hungary.

---

19   The first letter for its Russian designation, the M-4.
20   Although the Valentine was quickly outclassed during the war by other designs, the Soviet High Command specifically asked for its continued production for their use.

The commander was *General der Infanterie* Otto Wöhler, and perhaps the most apt description of him would be competent. Blandly handsome, but with a care-worn face that reflected six years of war, Wöhler seemed an odd choice for such a high command. Most of his career had been spent as a staff officer. He was aged 51 in 1945, and had joined the German Army before the First World War. His first combat command came in 1942 when he led *Kampfgruppe Wöhler* in an unsuccessful attempt to save the garrison of Velikiye Luki. It's worth noting that few men who served under him ever spoke ill of him. But Otto Wöhler was not among Germany's pantheon of brilliant generals. He was no Guderian, Rommel, Heinrici, von Manstein or Model. His style of command was more management than active participant.

Even the *Waffen-SS* considered him a reasonable man, although he unquestionably sided with Hermann Balck in his squabbles with Sepp Dietrich and other SS commanders. As an indication of his ability to get along with people, Hitler kept him on as Commanding Officer of *Heeresgruppe Süd* long after he would have sacked others, despite Wöhler not being a Nazi Party member. At this late stage of the war Hitler looked more and more to fanaticism to fill the void created by lack of resources. The commander of *Heeresgruppe Mitte*, for example, *Generalfeldmarschall* Ferdinand Schörner, AKA Bloody Ferdinand, won the admiration of both Hitler and Joseph Goebbels by his orders to shoot anyone even suspected of shirking their duty. His brutality was legendary. Wöhler was nothing like him.

Wöhler, on the other hand, was an archetype of the German Army Command system. Although he was convicted after the war as a war criminal for cooperating with *Einsatzgruppe D* in Russia when he was *Stabschef*, Chief of Staff, for *11. Armee*, Wöhler was very much the staid, non-political German officer. The main quality recommending him for command of an army group, therefore, was that Hitler hadn't forced him into retirement as he had with more talented officers, such as *Generalfeldmarschall* Erich von Manstein. What Wöhler was not was a man to work miracles to stop the Red Army, but then again, neither was anybody else.

He was also not the man to impose his will on his subordinates, which had led to months of squabbling among his army commanders, the net result of which had influenced the disaster in Hungary. Yet by 1 April, none of that mattered. There was no strategy Wöhler could employ to save Vienna. Indeed, for the most part any orders he gave were obsolete by the time they were received. No German general could have stopped the Russians with the ruined units comprising *Heeresgruppe Süd* on that Easter Sunday.

* * *

Heeresgruppe Süd had four armies under its command. North of the Danube was *8. Armee*, commanded by *General der Gebirgstruppe* Hans Kreysing; then, south of the Danube near Vienna was the famed *6. SS-Panzerarmee*, with *SS-Oberstgruppenführer* Josef Sepp Dietrich in command; followed by *General der Panzertruppe* Hermann Balck's *6. Armee*; and finally *2. Panzerarmee*, commanded by *General der Artillerie* Maximilian de Angelis.

On paper this seems like a juggernaut of military power. In reality, those four armies were like rotten logs that appear solid from the outside, but whose interior has disintegrated into dust.

By 1945 the Germans sought to keep the number of panzers in their armored divisions higher by including non-turreted, tracked vehicles like the *Jagdpanzer IV/70*, a very effective tank destroyer, and various models of the *Sturmgeschütz*, or assault gun, in their panzer totals. Those machines were much cheaper to build than a Panzer Mark V Panther, or even an aging Mark IV, although not as effective as a true panzer with a rotating turret. Stop gaps such as the *Jagdpanzer 38(t) Hetzer* proved extremely effective and were built in huge numbers.

There's one last point to remember about German vehicle totals at this state of the war. Whether panzers or SPWs, the machines in the divisions had mostly likely already been repaired, some more than once, and many, perhaps even most, had been recovered from the battlefield after being damaged or knocked out. Barrels, sprockets and treads were worn out, cranky engines needed parts that weren't available and ammunition shortages made prolonged fighting impossible. German factories had all but stopped manufacturing new panzers and SPWs, so even the reliability of the remaining machines was in question. *Heeresgruppe Süd* had literally left most of its weapons behind in Western Hungary and those losses could never be made up.

The Russians

Third Ukrainian Front was the primary Red Army formation attacking into Austria, with half of Second Ukrainian Front supporting their right flank. At the start of the campaign most of Second Ukrainian Front stood north of the Danube River facing the German *8. Armee*, although it did have one army south of the river. As the fight progressed, however, the direction of Russian attacks turned to the northwest and all of Second Ukrainian Front's forces crossed to the north for the attack into old Czechoslovakia.

Marshal of the Soviet Union Rodion Malinovsky commanded Second Ukrainian Front. Malinovsky was every inch a warrior. Born in Odessa in 1898, Malinovsky grew up poor. His step father threw him out of the house at age 13 and he worked whatever jobs he could find to feed himself. When war broke out in 1914 the 15-year-old boy convinced an officer to let him join the army, even though he was too young. After being badly wounded and recovering, he went to fight in France as part of the Western Front Russian Expeditionary Corps. His continued bravery won him the coveted Croix de Guerre from the French Government.

After the First World War he signed up to fight for the Red Army in its civil war against the Whites, supporters of the late Czar and other anti-Communist forces. Once that war ended, and the Russo-Polish War after it, Malinovsky stayed in the army. After attending command school he rose through the ranks and volunteered to fight in Spain during the Spanish Civil War. This may have saved his life when the purges started in 1937. When Germany invaded the USSR in 1941, Malinovsky's skill at handling a corps on the southern end of the front bogged down and delayed German forces along the Black Sea coast, as well as inflicting heavy casualties on the invaders.

This brought him to Stavka's attention as a clever commander. Promotions followed, but as he rose through the ranks Malinovsky's consideration for his troops often put him at odds with Stalin, to whom losses were irrelevant. Fortunately for him, his remarkable successes kept him safe. As 1944 waned his command drove through Romania and Hungary toward Austria, and Malinovsky harbored a dream of driving down the Danube Valley all the way to Munich, thereby cutting the Reich in two and isolating Austria. He was a formidable opponent and certainly a more forceful commander than his counterpart *Generaloberst* Wöhler.

The commander of Third Ukrainian Front, Marshal Fyodor Tolbukhin, was cut from much the same cloth as Malinovsky. Aggressive in battle, his skills in organization helped him keep Third Ukrainian Front combat-ready despite its lower place on the supply chain than formations like Marshal Zhukov's First Belorussian Front. Also like Malinovsky he came through the purges of 1937-1938 unscathed, which if nothing else means he knew how to navigate the dangerous paranoia at the top of the Russian chain of command. It's instructive that during the Battle of Stalingrad, when other officers were being shot for failure, as Chief of Staff for the Fifty-Eighth Army Tolbukhin was singled out for praise by his commanding officer, Colonel General Andrei Yeremenko.

1

Sunday, 1 April

Not a single meter of ground is permitted to be given up anymore.
Adolf Hitler, 1 April 1945

Vienna

Hints of smoke swirled on the gentle winds of a bright Easter Sunday morning in Vienna, former capital of the Austro-Hungarian Empire. Bits of ash drifted around the grim faces of the people gathered at the Heldenplatz. A bitter smell hung over the city that had become all too familiar to its citizens. Around the sprawling metropolis buildings slid into the street as if the ground beneath them had liquefied, their facades and roofs smashed to ruins by the rain of American bombs that started the previous June and intensified in February and March. The powdered rubble and skeletal walls of buildings both magnificent and ordinary inflicted a shared and classless destruction the former capital of empire had never known before.

The Allies treated the Brown Plague, the derisive Viennese name for Nazism, like an infection needing high-explosive antibiotics, and were not shy about the dosage. After fifty-one previous attacks on all districts of the city, the attack on 30 March 1945 was the last. The Americans were finally done battering one of Europe's great cultural centers, because it was also one of Europe's great industrial centers. The destruction wrought by the B-24s and B-17s of the US Fifteenth Army Air Force left Vienna a broken shell of its former glorious self.

Vienna exists because of the Danube River. The area was conquered by the Romans during the reign of Augustus around 15 BCE. Except for brief periods when the Romans pushed northward into the Germanic territories, such as during the reign of Marcus Aurelius, the Danube marked the northern boundary of the Roman Empire. Vienna became an important center of trade and, eventually, capital of the empire of the Hapsburgs.

But the Danube could be temperamental. One branch ran through the city itself, and had a propensity to flood and erode its banks. To combat this, the Viennese worked the river branch into a canal with quays and reinforced sides, as well as several methods of controlling water levels and keeping the canal free of floating ice. Named simply the Danube Canal, it runs through the city and creates a huge island containing the Second District, Leopoldstadt, and the Twentieth District, Brittgenau.

After the joining of Germany and Austria in 1938, the *Anschluss,* Vienna was expanded from 21 to 26 districts, and today has 23, but the soul of the city has always lain within the Ringstrasse, the semi-circular boulevard around the *Innere Stadt*, the inner city, which was also the First District. Districts two through nine spiraled in a clockwise rotation around the First District, starting with the Second District, Leopoldstadt, across the Danube Canal and including the Prater, with the Ninth District adjacent to the First on its northwest corner. From there the numbering was more haphazard.

Contained within the inner city were the traditions which had always made the Viennese heart beat faster. The grand opera houses, the promenades, St Stephen's Cathedral, the Spanish Riding

23

School, the Parliament Building and, facing the city's most famous square, the Heldenplatz, which was the center of power of the Austrian Emperors who resided in the Hofburg. On 12 March 1945, a huge wave of bombers aiming for the Floridsdorf Oil Refinery instead bombed the inner city, causing massive damage.

On that Easter Sunday the normal bustle of the city was louder than usual as those who could leave, did. They fled in every imaginable type of vehicle, from sedans to garbage trucks. In quieter moments the faint thunder of artillery fire could be heard as the Red Army reached the Austrian frontier, but instead of heading east to fight for the Reich, as they urged and forced others to do, most Party officials were headed west wearing civilian dress and not their uniforms.

The Russians were coming and only the most delusional fanatic believed Vienna could be saved. Twice before had Vienna stood as the last bulwark of European culture and religion against invasion from the east, stopping Turkish invasions in both 1529 and 1683. Both times a mighty warrior had stepped forward to lead the defense, first in the person of the German Nicholas, Count of Salm, and later by John III Sobieski, King of Poland. To defeat the Russians in 1945 Vienna needed another such man to lead the defense, a hero of the people who could rally them to achieve the impossible. Instead, the man they got was the hated *Gauleiter*[1] of Vienna, Baldur von Schirach.

* * *

It wasn't just the citizens of Vienna who despised Baldur von Schirach; Joseph Goebbels loathed him, too. To be sure, Goebbels hated a lot of people, but the diminutive *Reichsminister* held a special contempt for the *Gauleiter* and *Reichsstathalter*[2] of Vienna that went back a long way. For years Goebbels had complained that von Schirach was, among other things, incompetent and unequal to the task of being a *Gauleiter*. Although he never put it this way, it was plain that he thought of von Schirach as an effete dilettante. It must have been cold comfort to be proven correct as the situation worsened and his opinion was borne out.

As broken German units streamed into Austria during late March of 1945, problems of command became almost untenable. *Gauleiters* had been given nearly plenipotentiary powers to resist the enemy, regardless of the brutality of their methods. This enforced the power of the Nazi Party in matters of defense, which sometimes made for a confusing chain of command. Hitler's method of staying in power was to have multiple layers of authority at all levels of government, so in Vienna von Schirach became the ultimate arbiter of all territorial disputes. That inherent inefficiency had crippled the war effort for years, including during the recent fighting in Hungary, and would rear its ugly head over and over again in the coming fight for Vienna.

Throughout the brief life of the Third Reich this relentless infighting drained the energy of the nation away from its primary task of fighting for survival. At every level, from Hitler's private war conferences to the lowest levels of civil service, full cooperation between rivals was hard to find.

This counter-productive bickering applied to Goebbels and most of the Nazi inner circle, and to von Schirach, too. Their rivalry dated from the early days of the Nazi Party. The handsome and urbane von Schirach was everything Goebbels was not. Goebbels joined the party in 1924 on the heels of the Beer Hall Putsch in Munich in November of 1923, and von Schirach joined in 1925.

Despite the crippling deformity of his right foot, the frail-looking *Reichsminister* was every inch the ruthless street fighter. He had clawed his way to the top of the Nazi hierarchy over the bodies of his enemies, both figuratively and literally. After the debacle at Stalingrad he called for Total War and showed no public empathy with the plight of the common folk. For him, the state towered

---

1   National Socialist Leader of a city or district.
2   Reich Deputy. This meant more or less the same thing as *Gauleiter*, giving the person control of a region's local governments.

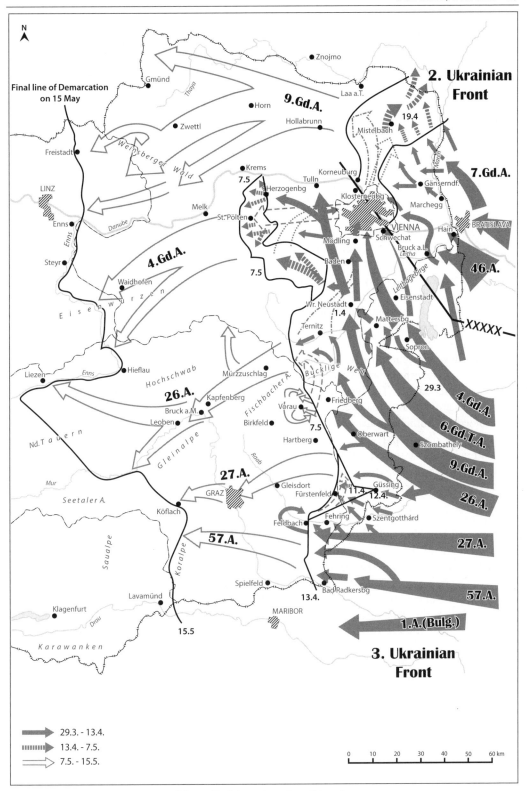

Map 1 Red Army invasion of Austria.

over the common people in importance, and he clearly saw that to stave off defeat would require every last measure the country could give. Only through a complete focus on war did the Third Reich have any hope of survival, and saving the Third Reich was his only concern.

By contrast, Schirach couldn't have been more different. Not only was he half American but three of his four grandparents were American. He was distantly related to two different signers of the Declaration of Independence. German was his second language, English his first. His marriage to Henrietta Hoffmann, the daughter of Hitler's personal photographer, Heinrich Hoffman, was blessed by the *Führer* and early in his career he became head of the Hitler Youth. Witty and polished, he was willing to prostitute himself to satiate his ambitions, while other similar early followers of Hitler, such as Putzi Hanfstaengl, were not. Von Schirach was everything most of the Nazi leadership was not. Gregor Strasser[3] referred to him as an effeminate aristocrat.

But von Schirach was also a combat veteran. In 1940 he volunteered to fight in France and was decorated for bravery, which didn't sit well with Goebbels, who never let a slight go unanswered, whether real or imagined, and any honor for a rival he saw as a personal affront.

As the *Gauleiter* of Vienna, von Schirach reveled in living an aristocratic lifestyle with his lovely and petite wife by his side. He loved fine dining, the opera, literature and art. He was anti-Semitic, yet also protested bad treatment of Jews and Eastern peoples. Goebbels often clashed with him on cultural matters, desiring that Berlin become the cultural center of the Reich, while von Schirach wanted it to remain Vienna. Since Goebbels was jealous of any intrusion on what he considered his areas of influence, this only made their relationship worse.

By extension, with von Schirach's tacit blessing Vienna's privileged class continued to live a luxurious lifestyle right until the end. A classic example is that of the Russian princess Marie Vassiltchikov, who attended a dinner party on the night of 7 March 1945, in a special room at the legendary Hotel Sacher. The hotel was famous for its *sachertorte,* a dense chocolate cake with an apricot filling, and was considered the pinnacle of fine dining and accommodation. Somehow it had avoided the bomb damage scattered over the inner city.

During the dinner party Vassiltchikov found herself attended by white-gloved waiters, ate pheasant personally hunted by her host and drank champagne kept chilled in silver buckets. There is no word whether von Schirach attended the dinner or not, yet it is exactly the sort of party he loved. Vassiltchikov left Vienna on 1 April.

* * *

For common folk Vienna had become a gray city of drifting ash and dust, but not for the ruling class. Winter had been harsh as a coal shortage left the city's citizens shivering in their flats, unless you had Party connections. The gas lines and electric grid had been badly damaged, turning those basic utilities into an unreliable luxury. Street cars ran only at midday. Ordinary people wandered the streets with one eye on the nearest air raid shelter, scrounging for the barest essentials of life. Yet reports from the Nazi secret services, chiefly the SD, the *Sicherheitsdienst,*[4] made it clear that while everybody was sick of the war, very few would act on their disgust. Most Viennese were simply exhausted. They were sick of the war and sick of their *Gauleiter.*

This, then, was Baldur von Schirach, a man out of touch with his responsibilities who, throughout his career, seemed to shoot himself in the foot with regularity, yet somehow survived in the vicious hierarchy of the Third Reich. In a famous visit to Hitler's home, the Berghof, in 1943, Henrietta von Schirach pressed Hitler about abuses of Jews she had seen in Holland. Furious

---

3   Strasser died on 30 June 1934, in the Night of the Long Knives purge of the SA leadership. In the early days of the Nazis Strasser was instrumental in organizing and expanding the party.

4   The SS Secret Service.

at being confronted with the truth of the Holocaust in his own home, Hitler left the room. And although the von Schirachs were thereafter banned from the Berghof, he remained *Gauleiter* of Vienna.

Nor was Hitler blind to his deficiencies. In his diary entry for 24 April 1943, Goebbels recounts a conversation between Hitler and *Reichsminister* Albert Speer concerning von Schirach's views on the conduct of the war: "Von Schirach hasn't the faintest idea about total war and tries again and again to torpedo it. The Führer…fears that Von Schirach has fallen into the clutches of the Viennese reactionaries and no longer sees the interests of the Reich clearly."[5]

Goebbels then showed how viciously petty he could be toward his enemies: "The Führer has a low opinion of von Schirach… He has not shown any political sense and is no grown-up Nazi. He now suddenly speaks with an American accent and rolls his 'rs' like an actor".[6]

Among his myriad failures, von Schirach had been responsible for construction of the Southeast Wall, the so-called *Reichsschutzstellung*. The plan was to have fortifications similar to the West Wall[7] along the Austrian border which retreating German forces could occupy and use to stop the oncoming Russians. Construction materials and manpower were in short supply but von Schirach only paid it lip service, anyway. It wasn't in his nature to pay attention to details, so by the time it was needed the *Reichsschutzstellung* was nothing more than a few trenches and tank traps. Goebbels' skeptical opinion of his leadership had proved correct.

* * *

The *Gauleiter* of Vienna made for a terrible Nazi. He was an early admirer of Hitler's, joining the party in 1925. Yet he didn't start learning German until age five. His father was a member of the German nobility, a theater director, ducal chamberlain and retired cavalry captain, Carl Baily Norris von Schirach.

He was a man of stark contradictions. Von Schirach undoubtedly had organizational talents, as his creation of the *Hitlerjugend*, the Hitler Youth, clearly shows. He was rabidly anti-Semitic, with 65,000 Jews deported from Vienna after he became *Gauleiter* in 1940. He was personally brave, yet terrified of air raids, which drew the scorn of the Viennese. They joked that he scurried into his fortified bunker and left them to fend for themselves.

Many in the Nazi hierarchy shared Strasser and Goebbels' opinion of him as a dilettante. Patronage of the arts was a major part of his life and fueled his feud with Goebbels, who believed Viennese cultural life fell under his jurisdiction but was opposed by von Schirach. In photographs he often had a startled look, like a mouse caught foraging in a pantry.

With the Red Army bearing down on Vienna, von Schirach's uncanny ability to make a bad situation worse did just that. Rumors had circulated for months that Vienna might be declared an open city, much like Rome, and would not suffer further damage through house-to-house fighting. So when, on 30 March, he declared martial law, it only served to panic the public, since the government already had all the power it needed to enforce order. Then, on 1 April, in a typical von Schirach move, he banned all private vehicles from leaving Vienna. This was not only unnecessary, it was stupid. By this point there effectively were no private vehicles left, and fuel for the handful remaining was unobtainable anyway. Government vehicles that did have access to fuel were not covered by the ban anyway, leading to an Easter Sunday where the roads leading west out of Vienna were already clogged as any government

5   Lochner, Louis, editor and translator, *The Goebbels Diaries* (New York: Popular Library, 1948), p. 392.
6   Lochner, *Goebbels*, p. 414.
7   Commonly known as the Siegfried Line, the Westwall was a series of fortifications built between 1938 and 1940 along Germany's western border.

functionary who could leave, did, in whatever vehicle he could scrounge, requisition or steal. So the practical effect of von Schirach's order concerning private vehicles was simply to panic the population further.

* * *

In a classic example of wasting resources, *Reichsführer-SS* Heinrich Himmler showed up in Vienna on board his private armored train. On Hitler's orders he had come to personally chastise Sepp Dietrich for his alleged failure during *Unternehmen Frühlingserwachen*, and to enforce the Cuff Band Order. Theoretically his confrontation would have inspired the *Waffen-SS* to fight hard enough to stop the Red Army, which shows how delusional Hitler's view of events had become; the *Waffen-SS* men looked to their combat officers for leadership, not the SS bigwigs, and their officers knew it. The loyalty of hard-bitten and heavily armed combat veterans now counted for more than that of sallow bureaucrats. In their eyes Himmler had largely become irrelevant.

Himmler met Sepp Dietrich on 28 March and the commander of 6. *SS-Panzerarmee* was in no mood to be understanding of Himmler's situation at *Führer* Headquarters. Dietrich arrived at the meeting accompanied by a mixed platoon of *Panzergrenadiers* riding in SPWs, and some *Wirblewinden*, the *Flakpanzer* with a turret mounted on a Panzer Mark IV chassis and four 20mm cannon.[8] The message was crystal clear; he, Dietrich, now had the firepower of the *Waffen-SS* on his side. Himmler is said to have paled at the sight.

Himmler lied to Dietrich and pretended to have defended him to Hitler, but Dietrich knew better. Hitler's personal SS adjutant, Otto Günsche, was a member of the *LAH* and had served under Dietrich when he commanded the division. Günsche let Dietrich know beforehand that Himmler groveled under Hitler's harangue and, in modern parlance, threw Dietrich under the bus. To a rough man of action like Dietrich there was nothing more craven than a lying coward.

But as he usually did, Himmler had ulterior motives for going south. After doing as Hitler had ordered and scolding Dietrich, Himmler took a detour to Vienna and tried to mitigate the crimes of the Holocaust in a ridiculous belief that the Allies would negotiate with him if something happened to *der Führer*. He spoke with von Schirach about evacuating Jews left in Vienna who worked in vital industries to nearby Mauthausen, but doing so in a humane way, with proper food and medical care, and by motor transport. Somehow, he believed their testimony would save him from postwar prosecution. This occurred during a brief period where Himmler had called a halt to all executions and issued new and drastically better orders for the treatment of Jews and prisoners throughout the Reich.

Not wanting to upset the head of the SS, von Schirach complied, but the Jews were evacuated on foot, not by transport. *Gauleiters* answered to the head of the Nazi Party, Martin Bormann, and the SS had no power over them without Bormann's blessing. At this stage, Bormann was actively scheming against everybody in Hitler's inner circle, including Himmler, so condemnation of a *Gauleiter* would have had to come from Hitler himself. Von Schirach knew all of this and wasn't about to waste precious fuel or transport on some scheme of Himmler's to try and save his own skin.

And so, as Himmler and von Schirach spent time scheming to save themselves, around them the Viennese mourned their ruined city. And the most egregious scar among all of the historic monuments and cultural achievements that had already been destroyed was the earthen mound erected

---

8   It was found that the 20mm guns didn't have enough killing power against the late-war fighter-bombers and bombers they encountered, but against infantry the four cannon were deadly.

in the Heldenplatz. It was a backdrop for target practice by the *Volkssturm* and *Hitlerjugend* units being organized to defend the city, which seemed the most hideous crime of all to the Viennese.

* * *

Wehrmacht Commandant of Vienna *Generalleutnant* Ludwig Merker had been appointed *Kampfkommandant,* Battle Commander, of the city on 26 March, a post he would hold for a week. Nothing shows the German penchant for overlapping authority more than this largely irrelevant position. A *Kampfkommandant* rarely had more than local forces under his control and couldn't do much to defend the city he'd been personally appointed to save, yet failing to fight to the last bullet during Nazi Germany's dying weeks could be a death sentence not only for the man on the spot, but for his family as well. In the weeks to come *Gauleiter* Fritz Wächtler of *Gau Bayreuth* would be shot for desertion, proving that even the highest Party official wasn't immune to the madness sweeping the dying Reich.

Being *Kampfkommandant* of Vienna was, therefore, tantamount to a suicide mission and Merker knew it. Fifty years old, he had commanded *35. Infanterie-Division* in Russia during the brutal winter of 1942-43, among other assignments, and was a brave, skillful officer. His relief was likely palpable when responsibility for defending Vienna would shortly be given to another unlucky general.

Falling bombs

Beginning in June 1944, and escalating throughout March of 1945, the US Fifteenth Air Force's campaign against Vienna crushed parts of the city into powder. Transportation and oil facilities were targeted, but bombs fell everywhere. For example, on 13 March both the Burg Opera House and the *Staatsoper,* the Vienna State Opera House, were smashed and rendered unusable as burned out hulks. Perhaps the greatest blow to Viennese morale was the loss of the Opera's huge costume wardrobe, an irreplaceable asset. People of all classes loved the Opera House and performances were a frequent topic in the city's countless cafes. The skies over Vienna rained explosives from June 1944 until the end of March.

But not all of the horror stories about the bombings are true. One myth that has lingered into the 21st Century concerns St Stephen's Cathedral being struck on 12 April by 22-ton bombs that destroyed most of the structure. Not only did this not happen, it was impossible for three reasons. First, the largest bomb of the Second World War was the 22,000 pound British Grand Slam. The claim of the cathedral being struck by 22-ton bombs appears to have come from an incorrect transposition of pounds and tons. Second, and unfortunately for this otherwise incredible story, the Americans never used this bomb, and the British never bombed Vienna. In fact it was only used on a few occasions, since only specially fitted Lancaster bombers could carry it. And third, by 12 April the Red Army had already occupied St Stephensplatz, where the Cathedral was located, so the Americans would have been bombing Russian territory. It wasn't bombing that destroyed the Cathedral, it was fires spreading from other causes.

Other churches throughout the city were hit, however, including Vienna's allegedly oldest one, the Ruprechtskirche, founded somewhere around the end of the Eighth Century.[9] The Neulerschenfeld Church was more or less totally destroyed, while the Salvator Church in the inner city showed evidence of damage from both aerial bombs and ground combat. The latter stands a

---

9   The debate about whether or not it truly is the oldest church in the city goes on to this day.

few blocks from the Danube Canal and photographic evidence shows what appears to be bullet damage around a balcony that would have made a perfect machine gun position.

The University of Vienna wasn't spared, either. Although its campuses were spread over the city, the main complex, affectionately known as *Die Uni,* sat in a prominent spot on the Ringsstrasse, adjacent the Rathaus,[10] and two blocks down from Parliament. Gaping holes were left in the main building and the Anatomical Institute, where the Lecture Hall was gutted. The Zoological, Law and Chemical Institutes all suffered heavy damage.

With historical irony to make even a hardened skeptic wonder if the gods of war might be inflicting their sense of humor on humanity, the balcony on the Hofburg from which Adolf Hitler spoke to the masses after the *Anschluss*[11] had sheared off during a bombing raid. The Hofburg was the Imperial Palace at one end of the Heldenplatz. Flanked by the incredibly well appointed Museums of Natural History and Art History, with the soaring statue of Archduke Charles in its center, the Heldenplatz was the crowning jewel of the Ringsstrasse, the worthy center of a mighty empire. But the Art History Museum had been struck by 24 bombs over the course of time, with the memorial statue of Viennese painter Moritz von Schwind having its head and limbs blown off. Fortunately for posterity, the Nazis had evacuated the art displayed in the museum and it was not damaged.

The world famous Donnerbrunnen fountain in the Neuer Markt wasn't so lucky. Baroque in design, with traces of ancient influences, it was one of two fountains sculpted in Vienna by Raphael Donner in 1737-39, and was near the Imperial Crypt in the Capuchin Church. It took a direct bomb hit and lay in pieces around the market.

The Viennese did not take their art lightly, and went to extraordinary lengths to protect what they could. Monuments too large to move were sometimes encased in bricks to protect them, such as the Prinz *Eugen* Monument. But some of their most cherished places could not be saved. The Imperial Palaces were all badly hit, with the front of the Schwarzenburg sliding downward like a lava flow and Schönbrunn looking more like ruins in the Roman Forum than the former residence of Emperor Franz Joseph. To the Viennese, however, nothing hurt worse than destruction to the Zoo, where more than half the animals died in the bombing and many more were let loose in the city. Many more succumbed to the hunger pangs of the population.

One loss that seemed appropriate was the Hotel Metropole. After the *Anschluss* it became Gestapo Headquarters, but when the bombers were done with it not one wall remained standing. The Rathaus and Parliament also took hits in the same attack that smashed the University, although the Rathaus Bells survived.

The city's utilities weren't so lucky. By 1 April the gas was shut off and electrical service was sporadic at best. The Municipal Gas-Works were a wreck, with the pipe-lines punctured in more than 2,000 places and even the largest underground pipes severed by bombs. The Municipal Electric Works were no better off with 90 percent of the grounds either damaged or destroyed, causing electricity to be off most of the time. This made cooking and storing food problematic, assuming there was food to be had in the first place. And the ground fighting was yet to come.

Garbage was no longer collected. The main building of the Vienna Fire Brigade took direct hits and three fire houses were destroyed, hampering the city's limited ability to fight fires. That no longer mattered, however, since the remaining fire fighting teams would be ordered out of the city. And the rail network had come in for particular attention by the bombers. Before it was all over

---

10   Town Hall.
11   The union of Germany and Austria in 1938. Ostensibly this was voted on by the Austrians, but in the eyes of the world it was a conquest by the Germans. This distinction would later lead to Austria's being treated as a liberated country, not a conquered one.

more than half of the passenger cars would either be damaged or destroyed, and the rail lines cut in countless places.

On that Easter Sunday, damage was apparent throughout the city, a constant reminder of the war. As far as the eye could see there were nothing but houses without roofs, or lonely chimneys stretching skyward like accusing fingers.

Even buildings showing little exterior damage could be burnt out hulks behind their facades, such as the Heinrichshof, across the street from the State Opera House. A nearby apartment block, the Philliphof, collapsed and buried some two hundred people. They are still entombed there to this day. Kärtnerstrasse, the city's famous shopping district, suffered more than most, where the opulent Hotel Grand Duke Charles was a total loss.

Fifty movie theaters were wiped out and damage to the fabled Prater, Vienna's park area, was nearly total. The Prater was then, as now, something of a tree-lined wonderland north of the Danube Canal in Leopoldstadt. Colorful pennants and striped awnings attracted the Viennese for a pleasant holiday outing, and under normal circumstances a sunny Easter Sunday, such as the one in 1945, would have attracted overflowing crowds. But that year Vienna had far more dangerous concerns.

An estimated 3,506 homes were destroyed in the bombing, and another 8,742 damaged. This doesn't include the military targets, such as rail yards and oil refineries, or the damage yet to come in the street fighting. Nor does it include the destruction of some of Vienna's most iconic landmarks.

The Zircus Busch, a multi-purpose structure opened in 1882 for a different purpose but converted to a circus in 1892, featured a variety of acts and stations, where the citizenry could see everything from a traveling Rumanian circus to plays. In 1895 Gabor Steiner created Venice in Vienna, which included an artificial lagoon to simulate the famous canals. But perhaps nothing symbolized the Prater more than the iconic *Riesenrad*, the giant Ferris wheel erected in 1897 which stood as the tallest in the world until 1985.[12]

On 30 March the Americans called off the bombings as the Russians approached. During the last raid the fire brigades were overwhelmed and couldn't fight all the fires as the streets were clogged with rubble. Even the Schwarzenburg Palace was hit. For the Viennese life underground in the air raid shelters had become common. Railroads and street cars shut down, or were overturned as makeshift tank barriers. A total of only 41 civilian vehicles survived the attacks.

* * *

Although the US Fifteenth Air Force was finished with Vienna by 1 April, it had other targets within Austria, most notably the transportation network behind German lines. On Easter Sunday that target was Bruck an der Mur, an important rail junction in Styria on the main line from Graz to Vienna.[13]

Twenty-seven B-24 heavy bombers took off from their base in Italy and crossed over the Adriatic in glorious spring sunshine. Over Yugoslavia they faced a building wall of clouds and circled as far east as Lake Balaton to try and get around it, but were forced to turn back and land with their bombs still aboard. For one small Austrian town, at least, Easter Sunday would pass in a peace its enemies didn't intend to happen.

Other targets throughout Austria weren't so lucky, as bombers struck marshalling yards in a number of places, and P-38 fighters shot up a railroad bridge and roamed the countryside looking

---

12 One of the most famous scenes in the legendary movie set in Vienna after the Second World War, *The Third Man,* takes place on the Riesenrad. Of note are the gondolas used, since none of the originals survived the war, and how quickly this attraction had been put back in service.

13 There are two towns in Austria named Bruck, both fairly close together. One is Bruck an der Leitha, near Vienna, but Burck an der Mur was the target on 1 April.

for targets to strafe. Twelve precious locomotives went up in flames under the guns and rockets of the marauding Fork-Tailed Devils.[14] With the Red Air Force also flying behind German lines, the air space over Austria was becoming crowded with Allied aircraft.

O-5 and the Austrian Resistance

Throughout Austria, resistance groups had sprung up like mushrooms as the war progressed, but particularly in 1944 and 1945. Most had no power to act, but within Vienna one did. O-5 was the generic sign of the Austrian resistance, and in Vienna it represented a coalition of civilians and *Wehrmacht* officers who wanted to avoid street fighting in the city. They believed the city was lost anyway and saw no point in having it further damaged.

The symbol O-5 represented the word *Österreich*, where the O was the first letter of the word and the 5 meant the fifth letter of the alphabet, E. Together, OE was the abbreviation in German for *Österreich*, Austria. By the middle of March O-5 was convinced Hitler would fight for Vienna instead of declaring it an open city, as had happened with Rome. If he declared it a *festung*, a fortress, as he had done with Königsberg and Breslau and dozens of others, it would lead to the city's total destruction. As fighting raged in Hungary and the splintered units of *Heeresgruppe Süd* dodged and weaved to avoid being surrounded, Major Carl Szokoll informed a meeting of O-5 that if Vienna were defended it would meet the same fate as Budapest, that it would be destroyed in the fighting, and the only way to save it was to allow the Red Army to seize it without a fight: "If they accept our terms, we must offer to hand over the city to them."[15]

Szokoll was assigned to *Wehrkreis XVII*, Military District XVII Headquarters, and was tasked with building the defensive line around Vienna. In such a capacity he had quietly placed several *Volkssturm* battalions loyal to O-5 in the Vienna Woods, south and west of the city. At the right moment he would simply order those units withdrawn, he explained, near the spa town of Baden fourteen miles to the south. The Soviets could then march through the gap straight into the city and take the remaining defenders from the rear. In return, the Russians would look upon O-5 as the new voice of Austria. This scheme was dubbed *Unternehmen Radestky*, Operation Radetsky. The *Volkssturm* battalions he raised for his plan were therefore called *Radetsky* units.

His plan was accepted with enthusiasm. Like so many others before and after them, the members of O-5 seemed to believe the Soviets could be trusted. As it turned out, they were wrong.

Although implicated in *Unternehmen Valkyrie*, the assassination attempt on Hitler on 20 July of 1944, Szokoll somehow talked his way out of being arrested and kept his job. With the Russians nearing Vienna, Szokoll got the last thing he needed to put *Unternehmen Radetsky* into action: the exact positions and passwords for *I SS-Panzerkorps*. He called an emergency meeting of O-5 leaders for the next night, 2 April.

In the meantime, at 10:00 p.m. on 1 April, *Feldwebel* Ferdinand Kas, Szokoll's top aide, left Vienna with a driver to make contact with the Russians concerning Szokoll's plan to help them take Vienna from the rear and avoid street fighting. Artillery flashed on the horizon like a distant thunderstorm, but unlike tens of thousands of others jamming the roads leading west, Kas and his driver rode toward the sound of the guns, not away from it.

---

14   The specific German nickname for the Lockheed P-38 Lighting. Fighter bombers in general, such as the P-51 or P-47, were generically referred to as *Jabos*, short for *Jagdbombers,* or, literally, hunter bombers.
15   Toland, John, *The Last Hundred Days* (New York: Bantam, 1967), p. 374.

Hitler Youth

Meanwhile, in Vienna, Ralf Roland Ringler, former Hitler Youth leader and a combat veteran, had been drafted to turn the Viennese Hitler Youth into squads organized for combat. Since the beginning of the year efforts to mobilize Hitler Youth for combat had intensified. Throughout the Reich the last drafts of the very young and the very old had begun the previous November, with the affected men and boys either filling out units of the *Volkssturm* or creating special Hitler Youth companies. This was all on orders of the *Führer*, who left no doubt that in his mind no one was exempt from battle, regardless of age, and driven forward by Goebbels, who understood the futility but did it anyway.

At 9:00 a.m. on that Easter Sunday Ringler marched one of the city's other Hitler Youth battalions, the *Panzerjäger-Bataillon*, along with the *Volkssturm*, all of them wearing clean uniforms, around the Ringstrasse to the Hofburg, rifles shouldered and at the ready, to be sworn in. The march was a solemn procession, as Ringler put it, to show the Viennese their presence and their determination to fight for the city. The activities began with the singing of a patriotic song:

> The Holy Fatherland faces danger,
> Thy sons shall be gathered round thee.

Gauleiter von Schirach then launched into a typically bombastic speech about the danger of the hour, the seriousness of the military situation and why the boys needed to put their lives on the line for Germany.

> The ceremony was the same as it had been for seven years: serried ranks behind bundled banners, martial music, patriotic songs about death and glory, von Schirach's speech about death, heroism and transfiguration in the *Führer*'s service.[16]

Ringler listened with scorn:

> "What do these homeland warriors know, when they speak of it, what it's like to die and fall with a joyous heart for their Fatherland? Nothing, absolutely nothing at all, do they know of the filth, the blood in the dirt, the tattered people.[17] Nothing but a bundle of filth is their pride for the gladly fallen men who have brought him here, so that they themselves do not become a mangled carcass. The political leader, the speaker with the pithy phrases, was certainly not a soldier. He sees his task as political and dogmatic.[18]

The speech was typical National Socialist hoopla of the type the boys would have seen repeatedly throughout their young lives, but it was also classic von Schirach, laden with bombast and slogans. The setting itself was impressive enough, despite the bomb damage that was obvious everywhere. A mere seven years before Adolf Hitler himself had chosen the Hofburg, former seat of Imperial Austrian power, for a speech before tens of thousands of newly Germanized Austrians. In 1938 the streets were lined with bunting, flags, posters and slogans, all proclaiming the glory

---

16   Weyr, Thomas, *The Setting of the Pearl: Vienna Under Hitler 1938-1945* (Oxford University Press, 2005), p. 276.

17   In fact, von Schirach had briefly served during the Invasion of France as a *gefreiter* in a combat unit, and won the Iron Cross. *Gefreiter* was the German equivalent of a British lance corporal. Typically, a *gefreiter* was a trusted subordinate who didn't have to perform menial tasks.

18   Ringler, Ralf Roland, *Illusion einer Jugend, Hitler-Jugend in Österrech* (St Pölten: Verlag Niederösterreichisches Pressehaus, 1977), p. 153.

of the moment. The very same Heldenplatz where the boys now gathered had been a sea of happy faces amid martial pomp. The similarities were obvious, even if the irony was not. On that early spring day in 1938 war was in the future, although few knew it besides the *Führer*. Now, that war had come home to Vienna with a vengeance. The very balcony where Hitler had stood was gone, sheared off in a bombing raid.

Instead of their beloved *Führer*, however, the boys were now lined up before a different authority figure, Baldur von Schirach, the first *Reichsleiter* of the Hitler Youth. They were organized into two battalions with 600-800 boys each. One had been training since January at the *Reichsschutzstellung* and was organized as infantry, while the other formed up in March and was the *Panzerjäger-kommando*, the tank hunters.

As they stood in radiant sunshine they were filled with ideas of glory in battle and of proving their loyalty to Hitler, and it would have been unusual if they were not. After all, much of their time in the Hitler Youth was spent learning that service to *Führer* and Fatherland was the only thing that really mattered, even unto death. Most of them could remember no life before the Nazis, except perhaps as a hazy memory and for the very youngest there had been no life to speak of without Hitler leading Germany. The Austrian youths might not have been quite as indoctrinated as their German brothers, but a 14-year-old boy would have been six or seven during the *Anschluss*, leaving his most impressionable years to be molded by the Hitler Youth. And if von Schirach's speech was a rehash of everything they had been told for most of their lives, with their mothers and grandmothers watching in fear and, in some cases, pride, they could not have known the difference. Their situation and duty were clear: the dreaded eastern horde was closing on the city from north, east and south, representing the communists and Jews they had been taught to hate for their entire childhood. No German, of any age, could permit such a thing. Not in the Third Reich.

When von Schirach became *Gauleiter* of Vienna in 1940, he lost control of the Hitler Youth to Artur Axmann, who made sure the Hitler Youth were actively engaged in combat operations in 1945. Axmann defended himself after the war by stating that he did so because the homeland had been invaded and every last available soldier had to fight, but that he insisted the boys be properly trained to fight tanks at close range and must never be committed as infantry, the implication being that somehow this exonerated him.

Yet in March Axmann had issued a proclamation to German Youth that said: "There is only victory or annihilation. Know no bounds in your love of your people; equally know no bounds in your hatred of the enemy. It is your duty to watch when others tire, to stand when others weaken. Your greatest honour is your unshakeable fidelity to Adolf Hitler."[19]

Axmann's proclamation is still chilling, even now. At its core, it makes it clear that since Adolf Hitler is in danger, and while you might only be boys, we expect you to do what others could not, namely, stop the enemy juggernauts. And if this is beyond your ability, then you must die trying. If this was not word for word what von Schirach said at the Heldenplatz that Easter Sunday in 1945, it surely echoed the tone; the professional soldiers with the best weapons couldn't stop the enemy, so now we look to you boys for salvation.

The Hitler Youth being mobilized were largely in their middle teens, 16 and 17-year-olds, in response to *Generalfeldmarschall* Wilhelm Keitel's order of 3 March 1945, conscripting all youth aged 16 and over. By spring 1945, however, most 16 and 17-year-olds were already engaged in one military capacity or another, any duty ranging from helping a *Flak* battery crew to serving in *12. SS-Panzer-Division Hitlerjugend* or, in the case of some 16 and 17 year old Hungarian *Volksdeutsche*, in the *37. Freiwilligen-Kavallerie-Division der Waffen SS Lützow* or even *31.*

---

19   Le Tissier, Tony, *Race for the Reichstag: The 1945 Battle for Berlin* (Barnsley: Pen & Sword, 2010), p. 25.

Freiwilligen-Grenadier-Division der Waffen SS. Arnold Friesen, one of the highest-scoring panzer aces of the war and then a Panther commander in *2. SS-Panzer-Division Das Reich*, soon to be a hero of the defense of Vienna, fought at Kursk in 1943 when he was 17. And the Hitler Youth of Vienna were chiefly born in 1928, making them already at least 16. Thus, boys of 16 and 17 were mostly mobilized already, so the practical effect of Keitel's order was minimal. More to the point, across Germany the true ages of Hitler Youth being brought into the fight were often much younger than 16, with some as young as 10 years old.

Ringler implies the Easter gathering was broken up by an air raid. If true, this was an attack by Russian aircraft, not American. The Americans were done with Vienna. Whether that happened or not, once von Schirach was done with his harangue he ordered the four assembled battalions of motorized *Volkssturm*, including the Hitler Youth, to the front. This order was not well received. What happened next shows just how far order had already broken down in a city the Nazis still controlled with an iron fist. Goebbels had filled up page after page of his diary discussing civil unrest in the West, but it was not only in the West.

Weyr describes the scene that followed this way: in 1944 one of the German security services recorded the following quote from a German woman: "It's always claimed that the *Führer* was sent to us from God. I don't doubt it. The *Führer* was sent to us from God – though not in order to save Germany but to ruin it."[20]

Having such sentiments as an undercurrent of the German population during the last year of the war is astonishing, considering the punishments they could bring and the security mechanisms in place to administer those punishments, but for women to express such thoughts expresses just how demoralized the Germans had become.

Vienna has always had its share of free thinkers and non-conformists. The Nazis did their best to expurgate those people but it was only successful to a point. After centuries of radicalism from both ends of the political spectrum, combined with a love of rich food and a lifestyle centered on opera, pageants and long talks in café bars, seven years hadn't been enough to wipe it out entirely. Food shortages and rising prices on basic staples only made civilian morale worse.

On 6 March 1945, quoting a document from *Wehrkreis VXII*, the military district of Vienna: "The mood here is very depressed. Everybody is tired of the war. Outright destructive tendencies are noticeable. Only a very few still believe in victory."[21] Factory workers had grown more and more resentful. The Viennese opinion of von Schirach had never been good but now plunged even lower. Nor did the complaints stop with their *Gauleiter*; not even Hitler was off limits anymore.

So when women, the non-political sex of the Third Reich, the silent sex that was supposed to do what it was told, rose up and demanded that the Nazis leave their city alone, and leave their men alone, it should have come as no surprise. The displeasure had been there a long while, but open rebellion was something new to Vienna.

The Viennese demonstrations, although moderate, showed just how little authority von Schirach commanded in the eyes of the citizenry. They were more afraid of the Russians, who were coming, than of their *Gauleiter*, who was still there. For any public disobedience to be displayed at all shows just how far Viennese morale had slipped; German civilians knew full well the consequences for disobedience. Ian Kershaw puts it this way, "the Nazi regime remained an immensely strong dictatorship…prepared to use increasingly brutal force in controlling and regimenting German

20 Rees, Lawrence, *7 Secret's of Hitler's Charisma http://www.huffingtonpost.com/laurence-rees/7-secrets-of-hitlers-charisma_b_3104664.html?icid=maing-grid7\main5\dl6\sec1_lnk3 percent26pLid percent3D304703#slide=2350753*, (accessed 29 April 2013).

21 Ringler, Ralf Roland, *Illusion einer Jugend, Hitler-Jugend in Österrech* (St Pölten: Verlag Niederösterreichisches Pressehaus, 1977), p. 272.

society at more or less every point. It left little room for opposition – recognizably as suicidal as it was futile."[22]

The mustering of the *Volkssturm* and the Hitler Youth throughout the Reich meant untold thousands of parents watched their boys marched off to war as this final levy was drafted for a final defense. But to what end, the mothers of Vienna wondered on that sun-splashed Easter morning? They were being asked to sacrifice their sons, but to what purpose? Could boys stop what veteran SS men could not? And what about the scratch conventional units being thrown together by whatever manpower could be found, how were they faring? Rolf Michaelis answers the questions this way: "During the fighting it was observed that the new units quickly lost their ability to resist. Again and again scratch units were formed from less capable personnel, Viennese policemen for example. Without training and equipment they suffered enormous losses."[23]

It was all futile, the sacrifices pointless, and the mothers of Vienna knew it. With the fate of their children hanging in the balance, some of them were no longer willing to knuckle under.

* * *

After the assembly on the Heldenplatz, Ringler met with his Area Leader to discuss various matters. He was told that conflicting orders between the *Gauleiter*, von Schirach, and the *Kampfkommandant*, made it hard to know whom to obey. Those two men bitterly fought about who commanded the *Volkssturm*, which also included the Hitler Youth, and each issued conflicting orders. Picking the wrong side was dangerous, so the Area Leader had so far picked neither.

An argument erupted when Ringler objected to the battalion's name *Werwolf*, fearing that if the boys were captured they would be treated as partisans, not prisoners of war. He put the response he received this way:

> Hans wipes this objection away – once they were captured, would it matter? They had to fight in such a way as not to be captured. Everything happening was irregular, and not to be judged by normal standards. If the boys were called Werewolves, they would take pride in it and fight like Werewolves.
>
> "Territorial Leader," I replied again. "That's what regular soldiers are doing."
>
> "Now they [the Hitler Youth] are too."
>
> "As if one could command such a thing."[24]

After an air raid alarm in the afternoon, Ringler sat up late into the night with his friends, making a list of everything they needed and trying to figure out how to procure it. Shovels, compasses and watches were near the top of the list, but mobility was number one.

Gasoline was scarce, even for high priority military purposes. To assure the battalion of reliable transportation, the chief of staff declared they would confiscate all the bicycles they could find on the basis of the *Reichsleistungsgesetzes,* the Reich Benefit Law, which allowed authorized state personnel to take any private property they deemed necessary for the defense of the Reich. To that end, flyers were printed up to hand out to anyone whose bike was taken, as a sort of receipt. After the war, the government promised to replace the bike. Cyclists would be stopped on the street and the bikes taken on the spot. Requisitions were scheduled to begin the next day, 2 April.

---

22   Kershaw, Ian, *The End: The Defiance and Destruction of Hitler's Germany, 1944-1945* (New York: The Penguin Press, 2011), p. 162

23   Ringler, *Illusion*, p. 135.

24   Ringler, *Illusion*, p. 154.

After the day's activities and the hours of planning, Ringler was exhausted, but was given some pills that had the magical effect of sharpening thinking and dispelling fatigue. Throughout the war the German armed forces had lived on methamphetamines, and now the Hitler Youth leaders would, too.

* * *

In the Slovakian capital city, Bratislava, one of the two Viennese Hitler Youth battalions had been trucked in and now stood in the front lines. The city's *Kampfkommandant, Oberst* von Ohlen, scattered the boys throughout the eastern region to aid and protect the flood of refugees pouring into the city. Von Ohlen had led a *Kampfgruppe* of the *178. Infanterie-Division* during the Slovak uprising the previous autumn, and was an experienced combat officer, but like most professional Army officers he was appalled at sending boys as young as 10 years old into combat and instead gave them jobs helping the troops.

The battalion had been sent into Bratislava to help build tank traps and fortify anti-tank guns behind field fortifications. They had been training along the Southeast Wall, the *Reichsschutzstellung*, since January. Once in Bratislava they were reinforced by heavy machine guns and anti-tank weapons. The total strength was around 800 men and boys but at least most of their group leaders were combat veterans. The rank and file carried light infantry weapons and *Panzerfauste*.

Among the other defenses of *Festung Pressburg*, Pressburg being the German name for Bratislava, were some 80 tanks and self-propelled guns of various makes, models and condition, a dozen batteries of Hlinka's Guard[25] of different calibers, Slovak Army anti-aircraft batteries and fragments and remnants of a number of German and Hungarian infantry divisions, largely stragglers who'd been collected and sent back to the front. There were even two German armored trains. In addition to those forces were a security division, some fortress troops, 23rd and 24th Hungarian Infantry Divisions, and shattered elements from five divisions that showed up during the fight, those divisions being the *27. Infanterie-Division, 98. Infanterie-Division, 211. Infanterie-Division, 287. Infanterie-Division* and *377. Infanterie-Division*. The *211. Infanterie-Division* remained cohesive after the battle, although depleted to a *kampfgruppe*.

On 1 April the Captain of the *Feuerschutzpolizei*, the Fire Protection Police, *Major* Walter Lentz, cobbled together an alarm battalion from *Luftwaffe* volunteers and miners evacuated from western Germany, with an approximate strength of around 300 men. Like most such units it had no heavy weapons and only a few machine guns. Before Bratislava fell, *Kampfgruppe Lentz* would suffer 23 dead and 40 wounded. The battalion was later attached to *Grenadier-Regiment 283* from *96. Infanterie-Division*.

The plan had been for the Hitler Youth to occupy positions until regular units retreating from the Gran Front could take them over. Like so many plans, this one didn't survive contact with the enemy. The Russians overran the Gran Front and shattered the defenders, and those ruined units flooded the city heading west. *Oberst* von Ohlen made no attempt to stop them because he knew that he couldn't. Other troops scheduled to replace them didn't arrive before the Russians did on 1 April, so there was nobody to take over the positions of the Hitler Youth. Only in the next few days would *Kampfgruppe Lentz* relieve the boys. Lentz's battalion would be deployed near the rail line to Pezinok, with the *Festung-Bataillon Herzog* on their right, and the two battalions of *Grenadier-Regiment 283* on their left. But that was in days to come.

On Easter Sunday the Russians attacked with Katyushas, infantry and tanks. The Katyusha was a multiple rocket launcher, usually mounted on a truck, as a Russian variation on the German *nebelwerfer*. On Bratislava's northern flank the attackers sliced through *Volkssturm* positions held by a contingent of old men and von Ohlen was forced to block them with the Hitler Youth.

---

25 The name for the Slovakian Militia, it was named for Andrej Hlinka, an important activist for the Slovak People's Party before the war.

Despite the tornado of fire and steel the Russians brought to bear, they were stopped by the boys with the loss of three tanks, while the Hitler Youth reportedly suffered no casualties. It was a hint of things to come.

* * *

The aggressive protests of the mothers of Vienna were by no means the only sign that order was breaking down; it was happening in the *Wehrmacht*, too, and the Nazi leadership took draconian steps to stop it. Stragglers and deserters mixed with refugees on the roads leading anywhere away from danger. This not only clogged the roads but also hampered the lines of communication of *Wehrmacht* units. As the front moved farther and farther west, German soldiers travelling behind the lines faced dangers of a different sort than Russian bullets or bombs. Valid travel papers were required for men behind the front and checkpoints were set up to verify and validate them on a daily basis. A man on required business with valid papers had to check in with local command posts and have his papers signed, dated and stamped, otherwise he faced the danger of encountering the *Ordnungspolizei*,[26] the *feldgendarmerie*,[27] the local police or some other security force appointed by this or that Nazi official or organization, or brutal *Wehrmacht* commander. If his papers were in order he might then draw rations from a local source and continue on with the mission at hand. Care had to be taken, however, not to appear as if you were taking a longer detour to avoid duty or delay return to your unit. Soldiers were being hung or shot for little or no reason, sometimes even with the proper papers. They would first be hauled before a flying courts-martial lasting a few minutes or less, then executed, sometimes shot and sometimes hung, usually with a placard hung around their necks declaring them a coward or traitor, and then forgotten.

Indeed, in some places fliers were posted declaring that soldiers wandering behind the front were enemies of the German people and that civilians were enjoined not to give them food or shelter, but instead to report them. Werner Mork served as a messenger further north in the area of Cottbus, but his experiences during this period were universal for German soldiers dispatched on such missions. He verifies that civilians were encouraged to despise their own army and look to their own defense in the form of the *Volkssturm*: "Citizens, many women in particular, were encouraged to think of German soldiers as slackers and deserters… These fliers made clear the general impression that the army, and by that we mean the regular army, not the *Waffen-SS*, was no longer trusted and that they would haphazardly show cowardice before the enemy."[28]

Nor did written orders from a valid command always protect a man. One man from *Jagdgeschwader 52* on a mission for his commanding officer, and possessing all necessary passes and papers, was shot anyway. As order crumbled within the Reich, the only things a man could absolutely rely on for safety were his close comrades and a loaded weapon.

* * *

With the Russians driving hard on Vienna from the northeast, east and south, and skirting west as had become their signature when attacking a major city with an eye to surrounding it, von Schirach went on the radio and introduced Sepp Dietrich to the population.[29] After years of the government glorifying the *Waffen-SS* Dietrich was well known, a household name that carried authority and reassurance. The previous December's attack in the Ardennes had been big news all

---

26   The much feared Order Police.
27   The Field Police, essentially the German version of the American Military Police, the *feldgendarmerie* often worked in close cooperation with the security organizations of the Nazi Party, such as the *Gestapo*.
28   Mork, Werner, translation by Setzer, Daniel H., *"Aus Meiner Sicht (From My View)", Excerpts from the Memoirs of Werner Mork* <http://www.dansetzer.us/Mork/Mork_EastFront_1945_Pt3.pdf> (Accessed 11 June 2017).
29   Sources disagree on what day this happened; some say 1 April, others the 2nd.

over the Reich and Dietrich was one of the two army commanders who got all the publicity. Also, as commander of *6. SS-Panzerarmee*, his name had been in the Vienna newspapers for weeks.

"I'm not a man of big words or polished speech," Dietrich said. "Besides, today deeds count for much, words for very little." He promised to do "everything humanly possible" to save Vienna. "More would be foolhardy. The battle will be hard, victory difficult."[30] In other words, and to those used to listening to the cautious, hedged comments of their leaders, Dietrich promised to do what he could, but warned not to expect much. Vienna was going to be overrun and there was nothing he could do about it.

Among the military, Dietrich's view of the situation was not a secret. Urban combat was coming to Vienna but in the end it would do no good; the city was going to be captured by the Red Army.

* * *

But Vienna was not defenseless against the coming Soviet onslaught. Because of its industry, port facilities and oil refineries the city had been heavily defended by anti-aircraft artillery, primarily the deadly 88mm multi-purpose gun, which could double as either fire support or anti-tank artillery. There were smaller caliber guns too, and there was one ace in the hole for the defense; the three *Flak* towers and their accompanying targeting towers. The towers had 88mm guns but also the fearsome 128mm cannon. Mounted in concrete casemates atop towers more than 100 feet high and up to nine feet thick, they could not be depressed to fire at specific land targets, however, like their counterparts in the Tiergarten *Flak* tower in Berlin, they proved excellent counter-battery or interdictory weapons. In the coming days they would ravage Russian columns on the southern fringes of the city.

The Germans built the large, expensive, expansive *Flak* towers in only three cities during the war: Berlin, Hamburg and Vienna. Why Vienna? Author Michael Foedrowitz explains it this way:

> The job of the *Flak* towers, in addition to coordinating anti-aircraft defense, did not consist primarily of shooting down enemy aircraft, but to hinder their flights over certain areas of the cities, whether the government buildings of Berlin, within the triangle of *Flak* towers built there or the cultural metropolis of Vienna, which Hitler classified as valuable.[31]

Certainly the Americans learned that flying over the towers was dangerous in the extreme. Of all the cities of the Reich that could have used the additional anti-aircraft defenses, whether the manufacturing centers of the Ruhr, the rocket testing grounds at Peenemunde or a transportation hub, it is indicative of the value Hitler placed on the capital of his homeland that they were built there. Was this only because of Vienna's industries and oil refineries? Or was there more to it than mere pragmatism? Given Hitler's love-hate relationship with the city, pouring so much in terms of time, money and scarce manpower and resources, to protect what he viewed as cultural treasures, does not seem outlandish, even for the *Führer*. Given his later decision to station his best forces in the south, near Budapest and Vienna, the *Flak* towers might be seen as a precursor to this decision, a clue that perhaps he valued the former capital of his homeland more than he wanted to admit.

* * *

Over the previous year numerous reorganizations of the panzer divisions had tried to compensate for dwindling numbers. The Allies' Strategic Bombing Campaign had a profound effect on not

---

30 Weyr, Thomas, *The Setting of the Pearl: Vienna Under Hitler 1938-1945* (Oxford: Oxford University Press, 2005), p. 275.
31 Foedrowitz, Michael, *The Flak Towers in Berlin, Hamburg and Vienna 1940-1950* (Atglen: Schiffer, 1998), p. 3.

only synthetic oil production but also construction of panzers. On that very Easter Sunday the Reich's most important industrial area, the Ruhr, had been surrounded by the meeting of the US First and Ninth Armies. Now not even the reduced factory output of the past few months would reach the front lines.

In response, considerable effort was expended in rewriting tables of organization to spread the few resources available over as broad a swath as possible. This was done by reducing the authorized strength of all panzer divisions, both in men and machines. On 1 March the SS Panzer Divisions were ordered reorganized according to the new Tables of Organization by 15 March, and on 1 April new regulations for the Army were issued. Panzer divisions too weak to be organized along the new lines were renamed *Kampfgruppe* Panzer Divisions, with their even further reduced authorized strengths. How unrealistic were these new tables? Even a *Kampfgruppe* panzer division was authorized to have 54 panzers and 22 *Jagdpanzers*.[32] No unit in the German inventory had anything close to those numbers.

The new SS regulations reduced the numbers of *Panzergrenadiers* and artillery. Germany had long since scraped the bottom of its manpower pool and artillery production suffered from the same issues of the manufacture of all such hard goods; lack of factories, raw materials, labor, transportation…the only thing Germany had too much of was enemies.

The timing of this reorganization was not merely pointless but showed a complete disregard for reality. To comply, the six major *Waffen-SS* formations attached to *Heeresgruppe Süd* would have had to either suspend operations in *Unternehmen Frühlingserwachen*, or make the changes while actively engaged with the enemy. They might as well have been told to use sorcery to make the Russians disappear, which, given Himmler's well-known mystic beliefs, probably would not have come as too much of a surprise.

North of the Danube

8. Armee

North and northeast of Vienna, in the Weinviertel, Austria's largest wine-growing region, *8. Armee* found itself desperately trying to find units to throw into the path of the Red Army. The lush countryside was the home of the *Grüner Veltliner* grape, the Green Veltin, which produced a very pure mineral wine of incomparable flavors. Whether made into a sparkling wine or a variety served with food, the versatile wine joined Rieslings and others from the region on many restaurant menus.

But Adolf Hitler was a teetotaler and concerned with a different fluid than wine; he was obsessed with oil, and for good reason. *8. Armee*'s mission was not only to prevent the forces south of the Danube from being outflanked on the north, but also to protect the very last sources of natural oil available to the Reich near Zistersdorf, in the state of Gänserndorf.[33] Given its critical importance, the expansion and reinforcement of the *Reichsschutzstellung* around the area from Dürnkrut to Zistersdorf and then Hohenau had been given priority. Tank traps, barricades, machine gun nests and bunkers were all hurriedly built.

To conquer this region, since 25 March the Russian offensive north of the Danube to take Bratislava and then Brno, in old Czechoslovakia, had driven the Germans back from their defensive positions along the Gran River. The attacking Russian formations were Seventh Guards Army,

---

32   Nevenkin, Kaven, *Fire Brigades: The Panzer Divisions 1943-45* (Winnipeg: J.J. Fedorowicz, 2008), p. 48.

33   In 1947 a nasty dispute broke out between the Russians and the British after the Russians stole some oil-drilling equipment from the Zistersdorf Oil Fields.

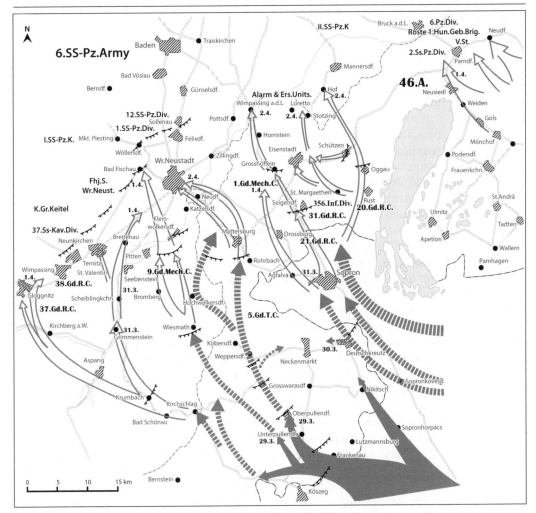

Map 2 Breakthrough south of Vienna.

Fifty-Third Army and 1st Guards Cavalry-Mechanized Group. One of the sub-units attached to Second Ukrainian Front, the Front attacking north of the Danube, was the 2nd Rumanian Tank Corps, a turncoat unit of men who formerly fought with the Germans. These formations contained a strange mixture of 205 tanks and self-propelled guns, which perfectly indicated how low on the supply chain Second and Third Ukrainian Fronts were. Among those numbers were 20 American M3 Stuart light tanks, 41 British Valentine Mark IX tanks,[34] 63 SU-76 self-propelled guns, smallest of all the Russian self-propelled guns,[35] 7 German Mark IV tanks, 8 German *Sturmgeschütz III* self-propelled guns, 9 pre-war Czech T-38 tanks built by the Germans and 24 pre-war French Renault R35/45 light tanks. Thus, of 205 total operational vehicles, only 33 were the latest model T-34/85 or SU-type SP guns, but in sheer numbers the Russians had an overwhelming advantage, not only in tanks but also in men, artillery and airpower.

---

34   The Valentine was not an impressive tank. The only reason the British still built them was at Russian request.
35   The German equivalent was the *Sturmgeschütz*.

On 1 April, Stavka ordered a continuation of operations and gave new lines of advance. Marshal Malinovsky was ordered to capture Bratislava by 5 or 6 April at the latest, and then to advance to the line Nove Mesto-Jablonica-Malacky. In addition Brno, Znojmo and Stockerau were to be taken. The area around Zistersdorf-Hohenau was a high priority, since the oil reserves of this area were the last in the Reich, and together with the Hungarian oil fields they achieved 80 percent distribution of their total production in March, even with the US Fifteenth Air Force bombing the refineries.

The Germans opposing them were a motley collection of shattered, newly raised and alarm units. Reserved to *8. Armee* headquarters were *Sturmgeschütz-Abteilung 325*[36] and *Sturmartillerie-Brigade 239*. The army commanded four corps, with *Panzerkorps Feldherrnhalle* northeast of Bratislava and *XXXXIII Armeekorps* to it south. *LXXII* and *XXIX Armeekorps* were also part of *8. Armee*.

On the army's left flank was the junction with *Heeresgruppe Mitte*. A gap existed between *8. Armee* and *6. SS-Panzerarmee* on its right flank, with no reserves to fill the undefended space. The Wienvertel had few natural defensive positions, being terraced and tilled for the extensive vineyards that gave the region its nickname of the Austrian Wine Country, but it did have some. Three significant rivers crossed the Russian line of advance, the Hron, Vah and March.

Since the autumn of 1944, Slovakia had also been included in the *Reichsschutzstellung*, which had its right-hand corner in Bratislava and then went northwards across the Little Carpathian Mountains. In addition, since February 1945, preparations had been made for the defense of Western Slovakia and South Moravia, which should have resulted in a coherent net of defenses. Along the Hron's south-west shore, the positions were extended from Ziar nad Hronom to the river mouth. To the north of Novy Tekov, the strongpoints were between 200 and 1,000 yards apart, which made them little more than trip wires, but south of them, the defenses were expanded. A second defensive zone was built from three to five miles behind the first. It also blocked access to the city of Nitra, and access to Handlova, Prievidza, and Pravno were all separately barred. Nitra and Nove Zamky had been made ready by trenches and tank traps. On the Vah and the Little Danube Rivers, only isolated guard positions were built.

West of the Vah River, the *8. Armee* exploited the mountainous terrain of the Little Carpathians, where defensive works ran north from Bratislava and were incorporated into the *Reichsschutzstellung*. That was in Slovakia. East of the Little Carpathians, as well as in the Austrian part of the *Reichsschutzstellung*, two trench systems, two to three kilometers away, had been dug, although these were of little value. Concrete obstacles had been readied to block roads, but these were stopgap measures that wouldn't delay the Russians for long. On the western side of the Little Carpathians, along the lower reaches of the March, *8. Armee* planned to take advantage of the existing Czech fortifications built to protect Czechoslovakia in the 1920s and 1930s.

As the fighting moved further west, the topography changed to hills and valleys, with stands of trees here and there, before finally becoming mountainous at the edge of the Little Carpathian Mountains. But without strong forces the rolling hills provided limited defensive advantages to work with, making the job of stopping the Russians almost impossible.

A week earlier, *8. Armee* had about 200 of what the Germans considered *panzers*, namely tanks, *Jagdpanzers* and *Sturmgeschütze*, self-propelled assault guns whose original purpose had been infantry support, but now substituted for actual tanks, with just over half that number operational. The army's ration strength was roughly 150,000 men distributed in 16 divisions, but only a third of those were combat troops.[37] Artillery tubes were well below the authorized number and

---

36 One source identifies this unit as a regiment, but no such regiment could be found in the *Wehrmacht*.
37 Rauchenstiener, Manfred, *Schriften des Heeresgeschichtlichen Museums in Wien Band 5 Krieg in Össterreich 1945* (Wien: Osterreichischer Bundesverlag Fur Unterricht, Wissenschaft und Kunst, 1970), p. 150.

the usual fuel problems afflicted movement. One week later, on 1 April, the number of panzers had dropped below 100 operational vehicles.

* * *

In early April *25. Panzer-Division* was in reserve for *Heeresgruppe Vistula* when, along with the *Führer-Grenadier-Division*, it was transferred by rail to Vienna. Between them the two divisions comprised half of the armored reserve for *Heeresgruppe Vistula*, to be used when Zhukov's inevitable and inexorable offensive against Berlin began. The *Führer-Grenadier-Division* crossed the Danube and went straight into action, but *25. Panzer-Division* never made it that far south and went into the reserve for *8. Armee* north of the Danube, with the mission of protecting the oil fields around Zistersdorf. Like so many German divisions, by this point *25. Panzer-Division* was nowhere near its full divisional strength.[38] After the severe mauling it took in Poland during January and February 1945 it had been rebuilt as a *Kampfgruppe Panzer-Division*, so on 1 April the division had some 45 operational tanks and assault guns, with another 20 under repair. Its *Panzergrenadier-Regiment 146* had a mere 1,000 men[39] and *Panzer-Artillerie-Regiment 91* only 16 guns.[40] And yet, owing to its 45 operational panzers, it was a relatively powerful formation compared to other German armored divisions.

As for the *Führer-Grenadier-Division*, although it had seen fierce combat and taken very heavy losses more than once, its status as a favored Army formation under Hitler's personal patronage meant that it was given priority for replacements in both men and materiel. Rauchensteiner reports that by early April the division was at full strength,[41] a claim backed up by von Bünau, which made it a rarity among German formations.[42]

Panzerkorps Feldherrnhalle

The history of German units named *Feldherrnhalle* is confusing. There was a *Kampfgruppe* by that name, a Panzer Brigade, a *Luftwaffe* contingent, a *Panzergrenadier* division, two Panzer Divisions, both of which were destroyed not once, but twice, and finally a *Panzerkorps*.

Like so many of Germany's premier units, *Panzerkorps Feldherrnhalle* had political patronage, representing the *Sturmabteilung*, the SA. They were the original brown-shirt bully-boys who provided security for early Nazi meetings and beat up opposition to the Nazis on the streets of Germany. The term *Feldherrnhalle* means Field Marshal's Hall, and refers to the monument on the Odeonplatz in Munich. Originally built in the 1840s to honor the Bavarian Army, it had been appropriated by the Nazis to honor the 16 men who died during the so-called Beer-Hall Putsch in 1923. In the ensuing years it became the spiritual center of Nazism.

Panzerkorps Feldherrnhalle was on the left flank of *8. Armee*. From north to south it deployed the following units to its front: *Kampfgruppe 101. Jäger-Division* on the left near Bukovac, Slovakia;[43]

---

38   By the standards of the 1945 Panzer Division, however, it was close to full strength.
39   About one full strength battalion.
40   Samuel W. Mitcham, Jr, *The Panzer Legions, A Guide to the German Army Tank Divisions of WWII and Their Commanders* (Mechanicsburg: Stackpole Books, 2007), p. 182.
41   Rauchensteiner, *Krieg in Österreich*, p. 115.
42   It should be noted that Nevenkin says the division was actually quite worn down, having few armored vehicles. As with so much from this period of the war it's hard to say for certain what the division's strength might actually have been. The author included the higher estimates based on the testimony of von Bünau, who was the source most in a position to know.
43   By 1945 two of the *101. Jäger-Division* battalions were *Osttruppen*, Eastern Troops. As discovered in Normandy, *Osttruppen* could be extremely unreliable.

Panzer Divisions *Feldherrnhalle 1*, then *Feldherrnhalle 2* and finally *Kampfgruppe 182. Infanterie-Division*.[44] Attached to the Corps headquarters were *Schwere-Panzerjäger-Abteilung 662, Schwere-Panzer-Abteilung 503* and *Sturmgeschütz-Brigade 382*. Other small remnants were parceled out to the front-line units, such as *Schwere-Panzerjäger-Abteilung 721, Sturmgeschütz-Bataillon 228* and a sprinkling of Hungarians.

All of the army's divisions were badly under-strength. The *46. Volksgrenadier-Division*, which was the recently renamed *46. Infanterie-Division*, a veteran unit, was also attached to the corps. At full strength a *Volksgrenadier-Division* should have had about 11,250 men. As an example of the size of the German divisions by this point in the war, on 24 March the rifle strength of *46. Volks-Grenadier-Division* was a sizeable 4,600 men, with a strong artillery component and eight *Sturmgeschütz III*. A regular 1944 *Infanterie-Division* should have had about 13,000 in total of all ranks. The combat strength of *357. Infanterie-Division* at this time was over 6,000 men, and its artillery detachment was even stronger than *46. Volksgrenadier-Division*. It even had a dozen *Jagdpanzer 38(t)s*, the famous *Hetzer* light tank-destroyer mounted on the modified chassis of a Czech T-38 tank.[45] Both divisions were depleted, but not shattered. However, both divisions suffered heavy losses in the Russian offensive through northwest Hungary and Slovakia which began on 25 March, so as the war moved into Austria both had shrunk quite a lot.

Most of *13. Panzer-Division* died in the siege of Budapest, but on Hitler's orders it had been partially reconstituted and thrown back into the fight for Hungary. On 23 March the rebuilt *Panzer-Division Feldherrnhalle* was renamed *Feldherrnhalle 1*, while the remnants of *13. Panzer-Division* became *Feldherrnhalle 2*. Combined with *Schwere-Panzer-Abteilung 503* on 24 March, *Panzerkorps Feldherrnhalle* was like most *Wehrmacht* formations of the day, short on tanks, fuel, ammunition and manpower.

Corps leadership was first rate. In overall command was *General der Panzertruppe* Ulrich Kleeman, winner of the Knight's Cross, veteran of the *Afrikakorps* and the officer in charge of the attack on Rhodes where the Germans fought the Italians after that country switched sides. *Feldherrnhalle 1* was commanded by veteran *Generalmajor* Günther Pape, and *Feldherrnhalle 2* was led by *Generalmajor* Dr Franz Bäke, who started as a panzer commander, became one of the top ten German panzer aces of the war, and then moved into higher command. Both men had fought through the *Konrad* attacks and *Unternehmen Frühlingserwachen*.

A stream of armored vehicles and SPWs were dispatched to the corps beginning on 23 March, but they came piecemeal and had to be committed to battle as soon as they arrived. Survivors of the two original divisions from which they took their cadres, *Panzergrenadier-Division Feldherrnhalle* and *13. Panzer-Division*, were combined with new SA recruits and various unit fragments to flesh out the sub-units. Despite the hurried nature of their formations, both divisions of the new *Panzerkorps* had the latest weapons and well-trained personnel, just not enough of them. Both were the size of brigades more than divisions. *Panzerkorps Feldherrnhalle* was, in reality, more of a reinforced panzer division than a corps.[46]

Desperate times forced every unit into the fray the moment it could move, often without any training whatsoever. According to one source[47] *Feldherrnhalle 2* reorganized itself on 31 March

---

44   Until 1 April this unit was known as the *182. Reserve-Division*.

45   The Germans themselves didn't use the name *Hetzer* for the vehicle. It's a postwar reference used by historians. It is used here because that is the name most people now know it by. More than 2,500 were built in the last year of the war.

46   Sánchez, Alfonso Escuadra, *Feldherrnhalle: Forgotten Elite, The Panzerkorps Feldherrnhalle and Antecedent Formations, Eastern and Other Fronts, 1942-1943* (Bradford: Shelf Books, 1996), p. 92.

47   Battistelli, Pier Paolo, *Panzer Divisions 1944-45* (Oxford: Osprey, 2009), p. 45.

according to the Panzer Division 1945 guidelines. If true the division didn't use the designation as a *Kampfgruppe* panzer division, as it probably should have given its rifle strength.

Operating near the ancient city of Nitra, on the north flank of *8. Armee* northeast of Bratislava, on 31 March *Feldherrnhalle 2*, still sometimes referred to as *13. Panzer-Division* until 20 April, reported a panzer strength of 10 Mark IVs and 12 Panthers, along with three motorized *Flak* vehicles, all of which were likely operational. The division's *Panzergrenadier* battalions were rated as either 'weak', or 'very weak', and its combat rating was given as IV. Weak battalions had somewhere between 100-300 men, therefore very weak battalions likely had 100 men or less.

Motorization was a paltry 40 percent, meaning less than half of the division had motorized transport, whereas panzer divisions were supposed to be 100 percent motorized. A week before its total manpower was 3,230, with a mere 1,013 men in the combat units, and by 1 April losses would have reduced that paltry number further. All artillery had either been lost or was under corps control, except for some mortars. And yet, far away in Central Germany at the Gotha Training Grounds, the division's heavy *Flak* battalion had been completely rebuilt and was at 100 percent strength in men and vehicles, and about 75 percent in materiel. Of course, that did the division no good; Central Germany was a long way from eastern Austria over a rail network under constant air attack and that powerful component would never serve with its parent headquarters.

Panzer-Division Feldherrnhalle 1, the rebuilt *Panzergrenadier-Division Feldherrnhalle*, was no better off than its divisional twin. The panzer regiment still had a few working machines: nine Mark IVs, eight Panthers, one *Jagdpanzer IV/70*, nine *Jagdpanzer 38(t) Hetzers* and one mobile *Flak*. Its infantry battalions were all rated as 'weak', while various attached formations were rated as either 'weak' or 'very weak'. The same strength return on 24 March as quoted for *Feldherrnhalle 2* showed ration strength of 6,530 and bayonet strength of 2,861. *Feldherrnhalle 1* still had two batteries of light howitzers, perhaps eight or ten guns, probably 105mm. Like its twin, the combat rating was IV, and it was 50 percent motorized.

Feldherrnhalle 2 dug into the foothills of the Little Carpathian Mountains at Smolenice, some 37 miles northeast of Bratislava, to allow a collection point for the Corps to gather and retreat. The remaining 31 Tiger IIs of *Schwere-Panzer-Abteilung Feldherrnhalle* formed a rearguard position to shield their withdrawal from the hard-charging Russians, who blundered into their line of fire and were badly shot up for their efforts. For all its many flaws, a Tiger II facing the enemy on flat ground with long sight lines and in the hands of an experienced crew, was a deadly opponent.

The *Panzerkampfwagen Tiger Ausb. B*, better known by its nicknames, the *Königstiger*, Royal Tiger in correct translation but known in America as the King Tiger or, as used in this narrative, the Tiger II, was the heaviest German panzer and only second to the monstrous *Jagdtiger* in total weight. It was very expensive to build and maintain. Arguments during the war and after have emphasized how many Panthers or *Jagdpanzer IV/70s* could have been built for every one Tiger II. But as will be shown throughout this narrative it could also dominate the battlefield in a way no other tank of the Second World War could.

Although *Feldherrnhalle* was technically an SA formation, its members had very little affiliation with that organization. For instance, *Schwere-Panzer-Abteilung 503* rarely used the term *Feldherrnhalle* in communications, since veteran members had been with the battalion for years. In a bizarre interlude, sometime in April the Chief of Staff of the SA, *Obergruppenführer* Wilhelm Schepmann, showed up without warning at Corps Headquarters so that he could spend the final days of the war "with his boys".[48]

But his boys ignored him; they had more serious work to do than entertaining some glory-driven Party official they'd never heard of before. *Schwere-Panzer-Abteilung 503*, in particular, was doing

---

48   Lochmann, *Goebbels*, p. 348.

everything it could to keep its Tiger IIs in the field, going so far as to send a group all the way to the factory in Friedrichshafen where their Maybach engines were built. The city was almost overrun by the French at that point, but somehow they not only acquired brand new engines for their panzers, but managed to get them transported all the way to the battalion's repair depot north of Vienna. Meanwhile, the remaining operational Tiger IIs, a dozen or so in all, dug in at Gerensker, west of Sered in Slovakia, and spent 1 April being heavily attacked by the Russians outside of Trvana.

That medium-sized town of some 50,000 people was representative of thousands more towns and villages like it in 1945, a historically Catholic settlement with a long, rich history, facing the flood of the officially atheist Red Army. Archeological evidence shows that human settlements on the site date back at least to the Neolithic Period and from the late Dark Ages onward it was an important center of trade. Because of its numerous Catholic Churches, Trvana was known as Little Rome. The city's name came from the Slovak word for thornbush, a plant which grew wild along the banks of the numerous small rivers in the region.

Schwere-Panzer-Abteilung 503 fought hard to defend Trvana, buying time for the refugees who flooded the city to stay one step ahead of the invaders, but by late in the day the Russians were attacking from all sides and the Tigers were surrounded. The only way out was through Trvana itself, which was already occupied by the Red Army, so the panzer crews revved their engines and pushed throttles to the firewall. The Tiger II had a top sustained speed of about 24 miles per hour but it's unlikely they were doing more than 20mph when the battalion clanked through Trvana, with machine guns and main battery firing at anything that moved. Blasting their way through they escaped the trap with no losses, but fell back toward the first escarpments of the Little Carpathian Mountains.[49] During their retreat and withdrawal, the Germans had to continually be alert for the Janko Kraf band of partisans who still roamed the hills after the Slovak Uprising of the previous fall.

XXXXIII Armeekorps
37. SS-Freiwilligen-Kavallerie-Division Lützow

One unit asked to hold back the Red Army in the Wienviertel was the newly formed *37. SS-Freiwilligen-Kavallerie-Division Lützow*. When Budapest was surrounded on Christmas Eve 1944, the two existing *Waffen-SS* Cavalry Divisions were trapped within the city, but like most divisions of the *Wehrmacht*, *8. SS-Kavallerie-Division Florian Geyer* and *22. Freiwilligen-Kavallerie-Division Maria Theresia* were scattered over a fairly large area. Elements of both units found themselves outside the Russian siege ring and cut off from their parent divisions.

One example of this was *SS-Untersturmführer* Heinz Schershel of *Florian Geyer*. Stationed west of Budapest, he received orders to report to the staff of *IX. Waffen-Gebirgskorps der SS (Kroatisches)*[50] on Christmas morning, but found himself stopped by the Russians, who surrounded Budapest the previous afternoon. Along with the scattered personnel from both divisions, including some veterinary staff, convalescent wounded, men returned from leave, supply elements and the few survivors of the Budapest breakout group who fought their way through the encircling Russians,

---

49   The Little Carpathians are a heavily forested range of low mountains in Western Slovakia. From a military standpoint they helped the defenders, because overland travel on the crowded slopes was nearly impossible for armor and restricted Russian vehicles to the roads.

50   In yet another bizarre German command situation, *IX SS-Gebirgskorps* had been formed as a corps headquarters for the two SS Muslim Mountain Divisions, *Handschar* and *Kama*. However, no mountain units were trapped in Budapest, but the two SS Cavalry Divisions were.

Schershel was assigned to newly forming *Lützow*. As a veteran officer he was given command of a company that saw heavy fighting throughout the rest of the war.[51]

By late March *Lützow* headquarters commanded the following combat elements: *SS-Kampfgruppe Ameiser*, whose main combat power was *SS-Kavallerie-Regiment 92*; a motorized Army infantry regiment; an Army machine gun battalion and the remnants of a Hungarian *Honved* division. The *Pionier* Battalion, engineers in American parlance, was the completely intact battalion from *8. Freiwilligen-Kavallerie-Division-der-SS Florian Geyer*, which had not been trapped in Budapest with the parent division. Rank and file came from SS Cavalry schools, as did NCOs and officers, as well as other sources. Many were *Volksdeutsch*. The artillery component was *SS-Artillerie-Abteilung 37*, formed at Beneschau in Central Bohemia starting in late January. Consisting of three batteries, these were parceled out with one assigned to the headquarters, one to *SS-Kampfgruppe Ameiser* and the other to *SS-Kampfgruppe Keitel*.

This organization is somewhat misleading, though, because *SS-Kampfgruppe Ameiser* was actually attached to other units for most of its brief career, although it does seem to have fought under its parent command for a week later in April. *SS-Kampfgruppe Keitel* never even served in the same army as its parent headquarters.

By 1 April *SS-Kampfgruppe Ameiser* was being shoved across the Nitra River into the area north of Bratislava, in company with the *96. Infanterie-Division*, as the Red Army launched new attacks from their bridgehead west of the Hron River.

On 27 March, *6. SS-Panzerarmee* reported that the other combat-ready elements of *Lützow* were being readied in the vicinity of Bratislava, per orders. With the crisis then forming south of Vienna the *Kampfgruppe* boarded six trains and headed for the critical area, where it detrained on 31 March near Wiener Neustadt.

The headquarters of *Lützow* was sent into the gap north of Vienna between *6. SS-Panzerarmee* and *8. Armee* at Znaim, with orders to stop the Soviet advance at all costs. The town itself sat atop a rocky outcropping along the Thaya River, a good defensive position for anything other than a rag-tag, thrown-together headquarters. But as bad as the situation was north of the Danube, it was worse to the south. So desperate was it south of the Danube that *SS-Kampfgruppe Keitel* had been sent to help *SS-Oberstgruppenführer* Sepp Dietrich's *6. SS-Panzerarmee* instead of staying with its parent headquarters. After unloading the day before on 1 April it was in the line at Neunkirchen near Weiner Neustadt. As things turned out, it never would rejoin its parent command.

Lützow was part of *XXXXIII Armeekorps*. The Corps reported its Order of Battle on that Easter Sunday as: *Kampfgruppen* of the *711. Infanterie-Division*, *356. Infanterie-Division* and *96. Infanterie-Division*, with *SS-Kampfgruppe Ameiser* attached to the *96. Infanterie-Division*, along with a machine-gun battalion. The corps also had a battalion from *6. Panzer-Division*; one Hungarian cavalry battalion; a *Kampfgruppe* of the *211. Volksgrenadier-Division* with one battalion from *Panzer-Division Feldherrnhalle 2* attached; a *Kampfgruppe* from *48. Infanterie-Division*, *Sturmgeschütz-Brigade 325*, *Sturmartillerie-Brigade 239* and the anti-tank battalion from *Panzer-Division Feldherrnhalle 2*. Clearly, the Corps was composed of fragments and remnants of once-proud formations, especially the famous *6. Panzer-Division*, whose illustrious alumni included such luminaries as Eberhard Raus.

---

51   Pencz, Rudolf, 'Waffen-SS Miscellany', p. 68.

SS-Kampfgruppe-Division Böhmen und Mähren

Scattered throughout the Protectorate of Bohemia and Moravia were schools for training *Waffen-SS* men in the various skills and duties necessary for service in a combat unit. South of Prague at Beneschau, the commandant of the SS Troop Training Grounds Bohemia, *SS-Oberführer* Wilhelm Trabant, was ordered in mid-March to begin the formation of three regimental combat groups of three battalions each, along with their associated specialist troops, such as engineers and artillery.[52] Individually, history would commonly refer to these formations as *Kampfgruppen Trabant I*, *Trabant II* and *Trabant III*; collectively they would be called *SS-Kampfgruppe-Division Böhmen und Mähren*.[53]

Untangling the history of this mostly unknown unit is fraught with perils for the researcher, as official records are incomplete and anecdotal stories don't give details of which element of which *Kampfgruppe* was where and when. Worse for the historian, the first two regiments fought in the same area of the Wienviertel at the same time, but most narratives simply refer to them as *SS-Kampfgruppe Trabandt*. To complicate matters further, Army records sometimes referred to them after the name of their *Kampfgruppe* commanders, or as simply *SS-Kampfgruppe Böhmen* or *SS-Kampfgruppe Mähren*.

The *SS-Kampfgruppe-Division* would reach the size of an average *Volksgrenadier-Division*, somewhere between 8,000 and 10,000 men, and while each regimental-sized component would have an artillery and engineer battalion attached, the larger unit would not have some of the components of a true division, such as a Signals Battalion or a Reconnaissance Battalion;[54] thus its designation as an *SS-Kampfgruppe-Division*. Nor was it counted among the 38 'true' *Waffen-SS* divisions, despite being larger in numbers than some of the very late-war divisions that are listed among those 38, such as *36. Waffen-Grenadier-Division der SS Dirlewanger*,[55] which only had about 4,000 men at its largest, and which disintegrated through desertions before ever being committed to battle.

If such a composite unit as *Böhemn und Mähren* was to have any chance in battle it needed proven commanders. *SS-Brigadeführer* Wilhelm Trabandt was a veteran officer, having fought with the *LAH* during the Battle of France in 1940, where he lost a bet over whether the Germans would conquer London first or Paris. It cost Trabandt 1,000 bottles of wine. After that he was assigned to the *1. SS-Brigade (mot.)*, which he commanded starting in October 1943, and finally to command the *18. SS-Freiwilligen-Panzergrenadier-Division Horst Wessel* when the brigade was upgraded to a full division in 1944. He was also a Knight's Cross winner, and was credited with having designed the divisional picklock symbol of the *LAH*.[56]

The Trabandt *Kampfgruppen* were drawn from the various *Waffen-SS* training schools scattered around the Reichs Protectorate for Bohemia and Moravia. One source also lists elements of *31. SS-Freiwilligen-Grenadier-Division* as part of the *Kampfgruppe*, which might explain how

---

52   As part of the *Kampfgruppe Division* there was a 'Northern Force' and a 'Southern Force'. The 'Northern Force' remained in the area of Prague in the zone of *Heeresgruppe Mitte* and therefore falls outside the scope of this book.

53   The three regimental-sized *Kampfgruppen* were also known by their commander's name instead of Trabandt's, making them *SS-Regiment Schulze*, *SS-Regiment Siegmann* and *SS-Regiment Konopacki*.

54   Landwehr, Richard, 'SS-Kampfgruppe-Division Bohemia and Moravia', *Siegrunen 38* (1985), p. 18. Landwehr states that the division had a bicycle reconnaissance battalion as well as a signals battalion, and that both remainded in Prague.

55   Some sources apply the honorific title of *Dirlewanger* to this division, since it was built around *SS-Sturmbrigade Dirlewanger*.

56   This clever symbol had two meanings. First, the emblem for the *LAH* was a key, or picklock, as a good luck symbol that opened all doors during a battle. The second meaning pertained to the division commander at the time, Sepp Dietrich. Dietrich is German for picklock.

the honorific title *Böhmen und Mähren* was sometimes erroneously attached to that division. Some sources list that division as *Böhmen and Mähren*, and great confusion reigned over to which specific unit the honorific applied. As previously mentioned it is often confused as being part of, attached to or in some fashion related to *31. SS-Freiwilligen-Grenadier-Division.*[57] Some sources even list Trabandt as taking over command of that division in April of 1945.

However, there is no relation between them. The *31. SS-Freiwilligen-Grenadier-Division* had the distinction of being the only *Waffen-SS* division without either an honorific title or an ethnic designation.[58] *31. SS-Freiwilligen-Grenadier-Division* did not include any of the aforementioned units.[59] In the chaos of retreat and destruction of records, the two divisions somehow became entangled and hopefully that is now cleared up.

Fragments of other units were also likely attached to Trabandt's division, and six *Jagdpanzer 38(t) Hetzers* had been assigned from Army depots. Those were assigned to the *Panzerjäger* company of *SS-Kampfgruppe Trabandt I*. Most of the manpower came from various *Waffen-SS* training schools scattered around old Czechoslovakia, renamed by the Germans as the Protectorate of Bohemia-Moravia.[60] The artillery component consisted of two field artillery batteries, and two truck-mounted *nebelwerfer* batteries of unknown size; the artillery commander was the veteran *SS-Obersturmbannführer* Dr Arthur Curtius. From January to March 1945, Curtius had been the commander of *SS-Schwere-Artillerie-Abteilung 503*, of *III SS-Panzerkorps (Germanisches)*, before being ordered to form his new artillery unit as part of *Böhmen und Mähren.*[61] The artillery *Kampfgruppe* was fleshed out by both instructors and students from the *SS-Artillerie-Schule II Beneschau*. One source lists *SS-Wach-Bataillon Prag* as part of the division. In addition to men from the various SS schools and formations, there were also men from the Slovak Army and the Slovak Hlinka Guard Militia.[62]

The three SS-Regiments were unofficially known to the Army by the name of their commanders, but are better known to history named after the division commander, *SS-Brigadeführer* Trabandt. The alternative titles were *SS-Panzergrenadier-Regiment Schulze* for *SS-Kampfgruppe Trabandt I* and *SS-Panzergrenadier-Regiment Konopacki* for *SS-Kampfgruppe Trabandt II*, which together formed and were referred to by some Army staff officers under whom they served by a third name, *SS-Kampfgruppe Böhmen*. *SS-Panzergrenadier-Regiment Siegmann* was also *SS-Kampfgruppe Trabandt III*, which was sometimes referred to by Army staff officers as *SS-Kampfgruppe Mähren*. Each Regiment had elements of the artillery battalion and the pioneer battalion attached. In addition, the survivors of *SS-Panzerjäger-Ausbildungs-und-Ersatz-Abteilung 1*, aka *SS-Kampfgruppe Kiss*, were also added.[63]

---

57   To this day there is no agreement over the exact order of battle for this unit. Some sources cite up to 5 regiments split between the Northern and Southern Forces, some have multiple regiments titled 'Böhmen' and 'Mähren'… the one used here accepts that the first two regiments, *Trabandt I* and *II*, were collectively known as *Böhmen*, while the third regiment, *Trabandt III*, was also known as *Mähren*. But even original sources seem confused as to which was which.

58   Some sources refer to that division as having the honorific title *Batschka*.

59   For a definitive discussion of this still-debated point, the curious reader is referred to Rudolf Pencz's exhaustive study of *31. SS-Freiwilligen-Grenadier Division*, titled *For the Homeland*.

60   Landwehr, 'SS-Kampfgruppe-Division', p. 17. Landwehr states that part of *SS-Grenadier-Ausbildungs-und-Ersatz-Abteilung 10* from Brno was incorporated into *SS-Kampfgruppe Konopacki*.

61   *III SS-Panzerkorps* was evacuated from the Courland Pocket only in late January 1945, when it was attached to Felix Steiner's *11. SS-Panzerarmee* on the Oder Front and participated in *Unternehmen Sonnenwende*. However, both Curtius and his battalion wound up in Austria, as *Schwere SS-Panzer-Abteilung 503* was added to *SS-Artillerie-Abteilung-Curtius* in late April.

62   Landwehr, 'SS-Kampfgruppe-Division', p. 17.

63   Richard Landwehr states two that additional regimental-sized *Kampfgruppen*, confusingly also named *Böhmen* and *Mähren*, under the command of *SS-Brigadeführer* Pückler-Burghaus, were formed in April 1945. This may

Böhmen und Mähren was the 39th *Waffen-SS* unit to be designated as a division. The qualifier of *Kampfgruppe* is one of those oddities of German military nomenclature, where this term can mean anything from twenty men to ten thousand. It was appended here because the unit didn't have all of the organic components a true division was authorized to have.

The new recruits and students at the various schools were almost all quite young, some no older than 15 or 16, and while all youth in the Third Reich had had some type of preliminary military training, there was no substitute for the maturity that came only with age and combat experience. Many of those young teenagers were issued ill-fitting tunics and helmets that slid around on their heads because they were too large. As combat reports noted, soldiers of this age typically froze when exposed to artillery fire.

The instructors, on the other hand, were mostly combat veterans, often disqualified from front-line service because of wounds. Forming these mismatched elements into the various squads, companies, battalions and regiments that made up a division-sized unit would have been difficult enough under ordinary circumstances, but making them combat-ready in a matter of days before they were thrown into action against seasoned Russian troops was impossible. Almost as soon as the organizational tables were finalized and the personnel assignments finished, the various elements were committed to battle, usually assigned to existing Army commands, with the result that the unit never fought as a unified entity.[64] By 1 April the various *Kampfgruppen* were either in combat, or about to go into action. Ready or not, there were simply too many holes in the defense; regardless of quality, the Germans needed bodies to throw in the path of the hard-charging Red Army.

The regiments weren't the only units under the Trabandt umbrella of formations, however. The least known, but potentially most interesting, was *SS-Kampfgruppe Röhwer*. It was constructed from the Panzer Close Combat Inspectorate at Breschan, Panenské Břežany in old Czechoslovakia, and also the *Aufklärung-Ausbildungs-und-Ersatz-Abteilung Bukowan*, Bukovany to the Czechs. The commander was *SS-Hauptsturmführer* Hans Rohwer, a former member of the *LAH* who had been severely wounded and, once recovered, been assigned to a training position. The *Kampfgruppe* was armed with captured Russian and American vehicles, which probably had been rebuilt for use at the schools to familiarize the students with enemy armor and vehicles.

Luftkriegsschule 7 at Langenlebarn Air Base at Tulln, and *Kampfgruppe Volkmann*

Tulln was a town west of Vienna on the south bank of the Danube. By 1945, the airfield at Tulln had long been critical to the *Luftwaffe* as not only an outlying airfield for the defense of Vienna, but also as a field for the training of new air crews. Since 1943 its commander had been *Generalmajor* Dietrich Volkmann. The US Fifteenth Air Force had bombed the field many times and wreaked much havoc, but it was only with the approach of the Russians that the school shut down for good. The air base nevertheless maintained its importance for *Luftwaffe* support of ground operations. Just two days before the 101st Hungarian Fighter Squadron had transferred there with 30 Messerschmidt ME-109s. Before the day was over the Hungarians flew strafing sorties against Russians in the Neuseidlersee area.

The day before, 31 March 1945, three small and very strange-looking jet fighters landed at the airfield. They looked nothing like the now familiar Messerschmitt ME-262, but instead were

---

have been the so-called Northern Force.

64   Pencz, Rudolf, 'Combat Formations of the SS-Kampfgruppe Div. Böhmen-Mahren', *Siegrunen 69*, (2000), pp. 6-8.

slender, with short wings, upward canted tail planes and a turbojet mounted atop the fuselage aft of the cockpit. Made mostly of wood, they were one of the vaunted *wunderwaffe*, wonder weapons, that Hitler had been promising, the Heinkel HE-162. Unfortunately, all three subsequently crashed. After the war the HE-162 was initially judged a total failure until extensive testing showed the opposite was true, that in fact it had been the revolutionary airplane that might have changed the air war in Germany's favor. But it was too little, too late.

The three Heinkels were refugees from the factory airfield at Schwechat, which lay in the path of the Red Army. The HE-162 had been rushed into production within weeks of the design competition ordered by the *Luftwaffe* in September of 1944. Unfortunately for the Germans, the factory which made the glue used to hold the planes together had been knocked out of action by the RAF and the substitute tended to dissolve the wood rather than bind it. But at that point in the war every risk had to be taken, including overlooking design flaws.

Much like the human flotsam clogging the roads out of Hungary, aircraft of all kind landed at Tulln throughout the day. Now other Hungarian planes, trainers of all types, and even a captured American B-24 Liberator landed at Tulln. The bomber was parked right next to one of the HE-162s. Also around the beginning of April, the *9. Jagdstaffel* and *10. Jagdstaffel*, from *III Gruppe, Jagdgeschwader 52*, transferred to Tulln to fly in defense of *Heeresgruppe Süd*.

With the dissolution of the school the previous day, the staff and instructors were formed into three alarm battalions. Exact numbers aren't available, but estimates of 300-400 men per battalion are likely on the mark. Not enough modern weapons could be found to arm them all, even after trucks were sent into Vienna to forage for weapons. Some *Panzerfauste* turned up, the mass-produced single-use anti-tank rocket tipped with a hollow charge, and ammunition for the 300 modern rifles on hand, but the rest of *Kampfgruppe Volkmann* received old Czech and Austrian weapons.

US Fifteenth Air Force

No city had benefitted more from the Third Reich's building program than Hitler's favorite town of Linz. Linz had once been a sleepy provincial capital, but construction of such massive facilities as the Hermann Göring Steel Works, and improvements in the roads and railroads leading into and out the city, had turned Linz into an important center of production and transportation. The population prospered.

And then the bombers came. And came, and came again. They came on 1 April, B-24 Liberators of the US Fifteenth Air Force flying from bases in Italy and loosening their bomb loads on hapless Linz, aiming for the railroad complex to cut supply lines to *Heeresgruppe Süd*. Further south, at Villach, more bombs fell to hurt *2. Panzerarmee*'s supply network. The Americans did everything they could to help their Russian allies by crippling *Heeresgruppe Süd*'s ability to keep its armies in the field. They would continue bombing targets in Austria until the last days of the war.

South of the Danube

With the front moving closer by the day, 15,000 prisoners of war marched out of *Stalag 17A*, headed west. The camp's location was Kaisersteinbruch, near Brück an der Leitha. In the coming weeks they would wander the battlefield looking for a place of safety.

6. SS-Panzerarmee
II SS-Panzerkorps

Like its parent formation, *6. SS-Panzerarmee*, *II SS-Panzerkorps* had split into several components during the retreat from Hungary. While one of its three divisions, *9. SS-Panzer-Division Hohenstaufen*, got shoved south into the area of *6. Armee*, the rest of the Corps retreated north around the Neuseidlersee. Once past that body of water *2. SS-Panzer-Division Das Reich* moved southwest to secure the junction with *I SS-Panzerkorps*, while *6. Panzer-Division* stayed close to the Danube.

6. Panzer-Division

Few German divisions had a more storied career than *6. Panzer-Division*. In its own way this division's reputation rivaled that of the better-known *Waffen-SS* formations. Its most famous commander, *Generaloberst* Erhard Raus, was considered by friend and foe alike as Germany's finest tank mind, above even Heinz Guderian and Erwin Rommel. During many desperate battles on the Eastern Front Raus and his veteran division performed miracles in attack and defense against impossible odds. To the Americans Raus "was one of the recognized masters of the mechanized art, highly sought after by the US Army after 1945 for his analysis of the fighting in the East".[65]

According to its strength returns for 1 April, the famed division was as strong as any unit left in *Heeresgruppe Süd*. All army panzer divisions were ordered to reorganize as Type 1945 Panzer Divisions, with total ration strength of 11,422 all ranks, 54 Panzers including flame and command panzers, and a mere 90 SPWs. The *Panzergrenadier* regiments were supposed to equip most of the infantry with bicycles.

In practice some divisions weren't strong enough to even achieve these modest numbers and were renamed *Kampfgruppe Panzer Divisionen*, with lower authorized numbers across the board. But *6. Panzer-Division* had a different issue, as it was over-strength for the new regulations and it doesn't appear to have carried out this reorganization. Given the never-stop nature of the fighting withdrawal from Hungary it's hard to imagine when the division would have had time to do this.

So on that bloody Easter Sunday *6. Panzer-Division* hugged the south bank of the Danube with ration strength of close to 14,000, a total of 31 panzers operational, including Panzer Mark IVs, Panthers and *Jagdpanzer IV/70s*, with another 32 panzers in repair. The serviceable SPW count stood at the full authorized strength of 90, with another 107 in for repair. Likewise, the artillery component was very strong. But while the division reported itself as 100 percent mobile, its combat rating only stood at *III*, probably because of the panzer total and the low quality of training for the replacements.

One example to show the effects of the retreat in March can be seen in the division's Panther numbers for 1 February. Eighteen Panthers were reported ready for action with 43 more in repair, for a total of 61. That more or less represented a full-strength Panther battalion. But in April it had 17 Panthers operational with 14 more in repair. In other words, 32 Panthers had been written off during February and March. It isn't known, but can safely be assumed because of similar experiences in other divisions, that many were destroyed by the Germans themselves during the retreat across Hungary, either from lack of fuel, or the means to transport damaged panzers out of the path of the Red Army advance.

---

65   Robert M. Citino, 'The 6. Panzer-Division', online <http://www.historynet.com/the-6th-panzer-division.htm>, (Accessed 3 January 2018).

2. SS-Panzer-Division Das Reich

Likewise, *2. SS-Panzer-Division Das Reich* was in better condition than most of the German formations. On 28 March, at the Györ, Hungary, train station, 2,800 replacements intended for *12. SS-Panzer-Division Hitlerjugend* were instead ordered off their trains and added to *Das Reich*. Whether these men were shanghaied by *Das Reich* officers, as some sources allege, or they joined the division because they couldn't get through to *Hitlerjugend*, as Weidinger states in his history of *Das Reich*,[66] the fact remains that while these men were untrained in ground combat, *Das Reich* had a massive infusion of young, fit men, mostly from the *Kriegsmarine*. At the end of March it was 60 percent motorized and classified with a *III* rating, making it relatively powerful among formations of *Heeresgruppe Süd*.

On 1 April found *Das Reich* was pulling back ever closer to the Neuseidlersee and Danube narrows, closely pursued by the Forty-Sixth Army of Second Ukrainian Front, so the Germans had no chance to rest or consolidate a position. At 10:00 p.m. the division began another withdrawal through Wallern.

On the left flank, across the Danube, *8. Armee* was also in a fighting retreat westwards. Like the SS they had been receiving orders from Hitler not to retreat one step backward, but the orders were moot by the time they were received, the positions having been lost well before. The *II SS-Panzerkorps* and *8. Armee* stayed in close contact so neither pulled back and left the other with an open flank facing the river.

One of the two *Das Reich Panzergrenadier* battalions, *SS-Panzergrenadier-Regiment Der Führer*, began the day headquartered in Andau but Russian spearheads closing in on Halbturn, five miles to the northwest, threatened to cut their retreat route. Late in the afternoon the regiment pulled back to Halbturn. Before midnight it was forced back again due to Soviet penetrations, this time to Parndorf, a few miles north of the Neuseidlersee. *Das Reich* had reached the Danube narrows, the only natural defensive position in the region. With the Danube close by on its left flank and the Neuseidlersee on its right, the division had one last chance to make a stand.

Weidinger makes the point that the division had been in continuous combat for twenty-six days, with sixteen of those spent continuously fighting and moving to keep from being surrounded, yet at no point did *Das Reich* loses its cohesion. The division's combat strength diminished due to losses in personnel and materiel, but its discipline under fire never wavered.[67] Based on its record to date, and the fighting it would yet do in Vienna, Weidinger was right.

3. SS-Panzer-Division Totenkopf

In the confused mess of the German front lines, *3. SS-Panzer-Division Totenkopf* had become separated from *IV SS-Panzerkorps*. Finding itself in the sector of *6. SS-Panzerarmee*, the division tried to organize some defense near Weiner Neustadt. On 23 March the division's *I./SS-Panzer Regiment 3*, the battalion armed with Mark IVs, was forced to abandon and destroy all of its remaining vehicles near Pénzezkút, Hungary. With no fuel left and the Russians constantly threatening to surround them, the tankers had no choice. The battalion had no officers left at that point, so it was dissolved and an infantry *Kampfgruppe* formed from the surviving members. Led by *SS-Untersturmführer* Wolfgang Barth it was known as *SS-Kampfgruppe Barth*. With a rifle strength of 84 men divided

---

66   Weidinger, Otto, *Das Reich, Volume V: 1943-1945* (Manitoba: J.J. Fedorowicz, 2012), p. 358.
67   Weidinger, *Das Reich*, p. 364

into three platoons, it deployed at Oggam Neuseidlersee where 80 men of the *Volkssturm* joined them. They carried no heavy weapons but did have 60 *Panzerfauste*.[68]

Totenkopf differed from other panzer divisions by having an organic heavy tank company. On 1 April this company retrieved six Tiger I panzers from the Vienna Arsenal, where they had been undergoing long-term repairs. Production of the Tiger I had ceased in February of 1944 but many were still in service, given the overall small numbers of Tigers IIs then available. *Das Reich* had once also had their own Tigers but gave them up in 1944. A Tiger II was also picked up that had been in repairs from *SS-Schwere-Panzer-Abteilung 501*.

The division also had *III. Bataillon* from *SS-Brigade Ney* attached, for the duration of the war as it turned out. This highly unusual SS formation was Hungarian and made up of diehard anti-communists, led by veteran commander *SS-Obersturmbannführer* Karoly Ney. By April this little-known unit had been fighting for four months. Its record in combat was so good that Hitler approved the rare honor of allowing the men their own cuff title, *Ney*. Morale was high and they were a very effective force.

SS-Brigade Ney began as a training formation for *22. SS-Freiwilligen-Kavallerie-Division Maria Theresa*. When that division was surrounded in Budapest, Ney's command was attached to *IV SS-Panzerkorps*. In the coming months its component battalions were parceled out to formations that were desperately short of infantry, such as *Totenkopf*. In all likelihood this battalion numbered at least 500 men and throughout the rest of the war their fighting record was excellent.

Elements of *Totenkopf's Panzergrenadier Kampfgruppe* now tried to stop the Russians at Bad Erlach, six miles south of Wiener Neustadt, along with cadets from the *Kriegsschule Wiener Neustadt*. Those *Fahnenjunker* were in training for both *Jäger* and infantry roles and were divided into two battalions of four companies, with total strength of around 500 men.[69] Several other blocking groups were set up also, such as one of about 100 men ordered to defend the road south.[70]

* * *

The city of Wiener Neustadt teemed with foreign refugees and Jews who had been forcibly evacuated from elsewhere. The last shops had closed two days before on Good Friday and on Easter Sunday heavy explosions rocked the city, knocking out both water and lights and leaving the populace desperate. As a major manufacturing and transportation hub for the Germans, Wiener Neustadt had endured multiple air attacks in the past year, and wreckage filled the streets.

At ten in the morning on 1 April the Russian 99th Guards Rifle Division assaulted the town from the south. The fighting was bitter, a harbinger of all that was to come. Most of the defense was put up by the *Fahnenjunkeren*, the officer cadets, of the *Kreigsschule*. They fought with energy and ferocity, and inflicted heavy losses on the attackers. In return, they were chewed up by the Red Army meat grinder. The men of the *Kriegsschule* suffered 200 killed and 800 wounded. When the fighting ended 33 German soldiers were buried on the city's southern periphery, and 205 more in the north. The survivors joined other units.

Two companies defending Erlach on the south were nearly outflanked before retreating north to the Lanzenkirchner Trift, a large meadow overlooking Lanzenkirchen on the northwest. Elsewhere, two more companies defended Lanzenkirchen and were also driven back, leading some of the Russian elements to attack the left flank of the two companies at Erlach. This was the move that nearly caved in their flank and forced them to retreat, too.

68   Ian Michael Wood, *Tigers of the Death's Head* (Mechanicsburg: Stackpole Books, 2013), p. 247.
69   Instead of companies, these were called Inspektions.
70   Brettner, Friedrich, *Die Letzten Kämpfe des II. Weltkrieges, Fotoband I* (Berndorf: Kral, 2014), p. 135.

By three in the afternoon it was over. The Russians had taken both Erlach and Lanzenkirchen, and captured some of the cadets. The Russians noted these men were in their late twenties. More than 20 civilians died in the fighting at Lanzenkirchen. According to Ian Michael Wood, the Russians reported capturing "nine trucks, six MGs, four store houses, two 7.5cm anti-tank guns and 35 railway wagons".[71] With the clarity of hindsight, the loss of the railway wagons may have been the biggest blow. One German company, the *5. Inspecktion* from the *Kriegsschule*, lost no less than 40 men in the fighting, not counting wounded or missing, and the injured commander was left with one man after the battle. As for the invading Russians, they lost a large number of tanks and, while they sliced through the disorganized, makeshift German defenses quickly, they nonetheless took heavy casualties in doing so.

* * *

Totenkopf's heavy tank company, *9./SS-Panzer Regiment 3,* had a mere three machines operational on 1 April. After helping *III./SS-Panzergrenadier-Regiment 26* rescue an encircled *Wehrmacht* regiment the day before at Hortischon,[72] the next day three of the company's precious remaining Tiger IIs moved back through Erlach and headed to Ofenbach with the Russians close behind. One of them broke down with engine trouble on the way to Lanzenkirchen. The crew bailed out and ran across open fields to avoid being killed or captured, without destroying their tank, leaving only two machines in operation.[73]

Totenkopf still had a few Panthers left, but all of them were under repair. The division also had two Tigers left operational from its organic heavy company. Meanwhile, the rest of the infantry *Kampfgruppe* tried to hold the village of Lanzenkirchen, less than two miles from Erlach, but were forced out with the loss of eight men killed. By the end of the day the *Kampfgruppe* was down to less than two hundred men.

I SS-Panzerkorps

When the Russians launched their Vienna Offensive in mid-March, *I SS-Panzerkorps* had already worn themselves down battering against the dug-in Russian defenses southwest of Stuhlweissenberg. By sheer skill, bravery and blood, the Corps, and the *LAH* in particular, had crossed the Sio Canal and partly taken Simontorya, a remarkable feat with all things being considered. But they were still far stronger than they would be a fortnight later.

After the Ardennes Offensive the corps had been refitted with armor at the cost of the rest of the *Wehrmacht*. During the chaotic retreat out of Hungary both divisions of the corps, *1. SS-Panzer-Division Leibstandarte Adolf Hitler (LAH)* and *12. SS-Panzer-Division Hitlerjugend*, lost most of those precious panzers.

One such example comes from Ian Michael Wood, who mentions in passing that also on 23 March *12. SS-Panzer-Division Hitlerjugend* abandoned six panzers and 10 self-propelled guns, *Sturmgeschütze,* near Zirc.[74] The loss of 16 panzers in battle would have been devastating to any armored division, as this was about eight percent of its authorized strength. Being forced to leave

71   Ian Michael Wood, *History of the Totenkopf's Panther-Abteilung* (Keszthely: PeKo Publishing, 2015), p. 102.
72   Ian Wood cites this as having been *Grenadier Regiment 587*, but that unit belonged to *320. Infanterie-Division* which was in Czechoslovakia. It is unknown whether this regiment had been detached from its parent division for service in Austria.
73   Ian Wood, *Tigers of the Death's Head* (Mechanicsburg: Stackpole, 2013), pp. 99-100.
74   Wood, *Tigers,* p. 100.

them behind by lack of fuel shows how devastating the lingering after-effects of *Unternehmen Frühlingserwachen* were. Once again Hitler's folly had cost Germany dearly.

The corps faced immensely strong Russian forces as the Fourth and Ninth Guards Armies, supplemented by the powerful Sixth Guards Tank Army, swept south of Neuseidlersee. It had only *Kampfgruppen* to stop them.

* * *

The *I SS-Panzerkorps* discovered that night brought no relief from Russian pressure. On the Corps' far right flank, attacks took Lanzenkirchen, an ancient market town due south of Wiener Neustadt on the western bank of the Leitha River. The Corps was being inexorably pushed westward into the foothills of the Alps. As events would turn out, this was the best thing that could have happened for them, for Austria, and perhaps for the future of Europe and the world. Marshal Tolbukhin, commander of Third Ukrainian Front, had his eyes on a bigger prize than either Vienna or Austria. He wanted to follow the Danube straight into Germany, and if *I SS-Panzerkorps* had moved into Vienna there would have been nothing to stop him. As it was, the Russians cut the Sopron-Vienna road to deny its use to *Hitlerjugend,* while *LAH* couldn't use the road to Vienna from Weiner Neustadt. Both divisions were shoved, side by side, into the narrow valleys and limited roads of the Alpine foothills. This put the depleted SS Corps in exactly the right place to stop Tolbukhin's dream from happening.

1. SS-Panzer-Division Leibstandarte Adolf Hitler

The most famous *Waffen-SS* division of them all was *1. SS-Panzer-Division Leibstandarte Adolf Hitler,* or simply the *LAH.* Since October 1944 some personnel from its panzer regiment had been languishing in the picturesque town of Osnabrück in northwest Germany, far from any of the battle fronts and about as far from its parent division as was possible in the shrunken Reich. It was the birthplace of Erich Maria Remarque, of *All Quiet on the Western Front* fame. Around 1 April the men were organized into an ad hoc infantry battalion of six companies and shipped to Austria.[75] To the amazement of all, after riding the failing Reich railway system for 11 days they arrived safely and rejoined the division on 12 April.

Like every other German unit, the *LAH* was a shattered shadow of what it had been a month before. But what exactly did that mean? Exact numbers are no longer available. However, a reasonable estimation can be made by using what figures are available then extrapolating. The *LAH*'s authorized manpower was approximately 19,000 men, divided into combat elements that included one panzer regiment of two battalions, two *Panzergrenadier* regiments each with three battalions, one artillery regiment, one reconnaissance battalion, one *Flak* battalion, one *Sturmgeschütz* (assault gun) battalion, one *Panzerjäger* (tank destroyer) battalion, one *pioneer* (engineer) battalion, one signals battalion and one *ersatz* (replacement) battalion. Non-combat elements included the division command headquarters, security, supply, medical and veterinary elements. Included in those are such vital services such as processing mail, cooking food and maintaining the field kitchens.

The *12. SS-Panzer-Division Hitlerjugend* was organized in similar fashion. By comparing the numbers we have from later in the month for both the *LAH* and *Hitlerjugend,* and those from 8-9 May when both divisions surrendered, a ration strength of 13,000 and rifle strength of 8,000

---

75   Although exactly how strong this battalion was isn't known, six companies would indicate a number somewhere between 360-600 men, and probably somewhere around 475.

on 1 April should be close to the actual number. We also know that on 1 April the *3./SS-Panzer Regiment 12* received ten brand new Panzer Mark IVs while in Wiener Neustadt.[76]

On 30 March it moved into the *Reichsschutzstellung* near Deutschkreuz and discovered that the fortifications were little more than a very long trench. Most of the division's armor was gone and what remained was in urgent need of repair. In particular, the treads on all tracked vehicles were either worn out or missing altogether, along with the rubber blocks, limiting mobility even more than the shortage in transport vehicles and fuel already had. On sharp turns the treads tended to work loose, usually leaving the vehicle disabled on the side of the road. With the supply system in chaos there was no way to get treads or blocks through regular supply channels, so in desperation the commander of the division's reconnaissance battalion did what other units, such as *Schwere SS-Panzer-Abteilung 503*, did. He scrounged what he needed. *SS-Hauptsturmführer* Emil Wawrzinek ordered Herbert Kühl to drive to Vienna to see if he could find replacements there. Taking six trucks and orders for 40 sets of treads, Kühl found the replacement depot in Vienna in the Prater but was put off by an officious *Feldwebel*, a sergeant, who told him that without authorization from either *OKH* or *Generalkommando XVII* he could not issue the requested parts. Kühl may not have known of the British quartermaster at the Battle of Isandlwana, who wanted proper requisition forms before parceling out ammunition to the riflemen on the firing line, but the similarities were eerie.

Disgusted, Kühl drove through rubble-clogged streets to the *Generalkommando XVII* headquarters on the Stubenring but found that much of it had already evacuated to Linz, leaving doors and windows open and secret papers blowing in the wind down the Ringstrasse and into the nearby Danube Canal. There was no one to sign authorization papers so Kühl drove back to the Prater where the same Sergeant now told him to take whatever he wanted, because they were getting ready to pull out to the west.

Kühl found mountains of treads and rubber blocks for every imaginable type of vehicle, from Tigers IIs to *Kettenkrads*, and loaded up everything they needed, plus extras. His little convoy then headed back to Deutschkreutz at the quickest possible speed. Once the treads and blocks had been installed, every vehicle was fixed and ready to move.[77]

Spare parts had always been in short supply for the *Wehrmacht*, but nothing illustrates the collapse of the German supply structure better than this incident. To abandon a huge depot of precious treads that were vital to keeping the armored divisions in the field shows how desperate things had become.

* * *

On 31 March the division found the Russians had already moved around to the west and they were again in danger of being cut off. As elements passed the airport at Weiner Neustadt they saw rows of ME-262 jet fighters[78] lined up intact, but no *Luftwaffe* personnel. Using machine guns and hand grenades they destroyed the aircraft, but it took much longer than they had hoped. Fortunately they also found enough fuel to top up all of their vehicles. The SS men thought their *Luftwaffe* comrades had given up and run for safety.

But the men of the *Fliegerhorstes Wiener Neustadt*, Air Base Wiener Neustadt, hadn't fled. Instead they had picked up weapons and gone to fight as infantry. After the Russians showed up in the early afternoon they attacked the positions of *Luftwaffe* bomber units fighting as infantry

76 Michael Reynolds, *Men of Steel, I SS-Panzerkorps, The Ardennes and Eastern Front 1944-45* (Staplehurst: Sarpedon, 1999), p. 261.
77 Michaelis, Rolf, *Panzer Divisions of the Waffen-SS* (Atglen: Schiffer, 2013), pp. 53-54.
78 According to Brettner, these aircraft were ME-109s, not ME-262s. Either is possible, or even both. Austrian factories in the area produced both types. Brettner, *Die Letzten Kämpfe Band I*, p. 162.

about a mile south of the road from Wiener Neustadt to Erlach. The airmen fought hard, and were supported by a Hungarian *Kampfgruppe*, but they couldn't stop the overwhelming Russian infantry attack supported by tanks. The Germans were driven back to the southern edge of Wiener Neustadt, including some of the *Kriegsschule* cadets. After the fall of the city the best surviving men were farmed out to other units, while 60 older men remained with the original *Kampfgruppe Fliegerhorstes Wiener Neustadt* and wound up at Horsching.[79]

That night the *Festungkommandant* of the Lower Danube, the man responsible for defending Wiener Neustadt, cobbled together as much of a defensive line as circumstances allowed. Instead of a continuous line of trenches or bunkers, the defenders created strongpoints using the elements of *LAH* that arrived in time, *SS-Kampfgruppe Keitel*, students from the Wiener Neustadt War Academy,[80] parts of *356. Infanterie-Division*, some miscellaneous mountain troops and *Volkssturm*. By immense good fortune, *LAH* found reinforcements in Wiener Neustadt. First, ten brand new Mark IVs on railroad flatcars were turned over to the division's *3. Panzer-Kompanie*. How they avoided destruction along the way must have seemed miraculous. The US Air Force had pounded the marshaling yards for more than a year, with the last attack coming on 26 March. That trains could still run into the city was a miracle of ingenuity and damage repair. The panzers' crews came with them too, from Linz. Then a platoon of Army Panthers joined the company, along with some mountain troops. This brought the total number of operable panzers to between seventeen and twenty-two, a veritable juggernaut by the standards of the day.

During the morning Sixth Guards Tank Army launched attacks from the Mattersburg area and drove the defenders back to Neudörfl, just outside Wiener Neustadt itself. More attacks came from the conquerors of Erlach and Lanzenkirchen, from the south, and broke through. They moved on Katzendorf, south of Neudörfl, virtually cutting off all Germans east of Wiener Neustadt. Only an immediate counterattack by the newly reinforced panzer force drove them back. *LAH* was then ordered to block all roads leading into the city from the southwest. It did so using the Panther platoon, which drove away all Russian spearheads for the rest of the day.

Parts of *LAH* were scattered all over the battlefield. In the morning, more Russian probes moved north of the city trying to cut it off from behind by taking Felixsdorf, due north of Wiener Neustadt. Prompt attacks by *SS-Aufklärung-Abteilung 1* stopped them for the moment. The battalion then sped south to Steinbrückl, 45 minutes from the city, and set up a defensive perimeter. Soon after, a slow-moving column of Russian panje wagons coming down the road from Wiener Neustadt was engaged at long range by two *Flakpanzer IV Wirblewinden*, Whirlwinds, the nickname for the four-barreled, self-propelled *Flakpanzer IV*. With a rotating turret and four 20mm guns, the *Wirblewind* was a precious commodity. The number built was small, between 87 and 105, and only the highest-priority units got that most coveted asset.

In return for the *Wirblewinden* chewing up the Russian infantry, the Russians deployed mortars and a few shells landed in the battalion's positions. By chance or great skill, one hit a house where the battalions' officers had gathered around a table. The roof collapsed, killing all but one of the men inside, including the battalion's commander, *SS-Hauptsturmführer* Emil Wawrzinek. He was typical of the division's dwindling number of veterans, the men who prevented *LAH* from disintegrating in the flight across Hungary. Wawrzinek joined the *Waffen-SS* in 1936 and was severely wounded more than once, having fought his way across Russia and back, been transferred to *Hitlerjugend* and then back to *LAH* as a battalion commander. Every successful army throughout

---

79   Brettner, *Die Letzten Kämpfe Band I*, p. 159.

80   One of the battle groups from the War Academy would be almost wiped out in the fighting. We know this because of the testimony of one man who survived, *Fahrenjunker* Medenwald. Along with another comrade he slipped through the Russian lines and made it all the way to Semmering, where he joined *Kampfgruppe Semmering* and told his story. Other groups would also survive, however.

history has had such men as the backbone of its formations and the *Waffen-SS* was fast running out of them.

After the death of most of its command staff, the Russians brought up tanks and the reconnaissance battalion was outgunned. Incoming Russian tank fire then forced the battalion to hastily evacuate Steinbrückl.[81]

With pressure coming from all sides, what was left of the division's artillery retreated to safer positions in the valley of the Piesting River near the *Wienerwald,* the Vienna Woods. In happier times this bucolic setting allowed Austrians to escape the stresses of big cities like Vienna or Wiener Neustadt, and hike among the jagged mountains and forested valleys, where ruined castles clung to the slopes like ivy vines on old trees. Now the Alpine foothills echoed with the boom of 105mm howitzers giving fire support to the outnumbered defenders of Wiener Neustadt. But not too much support; ammunition supplies had reached critically low limits.

Southwest of Wiener Neustadt *SS-Panzer-Regiment 1* deployed 17-22 panzers in a mixed company of Mark IVs and Panthers. These were doled out singly to support the infantry by giving them a heavy weapons presence. There was no pretense they could stop the Russians, but slowing them down with blocking groups seemed feasible.

It wasn't just their own situation that *LAH*'s commander, *SS-Brigadeführer* Otto Kumm, had to worry about, however. To their north, the left flank, *12. SS-Panzer-Division Hitlerjugend* was driven back again and again. By nightfall it was behind the Leitha River, northwest of Wiener Neustadt, astride the main roads leading to Vienna.

12. SS-Panzer-Division Hitlerjugend

When night fell on 31 March *12. SS-Panzer-Division Hitlerjugend* found itself surrounded near Sopron, situated on the slice of Hungary on the southeast bank of the *Neuseidlersee,* Lake Neusiedl. At heavy cost the division fought its way through the town to what was supposed to be the German front lines, but in fact the Germans didn't have a front line. The *Reichsschutzstellung* was supposed to be occupied by fresh forces to let the retreating SS men get a breather, but the positions were empty. This left the worn-out men of *Hitlerjugend* no choice except to occupy the positions themselves. Worse, the Russians had already breached the line further south.

Hitlerjugend typified how illusory were the pins in the maps of the high command when it came to unit strength. According to the division's former commander and historian, Hubert Meyer, "from April 1 onward, at the latest, one could only speak of a divisional *Kampfgruppe* which, in reality, had the strength of two medium-sized battalions."[82] This seems hyperbolic. In all likelihood, *Hitlerjugend* had roughly the same number of men as the *LAH*. On 13 April it is listed as having 7,731 men. Since more than 10,000 men surrendered to the Americans, that number almost certainly had to be the combat elements.

Some sources say three panzers were operational, with a few more in repair near Sankt Pölten, while the highest estimates put the combat-ready numbers as 13 of all models, with one or two *Flakpanzers* operational, and 35 panzers of all types in repair. By this point keeping the vehicles running had become a heroic task as the delivery of spare parts had more or less stopped. As seen earlier scrounging, stealing or scavenging wrecks had become the norm. The remaining artillery

---

81   Tiemann, Ralf, *The Liebstandarte IV/2* (Winnipeg: JJ Fedorowicz, 1998), pp. 278-279.
82   Meyer, Hubert, *The 12th SS, The History of the Hitler Youth Panzer Division: Volume Two* (Mechanicsburg: Stackpole, 2005), p. 461.

and mortars were hampered by lack of ammunition. The attached *Panzerjäger-Abteilung 560* had one *Jagdpanzer IV/70*, one *Jagdpanther* and three *Flakpanzer IVs* ready to fight.

The division assembled near Baumgarten, a few miles northwest of Sopron, and moved to nearby Zagersdorf, a town of less than one thousand people. That northern region of Burgenland, which included Zagersdorf, had seen combat and conquest for two millennia, and was about to see it again.

The two *Kampfgruppen* split further and took up positions in the last *Reichsschutzstellung* position at Zagersdorf, in the front lines, in a rearguard position at Wulkaprodersdorf two and a half miles northwest of Zagersdorf, and finally in a blocking position on the roads to Wiener-Neustadt and Vienna. In other words, a thousand or so fighting men were divided between four major defensive positions, and the Red Army was on the way.

Those dispositions didn't last long. The Russians attacked from Sopron down the road to Vienna and there wasn't much the *Panzergrenadiers* could do about it. They had no heavy anti-tank weapons, aside from a few *Panzerfauste*, and by noon had been driven back to the rearguard position at Wulkaprodersdorf. A precious 88mm gun was destroyed by a direct hit from a tank, stripping the position of its main anti-tank weapon. Digging in behind a creek they hoped to at least delay the Russians, but like had happened so many times in the past two weeks there were too many Russians and not enough Germans. In short order the SS men were being flanked on both sides.

Once again retreat was necessary, this time to Müllendorf, on the direct road to Vienna. Fighting continued with attacks and counterattacks. Even the divisional staff got into the combat. Around 3:00 p.m. another position was taken up at Hornstein, a small town tucked away in the woods north of the road to Vienna. Here, the division had come together with the staff headquarters and the remaining armor and SPWs to repel heavy Russians attacks featuring infantry mounted on tanks. The defenders knocked out two T-34s and two APCs, and stopped the Russian infantry in the gardens outside of town, but this respite was short-lived.

When night fell, another withdrawal behind the Leitha River brought the scattered *Kampfgruppen* together, but the *Kampfgruppe* formed around the survivors of the *SS-Panzergrenadier-Regiment 26* had suffered heavily and was dissolved to make one larger *Kampfgruppe*. But yet again a move was necessary, since the Russians had already crossed the Leitha at Pottendorf.

* * *

The month of April began with a huge hole torn in the front between the right flank of *6. SS-Panzerarmee* at Mattersburg and the left flank of *6. Armee* at Rechnitz, a gap more than thirty miles wide. As the sun set on that glorious Easter Sunday, by the barest margin the gap had been plugged by the unlikeliest of units.

6. Armee

General der Panzertruppe Hermann Balck's *6. Armee* had been shoved far south as it retreated west, and by 1 April it had taken position in the prepared fortifications, such as they were, of the *Reichsschutzstellung*. The ruined and exhausted units hoped for a momentary reprieve to rest, reorganize and heal but they didn't get it.

Balck faced crises on both of his flanks. South of Steinfurt, the Russian 18th Tank Corps drove *IV SS-Panzerkorps* back into Austria and tore open the seam between it and the *I Kavallerie-Korps*, the northernmost corps of *2. Panzerarmee*. The Russians sped westward into the gap while *IV SS-Panzerkorps* retreated on a parallel course and it became a race to see which side could beat the other to the west.

The *IV SS-Panzerkorps* commanded *5. SS-Panzer-Division Wiking*, *1. Panzer-Division* and *3. Panzer-Division*. The Germans barely won the race, deploying into the area between Fürstenfeld and Lafnitzel on 1 April, and thereby protecting the flank of *III Panzerkorps* nearby on the east. On *IV SS-Panzerkorps'* right flank was *SS-Ausbildungs-und-Ersatz Bataillon 18* near Kirchberg an der Raab. But the 18th Tank Corps kept going west instead of turning north to attack *IV SS-Panzerkorps*, and by 1 April had thrust deep into Austria at Feldbach and beyond. Like much of the *Wehrmacht* on that Easter morning, *6. Armee* was in serious danger of being encircled.

* * *

More than 200,000 refugees had followed the army into Styria and also paused to rest, in the belief they were safe inside the borders of the Reich. Mountain passes blocked by snow didn't really give them much choice anyway. Mixed into the mass of humanity were the troops of the Hungarian Second Army who, theoretically, were still under Balck's command. From the distance of more than seventy years it's hard to imagine what could have motivated the Hungarians to keep fighting, since their country had been totally overrun. As events would prove, the answer was simple – nothing.

Hermann Balck had no doubts why the gap existed on his flanks, both between his army and that of Sepp Dietrich and where he'd lost contact with *2. Panzerarmee*; it was all the SS's fault. That was his default position when something went wrong. Balck had ordered Otto Gille's *IV SS-Panzerkorps* not to lose contact with *I Kavallerie-Korps* by retreating into the very area now occupied by the Russians, and ignored the inconvenient fact that the Russians had beaten them there. When Gille was unable to go to the positions assigned because he had no way of ejecting the Red Army from them, Balck took this as a sign of disobedience.

Kampfgruppe Semmering

One of the most pivotal actions in the entire campaign was fought at the Semmering Pass by a thrown together German *Kampfgruppe* with members from the *Heer*, *Waffen-SS*, *Kriegsmarine* and *Luftwaffe*. In one of his few comments about the *Kampfgruppe* the usually self-aggrandizing Hermann Balck paid credit to the defenders in this battle. From the time combat commenced in early April until the end of the war not one day went by without Russian attacks on the Semmering Pass, but despite terrible casualties the Germans held this vital position with a scratch force. Indeed, their defense was so rigid that the ragged *Kampfgruppe* grew into an actual division, and if anything shows the potential defensive capabilities of an Alpine Redoubt, it's this battle.

Everywhere along the so-called front lines there were gaps with no defenders, but the most dangerous point was the aforementioned junction with *6. SS-Panzerarmee*, where no units filled the gap. The terrain was rugged and not suited for maintaining an advance overland, which made the strategic passes like those at Wechsel and Semmering even more critical. Mountains flanked the winding Semmering Pass valley that led into the heart of Styria, with the best road more or less paralleling the *Südbahn* railway line. The setup was very much like a walled medieval city with Semmering Pass acting as a drawbridge.

Its loss would have been catastrophic for the Germans. If the Russians had seized the pass then Styria would have been indefensible. Moreover, the left flank of *1. Volks-Gebirgs-Division* would have been turned and the entire position of both *6. Armee* and *2. Panzerarmee* would be unhinged, jeopardizing not only half of *Heeresgruppe Süd* but all of *Heeresgruppe E*. Despite the gradual withdrawal of their best assault units being sucked into the battle for Vienna, the Russians never stopped attacking along this sector. According to Balck *Kampfgruppe Semmering*, which was shortly renamed *Kampfgruppe Raithel*, comprised the following elements: "Mountain

Training NCO School, Mittenwald; Mountain Artillery School, Dachstein; SS Mountain Reserve Battalion, Leoben; Bomber Wing Bölcke; One *Flak* Battalion, One Infantry Battalion; Two Quick Reaction Battalions and *Volkssturm* personnel used as ammunition and ration porters."[83]

Specifically these were local *Volkssturm* men who were guarding their homes around the Semmering Pass and regular *Landser*, soldiers, from the above-discussed *SS-Gebirgsjäger-Ausbildungs-und-Ersatz Bataillon 13 Leoben*; *Gebirgsjäger-Unteroffizier-Schule Admont*; men from *Gebirgs-Artillerie-Schule Dachstein-Obertraun*; two *Reichsarbeitdienst (RAD)*[84] brigades; *HeimatFlak Wiener Neustadt*; *Gebirgsjäger-Regiment 136*; surplus *Luftwaffe* ground personnel from *Kampfgeschwader 27 Boelcke*[85] and, later in the month, the so-called *Schatten-Division Steiermark,* or Shadow Division Styria. It would eventually have *Gerbirgsjäger-Regiment 154* (with 3 battalions) and *155* (4 battalions!), *Gebirgs-Artillerie Regiment 56*, *Landschützen-Bataillon 851*[86] and an anti-tank company.

On 1 April *Oberst* Heribert Raithel became commander. He was highly decorated for bravery and his most recent assignment had been commandant of the *Gebirgs-Artillerie-Schule Dachstein*. He turned out to be like a chess grandmaster in moving his disparate, outnumbered and outgunned fragments to the point of greatest need, blocking the Russians for more than a month and denying them the use of the Semmering Pass. And yet despite his few positive remarks, Balck was overall dismissive of this *Kampfgruppe* and the month-long battle it fought, which is bizarre considering in May he would award *Oberst* Raithel the Knight's Cross. From the German defensive standpoint its defense was nothing short of heroic.

* * *

The unit's formation began on 30 March when *Panzerjäger-Ausbildungs-und-Ersatz-Abteilung 48*[87] moved to block the Semmering Pass by sending a company of men and seven 75mm *PAK 40*[88] guns, under the command of *Leutnant* Adolf Povlika. His orders were to hold the passes at Semmering and Preiner Gscheid and not allow any Russians into Styria.[89] At least 14 Hetzers and Marders[90] were detached from the battalion and sent to Feldbach.

Another one of the units in the vicinity was the partly trained *SS-Gebirgs-Ausbildungs-und-Ersatz-Abteilung 13,* based in Leoben. Members of this unit were *Volksdeutsch* from the Balkans, although their officers and NCOs were veterans. The SS battalion had no heavy weapons and no transport. Reaching the front meant marching at the head of a pack train of mules when time was of the essence. To solve that the battalion's Commanding Officer seized every vehicle he could

---

83   Balck, Hermann, Edited and Translated by Major General David T. Zabecki, USA (Ret.), and Lieutenant Colonel Dieter J. Biedekarken, USA (Ret.), *Order in Chaos, The Memoirs of General of Panzer-Troops Hermann Balck* (Lexington: The University Press of Kentucky, 2015), p. 428.

84   The *Reichsarbeitdienst* was the German Labor Service. This was a compulsory duty that initially centered on public works projects, but in the latter stages of the war became little more than a training ground for the *Volkssturm*. Six RAD Brigades saw fierece front-line action during the war, including with the so-called *Schatten-Division Steiermark*.

85   *Kampfgeschwader* or KG 27 fought from the beginning of the war until the end, but by late 1944 it had more or less run out of Heinkel HE-111s, the obsolete bomber it had flown throughout the war. Plans were drawn up to convert it to a fighter group, and while its unit designation was changed the ME-262s it was supposed to fly never materialized. The veteran and highly trained personnel were then handed rifles and sent to the front.

86   The *Landschützen* Battalions were part of the *Volkssturm*.

87   At least one source lists this unit as *Kampfgruppe* Lang, after its commander *Oberstleutnant* Ludwig Lang.

88   *Panzerabwehrkanone*, an anti-tank gun.

89   Brettner, Prof. Friedrich, 'Semmering, April 1945 – Die Kämpfe um die Südbahn-Meierei', <http://www.bundesheer.at/truppendienst/ausgaben/artikel.php?id=94>, (Accessed 18 January 2018).

90   Marders were a series of German *jagdpanzers* based on either foreign or surplus German tank chassis, mounting either a German 75mm *PAK* 40 or captured Russian 76.2mm gun.

find, regardless of what it was or to whom it belonged. Officers fleeing the front found themselves suddenly walking, but facing armed men and fear of the notorious SS Flying Courts-Martial made them comply. Everywhere behind the front was evidence of men who had been killed because they had supposedly fled from combat. Sometimes they hung from utility poles or trees with signs around their neck declaring their crimes, and sometimes they lay face-down in a ditch.

But that wasn't enough, so the determined battalion commander, *SS-Hauptsturmführer* Horst Grunwald, seized vehicles belonging to the Budapest Fire Department that had accompanied Ferenc Szálasi into exile.[91] Grunwald was not a man to be denied. He had fought from the first day of the war and won both classes of the Iron Cross, the Infantry Assault Badge and the German Cross in gold. His previous service was with the *7. SS-Gebirgs-Division Prinz Eugen* and after the war he served in the West German Border Police, achieving the rank of colonel. Throughout the coming battle Grunwald more often than not ignored orders coming from higher headquarters, when those orders bore no resemblance to the reality of the fighting in the mountains. In fighting of that kind, where trees and underbrush limited sight lines and hand-to-hand combat was frequent, orders became irrelevant. The solidness of the defense depended solely on the willingness of the man on the spot to stand fast and not give up his position. No orders, threats or cajoling could influence that determination.

Three of the battalion's companies set off for the front on 30 March. Counting the command staff the group probably numbered around 300. But by 1 April the Russian 103rd Guards Rifle Division, from Ninth Guards Army, had captured Gloggnitz without opposition. The Germans were shocked at the loss of Gloggnitz, but the speed of the Russian advance caught everyone by surprise. Only a few hours after the Red Army took the city, American B-24 bombers of the Fifteenth Air Force began bombing the rail facilities there. The Russians fired from every available tube to get their attention, and after the lead bombers had dropped their loads the rest of the formation got the message and turned away.

The loss of the city cut the Gloggnitz-Neunkirchen railway, which crippled efforts to transport troops along the front. It also put the Russian due north of the Hochwechsel, a potentially strong defensive position that would see bitter fighting before the month ended.

Therefore, at dawn Grunwald got the call to bring the rest of the battalion to the Semmering area. The various companies were scattered all over the area around Leoben and moved to Semmering independently. They took up positions at Bärenwirt, which literally means 'the bear's host', a 3,000 foot mountain in the Semmering Pass area.

By the end of the day a hastily thrown-together fighting line had been established. The *Kampfgruppe* command post was established in the Südbahn Hotel, the grand fairytale structure built to resemble a romantic castle. Its pristine grounds would shortly be the scene of several rounds of vicious fighting.

* * *

As more and more men poured into the area, the polyglot unit was called *Kampfgruppe Semmering* after its location, and the commander was the energetic 35-year-old *Oberst* Heribert Raithel, who would be awarded the Knight's Cross for his brilliant defense of the pass.[92]

The people of Styria knew the Russians were coming, and had seen the newsreels about the raping and pillaging that came along with them, but it was only on 1 April that the truth

---

91   Lucas, James, *Last Days of the Third Reich, The Collapse of Nazi Germany, May, 1945* (New York: William Morrow and Co., 1986), pp. 100-104.

92   The award was given on 19 May, while in captivity, by the former General der Panzertruppe Hermann Balck. Its legitimacy is questionable because *Grossadmiral* Dönitz ordered that no more awards could be given after 8 May, but the citation on Raithel's Knight's Cross was dated 20 April.

confronted them face to face. Hungarian refugees pouring into Austria related tales of horror and bestiality, and the Austrians suddenly realized that for once Goebbels had not been lying and hell was upon them. Some looked to the shattered *Wehrmacht* to somehow turn back the Russian invasion, while others saw no chance of avoiding the coming storm and only wanted it to be over with. A few Communists or Socialists who had escaped seven years of Nazi rule even looked forward to a Russian occupation.

III Panzer-Korps

It wasn't just Balck's flanks that were in danger. By 1 April, four Russian Corps had cut *6. Armee* in half starting at Lafnitztal, with penetrations as far west as Kirchberg an der Raab. North of that breakthrough area was *III Panzerkorps*, commanded by the brilliant *General der Panzertruppe* Hermann Breith. Instead of the panzers he was trained to lead and his corps was named for, Breith commanded *1. Volks-Gebirgs-Division, Divisionsgruppe Krause, Arko 3* and *Sperrverband-Motschmann*. This force totaled about 20,000 men.

Divisionsgruppe Krause

Knight's Cross winner *Generalleutnant* Walther Krause was ordered by Balck to form a *divisionsgruppe* on the southern flank of *Kampfgruppe Semmering*. Some sources refer to his rag-tag formation as a corps, others simply as a *Kampfgruppe*. It certainly never approached the strength of a division, or probably even a full-strength brigade until other divisions were subordinated to its command later in the month. To Krause's south was *1. Volks-Gebirgs-Division*.

Krause's command was called a *divisionsgruppe*, another amorphous term for a German unit. The original intent of such a formation had been to maintain the cadres of divisions wrecked in battle that could then be rebuilt, but morphed over the years into something akin to a large *Kampfgruppe*. The idea was to form a headquarters staff that could manage anything up to and including a division-sized unit, or even larger. Krause's beginning order of battle included *Feldersatz-Bataillon 75* from *3. Panzer-Division*, a *nebelwerfer* battalion, a *Kampfgruppe* from *Stellvertretendes-Generalkommando XVIII Armeekorps*, the full name of the command organization of *General der Gebirgstruppen* Julius Ringel operating out of Graz, two heavy artillery battalions and three 88mm *Flak* batteries. It wasn't much to stop an enemy flood of tanks and cavalry.[93]

Krause's command was much like other German *Kampfgruppen* of the period, a thrown-together mix of whatever men were available who could hold a rifle. Other small units were soon added. Some of the men put under his command were heavily engaged and could only move into position on his northern flank after dark; this included both battalions of the *werfer* brigade which only numbered about 100 men and which were already formed and ready for combat; a *Flak regiment* with two battalions of 88mm guns and one of lighter calibers, which were then divided into troops of three guns each, with a very good ammunition supply on hand; an *SS-Ausbildungs-Bataillon* with a strength of about 900 men, most of whom were Dutch or Norwegian *Volksdeutsche*, with German officers (these troops were rated as being very good in combat); a *Gebirgs-Jäger-Ausbildungs-Bataillon* of 400-500 men, with no heavy weapons or machine guns; a *Gebirgs-Ersatz-Kompanie* of

93   Brettner, Friedrich, *Die Letzten Kämpfe des II Weltkrieges, Pinka-Lafnitz-Hochwechsel-1743 m: 1 Gebirgsdivision – 1 Panzerdivision – Divisionsgruppe Krause – 117. Jägerdivision – Kampfgruppe Arko 3* (Eigenverlag Friedrich Brettner: Gloggnitz, 1999), p. 17.

150 men with no heavy weapons, machine guns or combat value (they had been trained to handle and treat horses, and to help veterinarians); and a cavalry squadron of about 180 men, again with no machine guns and of low fighting value.

None of those units were set up for combat, as they had no means of transportation, or even field kitchens. Most of them were simply warm bodies. The lack of the basic essentials needed to keep a unit in the field would later cause serious difficulties for the *divisionsgruppe*.

Sperrverband-Motschmann

Sperrverband was a German term meaning 'blocking group'. In literal German fashion it meant exactly that, a small *Kampfgruppe* put in place to prevent enemy movement through an area. *Sperrverband-Motschmann* was formed around *SS-Polizei-Regiment 13*, whose roster included mostly older *Volksdeutsche* and Croatians. Although it did have an artillery battery, overall it was ill-equipped and without combat experience, and had low combat value compared to actual units designed for battle. But with a rifle strength of around 1,000 men it was thrown into the fight out of sheer desperation.

* * *

Beside Breith's corps on the right was *IV SS-Panzerkorps* near Fürstenfeld, with three ruined panzer divisions: *1. Panzer-Division*, *3. Panzer-Division*, and *5. SS-Panzer-Division Wiking*. Defending Kirchberg was *Fahr-Ausbildungs-und-Ersatzbataillon 18*.[94] South of the hole ripped in the front was *I Kavallerie-Korps*, with *297. Infanterie-Division*, *Köruck 582* and the *Flak* battalion from *16. SS-Panzergrenadier-Division Reichsführer-SS* in the immediate vicinity of the breakthrough line.

Arko 3

The term *Arko* is a German abbreviation for *Artillerie Kommandeur*. An *Arko* commanded artillery attached to a corps, army or army group. The *Arko* had a small staff of his own that, when attached to a smaller unit such as a division, supplemented that unit's staff. In this case, the *Arko 3* was part of *III Panzerkorps*.

The *Arko 3* commander was *Oberst der Reserve* Gerhard Semmer. Little is known of the exact composition of this *Kampfgruppe* by the beginning of April, but it probably contained *Heeres-Sturmartillerie-Brigade 303* and some of *Artillerie-Brigade 959*, and perhaps a few other small units.

Kampfgruppe Schweitzer

Rechnitz was the key position in Balck's sector. Roads leading west from the town led to Oberwart, the loss of which would drive a wedge into the gap between *6. SS-Panzerarmee* and *6. Armee* that

---

94   *Fahr-Ausbildungs-und-Ersatzbataillon* translates in German military nomenclature as "Driving Replacement and Training Battalion". These units taught a variety of skills for transport and supply personnel, including repair of gasoline-powered vehicles, the handling of horses, driving various military trucks and accounting for supplies.

couldn't be dislodged. There was no choice except to attack and retake Rechnitz, but Balck had no forces to carry out the assault.

Gauleiter Siegfried Ueberreither had no intentions of allowing his *Gau*, Styria, to be overrun without a fight. As committed a Nazi as still existed in the Third Reich, Ueberreither knew that with the field armies reeling backward into Austria he had to mobilize every possible resource to stop the Red Army. One of the first was the *SS-Ausbildungs-und-Ersatz-Abteilung 11*, based at Graz.[95] This unit supplied trained replacements to the *11. SS-Freiwilligen-Panzergrenadier-Division Nordland*.[96] Most of the men of the battalion fell into one of two categories. First were the officer and NCO instructors, combat veterans sent back to train new replacements, usually while recovering from wounds, and second were the recruits, in this case mostly 16 and 17-year-old Dutch teenagers. A few convalescent wounded and ethnic Germans rounded out the battalion. It was divided into six companies and fielded about 800 men.

Also part of the *Kampfgruppe* were *Volkssturm Bataillon 31/191*,[97] with 300 men, and a replacement troop for *3. Kavallerie-Division*, which added another 120 men. What it didn't have was heavy weapons of any sort, aside from a few mortars, being armed strictly with infantry weapons, rifles and sub-machine guns. The commander was *SS-Sturmbannführer* Willi Schweitzer, as hard-bitten a combat veteran as could be found in all of Austria. He joined the *LAH* in 1934 and participated in the war from the first moment the *Wehrmacht* marched into Poland, fought in Russia with *7. SS-Gebirgs-Division Prinz Eugen* and later took part in the destruction of the Warsaw ghetto. Also part of the *Kampfgruppe* were at least two Swedes who had been recovering from wounds at a hospital in Graz, neither one of whom would ever return to Sweden.

Some sources also include the orphaned *I./SS-Panzergrenadier-Regiment 23 Norge*, part of *11. SS-Freiwilligen-Panzergrenadier-Division Norge*. This unit had fought as part of *Heeresgruppe Süd* since January and had suffered terrible losses during *Unternehmen Konrad 1*, the first relief attempt aimed at Budapest. Its commander at the time, *SS-Hauptsturmführer* Fritz Vogt, won the Knight's Cross for his actions during that period, but by 8 January the battalion's effective strength was down to 40 men and probably numbered no more than 200 by 1 April.

Another significant addition to this force was *I./ SS-Brigade Ney*. The men had fought in the Konrad offensives to relieve Budapest in January and *Unternehmen Frühlingserwachen* in March, and were heavily engaged during the retreat from Hungary, their homeland. They likely numbered somewhere between 600-800 tough combats veterans with nothing to lose.[98]

After being activated on 30 March, *SS-Kampfgruppe Schweitzer* headed to the front in trucks borrowed from the postal service, with the mission of retaking Rechnitz and patching the hole in the German lines. The attack seemed suicidal: 2,100 men with no artillery or armor, and with more than half the men new to combat, were supposed to attack and recapture a town from a Red Army who suffered under no such handicaps.

Fleeing refugees and military units jammed the narrow mountain roads. Instead of attacking at first light on 31 March, *SS-Kampfgruppe Schweitzer* couldn't get organized enough until 11:00 a.m. on 1 April. When they set off in broad daylight the chances of surprising the enemy seemed slim, yet hidden behind the hills and mountains the Russians didn't notice their approach. The unit

95   Exactly who ordered the battalion to form up for battle has been lost to history. The author here assumes it was Ueberreither because in the following days he sent a steady stream of similar units to the front under his authority as *Gauleiter*.

96   Some dispute this was the replacement and training battalion for Nordland, but instead supplied *III SS-Panzerkorps* as a whole, or Nordland and *23. Freiwilligen-SS-Panzergrenadier-Division Nordland*. Most sources agree on it being strictly tied to Nordland, although most of its recruits were Dutch.

97   31 was the Gau number for Styria, while 191 means it was the 191st *Volkssturm* battalion raised.

98   Men of the brigade are known to have executed downed American airmen on 13 March 1945.

holding Rechnitz belonged to 37th Guards Rifle Corps, a veteran front-line formation awaiting relief by follow-on forces of the Twenty-Sixth Army, when it would return to its parent Ninth Army. After chasing the Germans across Hungary for two weeks the last thing they expected was to be attacked by a scratch force with no artillery or air support.

The terrain to Rechnitz's north and northwest is mountainous and heavily forested. This shielded *SS-Kampfgruppe Schweitzer* and allowed them to achieve total surprise and, against all odds, drive the Russians out of Rechnitz. Casualties on both sides were heavy but the impetus of the German attack even carried them past the town and back to the entrenchments of the *Reichsschutzstellung*. Along the way they found the bodies of executed men and raped women in streets littered with loot either discarded or dropped by the rampaging Russians.

The commander of the Russian Twenty-Sixth Army, Lieutenant-General Gagen, didn't immediately know how large the force was that had counterattacked, or that somehow the broken front line had been plugged by a small, ragged but well-led force. He also didn't know that the two German armies still weren't connected, or that a force no bigger than a regiment was responsible for retaking Rechnitz. All he knew for certain was that the road network through Rechnitz was again in German hands.

* * *

During the war *Reichsführer-SS* Heinrich Himmler lavished immense resources on foreign SS units in the hope of making the war with the Soviet Union a pan-European crusade. Some of the experiments were a success, such as *5. SS-Panzer-Division Wiking* and *11. SS Freiwilligen-Panzergrenadier-Division Nordland*, the Belgian troops under Leon Degrelle, the French volunteers and others. Most were far less successful. The *13. Waffen-Gebirgs-Division der SS Handschar* and *14. Waffen-Grenadier-Division der SS Galizien*, both had notable successes along with major disappointments. Others were outrights disasters, such as *23. Waffen-Gebirgs-Division der SS Kama*, which was disbanded shortly after being activated because many of its Bosnian Muslims mutinied. But undoubtedly the biggest waste of resources was the Hungarian SS Corps containing *25. Waffen-Grenadier-Division der SS Hunyadi* and *26. Waffen-Grenadier-Division der SS Hungaria*. Both divisions were in southeastern Germany and western Austria eating SS food, burning SS fuel and holding SS weapons that for the vast majority would never be fired in anger.

SS-Brigade Ney

As previously mentioned, one of the most successful of the foreign SS units was *SS-Brigade Ney*. The brigade was formed in 1944 by *Honved* veterans to fight the Russians then invading their country. The unit fought so well during the *Konrad* operations that Hitler awarded them their own cuffband to honor the unit's founder, Karoly Ney.

Now, on 1 April, the Hungarians had been completely driven out of their own country. After fighting in the area of Rechnitz for several days, the brigade staff was ordered to Birkfeld in Styria, where the brigade was once again parceled out to units in dire need of infantry. As part of *SS-Kampfgruppe Schweitzer,* which included the *SS-Panzer-Grenadier Ausbildung und Ersatz Abteilung 11*,[99] with a strength of some 800 men;[100] a squadron of some 120 cavalry from *3.*

---

99   Some sources say it was *SS-Panzergrenadier-Ausbildungs-und-Ersatz-Abteilung 18*, but *SS-Panzergrenadier-Ausbildungs-und-Ersatz-Abteilung 11* was based in Graz and makes more sense.

100   Sources disagree on including the battalion from SS-Brigade Ney in the Kampfgruppe. It seems possible that the 800-man strength of the SS-Panzergrenadier-Ausbildungs-und-Ersatz-Abteilung 11 might also include the men from Ney.

Kavallerie-Division and a *Volkssturm* Battalion of some 300 men, the *I./SS-Brigade Ney* counter-attacked at Rechnitz and retook the town, but suffered heavy casualties doing so. The *Kampfgruppe's* commander was badly wounded in the attack.

SS-Obersturmbannführer Ney had somewhere found the men to form a fourth battalion. The *II.* and newly formed *IV. Abteilungs* were attached to *III Panzerkorps* in the area of Birkfeld-Styria; that corps then assigned them to *1. Panzer-Division*. Another battalion was subordinated to *Arko 3* defending the *Reichsschutzstellung* defensive positions near Dürnbach.[101] In the previous 16 days the Brigade had suffered 75 men killed, with 94 missing and many more wounded.[102]

Other broken units were also wandering all over the battle area. In early January a volunteer SS formation, the *1. Ungarische-Sturmjäger-Bataillon*, had been stronger than many regiments, with approximately 1,500 men, but three months of fighting had bled the unit white. By late March the remnants, now little more than an average-strength battalion and likely no more than 500 in number, split up into two *SS-Kampfgruppen*. *SS-Obersturmbannführer* Rideph lead the *1. Kompanie* and *3. Kompanie* of *I./SS-Brigade Ney* and the *6. Kompanie* of *II./SS-Brigade Ney*. The group was immediately attached to a Hungarian mountain brigade. The other group was commanded by *SS-Hauptsturmführer der Reserve* Dr Lenk, consisting of *2. Kompanie* and *4. Kompanie* of *I./SS-Brigade Ney* and *5. Kompanie* of *II./SS-Brigade Ney*, the inference being that *I./SS-Brigade Ney* still had 4 intact companies, while *II./SS-Brigade Ney* only had 2 companies left. Lenk's group was attached to *1. Volks-Gebirgs-Division* of *III Panzerkorps*.

As the calendar turned to April, somewhere near the town of Szombathely, just inside the Hungarian border with Austria south of Sopron, 62 miles from Vienna and 73 from Graz, *SS-Kampfgruppe Lenk* was attached to *IV SS-Panzerkorps*. Happily, the Hungarian ski troops actually found themselves subordinated to their countrymen in *SS-Brigade Ney*, which was also attached to *IV SS-Panzerkorps*. *SS-Brigade Ney* had moved with as much speed as possible down the main highway heading west, and had wound up near the Austrian border in the area of Rechnitz, under the direct command of the 2nd Hungarian Armored Division. Later, however, the brigade was parceled out to *III Panzerkorps*, then *6. Armee* and finally *I SS-Panzerkorps* of *6. SS-Panzerarmee*.

All of the Hungarian SS men were now without a country and most knew their fate was sealed. The *Waffen-SS* in general could expect no mercy from the Russians, but foreigners who swore allegiance to Hitler were doubly doomed, since the communist regimes in their home countries would not only execute them, but would make a spectacle of the affair, too.

1. Volks-Gebirgs-Division

Over the coming five weeks, no division in *Heeresgruppe Süd* would endure heavier fighting and bombardment than *1. Volks-Gebirgs-Division*. On a daily basis the dug-in mountain troops fought on the steep slopes of the Alpine foothills while being pounded by limitless mortar, artillery and rocket barrages. But there were no set-piece battles or rapid movements. Instead, it was like two heavyweight fighters bent at the waist, head on their opponent's shoulder, slamming away at the other's torso.

Commanded by *Generalleutnant* August Wittmann, winner of the Knight's Cross and the German Cross in Gold, the division had been formed in 1938 and had always been considered

101 'RFSS-Brigade "Ney"', <http://www.hunyadi.co.uk/page5.php>, (Accessed 14 October 2018). One source says that the brigade's *I. Abteilung* was involved in the attack to retake Rechnitz as part of *SS-Kampfgruppe Schweitzer*, enduring heavy casualties in the assault. And while the attack was successful, the town could not be held for long.

102 Pencz, Rudolf, 'The Story of the Hungarian Volunteer Brigade "Ney"', *Siegrunen 76* (2004), p. 22.

one of the *Wehrmacht*'s elite formations. Originally it had three *Gebirgsjäger* regiments, but *Gebirgsjäger-Regiment 100* was transferred in 1940 to *5. Gebirgs-Division*, leaving Wittmann's command with only *98. Gebirgsjäger-Regiment* and *99. Gebirgsjäger-Regiment*.

Like the rest of *Heeresgruppe Süd*, *1. Volks-Gebirgs-Division* lost heavily in the retreat from Hungary. It reached the frontier of the Reich on 31 March in the area south of Rechnitz with its regiments aligned with the *99. Gebirgsjäger-Regiment* on the left, or north, flank and the *98. Gebirgsjäger-Regiment* on the right. The division to its right was *1. Panzer-Division*, but Wittmann's left was unsupported, with only the forming *Kampfgruppe Semmering* at the Semmering Pass too far away for mutual support, so he spread his front over a long area and bent it backward to the left.

Russian attacks followed quickly, with most of the pressure coming on the division's left flank in the direction of Oberwart. The gap between *Kampfgruppe Raithel* and *1. Volks-Gebirgs-Division* meant not only that Oberwart couldn't be held, but also threatened an immediate Russian breakthrough.

* * *

As an example of preparations behind the lines, in the sector of *1. Volks-Gebirgs-Division* a number of units had already been mobilized for defense. Such measures had been taken throughout all of the threatened areas in the zone of *Heeresgruppe Süd*. Each town was organized into a *Kampfabschnitt*, literally 'battle section', which contained all of the units readied for defense of that town.

As one example of what this looked like, *Kampfabschnitt Rechnitz* was commanded by a mere captain but had *Volkssturm* battalions from Oberwart, Bruck an der Mur and Leoben, two companies from *Baupionier-Bataillon 730*, a company of 60 men from the border security police, a *Flak* company made up of men and guns from Dürnbach, Hannersdorf and Neuhodis with two 88mm and three 37mm guns, another platoon from *Baupionier-Bataillon 730* and *Volkssturm-Bataillon 31/815*.[103] The total manpower of this force may have approached 1,500 men, but aside from the *Pioniers* and *Flak* crews *Kampfabschnitt Rechnitz* had little combat value. Other *Kampfabschnitt* had been established at Kohfidisch, Güssing, Lafnitztal, Raabtal and Kalch, but none had even the fighting capacity of *Kampfabschnitt Rechnitz*.

* * *

Training in the picturesque town of Güstrow in Mecklenburg, Northeast Germany, in early April, *SS-Hauptsturmführer* Emilian, of the still forming Rumanian SS division,[104] along with his classmates heard the sound of Russian guns in the distance and watched refugees streaming through the town. The masterpiece of Renaissance architecture, Güstrow Palace, and the Gothic Dom, the cathedral housing Barlach's Floating Angel sculpture, were both in the path of the Red Army. But instead of having the Rumanians help defend the town, as would usually have happened, they were immediately ordered to Berlin for reassignment. Once there, Emilian was sent back to Austria to rejoin his unit. Further building of the Rumanian division was halted and the components that had been assembled were placed at the disposal of Sepp Dietrich and *6. SS-Panzerarmee*. Rumania had long since been overrun by the Russians and switched sides, so, like their Norwegian or Danish comrades in *Wiking*, Emilian and his countrymen were under no illusion about the fate awaiting them at home.

* * *

---

103 Brettner, *Pinka*, p. 9

104 A Rumanian SS division did not actually exist, although plans had long since been laid to form one. Emilian and his fellows were being trained as officers for that division when the situation demanded their return to the front.

Southeast of Weiner Neustadt, the detachments from the SS Officer's Academy had taken heavy casualties defending Deutschkreuz and Nikitsch the day before, and withdrew to new positions at Frohsdorf and Walpersbach. They were reinforced by the supply company for *SS-Panzer-Regiment 3*. A hodge-podge of other units was thrown out to screen the city elsewhere, including three *Volkssturm* battalions and two police battalions at Neudorfl, none of which had uniforms or even basic military equipment. A *Kampfgruppe* from *356. Infanterie-Division* joined *SS-Kampfgruppe Keitel* at Neunkirchen, just southwest of the city. The commander was *SS-Obersturmbannführer* Karl-Heinz Keitel,[105] son of Hitler's military adviser *Generalfeldmarschall* Wilhelm Keitel.

During the night of 31 March-1 April heavy attacks were launched on the SS positions at Walpersbach and Frohsdorf from the south, southeast and east, by tanks, artillery and infantry of IX Guards Mechanized Corps. With few heavy weapons the Germans were thrown back and retreated down the road to Weiner Neustadt. Instead of following, the Russians moved to secure crossings over the Leitha River in accordance with the now standard practice of first trying to surround a city before assaulting it. They moved so quickly that elements of *I SS-Panzerkorps* retreating from Sauerbrunn three miles east of Weiner Neustadt had to detour around them at Lichtenworth, a few miles due north of the city. Moving through the city itself was out of the question, since the roads leading from the east were under imminent danger from Russian spearheads. Had *I SS-Panzerkorps* waited even hours longer they would have been surrounded. Weiner Neustadt would be seized by V Guards Tank Corps, with only men of the *SS-Junkerschule* to defend it.

232. Reserve-Panzer-Division

During the Slovakian uprising of August 1944, a scratch force named *Panzer-Division Tatra* had been assembled around twenty-eight obsolete Panzer IIIs and IVs and three Tiger Is. Once the fighting was over, the division was re-formed into a training division. With the Russians closing in, in March of 1945 it was reorganized again as the *232. Reserve-Panzer-Division* and immediately sent into reserve for *Heeresgruppe Süd*. In turn, the Army Group assigned it to *8. Armee* and it went into the line near Marcaltö, Hungary, southwest of Győr. The area was one of rolling hills and farmland, with no natural defensive barriers behind which *232. Reserve-Panzer-Division* could make a stand. It came under attack immediately and fought well, but was pushed north anyway.

The division commander, *Generalmajor* Hans-Ulrich Back, was badly wounded on 29 March and the division took severe losses while trying to hold at Raab on 31 March. Because of his wound Back survived the fighting and wasn't captured, which is a better fate than befell his command. By 1 April the *232. Reserve-Panzer-Division* dissolved under the weight of heavy casualties and repeated Russian hammer blows. It ceased to exist as a cohesive formation and was written off the German Order of Battle. The remnants who escaped the destruction fled northwest.

With *232. Reserve-Panzer-Division* written off the rolls, the remaining members of the division had no way to draw supplies. In other words, they could not officially get food, fuel or ammunition. This required attachment or reassignment to a parent formation. A small group of survivors wound up attached to *3. SS-Panzer-Division Totenkopf*. Two *Kampfgruppen* were formed around the other remnants. The first one, numbering about 750 men and fully motorized, wound up attached to *6. Panzer-Division*. The other *Kampfgruppe*, some 400 men, was absorbed into *Panzerkorps Feldherrnhalle*.

---

105 A few sources put his rank as *SS-Standartenführer*.

Kampfgruppe 1. Panzer-Division

Near the southern end of the Vienna Woods at Heiligenkreuz, the storied *1. Panzer-Division* regrouped and counted its losses. The town had long been an island of solace close to Vienna, with a backdrop of firs and pines to ease the pressures of the capital. The ancient Cistercian Abbey had been continuously occupied since the 12th Century and was not abandoned even as war approached its gates.

Typical of the time, *1. Panzer-Division* was assigned to whatever corps headquarters made sense at the moment. At the beginning of April that was *IV SS-Panzerkorps*. A strength return on 1 April indicated how devastating the materiel losses had been during the retreat across Hungary. Total manpower, i.e. ration strength, remained high at 11,473 men. But the equipment ready for combat tells the true story. A mere three Mark IV panzers were on hand but none were operational, while a whopping 39 Mark V Panthers remained on the rolls but just a single tank could fight. The SPW numbers were about sixty percent of authorized.[106] The division's heavy *Flak* regiment was reorganizing at Bratislava, where it got caught up in the fighting and the flood of war washed it away.[107]

Kampfgruppe 3. Panzer-Division

Also near Heiligenkreuz was *Kampfgruppe 3. Panzer-Division*, which was in even worse shape than *Kampfgruppe 1. Panzer-Division*. With so many vehicles lost *Kampfgruppe 3. Panzer-Division* did what the other divisions did, organized the surplus personnel into Alarm Companies to fight as infantry. Armor ready to fight consisted of one command Mark III and one Mark IV. It also had five *Jagdpanzers* operational, with 5 more in repair. Even counting these, the entire armored strength of the division only reached 20 panzers. The SPW count was 119 vehicles ready for combat.

An interesting footnote for this division was that in March it received between 10 and 12 Panthers armed with the new infrared (IR) night vision system.[108] The system itself was heavy, cumbersome and cantankerous, but effective when it worked like it should. The Panthers were assigned to the division's *Panzer-Regiment 6* as its *3. Kompanie*. It's unknown if any of them actually fought in either Hungary or Austria, and there's some debate whether they were ever shipped to the division at all. Russian reports do mention them as being present near Berlin and American after-action reports also claim that Panthers equipped with IR devices were used on the Western Front, although during daytime. Nor was Germany the only country working on IR technology; Russia and the Allies were too, and had workable systems on the verge of mass production.

During the retreat from Hungary formations that held together, such as *Kampfgruppe 3. Panzer-Division*, attracted stragglers who were separated from their units and wanted a functioning headquarters from which to draw food and supplies. In the month following the 1 March strength return, *Kampfgruppe 3. Panzer-Division* reported 2,008 casualties and only 615 replacements, yet under the new table of organization the division was 73 men over-strength. Its combat rating was IV, the lowest possible.

---

106 Under the new table of organization for the Panzer Division 1945, which went into effect that day, the division was over its allocated strength of 90 SPWs.

107 Nevenkin, Kamen, *Fire Brigades: The Panzer Divisions 1943-1945* (Winnipeg: J.J. Fedorowicz, 2008), p. 85.

108 Nevenkin, *Fire Brigades* p. 137.

Both *1. Panzer-Division* and *3. Panzer-Division* had been reduced to *Kampfgruppe*. On Easter Sunday morning the two panzer divisions scratched together *Kampfgruppen* from the last of their tanks, *Jagdpanzers*, assault guns and SPWs. A reconnaissance needed to be made into the valley of the Raab River but neither division was strong enough on its own so they combined their efforts. From day one of the war both divisions had won accolades on every battlefield in Europe, but now, at the last, they were a mere shell of their former selves.

The *1. Panzer-Division* built their group around the remaining armored elements plus *Panzergrenadier-Regiment 113*, while *3. Panzer-Division* used all of the remaining panzers and SPWs. The latter was commanded by *Major* Medicus of *Panzerjäger-Abteilung 543*.

The *1. Panzer-Division Kampfgruppe* retook the lost town of Feldbach, at the apex of the Russian penetration down the Raab Valley, while *Kampfgruppe Medicus* did the same over the Hungarian border at Vasszentmihály, south of Heiligenbrunn, at the valley's eastern end. Along with the assault at Rechnitz from *SS-Kampfgruppe Schweitzer*, the sudden counterattack in the Raab Valley stopped the Russian drive and forced them to shift forces against this incursion, even though the fuel shortage meant that both German groups had to withdraw again. Nevertheless, the attacks served their purpose in halting the headlong Russian drive to the west.

Graz

Headquartered now in Graz, *Gauleiter* of Styria Dr Sigfried Ueberreither had the ultimate power to do whatever was necessary to defend his *Gau*, and he was determined to do just that. Ueberreither saw combat in Norway and held the rank of *SS-Obersturmbannführer* in the SA. In addition to being the *Gauleiter* he headed up the *Volkssturm* for his *Gau*.

He was aided in his efforts by the energetic *General der Gebirgstruppe* Julius Ringel. Both men were determined to keep the Russians out of Styria, but the question they had to answer was, defend it with what units? The mountainous and heavily forested terrain gave the defenders most of the advantages, but that presumed there were defenders. When Ueberreither and Ringel looked around in late March all they could find to throw into the line were training units.

IV SS-Panzerkorps

The focus of Hermann Balck's hatred for the *Waffen-SS* was *SS-Obergruppenführer* Herbert Otto Gille, the commander of *IV SS-Panzerkorps*. The two men became mortal enemies the previous year during the German breakout from the Cherkassy Pocket and both of their staffs echoed the feelings of the commanders. But Gille was a highly decorated officer, having won the Diamonds to his Knight's Cross with Oak Leaves and Swords, a rare honor. He'd been under Balck's command since the beginning of the year, not long after Balck had been demoted from command of *Heeresgruppe G* on the Western Front. Since then, the mistrust and mutual dislike plagued relations between the two men and adversely affected their respective commands.

* * *

Yet another orphaned unit was the Panther battalion of *24. Panzer-Division*, which was attached to *IV SS-Panzerkorps*. The battalion had fought in Hungary since January and was down to 15 percent of its authorized strength. Its handful of Panthers made little difference.

5. SS-Panzer-Division Wiking

No SS division ostensibly built around volunteers accomplished more than *5. SS-Panzer-Division Wiking*. Whenever German propaganda needed evidence of a pan-European movement it featured the men of *Wiking*. And early in its history the division had indeed been staffed by a wide variety of European volunteers, but by 1945 most of those men were long gone, either dead, wounded or missing, and with the turn in the fortunes of war recruiting in the occupied countries had dried up. In 1945, therefore, only about 5 percent of the division's ranks were foreign volunteers.[109] The rest were either Germans or *Volksdeutsche*.

And by 1 April, *Wiking* had ceased to exist as an armored force. During the fighting in Hungary during the second half of March, the division stood fast at the small town of Székesfehérvár to give *6. SS-Panzerarmee* time to withdraw from the trap it had found its way into. In doing so, the already shattered *Wiking* lost most of the heavy weapons it had left.

Withdrawal across Western Hungary meant constantly being without flank protection, in imminent danger of being surrounded. Instead of withdrawing due west, as their commander Balck had ordered, *Wiking* had to withdraw northwest instead; the positions they had been ordered to occupy were already in Russian hands.

A condition report exists for *Wiking* dated 1 April. Its defiant stand at Székesfehérvár and subsequent retreat cost the division 4,471 men killed, wounded or missing, while it only received 1,724 replacements, including convalescents. It also had 5,917 men on the eight-week sick and wounded list. Its combat readiness was given as IV. From an authorized strength of 114 Mark IVs and 79 Panthers, totaling 193 panzers, the division had two Panthers combat ready, with nine more undergoing repair. The entire division had a paltry 51 SPWs operational, with 53 more down for repairs. Total motorization was a mere 36 percent.

The combined authorized manpower total for the panzer regiment was just over 2,000 men, although losses had diminished that number. Roughly 150 men were in Germany for training. But with no significant mechanized component left, and little prospect for replacement vehicles, much of *SS-Panzer-Regiment 5* was reorganized to fight as infantry. Klapdor reports there were four companies, with each platoon having three squads of 10-15 men each. The company strengths were between 80-100 men, so the battalion likely had a total strength of around 400-450 men. A heavy weapons company was also formed, with a heavy machine gun platoon, an 81mm mortar platoon, a flamethrower section and a tank destroyer section armed with *Panzerschrecks*.[110] Once considered the armored fist of the pan-European anti-communist movement, *Wiking* had been reduced to little more than a depleted infantry *Kampfgruppe*.

When the time came to fight again, however, they fought like the seasoned veterans they were. And though they were few in number by this time, *Wiking*'s non-German volunteers knew the fate awaiting them in their home countries once the war ended in Germany's defeat.

2. Panzerarmee

In late March Hitler ordered the commander of *2. Panzerarmee*,[111] *Gendeneral der Artillerie* Maximilian de Angelis, to hold in place at all costs. *Heeresgruppe E* was fighting its way out of the

---

109 Michaelis, *Panzer Divisions,* p. 203.
110 Klapdor, Ewald, *Viking Panzers, The German 5th SS Tank Regiment in the East in World War II* (Mechanicsburg: Stackpole, 2011), p. 435.
111 Despite its name, *2. Panzerarmee* had few panzers and only a handful of *Sturmgeschütze*.

Balkans and unless de Angelis held open a supply and escape corridor, the Army Group would be surrounded and destroyed. For de Angelis it was already too late to stand fast. Disobeying Hitler's direct orders he withdrew to the partially completed positions of the *Reichsschutzstellung*. Many officers had been shot for less, but somehow de Angelis suffered no consequences for ignoring a *Führerbefehl* and doing what was militarily sound.

I Kavallerie-Korps

As 18th Tank Corps moved west into the seam south of *IV SS-Panzerkorps*, two more Russian Corps slammed into the northernmost of de Angelis' forces, *I Kavallerie-Korps*, and kept it from counterattacking north into the breach between the two armies. The 30th Mechanized Corps was followed by 5th Guards Cavalry Corps, driving the Germans westward. By 1 April a dangerous gap had been ripped between *IV SS-Panzerkorps*, on *6. Armee*'s far right flank, and *I Kavallerie-Korps*, on *2. Panzerarmee*'s far left flank.

   I Kavallerie-Korps included *Kampfgruppe 3. Panzer-Division*, *3. Kavallerie-Division*, *4. Kavallerie-Division*, *16. SS-Panzergrenadier-Division Reichsführer-SS*, *297. Infanterie-Division*, *Divisionsgruppe Krause*, also known as *Köruck 582*,[112] two new addition as of 31 March. The first was a huge division of questionable reputation among Army officers, the *14. Waffen-Grenadier-Division der SS Galizien*, and the second, a burned-out division of unquestioned valor in combat, *9. SS-Panzer-Division Hohenstaufen*.

   Neither *I Kavallerie-Korps* or *IV SS-Panzerkorps* had reserves to close the gap, so in desperation the *Oberkommando des Heeres, OKH*, in overall command of the Eastern Front, decided that the time had come to see if one of Himmler's expensive experiments with non-German volunteers might yet pay off. If *Galizien* couldn't restore the situation, there was nobody else who could.

9. SS-Panzer-Division Hohenstaufen

9. SS-Panzer-Division Hohenstaufen was no better off than the other formations, and worse than some. The division was delayed in withdrawing after the Ardennes Offensive the previous December and was never fully reorganized. Parts were left behind near Györ when *Hohenstaufen* went back into action with *II SS-Panzerkorps* during *Unternehmen Frühlingserwachen*. Like *Wiking*, *Hohenstaufen* stood fast while others escaped in the aftermath of the failed offensive, and holding the escape corridor open for *6. SS-Panzerarmee* cost it dearly. Afterward the scattered parts fled west as best they could.

   The reconnaissance battalion wound up attached to *6. Panzer-Division*, now far to the north, while elements of the artillery regiment joined *Das Reich*. The Panzer Maintenance Company was later attached to *Korps Schultz* and is reported to have fought as infantry during the Battle of Vienna. If nothing else shows how bad things had become, this last part should. A panzer division that gave up the men who kept its panzers running was no longer a panzer division.

   The rest of the division wound up in *2. Panzerarmee*, far to the south, attached to *I Kavallerie-Korps* with *16. SS-Panzergrenadier-Division Reichsführer-SS* on its right. The division had eight Panthers from *SS-Panzer Regiment 2* attached. This stemmed from a shootout at the train station

---

112 *Köruck* was a German abbreviation for *Kommandant des ruckwartigen Armeegebietes*. This is a typically German term meaning Commander of the Rear Army Area. Such a commander had absolute control of the area assigned to him. His responsibility was to ensure security of the rear areas and supply routes.

in Veszprem on 20 March. As *Hohenstaufen* stood outside the town holding back the Russians, *Das Reich*'s panzer regiment was more than half loaded on flatcars when a Russian armored column broke through and attacked without warning. The Germans drove them back but one company of panzers hadn't arrived when the train had to pull out. Suddenly without a division, the orphaned panzers were taken in by *Hohenstaufen*. Among those panzer commanders was the legendary Ernst Barkmann, one of the top ten German panzer aces of the war and a man whose story will re-enter this narrative later.

14. Waffen-Grenadier-Division der SS Galizien (Ukrainisches Nr. 1)

The time had come for one of Himmler's pet projects to go into combat against the rampaging Russians. The *14. Waffen-Grenadier-Division der SS Galizien* (Galicia)[113] had been formed in 1943 following the Stalingrad catastrophe from Ukrainians who hated Russia and longed for their own country. The idea of tapping a vast manpower reservoir of anti-communist Ukrainians appealed to Himmler. Hitler wasn't so sure.

The Ukrainians' motivation for swearing allegiance to Adolf Hitler had nothing to do with a fondness for Nazism, and everything to do with their hatred of Russia. The men themselves either remembered the brief period when Ukraine was its own nation, 1917-1920, or were children whose parents never ceased telling them about the glory days when they were a free and independent nation. Then Lenin launched the Russo-Polish War of 1920, a fierce and bloody conflict largely unknown in the west, after which the nation of Ukraine was divided between Poland and Russia.

Ukrainian nationalism could not be so easily crushed, however, despite harsh years under Polish rule. Then, when Germany conquered Poland in 1939, Russia gobbled up huge swaths of Polish territory in the east. The Poles had treated the ethnic Ukrainians harshly, but the coming of the Soviets resulted in a bloodbath. Stalin brooked no resistance to his regime, not in thought, word or deed. Oppression, repression and punishment were the orders of the day.

In the portions of the Ukraine given to the USSR after the Russo-Polish War, some 5,000,000 Ukrainians died of starvation during the famine of 1932-33.[114] Known today as the Holodmor, it has been recognized since 2006 as genocide carried out on Stalin's orders. The hatred of the SS Ukrainians toward the Russians was well-earned and reciprocated, nor was it lost on anyone that the Ukrainian *Waffen-SS* men faced off against Third Ukrainian Front.

When the Germans overran the Ukraine in 1941 they were greeted as liberators, not conquerors. Much like in the Baltic countries, Ukrainian nationalists threw in their lot with the Germans. It was hoped Hitler would eventually grant them independence and they, in turn, would be loyal allies. Unfortunately for all involved, German policy in the east had nothing to do with looking for friends among the native population and everything to do with treating them as chattel, if not outright slaves.

Despite Hitler's staunch opposition to granting the Ukrainians their own country, the area was ruled by a rare German administrator who wanted cooperation, not blind obedience.

---

113 Hitler strongly opposed any underlying nationalist movements within the *Wehrmacht*, particularly from Slavs, no matter how friendly or loyal they might be. He intended to rule the conquered east as a sort of supersized East Prussia, with vast estates overseen by worthy families who proved their mettle during the war. Galicia was the German name for part of the Ukraine that had Germanic history, having been part of the Austro-Hungarian Empire, and thus was palatable to Hitler.

114 The highest estimates put this number at 12,000,000.

SS-Brigadeführer Otto Wächter tapped into the pro-German sentiment and ruled with a light hand, and it paid off. The Ukraine remained far more peaceful than most other occupied territories.[115]

This directly led to large numbers of volunteers to aid the German war effort, and it's from these men that *Galizien* sprang. Many of the division's Ukrainian officers had combat experience from the First World War. The men, however, did not. Although enthusiastic, they had no military experience.

Much worse was that the division's German officers never quite believed the men would fight when the time came, particularly the division commander, *SS-Brigadeführer und Generalmajor der SS* Herman Freitag. Freitag was disliked and distrusted by most people who knew him. He was considered a schemer who would do or say anything to get ahead. This held true for many of the division's other officers, too, who were supplied by existing formations to provide a cadre for *Galizien*. By and large they were men considered expendable by their former units, who were often glad to be rid of them.

Nevertheless, the division came into existence and was soon gaining strength with volunteers. When the call went out between 70,000 and 100,000 men signed up, so the division got the pick of the litter and the average recruit was young and fit. Equipment and materiel badly needed elsewhere was supplied to the Ukrainians. Combat-ready elements fought partisans behind the German lines in 1943, but final training and expansion to full authorized strength didn't occur until early 1944. April found the division at the Neuhammer training grounds in Silesia, where the opinion was that *Galizien* showed promise, but would need several more months of training before being ready to fight. Freitag's relentless negativity didn't help, and Hitler's inherent disregard for the fighting qualities of Slavs left *Galizien* with a lingering question mark beside its name.

The situation facing the Germans on the Eastern Front as summer 1944 approached could fairly be described as desperate. *Heeresgruppe Mitte* occupied a huge bulge in the line and Hitler would allow no withdrawals, not even to straighten the line and free up reserves or to find better natural defenses. The Army Group's divisions were depleted and lacking reserves, so when the blow fell on 22 June, the Russians quickly penetrated the German lines and rampaged westward.

Although not yet combat-ready, the dire situation called for the commitment of every man and machine. *Galizien* found itself attached to *XIII Armeekorps* in *Heeresgruppe Nordukrain*, commanded by Hitler favorite *Generalfeldmarschall* Walther Model. Then in July came the Battle of Brody. It began when Marshal Konev's First Ukrainian Front slammed into *Heeresgruppe Nordukrain*. *Galizien* was ordered to counterattack a Russian breakthrough in the area around the city of Brody, and did so with some success. Only the arrival of the Red Air Force drove the Ukrainians back with substantial losses. Vicious hand-to-hand fighting ensued and *Galizien* was forced westward.

In the days that followed *XIII Armeekorps* became surrounded and had to fight its way out of the encirclement. The results were devastating. After starting the battle with more than 15,000 men, when it ended *Galizien* had 3,000 men left. During the fighting Freitag suffered a breakdown and asked to be relieved of his command, but was denied.

The division was rebuilt using men from anywhere they could be found, including ethnic Germans from various countries, Ukrainian refugees who fled west with the Germans and Ukrainian police units. By October the rolls had swelled to a staggering 22,000 men, at least 8,000 over its authorized strength. *Galizien* had, more or less, become a partly trained and equipped corps.

---

115   The light hand Wächter ruled with is relative to other Germans in the east. He helped set up the Krakow Jewish ghetto and persecuted Jews as harshly as any other Nazi. Where he differed was in his treatment of the non-Jewish Ukrainians.

The division was soon in action again when it took part in crushing the Slovak rebellion in late summer and autumn 1944. It was still looked upon as a questionable unit, no doubt in part because of Freitag's continuing efforts to be transferred elsewhere and continual degrading of his command. Because of this widespread viewpoint, the massive division next found itself fighting partisans, who plagued the German rear areas, in Slovakia into January of 1945, even after the official rebellion had been put down. *Galizien* used captured weapons stores to alleviate its equipment shortfalls.

In December 1944 part of the division went into action to stop a Russian breakthrough in southern Slovakia and fought well. In January 1945 in the middle of winter, the division was ordered to march 500-600 miles through Austria to Slovenia, almost entirely by foot. Once there they engaged in anti-partisan operations, mostly against the well-organized communists under the command of Tito.

The early morning of 20 March 1945 brought another shock from Hitler's headquarters in the form of an order for *Galizien* to completely disarm itself and turn over all weapons to forming German units. During a conference the *Führer* declared astonishment at having just discovered a group of armed Ukrainians behind German lines in the south. Given Hitler's micro-management of every part of the war in the east, and *Galizien*'s prominent role at Brody, and again in Slovakia and Slovenia, for him to have suddenly discovered the division's existence is hard to believe. Regardless, long negotiations and conflicting orders gave way to the reality of the situation: the Russians were closing in on the Reich. *Galizien* kept its weapons, although final confirmation of this didn't come through for a few more days.

But without ammunition resupply the weapons were useless, and Slovenia was at the end of the logistics chain. Maybe needed supplies would show up and maybe they wouldn't. Waiting for orders the Ukrainians welcomed a Hungarian artillery unit that showed up out of nowhere. Then, as the Russian Fifty-Seventh Army, First Bulgarian Army and part of the Twenty-Seventh Army drove a dangerous wedge into the junction of *6. Armee* and *2. Panzerarmee*, specifically between *IV SS-Panzerkorps* and *I Kavallerie-Korps*, and were about to cross into the Reich itself, on 30 March *Galizien* received orders to cross into Austria. The relief was palpable. There were few partisans in Austria and supplies usually got through.

On 31 March the division was put under command of *I Kavallerie-Korps*. *Galizien* was still huge, with 14,000 men in the division itself and a staggering 8,000 in *Feldersatz-Bataillon 14*. In other words, the replacement battalion was literally larger than many divisions. As the divisional Chief of Staff, *Heer Major* Wolf-Dietrich Heike[116] wrote when speaking of *General der Kavallerie* Harteneck, commander of *I Kavallerie-Korps*, "it had been a long time since his army saw as strongly manned and armed a division as the Ukrainians."[117]

But the German situation was desperate and no time was given for the Ukrainians to acclimatize to their new situation. They were thrown into the attack immediately, the very next morning, because the gap between *6. Armee* and *2. Panzerarmee* had to be closed before the Russians could widen it further. The division had been spread over a wide area and with no motorized transport available, its massing for attack took place on foot and at night, to avoid air attack. The skies had become doubly dangerous now, since they no longer harbored only lurking Red Air Force aircraft. The southern end of the front was in range of American *Jabos*, the abbreviation for *Jagdbombers*, or ground-attack aircraft. Unlike the Red Air Force which usually flew no more than 20 miles deep

---

116 The major was on permanent loan from the Army, a very unusual situation. Unlike the commanding officer, Heike was very proud of the Ukrainians.

117 Heike, Wolf-Dietrich, *The Ukrainian Division 'Galicia' 1943-45* (Toronto: The Shevchenko Scientific Project, 1988), p. 115.

into German territory, American *Jabos* ranged hundreds of miles into the Reich air space looking for targets of opportunity, so that road and rail movement by day had become almost suicidal.

After forced marches to get into their jumping-off positions, at 6:30 a.m. on Easter Sunday, *Galizien* pushed off in an attack toward Gleichenberg, home of the world-famous thermal springs at Bad Gleichenberg. *Waffen-Grenadier-Regiment der SS 29* attacked toward Gleichenberg itself, while its sister regiment, *Waffen-Grenadier-Regiment der SS 30* veered northeast at Straden, heading for Merkendorf. Behind the two advancing regiments, *Waffen-Grenadier-Regiment der SS 31* came on in reserve.[118] On *Galizien*'s left was *SS-Ausbildungs-und-Ersatz-Abteilung 18* and elements of *Wiking*. On its right was *3. Kavallerie-Division*, which attacked to the northeast alongside *Galizien*.

After the scare of being disarmed and abandoned the Ukrainians were eager to prove their worth on the battlefield. To a man they realized that if Germany lost the war they could expect no mercy from the Russians. Worse, the troops facing them were those of Third Ukrainian Front, their countrymen, who bombarded them with propaganda broadcasts and leaflets in their own language. Thus motivated, they attacked with a vigor not often seen from German troops in 1945, when sheer fatigue dragged at the willingness to fight, an exhaustion that was as much mental as physical.

Facing the Ukrainians' of *Waffen-Grenadier-Regiment der SS 29* were troops of the crack 3rd Guards Airborne Division, among others. Despite that, the attack took the Russians by complete surprise and went well. The hilltop village of Straden was captured and provided a wide view of the battlefield area, enabling the attackers to better direct their movements. After a brief, sharp fight, including increasingly rare German artillery support, Gleichenberg town was retaken, and also nearby Trautmannsdorf to the west. Another battle ensued for Castle Gleichenberg, the 12th-Century fortification just north of the town, where a large force of Soviet infantry with armor support had to be forced out of their positions in a vicious firefight. Like most medieval fortifications it had been built on a jagged promontory and situated for defense. The already ruined castle was nearly destroyed in the fighting.

With *Wiking* attacking south from their positions, the two SS divisions stopped what could have been a fatal Soviet breakthrough and, for that one day, stabilized the front between *6. Armee* and *2. Panzerarmee*. So fast had the Ukrainians moved that they captured six heavy artillery pieces and found breakfasts set in several houses for the now departed Russians.

For a brief moment Himmler's investment had paid off. Although he criticized the division the previous autumn, the Russians had been stopped by the only unit available to stop them. As things turned out the locals were not universally pleased by this. Supplies didn't reach the front lines and the SS men grew hungry. They foraged local homes and found some of the inhabitants deriding them as *Kriegsverlänge*, war prolongers.[119] Given that they wore the SS runes this indicates the state of thinking of these simple folk whose quiet corner of the world suddenly became a battlefield, and whose fear of the SS was outweighed by fear for their homes. Most of the locals, however, greeted the return of German units as liberators.

---

118 Once again sources disagree on various points about this attack, including the timing. One source has *SS-Waffen-Grenadier-Regiment 30* in Maribor on the day of the attack, and a different source has *SS-Waffen-Grenadier-Regiment 31* still in Slovenia and marching north. The author believes the version presented here to be the correct one.

119 This stands in contrast with liberated German towns elsewhere, most of which were all too glad to have the Russians kicked out, even for a brief while. The mass rapes and looting so characteristic of the Russian drive across Europe had apparently not caught up to southern Austria yet.

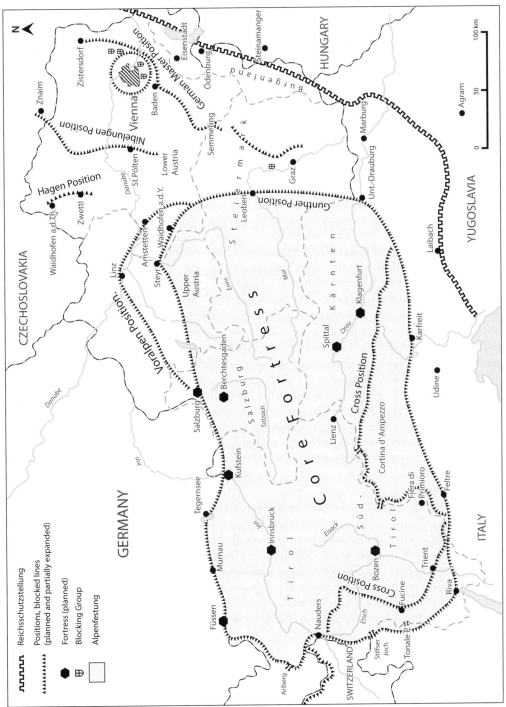

Map 3 The National Redoubt, or *Alpenfestung*.

Kampfgruppe 3. Panzer-Division

Nicknamed the Eiffel Tower Division because it had been formed in France, on the far southern end of *Heeresgruppe Süd*, the veteran *Kampfgruppe 3. Panzer-Division* started April with something it didn't have a few days before: an armored group.[120] The division repair company had worked miracles and put five Panthers, four Mark IVs, two *Jagdpanzer IV/70s* and a *Sturmgeschütz* back into service. But for the moment the division's main concern was avoiding encirclement, as Russian spearheads had penetrated far to the northwest on its left flank, almost severing contact with *I Kavallerie-Korps*.

The division was in the extreme southwestern tip of Hungary, the very last bit of that country still in German hands, with its main line of resistance facing east. Now, however, it would have to do an about-face and attack west to save itself. The region was dotted with small towns and villages centered in the forested hills, with Alpine foothills lining the western border. The assembly area was the village of Guterfölde, which was crowded with vehicles of all types and refugees, making it hard for the combat elements to deploy.

At 8:00 a.m. on 1 April the attack began on the nearby village of Csömödér with the armored group out front, followed by a battalion of *Panzergrenadiers* from *Panzergrenadier-Regiment 126*. One Panther was hit immediately by a Russian 76.2mm anti-tank gun but while some of the attackers peeled off to deal with this threat, the spearhead didn't slow. The division had no choice but to either reconnect with German lines or be destroyed.

Along the way the lead elements ran into some Hungarians, who said Csömödér was in Hungarian hands, but this turned out to be a ruse. Nevertheless, with only three panzers, one officer and seven *Panzergrenadiers*, the Germans drove a sizeable force of Russian infantry out of the village and to the north. A lot of the ubiquitous panje wagons were taken, presumably with loot or supplies in them, and by late afternoon the Germans had made it to Hernyék, another village about five miles north of Csömödér.

The division's other *Panzergrenadier* regiment, *Panzergrenadier-Regiment 128*, advanced north on a different axis to the right of the first one, while the rest of *Panzergrenadier-Regiment 126* stood as rearguard. Nova would be the next target, a few miles to the northeast, to block the Red Army advance to the southwest, but a nighttime patrol found them already there.[121]

LVIII Armeekorps
13. Waffen-Gebirgs-Division der SS Handschar (Kroatische Nr. 1)

Heinrich Himmler's first project to create combat units from non-Aryans started in 1942, when Hitler agreed to the formation of an SS Mountain Division composed of Croatian and Bosnian Muslims. Thus was born *13. Waffen-Gebirgs-Division der SS Handschar (Kroatische Nr. 1)*.[122] In the years that followed the divisional history was that of desertion and mutiny and poor leadership on the part of its German NCOs and officers, combined with some successes fighting communist partisans in Yugoslavia. By April 1945 it was in the front lines facing Third Ukrainian Front as

---

120 The division's commander, *Generalleutnant* Josef von Radowitz, had the distinction of being turned down for the Knight's Cross on the day after Adolf Hitler committed suicide, 1 May 1945. The *OKW* still bothered with such things even then, and it was determined by a staff officer that von Radowitz had not met the criteria for the award.

121 Rebentisch, Dr Ernst, *To the Caucasus and the Austrian Alps: The History of the 2Kampfgruppe 3. Panzer-Division in World War II* (Winnipeg: J.J. Fedorowicz, 2009), p.463.

122 *Handschar* was the name for the knife carried by Turkish policemen of the Ottoman Empire.

part of *2. Panzerarmee*, not because of its combat prowess but because there was nobody else to put in those trenches.

At one point in September 1944, *Handschar*'s ration strength surpassed 14,000 men and officers, but those days were long gone by that Easter Sunday. Killed, wounded, missing and desertions had left the division badly under strength, until an influx of *Luftwaffe* and Army Supply Troops brought its combat number to 3,601 on 17 March, with ration strength of 9,228.[123] However, by this point none of the men in the division were Muslims, since they had proved notoriously unreliable, and they had all been replaced by ethnic Germans. This led to a drastic improvement in the unit's combat capabilities. While primarily a Muslim division it showed a propensity for abusing not only Jews and partisans, but Christian Serbs as well, and gained a reputation for brutality. Once filled up with Germans it became a marginally effective division.

On 29 March the Red Army broke through German defenses around Nagybajom, a small town south of Lake Balaton. This was on the left flank of *Handschar* and like the rest of *Heeresgruppe Süd*, the division had no choice but to retreat to the northwest, in the direction of Naykanizsa and the Hungarian oil fields. With no armor and few heavy weapons, *Handschar* had no chance to counterattack and could only fall back along with the rest of their comrades.

The Americans

The specter of brutal, costly and prolonged mountain fighting in Austria stood foremost in General Dwight Eisenhower's mind as March passed into April. The 1 April intelligence summary for Supreme Headquarters Allied Expeditionary Force, SHAEF, included a diagram of Germany's so-called National Redoubt, a huge and heavily fortified area in Southern Germany, Austria, Northern Italy and Yugoslavia. The Redoubt was said to encompass most of the German-held Alps, from the Swiss border to the foothills west of Graz, with a northern border stretching from Lindau east to the area near Mariazell and a southern flank from the region east of the Lenzerhorn past Klagenfurt toward Maribor. Aside from the inherent strength given the defender in such rugged terrain, the German's western flank was protected by the Bodensee and the Swiss border. Allied attacks into the Redoubt would have to come primarily from the north, with supporting attacks from American-held fields in Northern Italy. Russian attacks from the east were expected to continue.

Since the summer of 1944 OSS (American Office of Strategic Services) agents in Switzerland had been warning that the Germans might attempt to prolong the war by fortifying and retreating into the Alps with their best remaining units, mostly the older *Waffen-SS* divisions mixed with a few elite Army units. Although the Russians shared very little tactical information with their American allies, it was known at SHAEF that most of the SS divisions were fighting at the southern end of the Eastern Front. In this they were correct. No less than 16 *Waffen-SS* divisions were then in combat in Austria, Italy and the Balkans, and while none was anywhere near full strength the American intelligence had no way of knowing the extent of their actual weakness. All of those SS flags on American maps made for a frightening endgame scenario. A quarter million tough, well-armed SS veterans defending the rugged Alpine terrain in concrete bunkers, with all of the food and ammunition needed to survive a multi-year siege, became a pervasive fear that infected SHAEF intelligence like a self-perpetuating and incurable virus.

---

123 Munoz, Antonio J., *The East Came West, Muslim, Hindu, and Buddhist Volunteers for the German Armed Forces 1941-1945* (New York: Axis Europe Books, 2001), pp. 272-273.

In defense of the American intelligence services, the German High Command was even telling their own soldiers that the National Redoubt was real and ready to fulfill its function as the last bastion of Nazism. On 30 March one of Hitler's favorite people, *SS-Obersturmbannführer* Otto Skorzeny, was ordered south by the *OKW* to take command of the Alpine Fortress, which he was assured was finished. Once he arrived in the mountains Skorzeny found out it was all a lie.

At least, it was all mostly a lie. Some work actually had been done on improving fortifications in the area of Bregenz to Feldkirche by 2,000 men of the *Organisation-Todt*, along the Swiss border with Austria. The *Gauleiter* for Tyrol-Vorarlberg, Franz Hofer, had been pushing for a National Redoubt for months and in January received permission for limited work to go forward. But only limited work; full-scale fortifications work was not yet approved and on 1 April there were only some ditches and bunkers, nothing close to the feared *Alpenfestung*.

On 28 March 1945, however, on his own initiative and without asking permission of his commander, Eisenhower opened a direct dialogue with Stalin that culminated with his decision to allow the Russians to take Berlin while the Allied armies turned southeast to attack the National Redoubt before the Germans could retreat into their formidable defenses. It was only after the fact that he discovered the whole thing was a myth.

Well after the fact Eisenhower downplayed the extent of the Americans' gullibility. In *Crusade in Europe* he wrote: "The evidence was clear that the enemy intended to make the attempt [to retreat into the National Redoubt] and I decided to give him no opportunity to carry it out."[124] As things turned out, Eisenhower had made the right decision for the wrong reason.

---

124 Eisenhower, *Crusade in Europe* (New York: Doubleday & Co., 1948), p. 397.

2

Monday, 2 April

The breakdown of the German war effort accelerated with each passing day. Orders to stand fast were routinely ignored by veteran units unless it served an immediate tactical purpose. For many division commanders it became a matter of 'hold as long as possible and then get out'. Sacrificing veterans you'd served with for years because the *Führer* ordered it had lost much of its authority, especially among the SS units. A *Führerbefehl*, an order from Hitler, was still by and large obeyed, but the damage done by the Cuff Title Order could not be undone.

Understanding Hitler's reasoning in military matters has never been fully articulated, probably because it's impossible. But one difference in how he came to different conclusions than the generals advising him was that he "had an undying suspicion of the documents presented to him".[1] Hitler's paranoia infected every aspect of his life, including his conduct of military affairs. For example, if someone told him that a unit couldn't attack because it didn't have fuel, he might or might not believe it. And if he didn't believe, then he often accused officers in such situations of cowardice and not wanting to attack.

Unfortunately for those who argued such things with him, Hitler also had an uncanny memory for figures and statistics, which was often mistaken for genius. He could remember the latest fuel stocks report for a given army, and if it then claimed not to have fuel to carry out an operation he could calculate whether that was probable or not. Of course, that would be predicated on him believing the fuel report in the first place.

Heeresgruppe Süd

The 2nd of April was a day of disaster for the reeling Germans. Both north and south of the Danube the Red Army gobbled up land. So far in pursuing the Germans across the tank-friendly terrain of western Hungary, both Second and Third Ukrainian Fronts had moved in a westerly direction. But topography always dictates the terms of battle, and what the Russians now wanted to do more than anything else was move fast. The Americans were still far from Austria's western border but the speed of their advance from the Rhine had been impressive, so if the Red Army was going to capture all of the country it had to maintain a rapid pace. The foothills of the Alps lined eastern Austria like the walls of some giant medieval fortress, and to maintain speed through them the Russians had either to move through the valleys of Burgenland, Lower Austria and Styria, or shift to a northwest axis and follow the Danube Valley. If they could capture western Austria fast enough, they could block the Western Allies from entering and bring Churchill's greatest fear into being, namely, installing a pro-communist government in Austria. Stalin had pledged not to do that, but he had also pledged to hold free elections in Poland.

---

1   Maier, *Drama*, p. 379.

North of the Danube

8. Armee

Spring arrived in Austria as the temperature warmed into the low sixties Fahrenheit. Bright sunshine lit the crocus and cowslips which brightened the green fields in the whites, yellows and purples of the season. Road conditions were good, even in rural areas, and men moved more easily without the killing cold of winter to sap their energy. The idyllic world of the Wienvertiel got ready for another season of growing grapes for the region's famous wines.

Then war rolled over the country.

The Red Air Force flew sorties at will while the *Luftwaffe* limited activity to the area south of the Danube. It was exactly the sort of weather the German defenders didn't want to see.

* * *

The 8. *Armee* had four corps under its command: *XXIX, XXXXIII* and *LXXII Armeekorps* and the newly created *Panzerkorps Feldherrnhalle.* In a report dated 1 March 1945, the US Army Intelligence Order of Battle Summary listed two Hungarian infantry divisions on its rolls, the 5th Hungarian Reserve Division and the 24th Infantry Division. On 12 April neither one was still listed. According to Hermann Balck, on 25 March "there were signs that the 24th Hungarian Infantry Division was disintegrating…the commander of a Hungarian infantry division declared that he could no longer accept the responsibility of his troops having to fight in such difficult mountain terrain under such difficult logistical challenges."[2] Once the front moved out of Hungary itself much of the *Honved* melted away and wandered the back roads looking for food.

* * *

The 8. *Armee* front lined up on 2 April as follows: on the army's far left was *Deutscher-Befehlshaber-Slowakia*, or German High Command Slovakia. This was another of those amorphous German formations formed for a special purpose. Its commander was *SS-Obergruppenführer* Hermann Höfle. The headquarters had been formed the previous summer to deal with the Slovak Uprising, when elements of the Slovak resistance, backed by a few communist partisans, tried to overthrow the pro-Nazi government of Josef Tiso. *Deutscher-Befehlshaber-Slowakia* was created to coordinate the units sent to deal with and crush the rebellion and once that was done it stayed on the scene to keep another uprising from occurring.

* * *

Second Ukrainian Front kept up the pressure as their objective became clearer to German intelligence. Marshal Rodion Malinovsky's command was attacking on both sides of the Danube, although the Germans assumed those operating on the southern bank would cross the river and continue the attack from there, which they eventually did. Those were the Forty-Sixth Army, 23rd Tank Corps and 2nd Guards Mechanized Corps. Other units would aim to make inroads into the Little Carpathian Mountains before the Germans could solidify their defense. That 60-mile-long range runs northeast from the outskirts of Bratislava. Although low compared to the Alps, they're still rugged and heavily forested and could have proven hard to fight through if the Germans had had time to organize themselves. Once past them, the road was open to move northwest to Brunn and west along the Danube Valley, where the land was flat and harder to defend.

---

2   Balck, *Order in Chaos*, p. 418.

Russian divisions and corps were of different sizes than German. For example, a Guards Mechanized Corps had fewer men but slightly more tanks, tank destroyers and assault guns than did a *Waffen-SS* Panzer Division. At full strength the SS division would have had approximately 183 panzers and *Jadpanzers*, significantly fewer than the 230 for the Russian unit, and 250 for a Guards Tank Corps. However, the German division totaled about 18,500 men while the Russian corps had just over 16,300. On paper the difference in divisions was also large, but in reality much less so.

A Russian rifle division contained roughly 9,600 men of all ranks. A German infantry division should have been much larger than that, but the newly organized *Volks-Grenadier* divisions were only marginally larger than their Russian counterpart, and a Guards Rifle Division was about the same size. Of course, these are authorized numbers and few Russian and no German formations were anywhere near that strong. The Germans, in particular, lacked their assigned armored vehicles, prime movers and trucks.

* * *

At Bratislava, the Russians had arrived in force, and remnant German units had orders to stand fast at all costs. Parts of the Russian 25th Guards Infantry Corps took the Sprinzl farmhouse complex on the city's northern edge and pushed on toward the railway station at Rača, where there was heavy fighting.

On the city's eastern edge, the Russian 23rd Infantry Corps overran the outlying villages of Podunajské Biskupice and Vrakuňa, and as night fell they crossed the Little Danube River. Their main objective for the next days were the Rača station to prevent German units either reinforcing or withdrawing from the area, and the Koliba Height overlooking the city from the north. After fighting in their sector during the day, the Hitler Youth Battalion was withdrawn to the western edge of the city.

Vienna

Throughout the city the obligatory posters and graffiti plastered everywhere by the Nazi Party declared that *Festung Wien* would fight to the last man. Never one to pass up a chance for bombast, *Gauleiter* von Schirach had been exhorting the Viennese to fight back against the Asian hordes, and the Polish King Sobieski's 1683 salvation of the city cropped up frequently in his harangues. But for the more cynical among the Viennese, which was most of them, there was no doubt what all of this meant; the city was about to become a battleground. They need only listen for themselves, after all, since Russian artillery fire rumbled in the distance like a slow-moving thunderstorm.

For years now the German newsreel service, *Die Deutsche Wochenschau,* had gloriously displayed images of burning Russian towns and cities, and the Viennese were savvy enough to realize that German cities burned just as easily as Russian ones. For those left behind, however, there was nothing they could do to get out of harm's way. The Nazis were fleeing and with them went the civil servants and bureaucrats who made the city function. Soon the only things left of the Party functionaries were the posters, slogans and empty promises they left in their wake.

But while most Viennese looked ahead with fear, 2 April was a stellar day for one man. *Generalleutnant* Ludwig Merker had been *Wehrmacht Kommandant* of Vienna since the previous September and a week earlier had been named *Kampfkommandant* of the doomed city. Merker had won both the Knight's Cross and the German Cross in Gold for leading combat units in action and certainly knew the hopelessness of his situation. As with any German commander, however, he had to stand and die lest his family be arrested for his actions. Then, out of the blue, his deliverance came in the form of a slender, hard-bitten veteran with a leathery face and a hand grenade in his belt.

On 2 April Vienna was officially declared a *Festung*, and *General der Infanterie* Rudolf von Bünau was appointed by the *OKW* to take over Vienna's defenses.[3] We can assume that Merker breathed a sigh of relief at no longer being responsible for defending the indefensible and going down in history as the man who lost Vienna. That legacy would now fall on von Bünau.

Unfortunately for him he was not given command of the Vienna area, meaning he could not command the field forces but only the scattered alarm units, various training formations and civilian forces within Vienna itself. Like so much of the byzantine Nazi bureaucracy there was no clear-cut chain of command or responsibility; even as the Reich was being overrun, petty jealousies dictated that bureaucrats protect their fiefdoms. He was informed of his new command by a single telephone call from the Army Personnel Department, with no follow-up calls, written orders or details about what he was supposed to do, and no clear instructions about what troops he would command. Like commanders throughout the shrinking Reich, von Bünau was expected to conjure defenses from thin air.

Von Bünau did not look the part of a highly decorated combat veteran. Slight of build, with a square face, high forehead and long nose, he could easily have been mistaken for a schoolmaster or librarian; by the spring of 1945 his slim physique had become gaunt, his face gouged with deep lines like cracks in a granite cliff-face. A photo of him during this time shows a non-descript *Landser* with a stick grenade in his belt, looking more like a new levy for the *Volkssturm* than a man wearing Germany's highest honor.[4]

Looks were deceiving, however; von Bünau was every inch a warrior. He was brave and experienced, and if what was needed was a man to lead well-armed forces in a stubborn and spirited defense, then his selection would have been a good choice. But that was not what he was being asked to do. Instead his mission was to work a miracle.

Six years of war had taken its toll on the man. At 54 years old, von Bünau had seen considerable action in the trenches during the First World War, then served in the greatly reduced interwar *Reichswehr* and had lost both sons in combat during 1943,[5] yet he continued fighting with distinction, winning the Oak Leaves to his Knight's Cross on 5 March 1945, while commanding *XI Armeekorps* on the central front. He had also served as Commanding General of *IX Armeekorps* in *1. Panzerarmee*.

Unfortunately for von Bünau his assignment was hopeless. The few forces available to him were odds and ends, with no seasoned ground combat units among them, and no time to organize them before the Russians were at the gates of the city. Ordered to defend Vienna at all costs, von Bünau knew the situation could not be saved but did his best anyway: "I did not have the authority to

---

3   Once again sources differ on exactly when von Bünau was appointed to command Vienna's defenses. Some say 1 April, Michael Reynolds claims 4 April and yet others list his appointment as late as 6 April. Weyr says it was on 2 April, and this seems in accord with von Bünau's own postwar interview as written by the Historical Division of the United States Army. Von Bünau does not specifically give the date that he was appointed, but he does say that Vienna was declared by the *OKH* to be a defense area on 2 April. Thus, he could not have been appointed on 1 April unless he was told in advance of Vienna's status change, and by 4 April he was already in Vienna as commander.

4   Wiegrefe, Klaus, 'Nazi Veterans Created Illegal Army', <http://www.spiegel.de/international/germany/wehrmacht-veterans-created-a-secret-army-in-west-germany-a-969015.html>, (Accessed 20 May 2014). Documents released in 2014 tell the story of an underground postwar army in West Germany that was formed to fight in case of attack from the East. It is now clear that the German government knew of this army and tacitly allowed it to exist. Many of its members later went on to top ranks with both the West German Army and NATO. One man who led a 'group staff' in Stuttgart was none other than Rudolf von Bünau.

5   One of whom, his namesake Major Rudolf von Bünau, was killed only a week after winning the Knight's Cross.

decide whether the battle of Vienna should or should not take place. When the battle was ordered, the only possibility, for command and troops, was wholehearted fighting."[6]

According to Maier, von Bünau arrived in Vienna in the afternoon of 3 April.[7] Even as von Bünau prepared to do what he could to defend Vienna, this is the day that Sepp Dietrich supposedly was introduced to the people of Vienna as their defender, using the speech quoted by Weyr.[8] Toland says that during his radio speech, Dietrich said, "It's not for us, it's for the Party! Heil our *Führer!*" Also according to Toland, the 'Little War-Newspaper' stated: "Hate is our prayer, revenge is our password."[9] Vienna Radio also responded to rumors that Vienna had been declared an open city by saying that the city would be defended vigorously.[10] So the confused command situation already in place as the jumble of German units being pushed into Austria were sorted into something resembling an order of battle, became even murkier as von Bünau and Dietrich were both given the same task with no clear delineation of duties.

* * *

The two Russian armies homing in on Vienna were the elite Fourth and Sixth Guards Armies. The designation of 'Guards' could only be given to units that distinguished themselves in combat. In many ways it was comparable to the American Presidential Unit Citation. Men who served in a Guards unit were referred to as Guardsmen. All rank designations had the term Guards placed before their rank, such as Guards Private, Guards Sergeant, etc. They were also permitted to wear the Guards badge on their uniform. All of this was honorary, and while it automatically identified the man as being part of an elite unit, it carried no preferential treatment within the Red Army.

Both Fourth and Sixth Guards Armies were tough, veteran formations. Losses during the pursuit across Western Hungary had been significant but not as heavy as those of the Germans. From Tolbukhin and Malinovsky down to the lowliest Guards Private, all of them wanted to capture Vienna as quickly as possible. For the high-ranking officers it was a matter of winning battle honors while there was still time. For the rank and file the road to home led through Vienna.

* * *

Carl Szokoll found what were thought to be the final positions and passwords for *6. SS-Panzerarmee* around Vienna and called for an emergency meeting of *O-5*, hiding in plain sight at the Headquarters for *Generalkommando XVII* on the Stubenring. As Herbert Kühl had already discovered, the Headquarters was nearly deserted so the chances of *O-5* being discovered were much less than had been the case. It was time to make contact with the Russians and Szokoll needed a volunteer he could trust. The obvious choice was *Feldwebel* Ferdinand Kas, a man he had known for more than a decade, and a man whose father had served in the First World War alongside Szokoll's father.

Armed with a faked pass and a small map, Kas set out to circumvent the battle area southeast of the city even as it was moving west and northwest. Exact knowledge of who was where was

6   The National Archives (TNA) M-1035 Fiche 365 B-160 Bünau, General der Infanterie AD Rudolf von *Combat in Vienna 29 Mar-16 Apr 1945* (Leavenworth: Historical Division Headquarters United States Army, Europe, 1946), p. 32.

7   Maier, *Drama*, p. 344.

8   Maier emphatically denies that Dietrich ever set foot in or anywhere near Vienna, and never left army headquarters. And Maier should know, since he was an eyewitness. Yet the bulk of the evidence supports the story that Dietrich did enter Vienna.

9   Toland, *The Last 100 Days*, p. 375.

10   Muddying the waters further on the issue of whether or not consideration had been given to declaring Vienna an open city, in his report on his role defending Vienna von Bünau states that he, von Schirach and Dietrich all made just such a request, but were turned down. See narrative for 4 April.

unknown even to the commanders on the spot, so Kas was in the dark about his precise route. Major Szokoll had given Kas his own driver, Corporal Johann Reif, in Szokoll's Opel. They headed south for Baden, then turned and according to Toland made for Weiner Neustadt, but turned to the southwest on small back roads before reaching the city, wandering about until they found the German front lines just before dawn on 3 April.

* * *

On 15 January 1945, Jenő Ruszkay was named Inspector General of all Hungarian *Waffen-SS* formations. He established his headquarters in the comfortable spa town of Baden, south of Vienna, more than 200 miles from the front lines in Hungary. But by 2 April the Russians were drawing too close to Baden for comfort, so *SS-Obergruppenführer* Ruszkay moved his headquarters far to the west, 35 miles northeast of Salzburg at Kremsmünster.

The picturesque town in Upper Austria had seen nothing of war yet. The ancient Kremsmünster Abbey had stood since 770 AD. The library contained more than 160,000 rare volumes, with the most famous manuscript being the *Codex Millenarius*, a Gospel Book created at the nearby Mondsee Abbey around 800 AD. This made it similar in age and content to the famous *Book of Kells* housed at Trinity College in Dublin. Another famous artifact which was crafted at the time of the Abbey's founding, the Tassilo Chalice, was still used in ceremonies even in 1945.

Trying unsuccessfully to contact the *SS-Hauptamt*, SS Main Office, Ruszkay went into Salzburg to see if that SS office was in contact with Berlin, since it was never a good idea to be out of touch with SS headquarters. In those chaotic days it was all too easy to be shot for alleged cowardice. As it turned out the SS office in Salzburg was in contact with Berlin and Ruszkay was ordered to report to the capital. In the meantime, however, he issued orders that all Hungarian detachments scattered at various training schools were to report to the main divisions still forming in Bavaria and Western Austria. To American intelligence this was more evidence for the existence of the National Redoubt, because yet more SS troops had been ordered into the Alps.

* * *

One of the few *Luftwaffe* units still operational over *Heeresgruppe Süd* in March 1945 was *III. Gruppe, Kampfgeschwader 4*, flying Heinkel HE-111 bombers. Five years earlier as the Germans finalized preparations for the invasion of France, this same group flew the same aircraft. During the intervening years Germany's enemies had developed new and drastically improved aircraft, while German pilots had to make do with whatever would fly.

The *Gruppe* flew relief missions during the Siege of Budapest and supported the ground forces during *Unternehmen Frühlingserwachen* and the subsequent Russian Vienna Offensive. When the front moved close enough that they could hear artillery fire the *Gruppe* withdrew west to the airfield at Wels. This grass strip had permanent hangars with concrete aprons and had been used mostly as a training and factory airfield.

One of the *Gruppe*'s members, a navigator and bombardier named Georg Zirk, wrote that upon arriving at Wels "we saw hundreds of brand new FW-190 fighters parked, but nobody was flying them. There was no fuel."[11] It's hard to credit the claim there were hundreds of newly manufactured Focke Wulfs sitting on the runway. On the other hand aircraft factories had been using the base for years. What makes the most sense is that Zirk saw rows of brand new aircraft and exaggerated their number. Taken together with the loss of the brand new ME-262 fighters on the airfield at Weiner Neustadt, what becomes clear is that Germany had continued producing first-class weapons of war even when they could no longer be flown for lack of gasoline.

---

11   Zirk, George, *Red Griffins Over Russia* (Mesa: Champlin Fighter Museum, 1987), p. 80.

South of the Danube

The Russians

Marshal Tolbukhin's path to the west was anticipated long before the war moved into Austria. As it had been throughout history, the south side of the Danube Valley acted as an invasion highway directly into south Germany, with Munich being the prize at the end of the road. Not only did he have the powerful Fourth and Ninth Guards Armies for such a drive, but he also had armored support from Sixth Guards Tank Army. The German forces opposing him appeared impressive on a map, especially *6. SS-Panzerarmee*, but as both sides knew the Germans had left most of their remaining artillery and armor in western Hungary. What Third Ukrainian Front faced were skeletons of divisions.

So far all was going according to plan. Wiener Neustadt was as good as captured. South of that city the way westward led into the mountains of Eastern Austria, where the only viable invasion routes were through the main valleys and mountain passes, such as the Semmering Pass. But north of Wiener Neustadt and south of Vienna lay the *Wienerwald*, the Vienna Woods, a favorite playground of the citizens of Austria's largest city. Although a heavily forested region of hills and mountains, the nature of the terrain wasn't nearly as rugged as the mountains to its south. Good roads ran through it, and beyond it to the northwest was the valley of the Danube River. And the only thing standing between Tolbukhin's spearheads and this highway to Germany were the remnants of once-mighty German divisions.

6. SS-Panzerarmee

Dietrich received word that the *Führer-Grenadier-Division* had been ordered to Vienna in its entirety. This came as welcome news for the depleted Army, since the division was at full strength and even had a significant panzer component. Ominously, however, orders were issued to ready the Danube bridges at both Vienna and Tulln for demolition.

Like Velikiye Luki, Stalingrad, Königsberg, the Courland Peninsula and scores of other locations before it, Vienna was ordered to be held to the last man. As indicated previously such suicidal *Führer* orders were now often ignored by the field commanders, including Hitler's long-time friend and follower Sepp Dietrich. Their friendship dated to 1928 when Dietrich joined the Nazi Party and became commander of Hitler's personal bodyguard. During the Night of the Long Knives on 30 June 1934, Dietrich commanded the SS firing squad at Stahlhelm Prison that executed five SA generals.

Dietrich served four years in the First World War and even won the Iron Cross First Class, a significant achievement for a man in the lower ranks, while being promoted to sergeant. After his involvement in the purge of the SA he rapidly rose through the ranks of the SS, which culminated with command of *6. SS-Panzerarmee*. His unquestioned loyalty and personal connection with Hitler allowed him to be more frank with the *Führer* than other generals could ever have been and survive.

Although many Army generals acidly commented that Dietrich had surpassed his level of competence when elevated beyond command of a division – *Generalfeldmarschall* Gerd von Rundstedt thought he wasn't too bright, although honest – Hitler never lost faith in his paladin. That was why the Cuff Band Order felt like such a personal betrayal to the doggedly loyal Dietrich. It is worth quoting Maier at length to portray exactly how this humiliating rebuff played out during the Battle for Vienna:

> The city of Vienna escaped the fate of Budapest...because the Commander-in-Chief of the
> 6. *Panzer Armee* was determined not to defend Vienna as a fortress. He intended to fight
> a delaying action as long as possible and with as few casualties as possible. There were not
> enough forces for anything else. Under no circumstances were the forces of the 6. *Panzer
> Armee* to get caught up in house-to-house fighting in Vienna.[12]

He goes on to mention that in the backs of their minds, some officers at Dietrich's headquarters began to observe the approach of American and French armies in southern Germany and to wonder if they would eventually find themselves surrounded.

Dietrich was a rough man who had loyally followed Hitler for almost two decades, but like all such men he expected his loyalty to be reciprocated. When he felt betrayed at the end of the war, his chief concerns shifted away from the war aims of the man he followed to the survival of those he led. That decision had major ramifications for the postwar world.

In their official histories the Russians went to great lengths to build up Vienna as a fortified city defended by strong SS forces, which posed huge difficulties for the attacking forces. Inflated numbers as high as eight panzer divisions, with various specialized brigades and battalions, were listed to show the valor of the Red Army in seizing the city. The truth was otherwise.

I SS-Panzerkorps

After holding on for as long as possible at Sopron and Mattersburg, *I SS-Panzerkorps* was obliged to pull back to Wiener Neustadt and the Leitha River or be surrounded, regardless of orders to stand and die in place. Blocking forces had fought hard to hold the passes heading west through the Rosalien Mountains, but they did not have the manpower, heavy weapons or mobility to stop the Russians indefinitely. The Russian tanks were about two-thirds American M-4 Shermans mounting a high-velocity 76mm gun, and one-third Russian T-34s with 85mm cannon. Through sheer bravery the German blocking forces knocked out four of the Russian tanks using *Panzerfauste*, but hand-held weapons alone weren't enough.

The strongest Russian attacks came from the south and cut behind the German positions erected east of the city, threatening to cut them off on the west. It soon became obvious that Wiener Neustadt could not be defended either, and during the night the Germans were forced to abandon that city too. The army's front extended from Gloggnitz in the south to Neunkirchen in the north, but there had been no time to build defenses. Instead the SS men tried to establish blocking positions to buy time.

Wisely, Russian attacks against 6. *SS-Panzerarmee* followed the terrain. Advancing over sheer and tree-covered slopes was hard enough with nobody shooting at them, and even if they did surmount a peak, supply became problematic. So the battle for the Austrian hinterland evolved into a fight for the few roads passable by heavy vehicles.

Smoking debris from an American air attack on 29 March still rose from the heavily damaged *Luftpark* in now-abandoned Wiener Neustadt. The city was the next prize in their sights, although the Russians didn't know the Germans had pulled out during the night. It is located on an elevated island completely surrounded by valleys, which are, in turn, overlooked by rugged peaks. One such valley, the Schwarz Valley, leads southwest to Gloggnitz, but that city sits in a cul-de-sac surrounded by heavily forested mountains.

---

12   Maier, *Drama*, p. 344.

The Russians weren't slow to recognize their opportunity. *I SS-Panzerkorps* had responsibility for that sector but didn't have the means to stop the enemy advance. Instead of attacking Wiener Neustadt directly, they drove both north and south using the valleys. *Oberstgruppenführer und Generaloberst der Waffen-SS* Sepp Dietrich told his commanders: "Gentlemen, there is nothing left to defend here."[13]

The southern pincer then branched both left and right, with the left-hand force driving south-west toward Gloggnitz by way of Edlitz and the right-hand group moving north to complete the encirclement of Weiner Neustadt. Following the path of least resistance, after the fall of Wiener Neustadt the northern force wheeled ninety degrees and headed for Felixsdorf and Sollernau on the direct road to Vienna.

Between Gloggnitz and Neunkirchen stood the regiment-sized *SS-Kampfgruppe Keitel*, part of *37. SS-Freiwilligen-Kavallerie-Division Lützow*, and from Neunkirchen to the area west of Weiner Neustadt was an obscure blocking unit named *Speerverbande Gross*, which had elements of *356. Infanterie-Division* combined with officer cadets from the *Kriegsschule Wiener Neustadt*.

Kampfgruppe I SS-Panzer-Division Leibstandarte Adolf Hitler

As units around it melted away without warning, the remnants of the division's panzer regiment found themselves on the wrong side of Weiner Neustadt. One Panther platoon fighting east of the city fired off all their remaining ammunition and then reportedly abandoned their panzers, presumably destroying them first. Others, fighting on the south side, suddenly discovered they'd been cut off from the north and west, while other Russian forces swept south of their position. There seemed no way out. But *SS-Obersturmführer* Werner Sternebeck, the *3./SS-Panzer-Regiment 1* veteran commander, led the survivors of his *Kampfgruppe* in a hell ride back through the newly captured city. Shooting at anything that moved while careening through rubble-strewn streets they made it to the western side before encountering significant opposition. When they came to a strong road block, Sternebeck's group barely slowed down as they blasted their way through and escaped.

There was more fighting once out of the city. The bridge over the Piesting River five miles north of Wiener Neustadt had already been blown up, so his group turned toward Wöllersdorf. But time was of the essence, since Russian tank columns had already taken Felixdorf just to the northeast. Fortunately for Sternebeck's group, they had the perfect flanking position as the Russian armored column moved out and destroyed up to 12 T-34s.[14]

SS-Kampfgruppe Keitel

The German Army had been primarily horse-drawn for years by this point in the war, but while horses remained the primary means of locomotion for transporting all types of wagons, guns, field kitchens, etc., even those animals were in short supply. For example, the *4.Panzerjäger-Kompanie* of *SS-Kampfgruppe Keitel* had no horses left by 2 April 1945, but in a bizarre twist it was fully motorized.

Many men of the still-forming cavalry division were veterans of either *8. SS-Kavallerie-Division Florian Geyer* or *22. SS-Freiwilligen-Kavallerie-Division Maria Theresa*, who had been wounded during the Battle of Budapest but were flown out and had since recovered. This was true for

13   Brettner, Friedrich, *Die Letzten Kämpfe des II. Weltkrieges, Fotoband I* (Berndorf: Kral, 2014), p. 147.
14   Brettner, *Die Letzten Kämpfe Band I*, p. 163.

both *SS-Obersturmbannführer* Karl-Heinz Keitel and *SS-Obersturmbannführer* Anton Ameiser. A few hundred had been lucky enough to survive the breakout attempt in mid-February, when the Russians massacred the last 17,000 Germans left standing from the garrison who tried to make it back to German lines. As many as 700 eventually filtered through.

Panzerjäger-Abteilung 37 arrived at Ebenfurth an der Leitha, and during the night of 31 March through to 1 April fought a mortar and artillery engagement against Russian troops bypassing Wiener Neustadt on the northeast. Other parts of the *Kampfgruppe* had fought to stop a Russian thrust at Schwarzau am Steinfeld, but after five hours the attackers broke through to the north-west, pushing the SS men aside. They retreated to the southwest and dug in near Eggendorf, but the Russians poured past their flanks and they withdrew again, this time to Pottenstein.

* * *

At Steinabrückl, five miles northwest of Wiener Neustadt, elements of the *Kampfgruppe* came under attack from the spearheads of 9th Guards Mechanized Corps. Twice the Russians launched assaults with tank support and twice they were repulsed. Throughout the region, as German units shifted and withdrew to try and establish a main line of resistance, time and again they discovered the Russians had already beaten them to their next destination.

II SS-Panzerkorps

Nowhere in Austria did chaos reign more than in *II SS-Panzerkorps'* area of responsibility. The *I SS-Panzerkorps, 6. Armee* and *2. Panzerarmee* had all retreated to the first foothills of the Alps, but the land approaching Vienna from the east and southeast was flat, with numerous good roads. Russian movements all along the front lines were beginning to flow northwest into the Danube Valley and the Vienna Woods, away from areas of stronger resistance and directly at *II SS-Panzerkorps*.

* * *

The misperception possible because of flags or designations on a map is nowhere more evident than with *II SS-Panzerkorps*. Seeing a map with *6. Panzer-Division, 3. SS-Panzer-Division Totenkopf* and *2. SS-Panzer-Division Das Reich* lined up side by side on a front 25 miles wide presents an image of fire and steel. At full authorized strength those divisions would contain more than fifty thousand men and 400 panzers, *Jagdpanzers* and *Sturmgeschütze*.

But in fact the manpower total was about half that and between all three they had fewer than 50 panzers operational. What they needed was time to repair damaged equipment and for exhausted men to rest and recuperate. What they got was more continuous combat.

* * *

Von Schirach's indolence toward construction of the *Reichsschutzstellung* was nowhere more evident than in the Bruck Gap, between the northern tip of the Neuseidlersee and the Danube River. What should have been an easily defended chokepoint was nothing of the sort.

The previous day's Russian attacks had captured most of the western shore of the Neuseidlersee, leaving the corps holding a thin line from the Danube to Eisenstadt. During the night of 1-2 April the Russians broke through but immediate counterattacks by *2. SS-Panzer-Division Das Reich* temporarily checked them. See-saw fighting ensued as *Das Reich* attacked from Mannersdorf to the north and Ebergassing to the northwest but the Russians proved too strong. The German attacks ultimately failed and the Russian spearheads advanced all the way to Münchendorf, a little town less than ten miles south of Vienna's city limits.

6. Panzer-Division

North of the Neuseidlersee along the south bank of the Danube, *6. Panzer-Division* acted as a blocking force to prevent Russian penetration of Vienna in a *coup de main*. Although no German units matched the definition of a panzer division in terms of strength, *6. Panzer-Division* still had more working panzers than could be counted on one hand. Only four Panzer IVs were combat-ready, but the division listed 17 Panthers and 10 *Jagdpanzer* IV/70s operational,[15] which gave it an armored strength virtually unknown by any other division. It also listed 29 artillery pieces on hand. Although still 100 percent mobile the division reported its combat readiness condition as III, meaning suitable only for mobile defense. Giving *6. Panzer-Division* much-needed extra firepower, *SS-Panzer-Aufklärung-Abteilung 9* from *9. SS-Panzer-Division Hohenstauffen* had been attached to the division.

Marshes and woodlands lined the banks of the Danube, making any incursion more than infiltration impossible. But inland from the river was farmland and orchards with only a few small towns, a difficult area to defend. Fields of fire favored whichever side had the greater firepower, which in 1945 was always the Red Army. Artillery observation made adjusting the fall of shots easier. German *PAK* weapons or panzers equipped with either a 75/L70 or the 88mm main gun still enjoyed a range advantage over most Russian tank and assault gun weapons. This advantage increased as the Russian armored units moving on Vienna increasingly drove American Sherman tanks equipped with a 76mm cannon, or the British Valentine tank. With adequate numbers of panzers, *6. Panzer-Division* could have put up a nearly unmovable defense, but while 27 panzers made the division relatively powerful among the divisions of *Heeresgruppe Süd*, they were inadequate to stop the onrushing Russians. All they could do was slow them down.

3. SS-Panzer-Division Totenkopf

The fearsome war machine that once had been *3. SS-Panzer-Division Totenkopf* fought on at a reduced strength of 25 percent of its authorized totals, roughly 5,000 men of all ranks. Working panzers could be counted on one hand. Because of this the division was reclassified as a *Kampfgruppe*. Separated from its parent *IV SS-Panzerkorps*, on 2 April the division was reassigned to *II SS-Panzerkorps*.

Despite its ruined state, elements of *Totenkopf* still stood on the western bank of the Neuseidlersee at Oggau, on the left flank of *Hitlerjugend*, with a *Volkssturm* detachment and a remnant of the destroyed *232. Reserve-Panzer-Division*. Rauchensteiner puts the number of SS men at 80, about a company's worth.[16] This unit was undoubtedly *SS-Kampfgruppe Barth*, which included men from the disbanded *I./SS-Panzer-Regiment 3* too. Including the *Volkssturm* the actual number was closer to 160.

The initial Russian attacks on Oggau am Neuseidlersee were repulsed with the loss of 16 tanks. *SS-Kampfgruppe Barth* was well armed with *Panzerfauste* but no other heavy weapons. Details of how and where these machines were destroyed have been lost to history, but it's likely this included tanks knocked out when the *Totenkopf* men retreated to the nearby Leitha Mountains later in the day for a cumulative total. Ian Michael Wood puts the number of tanks destroyed by the *Kampfgruppe* at two, with five *Volkssturm* men killed in action.[17] *Totenkopf*'s position grew

15   Nevenkin, *Fire Brigades*, p. 206.
16   Rauchensteiner, *Krieg in Österreich*, p. 90.
17   Wood, *Tigers*, p. 247.

increasingly precarious as Russian spearheads moved west along the Danube, pushing back *6. Panzer-Division* and threatening *Totenkopfs* northern flank, while along their southern and western flanks other enemy forces moved to cut them off. It became obvious to all that the question was when, not if, they would have to abandon the finger of land they still defended. Refugees clogged the road to Vienna while they could still get out.[18]

During the evening hours the surviving Germans pulled back across the tiny Wulka River running through a valley of the same name, but even in rugged terrain that position proved indefensible. Under attack by the 7th Airborne Division of 20th Guards Corps, they fell back again to join another group defending the nearby Rosalie Mountains. This small chain of low hills is separated from the Leitha Mountains to their north by the Ödenburg Gate. Together these rugged peaks could have been a formidable barrier if defended by significant forces. Unfortunately for the Germans all they had were small groups of under-armed men who were unsure of the situation in general, or even the security of their own flanks. Further attacks pushed the *Totenkopf* men northwest, toward Vienna, where a repaired Tiger II had been turned over to a crew from the division's *9./SS-Panzer-Regiment 3*.

2. SS-Panzer-Division Das Reich

With *6. Panzer-Division* on the corps' left flank and *Kampfgruppe 3. SS-Panzer-Division Totenkopf* in the center, *2. SS-Panzer-Division Das Reich* anchored the corps' right flank. If the German position had been solid *Das Reich* would have joined *I SS-Panzerkorps* in a cohesive front line, but even as early as 2 April that was a fantasy. The division's front bent to the west with its right flank up in the air and the Russians driving past it to the west. The Russian spearheads offered a tempting target for a counterattack, but the burned-out SS panzer divisions were in no position to take advantage of the momentary opportunity.

* * *

During the retreat from Hungary, parts of *SS-Panzer-Artillerie 9* that were in the Györ area refitting were attached to *Das Reich,* giving it added firepower at the expense of the regiment's parent unit, *Hohenstaufen*. In the desperate situation the division found itself in every little bit helped.

Another formation absorbed into *SS-Panzergrenadier-Regiment 4 Der Führer* was *SS-Kampfgruppe Hauser*, a collection of miscellaneous convalescents and students from the Motorized Vehicle Training School Vienna, commanded by *SS-Sturmbannführer* Hans Hauser. It was thrown into the gap between *SS-Panzergrenadier-Regiment 3 Deutschland* and *Der Fuhrer* and ordered to hold the town of Münchedorf at all costs. *Das Reich's* two *Panzergrenadier* regiments were stretched to the limit already and had no reserves to close the gap between them. Hauser was ordered to hold Münchedorf for three or four days.

They arrived just in the nick of time. Russian tanks immediately slammed into Hauser's command but it held its ground and prevented a dangerous penetration of the front. Such heroism had its cost, however, and the *Kampfgruppe* suffered very heavy casualties.

* * *

---

18 Rauchensteiner puts this fighting on 1 April, not 2 April. Maier's date is used here because his was the later scholarship and 2 April makes more sense in the overall flow of events. He was also on the spot when all this occurred. Most of *Totenkopf* was still in the Weiner Neustadt area on 1 April.

Throughout the day *Das Reich* continued withdrawing northwest toward Vienna. There was no thought given to holding in place, as ordered. The only way withdrawal was possible at all was by pulling back in stages, with a few panzers and infantry giving covering fire as their comrades retreated past them and set up positions so they could retreat in turn. At no point did the chance to make a stand present itself, although the ferocity of the SS men's defense made the Russians slow the speed of their pursuit. The division also noted fewer T-34s and more American Shermans in the Russian units.[19]

Knowing the precise location of neighboring units proved impossible in the fluid situation. The *Das Reich* command staff set up headquarters at Götzendorf, a few miles northwest of the Neuseidlersee, but this was more of a resting stop than a permanent location. Within hours it had moved again, this time to Trautmanndorf. Nobody thought the Russians could be stopped, although efforts to form a defensive line were made. Nor did the SS men ever consider surrender. Most of them believed that the immediate fate of captured SS men was a bullet in the head.

Even on a day with sporadic fighting the hemorrhaging of German blood continued. Like commanders have done throughout history, *SS-Sturmbannführer* Kesten, commander of *II./ SS-Panzer-Regiment 2*,[20] went out that morning to personally reconnoiter the best panzer positions in the wooded hills north of Baden. Such dangerous maneuvers often result in the death of the officer involved, from *General der Panzertruppe* George Stumme, commander of *Panzerarmee Afrika*, to Confederate General Stonewall Jackson, but despite the danger there is no substitute for a commander seeing the field of battle for himself. The Confederates lost the Battle of Pea Ridge in 1862 because two generals died reconnoitering Union positions before the battle even started. Like those men, when Kesten moved past the German front lines he was killed, although exactly how is not recorded. During a long career he had won the coveted Knight's Cross and the undying respect of those who knew him. Such men were scarce now in the German ranks and could not be replaced.

* * *

Word came that the Russians were already west of Vienna and the command post of *Der Führer* moved twice more that day, first to Moosbrunn and then to Gramatneusiedl. *II./SS-Panzer-Regiment 2* was charged with defending Moosbrunn when a major Russian attack slammed into the small town. There could be no retreat this time because that would endanger the entire German position southeast of Vienna, so the *Panzergrenadiers* stood and fought. Russian tanks got as far as the battalion command post where they wiped out the entire battalion command staff, except the commander who had been out inspecting positions. Against huge odds the battalion hung onto Moosbrunn, but to no avail. Heavy Russian attacks also hit *I./SS-Panzergrenadier-Regiment 4* at Gramatneusiedl and drove it back, ruining the attempt to maintain a defensive line.

As night fell the roads to Vienna were clogged by the flotsam of war. Civilians led wagons overloaded with their possessions, German troops from broken units stumbled onward, deserters from the *Wehrmacht* and the *Honved* avoided the field police, Hungarians terrified of the Russians limped forward and hoped to find sanctuary somewhere in the Reich and the *Waffen-SS* units still trying to halt the Russians pushed aside any who got in their way. *Das Reich* formed an armored rearguard to protect them against surprise night attacks, using elements of the *Flak*, reconnaissance and tank destroyer battalions.

* * *

19   Weidinger, *Das Reich*, p. 364.
20   *Das Reich* had recently folded the remnants of the *I.Abteilung* into *II. Abteilung*, so the Regiment only had one battalion at this point, but it's official designation remained *II./SS-Panzer-Regiment 2*.

South of the Danube there was no German front at all, there were only pockets of resistance, like debris washed ahead of a rising tide that gets caught on a submerged rock or log. Six of the seven *Waffen-SS* panzer divisions were concentrated along Austria's eastern border, excepting only *10. SS-Panzer-Division Frundsberg*, and yet between all six they didn't have a full battalion's worth of panzers, *Jagdpanzers* or *Sturmgeschütze*. With their *Panzergrenadier* regiments depleted and most of their armor and artillery lost in the retreat from Hungary, it was impossible to stand and hold territory. None of *SS-Oberstgruppenführer* Sepp Dietrich's divisions was strong enough to keep contact with the neighbors on their flanks, so inevitably the Russians would filter past and threaten to surround them.

I SS-Panzerkorps

The situation was particularly bad for *SS-Gruppenführer* Hermann Preiss' *I SS-Panzerkorps*. Although *Totenkopf* was still technically part of his corps, in reality it had been virtually surrounded due west of Pottendorf and its only escape route was to the northwest, toward Vienna. With *Das Reich* on its right flank, it was sandwiched between the two divisions of *II SS-Panzerkorps*, with *6. Panzer-Division* being the other. That left only *Kampfgruppe 1. SS-Panzer-Division Leibstandarte Adolf Hitler*, *Kampfgruppe 356. Infanterie-Division* and *Kampfgruppe 12. SS-Panzer-Division Hitlerjugend* covering a long front from north of Wiener Neustadt to the south, where a huge gap had opened with *6. Armee*.

12. SS-Panzer-Division Hitlerjugend

Nine miles northeast of Wiener Neustadt, *Hitlerjugend* tried to make a stand in the area of Neufeld an der Leitha and Ebenfurth, but Sixth Guards Army slammed into their position with strong armored support and drove them backward to Blumau-Neurisshof, eight miles to the west-north-west. That was the area of the Danube Valley leading south of the city of Vienna to the Vienna Woods, and was excellent tank country.

Various parts of the division were incorporated into a *Kampfgruppe* at Grossau, including *SS-Panzergrenadier-Regiment 26*, and *SS-Sanitäts-Truppen 12*, which was the medical detachment and had two army *Flak* cannon on hand. This *Kampfgruppe* was in position to block entrance to the Triesting Valley and repelled the initial Russian attacks on its position. Ultimately, though, Grossau couldn't be held.

1. SS-Panzer-Division Leibstandarte Adolf Hitler

Sixth Guards Army pushed through Wiener Neustadt toward Konningbrunn, shoving the *LAH* even further south and west. The division wasn't strong enough to stand and slug it out and so it blocked the mountain passes from Wollersdorf to Bad Wischau using anyone who could hold a rifle. This included mobilizing men of the artillery regiment and *Flak* battalion without their heavy weapons to fight as infantry.

Where retreat wasn't feasible they stood their ground against heavy armor-supported infantry attacks, combined with mortar and artillery fire raining on their positions, and held the Russians back as long as humanly possible before being forced to retreat to Dreistetten. Fifty-five Germans died in the fighting along with 27 Russians and 28 civilians. A further 27 Germans had been captured, but were immediately shot.[21] Thus began the battle for the entrance to the valley of the Piesting River, which would last until 6 April.

The casualty list shows just how desperate the German defense was, with *8./SS-Panzergrenadier-Regiment 2* suffering more than 100 men killed, wounded or missing, which was nearly 100 percent of its roster, and the *7./SS-Panzergrenadier-Regiment 2* suffering 22 casualties. Those weren't simply heavy losses, they were catastrophic and unsustainable losses.[22]

The *Nebelwerfer* battalion was assigned to defend the Hohe Wand, a broad, rugged area that would see intense combat in the weeks to come, while the last of the *Flak* guns were placed near Felixdorf. There were only five 88mm, three 37mm and two 20mm guns left.[23] By also incorporating the surviving *Fahnenjunkeren*, the young officer cadets of the *Kriegsschule Wiener Neustadt*, the division cobbled together something resembling a front line.

Meanwhile, the remnants of the panzer regiment had to fight their way out of a trap southeast of Wiener Neustadt. As part of a mixed battle group from different units, the *LAH* panzers defended a hill with a platoon of Panthers on one flank and a company of Mark IVs on the other. Strong Russian attacks were repulsed time and again, until without warning the supporting infantry disappeared. Then the Panthers ran out of ammunition and the crews abandoned them, leaving the Mark IVs to fend for themselves. A courier was sent to the Wiener Neustadt Military Academy, riding a bicycle since there were no motorcycles or cars left operational, only to discover that the Russians had already taken the city. They were surrounded.

Eight surviving Mark IVs decided to run the Gauntlet through Wiener Neustadt at full speed, surprising the Russians who were too stunned to react. On the far side of town they had time to set up a barricade but the Germans simply drove through it. Once west of the city they blasted some Russian anti-tank guns near Felixdorf before they could unlimber, then drove to an area northeast of Wollersdorf, closely pursued by armored elements of the Red Army. From ambush they shot up the Russian spearheads, destroying up to 12 T-34s.

The intense combat and retreat across Hungary left *LAH* a shell of its former self.

* * *

On Easter Sunday the alarm had gone out to both Puchberg am Schneeberg and Grünbach am Schneeberg that Russian tanks were approaching. The *Volkssturm* was called up and three companies of Hungarian soldiers passed through Grünbach on their way to Puchberg, although what unit they belonged to isn't known. These were probably the men who were later disarmed by *SS-Kampfgruppe Keitel*. Later that afternoon a small SS unit also went through Grünbach, also probably from *SS-Kampfgruppe Keitel*. This caused great anxiety among the population and some decided the time had come to flee west.

6. Armee

The Russian high command had realized that easy prizes and rapid advances were coming to an end against Austria's greatest natural defenses, the Alps and their foothills. They were butting against the eastern edge of that mythical fortress area the Americans called the National Redoubt. And while the German preparations for a last-stand *Götterdämerung* existed mostly in the minds of American intelligence personnel, the formidable mountains they were supposed to inhabit were

21   Brettner, *Die Letzten Kämpfe Band I*, p. 166.
22   Brettner, *Die Letzten Kämpfe Band I*, p. 163.
23   Tiemann, *The Leibstandarte IV/2*, p. 281.

all too real. Because of this, and unnoticed by German intelligence, Second and Third Ukrainian Front's avenues of advance began taking a decided turn to the northwest toward the Danube Valley.

* * *

April was a month of gory stalemate for *6. Armee*. The fight for the passes into Styria barely gets a nod in Balck's memoirs or in the few histories that even mention the Battle for Austria. Yet nowhere else in the entire Reich was there sustained fighting on such a scale for the entire month of April. Events in the Ruhr and the battles for Vienna and Berlin certainly involved much greater numbers of men and weapons, but only the fight for the passes resembled the continuous bloody stalemate reminiscent of the First World War. The Russians used their massive superiority in artillery and Katyusha rocket launchers to drench the Germans in exploding metal, while the Germans knew that if the Russians captured ground only an immediate counterattack could stop them from exploiting their gains.

* * *

From his office atop the Schlossberg in Graz, Austria's second largest city, *Gauleiter* Siegfried Ueberreither vowed to stop the Russians and hold Styria as long as humanly possible. Born in Salzburg in 1908, Ueberreither was an energetic 37-year-old true believer in Nazism. His nickname was *Übereifer*, 'overly zealous'. He'd fought in Norway as a *Gebirgsjäger* before being mustered out after the fall of France.

*Gauleiter*s had virtually unlimited powers within their *Gau*s when it came to defense matters and Ueberreither was determined to use them all. He publicly declared to defend Graz house by house, to the last man and the last bullet. It was eerily reminiscent of the bombast of von Schirach, except that Ueberreither put his considerable energy into mobilizing his *Gau*. But like his fellow *Gauleiter* in Vienna, when it became his time to fight or flee, Ueberreither took the option he didn't give to his fellow Austrians and fled.

As leader of the *Volkssturm* he mobilized them and tightened conscription rules for the remaining men. Any man who could walk was handed a rifle or *Panzerfaust*, and many were sent to the front as replacements for the regular units. In addition to the various *Volkssturm* battalions were various small *Flak* units distributed throughout the region, with their own guns and ammunition supplies.

The women and children were finally evacuated. Defenses were built and barricades erected at crossroads and on critical streets. Slogans were printed up extolling any sacrifice necessary to stop the Russians. Everything that could be done was done.

But another man lived in Graz who also wanted to defend Styria. Like Ueberreither, Knight's Cross with Oak Leaves winner and *General der Gebirgstruppe* Julius Ringel was also a native Austrian, and the local troops at the front were put under his overall command. For the time being the two men's fates were intertwined and they dedicated themselves to keeping the Russians out of the interior of Styria.

* * *

The Germans often joked that the safest place during a Red Air Force bombing attack was on the target, but what the Russians lacked in precision they made up for in numbers. Balck's command counted more than 200 Russian bombers with fighter escorts over their lines on 2 April. The *Luftwaffe* could do nothing to interfere with these operations, but did fly 70 sorties against targets around Weiner Neustadt.[24] They had no significant effect on Russian operations except to inflict

---

24   Maier, *Drama*, p. 343.

losses, the cumulative effect of which did force them to transfer units from the stalled southern operations to the attack along the Danube valley.

With air superiority bordering on air supremacy the Russian bombing accuracy was good enough to claim yet another SS veteran officer. The commander of *SS-Panzer-Aufklärung-Abteilung 5*, the highly decorated Munich-born *Sturmbannführer* Fritz Vogt, whose actions leading *I./SS-Panzegrenadier-Regiment Norge* during *Unternehmen Konrad I* had been either heroic or self-serving, depending on the source, was mortally wounded in a strafing attack. As the war wound to a close the loss of men such as Vogt crippled the *Wehrmacht*. Such experience simply could not be replaced.

III Panzekorps

III Panzerkorps commanded the left, or northern, wing of *6. Armee* and caught the brunt of the day's attacks and was unable to prevent some minor penetrations into the front positions, some of which were in the *Reichsschutzstellung*. For the most part, however, the defense held. Some reports even claimed retrograde movements on the Soviet side. Hermann Balck and his staff believed the Russians were reorganizing to put pressure on *IV SS-Panzerkorps*, but this was wrong. Unknown to the Germans the weight of the Russian advance was shifting north.

* * *

Commanded by the well-respected *General der Panzertruppe* Wilhelm Breith, *III Panzerkorps* began April with an order of battle of *1. Volks-Gebirgs-Division*; *Divisionsgruppe Krause*, another ad hoc formation created to deal with the breakthrough northeast of Graz in the Oberwart region – it was this unit that was the parent formation for *SS-Kampfgruppe Schweitzer*; *Arko 3*[25] commanded by the Corps Artillery Commander, *Oberst* Semmer; and finally *Sperrverband*[26] *Motschmann*, a small unit based on a battalion from the *118. Jäger-Division*. Later in the month it would be heavily reinforced.

Bits and pieces of divisions were also used to bolster its numbers, including the replacement battalions of both *1. Panzer-Division* and *3. Panzer-Division*, *Volks-Werfer-Regiment 24*, *Beobachtungs-Abeitlung 34*, some Army artillery and smaller units. The only armored component at this point was the badly damaged *Schwere-Panzer-Abteilung 509*, which fielded Tiger IIs. The closer the combat range, the less effective those monstrous tanks became, so deploying them had to be done with great care.

Forwarded to the threatened Oberwart area from Graz was the *SS-Panzergrenadier-Ausbildungs-und-Ersatz-Abteilung 11*, part of *11. SS-Freiwilligen-Panzergrenadier-Division Nordland*, which was part of *Heeresgruppe Vistula*. This battalion was near full strength with 900 men. Another training battalion sent to the front was from *3. Gebirgs-Division*, the *Gebirgsjäger-Ausbildungs-und-Ersatz-Bataillon 138*, with about 500 men.

Despite its title as a *Panzerkorps*, and Breith's shining record as a panzer commander, in reality he commanded one regular division and a hodge-podge of countless alarm units, the composition of some of which are still unknown. Combat strength is also lost, but perhaps at the beginning of April the corps fielded a total of 40,000 men, with no more than 20,000 in the most threatened area on its left flank. But numbers alone don't paint an accurate picture. Few of these formations were designed for front-line combat. Their officers and *unteroffiziere* may have been combat

---

25 Arko stood for *Artillerie Kommandatur*.
26 Blocking Force.

veterans, but the men weren't, and their weapons were whatever could be scrounged. Some of them fought well, while others deserted at the first opportunity. There was no way of knowing ahead of time which man would run and which wouldn't.

At the top of the list of things the *Panzerkorps* didn't have were panzers.

The Russians

The main Russian force attacking *III Panzerkorp*'s left flank was the Twenty-Sixth Army. As an indication of the comparative forces, while the Germans might have fielded 20,000 men at the front line in various splinter groups, the Twenty-Sixth Army probably numbered around 100,000 men in three rifle and one cavalry corps. Nor were they hampered by a shortage of supplies and ammunition.

Kampfgruppe Semmering

Throughout history the avenues of invasion into and through Austria have remained unchanged. Even when Augustus' legions marched through the region, the only feasible routes were through the mountain passes, relatively flat valleys between wooded and towering peaks. An invading army could go over the mountains for short distances, but maintaining a supply line across steep, jagged and heavily wooded peaks was impossible even in the non-motorized days of horse and donkey power.

Armies moving into Austria from the east, such as Second and Third Ukrainian Fronts did in April of 1945, had no better options than did Attila. The Austrian state along the border with Hungary was Burgenland, while north of the Danube it was Lower Austria. The best avenue of invasion from either east or west was through the Danube Valley, which ran from Upper Austria to Lower Austria and Burgenland. The valley itself is marshy north of the Danube, but arable and easily traversed on the south side.

Burgenland ran north to south, and was much like the plains of Western Hungary, a rolling land of farms and vineyards. Those fertile lands have always been at risk of invasion because of the relative ease with which large forces could move across them. This was particularly true of the mechanized units of the Red Army in 1945, and it's why Marshals Malinovsky and Tolbukhin dreamed of a thrust straight down the Danube Valley toward Germany itself.

But for invaders of Styria, the Austrian state due west of Burgenland and south of Lower Austria, it was a very different matter. Like the towering ramparts of some mighty kingdom, the foothills of the Alps formed a protective wall from which determined defenders could extract a ruinous cost from attackers. Aside from trudging up and down jagged and heavily forested slopes, which was not an option that most military commanders would take, the only way for an invader to penetrate these protective barriers was through the mountain passes.

Three main valleys allowed access into Styria. The most important pass of the outer line of mountains was the Semmering Pass, which starts at Gloggnitz, winds through Eichberg, Schottwien, Breitenstein, Semmering, Spital am Semmering and ends at Mürzzuschlag. A critical railway line runs through the pass.

Another was the Preiner Gscheid Pass between Prein and Raxen. The third, south of the Semmering Pass, was the Feistritzsattel between Feistritzbachtal and Trattenbach. *Kampfgruppe Semmering* was responsible for all three. On the north its front ran from Gahns, overlooking the pass west of Gloggnitz near Payerbach, to Feistritzwald in the south, where the boundary was with *1. Volks-Gebirgs-Division*.

* * *

By 2 April the Russians had already taken Gloggnitz and begun moving through the pass. The leading unit, 103rd Guards Rifle Division, was filled with hardened veterans subordinated to another experienced unit, 37th Guards Rifle Corps. They knew how to fight and win battles against Germans, and were highly motivated to do just that. Moreover, Stalin turned a blind eye to the excesses of his men in conquered territories, believing it was their right to rape and pillage on foreign soil, which only added to the invaders' motivation. Styria was a prosperous land with plenty to offer a conqueror, and the only things standing in their way were the handful of rag-tag units that made up *Kampfgruppe Semmering.*

Some of the leading Russian units followed the railway line or moved overland north of Semmering itself, through Schottwien into the villages of Adlitzgraben and Breitenstein. With such limited forces for defense, there wasn't much the Germans could do. But travel along the railroad wasn't easy. In the area there were 16 viaducts over deep gorges and 15 tunnels blasted through the living rock.

* * *

In another example of the overlapping command structure of the Third Reich, *General der Gebirgstruppe* Julius Ringel, the dashing former Commander of *Generalkommando XVIII*, aka the Salzburg Military District, ordered the formation of yet another *Kampfgruppe* under *Oberstleutnant* Ludwig Lang, using whatever troops were available from the various schools and training units in the area. Ringel was now commander of *Armeekorps Ringel*, which appears to have been a headquarters with a plethora of alarm units under its command. Lang's *Kampfgruppe* was ordered into the Semmering Pass.

The Mountain NCO school Balck mentioned was at Admont, 88 miles from Semmering, famous both for the lush beauty of the area and for its thousand-year-old Abbey with its magnificent library. Under the command of a captain, the battalion moved into the line on 2 April and relieved the *Gebirgsjägers* on the Bädenwirt. Like many of the units they quartered at the Grand Hotel Erzerhog Johann, a luxury hotel that had seen everyone from kings to international chess grandmasters pass through its front doors.

By nightfall a diverse collection of men had assembled from every branch of the *Wehrmacht* except the *Kriegsmarine*. There were regular troops from the Army, students from Army and *Waffen-SS* schools, pilots and ground crews from the *Luftwaffe*, NCO candidates and both children and old men from the *Volkssturm*. One unit was formed from the personal men of an army lieutenant and had seven *PAK-40* antitank guns. The overall commander was Knight's Cross winner 34-year-old Colonel Heribert Raithel. They were known initially as *Kampfgruppe Semmering,* but would shortly earn the sobriquet *Kampfgruppe Raithel.*

* * *

The *Kampfgruppe* had to defend a front of 22 miles. One of the dominant positions was the Sonnwendstein, a 4,600 feet-high peak which dominated the pass opposite the town of Semmering. It was by no means the only important tactical position in the area, however. Similar peaks rose elsewhere along the pass.

* * *

The sprawling Südbahn Hotel had seen countless VIPs during its history. Its glorious setting was matched only by the level of service it provided to guests. Built in 1882 to service patrons of the Southern Railway Company, after expansion and renovations it had been, in every respect, a grand hotel. Now, in early April 1945, it became the headquarters for numerous units of *Kampfgruppe Semmering*.

One such formation was the unit sent forward by Ringel, *Panzerjäger-Ausbildungs-und-Ersatz-Abteilung 48* from Cilli, under the command of *Oberstleutnant* Ludwing Lang. Lang received orders to build a *Kampfgruppe* in the pass and made his headquarters in the Südbahn Hotel. Another ad hoc formation ordered to Semmering which drove all the way from Wolfsburg, in Carinthia, was the replacement batalion for *Gebirgsjäger-Regiment 136*, from *2. Gebirgs-Division*, which was a highly valued formation of the regular army. The battalion's parent division had begun life as the Austrian *6. Armee-Division* but joined the *Wehrmacht* after the *Anschluss*. The division had been crushed fighting on the Western Front, and its *Ausbildungs-und-Ersatz-Abteilung* had returned to Austria to train new recruits in mountain warfare. Now they would get the chance to fight in terrain they'd been trained for.

Sperrverband Motschmann

Wedged between *Kampfgruppe Semmering* and *Divisionsgruppe Krause* was *Sperrverband Motschmann*. The concept of a 'blocking group' was another of the *Wehrmacht*'s many ad hoc unit designations, like *Kampfgruppen* and alarm battalions. Led by *SS-Hauptsturmführer* Motschmann, this unit consisted of the veteran *SS-Polizei-Regiment 13*, the headquarters staff of the above-mentioned *Gebirgs-Ausbildungs-und-Ersatz-Abteilung 136*, a signals platoon, tank destroyer platoon, bicycle reconnaissance troop and *Gebirgs-Pionier-Ausbildungs-und-Ersatz-Abteilung*.

This unit was intended for defensive purposes only, but it should be noted that like all German splinter formations, the attempt was made for it to be self-contained. That is, it contained an organized staff who knew each other, a signals platoon to handle radio and field telephone communications, a specialized anti-tank platoon and even a small number of men on bicycles to scout the area.

1. Volks-Gebirgs-Division

The recently renamed *1. Volks-Gebirgs-Division* was in its element in the mountains of Styria. A mere two and a half years earlier, during *Fall Blau*, the German drive to Stalingrad and the Caucasus, *1. Gebirgs-Division* planted the swastika atop Mount Elbrus, the highest peak in Europe. Most of those men were gone by now, but not all. It was easily the best division in the corps.

In particular the *Gebirgsjäger-Regiment 99* would distinguish itself in the coming fight. But for the moment *Generalleutnant* Wittmann had a more immediate problem. The Russians launched numerous heavy armor-supported attacks east of Burgau which resulted in a breakthrough on his left flank. With no pressure on his right flank, Wittmann ordered *Gebirgsjäger-Regiment 98* to march behind his line and shift to his left. Before they could get there heavy fighting nearly broke the line. Around Neudau, and the Sauberg to its west, *Gebirgs-Pionier-Bataillon 54* held against Russian pressure all day, absorbing extra casualties instead of retreating.

Graz

It had become obvious that Graz was a major Russian objective, and plans were underway to see to its defense. *Gauleiter* of Salzburg Siegfried Ueberreither worked night and day to mobilize his *Gau* for the defense of Styria. One alarm company was formed from *Luftwaffe Flieger Schule 14*, mostly pilots-in-training with no aircraft to fly, or fuel for the few operational planes left. Within a few days it was off to join *Kampfgruppe Semmering*.

Elsewhere, the commander of *SS-Gebirgsjäger-Ausbildungs-und-Ersatz-Bataillons 13*, *SS-Hauptsturmführer* Horst Grunwald, received a phone call from the *Korück 593*, the rear area commander for *6. Armee, Generalmajor* Fritz Krause. Grunwald was told to ready his battalion for combat as an alarm unit, and to report to the headquarters of *Generalmajor* Bormann at Bruck an der Mur. In yet another duplication of effort, it was Bormann's job to protect the railway through the Semmering Pass. After meeting Bormann, Grunwald was ordered to take his battalion to defend the pass, and for all follow-on forces to do likewise. As the SS men moved off, a feeling of doom hung over the battalion.[27]

IV SS-Panzerkorps
Kampfgruppe 1. Panzer-Division

With no significant panzer force operational, and with its supply company reorganizing at Erfurt and its heavy *Flak* battalion caught up in the fighting in Bratislava, *1. Panzer-Division* was in dire need of reorganizing. Starting the day deployed near Heiligenkreuz, the division withdrew to Feldbach, southeast of Graz, to rest, let the wounded recuperate and to train new replacements. It would not be out of the battle for long.

Kampfgruppe 3. Panzer-Division

The men of the division saw aircraft approaching their positions from the north. Hundreds of aircraft in tight formations, which meant they couldn't be Russians and certainly weren't German; all of *Luftflotte 4* couldn't muster that many aircraft, not any more. Which meant they could only be…American? Yes, American bombers, 268 of them, but the men gaped in stupefied horror. Their target could only be the positions of the badly depleted *3. Panzer-Division*, but what were US bombers doing flying tactical missions on the Eastern Front? As the bombs rained down from this overhead nightmare there was nothing the men could do except hunker down, pray and wonder exactly how the attack came about.

Despite the damage done by the bombers the division counterattacked again during the afternoon and once again the Russians were caught off-guard. The slaughter was wholesale. Columns of trucks and wagons caught on the Raab Valley road were shot to pieces and the Germans rolled over them. They once again recaptured Vasszentmihály, plus Rátot, Gastony, Renck and Alsö, and drove the Russian garrisons out in panicked flight. Captured supplies were a welcome treat for the *Landser*, particularly 7,000 cigarettes. Fifty Hungarian women and girls were released from a basement where they were being held for shipment elsewhere.

The success of their attacks on 1 April had caught the Germans off-guard. This time they were ready to stay at Vasszentmihály and hunkered down, knowing that as long as they held that town it would cut off any drives into the Raab Valley.[28]

---

27   Brettner, *Die Letzten Kämpfe Band I*, p. 87.
28   Veterans of the 3. Panzer-Division, *Armored Bears Volume Two, The German 3. Panzer-Division in World War II* (Mechanicsburg: Stackpole Books, 2013), p. 283.

5. SS-Panzer-Division Wiking

Maintaining combat strength in the divisions remained a priority for the SS departments in Berlin, but finding bodies was the hard part. Germany was scraping the bottom of the manpower barrel, so the holes in *Wiking*'s roster were filled by men in their 50s and 60s, or teenage *Flakhelfer,* children who helped out with the anti-aircraft defenses. The combat value of these replacements was nil, since they had no training in ground combat and were physically incapable of withstanding the rigors of anything more than static defense. Instead *Wiking,* and presumably the other SS divisions, used these men in supply jobs or as orderlies, thus relieving trained men to fight as infantry.

2. Panzerarmee

Viewed on a tactical map it is almost impossible to understand now how the Germans saved Graz from being captured on 3 or 4 April. Such an event would have irreparably shattered *2. Panzerarmee*, as it would then have been nearly cut off from the Reich, along with *Heeresgruppe E* and much of the German Army in Italy. The gap between *6. Armee* and *2. Panzerarmee* spanned more than 40 miles, while the Russian 18th Tank Corps had already penetrated within 25 miles of Graz and there were no German forces available to stop them. In retrospect it seems impossible that the German front could be repaired, but somehow that happened.

* * *

The *2. Panzerarmee* had one, and only one, panzer division, *23. Panzer-Division*, which was equally battered by this point. Magnifying the lack of heavy weapons was the army's place at the far end of *Heeresgruppe Süd*'s supply lines.

The army's front extended into northern Croatia at the juncture with *Heeresgruppe E*, which itself had only seven infantry divisions, two *Kampfgruppe* and five infantry brigades. Like all German units of this period none of them were at full strength.

* * *

Russian attacks concentrated on the junction of the two army groups. Rough terrain and poor roads in Croatia and Slovenia made rapid movement difficult. *General der Artillerie* de Angelis had to cast a nervous glance at the map as Russian attacks pushed both his left and right flanks, while behind him to the southwest were the British and Americans fighting through northern Italy. Moreover, if he lost contact with *Heeresgruppe E* those units could be trapped against the Adriatic Sea.

After the Russians ripped a seven-mile-wide gap in the army's front lines they penetrated deep on its right flank. On 2 April it found itself clinging to two tiny bridgeheads on the eastern bank of the Mur River in the far southwestern tip of Hungary, about ten miles west of the lost oil fields around Nagykanizsa. The river there is wide enough to be a significant barrier, with hills tall enough to give the defenders an advantage.

I Kavallerie-Korps

Genderal der Artillerie Maximilian de Angelis possessed arguably the weakest German Army on the Eastern Front. The army had few heavy weapons left among its polyglot units, with *I Kavallerie-Korps* in particular being intrinsically weak in this regard. The two cavalry units of the corps, *3.Kavallerie-Division* and *4. Kavallerie-Division*, were partly motorized but most of their combat troops rode horses into battle. By their very nature they couldn't deploy much heavy artillery or many anti-tank guns.

Both divisions were organized in the same way. Each had two regiments of cavalry divided into two squadrons, the equivalent of two battalions. The artillery regiment had three battalions, but these only had eight 105mm guns each and no 150mm guns. As partial compensation they had 24 120mm mortars and 30 81mm ones. They also had 39 anti-tank guns of mixed 75mm and 88mm calibers. The anti-aircraft component was weak, with 19 20mm guns.[29] They also had an armored component, with at least three *Sturmgeschütz*, or assault gun, companies, an armored infantry company mounted in SPWs, a motorized infantry company riding in trucks and a pioneer company, which western armies called engineers.

But the corps commander, *General der Kavallerie* Gustav Harteneck, was a Knight's Cross-winning veteran with an excellent reputation. If competence could make up for a lack of firepower, *I Kavallerie-Korps* was better than it appeared on paper.

23. Panzer-Division

The veteran panzer division had been in Hungary during all of 1945, and fought in all three *Konrad* operations as part of *6. Armee*. Like most German divisions it was under-strength before *Unternehmen Frühlingserwachen* and lost heavily in the flight across Western Hungary. *Panzerjäger-Abteilung 128* entered the battle with 20 *Jagdpanzer IV/70* tank destroyers. During combat three were destroyed by Russian fire, another three by friendly fire from *12. SS-Panzer-Division Hitlerjugend*, and 11 had to be destroyed by their crews during the retreat from Hungary due to lack of fuel. Pushed south by circumstances, *23. Panzer-Division* wound up attached to *2. Panzerarmee* in the area northwest of the Hungarian oil fields at Nagykanizsa.

Like the other German panzer divisions, deliveries of new panzers from the factories were few and far between, so the only operational machines were those put back into service by the maintenance teams. At the beginning of April it had a small armored group of five Panthers, four Mark IVs, two *Jagdpanzer IV/70s* and a solitary *Sturmgeschütz*. As the *Kampfgruppe* approached the Reich border early on 1 April the leading Panther was hit by a Russian 76.2mm anti-tank gun; once again the Russians were ahead of them. The surviving panzers attacked and destroyed the Russian guns.

But everywhere they turned it was the same story; the Russians were to the Germans' west and they had to fight their way out of trap after trap. A *Honved* officer told them that a village on the *Kampfgruppe's* line of march was under Hungarian control, and the leader of the Germans sent out two vehicles to reconnoiter ahead, a Mark IV and the lone *Sturmgeschütz*. When the Germans arrived all they found were Russians and their ubiquitous anti-tank guns.

A firefight ensued but without infantry support there was nothing the two German panzers could do, especially against the dozens of Russians who took up defensive positions. After destroying the anti-tank guns the vehicles could only idle and ask for reinforcements. In response to their urgent request a single *leutnant* showed up leading the last seven survivors of a *Panzergrenadier* company. The odds of eight men and two panzers driving off scores of Russians seemed absurdly long, but there was nothing else to do. The road to the west led through that village, Csömöder, and so they had no choice except to clear out the Russians. Pouring fire into the Russian positions as they clanked forward, the two armored vehicles went first while the eight infantrymen followed.

---

29   *German Horse Cavalry and Transport,* Intelligence Bulletin, March 1946, http://www.lonesentry.com/articles/germanhorse/index.html, (Accessed 6 February 2018).

Fortunately for the Germans, the Russian infantry had no stomach for facing cannon fire without their anti-tank guns. A stream of panje wagons moved north and the Germans pursued them. The group finally laagered for the night north of Csömöder, where *Panzergrenadier-Regiment 126* and *Panzergrenadier-Regiment 128* caught up with it. Both had been bled white by this point.

The next day the operational elements were ordered to attack north and take the town of Nova, thereby cutting off the Russian line of advance and relieving pressure on the rest of the division, which at that point was west of Nova. Of course, this was ninety degrees off the axis that would move them toward the relative safety of the vaunted *Reichsschutzstellung*, but it was necessary to save the divisional columns of *23. Panzer-Division*. Before dawn on 2 April, therefore, the Germans attacked in great strength, at least relative to their overall remaining forces. All of the surviving armor, *Panzergrenadier-Regiment 128*, the division replacement battalion and the replacement battalion for the *79. Infanterie-Division*, supported by two battalions from *Panzer-Artillerie-Regiment 128*, participated in the attack.

The Russians fought like their backs were to the wall, refusing to retreat no matter how hot the fight became. The Germans intercepted a radio message to the commander of Russian forces in Nova from his army commander, which explained the tenacity with which they defended the town. He was told, in no uncertain terms, that if he lost the town he might as well not survive the battle. The fight for Nova went on for hours until Russian tank support arrived and, with no recourse except to stand and fight, they eventually drove the Germans back with heavy losses. In particular, the armored group was whittled down to five operational panzers. Having failed in its attack, the unnamed *Kampfgruppe* hunkered down for the night at Iklódbördőce.

Kampfgruppe 9. SS-Panzer-Division Hohenstaufen

No division of *Heeresgruppe Süd* suffered more in the aftermath of *Unternehmen Frülingserwachen* than did *Hohenstaufen*. At the time it had been the 2nd division of *II SS-Panzerkorps*, along with *Das Reich*. The corps had not been able to get into its jump-off position in time to start the offensive, which might have been a blessing in disguise. Little progress was made during the nine days it lasted, which shortened *Hohenstaufen's* line of retreat. Then when most of both *6. Armee* and *6. SS-Panzerarmee* were in danger of being trapped, it was *Hohenstaufen* that stood as a breakwater between the Russians and the withdrawing German columns. Under the command of *SS-Brigadeführer* Sylvester Stadler they held their ground but took ruinous casualties by doing so. More losses followed in the retreat across Western Hungary, when they became separated from *II SS-Panzerkorps*, although the depleted and disorganized division was still credited with destroying up to 80 Russian tanks during that period.

Now, on 2 April, the shattered remnants stood southwest of Söjtör as part of *I Kavallerie-Korps*. On their left flank somewhere were *23. Panzer-Division*, *3. Kavallerie-Division* and *297. Infanterie-Division*, none of which were anywhere close to full strength. To the south the only cohesive formation was the *118. Jäger-Division*, along with disorganized remnants, until the far right flank of *Heeresgruppe Süd* was held by *13. Waffen-Gebirgs-Division der SS Handschar*.

16. SS-Panzer-Grenadier-Division Reichsführer-SS

The *16. SS-Panzer-Grenadier-Division Reichsführer-SS* was the most powerful unit in *2. Panzerarmee* at the time, with a strong assault gun battalion. The division had been formed in November, 1943, from the cadre of an assault brigade. The *Waffen-SS* didn't allow honorifics named after living persons which is why the division wasn't named after Himmler.[30] Although it had been in almost continuous combat since becoming operational, *Reichsführer-SS* was continually reinforced and upgraded because of Himmler's personal patronage, which is why it was still so strong.

Strong is a relative term, though. In comparison to its authorized strength, *Reichsführer-SS* was barely over half strength before the Russians attacked in late March. The division had been *2. Panzerarmee*'s chief assault force during that army's participation in *Unternehmen Frülingserwachen* on 6 March. Prior to the attack the division was close to full strength, with more than 60 assault guns in *SS-Sturmgeschütz-Abteilung 16*. Authorized manpower topped 14,000 men of all ranks. By late March that number had fallen below 10,000 men, with rifle strength of around 3,000, or less than half of what was authorized, because even Himmler's patronage could only do so much.

The Americans

In July 1944 the *Oberkommando der Wehrmacht, OKW*, the High Command of the Armed Forces, commissioned a group of engineers to survey the Alpine region in southern Germany and Austria about the possibility of erecting a line of defense there. Many of the positions created by the Austrians during the First World War still existed, mostly in the south for use in their war against the Italians. By September 1944 the German war situation seemed bleak enough that either the Western Allies or the Russians might potentially overrun the Reich by the end of the year.

Anticipating the need for emergency fortifications, in September *OKW* established a 39-man group in Innsbruck, led by *Generalmajor* August Marcinkiewicz. His mandate was only to conduct surveys and take measurements, not to build any fortifications. With interruptions for avalanches and snowstorms during winter, Marcinkiewicz continued this work until nearly the end of the war.

It was around this time that the OSS, the American Office of Strategic Services, forerunner of the Central Intelligence Agency, began picking up hints of field fortifications work in Austria. No one was sure of exactly what kind of building was being done, but the Americans had witnessed for themselves the impressive fortifications built by the Swiss in 1941 and 1942. The nightmare of a huge section of Alpine Austria with such defensive works, manned by heavily armed and fanatical SS men, with underground factories and supply dumps, fired their imaginations.

Also in September German intelligence intercepted an OSS report written by Allen Dulles concerning the potential of a National Redoubt. In the report, Dulles estimated that in a properly organized alpine region, with sufficient food, munitions and underground manufacturing systems, the German could potentially hold out another two years. It even broached the German belief that a prolonged war might spark conflict between the Western Allies and the Russians.

The actual document was passed to the Germans at Bregenz, near the Swiss and Austrian border. A copy wound up in the hands of Franz Hofer, the *Gauleiter* of the Tyrol and Vorarlberg, who thought a National Redoubt sounded like a splendid idea. Someone else who knew about the report was Joseph Goebbels, who knew a great propaganda idea when he saw one. In a masterful campaign that has rarely been matched, Goebbels dripped information through hints and innuendos in a way that American intelligence services, in particular the OSS, found very convincing. In a brilliant bit of disinformation, Goebbels called together the German press for a secret meeting, and admonished them not to mention the National Redoubt. He knew leaks would inevitably show up in articles and allowed them to be printed, while Allied spies within the Reich also got wind of the meeting. The OSS lapped it up.

---

30   As with everything in the Third Reich, Adolf Hitler was the exception to this rule.

On 12 November 1944, America's most authoritative newspaper, the *New York Times*, ran a story titled 'Hitler's Hideaway', in which the idea of a National Redoubt was brought to the public. The article combined truth with the types of rumors that are common during wartime to paint a scary picture of tunnels and fortifications blasted out of the living rock, and guarded by hundreds of thousands of fanatical SS men ready to fight to the death. As time went by other major American media outlets, such as *Collier's* magazine, ran similar articles. The specter of guerilla warfare extending into the indefinite future painted a terrifying picture.

That same month of November Hofer wrote Hitler a memo outlining a plan to build a National Redoubt in his *Gau*. As head of the Nazi Party, from which the *Gauleiters* derived their power, *Reichsleiter* Martin Bormann received the document but didn't present it to Hitler until late January 1945. The *Führer* had been busy planning the Ardennes Offensive which, if it worked, would make a National Redoubt superfluous. When the offensive failed Bormann belatedly passed the memo on to Hitler.

* * *

Meanwhile, Eisenhower paid attention to a growing body of evidence pointing to the existence of the Redoubt. Now, one of the big differences between the philosophies of British and American armed forces rose to play a critical role in world history. Unlike their British comrades, American officers only cared about achieving military objectives. Political considerations did not enter into their calculations. The British, however, considered political ramifications as an equal factor to military and economic ones. Berlin had long been agreed upon as the ultimate objective for the Allied Expeditionary Force, but on the night of 27-28 March General Eisenhower changed all of that. After thinking about it for weeks, he decided that the military objective of capturing the National Redoubt took precedence over the political objective of Berlin, particularly since Berlin had already been put in the Soviet zone of occupation as agreed to at Yalta.

The next morning he composed the famous message to Stalin in which he changed the course of America's armies from northeast toward Berlin, to southeast into Austria. He did this without asking permission from anyone. To say that Eisenhower's direct communication with Stalin infuriated Churchill would be understating the case. The Prime Minister was livid. He immediately protested to the dying President Roosevelt, who deferred to his Chief of Staff General George C. Marshall, who in turn backed up his Supreme Commander. Churchill had to face the unpleasant fact that Britain was now a junior partner in the alliance.

Eisenhower believed his decision was the correct one and nothing happened to change his mind. An early April OSS report on the National Redoubt went so far as to outline four general areas of resistance containing most of Western Austria and a small slice of Bavaria. The reports invoked the one name most feared among Allied planners: Otto Skorzeny. Since the Ardennes Offensive the Americans had been convinced that the true mission of *Panzer-Brigade 150*, Otto Skorzeny's secret commando unit created to carry out Operation *Greif*,[31] was the assassination of Generals Omar Bradley and Dwight Eisenhower. Skorzeny had training schools at Santhofen and Bad Tölz that were assumed to be training *Werwölfe*, werewolves,[32] for use in a last stand. More evidence was given as the number of SS units flowing into the region. Of course, those units were not so much moving into Western Austria as being shoved there by the advancing Allied and Russian armies.

---

31   *Unternehmen Greif* was the deception plan, using English-speaking Germans posing as American GIs, used during the Battle of the Bulge to spread chaos behind American lines.

32   This program was designed to unleash thousands of guerilla fighters in Allied occupied areas. In fact it achieved almost nothing, although the American-appointed mayor of Aachen was assassinated.

On a map, however, all the planners at Supreme Headquarters Allied Expeditionary Force, SHAEF, saw were flags labeled *1. SS-Panzer-Division Adolf Hitler* or *12. SS-Panzer-Division Hitlerjugend*, with the implication that each still had strong panzer regiments and veteran infantry. The remnants of *17. SS-Panzergrenadier-Division Götz von Berlichingen* were in Bavaria after the battle for Nuremberg and also appeared close to the National Redoubt. So many SS units heading in the same general direction lent verisimilitude to the intelligence reports. And in the map room at SHAEF headquarters, the area marked National Redoubt was studded with symbols portraying supply, fuel and food dumps, barracks, underground factories, military defensive positions and other facilities needed to maintain a defense for a prolonged period. Everything added up to a nightmare scenario.

Eisenhower's biggest fear was that guerillas would hide in the mountains and come out to fight a year or two after the war ended, and that within their protected fortress he would have to dig them out using siege tactics. He associated the *Werwölfe* program, wherein Germans behind Allied lines would attack their occupiers, as being part of the National Redoubt. If allowed to happen, that could entail keeping an American combat force in Europe for years and could generate tens of thousands of casualties. But more than just the fear of guerillas, "Eisenhower had never forgotten that Skorzeny was the man who had ruined his 1944 Christmas by threatening to capture or assassinate him".[33] Skorzeny was the boogey-man of the Americans. In modern parlance he lived in Eisenhower's mind, so the general was predisposed to believe almost any wild scheme that had the *SS-Obersturmbannführer*'s name attached.

Of course, while Skorzeny was Austrian, he was never particularly mentioned as being associated with the National Redoubt by the Germans. That was an American fantasy. Nor did it matter that Skorzeny never targeted Eisenhower and that was simply a rumor; in the atmosphere of 1945 the Germans were thought capable of all manner of irregular operations.

And so by 2 April the die had been cast. One of the most momentous political decisions of the 20th Century had been set in stone, despite Winston Churchill's vehement objections. To Churchill's way of thinking, by capturing Berlin the Allies would have had a major bargaining chip to ensure that Stalin kept his word about the postwar world and the fate of Austria was uppermost among his worries. But in one of those ironies of history that can only be seen with the clarity of hindsight, Churchill's worry about Austria becoming a pro-Soviet puppet was rendered moot by the very decision he opposed with such vigor.

---

33   Infield, Glenn B., *Skorzeny, Hitler's Commando* (New York: St Martin's Press, 1962), p. 114. This wasn't true, but the Americans believed it completely. Thus had Skorzeny's mere reputation imprisoned the highest-ranking Allied General in Europe inside of his own headquarters.

3

Tuesday, 3 April

Heeresgruppe Süd

Once again the weather favored the Russians as the day dawned sunny and warm, with a high temperature of 61 degrees F. Further south on the mountain tops of Styria it was a different matter. Sleet and snow were the order of the day for much of the next month.

Fleigerhorst Langenlebarn Tulln and *Kampfgruppe Volkmann*

Regarding the air war the perception seems to be that Russia achieved air supremacy in the east, with the *Luftwaffe* having already been destroyed. In fact the German air force fought to the very end despite being badly outnumbered. On 3 April *Generaloberst* Otto Dessloch's *Luftflotte 4* took advantage of the fine conditions to interdict Russian armored and supply columns moving into the Vienna Woods from south and southwest of the city, flying more than 100 sorties. However, this once mighty air fleet had formerly flown thousands of sorties in a day, and so, while their efforts in April slowed the Russians down, they were a weak reminder of the overwhelming force that had once dominated the battlefield.

Many of those sorties were flown out of *Fliegerhorst Langenlebarn Tulln*, Air Base Langelbarn Tulln, using Messerschmidt ME-109s and Focke-Wulf FW-190s. More HE-162s also rebased there but didn't fly combat missions. Nor did all of the aircraft landing there have parent formations. Like the people crowding the roads leading west, they were refugees fleeing the Russians. All manner of planes filled with all manner of people showed up at Tulln, from JU-52s crammed with Hungarians to Fiesler Storchs carrying German officers of high-enough rank to rate their own aircraft.

Nor did all of the refugees arrive by air. In the chaos of the day, thousands of people showed up on foot until the air base was packed. Some were Nazi officials, some were military bureaucrats trying to avoid combat and some were simple peasants leading carts filled with as many of their possessions as they could pile on board.

Among the flood were the personnel of *Luftgaukommando XVII*, the department in control of *Luftwaffe* activities within *Werhkreis XVII*. Commanded by *General der Flieger*, General of Aircraft, Egon Doerstling, their permanent headquarters in Vienna's 6th District, Mariahilf, had come too close to the front lines for comfort. So, like nearly every other *Wehrmacht* officer or Nazi bureaucrat with the pull to get out of the city, they fled. Train transportation was supposed to be made available but the train never showed up. Despite the general lack of motor transport, however, and the critical shortage of gasoline, the local *Luftwaffe* command had their own resources and rode to Tulln in trucks. Once there, Doerstling decided the airbase was too overcrowded for his command to carry out its functions and wasted no time moving further west to Aigen, in the valley of the River Enns.[1]

---

1   Prigl, Dr Mag. Hubert, *Die Geschichte des Fliegerhorstes Langenlebarn von 1936 bis 2000 Kurzversion aus der Dissertation von Herrn Dr.Mag. Hubert Prigl* <http://www.gotech.at/lale2/langenlebarn_2.html>, (Accessed 10 October 2018).

* * *

On 3 April *Generalmajor* Volkmann officially received orders naming him the *Kampfkommandant* of the Tulln area. Henceforth, ground forces under his command would be known as *Kampfgruppe Volkmann*. That gave him all the authority he needed to defend the critical Danube River crossings at Tulln, now all he needed was troops.

North of the Danube

Across the river from Bratislava, during the night of 2-3 April the Germans blew up the last bridge over the Danube to prevent a fast Russian thrust into the rear of the city's defenders. Then came the final death blow; the Russians crossed the river anyway. The Russian Danube flotilla had taken control of the river and landed troops behind the Germans to capture the northern bank. With no forces to counterattack, *Kampfkommandant Oberst* von Ohlen was helpless to react and, thus outflanked on the river side, knew there was now no hope for saving the city.

At daybreak Russian attacks on the Slovakian capital began with a half-hour artillery bombardment which concentrated on the Dynamite-Nobel factory in Nove Mesto, in the southeastern section of the city, on the Rača railway station in the northeast, and the Koliba Height to the north. Near Rača the Germans committed fifteen panzers and the two armored trains to try and stop the Russians, which represented a major attempt to bolster the defense. *Oberst* von Ohlen shifted his forces to meet each crisis as it came up, but his options were limited.

Fighting at the Dynamite Factory raged particularly bitter, with some calling it a *kleine Stalingrad*, little Stalingrad, because of the resemblance to combat in the Tank Factory there. But the heaviest fighting was in the area named Prievoz, in the far southeast area near the Danube. Each house was fought over, but the Russian pressure was too great. First they pushed the Germans out of Prievoz, then through the adjacent industrial area, into downtown Bratislava. This penetration threatened the defenders still fighting in Nove Mesto and around the Rača station with being surrounded.

Vienna

General der Infanterie Rudolf von Bünau arrived in Vienna to find what German commanders in those last weeks of the war were finding at almost every turn: chaos. According to von Bünau, the former commander of the city, *Generalleutnant* Merker,[2] was still on the scene as was the provisional commander, longtime *Inspektor der Panzertruppe* for *Wehrkreis XVII Generalmajor* Hans Koelitz, with their headquarters at the Vienna Military Headquarters on Universitätstrasse.[3] No doubt Merker was ecstatic at being relieved of responsibility for fighting an unwinnable battle and defending an indefensible city.

During the glorious victories of the early years the biggest advantage the *Wehrmacht* had over its opponents was its sophisticated command and control system. In the French campaign of 1940, during the first years of the war with Russia and in the deserts of North Africa, the Germans were almost always outmanned and outgunned. Fewer men, fewer and often lesser quality tanks and,

---

2   Merker had been *Wehrmacht Kommandant* of Vienna since the previous September and his rank was equal to von Bünau. Why more had not been done by him to prepare Vienna for combat is not clear, nor why Hitler or his advisers thought he should be replaced by von Bünau, since Merker would have been much more familiar with the resources available in Vienna, including stores of weapons and ammunition, and the merits of the personnel on hand.

3   Von Bünau, *Combat in Vienna*, p. 11.

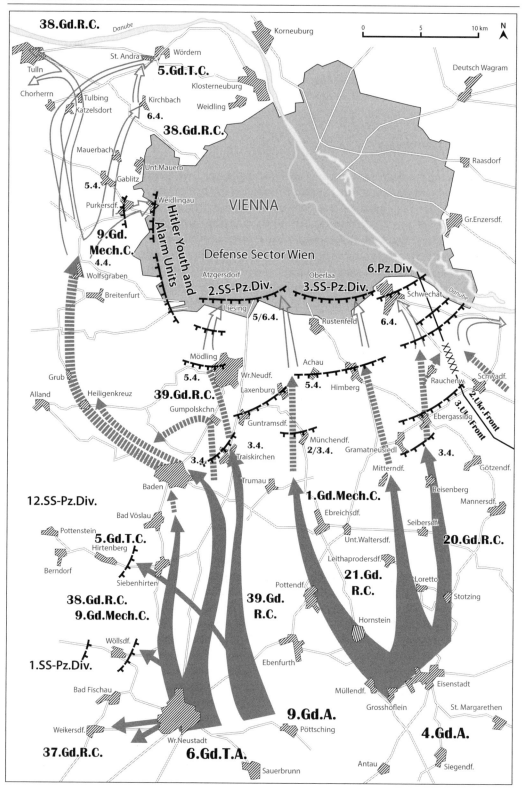

Map 4 Russian advances to the Vienna city limits.

in many cases, fewer aircraft; all of these disadvantages and more were either overcome or minimized because German command and control functioned faster, more efficiently and with more imagination than that of its enemies. Now, with every unit crucial to whatever small hope the Third Reich might still have for salvaging something from disaster, the very thing that had characterized its victories fell apart in its defeat. Confusion reigned in the German chain of command, frequently leading to contradictory or obsolete orders being issued by overlapping headquarters and government bureaus. Entropy was the order of the day, with *14. Waffen-Grenadier-Division der SS Galizien* being a prime example. *General der Infanterie* von Bünau was another. Put in command of Vienna's defenses, he was given virtually no troops to defend it with and no authority over the only combat troops who could.

What he did have were Vienna's heavy anti-aircraft defenses, arranged in three belts around the city to protect the oil refineries and other industrial targets. The first ran from Mödling on the southern edge to Wilhelminenberg in the west. A second line was closer in to the city center. Most of these guns were 88mm but there were also the three monster *Flak* towers armed with the devastating 128mm cannon.

Throughout the war Vienna had been the headquarters for the *177. Ersatz-Division*, but this unit existed to enforce the conscription laws and ready men for the army. Whatever numbers it may have possessed in 1945, it played no part in the fight for Vienna as a separate unit, although its members may have been incorporated into other units.

Because of the critical importance of Vienna's oil refineries the various anti-aircraft guns numbered in the hundreds and had adequate ammunition supplies. As the battle unfolded they were effective in interdicting Russian columns approaching the city. But in many cases their mounts were concrete and the guns were immobile, so even as they took a heavy toll on the attacking Russians, once the defending infantry withdrew they were lost.

* * *

Aside from the generally disastrous military outlook, the command situation in Vienna was a mess because no formal orders were ever issued by the *OKW*. Von Bünau discovered his new assignment by a single phone call, with no clarification given of his duties or of the forces he would command, either verbally or in writing.[4] In his mind he would lead:

> all units and commands of the Replacement Army stationed in the defense area which had not yet been shifted or were in the process of being shifted west; all units of the field forces withdrawing to the defense area; all air force units detailed for ground fighting; the police, the military units of the 'Party' (organized in the *Volkssturm*), and the civilian administrative agencies of the city.[5]

In other words, he would command everybody in the metropolitan Vienna area, including *II SS-Panzerkorps*. That was what he thought would happen. In reality, von Bünau would never have more than alarm units such as training, irregular and ad hoc formations to command. With no written orders delineating responsibilities or chain of command, the veteran SS combat formations were not about to answer to someone other than their own commanders, and Sepp Dietrich was not inclined to take orders from a *Wehrmacht* general that he outranked:[6]

---

4   There is no indication of how Merker was told of his relief by von Bünau.
5   Von Bünau, *Combat in Vienna,* p. 1.
6   As an *SS-Oberstgruppenführer*, Dietrich's equivalent Army rank was *Generaloberst*, whereas von Bünau was a *General der Infanterie*, one rank below *Generaloberst*.

Bünau had ostensibly been put in charge of the defense but could not dispose of all the troops theoretically under his jurisdiction. After a quick survey of the situation, Bünau wrote in his diary that Vienna was indefensible – a conclusion Dietrich and others had also reached. But Bünau was bound by Berlin directives: should he fail to hold the line he would be put before a military court and his family held hostage. In the end he and his soldiers were put under Dietrich's command.[7]

For the time being von Bünau would hold a separate command from Dietrich, but only until 7 April when he was formally subordinated to *II SS-Panzerkorps*. The so-called *Kampfkommandant* of Vienna would only command all forces in Vienna, including *II SS-Panzerkorps*, for one day, 13 April, when the vast majority of the city was already in Russian hands. For most of the rest of his brief tenure the chain of command would be reversed. He would organize the motley collection of formations that could be scraped together to throw into the path of whatever Russian threat seemed greatest at the moment, but would do so after 7 April under the command of *II SS-Panzerkorps*.

From his point of view, this was the best outcome von Bünau could hope for. As Goebbels wrote in his diary, Hitler had issued clear orders that Vienna must be held at all costs, else heads would roll.[8] That put von Bünau clearly in Hitler's crosshairs, but now he had a scapegoat if Vienna could not be held, and he was confident that Vienna could not, in fact, be held: "The idea of a successful or even prolonged defense of Vienna had to be rejected from the beginning."[9] And while it might then be Dietrich's head on the chopping block if Vienna fell, Dietrich had the advantage of having well-armed, hard-eyed veterans protecting him, while von Bünau was essentially alone.

Muddying the situation even more, von Bünau had one more person between him and control of the coming battle: Baldur von Schirach. "My authority was limited by the necessity of obtaining the agreement of Reich Defense Commissioner von Schirach for every important measure",[10] so the man officially named as the *Kampfkommandant Wien* had no meaningful combat forces to command, was mostly under the command of another headquarters and could not issue significant orders on his own authority. When he did want to issue an order, it had to first be cleared by von Schirach. Nor was he given even rudimentary instructions on what he was supposed to do, aside from defend the city. His only guidelines were standing orders concerning combat and his own instincts on what should be done. At a time when speed and decisiveness of command mattered most, the Germans devolved into a maelstrom of orders, counter-orders and threats.

However, the issue of responsibility only concerned the officers involved. Regarding the coming battle for Vienna it was all a charade anyway, as it did not matter who was in command and who was not. The city could not be held.

The only major formation in position to defend the city was the mangled *II SS-Panzerkorps*, which was desperately trying to stop Third Ukrainian Front before it reached the city. But Bittrich's command had been very badly damaged in the previous month's fighting, *2. SS-Panzer-Division Das Reich* had lost most of its armor, *9. SS-Panzer-Division Hohenstaufen* had been replaced with the veteran but depleted *3. SS-Panzer-Division Totenkopf*, and *6. Panzer-Division* was a mere shadow of its former self. The few alarm *Kampfgruppen* and anti-aircraft units that were scraped up could not fill the gap where divisions were needed, and even the forthcoming addition of the *Führer-Grenadier-Division* would not bolster the defense enough to stop the Russian steamroller.

---

7   Weyr, *Twilight*, p. 276.
8   By this point German commanders knew the price of failure was execution of the officer involved and punishment for his family, imprisonment at the very least.
9   Von Bünau, *Combat in Vienna*, p. 5.
10   Von Bünau, *Combat in Vienna*, p. 2.

6. SS-Panzerarmee

By now the Russian path of attack had become obvious in Sepp Dietrich's sector, as the hard-hitting Russian armored columns turned northwest after the capture of Weiner Neustadt. The nature of the terrain changes abruptly at the Danube Valley. The relatively flat lands along the river are separated by an escarpment extending for many miles from the mountains to the south. In the same way that the walls of the American Grand Canyon funnel the Colorado River along its course, the Danube and its valley are directed by mountains.

With *I SS-Panzerkorps* reduced to less than the strength of a single division, the *356. Infanterie-Division* marched to the army's right flank to try and give the army time to regroup. The *356. Infanterie-Division* had never been considered a first-class division, having been formed around reservists in 1943, but the urgencies of war had pushed it into the front lines in Italy and again in Hungary in 1945. Fighting at Stuhlweissenberg in February and March the division had been mauled and reduced to a *Kampfgruppe*. After a brief period of reorganization it was again facing the Russians.

* * *

Things had become so chaotic that on 3 April Dietrich ordered a straggler line to be established to collect any men who had been separated from their units. In the same order he commanded that no man could leave the front lines or head to the rear, under penalty of martial law, which was a euphemism for immediate execution. Unlike the commander of *Heeresgruppe Mitte*, *Generalfeldmarschall* Schörner, Dietrich did not relish the idea of shooting his own men but made it clear that he would if he had to.

I SS-Panzerkorps

The Corps' front-line units for this day consisted of *Kampfgruppe 12. SS-Panzer-Division Hitlerjugend, SS-Kampfgruppe Keitel, Speerverband Gross,*[11] *Kampfgruppe 1. SS-Panzer-Division Leibstandarte Adolf Hitler,* and the remnants of the Hungarian 2nd Armored Division, along with a few smaller attached units.[12] Its defensive front stretched from the Neuseidlersee down to Neunkirchen, but south of that town was a 35-mile gap between *I SS-Panzerkorps* and *6. Armee*, with no reserves to plug the hole. This was the Russians' opportunity to carve up *Heeresgruppe Süd*. All of Austria lay open to invasion. If they moved fast enough they could drive all the way to the Swiss border.

12. SS-Panzer-Division Hitlerjugend

As if the gaps between *6. SS-Panzerarmee* and *6. Armee*, and *6. Armee* and *2. Panzerarmee* weren't bad enough, Sixth Guards Tank Army drove through and past *12. SS-Panzer-Division Hitlerjugend*, ripping open the front of *6. SS-Panzerarmee* from Baden bei Wien to Alland. Sepp Dietrich had nothing to plug that ten-mile hole and the Russian spearheads were only stopped

---

11   *Sperrverband* means 'blocking formation'. In this context it means a unit named *Gross* had been formed to block a particular road or avenue of advance.

12   Maier, *Drama*, p. 345.

by *SS-Aufklärungs-Abteilung 12* after making huge advances. Attacks against Gainfarn from near Bad Vöslau were repulsed.

Once again the depleted division had been forced to break into small groups to defend key points, but the progress by Sixth Guards Army on 3 April cut *Hitlerjugend* off the direct route from *Das Reich*, necessitating a long detour through Vienna to maintain contact. Slowly but surely the two SS corps were being pushed aside as the Russians cut a swath toward the Vienna Wood: *6. SS-Panzerarmee* itself was being sliced up and there appeared to be no stopping the Russians.

In the Triesting Valley the town of Hirtenberg became a front-line settlement after relentless armored attacks drove the *Hitlerjugend* men to the west. The valley led into the heart of the German defenses south of Vienna and *Hitlerjugend* would fight bitterly to hold the area in the coming weeks. It had two entrances that converged at Berndorf, one of which passed through Hirtenberg, and the other through Grossau. Another road led to higher elevations around Schwarzensee, which would soon see some of the bitterest fighting of the entire war. The defense of Hirtenberg was conducted by *Kampfgruppe SS-Panzergrenadier-Regiment 25*, which by this time was as disorganized as it was bled out. The regiment held for a while but eventually was in danger of encirclement and fell back to the vicinity of Berndorf.

Some of the worst fighting happened at Leobersdorf, where *III./SS-Panzergrenadier-Regiment 26* refused to retreat and both absorbed and inflicted terrible casualties. The longer they stood in place, the greater was the danger of being outflanked or even trapped. So when the battalion commander fell dead under a sniper's bullet the hard-pressed battalion also fell back to the hapless town of Berndorf. *SS-Hauptsturmführer* Joseph Riede was the sort of man who the Germans simply couldn't replace. He'd joined the fledgling *SS-Verfügungstruppe*, forerunner of the *Waffen-SS*, in 1934 and had fought in every campaign since. Seasoned officers like him were a vanishing breed in both the German and the Russian armies, but with the Germans reduced to putting untrained men in the front lines, the experience of men like Riede was an order of magnitude greater than when all troops had undergone basic ground combat training.[13]

* * *

Hirtenberg had a small satellite camp of the Mauthausen system, housing women forced laborers for the nearby ammunition factory, the Gustloff Works Hirtenberg. Its chief product was infantry ammunition, which the SS men no doubt found useful.

The shape of the Russian offensive began to resemble the channel dug by a flash flood. The southern shoulder ran roughly from Loebersdorf in the east to Pottenstein in the west. Like the water in this metaphor, Russian attacks aimed to broaden the breakthrough channel by driving the Germans to the west and south.

Death and destruction littered the battlefield everywhere the fighting swept through. When combat came to Pfaffstätten 18 people died, at Loebersdorf another 13 were lost. Homes, factories and shops burned. In a region with many bridges most were destroyed. West of Wöllersdorf, the Russians captured Oberpiesting next and the fighting moved into the Vienna Woods. These heavily forested highlands have long been a favorite recreation spot for the Viennese. The area is about 28 miles long and varies from 12 to 19 miles wide. Four rivers loosely define its boundaries: the Piesting, Traisen, Gölsen and Danube. Although the hills aren't as jagged as some in the Alps, it should have been ideal defensive terrain. But the Germans never had a chance to set up a defense in depth, or properly deploy what heavy weapons were left. Most of the time there wasn't even time

---

13   Meyer, Hubert, *The 12th SS, The History of the Hitler Youth Panzer Division: Volume Two* (Mechanicsburg: Stackpole Books, 2005), p. 467.

to fell trees to block the roads. All they could do was turn, fight when the Russians got too close, and retreat again. Inevitably, *Hitlerjugend* began to bend to the southwest and south as the Russian spearheads sped past them toward Tulln.

1. SS-Panzer-Division Leibstandarte Adolf Hitler

After speeding through enemy-occupied Weiner Neustadt the night before, the *1. SS-Panzer-Regiment* found itself in a mousetrap north of the city, with Russian tanks all over the area, in particular blocking the way to the west. Keeping control of the Wöllersdorf-Steinabruckl area was critical to the *LAH*'s position and it was defended by *SS-Panzergrenadier-Regiment 2*, part of the panzer regiment and the reconnaissance battalion. The SS men had fought hard the day before but it wasn't enough and the battle group had been pushed back to Dreistetten. Worse, to their west Oberpiesting fell, putting Russians on three sides of Dreistetten.

The loss of the Wöllersdorf-Steinabruckl area had left the defenders of Bad Fischau, four miles northwest of Wiener Neustadt, with an open left flank. The defenders consisted of more *Panzergrenadiers* from *SS-Panzergrenadier-Regiment 2*, some artillery crews fighting as infantry and the Wiener Neustadt cadets. Four miles south of Wöllersdorf, the threat of attack from the north complicated their defense. The Russian attacks came in one after another, and were supported by large tank formations. Bad Fischau couldn't be held.

* * *

A counterattack by part of the *Fahnenjunker-Bataillon* on Wöllersdorf overran an air-raid bunker where 10 women had been beaten and repeatedly raped by the Russians who captured the town. Infuriated, the men evacuated the women back to their positions. Six Russians were killed in the attack. But the Russians had dug in behind the Piesting River, which flows through the center of Wöllersdorf. The *Fahnenjunkeren* were pulled back and replaced by *II./SS-Panzergrenadier-Regiment 2*, and were redeployed southwest of the town.

SS-Kampfgruppe Keitel

Situated southwest of Wiener Neustadt, *SS-Sturmbannführer* Karl-Heinz Keitel's regiment-sized command had only existed for five days. Formed on 30 March, it was immediately transported to the Gloggnitz area and attached to *I SS-Panzerkorps*.

No soldier in the *Wehrmacht* had a more powerful father than *Generalfeldmarschall* Wilhelm Keitel, but the son joined the *Waffen-SS* instead of the Army, and was a well-respected officer. Defending the mountainous area south of Bad Fischau, along with *Sperrverband Gross*, *SS-Kampfgruppe Keitel* had set up in the area north of Neunkirchen but couldn't hold. A valley ran north-northeast from Neunkirchen to Bad Fischau, a lowland stretch of small hills and farms that was perfect tank country. Holding this with a stretched-out force the size of a regiment, and without enough heavy weapons, proved impossible. Russian attacks pushed the *Kampfgruppe* back to a line running from Puchberg am Schneeberg through Willendorf to Muthmannsdorf at the Hohe Wand.[14]

Two days earlier, on Easter Sunday, the parish church of Puchberg reported that 100 Hungarian soldiers attended mass and collectively said an 'Our Father' prayer for their loved ones at home

---

14   Tiemann, *The Liebstandarte IV/2*, p. 284,

in their native language. Exactly which unit they were from is unknown,[15] but since Keitel's men disarmed them on 2 April they must have been from the *Honved*, the regular Hungarian Army.

The townsfolk were urged to evacuate and the town square filled up with cars and trucks that came for them, but many refused to leave. Like refugees in every country ever touched by war, they had to decide between the dubious safety of joining the endless columns trudging west and staying home to protect their property, in the hope that the Russians would treat them with respect. Goebbels' propaganda made them aware of what the Red Army did to those it captured, but many people no longer believed anything the diminutive Propaganda Minister said.

* * *

Russian troops had already reached both Würflach and Willendorf, which prompted the first artillery duel with German batteries in and around Grünbach. This was quickly followed by armor-supported infantry attacks on the German positions blocking the road to Grünbach. That town was the key point to capture before the attack could begin on Puchberg and the Schneeberg itself, a towering mountain used by the Germans to train ski troops. The Russians were determined to take it, and the Germans were just as determined not to give it up. Altogether, 32 of them fell defending the town.

* * *

SS-Panzerjäger-Abteilung 12 had become separated from the main body of its parent *Kampfgruppe*. Leaving Pottenstein it moved over the *Hals Sattel*, Neck Saddle, into the valley of the Piesting River. Along the way men came across a supply dump loaded with food and, over the vehement protests of a supply officer, grabbed as much food as they could possibly carry. Even the local civilians helped themselves. But when they arrived at their destination they once again found the Russians had been faster and had to drag their anti-tank guns overland through the woods.[16]

II SS-Panzerkorps
3. SS-Panzer-Division Totenkopf

The Workshop Company for *II./SS-Panzer-Regiment 3* had set up at Sankt Egyden am Steinfeld a few miles north of Neunkirchen, thinking this was far enough behind the front to safely work on damaged vehicles. It wasn't. A Russian tank force attacked and, while the Germans reportedly knocked out four T-34s, the proximity to the fighting caused another move, this time to Judenau. A repair shop was set up there but that wouldn't last long, either. Eventually they would move far to the west beyond Sankt Pölten and be cut off from the battalion they were supposed to support.

By now the division's *Schwere-Panzer-Kompanie* had a number of crews with no prospect of ever getting another panzer. Therefore, twenty trained Tiger crewmen were trucked into Vienna, unloaded at the West Railway Station and sent directly into battle. The men fought all the way back through Vienna during the course of the next ten days.

But one lucky crew did find a tank. The Vienna Arsenal turned over yet another Tiger II that had been repaired. This one had a brand new main gun, road wheels and tracks and would fight for the rest of the war.

15   Brettner, *Die Letzten Kämpfe Band I*, p. 194.
16   Brettner, *Die Letzten Kämpfe Band I*, p. 162.

2. SS-Panzer-Division Das Reich

To understand how under-strength the SS Panzer Divisions were at this point, it's instructive to look at *Das Reich* manpower strength before the Normandy fighting, in June 1944. The *Stab/SS-Panzer-Division 2*, division headquarters company, numbered about 150 men. Each of the two *Panzergrenadier* regiments had 3,200 men, broken into three *Abteilung* instead of two as in the smaller Army regiments. The panzer regiment numbered 2,400 men and the *SS-Panzer-Artillerie-Regiment 2*, 2,200. *SS-Pioneer-Abteilung 2* had 1,000 men, *SS-Panzer-Aufklärungs-Abteilung 2* numbered 950 and *SS-Panzerjäger-Abteilung 2* and *SS-Nachrichten-Abteilung 2*, the signals battalion, another 510. The *SS-Flak Abteilung 2* had grown by this time to 820 men. In addition to the artillery, the division had a *nebelwerfer* battalion of 480 men and *SS-Sturmgeschütz Abteilung 2* of 350 men. The remaining ration strength was in supply, veterinarian, postal, medical and other services, totaling 3,400 men.

In terms of armor, in June 1944 the division's panzer regiment had two battalions of 60 panzers each. One battalion had aging Mark IVs and the other was equipped with Panthers. The Assault Gun Battalion had 18 *Sturmgeschütze 40s*, and one *Panzerjäger Kompanie* had 12 *Jagdpanzer IV/70*, for a total of 150 panzers.

By April 1945, *Das Reich* had been crushed not once, not even twice, but more than three times and veterans of the original roster were few and far between. First were the horrific casualties suffered on the Russian Front during 1942 and 1943 and then the debacle of the Falaise Gap in summer 1944, followed by the badly planned Ardennes Offensive and finally the catastrophic *Unternehmen Frühlingserwachen* and subsequent retreat across Hungary. The fact that *Das Reich* maintained even minimal cohesion through massive infusions of new members is remarkable, but none of that mattered to Adolf Hitler. The only thing he wanted was the impossible.

* * *

The Vienna rail system was in a shambles but trains still operated sporadically. One train that rolled into the city contained men returning from leave, convalescents cleared to return to the front and replacements. On the direct order of the *Das Reich* commander, SS-Standartenführer Rudolf Lehmann, those men were pulled from their rail cars and incorporated into the division on the spot, regardless of their destination units or branches of service. This marked the second time Lehmann had issued such orders, having appropriated replacements meant for *12. SS-Panzer-Division Hitlerjugend* the previous month in Hungary. Many of the men died before the day was over.

More men were added to the rolls by straggler lines. These were collected behind the lines and represented men separated from their units or perhaps deserters who avoided being shot if they returned to combat. Other men came from other sources and even the *Kriegsmarine* contributed 50 men to *Das Reich* rolls. Unfortunately for those men most didn't survive the subsequent fighting. Casualties were so high the division no longer kept up with the names of its members, but only the numbers killed, wounded, missing or available for combat. There was no time for anything else.

Along with those men, the remnants of *SS-Kampfgruppe Hauser*, still holding Münchedorf despite frantic Russian efforts to eject them, found themselves absorbed into the *I./SS-Panzergrenadier-Regiment Der Führer*. Hauser would shortly be named to replace that battalion's commander, SS-Hauptsturmführer Engelmann, who had been killed in action.

The *Flak* battalion also kept its numbers up by absorbing orphan units. Several light *Luftwaffe* batteries without a parent unit gladly joined, but the SS men even unshipped some 88mm guns in fixed emplacements and used their own transports to move them. The crews, abandoned to their fate by their parent headquarters, were only too glad to latch onto *Das Reich*. If anybody in the *Wehrmacht* was going to be fed, it was the *Waffen-SS*.

* * *

According to Otto Weidinger, on the morning of 3 April the commander of *Das Reich*'s *Flak* battalion, *SS-Hauptsturmführer* Dreike, was asked by an Army detachment for help putting down some sick horses they'd been caring for. To his amazement, Dreike recognized them as Lippizaner stallions from the Spanish Riding School's stud farm. The horses had been painted green and brown to hide them from prowling Russian aircraft. Instead of killing them Dreike requested help from the division's veterinarians, which was promptly granted.[17]

Das Reich formally asked for help from Party members who knew Vienna and could help them establish firing positions and defensive lines. The brown-shirted functionaries carried weapons and *Panzerfauste* the front-line troops desperately needed, but no help was forthcoming. Like many chest-thumping Nazi Party officials across the Reich, the guiding principle of the men who had urged others to fight to the death seemed to be "every man for himself".

O-5

South and southwest of Vienna, with the pass and map given them by *Major* Szokoll, *Feldwebel* Kas and *Unteroffizier* Reif had found a quiet sector through which they intended to make a dash for the Soviet lines. It was dangerous, of course. If the Germans did not shoot them exiting German territory the Soviets might do so as they entered Soviet lines. Yet it had to be done. And since they were already engaged in high treason, what was one more danger? They were probably going to wind up getting shot no matter what happened. Without the success of their mission, however, all of the work and planning of O-5 would be in vain. It was up to them and them alone to save Vienna from destruction.

As dawn lightened the world around them they sped through the German front lines safely but the guards at the last checkpoint fired as they roared by, hitting the Opel and disabling it. Several hundred yards down the road it coasted to a stop. Kas and Reif jumped into a ditch as bullets whizzed around them. Then "a Russian wearing a fur cap and holding a balalaika stepped from behind a tree and said 'rukiv verkh!' (Hands up!)"[18]

O-5 and its naive leaders had not considered that the Soviets might see them as a *ruse de guerre*, two spies sent to lead the Red Army into a trap. But the Soviet Union was a nation ruled and guided by paranoid terror of unwarranted arrest and torture, and its citizens viewed each other suspiciously, to say nothing of their known enemies. Two German soldiers claiming to be representatives of a heretofore unknown resistance group willing to lead the Red Army secretly through German lines and into Vienna raised every paranoid hair on the Soviets' necks. This was too good to be true; therefore it must be a lie.

No Red Army officer would knowingly accept responsibility for such a grave matter without clear orders from above; political initiative almost always proved fatal.[19] Therefore the two Germans were handed from one unit to another until, late in the evening, they reached the headquarters of Third Ukrainian Front in the village of Hockwolkersdorf, in the wooded hills southwest of Weiner Neustadt, near Gloggnitz.[20] On the Soviet side the senior officer present was trusted commissar

---

17   Weidinger, *Das Reich,* p. 366.
18   Toland, *The Last 100 Days,* p. 376.
19   By 1945, military initiative in certain tactical situations was tolerated, as hard-won experience taught the value of letting seasoned veterans make decisions in real-time based on battlefield circumstances. Political initiative, however, was almost by definition treasonous.
20   There is a memorial in the village now, the Gedenkraum 1945, to commemorate the negotiations held there.

Colonel General Alexei Zheltov, an NKVD operative and a physically imposing man of some 220 lbs.[21] He would come to be hated by the Viennese after the war as Konev's second-in-command, a brutal enforcer who showed no mercy. He was not a man given to caring about O-5's concerns for Vienna, but neither was he a man to act without orders.

* * *

Kas gave an outline of Szokoll's plan, along with the demands that all Allied air attacks against Vienna must be stopped, members of O-5 would not be arrested and Austrian prisoners of war would be released first. Toland describes the Russian reaction:

> Annoyed by the Austrian demands, the staff officers showed far less courtesy than Zheltov and started bombarding Kas with questions: What is O-5? Do they have arms, ammunition, troops? Who are the leaders? What are they – Social Democrats, Socialists, Communists, Fascists? What is the political situation in Austria?.. Aren't all Austrians Nazis? If not, why did they shout so enthusiastically when Hitler marched into Austria? Kas knew a trap when he saw one and dodged their questions. Soon enough a map was produced and when he indicated their current position at Hockwolkersdorf the Russians demanded to know how he knew that. 'There's a sign over the firehouse,' he answered, and everyone laughed.[22]

He then marked down all the current German positions and marked out the suggested Red Army path of advance: north to Baden, then northwest to the Vienna Woods, where units loyal to O-5 would lead them by the back door into Vienna. Ever suspicious, the Russians wanted to know why they should trust him. Kas volunteered to ride on the lead tank and this seemed to satisfy them. He was packed off to await word from higher authority whether his offer would be accepted or not. If not, his immediate future was bleak, but Kas was too tired to care.

* * *

Even without the unexpected assistance of O-5, Third Ukrainian Front's attack plans for the capture of Vienna began to unfold on 3 April, as multiple Russian armies poured through the hole torn in the German defenses around Weiner Neustadt, capturing that city and lunging forward to block the Semmering Pass rail line near Gloggnitz. Severing rail links that supplied German forces to the south and southwest of Wiener Neustadt was a blow to the defenders, but Vienna was the main prize in the short term, and to capture it the overall direction of the Russian attack would have to pivot from a west-northwesterly direction, to north-northwest, directly toward Vienna and the Danube to its west. In places the Red Army attack was advancing quickly against little or no resistance, and so even as Wiener Neustadt faded in their rear the Russians sped toward Vienna.

To counter this rapid thrust the Germans were trying to pull back to a line running from Mariabrunn-Mauer-Liesing-Ensersdorf-Mödling-Wendorf-Himberg, but the forces available were inadequate to properly defend such a line from the massive Soviet attack. Starting from just south and west of Baden, Sixth Guards Tank Army headed almost due north for Tulln and its bridge over the Danube, with three corps moving abreast. According to Rauchensteiner, on the western flank was 38th Guards Rifle Corps,[23] with 5th Guards Tank Corps in the center and 9th Guards Mechanized Corps on the eastern flank. This movement was designed to sever the western

21   Zheltov is remembered as the brutal Soviet deputy high commissioner in occupied Austria who laughed off his soldiers' crimes toward Austrians, in particular the rape of women.

22   Toland, *The Last 100 Days*, p. 376.

23   The German term for these formations was *schützen*, which variously meant motorized infantry or *Panzergrenadier* or simply riflemen; this term is used for the Russian version of this type of soldier.

approaches to Vienna and cut the city off south of the Danube, outflanking it and allowing a direct assault from the west, where German defenses were the weakest.

Close on Sixth Guards Tank Army's right flank was Ninth Guards Army, starting a few kilometers east of Baden and taking a route just west of Mödling and Liesing, with its main unit being 39th Guards Rifle Corps. During the evening of 3 April, Russian spearheads ran into German blocking forces south of Mödling near Laxenburg in the form of the *4. Panzer-Ausbildungs-und-Ersatz-Abteilung* and *33. Panzer-Ausbildungs-und-Ersatz-Abteilung*.[24] Despite their name, neither of these battalions had armor, artillery or anti-tank guns, being armed strictly with light infantry weapons. They were well lead, however, and fought valiantly, but could not do much to slow down the Russian juggernaut. Because of the imminent danger, *2. SS-Panzer-Division Das Reich* was shifted into the area and absorbed both of the training battalions into the division. Its chief responsibility was to block the main highway leading fromWiener Neustadt directly into the heart of Vienna. *Das Reich* deployed in the area from Guntramsdorf to Laxenburg, virtually within the city limits of Vienna.

Finally, just east of Ninth Guards Army and with the most direct route into the Vienna metropolitan area, was 4th Guards Army, which deployed three corps, listed here in order from west to east: 1st Guards Mechanized Corps, aimed directly at Central Vienna; 21st Guards Rifle Corps on a path to the Arsenal area; and 20th Guards Rifle Corps moving in the direction of the Prater. With Russian spearheads well beyond Wiener Neustadt on the west and driving past the northern tip of the Neuseidlersee, the defense of Eisenstadt had become untenable and that city became the latest to be swamped by the Russian tide. North of the Danube, Vienna's northern suburbs were threatened by 46th Army of Second Ukrainian Front after it had overrun Bratislava.

SS-Kampfgruppe Keitel

After fighting at Wiener Neustadt, *SS-Kampfgruppe Keitel* retreated west to defend a line from Teinitz to the Siering stream and Winzendorf Valleys. This industrial lowland was the gateway to the densely forested mountains to the west, south of Rohrbach an der Gölsen. As the *Kampfgruppe* retreated west it lost contact with units on both flanks. Over the next few days it fought dozens of small, vicious firefights trying to establish an outpost line to connect with its neighbors. Once such fight occurred beginning at 5:00 a.m., when new Russian assaults hit Steinabrückl. Twelve *Landser* fell in the vicious fight for the town.

6. Armee

The Russians kept up the pressure of attacking north toward Aspang to widen the gap on *General der Panzertruppe* Hermann Balck's right flank with *2. Panzerarmee*. Likewise, the immense hole in the front north of *6. Armee* loomed as a disaster in the making. Over the course of the next five weeks the fighting on the eastern edge of Styria would be constant, bloody and bitter. In many ways it would resemble the static warfare of the First World War. Thousands would die on both sides. In places the combat would be nearly constant.

The terrain along and west of the border of Styria and Burgenland had large areas of cultivated rolling hills, with impressive and wooded mountains rising throughout the region. Those were the foothills of the Alps, and the further west the fighting went the more rugged it became. For snipers

24   Von Bünau, *Combat in Vienna*, p. 3.

of both sides this was the perfect killing ground. Hidden among the rocks and boulders they were not only invisible to the enemy, they were also shielded from return fire. Only mortars and heavy artillery could dig them out, but by that time the sniper was long gone.

Where the mountains were not sheer or broken, stands of dense forests stood among open, steeply sloped meadows. Men charging across that open ground made perfect targets. They fell in their hundreds.

Yet the myth has arisen that for the duration of the war nothing happened on the southern half of *Armeegruppe Süd's* front. The truth is that it was dirty, grinding warfare of the most primal sort, between relatively small numbers of men who lived and fought in the worst conditions possible. There were no sweeping tank movements and none of the battles will ever be studied in war colleges. It was kill or be killed at its most basic level. From the German side, added to food, fatigue and ammunition shortages was the frequent and sometimes constant exploding of mortar, artillery and rocket shells.

The most significant of the actions will be detailed so the reader can understand the broader picture. But the idea that the Russians reached the Alpine foothills and stopped because it was in the acknowledged British zone of occupation is contradicted by the huge losses they suffered trying to overrun Styria.

SS-Kampfgruppe Schweitzer

After the shocking success of *SS-Kampfgruppe Schweitzer* on the first, the Russians regrouped and prepared to retake Rechnitz. The situation for the Germans was precarious, much like an island with a waterfall on either side. To the north the enemy spearheads had moved far to the west with *6. SS-Panzerarmee* unable to stop them. To the south *6. Armee* resistance had stiffened in the Alpine foothills but hadn't closed the gap with *SS-Kampfgruppe Schweitzer*. Having no other realistic choice if he was going to hold Rechnitz, *SS-Sturmbannführer* Schweizter launched a surprise attack to the south. Once again tactical surprise led to rapid advances, only this time Russian tanks were in the vicinity and counter-attacked immediately. With nothing more than a few *Panzerfauste* they had no way to fight this new threat and fell back to their start lines, leaving scores of bodies on the field.

Kampfgruppe Semmering

In Roman days this part of Lower Austria had been known as *Noricum*, a prosperous and important province for supplying the Empire with produce of all kinds, but especially apples. Some of the crags were impassable pinnacles of stone, while others had forest paths winding up high-angled slopes covered in dense forest.

The *Kampfgruppe* had deployed around the region of the pass in smaller groups, not in a continuous line of fortifications. There weren't enough men for the latter. Two such groups flanked the road through the pass, one behind the other oriented east to west. Another held the high ground south of the pass, while the fourth one screened Russian forces in Breitenstein. At this early stage the whole of *Kampfgruppe Semmering* was small and composed of fragments from every conceivable military branch, from regular and training formations, to *Volkssturm*, Hitler Youth and even a *Luftwaffe* construction battalion.

* * *

Late in the afternoon of 3 April, both *3./SS-Gebirgsjäger-Ausbildungs-und-Ersatz-Abteilung 13* and *7./SS-Gebirgsjäger-Ausbildungs-und-Ersatz-Abteilung 13* got their first glimpse of the advancing Russians and what they saw caused their jaws to drop. Instead of a preliminary bombardment of artillery shells and Katyusha rockets, the quiet of the mountains was broken by the squeal of a harmonica.[25] From their dug-in positions above the valley the Germans looked down as a bedraggled Russian infantry column advanced up the road oblivious to the guns pointing down at them from the heights above. They'd come from the direction of Breitenstein, a nearby village north of Semmering Pass that was also on the rail line. German fire discipline was excellent. Only when all the Russians had entered the killing zone did they open fire, wiping them out to the last man.

During the night of 3–4 April, a small troop of men, along with the *5. Kompanie* machine gun platoon of the *Gebirgsjägers*, reinforced the tank barrier above Payerbach, east of Reichenau, at the eastern end of the pass. While moving there, the Germans saw a truck parked in Reichenau with only one guard, filled with several cubic meters of Hungarian currency from the National Bank of Hungary. With Hungary overrun by the Red Army, money from either Horthy's regime or that of his successor, Ferenc Szálasi, had absolutely no value beyond toilet paper.

* * *

Meanwhile near Semmering, at the nearby Pertl farmstead the family had been up before sunrise baking bread. The large home rested on the side of a steep hill, accessible by a narrow driveway off of the Adlitzgrabenstrasse. This was north-northeast of the Semmering Pass. Like so much of the region an apple orchard flourished on the grounds and the Russians set up three anti-tank guns under the trees.

Around 5:00 a.m. the Russians came through the valley and smelled the mouthwatering scent of fresh bread, a smell that people around the world would all recognize. For the attackers, supplying troops fighting in the mountains meant hand carrying everything from food to artillery pieces to the forward positions, so the promise of hot bread drew the Russians like sharks to blood. They ate everything in sight and asked the family for directions to Spital am Semmering.

The Germans could not allow this to stand and launched a counter-attack that was typical of the fighting to come. Led by an *SS-Untersturmführer* the attack group consisted of the candidates from the NCO school at Admont. Before leaving the Südbahnhof Hotel they sampled vintage wines from the hotel's cellar, probably to stiffen their resolve. Divided into three elements, one group charged on either flank and the third went straight across a valley through which ran the Adlitzgrabenstrasse. The sun was fully up by the time the attackers reached the building. Someone spotted a machine gun sticking out of a window and fired a rifle grenade through it, which killed the gunner. A firefight broke out and the Germans tossed more grenades inside. The family ran to a cider cellar built into the side of the mountain and didn't came out for days. It had a ventilation shaft coming out further up the hillside, which allowed them to survive the coming nightmare.

Other Germans overran the anti-tank guns and drove off their crews. There was no chance to capture the guns so they shoved grenades down the barrels and destroyed them. More Russians were on the mountain above the homestead and the Germans were too few to try and hold the recaptured ground, so all three groups retreated back to their starting point across the valley. The surprise nature of their attack meant they suffered no casualties until they were retreating, when Russians reinforcements fired at their backs.

---

25   Other sources say it was an accordion. If so it was probably looted, as carrying an accordion on campaign would have been difficult.

But while they had been attacking one way, other Russians had infiltrated their side of the valley, and set up a machine-gun nest to cover a series of steps cut through the forest. Visibility was limited underneath the dense green canopy. Invisible in the undergrowth, the gun cut down three Germans before being destroyed in turn by a *Panzerfaust*. The survivors carried their wounded to the Südbahnhof Hotel.

The fighting wasn't over for the day, though. A battalion from *Gerbirgsjäger-Regiment 136* arrived during the day from Wolfsberg under the command of *Hauptmann* Rudolf Dickerman. The battalion's parent division, *2. Gebirgs-Division*, was in Denmark after being withdrawn from Norway, but its home base was Innsbruck, in *Wehrkreis XVIII*. The battalion contained all of the regiment's non-essential personnel, including the regimental band, so their combat value was only fair. But with the Russians pouring into Austria anybody who could carry a rifle qualified for front line duty.

The Südbahnhof Hotel Dairy Farm would be the scene of bitter fighting for weeks to come, along with the hotel's golf course. Built in 1926 on the site of the hotel's ski jumping and training area, it was the first golf course in the region and the open ground made it ideal for defenders. A dairy operation was also constructed. The position sat on the Germans' far left flank, a mile north-east of Semmering, on the south side of the valley through which ran the Adlitzgrabenstrasse.

The Russians had already captured the dairy, threatening the entire German position, so it had to be retaken. With daylight fading Dickerman led one of his companies in an attack, supported by a mortar and a platoon from *SS-Gebirgs-Ausbildungs-und-Ersatz-Abteilung 13*. It failed, not least because of the inexperience of his troops. They fought hard and died well, but their mission wasn't to die, it was to retake the dairy. Courage could only do so much to compensate for lack of experience.

The company commander and five men died, while 18 men were wounded and two were missing. The losses necessitated the establishment of a cemetery and the fallen were buried on a grassy slope on the Styrian side of Semmering Pass. Others would soon join them.

3. Panzer-Division

After a quiet night at Vasszentmihály, nearer the eastern terminus of the Raab River at Györ, the Germans woke to find Russian trucks approaching the town. They appeared to have no idea that Vasszentmihály was in German hands. The *Panzergrenadiers* waited until the trucks were too close to miss and opened fire. Suddenly the blast wave from a massive explosion knocked the Russians down and destroyed several houses, as the closest truck blew up. It had been loaded with mines.

After a few seconds of shielding their eyes, German machine-gun fire raked the column. Russians tried to turn around and flee, but those who couldn't turn their trucks panicked and abandoned them. When the Germans investigated they found them loaded with precious fuel, which at that moment was more valuable than food.

1. Volks-Gebirgs-Division

All of the pressure on *Generalleutnant* Wittmann's division came north of Deutsch Schützen, where Marshal Tolbukhin saw a chance to drive a fatally damaging wedge between *6. SS-Panzerarmee* and *6. Armee*. Wittmann's *Gebirgsjägers* had been giving ground slowly, making the Russians pay in blood for every yard they went forward. But his men's stubborn resistance actually increased their danger of being outflanked, since beyond his left flank were only the two *Kampfgruppen* of *Raithel* and *Semmering* and *Divisionsgruppe Krause*. And north of them was the gap with *SS-Kampfgruppe Keitel*. He had to bend his left flank to deny the Russians his rear areas and the further they drove west, the longer his flank protection had to be. It was only his prescient shift of *Gebirgsjäger-Regiment 98* from right to left that had it arriving southwest of Oberwart just in time to shore up the defenses there.

2. Panzerarmee

Russian attacks south from the divide with *6. Armee* had the objective of rolling up the left flank of *2. Panzerarmee*. Aside from merely trying to capture more of Austria for postwar bargaining, the Red Army was spurred on by Tito's claims to southeastern Austria as part of the future Yugoslavia. Driving the right flank of *Heeresgruppe Süd* back from the Mur River to the Drava River was the first step in that objective. If that could be accomplished it would make the evacuation of German units still in the Balkans all but impossible.

The day before the army had tried to build a defensive position shielding the Nagy Kanisza area, running from the confluence of the Mur and Drava rivers, skirting the western edge of the Nagy Kanisza oil complex to a point near Lake Balaton and then swinging westward. But the German fantasy of hanging onto the oil fields proved futile. The Russians looked for weak spots in the line and found some. German units were strung along the Mur River deep into Slovenia, with multiple enemies in close pursuit: not simply the Russians and Bulgarians, but also the well-organized Slovenian partisan army, part of Tito's forces. By early April the Germans had already reached the only defensible river line across their path of retreat, namely the Mur, where it flows southeast from Austria into Slovenia.

23. Panzer-Division

The Eiffel Tower Division, so named because it was formed and trained in the region of Paris in 1941, was strung out from the Reich border to well within Hungary. The *Kampfgruppe* at Iklódbördőce acted as a blocking force for Russian troops moving west in the wake of the remainder of the division, and consequently caught the full brunt of their fury. After the customary artillery bombardment a strong attack supported by tanks drove back the *I./Panzergrenadier-Regiment 128* and, despite an immediate counterattack, the Germans were unable to restore the line. With Russian pressure increasing there was no choice but to disengage and run, which the *Kampfgruppe* did during mid-afternoon. The rearguard company consisted of a mere 15 men, few of whom made it out alive. Their defense inflicted numerous casualties on the Russians, however, which bought the rest of the *Kampfgruppe* time to form a new line of resistance further to the west.[26]

---

26   Rebentisch, *To the Caucasus*, pp. 463-464.

4

Wednesday, 4 April

Heeresgruppe Süd

A cold front moved in from the northwest bringing heavy rain to parts of the battlefield and snow to higher elevations. Nevertheless *Luftflotte 4* again flew against Russian targets in support of *I SS-Panzerkorps* south of Vienna.

The Army Group's orders for the day were to counterattack and close the various gaps in the front lines while not retreating anywhere, but the directives were obsolete before ever being issued. Lack of reserves, supplies and tactical immobility made them impossible. Maier wrote that "no attention was paid to them as they were meaningless."[1] All the Germans could do was to survive and try to maintain unit cohesion.

The Russian attack plan for capturing Vienna had become crystal clear. Second Ukrainian Front would drive along both banks of the Danube, to dislodge the Germans from their anchor on the river. Meanwhile Third Ukrainian Front would attack the city from the southeast with part of its strength to fix the defenders in place. Another spearhead containing very strong armored forces would pour into the Vienna Woods to cut the city off on the west. All of these movements had the ultimate objective of cutting off and destroying any German forces defending the city, including *II SS-Panzerkorps*.

Otto Wöhler had seen this before. In 1942 he had led a relief force trying to break through to the doomed garrison at Velikiye Luki, an effort that failed to save the city, and he knew that once Vienna was surrounded the defenders would be doomed. The example of the Budapest Garrison was only the latest in a long string of such encirclements that also included Stalingrad. But there was not much Wöhler could do about it with the forces on hand, and his time for doing anything was over anyway. *Generaloberst* Dr Lothar Rendulic was on his way to replace Wöhler as commander of *Heeresgruppe Süd*, soon to be renamed *Heeresgruppe Ostmark*.

North of the Danube

8. Armee

The defenders of Bratislava found themselves pressed harder and pushed back farther with each passing moment. Russian infantry fought their way forward until reaching a strongly held position, then called in self-propelled guns and artillery for direct fire to destroy them, and the Russians had a smorgasbord of such weapons to call on. The SU-76 and SU-100 assault guns were both ubiquitous in the Soviet ranks, but if a bigger gun was needed they could call on the devastating SU-152, with its 152mm main gun. That was the same size gun mounted by light cruisers in navies around

---

1   Maier, *Drama,* p. 347.

the world, and one shell could bring down a multi-storey building. This happened over and over again and there was nothing the Germans could do to prevent it.

Around noon they seized the Koliba Height, which overlooked the entire city, and immediately headed west. Not only did the Soviets now have a clear view of the city, but their spearheads planned to turn south and trap the Germans against the river. After that they could destroy them in detail, exactly as happened at Budapest. Their target was the main railway station. By evening it was all over. Some Germans escaped, others were captured, but by evening Pressburg was in Russian hands and once again became Bratislava.

Casualties in the fighting are hard to verify. A commonly calculated number for German losses is 5,500 men and the Russians only 800. If the German figures included wounded and captured, those seem plausible.

With the fall of Bratislava most of Slovakia was in Russian hands and the ultimate objective of Second Ukrainian Front began to crystallize as being Korneuberg, across the Danube from Klosterneuberg, west of Vienna. Getting there meant driving across the mostly flat ground north of the city, a floodplain named the Marchfeld, with good roads helping the attackers and only urban areas to aid the defenders. And with that the race was on to trap *II SS-Panzerkorps* between Second and Third Ukrainian Fronts, thereby destroying the hated *Waffen-SS* formations once and for all.

But the tactical ramifications were even worse. The most significant terrain feature in the *8. Armee* area was the Little Carpathian Mountains, a densely forested line running northeast from Bratislava. West of the mountains was a land of farms and vineyards, with few natural defensive obstacles. But with Bratislava gone, any defensive stand Kreysing might have contemplated was already outflanked on the south: *8. Armee* now had no choice but to retreat or die.

* * *

Vienna wasn't the only city asked to sacrifice its children for the *Führer*. At Korneuberg, close by on the north bank of the Danube, the city's Hitler Youth assembled at a local school and then marched to the river where they took a ferry and joined the defense of Vienna.

Vienna

To Sepp Dietrich's horror, on 4 April *OKH* put the Vienna Defensive Zone under the command of *6. SS-Panzerarmee*. *Kampfkommandt* and *General der Infanterie* Rudolf von Bünau dutifully turned up at *6. SS-Panzerarmee* HQ to find out what Dietrich wanted him to do, and Dietrich's response was that he wanted von Bünau to give up the notion of defending Vienna and stay there with him at *6. SS-Panzerarmee* headquarters. That violated both of their orders but Dietrich no longer cared about such things and stated that he would not order his army to fight for Vienna.

As a witness to the encounter, Maier adds that von Bünau made it clear that threats had been made against his family if he didn't defend Vienna. Dietrich offered him sanctuary and armed protection and, although von Bünau refused, the time would come when the tough *Kampfkommandant* would take him up on that offer.[2]

With the battle lines being shoved backward into metropolitan Vienna, von Bünau returned to the city and surveyed his new command to see exactly what defense forces were on hand, and what *Gauleiter* Baldur von Schirach had done to prepare the city for a Russian attack. What he found was depressing: "In short, no preparations whatever had been made for the defense of the city."[3]

---

2   Maier, *Drama*, p. 47.
3   Von Bünau, *Combat in Vienna*, p. 5.

The complacent von Schirach had done little to ready Vienna for battle, despite Hitler's frequent and direct orders to do just that. As for the defending combat forces, those could be divided into two distinct groups. First was *II SS-Panzerkorps*, which despite Dietrich's vow they would not fight in Vienna increasingly appeared to have no other path of escape except through the city, and second was a motley collection of miscellaneous formations under von Bünau's direct command.

* * *

One strange story concerns *SS-Sturmbannführer* Hans Hauser. Hauser received orders to report to *13. Waffen-Gebirgs-Division-der-SS Handschar* to command a regiment. *Handschar* was one of the first non-German SS divisions and had been operating with *2. Panzerarmee* after fighting partisans in the Balkans. It contained Muslims, Catholics and ethnic Germans and had the distinction of being the only SS division to ever mutiny.

In mid-March, as Hauser entered the *Heeresgruppe Süd* area he was rerouted to Vienna reportedly on orders of *SS-Obergruppenführer* Felix Steiner. As the story goes Steiner ordered him to form a *Kampfgruppe* from students at an SS Technical School, plus any recovering wounded and troops on leave he could round up.[4] When the Russians poured over the frontier, *SS-Kampfgruppe Hauser* moved to defend Münchendorf, a small town just west of Mödling.

Around 3 April three T-34s unsupported by infantry approached the town, unaware of the German defenders. Hauser's group was small but experienced. In addition to small arms, the unit no doubt possessed the ubiquitous *Panzerfaust*. The first tank nosing toward the bridge into the town was destroyed. More attacks came and were beaten off, although both Hauser's adjutant and orderly were killed.

II SS-Panzerkorps

In light of the reality of the tactical situation, Dietrich altered the orders to *SS-Obergruppenführer* Wilhelm Bittrich concerning Vienna. The *II SS-Panzerkorps* was to hold its defensive positions as long as possible, including by means of frequent counterattacks, but in no circumstances was it to become surrounded in the city. Before that could happen the corps was ordered to abandon Vienna in direct contradiction of Hitler's orders to stand fast with no retreats allowed.

Exact strength returns for *II SS-Panzerkorps* in this last phase of the war are hard to determine, but some approximations can be made. The figures probably represent men actually on hand. Stragglers and wounded are likely excluded. For the defense of Vienna the corps had four divisions under its command, but only the newly arrived *Führer-Grenadier-Division* was anywhere close to full strength, and even it wasn't close to authorized materiel numbers. All of the best sources agree that *6. Panzer-Division* and *3. SS-Panzer-Division Totenkopf* were both reduced to a quarter of authorized strength in men and materiel, and *2. SS-Panzer-Division Das Reich* was at half strength.[5]

---

4   If Steiner actually did this then exactly why isn't known, since he wasn't Austrian and at the time was stationed north of Berlin and, if we presume he was scrounging for any reinforcements he could find for his undermanned unit on the Oder Front, then why did he worry about some small *Kampfgruppe* in Vienna? If he intended to transport Hauser's *Kampfgruppe* so far north is anybody's guess. Yet this report persists in the sources and however it came into existence, Hauser's *Kampfgruppe* was quite real.

5   Von Bünau agrees with Rauchensteiner about this, although it is possible that Rauchensteiner used von Bünau as a source. Nevertheless, the percentages for all three divisions are generally agreed upon. One reason that *Das Reich* was so much stronger than *Totenkopf* was the contingent of more than 2,800 replacements the division had appropriated that were on the way to *Hitlerjugend*, as well as the absorption around this time of the *Panzer-Ausbildungs-und-Ersatz-Abteilung 4* and 33. These replacements might have skewed the figures but their combat value could not have been as high as the men they replaced.

Extrapolating exact numbers from these percentages is not easy. Was *6. Panzer-Division* at 25 percent of a Type 1944 Panzer Division or a Type 1945?[6] Moreover, in *6. Panzer-Division*'s case we know this only refers to machines, not personnel, so is that also true for other divisions? Sources give no guidance. Still, in approximate numbers this puts the strength of *Totenkopf* at between around 5,000 ration strength and *Das Reich* about double that, about 10,000. The total strength of *II SS-Panzerkorps*, therefore, including the *Führer-Grenadier-Division*, can be estimated in the range of 35,000-40,000 men counting independent units attached to the corps. This was a very small number when defending a huge metropolis under attack from three directions, however depleted the Soviet forces may also have been.

As for the alarm, *Volkssturm* and civilian formations, they consisted of various units that wound up having some value in combat: the best of them was the Hitler Youth Battalion, three companies strong and armed with both small arms and *Panzerfauste*. No unit would earn more praise for fighting heroically than the Hitler Youth. The afore-mentioned alarm units of the *Panzer-Ausbildungs-Abteilungen 4* and *Panzer-Ausbildungs-Abteilungen 33* are assumed to have numbered personnel somewhere in the two to three company range or perhaps 250-300 men each, using only light infantry weapons, although they fought well along the southern edges of the city. Alarm units from *Aufklärungs-Ausbildungs-Abteilung 11* were at full strength. This unit's strength was listed as two troops, which would seem to indicate these were mounted cavalry armed with small arms and a few machine guns; a cavalry troop had an authorized wartime strength of about 224 men,[7] and this formation performed reasonably well in the fighting. *Panzerjäger-Ausbildungs-und-Ersatz-Abetilung 17* provided one company with four motorized and three towed 75mm anti-tank guns, while *Artillerie-Ausbildungs-und-Ersatz-Abteilung 96* contributed one battery of four 105mm howitzers that were attached to *6. Panzer-Division*. *Pionier-Ausbildungs-und-Ersatz-Abteilung 80* and *Pionier-Ausbildungs-und-Ersatz-Abteilung 86*[8] contributed three companies armed with light infantry weapons and fought well.

The *24. Flak-Division* detailed two regiments of about 75 percent strength for ground fighting, along with their guns.[9] This would have been a fairly powerful force, with a mixture of 20mm, 37mm and 88mm guns, both towed and self-propelled.[10] Regiments of *Flak* would typically have four battalions each, so at 75 percent strength that would be three battalions. Each battalion should have had four heavy batteries each containing four–six heavy guns, usually the ubiquitous dual-purpose 88mm, with two 20mm light guns for close support; five mixed batteries of both heavy and light guns, with some combination of 88mm, 37mm and 20mm cannon, with a light battery having 12-16 guns of either 37mm or 20mm; and three–four light batteries, as well as three–four searchlight batteries with an average of one searchlight per platoon.[11] Without supporting infantry the *Luftwaffe* men would have had a hard time fending off ground attacks in an urban environment. Von Bünau lists their combat efficiency as average to good, but with the Red Air Force bombing and strafing at will they would have been a welcome addition to any combat unit, not to mention the anti-tank capabilities of the 88mm guns. A final fragment was one company

---

6   *6. Panzer-Division* is the only panzer division known to have absolutely reorganized under the 1945 guidelines.
7   Peacetime strength for a troop of mounted cavalry was 205 men, but there is no way now to know the exact total for these troops.
8   One source lists the two engineer training formations as *Panzer-Pionier-Ausbildungs-Bataillon*.
9   Von Bünau lists their commander as *Generalmajor* Grieshammer.
10 As *Das Reich* pulled back into the city, it encountered a *Luftwaffe Flak* unit that was all too glad to be attached to a *Waffen-SS* division like *Das Reich*, and parts of *24. Flak-Division* seem the most likely candidate.
11 These numbers are authorized strengths; the actual numbers present in Vienna are impossible to determine this long after the fact. If von Bünau is right, however, then even if four battalions were present the number of guns should be reasonably accurate.

from *SS-Panzer-Instandsetzung-Abteilung 9,* the panzer repair battalion of *9. SS-Panzer-Division Hohenstauffen*. During the retreat from Székesfehérvár in March, those men wound up in the Györ area and were swept west as the Red flood rolled toward Vienna. They wound up fighting in the city streets of Vienna, most likely under von Bünau's command.[12]

Of less value were the other alarm formations, few of which were worth the trouble it took to organize and arm them. These included alert formations from the *Administraiv-Ausbildungs-und-Ersatz-Abteilung 17,* Administrative Replacement and Training Battalion 17, of about company strength, plus various walking wounded, men returning from leave and stragglers that von Bünau gives as a strength of eight battalions armed with light weapons; three battalions of *Luftwaffe* personnel with small arms; a large force of Police divided into a regiment with three battalions, with small arms and one tank of undetermined type; various *Volkssturm* units of unknown composition; an under-strength but eager company from the *Nachrichten-Ausbildungs-und-Ersatz-Abteilung 17,* the Signal Replacement and Training Battalion 17, poorly equipped with arms and radio equipment; and lastly, various police and constable groups that were unreliable and tied into O-5, as likely to join the Russians as to fight them. As for supply troops, there were none, meaning that the irregular and alarm formations had no reliable means of drawing supplies outside of those given to them by the regular and SS units in the field.[13]

The *Alarm-Bataillon 1* from *Luftkriegschule 7,* 7th Air Warfare School, based at Tulln, had already been deployed on a mountain called the Laaer Berg as infantry support for various caliber anti-aircraft guns dug in on the mountain. The main highway leading into Vienna from the east passed over the mountain, so it was a critical position. The school's *Alarm-Bataillon 2* was loaded down with schnapps, cigarettes and food for their upcoming use in the city. As things turned out they would march to Floridsdorf to guard the *Flak* guns there.

As the fighting progressed all of the alarm formations got swallowed up by the regular divisions of *II SS-Panzerkorps*. Such incorporations could have, and probably did, take place when a higher-ranking SS officer informed this or that training or alarm formation they were now part of the *Waffen-SS*. Maybe the paperwork was filled out later and maybe not, but many of those formations simply disappeared without a trace. Given the supply situation as discussed above, most were probably happy to be part of a regular formation, although having a *Waffen-SS* stamp in their *Soldbuch* probably wasn't appreciated as much.[14]

As mentioned previously, von Bünau could also count on the heavy anti-aircraft guns mounted on Vienna's three *Flak* tower complexes,[15] located in the Augarten, Arenberg Park and the Stiftskaserne. In a very real sense the towers were like small cities unto themselves. The monster structures were only built in three cities in all of the Reich: Hamburg, Berlin and Vienna, showing the importance Hitler still felt for his one-time home. The towers had been built in a triangle to protect the Old City from bombing attack, and the approximate center of the triangle was St Stephan's Cathedral. In the truest sense of the word the towers were fortresses, with outer walls up to two meters thick and roofs up to 10 feet: "A very hard type of concrete, reinforced with spirals,

12   Nevenkin, *Fire Brigades*, p. 874.
13   Von Bünau, *Combat in Vienna*, pp. 36-39.
14   The *soldbuch* or 'soldier's book' was a man's identification papers. It listed all units he had served with, his rank, had his photo, list of awards, wounds, etc. Men who lost their *soldbuch* could get it replaced, but being caught without one behind the lines was a fast way to get a bullet in the head.
15   There were six towers in total. Each location had a Gun Tower, known as the G-Tower, and a Command Tower, known as the L-Tower, which housed the range-finders. The two towers were connected by an underground cable.

was used…the crews of the 128mm *Flak* guns were somewhat safe from splinters and light bombs hitting the roof because of the fact that the guns in the towers were protected by steel cupolas."[16]

The various towers had incurred minor damage during the war, and every tower in Vienna suffered countless hits from Russian artillery, but in the fight yet to come only a single high-caliber Russian shell would penetrate the Augarten tower high on one wall above the lower platform.[17] Only Vienna's sewers offered more protection than the *Flak* towers.

Each complex had two towers, one for the guns and one for the targeting personnel. In addition, each had its own water supply and power-plant, bomb shelters for up to 15,000 people,[18] as well as storage facilities for valuable cultural artifacts and offices for the military and civilian government. More important for the looming battle, each tower also had a hospital with up to 800 beds. There were even small factories in the towers producing ammunition, aircraft engines and other electrical components.

The *Luftwaffe* and female helpers at the towers had already been released from their duties as combat came closer. The *Flak* batteries were armed with the devastating 128mm heavy *Flak* gun. This massive high-velocity gun had a range of nearly 8.5 miles or 50,000 feet, but their angle of depression downward was severely limited, meaning they were only of use at longer ranges. Once the Russians had penetrated into the city they could not depress far enough to engage targets. Smaller *Flak* guns were intended for use against low-flying attacks but seem never to have been installed.[19]

The *2. Batterie*, located on the tower in the Stiftskaserne, fired on targets in Laxenberg, Hennersdorf, Perchtoldsdorf, Rodaun and Mauer, while the *1. Batterie* on the Arenberg Park tower fired at targets in southern Vienna. The Arenberg Park tower had eight 128mm guns, four in single and four in double mounts. The Stilfskaserne and Augarten towers both had eight 128mm guns in double mounts, with the *3. Batterie* at the Augarten Tower also having eight 128mm guns. All of the towers had smaller-caliber 37mm and 20mm guns as well.

Beginning on 4 April they began engaging targets to the south, southeast and west, chiefly Russian troop concentrations of the Third Army, Ninth Guards Army and the Sixth Guards Tank Army. Once the guns opened fire, "the air pressure broke windows in the surrounding area, and the window frames were loosened in the [Rossau] barracks"; although hindered by the dense canopy of trees that made target acquisition difficult, "firing continued steadily for four days and nights".[20]

Von Bünau had also been promised reinforcements from *Wehrkreis XVII*, two light and two heavy batteries of artillery and an anti-tank company, but he only got the *Panzerjägers* and one light battery, both are which were assigned to 6. *Panzer-Division*. Regardless of which formations were available, their combat value would be nil unless they could be armed with weapons, ammunition and other equipment from depots around Vienna. Arrangements should have, and could have, been made before he took command, but they were not. Unfortunately for von Bünau, this was not easily accomplished in the confused situation inside the city as the Russians closed in and resistance forces tried to hamper the defenses. Finding the desired stores, then transporting them

---

16   Foedrowitz, Michael, *The Flak Towers in Berlin, Hamburg and Vienna 1940-1950* (Schiffer, 1998), p.38.

17   In Berlin, where the towers were very similar to those in Vienna, the Russians found that not even their massive 203mm artillery guns could do more than chip the outer wall. The only penetration of a tower in Vienna was at a low level, where the wall was only three feet thick.

18   The shelters were not intended for such a huge number, but when the bombs were falling the fetid, standing-room only conditions inside were preferable to being killed or buried under rubble outside.

19   Sources are divided on whether the 20mm light *Flak* guns were ever installed, but the preponderance of the evidence seems to indicate they were not.

20   Foedriwitz, *Flak Towers,* p.38.

to the men who needed them in time for those men to deploy was a massive nightmare that was never completely overcome; many transport vehicles had already been confiscated by anyone with clout who had fled the doomed city. All remaining motor vehicles within Vienna were ordered commandeered but the coordination necessary for such a massive effort to be put into place with no plans or practice was simply too much to ask; the distribution of supplies to the alert formations and *Volkssturm* was, therefore, haphazard at best. Likewise, von Bünau tried to impose military authority over the civilian agencies and public services, but with no time or means of enforcing his authority all he could do was ask them to stay at their posts as long as possible and do their best.

During a meeting on 4 April between von Bünau, Dietrich and von Schirach, it was agreed that defending Vienna for a prolonged period was not possible. Not only had no defense measures been taken for doing this, but there were insufficient forces to prolong the battle for long. The three men agreed that Vienna was going to fall to the Russians, the only question was when;[21] later, they even requested that Vienna be declared an open city, a request which was summarily rejected.

And so, with no other choice, von Bünau endorsed the order to defend Vienna: "The decision for or against fighting was not mine to make."[22] Given the motley nature of the forces under his command, fulfilling his mission was more fantasy than reality. Since there were not enough forces to form a continuous front or time to prepare defense in depth, about all he could do was block the main arteries with static forces such as *Volkssturm*, assign bicycle-mounted anti-tank units the mission of destroying any Russian tanks that broke through, and give demolition missions to the various engineer units. Above all, the bridges over the Danube Canal and the river itself had to be protected from being captured, or, if that was not possible, to be prepared for demolition along with critical junctures and structures along the railways. As with everything else about his assignment, though, even issuing orders was hard for von Bünau; with a lack of radio equipment and personnel for the alarm units, most of the time messengers had to relay orders and information, and even the local phone system was employed while it still worked.

* * *

One thing no German commander could do anything about during the coming battle was Russian air supremacy and artillery dominance. Whenever a German vehicle or artillery battery showed itself Russian aircraft would invariably show up to strafe or bomb, especially when deployed in open areas, such as *6. Panzer-Division* would be in the Prater or traffic entering Pater Abel Platz at the south end of the Floridsdorfer Bridge. All bridge traffic during the day was badly disrupted. The actual casualties caused by the air attacks were not particularly heavy: most Russian pilots were notoriously bad shots, but they could not be ignored and disruption to German movements and communication was very damaging to the defense.

More significant was the damage caused by artillery and air attack to Vienna itself. German ammunition shortages limited the firing of artillery, and therefore damage inflicted on the city's infrastructure, but the profligate use of Russian shells and bombs resulted in numerous fires and heavy damage, just as the Austrian resistance groups had feared.

Also during the coming battle the veteran Russian units would demonstrate their mastery of tactics in ground attacks, especially in smaller engagements. Over time the tactics of the Red Army had evolved into a systematic approach to the attack. Infiltrators would move forward first, finding gaps in the defenses either in woods or urban areas. In the fighting for Vienna this proved

---

21   After the battle, von Bünau stated that given the relative strengths of the two sides the fall of Vienna could almost have been predicted on schedule, with only the influence of resistance groups influencing the timetable one way or another.
22   Von Bünau, *Combat in Vienna*, p. 6.

especially effective since the Germans did not have enough men to properly man contiguous defense lines and infiltrators could exploit the gaps. Armored reconnaissance units with infantry would then scout enemy positions; once found, the attack would take place with tanks covered by infantry and a profligate use of mortars and artillery, with crossfire from any infiltrators who were in position. If this was not successful the Russians would usually try another direction of approach to try and turn the Germans' flank; *Das Reich* would repeatedly face this threat in the coming days.

Even so, the Russian attack on Vienna was anything but a model of efficiency. Having huge numerical advantages in all categories, from men to artillery tubes to tanks and aircraft, should have meant the Red Army could roll over the defenders of Vienna quickly. This was not to be the case, Von Bünau reflected: "The general impression was that of a methodical and relatively slow, sometimes even hesitant, attack. This was surprising in view of the great superiority of the enemy, in numbers and material…This deliberate, cautious offensive was all the more inexplicable in view of the enemy's undoubted knowledge of our weakness."[23] Speculating after the fact, von Bünau wondered if the Russians might have hesitated because they were waiting on guides promised by the Austrian resistance, because no other explanation made military sense.

After the battle von Bünau would judge the Russian artillery to have been average in performance and the overall volume of fire less than might be expected, although there were times when heavy concentrations of fire were laid down, around the Ringstrasse and particularly once the defenders retreated behind the Danube Canal.

0-5

Ferdinand Kas was sound asleep after the exhausting day before. First, he took off from Vienna carrying an offer of surrender from a resistance organization with few members that nobody had ever heard of before. His improbable trek then involved maneuvering through German lines without getting killed, making it into Red Army lines without getting killed, then asking to be given a chance to tell his story to a room full of skeptical Russian officers without getting killed, then held all day while the Soviets contacted higher authorities who might order him killed anyway, then being driven all over eastern Austria to confuse him as to his whereabouts until finally being deposited in Hockwolkdersdorf in the room full of wary Soviet officers he had been seeking, who could order him killed at any moment. His story was preposterous and unless he convinced the enemy officers of his sincerity he would most likely be shot out of hand. Having avoided the many chances of being killed, and getting out his entire story in something approaching a coherent manner, he was told to wait for an answer. He then promptly fell asleep.

Early on the morning of 4 April he was awakened and given his answer. Remarkably, the Soviets accepted him, his story and all of his conditions. Kas made the agreement, was handed a telephone and told that on the other end was Field Marshal Alexander in Italy, who assured him that air strikes against Vienna would cease immediately.[24] The deal was struck. All he needed now was to survive the return trip to Vienna.

---

23   Von Bünau, *Combat in Vienna*, p. 29.
24   With the Russians so close to the city air strikes were suspended anyway, but Kas didn't know that.

6. SS-Panzerarmee

Sepp Dietrich's staff desperately tried to form a unified front line, but the Russians never stopped attacking. To stop them required the commitment of every available unit, so there was no chance to build a reserve, and even if a certain location was held it was impossible to build defenses while fighting.

II SS-Panzerkorps

SS-Kampfgruppe Rideph, one of *1. Ungarishes SS-Sturmjäger-Regiment*'s two battle groups, had taken a route north of its sister *SS-Kampfgruppe Lenk*, and found itself attached to *II SS-Panzerkorps*. For such a tiny force wandering such a huge and fluid battlefield this probably initially came as a great relief; at the least they were attached to a chain of command and, more urgently, supply. What they may not have realized is that *II SS-Panzerkorps* had jumped from one mortal danger to another by being the only significant force in place to defend Vienna, and that it had orders to stand fast regardless of losses. Even so, in the dead of night the Hungarians left their homeland and crossed the border into Austria near the small town of Mosonszentpeter.

6. Panzer-Division

The *6. Panzer-Division* was in a particularly dangerous position. It was still holding the southern bank of the Danube far to the east of where *Totenkopf* anchored its right flank. This gave it a long but shallow front. Russian attacks along the division's entire front made progress, with the imminent danger of a breakthrough to the river cutting off any elements east of the penetration. Nevertheless it fought hard to keep all of the ground it occupied. Like so many days before, it was a day of Russian attacks followed by immediate German counterattacks.

By the end of the day, *6. Panzer-Division* had been pushed back to Bad Deutsch-Alternburg and Petronell, the site of the Roman fortress town of Carnumtum. Rohrau also fell, but only after a bitter fight for every house and every yard. This put the Russians directly across the river from the hard-pressed German forces around Bratislava. Russian batteries could now direct fire north across the Danube, rendering the German position untenable.

3. SS-Panzer-Division Totenkopf

Fighting raged all day in the area of Rauchenwarth, which the Germans recaptured. Two of the Tiger Is picked up at the Arsenal on 1 April played a pivotal role in the action there. More house-to-house fighting raged at Wilfeinsdorf an der Lietha and Bruck an der Leitha, both of which suffered heavy damage as the Germans lost both towns, retook them and then lost them again. Combat at Bruck an der Leitha continued into the night.

When the Germans finally had to give up Rauchenwarth the two Tigers retreated to Himberg in a fighting withdrawal. How they wound up destroyed is unknown now, but when the Russians took Himberg they discovered both panzers on the northern edge of town, completely burned out.

* * *

During the night of the 4-5 April the Russians pushed through the Vienna Woods and made great progress toward Pressbaum and the vital western railway there. With fuel shortages, too few troops, clogged roads and a tangled command structure the Germans were limited to how they could react to this growing threat from the west. General von Bünau identified this as one of the three critical moments in the battle. With no significant combat forces in the Russians' path of advance the situation was dangerous in the extreme. "Therefore the danger that the sudden enemy advance toward the east into the city would penetrate to the Danube Canal and Danube bridge was very great."[25] Such a lightning thrust would have been disastrous to the Germans, making it problematic whether any of *II SS-Panzerkorps* could have escaped the trap.

One of von Bünau's police battalions was deployed on either side of the road leading to Pressbaum from the south, backed by the single police tank available, but this ad-hoc formation could not stop the veteran Russians; night-fighting was difficult enough for seasoned troops, much less men with no combat experience. Poorly led and with little enthusiasm for open combat, they neverthe-less managed to stage a rearguard defense that delayed the Red Army briefly before retreating to Huettendorf. At Huettendorf the police joined the full-strength Hitler Youth Battalion that made up for being ill-equipped with a fanatical fervor to halt the Russians short of Vienna. This was probably the *Panzerjäger* battalion of the Vienna Hitler Youth. When dawn came on the morning of 5 April, however, no amount of determination or desire could hide the fact that, with the excep-tion of a few minor roads, Vienna south of the Danube was cut off from the west.

With the danger from the west mounting, *2. SS-Panzer-Division Das Reich* now had to face threats to both flanks and from behind. The already over-stretched division was ordered to extend its right flank to the western rail line, north and northwest of its position near Mödling, but was given command of two small alarm units, cavalry from the *Aufklärung-Ausbildungs-und-Ersatz-Abteilung 11* and a single company from the *Pionier-Ausbildungs-und-Ersatz-Abteilung 80*, to help with the extension. Nobody expected that this makeshift force could stop the Russians for long.

2. SS-Panzer-Division Das Reich

Almost three weeks after the Soviet offensive began *2. SS-Panzer-Division Das Reich* was still trying to find a defensible line amid the chaos of retreat. Day after day, week after week, the division had been shifting and moving to avoid being surrounded and destroyed, with no end in sight. The defensive positions north and south of the Neuseidlersee had been overrun before they could be fully manned, with some alarm units being attacked before they had even reached their destinations. In the narrow strip of land between Lake Neuseidler and the Danube River, Russian spearheads broke through the thinly held frontier fortifications and headed for Bruck an der Leitha. There were no front lines, no order and no prepared positions. Bruck could not be held and it was quickly captured.

In that relatively short span of three weeks *Das Reich* had been shoved backward from the vicinity of Budapest to the city limits of Vienna. Losses had been very heavy and supplies were short, espe-cially fuel. On 4 April *Das Reich* found itself spread out near Mödling, with the *Kampfgruppe* of the mangled *3. SS-Panzer-Division Totenkopf* on its left flank near the Vienna airport.[26] The divi-sion's mission for the day was to stop the Soviet advance on the main road leading to Vienna from Wiener Neustadt, even while *O-5* went about bypassing that defense to the west. It became clear that while some Russian forces were driving directly at Vienna, others were moving northwest to

---

25   Von Bünau, *Combat in Vienna,* p. 30.
26   One source puts *Das Reich* as between 'Odling' and Andau. This almost certainly refers to Mödling, but makes little sense, as the distance between those two towns is approximately 40 miles. It is possible that *Das Reich* was strung out and moving west between those points, to wind up at Mödling, but it's probably an error.

the Danube Valley near Tulln. Just as it had against so many other major cities, Stavka planned to cut off the city from the west and surround most of *6. SS-Panzerarmee* trapped there, with the added inducement of perhaps infiltrating the city with the help of the German resistance.

The loss of Bruck meant that the positions *Das Reich* had occupied the day before were no longer tenable; its left flank was endangered because what was left of *Totenkopf* was too weak to make a stand and the Russians threatened to envelop both SS formations. The division once again pulled back to the line Mödling-Neudorf-Himberg; heavy fighting ensued as the SS men tried to make a stand somewhere, but the crisis on *Das Reich*'s left flank continued as the Russians kept pushing toward Vienna and a savage fight broke out for Rauchenwarth. It was readily apparent that the pressure on the division's left would shortly force yet another withdrawal, even as another Russian envelopment attempt developed on the right flank, from the direction of the Vienna Woods. Crippled by fuel shortages and too weak to stand fast, *Das Reich*'s only option was to hold a position as long as possible and then withdraw.

The quaint town of Gumpoldskirchen, near Mödling, came under heavy artillery fire. At Hinterbrühl fifty-three civilians died as explosions raked the streets.

Maier makes passing reference to *Das Reich* getting fire support from an unexpected source, the German Danube flotilla.[27] After the fall of Czechoslovakia in 1939 the Germans renamed the Czech river monitor *President Masaryk* the *Bechelaren*, and spent time and money modernizing the boat in 1940. Since the Danube acted as a water-highway into the Reich, both sides maintained flotillas to defend or attack the other side's ships. The *Bechelaren* mounted a 7.9inch naval gun and the entire fleet had a heavy anti-aircraft complement. The flotilla fought during the Siege of Budapest, even earning a brief segment on the German newsreel *Die Deutsche Wochenschau*.

Counterattacks near Laxenberg threw the Russians back to the east side of the Wiener Neustadt canal but this minor victory couldn't offset the day's lost ground. By nightfall *Das Reich*'s front lines ran from Heiligenkreuz through Sittendorf to Mödling, virtually inside Vienna. In the face of the relentless Russian pressure on the seam between *I* and *II SS-Panzerkorps*, and the current position of the latter, Dietrich's order of the previous day that no soldier of *6. SS-Panzerarmee* was to set foot in Vienna had been overcome by events.

During the day, *SS-Panzer-Regiment 2* received two Tiger IIs that had been in long-term repair at the Arsenal. Both originally came from *Schwere SS-Panzer-Abteilung 503*, but there was no point shipping them back to their parent unit when there would soon be fighting on the grounds of the Arsenal itself. Both panzers would eventually join *SS-Kampfgruppe Langanke*.

* * *

The Red Army advance was much like an ocean swell that washes flotsam and jetsam before it, as it had throughout Eastern Europe. The roads were choked with refugees pushing carts or leading wagons loaded with everything they could carry, Nazi Party Officials of every rank and organization, broken military units, bewildered *Volkssturm*, eager Hitler Youth, all milling about or fleeing westward by whatever means of transport were at hand. Combat units attempted to change positions in accord with confusing orders along narrow roads clogged with these hordes. Stragglers searched for lost units while the *feldgendarmerie* and flying courts martial complied with Dietrich's order of the previous day and pulled suspicious men from the herd and hung them as examples of cowardice. In many ways the German rear areas had more to fear than the front lines.

---

27   Maier, *Drama,* p. 346.

I SS-Panzerkorps

Five miles due west of Wiener Neustadt the Russians first captured the steep ridge named Hohe Wand and then lost it to an immediate counterattack. This position was the first of the Alpine foothills, with a peak over 3,000 feet high and heavily forested slopes.

1. SS-Panzer-Division Leibstandarte Adolf Hitler

After holding the Enzesfeld-Lindabrunn area in heavy fighting, *LAH* moved into the mountains to the south and came under immediate attack. Without flat ground for artillery-supported armored attacks, however, the weak division was able to repel the Russians on the tangled slopes.

But there was nothing to be done about the yawning gap with *6. Armee*, and the Russians took advantage of it. Moving through undefended country south of Gloggnitz they turned north and seized then passed Reichenau an der Rax and captured the Hohe Wand. An immediate counterattack retook the Hohe Wand, but now the pincers of the Russian attacks from north and south became clear, as did their intention to trap both the *LAH* and *Hitlerjugend*.

I SS-Panzerkorps had two choices: either to pull back the front line or counterattack. In typically aggressive *Waffen-SS* fashion, they counterattacked, with the *LAH* recapturing both Oberpiesting and Wöllersdorf. Further Russian attacks at Dreistetten and Markt Piesting were repulsed with heavy losses. The ruins of Starhemberg Castle in Dreistetten made an excellent observation post for German artillery, particularly the tower above the chapel, until Russian fire smashed it. Another cultural casualty was the 15th-Century Plague Tower, built to memorialize those who died in the Black Death.

Kriegsschule Wiener Neustadt Fahnenjunker-Bataillon

In its short life the battalion of officer cadets had seen fighting every single day. Relieved in Wöllersdorf the previous day, the battered *Fahnenjunker* instead dug in behind a stream running southwest from the town. Its marshy mouth ran northeast and emptied in the Piesting River at Wöllersdorf, with rugged mountains along its course. Nevertheless, this position stretched more than three miles and its left flank was up in the air. It was asking a lot of a few hundred half-trained officer cadets to hold this position against a far stronger foe.

In an effort to at least establish a continuous line of outposts the battalion sent patrols in the direction of Dreistetten, a few miles southwest of its far left flank. In the process, the battalion's *3.Kompanie* ran into a reconnaissance in force by 150 Russians which led to a fierce firefight. The Germans reacted fast and inflicted heavy casualties on the Russians, while probes against the battalion's *1.* and *2.Kompanien* were repulsed.[28]

12. SS-Panzer-Division Hitlerjugend

Meanwhile, *Hitlerjugend* took over the defense of Enzesfeld but *Kampfgruppe SS-Panzergrenadier-Regiment 26* got pushed out of the town. Retreating to nearby Berndorf, about four miles to the northwest, the SS men were able to stop the Russians there. Unlike Enzesfeld, Berndorf had

---

28   Brettner, *Die Lietzte Kämpfe Band I*, p. 164.

mountains on either side which made it impossible for the Russians to turn the regiment's flanks, so the attackers could only launch frontal assaults backed by artillery. Those failed with heavy Russian losses.

The division's other infantry strike force, *Kampfgruppe SS-Panzergrenadier-Regiment 25*, launched a surprise counterattack against Russian forces that had infiltrated eastern Sankt Veit an der Triesting, a community near Berndorf. As an example of how weak the division was, the only armored support that could be scraped together for this assault was one *Jagdpanzer* and one mobile single-barreled 37mm *Flak* cannon. Somehow the attack succeeded anyway.

With the three Russian corps speeding toward the Danube west of Vienna, *SS-Kampfgruppe Bremer*, which comprised the remnants of *SS-Panzeraufklärung-Abteilung 12,* moved to Alland to block them from turning southwest and also outflanking *I SS-Panzerkorps.* With the Germans now at Alland the Russians turned northwest and kept moving.

SS-Kampfgruppe Keitel

Having assembled at Marchfeld just to the northeast of Vienna, *SS-Kampfgruppe Keitel* was transported south and deployed in the area west of the line Weiner-Neustadt-Neunkirchen-Terwitz on 4 April. Why it had to be sent south to fight Russians must have seemed strange, since there were plenty of Russians heading right for them where they were. But the truth was that as critical as the situation was north of the Danube, it was even worse on the approaches to Vienna.

Numbering more than 2,000 men *SS-Kampfgruppe Keitel* resembled a self-contained brigade and had a high combat potential. It was on the right wing of *6. SS-Panzerarmee* and subordinated to *I SS-Panzerkorps.* Almost immediately the *Kampfgruppe* was involved in heavy fighting in the ravines and valleys around the Schneeberg, the 6,800 foot mountain that is the highest in Lower Austria.

Keitel's main mission was to block the Soviet west-northwestern advance on an axis north of Wiener-Neustadt, from Willendorf to Gruenbach to Puchberg, by Russian forces that were not committed to the attack on Vienna. They maintained this mission until late April, when the *Kampfgruppe* was finally forced to retreat to the Schwarzau area high in the mountains. Blocking the way west was of primary importance to preventing a breakthrough into central and western Austria. When Sixth Guards Tank Army turned northwest and made for Tulln on the Danube to cut Vienna off from the rest of Austria, it allowed *SS-Kampfgruppe Keitel* to hold the line for nearly three weeks against weaker Soviet forces.

6. Armee

General der Panzertruppe Hermann Balck's most pressing concern was the 31-mile gap between the left flank of his army and the right flank of Dietrich's *6. SS-Panzerarmee.* The *III Panzerkorps* held on *6. Armee*'s left but Gloggnitz was well to the northwest, with nothing between the two armies. This meant the Russians could drive down the main highway connecting Neunkirchen and Hartberg directly into the rear of *6. Armee.*

Intelligence also reported that the Soviet 18th Tank Corps had withdrawn from the Raab Valley to be used against Graz, but this proved incorrect. In fact Marshal Tolbhukin was reinforcing the success northwest of Wiener Neustadt in the Bruck Gap, by drawing off mobile assault forces further south and sending them against *I SS-Panzerkorps* as reinforcements. This dilution of forces allowed *6. Armee* to cobble together a defensive front to block the mountain passes into Styria.

* * *

Throughout history generals have taken a dim view of men who run away from their military units. A Roman unit that fled the field of battle would be decimated, that is every tenth man would be beaten to death by the rest of his comrades. At the Battle of Verdun in 1916, French commanders gave strict orders to shoot anyone who retreated without orders, while simultaneously at the Battle of the Somme the British had orders to shoot any man who didn't march across no man's land into fire from the waiting German machine guns. Stalin had many times ordered such draconian measures for men who ran from a fight.

The German Army was no different. The problem of desertion plagued every German army still fighting on every front, and *6. Armee* was no exception. So early on 4 April *General der Panzertruppe* Balck issued an order that any man caught more than three kilometers behind the front lines without specific orders to be there, would be summarily tried and shot by a mobile court-martial designed for that very purpose. This mattered more to *Kampfgruppe Semmering*, soon to be known as *Kampfgruppe Raithel* and eventually as *9. Gebirgs-Division*, since that unit had no mechanism for trying its own members.

When the mobile tribunal met in the Semmering area, it did so at the old schoolhouse in Steinhaus am Semmering. At least five men from the unit were convicted and shot on the school grounds, and three more elsewhere. Two more men from *Gebirgs-Aufklärungs-Abteilung 56* were executed in Breitenstein.

III Panzerkorps
Kampfgruppe Semmering

Skirmishes took place all over the Semmering Pass and continued throughout the month. One such happened on the eastern end of the pass three days after Easter. A German *PAK-40* entrenched behind a field fortification near the railroad bridge between Reichenau and Payerbach traded shots with a Russian 76.2mm ZiS-3, the ubiquitous multi-purpose gun the Germans had come to fear and hate.[29] The gun was so successful it had been even been mounted on a tank chassis as the SU-76 assault gun, but it was best known as the weapon of choice in Russian *Paknests*, or clusters of dug-in anti-tank guns. A line of such fortifications was a *Pakfront*.

In this case neither side drew blood.

* * *

Early in the morning Russian spearheads closed in on Breitenstein, which had the *4./Landesschützen-Bataillon 851* dug in shielding it. Rather than spending blood on a direct assault, the Russians brought up snipers, who took a terrible toll on the inexperienced Germans. Even veteran troops hated snipers, but watching Death strike down men all around them unnerved those considered too old or otherwise unfit for front-line duty.

* * *

The commander of *4./SS-Gebirgs-Ausbildungs-und-Ersatz Bataillon 13*, *SS-Obersturmführer* Harry Sinske, received orders to take his men toward Breitenstein and advance until he met the Russians, then stop and send word of their location. He made it to the village without encountering the enemy. Leaving a platoon on the Höhenberg overlooking Breitenstein to block the road, Sinske

---

29   Some 103,000 of the guns were made during the war, in all its variants.

occupied the Sanatorium on a nearby hill with his other two platoons, and immediately sent out reconnaissance patrols. They discovered Russians infiltrating the whole area.[30]

* * *

Deeper in the pass, the Germans knew the dairy farm northeast of Semmering had to be retaken if they meant to keep the pass, but with only emergency units to call on the situation was desperate. At 1:00 a.m. on 4 April a hastily composed group numbering somewhere around 80 men, including *Volkssturm*, made a night attack. Even veteran units with high cohesion found night attacks difficult to pull off and the results in this case were predictable. The assault failed, with heavy casualties.

A company of *SS-Gebirgs-Ausbildungs-und-Ersatz-Abteilung 13* was withdrawn from their positions at the pass and ordered to attack the dairy at 8:00 a.m. Under the trees the snowpack hadn't yet melted, so their boots grew soggy as they trudged through deep snow up steep slopes, slipping as the ground was beaten into icy slush and pulling themselves up by grabbing roots and trees. Going down was even more dangerous. The men didn't stagger to their jump-off points until 9:30 a.m. Their clothes were soaked, snow packed inside their boots and many were so tired they could barely stand. Once in place they scanned the open ground over which they would have to attack. They spotted nothing and heard nothing except the sounds of battle coming from the hotel laundry, where a small group had tried to seize that building and been shot to pieces.

Even after crossing open ground visible from the dairy it seemed to be a quiet spring morning. The first group set off over the fields and nothing happened. When enough time had elapsed the second group followed them and hadn't gone far when the shutters on the dairy flew open and machine guns ripped through their ranks. The attackers fell in heaps and the remainder hit the dirt, until an MG-42 machine gun from the woods behind them hosed the dairy with bullets. Under cover of this supporting fire the attack group withdrew, losing a few more men and dragging the badly wounded with them.

Safety for the attackers led back over the same open ground they'd crossed earlier, only this time the Russians didn't hold their fire. Some men were pinned down behind a concrete water cooler, while others crawled away up a steep slope, but the men carrying the badly wounded didn't have those choices. One by one, however, the group slunk away. Finally, other help arrived and rigged up a rope and sled system to pull the wounded to safety. The injured were taken to the Südbahnhof Hotel, which had been a military hospital in the previous two years.

Divisionsgruppe Krause

The Russians began to probe the middle of *6. Armee*'s front as their attacks increased in both tempo and scale. With the fall of Rechnitz the next significant town in the Russian Twenty-sixth Army's sights was Oberwart. Rechnitz had been defended by *Volkssturm* from Oberwart and other nearby towns and villages, and its fall left those places with little or no defense. Moreover, Rechnitz had been jammed with *Volksdeutsch* refugees, many of whom got out in time to flee to Oberwart. But now that town was on the front lines.

With *1. Volksgrenadier-Division* fighting hard just to its south, the Russians' best chance to drive that division backward was to threaten its flank, and Oberwart was the key. Attacking with ferocity, the Russians were opposed in heavy fighting by the rag-tag remnants of *Divisionsgruppe*

---

30   Brettner, *Die Letzten Kämpfe Band I*, p. 95.

Krause. A nearby *Flak* unit turned its 88mm guns on the Russian armor, and between them it was just enough to hold the town for the time being.

1. Volks-Gebirgs-Division

Guarding the right flank of *Kampfgruppe Semmering* was the steadfast *1. Volks-Gebirgs-Division*. On 4 April the vagabond Hungarian *SS-Kampfgruppe Lenk* was attached to the division in the vicinity of Sankt Michael im Burgenland. This was directly behind the front, a welcome addition to the hard-pressed mountain division. In the past four days its right wing had held its ground against only light pressure, but the left had been driven back from the Rechnitz area to west of Oberwart. The towns of Unter and Oberwart had been lost, along with Stadt Schlaining, Oberschützen and dozens of others. Grosspetersdorf was a front-line town. Casualties had been heavy and would only get worse as the division dug in and the fighting escalated.

* * *

SS-Kampfgruppe Schweitzer[31] was unable to hold Rechnitz any longer as the Russian pressure became too strong, and the Germans retreated all along the front. To stay longer would have meant complete destruction.

3. Panzer-Division

Having smashed a Russian supply column at Vasszentmihály on the previous day, the Armored Bears[32] of *Kampfgruppe Medicus* were ordered back over the Reich border into Burgenland. The Hungarian civilians hated to see them leave again, since they had twice been occupied by the Russians and knew what that meant, but *6. Armee* was simply too weak and fragmented to hold the area any longer. The ruptured northern flank threatened the entire army and *3. Panzer-Division* needed to be ready for anything at a moment's notice.

When the month started the panzer regiment had six panzers ready for action, with another 30 in long-term repair and classified as being not worth fixing. Earlier in the war these could have been shipped back to the factory for a complete refurbishing, but that was no longer possible. The signals and reconnaissance battalions were in similar condition, so all three combed out the surplus personnel to form infantry companies.

Along with sudden mortar and artillery barrages, another constant danger was air attacks, and on 4 April one strafing Russian ground-attack airplane dealt the division a terrible blow. Major Medicus, survivor of more than 200 battles, was killed instantly during one such attack. With its commander dead and no significant heavy weapons left, *Panzerjäger-Abteilung 543* was dissolved and the men formed into an alarm company.[33]

---

31   Reportedly with *I. Abteilung* of *SS-Brigade Ney* still attached.
32   Many German panzer divisions had nicknames, and *3. Panzer-Division* was called the *gepanzerte Bären*, the Armored Bears.
33   Veterans, *Armored Bears*, p. 284.

2. Panzerarmee
23. Panzer-Division

The division again pulled back to the west, this time to the area north of Mursko Središće, a town on the west bank of the Mur River. The division's new mission was to shield military units and refugees crossing the river. On its far left flank was the *4. Kavallerie-Division.*

It was slow going. Most of the columns plodding west were horse-drawn and moved no faster than the worn-out beasts could walk. Nor were the rickety wagons piled high solely with furniture, grandparents, children and chickens; many carried wounded soldiers, ammunition or field kitchens. Only after the last of the wagons crossed the river did *23. Panzer-Division* follow them to the west side. Pioneers did what they had done countless times during the past two years of retreat; they blew up the bridges behind them.

Digging in with the river to their front would give the exhausted men a chance to rest, clean weapons and repair uniforms. Once the new rifle pits were dug, at 3:00 a.m. on 5 April they fell into their new positions and slept.

* * *

Hungarians serving with the Germans officially became men without a country when the last bits of Hungarian territory were evacuated and occupied by the Russians. General de Angelis had finally had no choice but to disengage his army's left flank and pull out its bridgehead north of the Mur near Radkersburg, and the *Führerbefehl* be damned. He needed the forces released to defend Graz and to launch another attack to close the gap with *6. Armee.* But intelligence indicated that the Russian Twenty-Seventh and Fifty-Seventh Armies were regrouping for a drive on Graz and de Angelis had nothing to stop them with, which was the second reason for pulling back across the Mur.

The *2. Panzerarmee* had more responsibilities than simply holding down *Heeresgruppe Süd*'s right flank; it was the last remaining conduit for German forces to evacuate the Balkans. *Generaloberst* Alexander Löhr's *Heeresgruppe E* depended on *2. Panzerarmee* to hold open an escape route if and when the time came, otherwise Löhr's men would fall to Tito's merciless partisans. De Angelis knew it and was determined to do everything in his power to help Löhr.

But things weren't going well on his far right flank in Slovenia. On 4 April the Russians closed on the Mur River and began to bombard the town of Bad Radkersburg, a vital road junction for the two German corps fighting to the southeast in Slovenia. The town was filled with refugees and the shells ripped into the huddled groups and left torn bodies all over the streets.

Further south it was the turn of German positions near the town of Veržej. The area had been part of the Austrian state of Styria until after the First World War, when the town had been called Wernsee. Now it was defended by elements of both the *118. Jäger-Division* and the *297. Infantry-Division*, both of which were in a sorry state, worn out and depleted.

The Russians had no intention of letting the Germans slip away and prepared for a river crossing. Firing their artillery non-stop for two hours, the first boats put into the river while the German defenders were too stunned to repel them. Before long they'd built a pontoon bridge and thrown two battalions to the west bank against only minimal opposition. Those Germans not wiped out in the initial assault fell back.

But the command staffs immediately saw the danger. With Russians on the west bank of the Mur the river line itself became useless and any units on its eastern side were in imminent danger of destruction. They brought every available artillery tube to bear to try and destroy the bridge, but it was useless. More Russians crossed and fought their way through the second line of German defenses. It wasn't long before the entire 299th Rifle Division was in the bridgehead.

As the Russians closed in on the town itself the Germans did what they had always done best, they counterattacked. Even at the end of the war this doctrine of attacking the attackers before they could dig in remained the most common feature of German defensive tactics. *Panzergrenadiers* from *16. SS-Panzergrenadier-Division Reichsführer-SS*, supported by panzers from *SS-Panzer-Abteilung 16* and artillery, hit the infiltrating Russians on the edge of town and drove them back in vicious fighting. In response, they hammered hapless Veržej with heavy artillery and Katyushas.[34]

For the Germans it had been a close-run thing, but once again at the last moment bold action had saved their position. But while the fight for the line of the Mur was far from over, it would continue up and down the river for the next two weeks. On the far southern end of the line the Bulgarians had already outflanked it by crossing the Drava River, or the Drau in German. Although the numbers of Bulgarian troops involved was small, it nevertheless forced the Germans to hinge their front at a ninety degree angle from the Mur River line, and to set up a front facing southeast from Štrigova to Kog and then Šafarsko.

But the same conditions that hampered the Russians, Bulgarians and Slovenians from blasting the Germans out of their Mur River positions crippled them on that flank, specifically a lack of heavy weapons. For the next week a terrible infantry battle raged along that flank, with each side losing heavily but unable to power past the other.

---

34   Octavianus (2003) 'St Stefan over the Prekmurje province 1941-1945', Axis History Forum, <https://forum.axishistory.com/viewtopic.php?t=36612>, (Accessed 27 October, 2018).

5

Thursday, 5 April

Berlin & Munich

Nazi Germany had few newspapers uncensored by Joseph Goebbels' Propaganda Ministry, but one was *Das Schwarze Korps*, the *Black Corps*, the official publication of the SS. The editorial offices were in Berlin but the paper was actually published at the Nazi Party's publishing company, the Eher Verlag, in Munich. The *SS Hauptamt* made every effort to distribute this weekly paper to SS forces everywhere, both to keep up the men's spirits and to reinforce their belief in Nazism. Joseph Goebbels alternately praised and vilified the paper, but the second-to-the-last issue ever printed, the 14th edition of 1945, dated 5 April, gave him ample reason to rage against this mouthpiece of his hated rival, Heinrich Himmler.

The article openly said the war was lost militarily. From anyone else this would have prompted immediate execution. With the SS already heavily engaged on all fronts, the effects of the article can hardly be overstated. For the official organ of the SS to admit that the war was lost undermined everything the average man had been told, and this effect was magnified in the ranks of the *Waffen-SS* after the debacle of the Cuff Band Order. Men who had silently known that Germany had been defeated now had their beliefs verified, although voicing such an opinion in the wrong circumstances could still lead to a bullet in the head.

Heeresgruppe Süd

The day's weather remained excellent, with a high in the lower 60s and partly cloudy skies.

North of the Danube

8. Armee

Eight miles north of the Danube along the Morava River was the town of Marchegg. Russian troops were already over the river into a gap in the German defense, between Marchegg and Zwerndorf. The Germans in Marchegg blew up several bridges but that did nothing to stop the Russians on the west side. Trapped in the town was the *II./Grenadier-Regiment 283*, from *96. Infanterie-Division*. A *Kampfgruppe* from *101. Jäger-Division* tried to break through and relieve them but it was hopeless; the Russians were far too strong. It wouldn't be long before the Russians could launch an all-out attack on the *Grenadier* battalion and wipe it out. With no other options left, the battalion commander was ordered by the division commander to break out and rejoin German lines to the west. The attack was successful because of the help of a local leader who knew the area well. He led the men safely through the Russian ring and into the pastures beyond without a single casualty.

That's when the shooting started. Between 200 and 300 Russians spotted them and opened fire. Other Russians were heading for the position when *Kampfgruppe Lentz,* built around six *Sturmgeschütze* of *Panzerjäger-Abteilung 196* from *96. Infanterie-Division,*[1] hit the unsuspecting Russians and drove them back over the river. Fierce fighting raged throughout the night as the Russians regrouped and counterattacked.

To the south the rest of *96. Infanterie-Division*, with *SS-Kampfgruppe Ameiser* attached, crossed the Morava River to try and find the left flank of *6. SS-Panzerarmee*, taking up positions in the western corner of the Danube and Morava below Marshegg. This was a major setback, as the Morava was a wide waterway separating Slovakia from Austria, and so was also the border of the Reich. Properly defended it could have held up Second Ukrainian Front for days, even weeks. But the necessary troops weren't available.

The *8. Armee* had been ordered to extend its right flank and find Dietrich's command, thus sealing the gap that existed between the two. Three bridges over the river were taken under artillery fire while the *96. Infanterie-Division* crossed, and kept firing as the rearguards followed. They made it just in time, as shortly thereafter the Seventh Guards Army reached the east bank of the Morava along a broad front and the 25th Guards Rifle Corps established a bridgehead on the western bank.

North of this breach of the river line, the 24th Guards Rifle Corps crossed near Hochstetten, set up bridgeheads of their own and rushed reinforcements across. Early on the first troops across were vulnerable to a counterattack, but blankets of artillery fire kept the Germans back.

Meanwhile, adding to the confused situation, the headquarters of *Lützow* was given command of the *96. Infanterie-Division*'s reinforced *Infanterie-Regiment 284*, as well as *Panzergrenadier-Ausbildungs-und-Ersatz-Abteilung 82*, a fragment of the *232. Panzer-Division* that had escaped the division's destruction near Raab a week before,[2] and some *Volkssturm* units. The bizarre command situation thus meant that part of *96. Infanterie-Division* was attached to *Lützow* and part of *Lützow* was attached to *96. Infanterie-Division*.

The polyglot *Kampfgruppe* was assigned to protect the line from Grub to Marschegg. The rough terrain in the region, chiefly old-growth forest, meant that while *SS-Kampfgruppe Ameiser* had few heavy weapons to combat tanks, the Soviets could not use their tanks in the dense woods. Meanwhile at Markthof, near the confluence of the Morava and Danube Rivers, the Russians crossed the Morava during the night and made for the town. The Germans were determined to hold onto it, however, and the fighting would last for days.

* * *

Engelhartsstetten, which may be loosely translated as 'Behold the Angels', was a small market town in the fertile region of Gärnsdorf, just west of the Morava and north of the Danube. Most of the gently rolling lands are cultivated, with vineyards that produced some of the best Austrian wines predominant among the growers. In 1260 AD, one of the defining battles of the Middle Ages took place at nearby Kressenbrunn wherein a Bohemian army crushed a Hungarian one in a struggle for control of Austria.

On 5 April war once again came to Engelhartsstetten. Russian artillery and mortar fire slammed into the well-groomed and neatly laid-out streets of the little town three miles north of the Danube. The barrages were interdictory, not in support of an attack, because the main road

---

1   Brettner, Friedrich, *Die Letzten Kämpfe des II. Weltkrieges, Fotoband II* (Berndorf: Kral, 2014), p. 151.
2   Pieces of this short-lived unit showed up all over the theater. The previous day saw *232. Panzer-Division*'s former Chief of Staff killed while fighting with *2. SS-Panzer-Division Das Reich*. At the beginning of May a staff of this division would command troops in the line with *Korps von Bünau*.

feeding the forward elements of both *96. Infanterie Division* and *SS-Kampfgruppe Ameiser* led through Engelshartsstetten. Destroying the town was secondary to stopping the flow of supplies to the German front lines.

* * *

Several ferries over the Danube supplemented the bridges, with some for motor vehicles and others for people. In 1943 one of them was damaged when a show-boating *Luftwaffe* pilot tried to fly under the guide cable and didn't make it. But with the coming of war to the area the damaged ferry was pressed back into service.

On 5 April, 360 men crowded onto one ferry boat to escape the south bank just ahead of the Russians, headed for Altenbrug. They thought they'd gotten away until two mortar shells ripped into their ranks and blew the bottom out of the boat. It sank within minutes. The overloaded soldiers drowned in the freezing waters, while the Russians acquired a new target, a powered boat filled with 80 wounded men. They sank it, too. A *Wehrmacht* motor vehicle ferry was damaged but stayed afloat. More than three hundred men died. Fortunately for those who survived, the *Luftwaffe* showed up as bombers and fighters of *Jagdgeschwader 52* and *53* struck the Russian positions.[3]

* * *

With Bratislava lost *8. Armee* gained freedom of movement to adjust its lines. The Russians had already penetrated the Little Carpathians and kept up the pressure by thrusting for Malacky, in the western part of those mountains. Losing the high ground meant that *8. Armee* had to defend flat, open ground all along its front. Meanwhile, northwest of Bratislava the Red Army captured the key hinge town of Devinska Nova Ves and drove on Marchegg, which outflanked the Little Carpathians to the south.

Making *8. Armee*'s situation worse, a new Russian spearhead moved out from Malacky to the northwest and a heavily reinforced assault group headed west toward Stockerau. And as Army Commander General Hans Kreysing tried to figure out how to slow down the Russians with the forces to hand, *Heeresgruppe Süd* gave him yet another responsibility.

The Russians had broken through south and west of Vienna and were driving hard for the Danube. Weak counterattacks on their spearheads had been crushed and *6. SS-Panzerarmee* had no more forces to stop them. The big danger was the bridge over the Danube at Tulln. If the Russians crossed there they could not only trap *II SS-Panzerkorps* in Vienna, but most of *8. Armee*, too. Therefore, Kreysing was given responsibility for defense of the north bank of the Danube up to and including Tulln.

At Korneuberg the fires of Vienna filled the horizon with smoke. The first heavy explosions boomed in the distance and Red Army ground-attack aircraft strafed anything that moved. The day before the city officials had sent their children to war, now it was their turn to be shot at.

Kampfgruppe Volkmann

At the Tulln airfield the base commander, *Generalmajor* Volkmann, had already been warned of the Russian advance south of the Danube. He ordered all airworthy trainers to evacuate to Raffelding airfield, near Eferding. Most of the pilots were Hungarians, who stuffed the Siebel Si-204 twin-engine trainers with all of the food, fuel and other scarcities they could carry.

---

3   Brettner, *Die Letzten Kämpfe Band II*, p. 150.

Once his other duties had been wrapped up, Volkmann donned the mantle of *Kampfkommandant* of the Tulln area. His first duty was simple: keep the Tulln Bridge over the Danube open for retreating German troops. To accomplish this he relied on the *Alarm-Bataillon 3* from *Luftkriegschule 7*. Volkmann knew the men, and who he could count on in crunch time.

He reported to *II SS-Panzerkorps* because, even though his command was south of the Danube and the corps was north of it, the military situation made it inevitable that he would soon be forced north of the river, too. His authority allowed him to conscript any and all men he needed to defend the Tulln bridgehead. Among these was an *SS-Wachbattalion Himmler*.[4] In all likelihood this unit came from the nearby Mauthausen complex. Meanwhile, *Alarm-Bataillon 2* began its march toward Floridsdorf armed with old Steyer Mannlicher rifles, but along the way was able to replace them with first-class weapons discarded by retreating units, simply by picking them up from the side of the road.

Vienna

The Battle for Vienna truly began on 5 April, and was a pivotal day in the Battle for Austria. Tolbukhin's directive from Stavka was to capture Vienna as soon as possible, but that wasn't the only possibility. Another temptation played out in the Marshal's imagination, because the way west along the Danube Valley lay essentially unguarded all the way to Passau, a distance of 175 miles. Once there it was only another 120 miles to Munich, meaning the Red Army was only about 300 miles from sealing the Western Allies out of Austria. Such a bold move might have changed world history, but it would have been a dangerous thrust requiring tremendous logistical support, not to mention a complete change in Russian strategic considerations.

Instead the Russians began their offensive to capture Vienna from the south and west in earnest, with attacks along the entire front. They expected to pin down the Germans defenders, move through the Vienna Woods unopposed and then turn down unguarded roads into the heart of the city. That's what they agreed to with *O-5*. But like most plans this one didn't survive contact with the enemy.

For the citizens of Vienna two wars were about to merge into one. As Gerald Linderman said, "every war begins as one war and becomes two, that watched by civilians and that fought by soldiers".[5] But in the reverse of Linderman's observation, the citizens of Austria's former capital were about to find out that two wars were becoming one, that the war fought by soldiers was about to become the same one experienced by them when street fighting swept through the city. The battle would only last for a week, but the intensity and viciousness rivaled any urban combat of the war, including the bell weather for such comparisons, Stalingrad. The only mitigating factors which spared the city from an even worse fate were the escape route north, and the disobedience of the commanders on the spot to obey Hitler's death-sentence orders not to retreat another step.

Since war with the Soviet Union had broken out in June 1941, the non-Jewish Viennese had been largely untouched by its physical effects until bombs started falling on Austria in 1944, escalating in scale until the storm passed over them like a tornado. In total Vienna suffered 52 bombing raids, during which severe damage was inflicted, with upwards of 20 percent of homes in the city being destroyed. The terror of bombing raids had been the totality of the Viennese view

---

4   'Die Geschichte des Fliegerhorstes Langenlebarn von 1936 bis 2000', Kurzversion aus der Dissertation von Herrn DrMag. Hubert Prigl. Anmerkung: Das Hakenkreuz ist ein Symbol dieser Epoche und dient der historischen Korrektheit. <http://www.gotech.at/lale2/langenlebarn_2.html>, (Accessed 10 July 2018).

5   Linderman, Gerald, *Embattled Courage: The Experience of Combat in the Civil War* (New York: Free Press, 1989), p. 1.

of the war up to that point. But the damage inflicted by air attack could not approach that which would occur during urban ground combat, not only the physical damage but the psychological carnage wrought on civilians. Bombing raids might kill people and crush buildings, but it was not the personal sort of cruelty that accompanied the Red Army wherever it set foot in German territory. Stalin justified the wholesale rape, looting and murder of his soldiers as being revenge for German atrocities in occupied Russia.

* * *

One of the more curious units caught up in the fight for Austria was that the Croatian Replacement and Training Regiment, based in Stockerau. The unit had existed for several years with the mission of training foreign soldiers for service to the Reich. At various times not only Croats had been there, but also the ill-disciplined remnants of the *250. Infanterie-Division*, better known as the Spanish Blue Division,[6] well-mannered Hungarians and various other non-German troops.

Orders came through on 5 April for the non-combat-ready elements of the Croatian regiment to move west to Haslach, out of the path of the Red Army. Alarms went out for both sides of the Danube, warning of Russian tanks moving toward Tulln. Meanwhile, combat-ready Croatians of the 1st Battalion marched from Stockerau into eastern Vienna in preparation for defending the city. This group became known as *Kampfgruppe Oesterheld*. With them went at least one artillery battery. When Nazi authorities discovered the actions of O-5, however, suspicion immediately fell on the Germans in this obscure unit as possibly being resistance members.

Meanwhile, the 2nd Battalion, under the command of *Oberstleutnant* Hofer, consisted of 16 officers, 162 NCOs and 481 men. After arrival in Vienna one company was immediately sent to western Vienna. Another took over the watch at the headquarters of *Wehrkreiskommando XVII*, which would cast suspicion on the entire regiment before long. The rest of the 2nd Battalion took up positions at the Arsenal, where there would shortly be some of the fiercest urban fighting of the entire war.

* * *

Terror of bombing raids made the Viennese sensitive to the sounds associated with such airborne destruction, so when the crack of the 128mm guns atop the city's *Flak* towers boomed through the streets it must have sent more than a few of them fleeing to shelters. But this time the targets weren't American B-24s heading for the oil refineries along the Danube. This time the huge cannon aimed at Russian columns pressing west toward the Vienna Woods, and for those in the know it must have been even more terrifying than the thought of bombs raining down. It meant the Russians were within artillery range of the city itself.

* * *

O-5's plan to lead Tolbukhin's troops into Vienna through the western back-door fitted perfectly into the preferred Russian method of attacking cities: namely to pin down the defenders with direct attacks while cutting wide sweeps and by-passing the city to the south, and the north too, if possible, to finally attack from the west. The same strategy had worked countless times already, including at Velikiye Luki, Stalingrad and Budapest, and they were confident it would work in Vienna, too; if German resistance groups could lead them into the city without resistance, all the better. But if O-5's plan was going to work it would have to work soon. By 5 April, Sixth

---

6   These were survivors of the *101.* and *102. Kompanien* of the SS Spanish Volunteer Unit, who wound up in Stockerau and Hollabrunn after taking heavy casualties fighting partisans in Slovenia.

Guards Tank Army had reached the vicinity of Pressbaum and Purkersdorf, where the powerful 9th Guards Mechanized Corps made a 90 degree turn from a northerly axis to one almost due east, directly toward Vienna's western suburbs and the battalions commanded by men loyal to O-5. The only other significant units in the area were the Hitler Youth Battalion, the two troops from *Aufklärung-Ausbildungs-und-Ersatz-Abteilung 11* and a company from *Panzerjäger-Abteilung 80*.[7] With the Red Army closing in on Vienna from several directions, not just from the west, the hope of the resistance leaders was that if they assisted the Soviets in taking the city this would give them leverage with the new regime. That could only happen if their help was vital to the capture of the city without serious fighting.

But the Germans were aware that there were traitors in their midst:[8] "It is not only possible, but probable, that the enemy was directed occasionally by inhabitants of the city and perhaps even by guides who were adherents of the resistance movement."[9] Vienna had been restive for some while now and the security services knew communist sympathizers were just waiting for the right moment to assist the Red Army. Indeed, rumors of O-5's plot were rife within the city, including an accurate representation of the overall plan. Even if they didn't know the details, average citizens knew something was afoot and in Nazi Germany it never took long before the authorities knew such things, too. They were even suspicious of members of the military. *Major* Szokoll himself had been implicated in *Unternehmen Valkyrie*, the plot to assassinate Hitler the previous July, and had only just escaped with his life. Despite his narrow escape, security for the plot was loose. O-5 was playing with fire and was about to get burnt.

* * *

The coming battle would be marked by poor visibility and intelligence on both sides. Russian forces coming from the west were largely obscured by the Vienna Woods, while those from the south were in urban areas that blocked observation. Only from the southeast, along the banks of the Danube, and due east could accurate assessments be made on the movements of Red Army formations.

For their part the Russians were hampered nearly as much as the Germans were, even with air supremacy and even when they finally seized the Kahlenberg with its view over virtually the entire battlefield. Fires, smoke and drifting ash all got in the way, and while it affected combat troops at ground level more than observers higher up, overall visibility for the battle was still limited. "The terrain did not facilitate either side's observation for heavy infantry weapons and artillery."[10] The Germans did have to be especially wary of any movement during daylight that might bring Russian air strikes or artillery bombardments.

South of the Danube

Third Ukrainian Front

Even through the fog of war, Marshal Tolbukhin's maps would have shown how badly his Front had shattered the three German armies south of the Danube. There was no front line, as such: *2.*

---

7   In all likelihood Rauchensteiner means the detachment that von Bünau lists as being from the *Pionier-Ausbildungs-und-Ersatz-Abteilung 80* and probably *86*, too. The only *Panzerjäger* formation in the area was from the *Panzerjäger-Ausbildungs-und-Ersatz-Abteilung 17*.

8   The Austrian resistance members are seen as heroes today, but in 1945 they would have been considered traitors to the government in power, thus the use of that term here.

9   von Bünau, *Combat in Vienna*, p. 29.

10 von Bünau, *Combat in Vienna*, p. 30.

Panzerarmee had become separated from *6. Armee*, although the gap wasn't wide and the Germans were attacking to close it. The hole north of *6. Armee*, however, was huge, a major rupture between that army and *6. SS-Panzerarmee*. And then there was the breakthrough south of Vienna, where Sixth Guards Tank Army sped north toward Tulln, crushing or bypassing any German attempt to stop them. The Russians had long-since learned to reinforce success, and now the only question was which breakthrough to send their reserves into.

Studying the day's dispositions, Tolbukhin must have smelled blood. His wartime record in both world wars was outstanding and he understood how power worked in Stalin's paranoid utopia. Sixth Guards Tank Army was a formation of his Third Ukrainian Front and whatever glory they accumulated would be credited to Tolbukhin as their Front Commander. The army commander, Lieutenant General Andrei Kravchenko, was a skilled and aggressive master of tank warfare. Having twice been awarded Hero of the Soviet Union, now that his armor had broken through the German front Kravchenko pushed them to go for the kill, with his first objective being Tulln and its bridges over the Danube. Seizing those intact would have put his troops into the rear of the German *8. Armee* and unhinged the entire German front.

To that end no less than five corps attacked the breakthrough area, three of them being powerful Guards armored corps. The 5th Guards Tank Corps was the spearhead formation speeding toward the Vienna Woods, along with 9th Guards Mechanized Corps and 1st Guards Mechanized Corps. Three more rifle corps provided depth and flank security, the 20th, 21st and 31st Guards Rifle Corps.

Tolbukhin assumed this would be enough to seize Vienna, move west down the Danube Valley and cross to the north bank into *8. Armee*'s rear. He made this assumption because he expected the *Volkssturm* battalions defending the Vienna Woods to move aside and let his forces into Vienna by the back door. With any luck he could trap *II SS-Panzerkorps* in the city. O-5's plan would shave weeks off his timetable.

6. SS-Panzerarmee
II SS-Panzerkorps
6. Panzer-Division

Echeloned far forward of the rest of *6. SS-Panzerarmee*, *6. Panzer-Division* finally received orders to withdraw to a narrow ridgeline which extended from Enzersdorf an der Fischa to Fischamend. The division still held Hainburg, 22 miles east of their new position, but the powerful Forty-Sixth Army, part of Second Ukrainian Front, was launching relentless assaults. As *6. Panzer-Division* withdrew it blew up the tobacco factory and the road bridge to Altenburg. Overstretched as it was, the division was vulnerable to attack, and during its withdrawal that's exactly what happened. The Russians broke through in several places between Bruck an der Leitha and Petronell, and the Germans were hard pressed to seal these off.

Once the division occupied its new position the men saw the runways of the Vienna airport less than half a mile to the west. Through their binoculars they could see the famous Riesenrad, the giant ferris wheel, towering over the trees in the Prater. At Fischamend their flank rested on the southern bank of the Danube. There is no evidence that Hitler gave his permission for the retreat and it's highly doubtful that Dietrich asked.

Kampfgruppe 3. SS-Panzer-Division Totenkopf

With Russians attacking from north and south, Bruck an der Leitha fell after fighting that lasted most of the night. The loss of the town made *Totenkopf*'s position nearly impossible. No significant geographic features offered a ready-made defensive position short of Vienna, but if *Totenkopf* pulled back too fast then *6. Panzer-Division* would be isolated against the river. To save their Army comrades, then, the only thing the SS men could do was stand fast and spend their blood holding indefensible ground until *6. Panzer-Division* was out of danger. Oberlaa was one such place. Another of the Tigers repaired at the Arsenal ended its war there, near a brick factory.

2. SS-Panzer-Division Das Reich

As the remnants of *3. SS-Panzer-Division Totenkopf* and *6. Panzer-Division* withdrew under pressure toward Vienna, along with what was left of the security detachments of Military Headquarters Vienna that had been in the Schwechat area, this meant the left flank of *2. SS-Panzer-Division Das Reich* was once again threatened. But that was not the division's only problem. On the right flank, Russian forces were probing forward both north and south of the western railway and there were only blocking forces to stop them. On the north side of the railway the Germans were able to stop the advance, but not on the south side, which meant the Russians were advancing into *Das Reich*'s rear. *SS-Standartenführer* Rudolph Lehmann, the division commander, received orders not to retreat another step. With *Totenkopf* unable to anchor *Das Reich*'s left flank and almost nothing to protect its rear, obeying the order was tantamount to suicide.

The reaction to this order of the troops on the spot is hard to say, or what effect the cuff band order might have had on the *Waffen-SS* commander's willingness to obey such obviously suicidal orders. But such commands had been coming from Hitler's headquarters for years by that point, so 'threat fatigue' may have set in, the numbness and complacency that arose when impossible or unreal orders were repeated over and over again, backed by threats to ensure they are obeyed.

Whatever the SS men's actual feelings at the time, the order to stand and fight to the death was moot anyway as *Das Reich* commander Lehmann had no intention of letting his division be trapped by the Russians. The Red Army was rapidly moving north to the Liesing and Schwechat Rivers between Mödling and Schwechat; if they got across the Liesing they would threaten *Das Reich*'s right flank and force the division to retreat yet again.

Alarm units were committed on the north bank of the Liesing River atop the mountain called the Laaer Berg, including some *Flak* units that saw action for the first time and had substantial firepower. These were the combined elements of *24. Flak-Division* guarded by *Alarm-Bataillon 1* from *Luftkriegschule 7* and some police. The Laaer Berg was in the Favoriten District of Vienna and rose almost 700 feet at its highest point. This prominent landmark was a strong defensive position and it was hoped the *Luftwaffe*, alarm and police units deployed there could anchor that flank, but that hope was forlorn.

Das Reich had been forced back more than two miles since the day before, to a ridge running from Vosendorf to Leopoldsdorf. This meant that Mödling had to be abandoned to its fate. But that didn't solve the division's immediate problems. Finding itself in constant danger of being outflanked, that position could not be held for long either and at 8:00 p.m. Lehmann ordered the division to form a new line behind the small Liesing River running from Mauer through Liesing and Inzersdorf,[11] where fighting erupted. This was within the city limits of Vienna itself and a profound shock awaited the SS men from the population: civil unrest and out-and-out opposition.

---

11   General von Bünau's postwar debriefing on the battle has *Das Reich* withdrawing to 'Enzersdorf', which could possibly be Maria Enzersdorf. But to do this *Das Reich* would have had to actually advance and swing west. Instead, this is probably an error and should read 'Inzersdorf', which lines up perfectly with the division's known position earlier in the day. Von Bünau was not Austrian and wasn't intimately familiar with the area.

* * *

One of Joseph Goebbels' complaints about *Gauleiter* Baldur von Schirach was that under his leadership Vienna had never been properly Nazified. The strong communist element that existed before the war had been driven underground, but never stamped out. Now, after years of privation and air raids, the anger and fear that had been simmering there boiled over as the Red Army closed in on the city. Local residents as well as local defense forces argued with the SS men and generally treated them with disrespect and even contempt. This was dangerous behavior. Given the realities of life in the Third Reich these encounters show just how far civilian morale had fallen. The people were not disobeying politicians or bureaucrats, although that would have been dangerous enough. Those were not frumpy *Volkssturm* in mismatched uniforms or Hitler Youth on bicycles, or even Army troops they were standing up to; they were *Waffen-SS* men, members of one of the two most famous divisions in the entire SS pantheon of heroes, built into demigods over the years by Goebbels' powerful propaganda machine. They were desperate men fighting a deadly enemy.

The *Das Reich* veterans had seen plenty of death in their careers: they had killed and seen their friends killed in turn, they had faced death in battle and probable death if captured. They knew very well what would happen to the Viennese once the Russians took over and they were not men who were used to having civilians get in their way. Had they trained their guns on the Viennese under the guise of shooting those who were hampering their ability to fight there would not have been repercussions. Hitler would undoubtedly have approved. For anyone to argue with *Waffen-SS* men about anything shows just how desperate the civil population had become.

* * *

As *Das Reich* pulled back the *Luftwaffe*, alarm and police units on the Laaer Berg panicked and abandoned their strong positions without orders or permission, a heavy blow to the defense. They left their guns behind. The position had bridged the gap between *Das Reich* and *Totenkopf*, anchoring the German center, and the withdrawal further endangered *Das Reich*'s already worrisome left flank. German intelligence indicated a Russian buildup in the area between Kledering and Rothneusiedl, in other words in the area just exposed by the withdrawal from the Laaer Berg, an ominous sign of a Red Army attack in the seam between *Das Reich*'s left flank and *Totenkopf*'s right flank. If the Russians had struck quickly enough and driven their attack forward with sufficient determination, they could have split the German defense and crushed both divisions.

Elements of *Das Reich*'s *Flak* battalion quickly moved into the gap and set up anti-tank positions on the main road leading into Vienna over the mountain. Another railroad embankment provided excellent cover for the guns, which included some 50mm Hungarian *PAK* 38s. Weidling illustrates another problem the combat forces had begun to encounter when they approached Vienna, namely the interference of local military or civil officials protecting their area of responsibility.

Within the Third Reich every level of authority had multiple overlapping layers. This was a fundamental principle of Hitler's that had filtered down to the lowest functionaries, to funnel territorial disputes up to the leader. When the SS men had finished setting up their anti-tank defenses at the Laaer Berg, a Police colonel showed up with his staff and declared that since he outranked the *Das Reich* officers on the spot, he was in charge. Nor was his priority blocking the Russian advance into Vienna. He wanted the SS men to execute a bunch of deserters.

Sixty filthy, disheveled men sat around an outdoor restaurant named the Wiener Garten. Although surly and disrespectful, many wore battlefield decorations and were obviously combat veterans. Seeing a better use for these men than forming them up in front of a firing squad, they were given a choice: join *Das Reich*, fight honorably and take your chances on surviving, or get shot. Not surprisingly they all joined the SS.[12]

Not long after this a company of men dressed in immaculate Army uniforms marched up to the commander of *2./SS-Flak-Abteilung 2*, *SS-Hauptsturmführer* Franz-Josef Dreike, and announced they had been attached to *Das Reich*. Heavily armed with personal weapons and *Panzerfauste*, they could have stepped right out of a parade. These were the candidates and instructors from the *Heer Offizier Schule Wien*, the Army Officer's School Vienna, fully trained and ready to fight. Dreike put them into the line not a moment too soon. Within minutes the Russians launched tank-supported attacks across their entire front.

Many non-SS men were from the *Reicharbeitsdienst*, the RAD, or Reich Labor Service. With no military training their use in battle was quite limited. Without enough crews, Dreike and another officer manned an 88mm gun and opened fire, knocking out Russian tank after Russian tank. All through the day the Russians kept attacking, and kept being repulsed. For his leadership and courage Dreike earned the Knight's Cross.

Further south, Laxenburg changed hands three times with at least 200 dead from both sides, but at the end of the day *Das Reich* still held the town. A counterattack on nearby Vösendorf, which was reinforced by a *Volkssturm* company of men who lived in that town, disintegrated when the Russians turned captured German *werfer* batteries on the attackers. Like their own Katyusha rocket barrages, it took highly disciplined and motivated troops to keep attacking through the devastation caused by a *werfer* salvo. The men of the *Volkssturm* were neither.

The failure to recapture Vösendorf compromised *Das Reich*'s entire defensive front, since the little town lay between and west of Laxenburg and the Laaer Berg. This left a dangerous wedge between the division's two flanks, which made further withdrawal imperative. Lehmann had already disobeyed the *Führerbefehl* once and saw no reason to stand and die now. He gave the order to retreat.

* * *

The good news was that German reinforcements were on the way in the form of the *Führer-Grenadier-Division*, under the command of the young and energetic *Generalmajor* Hellmuth Mäder,[13] but they would not arrive in force for another day or more. This formation had recently been upgraded from a brigade and was favored by Hitler personally, which meant that it had priority in replacement of men and materiel. During the 27 January midday situation conference, General Jodl had given the brigade's strength as "4,227 men in daily strength [and]…60 tanks altogether [including those in for repair]".[14] It had been drastically strengthened in manpower since then.

As for armor, the strength report for 1 April would still have been accurate four days later, since the division had not been in combat during the interim. A few machines in repair may even have been returned to service. It reported nine Mark IVs in total and two operational; 22 Panthers, with seven combat-ready; 15 *Sturmgeschütze IIIs*, of which seven were ready to fight; 19 *Sturmgeschütze IVs*, and 18 of those operational; but no *Flak* panzers and only six heavy *Flak* guns, probably 88mm. Nevertheless, 34 combat-ready Panzers gave it a punch the other armored divisions had lost.

---

12   Weidinger, *Das Reich V*, p. 369.
13   Mäder was very well thought of by both Hitler and Goebbels, and was awarded the Knight's Cross with Oak Leaves and Swords, being awarded the Swords on 18 April 1945.
14   Heiber, Helmut & Glantz, David M., *Hitler and His Generals: Military Conferences 1942-1945* (New York: Enigma, 2004), p. 641.

1. SS-Panzerkorps
Kampfgruppe 12. SS-Panzer-Division Hitlerjugend

On the division's right flank, *Kampfgruppe SS-Panzergrenadier-Regiment 25* held Sankt Veit with the help of a few panzers against ever more violent Russian attacks. On the left flank, however, the *Kampfgruppe SS-Panzergrenadier-Regiment 26* was outflanked around the Haidlhof near Bad Vöslau. The Russians pushed on through the woods to the southwest toward Pottenstein, one mile northwest of Berndorf. If Pottenstein fell, then both *Panzergrenadier* divisions would be nearly cut off.

Division commander *SS-Obersturmbannführer* Hugo Kraas was fast running out of men to plug the holes in his lines. He ordered *SS-Kampfgruppe Taubert* to Pottenstein with orders to throw the Russians back. This unit was essentially *SS-Panzer-Pioneer-Bataillon 12* with some attached artillery, *Flak* and armored vehicles, probably *Jagdpanzers*. Taubert's command did its job and cleared the woods around Pottenstein of the Russian advance units, and then moved to defend the town.

Several new *Kampfgruppe* were formed from troops combed out of the supply, *Flak*, artillery and medical companies. The previously constituted *SS-Kampfgruppe Möbius* was reinforced by ambulance drivers with no vehicles to drive.

The overall situation in the sector of *Hitlerjugend* had worsened during the day. *Das Reich* had been flanked on the right and bent back to protect the approaches to Vienna, leaving only a few scattered units to try and stop 5th Guards Tank Corps' juggernaut attack south of Vienna. Worse, the far left flank of *I.SS-Panzerkorps* was held by *SS-Panzeraufklärungs-Abteilung 12* at Alland, but between that battalion and the rest of the division there were only pickets to warn of attacks. Against any determined Russian advance they could offer no resistance. With no reserves to throw in, Sepp Dietrich approved a redeployment of *Hitlerjugend* to a new defense sector further to the west.[15]

Kriegsschule Wiener Neustadt Fahnenjunker-Bataillon

The battalion once again tried to connect its right flank with the German defenders of Dreistetten. It wasn't until 8:00 p.m., however, that an actual main line of resistance was established along the Marchgrabens stream and through the forest and mountains. The commander of the officer cadets was wounded while mapping out the battalion's defensive positions. The units in this area lined up as following, starting southwest of Wöllersdorf and stretching to Dreistetten: *2./Kriegsschule Wiener Neustadt Fahnenjunker-Bataillon*, combined with some SS men, then the *1./Kriegsschule Wiener Neustadt Fahnenjunker-Bataillon*, *SS-Kampfgruppe Vogler*, which was essentially the *10.Flak-Kompanie/SS-Panzer Regiment 1*, and *3./ Kriegsschule Wiener Neustadt Fahnenjunker-Bataillon*. The force was renamed *Kampfgruppe Koch* after its previous commander, *Hauptmann* Widmer, was wounded.[16]

Kampfgruppe 1. SS-Panzer-Division Leibstandarte Adolf Hitler

Moving *Hitlerjugend* north meant the *LAH* would have to broaden their front without any additional troops. This was taking a serious risk, since the defense had already been reduced to mutually

---

15   Meyer, *The 12th SS*, pp. 468-469.
16   Brettner, *Die Letzten Kämpfe Band I*, pp. 164-165.

supporting strong points. Stretching it further risked infiltrators getting through and destroying the division piecemeal but it couldn't be helped. To cover this change the division's northern battle group had to move south from Oberpiesting to Berndorf, taking the route over the 1,700 feet-high Buchreigel, a forested mountain. This group consisted of men from the *SS-Panzergrenadier-Regiment 1, SS-Panzer Regiment 1, SS-Flak-Abteilung 1* and some artillery. Once in Berndorf they learned of a Russian move on Pottenstein and some of the men kept going to that town. They got there just as attacks came in from the north and the west and managed to stop them all, because if Pottenstein fell the Russians would be in the *LAH*'s rear.

Savage fighting around Pottenstein and Weissenbach an der Triesting went on for days and typified what would happen during the rest of the month. The German defenders gathered in groups to defend the roads, as armored cross-country attacks were impractical because tanks couldn't traverse the rugged mountain slopes. The remaining Panzer Mark IVs would hide behind a bend in the road until Russian attacks appeared and would then destroy them, blocking the road. Generally the country to either side couldn't support vehicles, so Russian infantry would have to attack and clear the Germans, who would then retreat to the next blocking point.

No sooner had the division command post redeployed to Pottenstein than Russian artillery fire raked their positions. The division security had to immediately attack a hill where the Russians had their observation posts, with heavy casualties to the Germans. Back-and-forth fighting eventually forced the defenders to retreat to Weiseenbach, after having first mined the roads and blown the bridges.[17]

One of the division's medical officers, *SS-Hauptsturmführer* Dr Knoll, related this anecdote about the chaos on 5 April:

> Regimental first aid station in Berndorf. Shortly thereafter Pottenstein fell under fire. Drove back like targets on a practice range. Treated new people. Redeployed to the rear. Under fire. Drove to the convoy, redeployment. Ambulance ran into a tree. Evening in Weissenbach.[18]

SS-Kampfgruppe Keitel

After their gains of the day before the Russians paused in their drive westward and began to shift forces to the north, where the unexpected breakthrough south of Vienna held the promise of becoming a deadly stroke. On the northern shoulder of the gap between *6. SS-Panzerarmee* and *III Panzerkorps* of *6. Armee*, weak Russian attacks and infiltrations were pushed back by *SS-Kampfgruppe Keitel*.

6. Armee
III Panzerkorps

Beginning on 5 April, the two battalions of *SS-Brigade Ney* that were attached to *III Panzerkorps*, the *III. Abteilung* and *IV. Abteilung*, were subordinated to *Kampfgruppe 1. Panzer-Division* for use in the area near Pöllau and Lafnitztal. With most infantry formations badly depleted by this point the additional two battalions were vital for defense, especially against infiltrators, in the broken country of the Alpine foothills. The brigade's *I. Abteilung*, part of *SS-Kampfgruppe Schweitzer*,

17   Tiemann, *The Leibstandarte IV/2*, pp. 286-287.
18   Tiemann, *The Liebstandarte IV/2*, p. 287.

would soon be absorbed into the larger *Kampfgruppe Semmering* near Friedberg, Austria, approximately 25 miles south-southwest of Wiener Neustadt.

SS-Kampfgruppe Schweitzer

The price for not having reserves to throw into the gap north of *6. Armee* finally had to be paid on 5 April. At 8:00 a.m., elements of the Russian Twenty-Sixth Army launched a massive attack south of Rechnitz against only weak and scattered defense. To their south they could see the flashes of Russian artillery pounding the positions of *Kampfgruppe Semmering* and *1. Volks-Gebirgs-Division*. The men of *SS-Kampfgruppe Schweitzer* could only listen and watch as the Russians filtered in west of the town, cutting them off.

Kampfgruppe Semmering

At this point *Kampfgruppe Semmering* had been reinforced by not only the battalion from *SS-Brigade Ney*, but also *Pionier-Bau-Abteilung 504*, Engineer Construction Battalion 504, the Panther Battalion from *Panzer-Regiment 24*[19] and *Sturmgeschütz-Brigade 303*.

As men continued reinforcing *Kampfgruppe Semmering*, higher-ranking officers came with them. One of those men was *Generalmajor* Josef Punzert, former commanding officer of the *4. Flak-Division* and winner of the German Cross in gold. As a native of Styria, Punzert was defending his own home in Voitsberg, a few miles west of Graz. Punzert had joined the Austrian Army in the First World War and fought through that war as an artillery officer, continuing to specialize in artillery throughout his career. On 5 April *General der Gebirgstruppe* Ringel gave him command of a *Kampfgruppe* to retake the dairy and laundry of the Südbahnhof Hotel, located at the golf course. It is illustrative of the desperation of those final weeks of combat that a *Generalmajor* led a battalion-sized battle group in a tactical assault.

It also shows that this time the Germans were determined to capture the dairy and secure the southern side of the pass. To help ensure success, they were willing to commit some of their precious few heavy weapons. One 75mm *PAK-40* and two 20mm *Flak* cannon were allocated, along with some mortars and machine guns. The 20mm cannon had proven extremely effective against dug-in infantry in the past, but the consideration now wasn't losing them in combat so much as it was expending precious ammunition. The troops in the attack would again be a mixture of SS men, NCO candidates, *Volkssturm* and *Gebirgsjägers*, but in much greater numbers than before. After meticulous planning the attack was launched and this time it succeeded in driving the Russians out of the dairy and the laundry, and back across the valley. Losses were lighter than expected.

But the Germans weren't satisfied with merely recapturing those places. As long as the Russians held the north side of the pass the German defense would be shaky, so they immediately pursued the defenders, who retreated in the direction of Breitenstein, to the northeast. Russians turned and fought from behind large boulders and thick trees. Bitter fighting took place at every house and barn in the area, destroying every structure. The Germans had already learned that if they gave the Russians any breathing room they would immediately dig in and then have to be rooted out. So they continued the attack until the Russians were driven back.

---

19   By this point *I. Abteilung* of *Panzer-Regiment 24* was effectively an independent unit with no parent division.

At the Pertl-Hof farm the family cowered in their cider cellar as fighting swept over their homestead. Not one structure survived the combat. This time the losses on both sides were staggering. One German company was reduced to 20 men after starting with 120.

* * *

Three miles south of the town of Semmering was the peak named the Fröschnitz, and the Fröschnitz *Sattel*, a pass that ran from Lower Austria past the peak itself and into Styria. If the Russians penetrated the German defenses there, they could then turn north and attack the Semmering Pass either from the south or even the southwest, outflanking the defenders. To stop that, *Oberst* Raithel ordered every possible unit to form a defensive line there.

* * *

South of Frösnitz was the Harterkogel, a peak east of the Kleiner Pfaff on the southern flank of *Kampfgruppe Semmering*, where a battalion from one of Austria's most beloved divisions launched costly attacks to stop a Russian breakthrough attempt. This was the z.b.v.[20] *Grenadier-Ausbildungs-und-Ersatz-Bataillon 44 Hoch und Deutschmeister*. The remnants of the battalion's parent division, *Reichsgrenadier-Division 44 Hoch und Deutschmeister*, which was fighting in both the *Wienvertiel* and Carinthia, could trace its beginnings back to 1696. After suffering horrific losses on the Eastern and Italian Fronts in the First World War, the regiment from which it sprang was disbanded until 1933, when it once again came to life.

After the *Anschluss* it became part of *44. Infanterie-Division*, which was totally destroyed at Stalingrad. Rebuilt in 1943, Hitler personally gave it the honorary title of *Reichs-Grenadier-Division*, along with its old regimental name. Because of its stellar combat record, in 1944 the division was allowed to wear a small, sky-blue enamel Maltese cross trimmed in gold, the old symbol of the regiment. Further, in early 1945 *Grenadier-Regiment 134*, which had been the number for the original Austrian cadre after the *Anschluss*, was given the privilege of wearing a cuff band with the *Hoch und Deutschmeister* name.

By April 1945 there wasn't much left of the division itself. Having been one of the assault divisions in *Unternehmen Frühlingserwachen*, Operation Spring Awakening, it not only suffered heavy casualties then, but also lost heavily in the retreat across western Hungary. Parts of the division were fighting in three different armies.

Although some of the division was also attached to *8. Armee*, and desperately needed more men, on 5 April the *5./Grenadier-Ausbildungs-und-Ersatz-Bataillon 44* found itself near the border of Lower Austria and Styria, attacking south of the Semmering Pass, and losing even more men while temporarily stopping a Russian advance. One of those killed was the company commander.

Sperrverband Motschmann, or *SS-Polizei-Regiment 13*

A key town in *III Panzerkorps'* area was Vorau, about seven miles west-southwest of Pinggau. Like countless other small Austrian towns it grew up around the Catholic Church, but the jewel of Vorau was the 12th-Century Monastery and its magnificent library. Vorau dominated a wide valley with roads leading off in all directions. It lay in the area between *Sperrverband Motschmann* and *Divisionsgruppe Krause*. It lay northwest of Krause's main line of defense around

---

20   *zur besonderer Verwendung*, commonly abbreviated as z.b.v. This designated a special purpose unit, or one with a special assignment.

Oberwart and points south, making its loss the dangerous threat to his flank that Krause had feared would come.

The fate of Vorau mirrored scores of other similar towns and villages. Some were luckier than others because there was little or no fighting to destroy the people's homes. Others weren't so fortunate. The inhabitants of Vorau began fleeing on Easter Sunday when it became obvious that the Russians couldn't be stopped. Like refugees in every war in every place and every time, they packed up whatever they could carry that was vital for survival, piled it onto whatever wagon or, in the case of the local Nazis, whatever vehicle they possessed, and plodded away from the only life they had ever known.

Refugees from Pinkafeld moved through the little town and clogged the roads leading west to Waldbach. Among the civilians were broken Hungarian military units who had no intention of turning to fight. On 5 April the last of the local Nazis pulled out with the Russians expected soon. The local hospital staff was dismissed and 22 sick and wounded patients were moved into the cellar for safety.

The town of Stegersbach was a crossroads for one of the main roads leading west. Situated a few miles east of the boundary with Styria in Burgenland, between Rohr im Burgenland and Ollersdorf im Burgenland, the populace watched as a large force of German armor, including both Tiger models, Panthers, Mark IVs, *Sturmgeschütze* and SPWs, withdrew through the town. Instead of lending a powerful image, however, the mass of vehicles appeared more bedraggled than fierce. Most had battle damage and none were fully operational. Horse-drawn columns trudged along in their wake.[21]

Divisionsgruppe Krause

The previous day's fighting had left Krause's unit exhausted but still in possession of Oberwart. He intended to hold as long as humanly possible to protect the center of *III Panzerkorps*, and the left flank of *1. Volks-Grenadier-Division*. But the Russians were equally determined to seize it quickly, and to do that brought up the 30th Rifle Corps to shove the Germans out.

In bitter fighting they did just that. What few reserves Krause had, or that *General der Panzertruppe* Hermann Breith at *III Panzerkorps* could give him, were committed to the defense of Grosspetersdorf. When 30th Rifle Corps broke through it took Oberwart with ease. Only with the Russians in sight did the last civilians flee the town.[22] Despite the ad-hoc nature of his command, and the stinging defeat handed it by 30th Rifle Corps, Krause managed to hold his *divisionsgruppe* together to establish a line of resistance between Oberwart and Markt Allhau, around Buchshachen.

1. Volks-Gebirgs-Division

On the division's left flank *Gebirgsjäger-Regiment 99* tried to hold its ground in the area between Grosspetersdorf and Oberwart against three Russian rifle divisions. The Russian advance blocked it from getting into the unoccupied sections of the *Reichsschutzstellung* in its area. *Aufklärungs-Abteilung 54* held its ground long enough, despite constant heavy attacks, to give the rest of the division a chance to pull back.

21 Brettner, *Pinka*, p. 116.
22 Brettner, *Die Letzten Kämpfe Band I*, p. 25.

Driven backward and stretched too thin, higher headquarters decided to shorten their front responsibility to allow a denser concentration of men in the front lines. This had no practical effect, however, as what the division needed were more men with guns, not empty gestures.[23]

2. Panzerarmee

The Russians kept up the pressure on *2. Panzerarmee's* left wing north of Radkersburg, which led to a series of attacks and counterattacks. At the end of the day General de Angelis's army sealed off any penetrations. Direct attacks on its main positions were pre-empted by the Germans' abandonment of all positions east of the Mur River, but the biggest danger seemed to come on its right flank where the Bulgarian First Army had three divisions south of the Mur. Yugoslav forces represented an ongoing threat to the rear echelon and supply lines. There was even a roving band of 200-300 deserters raiding farms to the west, and who wouldn't hesitate to rob the army's supply lines if they weren't well guarded.

All in all, however, the threat to the extreme right of *Heeresgruppe Süd* had lessened as the Russians began drawing off mobile forces for the breakthrough around Vienna.

23. Panzer-Division

As the Russians closed in on the Mur River from the north, the division redeployed its armored elements to the area east of Ljutomer, including *Panzer-Artillerie-Regiment 128* and *Heeres-Flak-Abteilung 278*. The only combat was light harassing mortar fire on the German trenches. Later in the day the infantry followed the vehicles and by nightfall they had rejoined the rest of the division. Once the division was whole again, it was resupplied and had a chance to sleep one night away from the front.

London

The Prime Minister of Britain should have been exultant as the Allied armies swept over the Third Reich, but Winston Churchill was incensed and worried. The war was obviously winding down toward an Allied victory, with the only questions being when it would end and how much more blood would be spilled before the fighting stopped. Churchill, however, had long since begun worrying about the postwar world and the containment of expansionist communism. Seeing Nazism as the greater evil that made an alliance with Soviet Russia palatable, he had nevertheless recognized that Britain had made common cause with a very dangerous potential enemy. Alone among the Allied leaders, Churchill recognized Stalin's insatiable appetite for power, which is why he ordered contingency planning for war with Russian that was code-named Operation *Unthinkable*.

With Yalta only six weeks behind them, Stalin was already breaking promises and Churchill could only wonder which ones could be next.[24] It was in this spirit of doubt and worry that he wrote Franklin Roosevelt one of the last letters he would ever compose to the soon-to-be-dead president, and one of his biggest worries was about the Red Army overrunning all of Austria:

---

23   Brettner, *Die Letzten Kämpfe Band I*, p. 36.
24   By this point free elections in Poland were looking less and less likely.

I may remind you that we proposed and thought we had arranged six weeks ago provisional zones of occupation in Austria, but that since Yalta the Russians have sent no confirmation of these zones. Now that they are on the eve of taking Vienna and very likely will occupy the whole of Austria it may well be prudent for us to hold as much as possible in the north.[25]

Clearly, Churchill's insight into Stalin's mind led to fear the Soviet leader would renege on his promise that Austria would be handed back to the Western powers if the Russians captured all or even most of the country. Of particular interest was Eisenhower's obsession, the area known as the National Redoubt, being the easily defensible Alpine regions in the west and southwest. Even if Stalin eventually did hand those areas over to the Western Allies they could be used as very valuable bargaining chips to gain concessions elsewhere. In a world far removed from that of the hungry, muddy foot soldiers fighting and dying in the grimy trenches, the game of Grand Strategy was afoot as the war came to a close.

Seizing areas in the Soviet zone of occupation would allow Churchill to have his own chips to force Stalin to turn over Austria, if the need arose, in exchange for whatever territories the western allies had captured, such as Berlin. It's why Churchill had been so incensed when General Dwight Eisenhower intruded on the high stakes poker game played by the Big Three, when he revealed the cards held by the Western Allies.

---

25   Churchill, Winston S., *Triumph and Tragedy* (Boston: Houghton Mifflin, 1953), p. 512.

6

Friday, 6 April

Heeresgruppe Süd

The end had come for *General der Infanterie* Otto Wöhler as commander of *Heeresgruppe Süd*. *Generaloberst* Lothar Rendulic officially received orders on 6 April to take over the army group and save Vienna or, if that couldn't be done, keep the Russian out of the Alps and the Danube Valley. It's unclear if American intelligence picked up on these orders, but if so it would have underlined their belief in the National Redoubt.

Rendulic inquired of the *Führer*'s headquarters how they envisaged the further course of the war, both in the immediate future and how it would end. He was told that politics would be used, and essentially that it was none of his business. Once he arrived to take over he discovered that the rail network was in terrible condition, much worse than he'd thought. Reinforcing *I SS-Panzerkorps*, the most critically threatened sector, could only be done at Tempo 1.[1] Nor could major formations move positions because of the fuel situation. His army was nearly paralyzed.

When judging Wöhler's performance as commander of *Heeresgruppe Süd*, his failings, chiefly a silent acquiescence to the denigration of the *Waffen-SS* units and officers under this command, which undermined morale and cooperation, materially contributed to the army group's recent failures. In particular there was a period where Hermann Balck refused to give up part of *1. SS-Panzer-Division Leibstandarte Adolf Hitler*, which had been attached to *6. Armee*, despite Wöhler's repeated direct orders to do so. Wöhler let Balck get away with ignoring his repeated orders, but then backed Balck when he asked Hitler how he, Balck, could be held liable for the retreat across Hungary when even the *LAH* couldn't stop the Russians, even though it was Balck and Wöhler who deprived the SS division of its reconnaissance battalion. Such prevarications and playing favorites created unnecessary friction in an emergency situation where tension already ran high.

On the other hand, Wöhler tried unsuccessfully to get *Unternehmen Frühlingserwachen* cancelled and did everything possible to support the offensive. Nor was the disintegration of Third Hungarian Army his fault and during the retreat across Hungary not one major German formation was cut off and destroyed. Considering the shattered state of the formations, and the helter-skelter nature of the retreat, that was a remarkable feat and as the overall commander Wöhler deserves part of the praise. If it's fair to blame Wöhler for things that went wrong, it's also fair to credit him for things that went right.

Wöhler was a competent general in the classic mode of German generals. He wasn't flashy, or a tactical genius or a visionary. He was a steady hand given an impossible mission who did the best he could with what he was given to fight with.

* * *

---

1   Tempo was the German measure of how fast a unit could move. Tempo 1 meant one train in a 24 hour period. Since a panzer division could require 80 trains to move, at Tempo 1 it would take 80 days for it to move.

The weather continued to aid the Russians, with clear skies and a high of around 57; more bad news for *Heeresgruppe Süd*. By 6 April the situation in Austria had deteriorated badly for the Germans: *8 Armee* barely had ground contact with *6. SS-Panzerarmee* and the most direct connection was about to be severed by the Russians pouring northwest through the Vienna Woods. Simultaneously the enemy was advancing on both banks of the Danube.

To all intents and purposes 6. *SS-Panzerarmee* was cut in two when *II SS-Panzerkorps* became entangled in the defense of Vienna, and now it was threatened with being surrounded, while *I SS-Panzerkorps* deployed only weak units to defend a long front. The army itself couldn't close a 30-mile gap between it and *6. Armee* on its right flank.

In its turn *6. Armee* had gaps on both flanks, and dangerous penetrations all up and down its front. A major Russian attack was underway against the weak left flank, and if the Russians broke through and widened the gap Balck's command would be in serious danger of being cut to pieces. Only the terrain and rapid mobilization of Styria had so far prevented disaster.

And finally *2. Panzerarmee* only had connections to the army group because the deep rear areas hadn't yet been overrun. Along the front its left flank was open and contact with *Heeresgruppe E* was tenuous.

* * *

With Germany literally scraping the bottom of the manpower barrel yet another trained unit not fighting was *Sturmpanzer-Abteilung 219*. The battalion had been formed from the disbanded *Sturmgeschütz-Brigade 237* and a company from *Sturmpanzer-Abteilung 216*. Regarding the latter unit, the intent had been for those specialized *Sturmpanzer* battalions to be equipped with the *Brummbär*, which mounted a 150mm infantry support gun in a boxy superstructure mounted on a Panzer IV chassis. By concentrating these in battalions the Germans could provide massive mobile firepower in support of infantry, either in attack or defense.

But there were never enough *Brummbärs* to go around. After being transferred to Hungary during the *Konrad* operations in January, the battalion wound up in Slovakia for reorganization while waiting for vehicles. On 6 April *Heeresgruppe Süd* reported that the battalion was in the process of becoming operational using 30 captured tanks, *Beutepanzers*, mostly T-34s. However, that process ended shortly thereafter because of a lack of ammunition for the foreign guns. It was then suggested the battalion be disbanded so the crews could be used as infantry, but that didn't happen either. So for the time being the crews without machines had nothing to do except eat, sleep and stay out of the way people who might shoot at them.

* * *

An overall survey of the combatants' deployments is possible for 6 April and might be useful to understand the scope of the campaign as well as the sheer number of units involved. The reader should keep in mind that Russian nomenclature differed from German and the strengths for various units types also differed. As a reminder a Russian army was the equivalent of a German corps, a Russian corps like a German division and so forth.

Likewise there were differences in how the two sides integrated replacements into existing units. Until late in the war, German divisions received replacements from depots and distributed them to whatever sub-formations needed them. Many divisions even had dedicated replacement battalions to prepare new members for service in the parent formation. This system is seen in this narrative by the various Replacement and Training battalions forced into the fighting.

A *Volks-Grenadier* division in 1945 had an authorized strength of about 10,300 men. Army policy called for replacements to join the division at the front, to keep it as close to full strength as possible. Divisions that had been badly depleted would then be withdrawn to integrate replacements and rest. By April 1945 this policy was impractical in most circumstances. As the story of

Heeresgruppe Süd makes clear, there weren't enough units to maintain the front as it was, much less to fill in while an exhausted unit was rested and rebuilt.

The Red Army, on the other hand, waited until a unit was almost destroyed before rebuilding it with replacements. A 1945 Russian rifle division was authorized to have approximately 9,300 men. Of those about 7,400 were in the rifle regiments. That division might be left in the field until its ration strength dwindled to 2,000 men or less before being withdrawn to accept replacements. The Russians gave these ruined formations no special designation, while the Germans referred to them with the nebulous title of *Kampfgruppe*.

North of the Danube

8. Armee

General der Gebirgstruppe Hans Kreysing won the Knight's Cross with Oak Leaves for actions under fire in Russia, so his personal bravery was never in question. That made no difference to the desperate situation facing his army, however. With all of his inadequate forces deployed forward to slow down the Russian juggernaut, he had nothing to blunt the threat to *8. Armee*'s rear areas by the Third Ukrainian Front's drive on Tulln. Desperate for any help he could get, he at least knew that the *25. Panzer-Division* was in transit.

In army reserve were the some of the survivors of the *44. Infanterie-Division Hoch und Deutschmeister*, the pride of Austria. The shreds of the division were split up during the retreat across Hungary, and part of it wound up with *8. Armee*. It was so ruined that some orders of battle that have survived from this period don't even list it, but sources also place it as part of three different armies during April. There is no evidence that it even had a general in command anymore, after *Generalleutnant* Hans Günther von Rost was killed in action on 23 March 1945. One researcher speculates that Rendulic listed it when interviewed after the war out of sentimentality, since he was Austrian.[2]

XXIX Armeekorps

On its far left flank *8. Armee* deployments from north to south found *XXIX Armeekorps* echeloned dangerously far forward to the east, where *Jäger-Regiment 28* of *8. Jäger-Division*[3] and *153. Grenadier-Division* stood in the area of Trenčín 80 miles northeast of Bratislava. With the desperate fuel situation it was an open question whether these units could fall back fast enough to avoid encirclement, if it came to that.

The army opposing them was the Russian Fifty-Third Army, commanded by Colonel General Ivan Managarov, the easternmost army of Second Ukrainian Front. It contained two corps. Facing *XXIX Armeekorps* was 57th Rifle Corps with the 6th and 227th Rifle Divisions, and the elite 1st Guards Air Landing Division.

---

2   Newton, Steven H., *German Battle Tactics on the Russian Front 1941-1945* (Atglen: Schiffer, 1994), p. 250.
3   The rest of *8. Jäger-Division* was attached to *Heeresgruppe Mitte*.

LXXII Armeekorps

The corps' most powerful unit was the *Kampfgruppe 271. Infanterie-Division* with three attached *Volkssturm* battalions, in the vicinity west of Trenčín. The division suffered terrible casualties in the fighting to come. On their right flank was the badly depleted *Kampfgruppe 182. Reserve-Division*, which suffered heavy casualties early in 1945.

In the lines opposite *LXXII Armeekorps* was the other corps of the Russian Fifty-Third Army, 49th Rifle Corps, which commanded 110th Guards and 203rd Rifle Divisions in the front lines, and the 1st Rumanian Volunteer Division 'Tudor Vladimirescu' in reserve.

Panzerkorps Feldherrnhalle

On the corps' left was *Panzer-Division Feldherrnhalle 1*, probably about as strong as its twin division listed below; in other words, about the size of a reinforced regiment. Next was *46. Volksgrenadier-Division*. Its last reports in late March gave it a total of 4,600 men, 25 88mm guns and eight *Sturmgeschützen* and it was the only division not officially listed as a *Kampfgruppe. Kampfgruppe 711. Infanterie-Division* was a veteran division that opposed the D-Day landings but was never intended for front-line use. Next in line was the renamed *13. Panzer-Division*, now called *Panzer-Division Feldherrnhalle 2,* totaling 2,861 men and 30 panzers in late March. Then came the strong but ineffective *357. Infanterie-Division*, which in late March had just over 6,000 men, 10 88mm guns and 12 *Sturmgeschützen*. This was a large total for that point in the war, but Lothar Rendulic gave it his lowest combat rating, which means it must have been poorly led, had bad morale and/ or was filled with untrained men. The division had only been in existence since March of the previous year, and had begun to disintegrate by this point under the pressure of three weeks of heavy combat.

Facing *Panzerkorps Feldherrnhalle* was a unique formation in the Red Army, 1st Guards Cavalry Group, aka Group Pliyev. This army-level group's commander, Issa Pliyev, had proven to be a master of cavalry warfare and went on to command a major formation in the Russian war against Japan. Against *8. Armee* he commanded IV and VI Guards Cavalry Corps, each with two Guards cavalry divisions and one regular cavalry division, three tank regiments and one self-propelled artillery regiment.

In Front reserve at Trnava was the powerful IV Guards Mechanized Corps, with three Guards mechanized brigades, one Guards tank brigade, three Guards tank regiments, one Guards self-propelled artillery regiment and two regular army self-propelled artillery regiments.

Deutsche Befehlshaber Slowakie

This position was essentially a liaison between the German High Command and what remained of the Slovakian military. The commander of this amorphous headquarters was Knight's Cross winner *General der Panzertruppe* Alfred Ritter von Hubicki. Although Hubicki is reported to have retired on 31 March 1945, the headquarters still shows up on tactical maps. Chances are these were remnant Slovakian forces with nowhere else to go who stayed with the headquarters even after the commander left, and headquarters personnel assigned to the command. Later it disappeared and was probably absorbed by *8. Armee*.

Third Hungarian Army

Although Hungary had been totally overrun by now, Hungarians who had attached their destiny to that of the Germans could either take to the hills and become bandits, or stay with remnants formations like Third Hungarian Army. Officially this army, which likely had fewer troops than a division, commanded the 9th and 23rd Reserve Hungarian Divisions. Their combat value was as low as it was possible to get.

XXXXIII Armeekorps

The final corps in *8. Armee* had few resources but the biggest responsibility, namely keeping the Russians from capturing the north bank of the Danube opposite Vienna before *II SS-Panzerkorps* could withdraw that way to safety. The corps' left-most unit was *Kampfgruppe 211. Volksgrenadier-Division*, with elements of *Panzer-Division Feldherrnhalle 2* attached. *Kampfgruppe 211. Volksgrenadier-Division,* had an approximate strength of 4,229 men of all ranks, 11 heavy anti-tank guns and seven *Sturmgeschütze*.

It was followed on the south by *126. Grenadier-Regiment*, of *48. Volksgrenadier-Division*. Like the *44. Infanterie-Division Hoch und Deutschmeister*, this division had been destroyed and rebuilt three times. Beside *Grenadier-Regiment 126* the rest of it was still reforming at Dollersheim, 65 miles northwest of Vienna.

Next in line came *Kampfgruppe 101. Volksgrenadier-Division* near Gänserndorf. The division's *Jäger-Regiment 228* hadn't arrived yet, and the division is another unit that doesn't appear on all tactical maps or orders of battle. It may have only been a regimental *Kampfgruppe* by this time, but on 6 April elements of *Jäger-Regiment 229* were definitely surprised by a Russian crossing of the Morava during the night, using a pontoon bridge, between Angern an der March and Mannersdorf on der March. Also in the area near Angern, guarding the river bridge there, was *II./ Grenadier-Regiment 284*, of *96. Infanterie-Division*. The Russians bypassed the Germans and cut the railway, and the units available for a German counterattack weren't strong enough to even try.

South of there, and holding the critical front on the direct route to Stockerau, was the remainder of *96. Infanterie-Division*, which had only crossed the Morava the day before, and that division was reinforced by *Panzer-Grenadier-Brigade 92*. The division happened to be in the crucial position of the entire front, not just because it blocked the shortest way to northern Vienna, but also because it had to fight on two fronts. To survive, it fought during the day but retreated to new positions during the night. In that way the commander hoped to save his division, but it also wore them out. They couldn't keep it up for long.

Although both were depleted by this point they represented the best units the corps had. Some sources mistakenly place the *97. Jäger-Division* in *XXXXIII Armeekorps*, but that division served in *1. Panzerarmee* in *Heeresgruppe Mitte* during all of 1945. Along the Danube was the 27th Hungarian Light Division with four battalions of *Volkssturm* and *Machinengewehr-Bataillone 117* and *118*. Although one of its two cavalry regiments was off fighting elsewhere as *SS-Kampfgruppe Keitel,* its other regiment, *SS-Kampfgruppe Ameiser*, had temporarily rejoined its parent division[4] and *37. SS-Freiwilligen-Kavallerie-Division Lützow* was in the line near *96. Infanterie-Division*.

Hammering at *XXXXIII Armeekorps* were, from north to south, 27th Guards Rifle Corps, 25th Guards Rifle Corps, 24th Guards Rifle Corps, 20th Guards Rifle Corps, 68th Rifle Corps, 2nd

---

4   Even while serving as part of its parent division, however, it was still referred to as *SS-Kampfgruppe Ameiser*, not as *SS-Kavallerie-Regiment 92*.

Guards Mechanized Corps, 18th Guards Rifle Corps and 23rd Tank Corps. This concentration of striking power made Russian intentions to clear the north side of the Danube Valley crystal clear.

* * *

Still thinking of counterattacks that could reverse the war situation, Hitler ordered *8. Armee* to defend the oil fields at Zistersdorf to the last. This was directly in the area of responsibility for *Kampfgruppe 211. Volksgrenadier-Division*. The fields were the final source of natural oil left under German control, although production had been shut down earlier as the Red Army approached. Isolated in the *Führerbunker* as he was, Hitler still had plans for them and knew to the barrel how much oil they could produce.

* * *

When *6. Panzer-Division* withdrew from Hainburg the previous day it left a long stretch of the Danube's southern bank in Russian hands, while *8. Armee* occupied the northern bank. This was tantamount to exposing a new flank to enemy attack and that's exactly what happened.

The Russian Danube flotilla ferried small forces to the north bank while others attacked in the area of Marchegg. The defending German corps in the area, *XXXXIII Armeekorps*, mustered enough forces to stop the attacks and seal off any breakthroughs. As testament to the ferocity of the combat, the cemetery at Hainburg contains the graves of 188 Russians who died in the fighting.

Kampfgruppe Volkmann

With alarms going out to all commands along the Danube that Russian armored forces were approaching, control of the Tulln bridge took on great importance and Russian tanks were reported at Sieghartskirchen, a mere five miles south of Tulln. Aside from threatening the chemical plants at Moorsbierbaum, the rampaging Russian spearheads also moved within striking range of the bridge over the Danube at Tulln. The defense of the bridge fell to the commander of the local *Luftwaffe* airfield and training school, *Generalmajor* Volkmann, who was named Battle Commander for the Tulln area.

Luftwaffe Luftkriegschule 7, Air War School 7, had been established at Tulln airfield in 1942 as a basic training facility for pilots. Under the command of the stern *Luftwaffe Generalmajor* Volkmann the base flourished and was considered a great success. Approximately 2,000 men were stationed there, with at least 60 officers and 120 flying cadets. The *Luftwaffe* classified the training aircraft types as light, such as double-wing Arado-66s and single-wing Focke-Wulf FW-140s. Multi-engine trainers were also on hand, like Junkers JU-52s and Heinkel HE-111s. Once cadets passed their courses at *Luftkriegschule 7* they moved on to more advanced schools elsewhere.

As part of their initial course, new recruits received infantry training at the Slovakian facility at Malacky, in the Little Carpathian Mountains north of Bratislava. The final exam involved storming up a steep, heavily wooded mountain about 2,300 feet high named the Kapellenberg, and doing so multiple times per day.[5] This no doubt helped in the fighting to come.

In 1944 and 1945 American fighters and bombers hit the airfield many times causing widespread destruction. German fighters based there often tangled with the raiders, with losses on both sides.

---

5   Prigl, 'Die Geschichte des Fliegerhorstes Langenlebarn', <http://www.gotech.at/lale3/langenlebarn_3.html>, (Accessed 07 August 2018).

On 31 March 1945 *Luftkriegschule 7* was dissolved and *Generalmajor* Volkmann named as *Kampfkommandant* of Tulln. The alarm battalions formed from the *Kriegschule* staff have already been mentioned, but the exact composition of the rest of his *Kampfgruppe* is unknown. The airfield had been heavily reinforced with anti-aircraft guns and at least some of them should have been mobile, even if only by towing, so he likely had good fire support. German 20mm and 37mm guns had proven deadly against ground targets, and the 88mm gun was the best anti-tank weapon in the *Wehrmacht* inventory. Along with the airfield staff and cadets, Volkmann would also temporarily get the Croatian Replacement Regiment, a Railway Field Engineer Battalion consisting of 14 officers, 82 NCOs and 202 enlisted men,[6] plus miscellaneous other alarm units.

Volkmann ordered the last of his Hungarian fighter pilots to scout the roads between Vienna and Krems for signs of the enemy. Upon returning they reported no signs of the Russians, but that the roads were clogged by retreating German military columns and countless refugees. He then ordered the Hungarians to fly their planes to the Raffelding airfield to the west.

At Stockerau, during all of the movements and confusion, the Croatian Regiment's food supply had been left unguarded, enough for 800 men. It was quickly plundered by civilians and hungry Croats. Another issue emerged, namely, what to do with the 540 Croats left behind who had been quarantined because of suspicions they were infected with typhus or other infectious diseases.

* * *

Volkmann might have been a *Luftwaffe* officer, but like other commanders in a similar situation he didn't hesitate to execute suspected deserters. This was made clear by the corpse of a young boy who'd been summarily shot and hung outside a local inn, with a note pinned to his uniform declaring him to be a coward.

* * *

A rare and fascinating American insight into Austria in general, and Langenlebarn air base in particular, can be found in an OSS debriefing memo dated 6 April 1945. On 26 March 1945 an American B-24 Liberator named *Bobbie Annie Laurie*, of the 464th Bomb Group, Fifteenth US Air Force, was shot down during an attack on the railroad yards at Bratislava. The crew bailed out and was captured. They were taken to the air base at Tulln where they saw JU-52s, ME-109s and even one example of the rarely seen Messerschmidt ME-210.

After being assigned cells some of the crew met a German pilot who was also in the stockade for a political offense. Only the pilot was confined in his cell. The rest of the crew were never interrogated and the Germans didn't pay them much attention. Indeed, they had liberty to wander wherever they wished. In an escape worthy of an adventure movie, four of the Americans stole a worn out JU-52 and the German pilot flew them out of Tulln into Yugoslavia. Ground fire nearly brought them down several times but eventually they made a forced landing in territory controlled by Tito's Yugoslav Partisan Army. A few days later they were handed over to the British.

When the OSS debriefed them all of the men stated that Austria was in a state of collapse. "Mobs of refugees were crowding the roads, and the bridge across the Danube near Tulln was overflowing with railroad traffic and refugees, all heading northwest."[7]

* * *

---

6   Schmidt-Richberg, E., *Das Ende auf dem Balkan*, 'Die letzten Monate der kroatischen Ausbildungsbrigade Von Rittmeister Reno Trippelsdorf', <http://www.znaci.net/00001/180_5.pdf>, (Accessed 07 August 2018).

7   Prigl, 'Die Geschichte des Fliegerhorstes Langenlebarn', <http://www.gotech.at/lale2/langenlebarn_2.html>, (Accessed 07 October 2018).

Three alarm battalions had been formed out of base personnel, but by 6 April the first two were already gone. On that very day, in fact, *Alarm-Bataillon 1* was in the process of retreating without orders from the Laaer Berg at Vienna, and the *Alarm-Bataillon 2* was marching over the Danube to guard the *Flak* guns there. That left only the *Alarm-Bataillon 3* to defend the airfield. During the dark, rainy night of 5-6 April, a single tank appeared out of the shadows. It turned out to be a lone German panzer that soon moved on.

The Russians approached Tulln from the east, south and southwest, through Langenrohr. The thunder of distant artillery fire echoed through the streets, followed later by gunfire. Around 2:00 p.m. the first shots fired at Tulln itself struck a *Volkssturm* battalion near a small bridge. The weather had cleared from the previous day, so that night, after dark, the entire horizon glowed red with fire.[8]

* * *

While battle conditions were out of his control, one thing Volkmann could control was the safety of his wife, Anitel. At one time more than 200 aircraft had called Langenlebarn home, but now Volkmann's wife boarded one of the last two flyable aircraft and took off for *Luftkriegschule 3* at Dresden. Unfortunately for him, the general's attempt to send his wife out of the path of the Red Army proved futile.

Vienna

After having marched into Vienna the day before, the I./Croatian Replacement and Training Regiment turned around and marched back out of the city. Their presence coincided with the planned launch of *O-5*'s plan to allow the Russians into Vienna and Croatian troops were deemed too unreliable to trust in combat. It was thought by *Wehrkreis XVII* that they might obey the conspirators. The artillery battery was dissolved and the guns turned over to an army unit. In classic German fashion they were even given a receipt for the guns and ammunition.

The leader of II. Battalion wasn't as fortunate. SS men took over *Wehrkreiskommando XVII* and *Oberstleutnant* Hofer was trundled off to face *General der Infanterie* von Bünau. Fortunately for Hofer he could produce proof of both his innocence and the ordering of both battalions into Vienna. Von Bünau accepted his explanation but ordered the two battalions to immediately leave the city and return to Stockerau. With more than 1,000 men ready for combat, it shows the depth of von Bünau's lingering suspicion of the regiment that he chose not to use them in the front lines. Except for the one company already committed to the front lines, that is. Those men fought through the entire battle for Vienna. When the city finally fell, four officers and ten men were all that survived.

O-5

During the night of 5-6 April, *O-5*'s plan went into motion. The Radetsky *Volkssturm* units were in place in the Vienna Woods, which on von Schirach's situation maps appeared to be legitimate defense battalions, but were in fact simply in place to speed up the Russians' seizure of Vienna. The agreed-upon signal exchange was for approaching Russians units to fire red flares, to which

---

8   Brettner, *Die Letzten Kämpfe Band II*, p. 40.

the Germans would answer with green ones. In the dead of night on the morning of 6 April that flare exchange lit the darkened sky and all seemed well with the conspiracy.

But conspiracies tend to be lax about security, and so it was with *O-5*. One slip-up proved fatal.

* * *

Major Karl Biedermann had joined the Austrian Nazi Party when it was illegal to do so and risen to command the Austrian *Heimwehr,* a sort of Austrian version of the German *Freikorps* who battled communists before the *Anschluss* with Germany. During the war he fought in France, the Balkans and on the Eastern Front.[9] Having fought in the First World War and later against communists in the Austrian Civil War of 1934, Biedermann was an Austrian Nationalist through and through, and joined Szokoll's group out of a love for Vienna. It must have been difficult for him to consider surrendering the city to the communist Russians, much less act on that decision.

Biedermann's responsibility was to seize the city center. *Hauptmann* Alfred Huth had been given the job of occupying the headquarters building of *Wehrkreis XVIII*, and *Oberleutnant* Rudolf Raschke was detailed to seize the radio station atop the Bisamberg. Other elements of the plot were to prevent destruction of the bridges over the Danube Canal and the river itself. A document was even drawn up for von Bünau to sign ordering the surrender of the city. Once these things were done a broadcast would be made to the Viennese asking them to welcome the Red Army as liberators.

But during the night of 5-6 April the conspirators got sloppy. When the flares were exchanged in the Vienna Woods, Szokoll phoned Biedermann with the news. *Leutnant* Walter Hanslik, a National Socialist leadership officer, overheard the conversation and immediately informed the *Gestapo*. Within hours the SS had arrested all of the major conspirators, except Szokoll. He had left to negotiate with the communist underground in Vienna. For everyone else, however, it was all over.[10] Torture quickly revealed the extent of the plans and both von Bünau and Bittrich took immediate measures to thwart the plot.

* * *

O-5 had arranged for the Radetsky units occupying the Vienna Woods to vacate their positions at 12:30 a.m. on 6 April. At 7:30 a.m. the Soviets began a comprehensive bombardment of the city using every available tube. In conjunction with the timetable, 39th Guards Rifle Corps launched relentless attacks from the south designed to not only break through into the city, but to also pin the defenders in place. By doing so, when the gap opened where the Radetsky units had been stationed the Germans would be unable to shift forces to block them. But when that didn't happen the viciousness of the fighting grew worse. The defenders only had two choices: stand and die, or conduct a fighting retreat from block to block. Bittrich had no intention of selecting the former.

In 1913, during his last year scraping out a meager existence on the streets of Vienna, Adolf Hitler could easily have passed Sigmund Freud, Leon Trotsky, Josep Broz Tito or Josef Stalin on the sidewalks of the capital of the Austro-Hungarian Empire. In an almost unbelievable conflu- ence of personalities, three of the men whose armies were fighting on the southern end of the

---

9   Biedermann was promoted to major in 1940 and never promoted again. Given the *Wehrmacht*'s severe losses among officers during the 5 years of war, that says much about the perception of his commanding officers.

10   The coincidence of Skorzeny being in Vienna on the day that *O-5* was shut down had led to reports he was in the city with orders to destroy the resistance. The author has been unable to find hard evidence of this. It makes much more sense that he was there to do as he wrote in his memoirs, see to the welfare of his men and make sure his family had been evacuated.

Russian Front all lived simultaneously in Vienna during 1913. None of the three future warlords had much money at the time, so they could easily have frequented one of the innumerable haunts where poverty-stricken men could eat a cheap meal, sip coffee or rent a cheap bed.

Vienna's famous café culture was an enervating environment in 1913, where the combination of coffee, cake and talk were considered an essential component of everyday life. Sigmund Freud was a regular at the elegant Café Landtmann on the Ringstrasse, near the University, the Rathaus and next door to the Burgtheater. Trotsky and Hitler preferred the nearby Café Central, although at the time it was usually referred to as the Chess School because so many people played chess there to pass the time. But unlike English pubs, patrons were not loyal to just one café. Reportedly in January 1913 Freud, Tito, Trotsky, Hitler and even Vladimir Lenin were patrons of Café Central; did any of these men ever sit next to each other? While that can never be known, it is quite possible that they did. In the smoky, noisy café did Hitler and Stalin lock gazes, if only for a moment, each man sizing up the other? Did Lenin ask Hitler to scoot his chair over so he could sidle past? There is a famous sketch made by Hitler's Jewish art teacher, Emma Lowenstramm, titled 'A chess game: Lenin with Hitler – Vienna, 1909', which was purportedly signed on the back by both men. Its authenticity has been debated by historians ever since. As the fighting approached streets that once echoed with the footsteps of so many giants of the 20th Century, one can only wonder if Tito, Hitler or Stalin thought of old friends and old haunts, many of which were already reduced to rubble.

* * *

SS-Obersturmbannführer Otto Skorzeny was told by someone on *Generalfeldmarschall* Ferdinand Schörner's staff at *Heeresgruppe Mitte* that Vienna's defense was in collapse. By this point Skorzeny needed no excuse to travel where he wished, but some of his commando units had gotten caught up in the fighting and he wanted to get them out. *Jagdverband Südost* and *Kampfgruppe Danube* were both units under his command. They weren't cannon fodder, they were highly trained special operations troops Skorzeny needed for the Alpine Fortress he'd been ordered to occupy. Thus he had a legitimate reason for heading into the path of the Red Army. Coincidentally, his wife, daughter and mother all lived in Vienna, too.

In his memoirs Skorzeny says that he went to Vienna on 10 or 11 April,[11] but the details he gives of the visit make it clear that date is wrong. By that point the German defenders had withdrawn behind the Danube Canal and Skorzeny would have been behind Russian lines. Based on the details he gives, the most likely date for his visit was 6 April.

Many *Luftwaffe* units had either begun pulling out of the city, or had plans to do so. For certain, *LuftGaukommando XVII* had already abandoned the city. On 3 April reports said that their *Luftwaffe* crews destroyed Vienna's searchlights. This dovetails with anecdotal evidence that the parent headquarters of many fixed batteries had already left. By 6 April the anti-aircraft guns and *Flak* towers were in action against ground targets, firing continually. There was no doubting the value of those 128mm guns in their impregnable fortresses, although plans were no doubt laid for how to evacuate when they were threatened with being overrun. To obtain trucks and gasoline required political and military influence of a high order, something few had, but the *Luftwaffe* was one of the few.

Skorzeny himself reported vividly on the chaos he found. Before he'd even crossed the Floridsdorfer Bridge he found evidence of the breakdown of discipline. Six horse-drawn wagons loaded with furniture clogged the road headed north, passing wounded men who lay in the ditches

11   Skorzeny, Otto, *My Commando Operations, The Memoirs of Hitler's Most Daring Commando* (Atglen: Schiffer Publishing, 1995), p. 429.

on either side.[12] Skorzeny disarmed the wagon drivers, turned the wagons over to the wounded and ordered the furniture thrown out and the injured men put in its place.

Proceeding into the Brittgenau Section of Vienna around dusk he heard the sounds of battle not too far away, but had no idea how close the Russians were. Driving to the Stubenring they found the War Ministry dark. No lights shone anywhere and a haze of smoke and dust hung in the air. Skorzeny found no signs of defenders, although there were some makeshift street barricades the Russians would simply push aside. A sentry told him the command post had been moved to the Hofburg so Skorzeny headed there. The only lights for his drive came from burning buildings and flashes on the horizon beyond the skyline.

Along the way he checked his brother's house but turned around at the Schwedenplatz because the rubble of the house had tumbled into the street. Finally reaching the command post for *Jagdverbände Südost* he found that its remnants and those of *Kampfgruppe Danube* had fled to an assembly point north of Krems. He found his mother's house also wrecked, but one of her neighbors told him she had fled several days before along with his wife and daughter.

Despite artillery flashes on the eastern and southern approaches to the city, Skorzeny made for the Ringsstrassee. At the Hofburg the courtyard was jammed with vehicles of all types. When he inquired about how the battle was going he was told the Russians were in the city but being engaged everywhere. Skeptical, Skorzeny decided to see for himself, so he drove toward the sound of the guns. When the noise of battle grew close he found the first manned defenses he'd seen in Vienna, a street barricade with two over-the-hill policemen. Driving back to the Hofburg after midnight, he was told that his information about seeing no defenders contradicted the reports that von Schirach had been getting. The *Gauleiter*'s adjutant ushered him into von Schirach's office to make a report.

In typical fashion von Schirach had adorned a candle-lit basement room with tapestries and plush rugs. Skorzeny found him having supper. He assured Skorzeny that an imminent counterattack would destroy the invading Russians and that he, personally, would never leave Vienna. He further told Skorzeny that two SS divisions were at his disposal, surely meaning *Das Reich* and *Totenkopf*, and that he had another panzer division crossing the Danube, which must have been the *Führer-Grenadier-Division*.

Skorzeny didn't believe any of this based on his own observations and twisted von Schirach's arm to call the *Führerbunker* and report the situation, which he did. Hitler supposedly ordered the immediate evacuation of his ancient weapons collection to the Obersalzburg.[13]

"Prevail or die," Skorzeny quotes him as saying.[14]

The 'Most Dangerous Man in Europe' left von Schirach's headquarters convinced that Vienna was doomed. After a quick stop at his own home in Döbling to take a few personal items, Skorzeny headed for the Alps. Baldur von Schirach followed him within a matter of hours.

6. SS-Panzerarmee

Across the battlefield army commanders increasingly resembled independent warlords as the German chain of command slowly dissolved. Death in battle was one thing, dying because of some unrealistic and pointless order was quite another.

---

12   Claims have been made that these were *Luftwaffe* men, although Skorzeny's memoirs don't explicitly state that.
13   Infield, *Skorzeny*, p. 116.
14   Skorzeny, *My Commando*, p. 431.

The Cuff Band Order had broken the SS bond with Hitler. Sepp Dietrich had made it clear who held real power when Himmler showed up to reprimand him but faced armed *Waffen-SS* men loyal to Dietrich protecting their commander. The following incident shows that Dietrich no longer feared retribution for doing as he saw fit to both protect his men and carry out orders.

On 4 April Hitler issued the infamous Nero Order, which directed that anything potentially useful to the enemy must be destroyed. This included all food supplies, utilities, sewer lines, bridges and everything else of value. Infrastructure topped the list. Maier reports this order only filtered down to Dietrich on 6 April because communications with *OKW* had become increasingly unreliable,[15] and that *Heeresgruppe Süd* added a specific order to blow up the Viennese Secondary Mountain Water Line, a pipe which supplied the city with its drinking water. "It ran just north of the field army command post…the Commander-in-Chief of the 6. Panzer-Armee [Dietrich] characterized such actions as 'insanity'. The order was…ignored."[16]

Dietrich had done terrible things in Hitler's name. During the Night of the Long Knives he'd ordered the execution of SA men who the day before had been his comrades. He'd led *Waffen-SS* formations throughout the war, many of which were alleged to have committed heinous war crimes. There can be no doubt he was a loyal paladin of his *Führer*, but Dietrich drew the line at killing helpless German civilians by cutting off essential requirements needed for survival for no purpose other than spite.

* * *

Stalag 17B was "a dingy, fleabag patch of hell for the Allied *Kriegies* who got stuck there".[17] Located in the idyllic Austrian countryside near Krems an der Donau, it should have been a comfortable camp surrounded by the beauty of nature. Instead it was a hideous place of double barbed wire fence and guard towers bristling with machine guns, that was so disgusting it inspired the American TV comedy series *Hogan's Heroes* in the 1960s.

On 6 April the Fifteenth US Air Force bombed nearby Krems and some bombs came dangerously close to the camp itself. The Americans had known something was up, since bombers flew overhead nearly every day. At night, flashes on the eastern horizon could only be artillery. But they hadn't known what would happen next. Would they be shot? Allowed by their guards to be rescued? Rumors were rife, not only in the American section but also in the French, British and other parts of the camp. So as the Red Army closed in from the east and the Americans from the west, the decision was made to evacuate the camp. First went the Russians, who left soon after the last bombs fell.

* * *

The 6. *SS-Panzerarmee* was in serious danger of being carved up and destroyed piecemeal. The Vienna Woods should have been a significant geographic barrier to the attackers, but while *O-5* might not have saved Vienna from urban combat, it did hasten the city's fall by labeling all of the *Volkssturm* battalions stationed in the Woods as unreliable in the minds of the German command. With the exposure of their plan, the so-called Radetsky units were withdrawn because of fears they would materially aid the Russians, but there were no units to put in their place.

---

15   As ridiculous as it sounds now, the *Führerbunker* eventually relied on one aerial antenna held aloft by a balloon to communicate with the outside world.

16   Maier, *Drama,* p. 350.

17   Ethier, Eric, 'Stalag 17-B The prison that inspired a movie and a TV comedy was a dingy, fleabag patch of hell for the Allied "kriegies" who got stuck there', <http://www.americainwwii.com/articles/stalag-17-b/>, (Accessed 27 July 2018).

For several days Third Ukrainian Front had been transferring mobile units from its southern wing to the north to reinforce the breakthrough between the two SS corps. Units such as 18thTank Corps, withdrawn from its drive down the Raab Valley toward Styria, finally got into the battle on 6 April. Those Russian mobile forces split off on three divergent axes of attack. The first prong attacked to the west to capture Sankt Polten and to tie down *I SS-Panzerkorps*, the second sprinted for the Danube at Tulln and, once there, planned to drive on Vienna from the northwest, while the third was already heading directly into the city from the west. The situation was desperate, but no matter how much Sepp Dietrich wanted to strike back at the rampaging Russians, there wasn't one damned thing he could do about any of it.

II SS-Panzerkorps

With each passing day the units defending Vienna became progressively weaker, shrinking the territory they could defend and making the manpower shortage even more acute. As day broke on 6 April and *II SS-Panzerkorps* was pushed back into Vienna, what Sepp Dietrich had vowed wouldn't happen, happened.

The wave of Russian units rolling into Vienna included 21st Guards Rifle Corps on the eastern edge, with 39th Guards Rifle Corps attacking from the south, while 1st Guards Mechanized Corps and 5th Guards Tank Corps moved in support of both rifle corps.

By 6 April the Russians drove a wedge between *II SS-Panzerkorps* and the rest of *6. SS-Panzerarmee*. In self-defense, that corps had no choice but to keep retreating into Vienna itself.

6. Panzer-Division

The German defensive line formed a rough arc starting at the Prater and running south-southwest, then northwest. On the eastern flank *6. Panzer-Division* was trying to regroup and defend in the Prater, backed up by the Panzer Regiment of the soon-to-arrive *Führer-Grenadier-Division* near the Stadium Bridge. The infantry component for *6. Panzer-Division, Panzergrenadier-Regiment 114*, was south of the Danube Canal screening the vital Gas and Electric Works even as the Soviet 80th Guards Rifle Division from 20th Guards Rifle Corps closed on the waterway and began looking for a way across.

Kampfgruppe 3. SS-Panzer-Division Totenkopf

On the right flank of *Panzergrenadier-Regiment 114*, parts of *Kampfgruppe 3. SS-Panzer-Division Totenkopf* stood just southeast of the Artillery Arsenal with the *Panzer-Pionier-Bataillon 124* from *Führer-Grenadier-Division*[18] in support and with *2. SS-Panzer-Division Das Reich* on *Totenkopf*'s right flank. *Totenkopf* briefly lost both the Arsenal and the East Railway Station in vicious fighting but retook them in a counterattack.

The little *SS-Kampfgruppe Barth* had spent the four previous days moving and fighting toward Vienna with no casualties, but by 6 April its weapons and ammunition were exhausted. After resupplying at the Arsenal the *Kampfgruppe* moved into the front line at the South Railway Station.

---

18   Panzer, in this case, is an adjective, not a noun, and translates as 'Armored'.

Das Reich was blocking Ninth Guards Army from moving into Liesing from due south, but its right flank was up in the air, with only minor units to defend its rear areas; there simply were not enough German units to defend Vienna on all sides. The western approaches were weakly held by a few small units, including some Hitler Youth, part of *Aufklärung-Ausbildungs-und-Ersatz-Abteilung 11* and a company from *Panzerjäger-Abteilung 80*, certainly not a force to stop a determined attack. Worse, this was the area where some of the units were commanded by members of O-5 and were prepared to allow the Russians to pass through their lines unopposed. The Russians knew this and prepared to take advantage of the Germans' desperate situation.

The bulk of Sixth Guards Tank Army had continued speeding north toward Tulln, but 9th Guards Mechanized Corps veered right through Pressbaum and Purkersdorf, aiming directly for Vienna's western districts and *Das Reich*'s rear. This was in accordance with O-5's plan, which the Russians didn't know was in the process of being discovered and thwarted.

The 9th Guards Mechanized Corps was a very powerful, fast-moving force. It deployed 18th, 30th and 31st Guards Mechanized Brigades, 46th Guards Tank Brigade, 83rd, 84th and 85th Guards Tank Regiments, and 252nd Tank Regiment.[19] A fast breakthrough would put *Das Reich* in dire straits. If the Russians could have sliced into Vienna's open western flank fast enough they could potentially have surrounded the city's defenders who were spread out in the arc on the southern side, with Austrian resistance members within Vienna tryng to bring about that very result.

That left two Russian corps to drive toward Tulln, 38th Guards Rifle Corps and 18th Tank Corps, with only the scattered weak forces of *I SS-Panzerkorps* to get in their way.

Within the city itself it's a mistake to think the Germans had front lines. They didn't. Instead, small unit commanders chose the most defensible positions and put their men there. If they were outflanked, as they inevitably were, the commander retreated to the next position he considered the best. Aside from being badly outnumbered, therefore, the defenders of Vienna were also constantly outflanked and betrayed.

The rest of the *Führer-Grenadier-Division* was moving into the city from the north bank of the Danube, but in the meantime the threat to *Das Reich*'s rear forced the division to pull back to near the Franz Joseph Bahnhof, exposing *Totenkopf*'s flank and forcing it to retreat in turn, first to, and then past, the Arsenal.

A major Russian attack was slated for 6 April to seize Vienna once and for all. Two armies had zeroed in on the city. Ninth Guards Army attacked from the south, while Sixth Guards Tank Army assaulted from the west and northwest. In Ninth Guards Army, 20th Guards Rifle Corps sent 20th Guards Rifle Division against the Prater, which was defended by the combat elements of *6. Panzer-Division*, other than *Panzergrenadier-Regiment 114*. Moving into support behind *6. Panzer-Division* was *Panzer-Regiment 101* of the *Führer-Grenadier-Division*. Across the Danube Canal, *Panzergrenader-Regiment 114* defended the gas and electric works against the elite Russian 5th and 7th Guards Airborne Divisions, which were also part of 20th Guards Rifle Corps.

In support of this push the Russians used loudspeakers to broadcast an appeal into German-held territory for the Viennese to help throw out the Nazis and save their city from destruction. The commander of Third Ukrainian Front, Marshal Tolbukhin himself, recorded the speech. It's hard to say for certain how much effect this propaganda had, but certainly the hostile acts of the population toward the defenders did not occur in a vacuum. Word had already spread that in Russian-occupied areas many citizens were helping the invaders by carrying ammunition or equipment.[20]

---

19   Rauchensteiner, *Krieg in Öserreich*, p. 97.
20   Reynolds, Major General Michael, *A Soviet Red Army Victory at Vienna*, https://warfarehistorynetwork.com/daily/wwii/a-soviet-red-army-victory-at-vienna/ (Accessed 4 December 2018).

To get into the Prater the Russians had to fight their way across the Danube Canal. The relatively open ground of the Gas and Electric Works gave clear fields of fire and made advancing costly. The combat there was savage.

The 21st Guards Rifle Corps sent all three of its divisions, the 4th, 62nd and 69th Guards Rifle Divisions, against *Totenkopf* southwest of the Arsenal. The SS men knew their fate if captured, even men who'd been drafted or transferred from other branches, which gave them courage born of desperation. In support behind them was the *Führer Grenadier Division*'s *Panzer-Pionier-Bataillon*.

Into the seam between *Totenkopf* and *Das Reich* drove the armor of 1st Guards Mechanized Corps. This powerful corps consisted of 9th Guards Tank Brigade, 1st, 2nd and 3rd Guards Mechanized Brigades and six tank and self-propelled assault gun regiments. To stop such a force required heavy weapons and large numbers of infantry armed with either a *Panzerfaust* or *Panzerschreck*, who were willing to get close enough to the Russian tanks to use them. The Germans had few of either. The 1st Guards Mechanized Corps fought their way to Prinz Eugen Strasse, on the western border of the Arsenal, on 6 April.

Next to 1st Guards Mechanized Corps on the west was 39th Guards Infantry Corps, which contained 100th and 114th Guards Infantry Divisions. That corps attacked the positions of *Das Reich* directly and drove them back. Mödling saw particularly heavy fighting as the SS men refused to give up the town. Casualties on both sides were extremely heavy. Eventually the Russians drove the Germans out by the sheer weight of numbers and followed them into Vösendorf, which fell and then was retaken in a counterattack.

The 750 foot-high Laaer Berg fell and was retaken several times on Vienna's eastern edge. The critical high point had been abandoned by elements of the *24. Flak-Division,* with the *Alarm-Bataillon 1* from *Luftkriegschule 7* for infantry support, but there is some indication those men returned to the fight. Regardless, as related earlier, *Das Reich* sent elements to take their place. The mountain's strategic position is shown because today the busiest highway in Austria runs into Vienna on its northern slope. After a day of bitter combat at least a dozen Russian tanks burned around it but by sundown the Germans still held the summit. The alarm battalion reportedly continued to fight through the whole battle for Vienna, then on the north bank of the Danube, and the survivors would eventually wind up in Krems to end the war.

* * *

Another armored Russian column broke through in *Totenkopf*'s sector at Rauchenwarth while a second group drove through the positions of *6. Panzer-Division* west of Fischamend. This was the flat ground around the Vienna airport and the geography offered no rallying point short of Männsworth. Following that Schwechat fell and the Russians penetrated into Simmering, reportedly aided by civilians. This penetration was dangerous in the extreme, and threatened to cut off *Das Reich* from the Danube.

With such a fluid situation *II SS-Panzerkorps* moved its headquarters north of the Danube. Everywhere its troops retreated they blew up things the enemy might find useful, such as power stations, bridges and even granaries, which had the effect of punishing the civilian population more than the well-supplied Russians.

* * *

Sixth Guards Army commanded 9th Guards Mechanized Corps driving in due west from the Vienna Woods. This was another armored formation, with 18th, 30th and 31st Guards Mechanized Brigades and 46th Guards Tank Brigade, with three Guards and one standard tank regiments. On paper this corps was a juggernaut.

But while German losses since the start of the Russian Vienna Offensive on 16 March had been appalling, the attackers hadn't fared much better. Many of the tanks of Third Ukrainian Front were American M4A2 Shermans. Soviet statistics from this era should be viewed with skepticism, but 9th Guards Mechanized Corps listed 153 Shermans combat ready on 16 March and by 5 April that number was down to 46, or about 30 percent of its starting strength.[21] Many Russian crews loved the *Emcha,* as they called the Sherman.[22] It was fast, reliable and the 76mm main gun was a substantial upgrade to the short-barreled 75mm cannon on the M4A1. But on the downside its high-profile made it an easy target, the armor was neither thick enough nor sloped, and the tank ran on gasoline, not diesel. Penetrating hits often led to terrible fires.

The corps faced parts of the still-arriving *Führer-Grenadier-Division,* along with various alarm units and the Hitler Youth Battalion, on *Das Reich's* far right flank.

Finally, driving southeast along the Danube was Sixth Guards Army's other corps, 5th Tank Corps, containing 20th, 21st and 22nd Guards Tank Brigades, 6th Guards Mechanized Brigade, 107th Guards Rifle Brigade, plus three Guards assault gun regiments and one Guards tank regiment. Against this the Germans could only muster some training battalions and the Hitler Youth Battalion. Seeing this danger, the commander of *II SS-Panzerkorps, SS-Obergruppenführer* Wilhelm Bittrich, ordered *SS-Panzer-Aufklärungs-Abteilung 2* to redeploy north to the area of the Floridsdorfer Bridge in support of the Hitler Youth.

2. SS-Panzer-Division Das Reich

In conjunction with this all-out effort, and while *Das Reich* was pinned in place by frontal attacks and had no flank protection, there is a story about a strong attack by a mixed-force Russian battle group aimed to slip around the SS division's right flank, penetrate to Vienna's center and seize the government quarter, along with bridges over the Danube Canal. The commander of the group was Captain Dimitry Loza of the I Battalion, 46th Guards Tank Brigade. For his attack he was given nearly half of the remaining Shermans, 18, along with three precious ISU-122 self-propelled guns to blow any barricades or strongpoints, and the depleted I Guards Battalion of 304th Guards Airborne Regiment riding on the 21 tanks, about 80 men. Among the Shermans were a number of Fireflies, Sherman tanks mounted with the deadly British 17-pounder gun. The striking power of that cannon made it the equivalent of the famous German 88mm gun and gave Loza's battle group a tank-killing component against anything the defenders could throw at them. It was a bold plan more reminiscent of *Wehrmacht* tactics than those of the Red Army. It had the potential to trap and destroy *II SS-Panzerkorps* in one fell swoop.

How much of Loza's story is strictly true, and how much isn't, is hard to say more than 70 years after the fact. Many of the dates do not match up to known events, but many of the incidents do, including several photos taken in the Heldenplatz showing Russian Shermans on the attack. The version told here has been adjusted to meet the historical timeline and, whether apocryphal or not, it is representative of the chaotic nature of street fighting in Vienna.

Loza had already tried to take his force into Vienna from the southwest and lost a Sherman for his efforts. He finally realized the attack would have to come from a different axis, so the force assembled west of the city center at Purkersdorf early on the morning of 6 April.[23] Once it pushed off again it hadn't gone far before meeting resistance. Barricades blocked the streets leading to a

---

21   Brettner, Friedrich, *Semmering, April 1945 – The battles for the Südbahn dairy* (Truppendienst: Episode 272, issue 5/2003), <http://www.bundesheer.at/truppendienst/ausgaben/artikel.php percent3Fid percent3D94&prev =search>, (Accessed 4 December 2018).

22   In Russian, the designation M4 was rendered as EM-chetyrye, or Emcha.

23   In his book Loza says this occurred on 8 April, but the date has been changed here because Loza's stated dates don't match up with the actual fighting.

bridge over the Wien River and provided cover for the Hitler Youth Battalion who defended that area. While attempting to crash through a Sherman was hit by a *Panzerfaust* round and destroyed.

Shifting to its right the battle group tried to cross the river from Hacking but found their way blocked by a long wall. The only way through it was through it, so a Sherman rammed the wall until it broke through. Loza says the Viennese they saw didn't recognize them as Russians and were going about their business, and that policemen waved them through at intersections, but this doesn't match up with other eyewitness accounts.

* * *

As the Germans pulled back under pressure, Red Army troops captured the Südbahnhof, the South Railway Station, right next to the Arsenal. There was little fighting there and so, unlike the other railway stations in Vienna, the Südbahnhof was captured with relatively little damage, aside from some broken glass. Employees of the *Reichsbahndivision Wien* hid in three sleeper trains and then were able to make their escape to the workshop named *Edelweiss* close to Sigmundsherberg. The loss of the *Südbahnhof* threatened the entire South Railway Station, threatened the entire Arsenal position of *Totenkopf,* the grounds of which were close by.

* * *

Much to his relief, in the gathering darkness of 6 April *General der Infanterie* von Bünau was placed under the command of *II SS-Panzerkorps.* Given the paucity of forces he commanded this was more symbolic than anything else, but surely von Bünau must have breathed easier. The fall of the city would no longer be his fault.

The general had only been in Vienna four days but the military situation forced him to order the demolition of the first bridges, the Freudenauer Hafenbrücke, the Ostbahnhofbrücke spanning the Danube Canal and the Stadtlauer Ostbahnhofbrücke. The 20th Guards Rifle Corps had been trying to force its way onto Prater Island and was dangerously close to those bridges. But it would only be a temporary delay, as von Bünau knew all too well.

* * *

By nightfall *Das Reich* held a ragged line just south of Schönbrunn Palace. The division's heavy artillery and some panzers set up on the grounds of the Palace itself, with at least one battery firing over the Gloriete and another blocking the northern gate in case of ground attack. Another of its batteries had set up in the grounds of the Prater, between the Danube and the canal. The division no longer fought as a cohesive whole but had become separated into its smaller components, trying to block all avenues at once.

The fall of night brought no relief, as Russian infiltrators sought gaps in the defense. Russian spearheads made it as far as the West Railway Station. Only Hitler Youth equipped with *Panzerfaust* and hunting in teams opposed them, but that was enough. They were stopped short of the station. Nevertheless, by midnight *Das Reich* had fallen back yet again, this time north of Schönbrunn Palace. *Das Reich*'s front stretched from the main square of the 13th District, Hietzing, on the right, to Matzleinsdorfer Platz on the left. The regal symbol of Austria's once-great empire and its beloved zoo were in Russian hands.

* * *

The SS units were battered, exhausted and hard-pressed, pulling back because there was no chance to organize a proper defense, and not enough units to defend such a large city, but they did not go quietly. Fighting could be intense. And as fighting within the city itself began its week-long progression toward a fiery climax, it became urban fighting at its worst. According to Mansoor, beneath the streets of Vienna was a labyrinth of tunnels and crawlways where the citizenry had broken through the walls of their basements. Smashing holes to create makeshift tunnels meant that during air attacks the people could move around like moles, and the German defenders made good use of these unseen roads. He described it this way: "The Soviets could control the street level for two blocks behind the German infantry who were still in the basement. The same situation applied to the upper levels of the buildings…the situation, put simply by one German who fought there, was 'a mess'."[24]

War underground was nothing new for the Viennese. During the Siege of Vienna in 1529 Turkish sappers had dug tunnels to the Carinthian Gate, with the intention to load explosives into the mine and explode them, breaching the defensive works so the Turkish Army could pour through. This was not unlike what the Union forces had done at the Battle of the Crater during the American Civil War. The Viennese had dug counter-tunnels to intersect the Turkish tunnels, leading to vicious and prolonged underground fighting. The clumsy guns of the day were useless in the confined spaces, so men killed each other with knives, rocks, fists, teeth, anything deadly that came to hand. The subterranean fighting continued for so long that weapons were actually adapted for use underground, including modified Turkish cavalry maces and Austrian spades. Forever after the Siege of Vienna earned the nickname The Siege of the Moles. And in 1945 history was repeating itself.

South of the Danube

Even as 9th Mechanized Corps veered off at a right angle to outflank the defenders of Vienna, Sixth Guards Army's two remaining corps kept heading north for the Tulln area. Known as The City of Roses, Tulln was occupied even in pre-Roman times and was a critical strongpoint for both Roman ground and river forces due to its strategic location on the high ground astride the Danube. When the Turks were besieging Vienna in 1683, Tulln acted as a collection point for the relief forces gathering to save the Austrian capital. In 1939, the *Luftwaffe* completed construction of Langenlebarn air base there, but as the Red Army closed in *Generalmajor* Volkmann ordered the base prepared for destruction. No one is certain now exactly who set the charges, except they were from the *Waffen-SS*.[25] Even more critical than the airfield, however, were the Danube bridges.

Crossing the Danube at Tulln would have been a shattering blow to the German position north of the river by driving into the rear of both *II SS-Panzerkorps* and *8. Armee*. By 6 April, 5th Guards Tank Corps had reached the river and began attacking Tulln with 21st Guards Tank Brigade. Not only did they attack west, however, but also sent strong forces due east along the south bank of the Danube toward Klostenburg and then Vienna. This force included 20th and 22nd Guards Tank Brigades, 6th Guards Mechanized Brigade, 48th Guards Tank Regiment and 1458th, 1462nd and 1484th Assault Gun Regiments, a fast force with a very strong punch.[26] Its mission was to roll eastward following the Danube, take Klosterneuberg and then to keep going until it reached Vienna, and the Germans had nothing to throw in its path to even slow it down.

---

24   Mansoor, 1st Lt Peter, *The Defense of the Vienna Bridgehead*, Armor Magazine, January-February 1986, <http://www.benning.army.mil/armor/eARMOR/content/issues>, (Accessed 4 December 2018).
25   Exactly which SS formation was responsible for the destruction of the airfield is not known.
26   An equivalent German force would be 2 Panzer regiments, 1 *Panzergrenadier* regiment, 1 Panzer battalion and 3 *Sturmgeschütz* battalions, a very potent force indeed.

I. SS-Panzerkorps

SS-Obergruppenführer Hermann Preiss' corps had been virtually severed from its sister *II SS-Panzerkorps* and with the strong Russian forces between them there would be no rejoining the two. Now facing Preiss' *I SS-Panzerkorps* along a broad front was 37th Guards Rifle Corps with three Guards rifle divisions. These were the screening forces for the metal juggernaut of Sixth Guards Tank Army. Meanwhile, the Russian spearheads began to split up to their different objectives. While 9th Guards Mechanized Corps headed into Vienna by the western door, 6th Guards Tank Corps passed west of Pressbaum and took Tulbing, a mere four miles from Tulln and the Danube; this was the group that moved on to attack Langenlebarn. A third force headed for Sankt Pölten and captured Rekawinkel, about five miles west of Pressbaum. Aside from some *Volkssturm* here and there, they rolled almost unopposed.

Although most of the Russian armor had moved into the breakthrough south of Vienna, assaults continued against the corps' whole front. Sometimes these came in company strength, other times by regiments, but it was clear the Russians were not through attacking due west.

Still, having to withdraw the unreliable Radetsky battalions of *O-5* from the Vienna Woods had left the corps fractured, depleted and with both flanks in danger of being turned.

SS-Kampfgruppe Staudinger

The artillery commander for *6. SS-Panzerarmee*, *SS-Gruppenführer* Walter Staudinger, had known Sepp Dietrich for years. He had commanded *SS-Panzerartillerie-Regiment 1* when Dietrich was commanding officer of the *LAH*, and he had served with him ever since. So when the desperate situation arose on the left flank of *I SS-Panzerkorps'* left flank Dietrich turned to his trusted colleague to block the Russian advance west along the Danube. Staudinger's *Kampfgruppe* consisted mainly of remnants, alarm units and *Volkssturm*, but his boss knew he'd do whatever he could to hold back the red tide.

Kampfgruppe 12. SS-Panzer-Division Hitlerjugend

The new boundary line between the *LAH* and *12. SS-Panzer-Division Hitlerjugend* was from the Haidlhof in the east to Weissenbach an der Triesting in the west. This allowed *SS-Gruppenführer und Generalleutnant der SS* Hermann Priess to form a north-facing front along the southern boundary of Fifth Guards Tank Army's breakthrough south and west of Vienna. The deployment of the two SS panzer divisions was tantamount to erecting a wall of sandbags to channel a flood away from valuable land. The Russians could keep moving northwest but couldn't turn south or southwest without encountering defenders.

Reacting to attacks along the front, a *Kampfgruppe* from *Hitlerjugend* drove north from the region north of Pottenstein with the objective of retaking Mayerling and sealing and cutting off the Russian spearheads already far to the west. They broke through scattered resistance and recaptured the high ground over the important road from Gainfarn to Raisenmarkt. This was the Hoher Lindkogel, a popular hiking area of steep, rocky terrain studded with trees that typified the Vienna Woods. Here and there, ruined castles and boulders made for excellent defensive positions. In this case, *Hitlerjugend* managed to patch part of gaping hole in the front, but not to close it completely.

Further west the news was even worse. Around Heiligenkreuz the Russians overwhelmed the badly depleted *SS-Kampfgruppe Bremer* and drove them back to Alland, further opening the road northwest to the Danube at Tulln. Those troops had been astride the breakthrough route and theoretically posed a threat to operations on the Danube. The attack further east by *Hitlerjugend* reinforced this fear. The Russians had no way of knowing that Sepp Dietrich was simply trying to cobble together a contiguous front. Dietrich recognized his opportunity, but he was so bereft of forces that launching an attack against the flank of their offensive was nothing more than a fanciful wish.

As night fell the Russians attacked both around Hirtenburg and at Alland. Despite being supported by 39 tanks, *Kampfgruppe SS-Panzergrenadier-Regiment 26* drove the Russians back with severe losses. One breakthrough near Grossau was sealed off and destroyed by *SS-Kampfgruppe Möbius*. But the assault on Alland succeeded in not only capturing the town but in driving *SS-Kampfgruppe Bremer* northwest toward Klausen-Leopoldsdorf.[27]

Kampfgruppe 1. SS-Panzer-Division Leibstandarte Adolf Hitler

The mighty *LAH* had been smashed twice in the previous ten months, first in the aftermath of Normandy in the Falaise Pocket and again after the Ardennes Offensive, and now for a third time it had been reduced to a *Kampfgruppe*. Marshal Tolbukhin knew the Germans were weak and kept up the pace of attacks, both to the northwest and the west. To feed the breakthrough south of Vienna he began to pull more and more units out of the central and southern sectors of the front.

Dreistetten, northwest of Weiner Neustadt, saw attacks come in from the north, most likely from 99th Guards Rifle Division. The picturesque little town of 500 people had been destroyed by invaders from the east when it resisted the Turkish invasion of 1683. The town boasted the ruins of a 12th-Century castle and Pffarkirchen Dreistetten had a choir loft dating to the early 14th Century. It was so typically Austrian as to be an archetype in its charm, but as they had done once before the demons of war came calling on the tranquil village. Nor were the scars left by the shells and bullets lessened or magnified depending on who had shot them. It fell to the Russians.

Regimental-strength attacks occurred all along the division's front as the Russians tried to take Pottenstein from the north and Berndorf to the south. Perhaps apocryphal, perhaps not, anecdotes of *Panzergrenadiers* arming themselves with clubs because they didn't have rifles arose from this time. Due to *LAH*'s depleted conditions breakthroughs occurred at a number of places, most notably west of Hirtenberg, where an immediate counterattack sealed the breach near Kkeinfeld, although another one in the direction of Neuseidl couldn't be sealed.[28]

Not even the *LAH*'s few remaining panzers could do much good when facing such over-whelming odds. With no hope of stopping the Russian drive on Tulln something had to be done about *I SS-Panzerkorps'* open left flank, so late in the day *SS-Aufklärung-Abteilung 1* was ordered from its position near Reichenau toward Pressbaum. The battered battalion wasn't much in the way of flank protection but it was all Hermann Preiss had to send, but in doing so it deprived division commander *SS-Brigadeführer* Otto Kumm of a critical component of his defense.

---

27   Meyer, *The 12th SS*, p. 470.
28   Tiemman, *The Leibstandarte IV/2*, p. 288.

Kampfgruppe Koch

The battered battalion from the *Kriegsschule Wiener Neustadt* was pulled away from the front by the headquarters of *SS-Panzergrenadier-Regiment 2* and ordered to assemble for transfer. Its ranks were filled out by *Volkssturm*, walking wounded and prisoners held for minor infractions. Some of its soldiers were very young, and some far too old for front-line combat. The SS provided trucks for transporting them to Markt Piesting where they were supposed to set off on foot for distant Neuseidl, on the eastern outskirts of Vienna.[29] It was far too late for that, however, as the direct route from *I SS-Panzerkorps* had been permanently severed. Instead, the battalion deployed to Dreistetten and the Hohe Wand area, where some of the *Fahnenjunkern* had fortified the ruins on the Starhemburg.

Kampfgruppe 356. Infanterie-Division

The much-reduced division had been split in two again, with a small *Kampfgruppe* of the combat elements being thrown into the path of the Russian drive toward Tulln, on *I SS-Panzerkorps'* left flank, which was a futile gesture. Against the might of an entire army this paltry force could do nothing and was brushed aside. On the corps' far right flank, close to the mountain passes into Styria and the boundary with *6. Armee*, a new enemy entered the fight against the headquarters *Kampfgruppe* of *356. Infanterie-Division*: partisans. Most likely they were deserters looking for food, although it's also possible they hoped to gain favor by fighting with or guiding Russian detachments through the heavily forested mountains. Regardless, rear area stores, convoys and sentries had to be careful of sudden attacks.

The Schwarzenberg is a 4,000 foot-high mountain in the Gahns region where one such clash took place. The Germans drove the partisans off but the threat remained of them raiding supply lines or aiding the Russians, but there was nothing to be done about that. Action took place all along this *Kampfgruppe's* front lines, when Russian probes sought for weak spots to exploit and everywhere they were thrown back with heavy losses. But now the weary *Landser* had to look for trouble from two directions.

SS-Kampfgruppe Keitel

The 2,000 or so men of *SS-Kampfgruppe Keitel* were on their own in the middle of the mountains southwest of *356. Infanterie-Division's* headquarters *Kampfgruppe* in the Gahns region. A few miles south was Gloggnitz and the gaping hole in the German front lines between *6. SS-Panzerarmee* and *6. Armee*. They defended a huge area and had only a few heavy weapons with which to do it, but fortunately for them the Russians had committed their breakthrough forces elsewhere.

Nevertheless, Gloggnitz had already fallen to the 103rd Guards Rifle Division and *SS-Kampfgruppe Keitel* wasn't strong enough to eject them. Between them and *Sperrverband Gross* they were able to wipe out a few small bands of infiltrators, but their right flank was completely unprotected. One Russian division could have rolled up the line and completely unhinged *1. SS-Panzer-Division's* defensive positions. But all of those units were now headed north.

---

29   Brettner, *Die Letzten Kämpfe Band I*, p. 165.

6. Armee

Hermann Balck moved the army headquarters to Gleisdorf, a picturesque town astride the equally picturesque Raab River that was directly in the path of the oncoming Russians. Establishing a clear picture of *6. Armee*'s left flank now is nearly impossible. One has to wonder if the same wasn't true for Hermann Balck in 1945, that he wasn't sure exactly what forces were where. Ad-hoc and alarm units sprang up, fought, died and disappeared without their names being recorded by history. Suffice it to say that an unknown number of *Kampfgruppe* of various sizes were atop the mountains at the border with *6. SS-Panzerarmee*, lonely men fighting a lonely war.

In addition to any unknown forces, by 6 April the efforts of the commander of *Wehrkreis XVIII*, *General der Gebirgstruppe* Julius Ringel, had begun to plug the gaps in the German lines. Hermann Balck singles him out for praise during this period but the holes were numerous and large, far too serious for one man to correct using alarm units. On 6 April the Russians captured the villages on the northern edge of the Hochwechsel for use as forward supply dumps. This highest peak in the Wechsel Mountains soared to nearly 5,500 feet, giving it a panoramic view of the entire region. It would see heavy fighting before the war ended.

Facing *6. Armee*'s extreme left wing was Ninth Guards Army's 37th Guards Rifle Corps, with three Guards rifle divisions. That Russian army's southern boundary line put it opposite the sparsely defended area between *SS-Kampfgruppe Keitel* and *Kampfgruppe Raithel*.

But the biggest threat to *6. Armee*'s flank came from the powerful Twenty-Sixth Army, with four rifle corps. This was the force that slammed into *Divisionsgruppe Krause* and *1. Volks-Grenadier-Division* on 3 April and drove them westward.

* * *

Due west of Rechnitz the Russians exploited one of those gaps and drove onward between Pinkafeld and Oberwart, forcing Hermann Balck to pull units of *6. Armee*'s right flank to send to the left, this at a time when progress was being made in closing the gap with *2. Panzerarmee* on the right. Even worse for the Germans, the attackers captured Friedberg near the Wechsel Pass. As at Semmering the only feasible way for the Russians to penetrate Styria was through the mountain passes and both sides knew it. But while both sides were approaching exhaustion from three weeks of continuous combat, the Russians had all the gasoline and ammunition they needed and let their superior firepower be their advantage.

Kampfgruppe Semmering

By this time *Kampfgruppe Semmering* had grown into a substantial force. It had had to become a substantial unit if a real defense of Styria was going to materialize, one that could hold. Because of *6. Armee*'s weakness the *Kampfgruppe* had to cover a front of 22 miles facing east, and another 15 miles facing south to protect its right flank. This was too much front for a full-strength corps, much less a cobbled together *Kampfgruppe*.

The list itself makes clear just how disparate the individual components were, and that makes their subsequent cohesion all the more remarkable. This is its composition up to and including 6 April, as far as is known.

The previously mentioned *SS-Gebirgsjäger-Ausbildungs-und-Ersatz-Abteilung 13* was filled by men who were *Volksdeutsch*, primarily from Romania, Hungary and Yugoslavia, and had been conscripted into the *Waffen-SS*. The instructors were veterans, chiefly from *7. SS-Freiwilligen-Gebirgs-Division Prinz Eugen,* although the battalion's original purpose was as the replacement battalion for *6. SS-Gebirgs-Division Nord*. Now the battalion was spread all over the Semmering area. Its *5. Kompanie*, the machine-gun company, had tracked vehicles.

Landesschützen Bataillon 851. These were usually men in the age range 35-45 who, for one reason or another, had not yet been called up. They were essentially a better-trained and equipped *Volkssturm*. Another little-known unit was *Luftwaffe-Bau-Ersatz-Bataillon 13*.[30]

An additional 200 SS men came from the *I./SS-Panzergrenadier-Regiment 23 Norge*, an orphaned battalion from *11. SS-Freiwilligen-Panzergrenadier-Division Nordland*. The seasoned veterans held down *Kampfgruppe Semmering*'s right flank at Rettenegg. Throughout 1945 this battalion had been detached from its parent division, now in the Berlin area, and had mostly served with *5. SS-Panzer-Division Wiking*. It had been shattered during *Unternehmen Konrad I* and had only recently become combat ready again, yet even as the men marched back into battle they heard bad news. *SS-Sturmbannführer* Fritz Vogt, Knight's Cross winner and commander of *SS-Aufklärungs-Abteilung 5*, but the former commander of *I./SS-Panzergrenadier-Regiment 23 Norge*, died of the wounds he suffered the day before in a Soviet air attack.

* * *

Luftwaffe personnel came from a number of different organizations, including airfields, schools and disbanded front-line units. Most were Germans although some Hungarians were also included. One group with three platoons came from the *Flugzeugführerschule Klagenfurt*, the Aircraft Leader School in Klagenfurt. They brought four machine guns with them. The total number of *Luftwaffe* personnel numbered somewhere between 250 and 300 men.

One machine-gun company came from the fortress battalion at Klagenfurt. Fortress battalions were static formations manning one particular defensive position and came in three variations; infantry, machine-gun and heavy machine-gun. This was likely from a heavy machine-gun battalion. This company was also posted to Rettenegg. Some 320 men from the *Gebirgsjäger-Ausbildungs-und-Ersatz-Abteilung 136* at Wolfsberg came in motorized vehicles.

Arriving on 6 April were the men and guns from the *Gebirgs-Artillerie-Schule Dachstein-Obertraum*. Their commanding officer, *Oberst* Heribert Raithel, would soon take over command of the *Kampfgruppe* and, when he did, the name would change to how it is known to posterity, *Kampfgruppe Raithel*. The men rode in buses to the front and along the way they stopped at the Böhler Bros Steel Works in Kapfenberg. This 75-year-old company was known for the quality of its light artillery guns, some of which Raithel ordered taken with them. A great number of the employees were conscripted as *Volkssturm* and added to the *Kampfgruppe*.

Sperrverband Motschmann

What happened in the rugged country south of Semmering Pass was typical of the fighting all around eastern Austria. Sometimes the numbers were much bigger, sometimes not, but it's illustrative of those days of confusion. In the previous week between 15,000 and 20,000 refugees had flooded the area of Friedberg, Pinggau, Mönichwald and other towns in the region. With them came stories of Russian war crimes that only heightened anxiety among the Austrians.

No one knew exactly where the Russians were so for the previous three days patrols had scouted the area around Markt-Aspang and Mönichkirchen. Like most of Styria it was mountainous, forested and cultivated wherever possible. The latter town was astride the border between Lower Austria and Styria. The SS men forced the men of the *Volkssturm* on the Styrian side to help fell

---

30   Some of the men are rumored to have been Bosnian volunteers.

trees across the main highway to set up a roadblock. Shortly thereafter, around 8:00 a.m., a group of Russians coming from Pinggau got hit with MG-42s and *Panzerfauste*.

Satisfied with having hurt the Russians the SS men melted into the forest. The Russians dragged civilians out of the local farms and made them clear the road, then they went after the Germans. The next nearest village, Schaueregg, fell without a shot being fired, but then the local *gasthof* burned down in a mysterious fire that killed two women. The Hotel Märzendorfer was used as a hospital and graves for the dead were dug around the town's war memorial.[31]

* * *

The Germans resisted everywhere they could but the Russian onslaught seemed unstoppable. In the area of Pinggau, Friedberg and Stögersbach alone there were some 20,000-30,000 Russians.

* * *

In the village of Lafnitz, for days the fires of Pinkafeld were visible in the night sky. As the front came closer the townsfolk who planned to evacuate began packing for the long, hard journey. On the morning of 6 April they began to leave. There was no *Volkssturm* left to defend the town because they had all been ordered to Friedberg on Easter Sunday.

Divisionsgruppe Krause, sometimes known as *Köruck 593*

Krause's command started with *Volks-Werfer-Brigade 19* attached, and he stationed it near Friedberg in anticipation of the coming Russian attacks. This brigade fought during the Ardennes Offensive and had been transferred to *6. Armee* as fire support during the fighting in Hungary, where it was attached to *III Panzerkorps*. It consisted of *Volks-Werfer-Regiment 23* and *Volks-Werfer-Regiment 24*. At full strength they brought a lot of firepower to the battlefield, but most of their men now fought as infantry. Stationed so far north, it caught the brunt of the Russian attack north of Pinkafeld. Its sister unit, *Volks-Werfer-Brigade 17*, was attached to *IV SS-Panzerkorps*.

The Russian 30th Rifle Corps moved west from Pinkafeld and shoved the *werfer* men out of the way and took Sparberegg, Ehrenschachen and Pinggau without a fight. The only place the *Volkssturm* resisted at all was at Schäffensteg, and the hard-bitten Russian veterans dealt with them in short order.

With the major breakthrough on his northern flank, Krause's division was also reinforced with two battalions from *Gebirgsjäger-Regiment 98* and one from *Gebirgsjäger-Regiment 99*, or roughly one third of the front-line strength of *1. Volks-Gebirgs-Division*, along with two light and one heavy artillery battery from *Gebirgs-Artillerie-Regiment 79* and two *Volkssturm* battalions.

* * *

West of Semmering itself was the town of Spital am Semmering. Dating back to its endowment in 1160 the town grew as a place of vineyards, but in more modern times was known for its ski slopes. Near the end of the first week in April 1945, 90 men from *Fliegerhorstkompanie E-218/VII* were bussed into the picturesque little town as a defense force. A *Fliegerhorstkompanie* was the umbrella organization for the men who ran an air base, such as the weather section, dental and medical group, air traffic controllers, workshop mechanics, ordnance personnel, photographers and fire fighters. Handing them weapons and telling them to fight didn't make them qualified for ground combat. Nevertheless, a few days later they were transferred to the Sonnwendstein, where parts of it were

---

31   Brettner, *Die Letzten Kämpfe Band I*, p. 26.

subordinated to *Gebirgsjäger-Regiment 134*, orphaned from *3.Gebirgs-Division* which was fighting in Silesia. Ready or not, the *Luftwaffe* men would see their share of combat in the coming weeks.

SS-Kampfgruppe Schweitzer

When surrounded, hundreds of German commanders before him had been ordered to hold until the last man, but *SS-Sturmbannführer* Schweitzer had no intention of allowing his *Kampfgruppe* to be wiped out. The densely forested mountains to the west and northwest of Rechnitz meant they wouldn't meet Russian tanks during a breakout, and offered the hope of being able to filter through enemy lines. At any rate, whatever the odds of them getting through, their collective fate was guaranteed if they stayed put.

The lightly wounded went with them, but the more seriously wounded were left behind to their fate. Between 300 and 400 men were gone from their ranks now, either dead, wounded or missing. *I./SS-Brigade Ney* was still with the *Kampfgruppe*, a veteran presence Schweitzer could rely on, since for the Hungarians surrender meant death. Two regiments of veteran Russian troops lay between them and safety. Three days of bitter fighting lay ahead before the exhausted survivors fought their way back to German lines. But by their sacrifice they had bought precious time for *6. Armee* to patch together a defense to protect Styria. The offensive toward Hartberg had to be delayed while the Russians drove Schweitzer out of Rechnitz.

III Panzerkorps

General of Panzer Troops Hermann Breith's corps was echeloned further east of its flanking neighbor, *IV SS-Panzerkorps*, but had no choice except to hold if it could. The problem was that Russian penetrations on the corps' northern flank had moved far to the west and there was nothing to seal the breach. The corps still had *Schwere-Panzer-Abteilung 509* attached but they were of limited use in the dense mountains.

Forcing *III Panzerkorps* backward was Twenty-Sixth Army with three rifle corps under its command, 30th, 135th and 54th, with a total of eleven divisions. With *6. Armee* effectively cut in two by the Russian breakthrough at Oberwart, Balck transferred *1. Panzer-Division* to Breith's command to take the Russian offensive in its flank.

1. Volks-Gebirgs-Division

The veteran division might have been the single strongest division in *Heeresgruppe Süd*, with 12,301 men, 4,738 of them in combat units, and 20 88mm guns. It did more than any other single unit to shield Styria from the Russian advance. On 6 April it faced no less than three Russian corps and six rifle divisions in the area around Deutsche Schutze and to the south. But its right flank had only scratch units somewhere in the mountains and Russian forces threatening its rear area. This was one of several danger points in *6. Armee*'s front, any one of which could prove disastrous.

IV SS-Panzerkorps

The valley of the Raab River acted as a highway for invaders from the east into the heart of Styria. The Russians had been rolling forward with 18th Tank Corps acting as the armored spearhead, until that unit was suddenly transferred north to exploit the gap between *I SS-Panzerkorps and II SS-Panzerkorps*. Without their firepower the Russian advance stalled under counterattacks by *IV SS-Panzerkorps*, but elsewhere new crises threatened the army's left flank.

Kampfgruppe 3. Panzer-Division

The Armored Bears held the corner position in the front line in the area near Güssing, before it bent west to prevent having the army's flank turned. To their southeast stood the Twenty-Seventh Army, with 35th Guards Rifle Corps commanding four divisions, including the elite 3rd Air Landing Division and a self-propelled artillery regiment.

Kampfgruppe 5. SS-Panzer-Division Wiking

Wiking's front faced south and southeast, not east, where the Russian 202nd Division lined up against it on the southeastern flank. Directly to the south was the Russian 33rd Rifle Corps, with at least four divisions in the gap between *6. Armee* and *2. Panzerarmee*. The wedge between them exceeded thirty miles west into German territory.

Kampfgruppe 1. Panzer-Division

On *Wiking's* right flank around Unterlamm the battered remains of *1. Panzer-Division* had bent backward under the Russian advance like a door being shoved open from outside. It was the last regular formation on that flank.

Kampfgruppe 9. SS-Panzer-Division Hohenstaufen

No SS division had come out of Hungary in worse condition than *Hohenstaufen*. A panzer division was designed to be 100 percent motorized, so that during a move every member rode in a truck, SPW, panzer or staff car. But after Hungary it only had 30 percent or fewer of its vehicles left. In practical terms that meant any move of more than a battalion would require the men to walk.[32]

XVIII Armeekorps

This was the official position of *Wehrkreis XVIII* in the German order of battle. One unit known to have been under its control was *Kampfgruppe Wolff*, of which little is known except it was commanded by *XVIII Armeekorps* and was divided into 18 groups. At least part of it was *Genesendenkompanie 278*, Convalescent Company 278, which consisted of men released from reserve hospitals who were being prepared for a return to the front. It fought in the area near Sankt Margarethen.

---

32   Newton, *German Battle Tactics*, p. 251.

10. Fallschirmjäger-Division

This newly formed division was on its way to *6. Armee*. Like so many of Hermann Göring's *Fallschirmjägers* the men were paratroopers in name only. It was composed of German paratroopers who had been fighting in Italy, along with surplus pilots and airbase staff from *Jagdgeschwader 101*. Despite their lack of ground combat training, the men of the division fought surprisingly well, although they never actually wound up in *6. Armee*. Instead they were sent further north, to reinforce the newly forming *Korps Schultz*.

2. Panzerarmee

Although Russian forces south of Vienna had been weakened by the transfer north of stronger assault forces, attacks continued nevertheless. North of the Drau in the vicinity of Varaždin strong Russian attacks pushed back *2. Panzerarmee*'s right wing. The effort to sever ties between Army Groups E and South became clearer with every day. On the left flank things went better as sporadic contact was made with *6. Armee*.

General de Angelis' army had three corps – *LXVIII Armeekorps, XXII Gebirgs-Armeekorps* and *I Kavallerie-Korps* – while in Army reserve was *Korps Gruppe von Rudno*, about which very little is known. Like the rest of the German front in Austria both of *2. Panzerarmee*'s flanks were imperiled, but unlike the rest of *Heeresgruppe Süd* the fate of *Heeresgruppe E* rested on the ability to maintain a physical link with its neighbor on the right.

14. Waffen-Grenadier-Division der SS Galizien

After their successful attack earlier in the month the Ukrainians held the line around Dietersdorf am Gnasbach. The division fought for three days and nights without stop. Nobody slept and meals were eaten on the march or with bullets whizzing around the men.

At the end of this period two sentries were discovered asleep. Since at least the days of the Roman legions sleeping on watch was cause for dire punishment, and so it also was in the *Waffen-SS*. A German *SS-Untersturmführer* in charge of the detail didn't listen to pleas for leniency from the Ukrainians, however, and condemned them to death. The two men were executed by firing squad, although alternate punishments were available.

This was a blow to the division's morale. The men knew the rules and understood the need for harsh punishment for the sentries, but they were friends from a homeland now occupied by their mortal enemies. Why should they fight for a supposed ally who treated them the same way the hated Bolsheviks did? Moreover, while these men were the last ones ever executed, there had already been more than 200 such killings before that incident.

The fact that *Galizien* fought as well as it did was surprising, given its terrible leadership. *SS-Brigadeführer* Fritz Freitag never missed a chance to disparage his command. He continually petitioned for a transfer and generally downplayed his division's combat value. Having once commanded *8. SS-Kavallerie-Division Florian Geyer* he saw his position as a demotion and punishment, and it probably was. Freitag wasn't liked within the *Waffen-SS* and was considered an ambitious schemer who pursued his own goals. There was no question of Freitag's personal abilities or courage, since he'd won the Knight's Cross, but his lack of confidence in the Ukrainians was an albatross around their collective necks.

* * *

Within a few days the division would hold a front of eight miles, from Feldbach south to Bad Gleichenberg. All three infantry regiments were in the line so reserves were limited. On its left flank, that is, to the north, was *Kampfgruppe 5. SS-Panzer-Division Wiking* and on the right was *16. SS-Panzergrenadier-Division Reichsführer-SS*. In a moment of fortuitous timing, 82 members of the division returned from schools where they'd been trained as *Unteroffizieren*, NCOs. Within the *Waffen-SS* lower-ranked officers and NCOs had been in chronically short supply for years, so this infusion was very helpful. Unfortunately the men had no combat experience.

Kampfgruppe 117. Jäger-Division

Although the division was badly hurt in heavy fighting against Tito's partisan army in Yugoslavia, it retained a Combat Rating of II, meaning suitable for limited offensive missions. Total manpower on 5 April was 8,940, with 6,015 of those men in the combat formations and strong artillery, anti-tank and *Flak* batteries.[33] On the army's right flank Bulgarian attacks on the southeast-facing line south of Veržej threatened to roll up their line on the Mur River. Casualties among the attackers were terrible but the intensity of the assaults was maintained. The Russians would spend as many Bulgarian lives as necessary to crack the German lines.

2. Panzerarmee

General der Artillerie de Angelis finally had a breathing space to begin cobbling together a front line: *23. Panzer-Division* moved from the Ljodomer area to north of Radkersburg, with *9. SS-Panzer-Division Hohenstaufen* on its right flank. By doing this, contact was re-established between *6. Armee* and *2. Panzerarmee* and, for the time being, a front had been cobbled together. Whether or how long it could hold was a different matter altogether.[34]

---

33   Axis History, '117. Jäger-Division', Updated 29 March 2014, <https://www.axishistory.com/list-all-categories/150-germany-heer/heer-divisionen/3871-117-jaeger-division>, (Accessed 16 December 2018).
34   Rebentisch, *To the Caucasus*, p. 464.

7

Saturday, 7 April

Berlin

Reverberations from the Cuff Band Order continued to shake the leadership of the Reich. *Reichsminister* Joseph Goebbels maintained his own extensive network of informants because he always wanted to know the truth for himself, regardless of how unpleasant it might be. Only by knowing the actual facts of a situation could he then mold them to suit his needs. To that end, he sent his own aides to investigate what really happened in Hungary and confided his feelings to his diary:

> The removal of their arm-bands from the crack SS divisions has had a devastating effect… members of them [the *Waffen-SS* divisions involved] said that Berlin was finished as far as they were concerned…I am most depressed over the *Führer's* action against the SS divisions.[1]

Despite the self-serving nature of these statements, at this point it is safe to say that Goebbels was far more concerned about the welfare of the SS men than was their commander, *Reichsführer-SS* Heinrich Himmler, who meekly acquiesced to the Cuff Band Order. It should have been his place to defend his subordinates, but not only did he not protest, he actually traveled to Austria to reprimand Dietrich in person. The fact that it backfired when Dietrich showed up with an armed escort only underscored Himmler's loss of influence with the *Waffen-SS*. However grotesque he may have been as a human being, Goebbels' outlook was at least grounded in some reality, whereas Himmler was already sliding into the fantasy world that led him to wonder whether he should give Eisenhower the Nazi salute or shake his hand.

With time running out to record invectives against his enemies, Goebbels couldn't resist a few parting shots at von Schirach concerning the battle for Vienna: "Riots have taken place in the former Red suburbs of the city and…von Schirach has been helpless. He let things take their course and then takes refuge with the soldiers…von Schirach has long been overdue for dismissal, but the *Führer* has not been able to make up his mind to despatch him to the wilderness."[2]

Heeresgruppe Süd

The weather across the battlefield had turned cool and rainy but this had no effect on the speed of the Russian advance. Compared to winters in Mother Russia it was downright tropical.

Army Group intelligence needed to identify the path of advance after the capture of Vienna, but so far there were no indications of Russian plans. The two choices were either to advance

---

1   Trevor-Roper, Professor Hugh, *Final Entries 1945: The Diaries of Joseph Goebbels* (New York: Avon, 1978), p. 390.
2   Trevor-Roper, *Final Entries*, p. 390.

west along the valley of the Danube, or turn northwest toward Prague. Whichever they chose the Germans could only sit and wait to find out. The days when the *Wehrmacht* held the initiative were long gone.

North of the Danube

8. Armee

The loss of the Morava River line was a disaster for *8. Armee*. Kreysing didn't have enough men to hold back the Russians as it was, but using natural barriers to their utmost he might have slowed them down. The multiple breaches left his army reeling. His job now was to both delay the Russian advance and avoid being surrounded.

One of the last towns still held in the center of the line was Hohenau an der March, but it wasn't to remain peaceful for long. Mortar rounds began impacting in the town on 7 April, a sure indication that infantry attacks would soon follow.

Around Angern the *101. Jäger-Division* committed a battalion to counterattack the Russian infiltration of the previous day, which sparked heavy combat near the Morava River. Other elements of the division took up positions to block any further Russian flanking maneuvers.

The *96. Infanterie-Division* fought its way backward step by step, often pausing to launch counterattacks with the *Sturmgeschütze* of *Panzerjägerabteilung 196*, or the men of its signals battalion. Attacks came from directly in front, that is to say from the east, but also from elements of the Forty-Sixth Army that were beginning to cross the Danube, and the division's only flank protection came from *SS-Kampfgruppe Ameiser*, still fighting at Stopfenreuth.

Sometimes German soldiers who were told to fight to the last man did so. At Engelhartsstetten, due north of Stopfenreuth, six men had established a machine-gun nest on the edge of town. The Russians had armored support, and the Germans apparently had no *Panzerfauste* to stop them. They stood their ground as a tank rumbled toward them, spraying it with bullets, until it crushed their position under its treads without wasting a cannon round.[3]

The Russian pontoon bridges over the Danube at Hainburg were protected by clouds of fighters, while ground-attack aircraft hit German targets further north, including *96. Infanterie-Division*. Late in the day the *Luftwaffe*'s own ground-attack aircraft returned the favor by hitting the Russian bridges, but this had little effect on troop movements.

Lost in all the reports of the fighting on the ground are the efforts of the *Luftwaffe* to help *Heeresgruppe Süd*. *Luftflotte 4* had very few aircraft compared to the Russians, but what they did have flew to the point of exhaustion. They were hampered as much by fuel and pilot shortages as lack of aircraft. The scores of brand-new ME-262s burned at Wiener Neustadt illustrate that perfectly. Dozens of jet fighters could have made a big difference in the air war over Austria, but for all Hitler's talk of *wunderwaffe*, the greatest weapon is useless if you can't use it.

Russian attacks continued along the entire lines of both Second and Third Ukrainian Fronts, although many units spent the day reorganizing and getting ready for the next phase of operations. Forty-Sixth Army in particular readied itself for offensive operations after moving to the north bank of the Danube.

---

3   Brettner, *Die Letzten Kämpfe Band II*, p. 153.

SS-Kampfgruppe Ameiser

SS-Kampfgruppe Ameiser,[4] with *Grenadier-Regiment 287* still attached, fought in the area of Stopfenreuth and Englehartstetten, west of Bratislava on the north bank of the Danube. German forces there were in serious danger of being outflanked and cut off from the south, as the Soviet offensive south of the Danube had penetrated much farther to the west by 7 April. Had the Russians crossed the Danube west of the city in the vicinity of Tulln on that day, instead of days later, they might have pocketed large numbers of German troops, thus making a drive westward through the Danube Valley a real possibility. The Soviet attacks in Vienna were aimed at conquering the city as swiftly as possible while hopefully capturing an intact bridge over the Danube. If they could accomplish this, the Red Army could then drive north to cut off units such as *SS-Kampfgruppe Ameiser*; as it was, Russian forces crossed the Danube just west of Hainburg on 7 April, driving northwest and threatening *8. Armee's* southern flank.

The people of Stopfenreuth hid in the cellar of a nearby hunting lodge as the SS men fought to hold the town. *SS-Kampfgruppe Ameiser* fought in the area until 9 April, when Russian units from the Forty-Sixth Army crossed the Morava River and threatened to cut them off from north, west and south, forcing Ameiser's *Kampfgruppe* to pull back yet again.

But at that moment on 7 April Stopfenreuth was a critical position to hold. When *6. Panzer-Division* was shoved westward on the south bank of the Danube, it gave the Forty-Sixth Army of Second Ukrainian Front nowhere to attack. The shrinking German defensive perimeter around Vienna left no room for it to advance on the city, so the army crossed to the north bank on pontoon bridges and prepared to drive westward toward Korneuberg. To do that it had to clear the north bank of the Danube, and their path led directly through Stopfenreuth and *SS-Kampfgruppe Ameiser.*

Vienna

When the Russians drew close enough many of the Viennese fled, hid or got conscripted. That, and a shortage of newsprint, led the city newspapers to cease publication. They were replaced by *The Little War Paper,* a one-sheet daily to filter the increasingly disastrous news through the Nazi propaganda system. The last issue was distributed on 7 April. A small number of copies were allegedly printed on the next day, but with half of Vienna in Russian hands there were few places left to distribute it.

* * *

SS-Oberscharführer Ernst Barkmann's Panther tank was under repair with his battalion's maintenance company, and if anybody had earned some downtime it was one of Germany's top panzer aces. During the previous month Barkmann's Panther company had become separated from its parent division and then fought its way across western Hungary to Austria with *Hohenstaufen,* before rejoining *Das Reich.* Barkmann had become known for never abandoning his panzer, regardless of battle damage.

But instead of resting while the workshop company got his Panther into fighting trim again, Barkmann grabbed a motorcycle and sped between *Das Reich* tank platoons carrying orders and

---

4   Authoritative sources about *Lützow* are few and far between. It appears the *Kampfgruppe* reunited with the parent headquarters for a few days, and then was detached again.

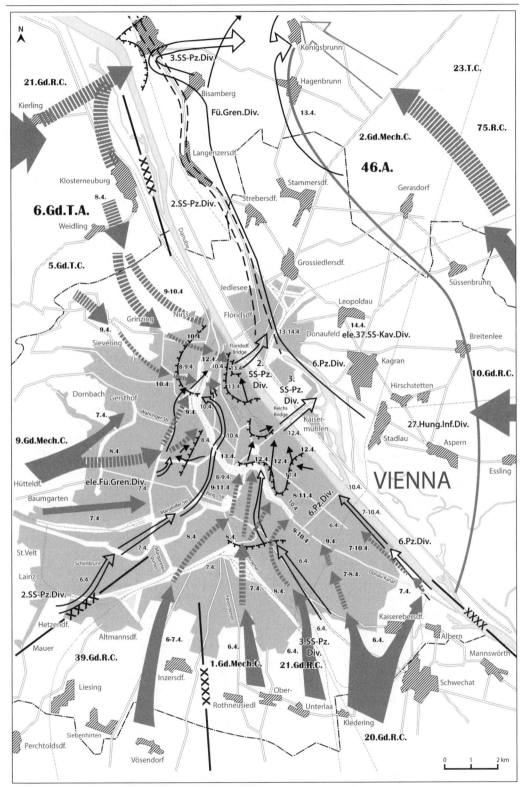

Map 5 The fall of Vienna and escape of *II SS Panzerkorps*.

news. Aside from the obvious dangers from Russian spearheads, artillery fire and ground-attack aircraft, he also had to avoid getting shot by nervous German sentries.

What amazed Barkmann was the Viennese attitude to the combat going on around them. While fighting took place several hundred yards down a road, the restaurants and nightclubs were filled with patrons drinking and dancing, as if the war was being staged for their entertainment. Most of those out on the streets were foreigners, he noted, not the Viennese themselves, either former French, Belgian or Dutch prisoners of war now freed, or Slavic workers from the Balkan countries. As fires lit the night with an orange glow, Barkmann steered his motorcycle through a scene reminiscent of a Hieronymus Bosch painting.[5]

* * *

The seventh day of April was a day of defeat for the *Wehrmacht* and disaster for the Viennese. At the top of the list was the capture of an essential part of Viennese life, the Anker Bakery in Favoriten. Founded by a pair of Jewish brothers in 1891, most Viennese got their bread from this bakery. After the *Anschluss* the founding family was hounded into leaving Austria and the bread factory became public property. Without the Anker Bakery producing their bread, starvation became a very real possibility for the Viennese. Looting caused severe damage to the production lines so that even after the Russians got it back up and running, the bread ration was two pounds or less per week.

* * *

As the Russians approached areas of the city they blew away the Nazi infrastructure like the gust front of a storm. There was always a brief interlude between the flight of the Nazi security forces and the arrival of the Red Army, and within that time frame chaos ruled. People desperate to flee the city crowded the remaining train stations and discarded Nazi pins, clothing and symbols of all kinds. Photos of Hitler lay about the streets in smashed picture frames. With the bread supply gone and no one to stop them, the Viennese looted stores of anything edible. News spread where fuel and food could be found and stocks were gone by the end of the day. If they were going to die, the Viennese wanted to do it on a full stomach.

Beyond food, anything of value was taken, with the hopes of later trading it to the Russians for essentials. In some places the Viennese even queued up as store owners gave away everything they had to keep the Russians from getting it.

* * *

It was probably on 7 April that the Russians captured one of most odious constructs of the entire Nazi state, the *Am Spiegelgrund*, Special Children's Ward, part of the massive Steinhof Hospital Complex in the Penzing, Vienna's 14th District. Of the 60 pavilions built on the grounds, after the *Anschluss* 13 were turned over to the vile T4 Euthanasia Program for use as both a reformatory and children's psychiatric ward. There, grotesque and horrifying experiments were conducted on living children, 789 of whom died during the war. Some of the perpetrators were tried after the war and sentenced to either death or imprisonment; some, but not all.[6]

* * *

---

5   Weidinger, *Das Reich*, p. 376.
6   'Am Spiegelgrund in Vienna Special Children's Ward 1940-1945', <http://ahrp.org/1940-1945-special-childrens-ward/>, (Accessed 10 August 2018).

O-5's plot to avoid street fighting may have been thwarted, but it was far from out of business. The survivors fled to a secret hideaway near Parliament and debated their moves, when from out of the blue Major Szokoll showed up. Having no other recourse to avoid execution he'd surrendered to the Russians, and then volunteered to return to the German part of Vienna to help *O-5* hinder the defense. The Russians saw no downside to this proposal and agreed.

Once back, a discussion followed about whether to try and free *Major* Biedermann, *Hauptmann* Huth and *Leutnant* Raschke, but in the end the resistance leaders decided nothing could be done. Instead, they began to think about forming a government after the Nazis were gone, thinking the Russians would reward them for their actions. That was a serious error in judgment.

* * *

Where the Red Army set foot, retribution was swift to follow. Most Nazis had wisely fled the city, but not all. Those who stayed behind soon came to regret it. Anti-Nazi Viennese were quick to point out their Nazi neighbors and the Russians wasted no time in shooting them, even if they weren't really Nazis. Old scores were settled through denunciations. One unfortunate young man was executed and his mother had to bury him in her garden. Many other people committed suicide, particularly the female family members of prominent men, whether they'd been Nazis or not. The GPU, the Russian Secret Police, showed mercy to none. Those not executed immediately could expect a long train ride east, to Siberia.

* * *

Nothing in the city worked anymore. Electricity was sporadic, phones didn't work, the gas was off and all services and utilities were in a shambles. With central authority gone, the streets reverted to a concrete jungle where no one was safe. Criminals suppressed by the Nazis no longer had anyone to fear and preyed on those foolish enough to venture outside, especially in the dark. An 8:00 p.m. curfew meant anyone out past that hour was risking instant death from the Nazi bully boys of a flying courts-martial. Packs of security men roamed the alleys and avenues looking for deserters, shirkers or anyone they felt like killing under the label of deserter. Constant danger, the stress of urban combat and the fear generated by Goebbels' propaganda machine about what would happen if the Russians came, left the citizenry exhausted and the women terrified. Their initial experiences with the front-line Russian soldiers reassured them Goebbels had merely been frightening them with tales of monsters, like they were children. Then they met the Russians who came after the combat troops moved on, and discovered Goebbels had been right after all.

* * *

Since 1 January 1945, no theater of war had received more support from Hitler than the southern part of the Eastern Front, and *Heeresgruppe Süd* in particular, and in his mind the end results had been disappointing in the extreme. Someone had to be the scapegoat for these failures, and Otto Wöhler was at the top of the list. Sacked for being unable to accomplish the impossible, Hitler appointed a fellow Austrian to succeed Wöhler and save the situation. Commanding *Heeresgruppe Courland* throughout most of the long, bitter winter, *Generaloberst* Dr Lothar Rendulic was chosen to be the savior of his native Austria in the hope that sheer will and determination could compensate for a lack of men and weapons. Rendulic was a long-time member of the NSDAP, and had won both the German Cross in Gold and the Knight's Cross with Oak Leaves and Swords. His best qualification, however, was that Hitler trusted him. Rendulic was one of Hitler's favorites because of his fervent support of Nazism.

Much like *Generalfeldmarschall* Walther Model, the *Führer* sent him into difficult situations and depended on him to stabilize the front. Time after time Rendulic had done just that. It was Rendulic who famously said: "When things look blackest and you don't know what to do, beat your chest and say 'I'm a National Socialist!' That moves mountains."[7] Because of his fanaticism, during 1945 Rendulic had the distinction of commanding three army groups: *Heeresgruppe Nord*, *Heeresgruppe Courland* and *Heeresgruppe Süd*.

Late on 7 April he arrived at Sankt Leonhard im Pitztal, just west of Sankt Pölten. The Pitztal Valley was beautiful during any season, but never more so than early spring, when the streams were filled by melting ice and flowers popped up through bright green grass and the blue sky provided a clean backdrop for packets of snow on the higher slopes. He must have found the warm sunshine energizing after the bleak gray months in Courland. But if the weather was to his liking, the military situation was not. Rendulic's stated intention was to save Vienna, a mission he was already far too late to accomplish.

* * *

After four days on the job as *Kampfkommandant* of Vienna, *General der Infanterie* von Bünau's command was officially subordinated by *6. SS-Panzerarmee* to *II SS-Panzerkorps*, with defensive responsibilities for the northern half of the city. Von Bünau equated this new position to that of a division commander, although he retained his title.[8] In fact he would soon officially become the commander of *Korps von Bünau* in *6. SS-Panzerarmee*'s Order of Battle.

Kampfgruppe Volkmann

Also subordinated to *II SS-Panzerkorps* was the local commander responsible for the defense of Tulln, *Generalmajor* Volkmann, and *Kampfgruppe Volkmann*. As in most places the defenses of Tulln were a hodge-podge of whatever troops and weapons were available. In Volkmann's case the backbone was the *Alarm-Bataillon 3* from *Luftkriegsschule 7* and whatever other troops he could scrape together. He also probably had at least the *I./SS-Kampfgruppe Trabandt II*, also known as *SS-Regiment Konopacki*.

The main defense line outside Tulln ran from Riederberg to Tulbingerkogel. A key position two miles southwest of the town was Langenrohr. On 2 April an SS company had replaced an under-strength Hungarian battalion garrisoning the village, and on 7 April a few panzers showed up to help the defense. When the Russians attacked during the day, the fighting was very heavy. A *Flak* contingent of 16 105mm guns northwest of the parish church added to the firepower of the defense. Other *Flak* batteries, including a twin-mounted 20mm gun, knocked out four T-34s. A German observation point in the parish church drew mortar fire, which damaged the structure. Other homes and two barns were set alight. As night fell the Germans still held the town.

* * *

In Tulln all stores and offices had closed up, although merchants had opened their stores to the local population to keep the Russians from plundering them. Workers who could fight were in the *Volkssturm*, along with government officials without the clout to merit evacuation. The streets leading west were clogged by columns of fleeing people, including prisoners, with *Flak* guns placed to protect them. Only the telephone exchange still worked.

There were never any realistic thoughts that Tulln could be saved from Russian capture. The soldiers would do what they could, but without enough heavy weapons Volkmann's ability to stop the Russian tanks was very limited. When the fight commenced at the outer defenses, using

---

7   Read, Anthony, *The Devil's Disciples: Hitler's Inner Circle* (New York: W.W. Norton, 2004), p. 863.
8   Bünau, *Combat in Vienna*, p. 17.

handheld weapons his men took a heavy toll on the attackers, but Russian attacks backed by armor couldn't be entirely stopped. Once they broke through at Nitzing they wasted no time in targeting Tulln. The attacking Russians included no less than two infantry regiments, 30 tanks and 14 self-propelled artillery guns, probably SU-100s.

Anti-tank barriers blocked the streets of Tulln and the troops had set up strongpoints, but the air base and the bridge were the main targets. Once the Russians got to the airfield, however, it was a different story. Unlike in the town, the airfield wasn't helpless. Heavy fighting erupted when Russian tanks tried to storm the field, only to be met with blistering fire from the numerous anti-aircraft batteries scattered around the runways and hangars. No less than ten Russian tanks went up in flames, while other sources put Russian losses as high as 35 tanks destroyed using *Panzerfauste*, teller mines and the air base's anti-aircraft guns. Infantry losses were as correspondingly high, and the remaining Russians retreated. It was a significant tactical victory, but despite that success Volkmann knew they'd be back. He also knew that he didn't have the men to hold the bridgehead much longer.

The stress of war caused people to make bad decisions they would never have otherwise made. Even as Russian shells landed on the runways during the fighting, a German pilot had loaded his family into a plane and took off, but didn't make it far. Ground fire over Muckendorf brought the plane down and Russian troops executed both the pilot and his wife.[9]

Later that night Russians crept unseen up to the bridgehead's southern outposts before being discovered, and General Volkmann knew the time to blow up the railway bridge was near. With the help of some railroad engineers the Germans moved as many locomotives and rolling stock to the north bank as possible, then blocked the line by derailing a train. Finally, the bridge itself went up in a great explosion. That left only the highway bridge as a lifeline for the defenders to reach safety on the north bank.

With combat moving into the city the time had come to also blow up as much of Langenlebarn air base as possible. There is no question it was SS troops who destroyed all except one hangar, but exactly what unit the men belonged to isn't now known. Some SS railway engineers were also in the *Kampfgruppe*, so these men could have been the ones ordered to destroy the air base facilities. Regardless, after a vicious fight the Germans lost the air base and retreated further into the city with it only partly damaged. At least three *Waffen-SS* men died in the fighting.

But the air base wasn't done being damaged. A few days later the *Luftwaffe* bombed it and destroyed many of the remaining buildings. German artillery continued shelling the area until the end of April, killing civilians and preventing a Russian buildup south of the Danube.

* * *

By 7 April it was apparent to anyone except Hitler that holding Vienna with the troops on hand was impossible, the same conclusion that von Schirach, von Bünau and Dietrich had come to days before. Three Soviet armies were attacking the city from the south, another from the west, and yet more Russians had reached the Danube near Tulln and were moving on the city from due west along the south shore of the river. Strong Russian armored forces were already nearing Klosterneuberg, including 20th and 22nd Guards Tank Brigades, 6th Guards Mechanized Brigade, 48th Guards Tank Regiment and 1458th, 1462nd and 1484th Assault Gun Regiments, and were opposed by the *Pionier-Ausbildungs-und-Ersatz-Abteilung 80*, a force that could not have numbered more than several hundred men, as well as four 75mm anti-tank guns; two that had been hurried up from Freistadt were placed on the southern bank, and two more on the northern bank.

9   'Die Geschichte des Fliegerhorstes Langenlebarn', <http://www.gotech.at/lale2/langenlebarn_2.html>, (Accessed 10 July 2018).

Meanwhile on the north shore a hodge-podge of miscellaneous German units was trying to hold open an escape corridor to the northwest. But time was running out for that, too: *II SS-Panzerkorps* and von Bünau's command were faced with danger on all sides, but orders from Hitler were to hold Vienna at all costs, orders that, if followed, were tantamount to suicide.

6. Panzer-Division

The military situation in Vienna on 7 April was dire. The defenses on the eastern flank were still anchored by the now badly depleted *6. Panzer-Division*.[10] Although not as famous as the SS divisions within the Reich, *6. Panzer-Division* had become a legend in the early months of the war in Russia. It had seen almost continuous fighting ever since, but as Erhard Raus' old unit was trying to hold the line in the Prater those days of glory were long gone. Few men were left from those who marched into Russia.

One way the divisions caught up in the horrific urban combat kept fighting was by swallowing fragments of broken or alarm units. One such were the shattered fragments of *232. Panzer-Division*. The so-called panzer division had been formed the previous year from odds and ends to deal with the Slovakian Uprising. What little armor it once had was a hodge-podge of anything that would run, and it was the only panzer division not authorized to have a panzer component! The division's peak strength was 2,315 men, although it was authorized to have more than 7,000.[11] In late March, as the Russians rampaged through western Hungary, the division disintegrated. One battalion was lost and the survivors dispersed.

But they kept fighting. An unnamed *Kampfgruppe* numbering 750 men fought near Vienna and seems to have acquired enough vehicles to be fully motorized, while a second group of 400 men was stationed near Lautersdorf, north of Vienna, and even had a *Hetzer*. Having fought beside *Kampfgruppe 3. SS-Panzer-Division Totenkopf* for the first week of April, on 7 April the remnants were absorbed by *6.Panzer-Division*. The second group would soon be used as replacements for *Panzerkorps Feldherrnhalle*.

* * *

The Russians had crossed the Danube Canal at its far eastern end and fighting in the Prater was heavy, but little by little the Russians pushed their way forward and *6. Panzer-Division* was forced back toward the Stadium Bridge. Still on *6. Panzer-Division*'s right flank, near the gasworks across the Danube Canal, was that division's *Panzergrenadier-Regiment 114*. Estimating how many men the regiment had left is difficult, but its combat value could not have been great. Not only did infantry units suffer the worst losses, but by that late point in the war the authorized strength of a panzer grenadier regiment was somewhere around 1,100 men, or about half of what it had once been. With the strength of its parent division estimated at only 50 percent, this means the regiment could likely field around 600 men, or about five companies. The opposing Russian units were also badly depleted but had superior firepower and command of the air to compensate for their weakened ground units.

The division's boundary stretched into the center of Simmering. Back and forth combat took place there all day, with buildings changing hands multiple times and casualties high on both

---

10   One source lists *6. Panzer-Division* as having the following strength on 7 April: 44 Officers, 229 NCOs, 962 men of other ranks, and 8 operational panzers.

11   Nevenkin, *Fire Brigades*, p. 604.

sides. The Russians had tank support and pressed their attacks but the Germans held on. The nearby Wiener Berg also held out against nearly continuous attacks.

While *6. Panzer-Division* was still in the Prater area, on its right flank *Totenkopf* and *Das Reich* were being pushed further and further into the city along the eastern and southern perimeter. The most immediate danger was from the west, where the Sixth Guards Tank Army was threatening to turn the Germans' right flank and slice into the city behind those units holding on south of the Danube Canal. Combined with the Russians fighting around the gas works and Arsenal it represented the very real threat of a pincer attack surrounding the elements of *II SS-Panzerkorps* in Vienna.

In reaction to this threat there was no choice except to shorten the lines by pulling back again and shifting forces to form a continuous front. *Totenkopf* had retaken the South Railway Station and was fighting hard around the Arsenal but received orders to withdraw further into the city while the newly arrived *Führer-Grenadier-Division* went into the line on that division's right flank just west of the Ringstrasse, replacing *Das Reich*. The idea was for the SS men to disengage and move behind the *Führer-Grenadier-Division* to the northwest from their position near Liesing to anchor that division's right flank in the vicinity of the Franz Joseph Bahnhof.[12] This would not create a continuous defensive perimeter, but instead a line of strongpoints with *Das Reich*'s right flank supported only by the alert units of *Pionier-Ausbildungs-und-Ersatz-Abteilung 80 and 86, Panzerjäger-Ausbildungs-und-Ersatz-Abteilung 17* and the Hitler Youth Battalion.[13]

But *Totenkopf* could not safely disengage. Combat at the Arsenal had become some of the fiercest fighting of all the war on the Eastern Front. Had the division tried to pull out of the line it risked being overrun. Helping in the fight was a Tiger I that had been in long-term repair and was finally returned to service. It would continue to fight throughout the battle for the city.

At the South Railway Station the Russians launched attack after attack at the positions held by *SS-Kampfgruppe Barth*, fighting beside another small *SS-Kampfgruppe* from *1. SS-Panzer-Division Leibstandarte Adolf Hitler* that must have become separated from its parent headquarters. The station itself became wrecked in the severe fighting. *SS-Untersturmführer* Barth became a casualty and was badly wounded, but he was one of the lucky ones. The medical evacuation services still functioned well enough to get him to a hospital in Linz, where he lay in bed until captured by the Americans. As for his *Kampfgruppe* it dissolved with his departure. Presumably the survivors joined another unit.

* * *

Well to the west, the two remaining operational Tiger IIs of *Totenkopf*'s *9./SS-Panzer-Regiment 3* had made it to Judenau. This small market town had so far been spared the ravages of war and allowed the exhausted tank crews some much-needed rest. After spending 6 April on maintenance, the twin monsters took up defensive positions and dug in. In support of the panzers were some 88mm *Flak* guns from the *Luftwaffe* and a scratch force of infantry.[14] The Tiger II had definite drawbacks when on the attack, but when sited behind strong fortifications it was deadly.

---

12   Rauchensteiner, *Krieg in Österreich*, p. 112.
13   By now the first Viennese Hitler Youth Battalion that fought in Bratislava may have rejoined the second in Vienna.
14   Rauchensteiner, *Krieg in Österreich*, p. 243.

Hitler Youth Battalion

The Hitler Youth Battalion had carried out its assigned mission of holding the rearguard at Hütteldorf and had then pulled out exactly as ordered. The attacking force they faced was the battle group led by Guards Captain Loza, heading for the center of the city, and the Hitler Youth inflicted heavy losses on them. Even as the Russians drove east the Hitler Youth continued to attack and inflict losses, but without heavy weapons they couldn't stop them. Baumgarten and St Viet both fell as the Russians moved toward the West Train Station. The most effective weapons the Hitler Youth had were *Panzerfauste* and they ambushed the column time and again, but the survivors pushed on. By noon the station had fallen but the Hitler Youth Battalion maintained its cohesion for the next fight.

The battalion then moved into the Hohe Warte area in the swanky 19th District of Döbling, sandwiched between the Vienna Woods in the west and the Danube in the east, and was given three 75mm guns that had previously been in the area of the West Station. The alert units were divided between its right and left flanks. The nearby Kahlenberg was held by a *Luftwaffe* alarm unit of dubious value.

2. SS-Panzer-Division Das Reich

The 9th Guards Tank Corps advanced toward the West Railway Station, forcing *Das Reich* to give ground on its right flank and cutting that division off from the hodge-podge of alarm units fighting in the northwest. The situation grew increasingly confused as the day went on, with the division fighting for its very existence against attacks along multiple corridors.

It was in that moment, as it appeared the Russians had broken through to the Danube Canal, that reinforcements arrived in the form of the *Führer-Grenadier-Division*. Moving into the gaps in the defense they stalled the Russians long enough for the defenders to sort out their confusion and maintain the semblance of a coherent defense.

With *Totenkopf* unable to redeploy the decision came for *Das Reich* to do so, moving behind the *Führer-Grenadier-Division* to its right flank.

* * *

After capturing the West Train Station, Guards Captain Loza's group moved further into the city. Suddenly the Russians faced foes more equipped to oppose them than Hitler Youth using *Panzerfauste*, in the form of Panthers from the *Führer-Grenadier-Division*'s panzer battalion. A close-quarters tank battle broke out and both sides suffered casualties, but the Russian momentum was stopped for the day.

* * *

During fighting on 7 April the Russians captured the Grinzing area, which was yet another dangerous penetration in the city. This area is adjacent to Döbling on the city's northwest side and Bittrich could see on his situation map that enemy spearheads were less than a mile from the Danube Canal, with only alarm units to stop them. Once across the canal they could cut off all of *II SS-Panzerkorps* still in Vienna. So now at least four major Russian spearheads threatened his corps, one each from the southeast, west and northwest, and another one on the north bank of the Danube. This left Bittrich with no tactical choices if he wanted to save his command. It was time to retreat across the Danube Canal and then blow up the bridges.

In anticipation of doing this the demolitions began. One by one the lifelines of the Viennese to the outside world exploded and collapsed into the water. Only two bridges were left standing, the Augarten and the Aspern. Those slim structures were all that stood between the defenders and capture or death.

Führer-Grenadier-Division

Panzergrenadier-Ausbildungs-und-Ersatz-Abteilung 10, with some 1,300 men, was ordered to join the *Führer-Grenadier-Division*.[15] The *Führer-Grenadier-Division*'s mission was more than just defensive: it was originally intended that it would counter-attack and recapture the West Railway Station, but it took all day and into the night for the division to fully deploy. By then the Russians were also building up their forces near the station, making a counter-attack unwise. Not that it would have mattered. The maneuvers were a desperate attempt to hold at least part of the city, but it was doomed from the start. The German formations were simply too weak to stop the Russians, much less push them back. But the planned counter-attack would put the men of the *Führer-Grenadier-Division* into position to hit the Russians hard in a surprise and unplanned blow.

The tactical movements through the streets of Vienna led to an incident that shows just how far Viennese morale had fallen by this point. According to Weyr, on 7 April some Viennese women began openly assaulting their own troops. He states that housewives poured hot water, whether boiling or not he does not say, onto soldiers of the "*Führer Division* crossing the Floridsdorfer Bridge".[16] This could only have been the *Führer-Grenadier-Division* as it shifted into the western part of the city. The division had recently been upgraded from a brigade and was then badly mauled during almost continuous fighting in the previous six weeks. It was rebuilt again before its transfer to Vienna.

While it's hard to know the exact reactions of those men to being abused by their own people, the *Führer-Grenadier-Division* knew better than most how civilians, and especially women, were treated by the Russians, having been part of the attack that recaptured Lauban the previous month. The effect on their morale of having hot water dumped on them by the people they were trying to protect must have been devastating, as the division had taken heavy casualties in liberating Lauban.

And Lauban was a stark warning of what awaited German civilians once the Red Army conquered them; Goebbels did not need his propaganda machine to magnify the scope of the threat facing anyone in a zone controlled by the Red Army. Widespread looting, rape and murder were common;[17] indeed, it was uncommon when they did not happen. The Germans recaptured very few cities or towns once the Russians had taken them, so the experience of seeing for themselves the atrocities committed by the Red Army had a profound effect on the men who witnessed the evidence of such brutality first-hand, such as those in the *Führer-Grenadier-Division*. They would have known the fate awaiting those women who dumped hot water on them once the Russians came, some to be gang-raped, others to be shot, or to see their husbands and children killed. It seems likely that the water-pouring incident took place south of the Danube immediately

---

15   Nevenkin, *Fire Brigades*, pp. 644-645. Nevenkin goes on to say this unit was also known as *Kampfgruppe Volkmann*, but as we have seen in the narrative this is in error. A possible explanation is that *Kampfgruppe Volkmann* was attached to the *Führer-Grenadier-Division* around the same time and, with the lack of extant records, the two units were simply mixed up.

16   Weyr, *Setting of the Pearl*, p. 279.

17   While it is beyond the scope of this study to inspect the Red Army's reign of terror on the territories it overran, it is important to note that such a threat existed and was known throughout Germany. Selected instances are mentioned where numbers and evidence exist.

after the troops had crossed the bridge, perhaps in Pater Abel Platz or its environs, or in some of the narrower streets it passed through on the way south. It is not recorded whether they took action against the offenders; presumably not, as the chaos inside the city may have prevented it, as well as the need to hurry to the front lines.

On paper the *Führer-Grenadier-Division* was a favored unit that had the backing of the Army at the highest levels. Its predecessor, the *Führer-Grenadier-Brigade*, had been formed from part of *Panzergrenadier-Division Grossdeutschland*, one of the most famous divisions in the German Order of Battle. Bled white not once but twice, first during the fighting in East Prussia in 1944 and again during the Ardennes Offensive, the brigade had been upgraded to divisional status in January 1945 by yet another infusion of men from *Grossdeutschland*'s replacement formation. Unfortunately, while the new recruits were generally of better than average physical stock, they were hastily trained and would not have been considered ready for combat had the situation not been so dire.

As seen earlier, its tank regiment, *Panzer-Regiment 101*, received 10 *Jadgpanzers* and 16 Panthers straight from the factories in early February, complementing what was already on hand[18] so that its strength was quite strong for a German division of the period. The division had been in almost constant action since February, participating in the counter-attack from Pomerania aimed at Zhukov's spearheads on the Oder, *Unternehmen Sonnenwende*,[19] and in the counter-attack to recapture Lauban as part of *XXXIX Panzerkorps*. But despite fighting hard during the Lauban offensive, the division received enough replacements to be rated at full strength when it reached Vienna.[20]

And so, as the *Führer-Grenadier-Division* went into the line southwest of the Ringsstrasse in Josefstadt, and *Das Reich* moved from their positions near Liesing to hold the line nearer Franz Joseph Station, chaos began to sweep over the city.

* * *

On 7 April, *Gauleiter* Baldur von Schirach ordered the entire complement of Vienna's firefighter force to evacuate the city. Some 3700 firefighters, along with 600 fire trucks and other vehicles, fled the city, leaving only 18 men and 3 damaged fire-trucks to fight fires during the coming battle. A trickle of reinforcements also came to Vienna on 7 April, as "two battalion commanders arrived from the Officer Replacement Pool in the Doellersheim Training Area, and 100 cadets were detached from the reserve officers training courses at Znojmo (Znaim)".[21] Most of the men were assigned to 6. *Panzer-Division* in the Prater, with a few going to *Das Reich* and a few more kept by von Bünau for his staff. Von Bünau had been trying to gather a functioning staff for days, but it was very difficult, since he came to Vienna alone and most of the previous staff had left. His only real choice was from officers assigned to *Wehrkreis XVII*, but most competent officers were already assigned to other duties, either in field commands or alarm units, leaving him only officers who were either too old to be of much use, had no experience or, more ominously, men with ties

---

18   Bishop, Chris, *Panzergrenadier Divisions 1939-1945* (London: Amber Books, 2007), p. 72. Bishop implies that the division started with 56 panzers before these factory additions. He claims that in early February the division incorporated all of its panzers into one battalion, with two companies of 14 Panthers and two companies of Mark IVs, for a total of 56 tanks. Adding another 26 to that total with the deliveries of 15 and 17 February bring the total to an impressive 82 Panzers of all types, which for the time period made this division very strong indeed.

19   This was the attack Guderian and Dietrich wanted 6. *SS-Panzerarmee* to be involved in after the Ardennes debacle.

20   Bishop, *Panzergrenadier-Divisions*, pp. 72-73. Bishop disputes this, saying the division was badly depleted by April.

21   Bünau, *Combat in Vienna*, p. 7.

to the resistance. He tried to impose some sort of military government control over the city, but by then it was far too late for such things. With the Russians already in Vienna and moving steadily forward, there seemed no hope of stopping them and measures to manage the civilian population were therefore superfluous. Likewise, von Bünau's request that the field divisions retreating through the city be put under his command was rejected out of hand.[22]

* * *

At Tulln airfield, rearguard *Waffen-SS* troops who had been destroying the facilities on the base were engaged by the advance elements of 5th Guards Tank Corps. The historic town was a vital link in the Germans' defense and the Russians were determined the capture it, Langenlebarn airfield and the remaining bridge over the Danube. After a short, sharp battle the defending SS withdrew and the Russians captured the airfield, which was not completely wrecked. All sources agree it was SS who defended the town but none note where they came from. The best guess would be from *I./SS-Kampfgruppe Trabandt II*, the rest of which was forming up in the general area.

By July, when it was handed over to the Americans, the field was again fully functional. The Russians also took the town, but the SS men retreated across the river and denied them the bridge crossing. Before going they blew up the halls and dormitories of the airfield and academy. Artillery batteries from both sides exchanged salvoes across the Danube. The Russians knew if they could cross the Danube in force, they could cut off not only the defenders of Vienna but the *8. Armee* too.

Tulln first drew military attention in Roman times. In the first century AD the Romans built a fort there, with stables for cavalry patrols into the neighboring barbarian lands. During the Second World War a major night-fighter base was established at Langenlebarn, in the city, along with a large *Luftwaffe* training school. The Allies bombed the area frequently, including 26 June 1944 when a huge air battle swirled over the city. The US Fifteenth Air Force sent 300 B-24 Liberator bombers with fighter escort against Vienna, and their homeward course took them over Tulln, where at least 40 ME-109s and FW-190s rose to meet them. Because of its importance the airfield had extraordinarily heavy *Flak* emplacements.

American losses were reported as a terrible 28 B-24s and one P-51, which was a very heavy price. The Germans reported three ME-109s lost.

6. SS-Panzerarmee
I SS-Panzerkorps

Having broken through to the Danube, Russian spearheads headed north, west and east. Against little initial resistance the leading elements moving west ran into a *Flak* group holding Michelhausen and took the town after a brief fight. This put Russians on the road to Krems while simultaneously outflanking *I SS-Panzerkorps* to the north. Dietrich's mangled *Panzerkorps* was in serious trouble.

During the fight for Langenrohr, three miles southwest of Tulln, 16 Russian tanks went into the assault and four were knocked out during the fighting. Even as the 43rd Guards Rifle Corps fought to eliminate the German bridgehead south of the Danube and east of Tulln at Neulengbach, Dietrich realized there was nothing to stop them driving west along the Danube Valley if that was their plan. And it was the obvious next step if they couldn't get over the Danube. In response the staff of *6. SS-Panzerarmee* began making plans to counter such a thrust, although with what units remained to be seen.

---

22   To the very last, the territorial nature of the German command bureaucracy made cooperation for the greater good very difficult.

Kampfgruppe 1. SS-Panzer-Division Leibstandarte Adolf Hitler

According to James J. Weingartner, the *Leibstandarte*'s strength had fallen to "fewer than 1600 officers and men and 16 tanks".[23] This must certainly mean combat elements and, if the numbers are accepted, it shows just how badly the SS formations had suffered during their three-week fighting retreat through Hungary and Austria. This didn't mean all of the missing men were dead, seriously wounded or captured, however. Many had probably become detached from the parent division and were stragglers, perhaps impressed into alarm units or other divisions, and others could have been lesser wounded in short-term convalescence. For example, it's known that a small number of men from the division got caught up fighting in Vienna. The numbers quoted simply accounted for men on hand when the count was taken. And yet for all their losses they remained formidable opponents.

The previous day in the area near Hirtenberg and St Veit an der Triesting a breakthrough had been sealed off by immediate counterattacks, so on 7 April the Russians assembled nearly 40 tanks and attacked Pottenstein again. This time elements of the *LAH*'s panzer regiment drove them back with the loss of 11 tanks. North of Pottenstein, see-saw fighting on a 1,400 foot-high mountain ended with the Germans finally taking the hill but having to immediately abandon it. The remaining artillery batteries supported the attackers but were hampered by the strict limits on ammunition expenditure. Despite this setback the Russian penetration at Dreistetten was blocked by a counter-attack.

Maier reports that a Russian attack with 13 tanks on Rekawinkel, west of Pressbaum, saw heavy fighting with unnamed elements of *II SS-Panzerkorps*,[24] with the defenders being pushed back several miles to the west. In all likelihood this unit was *SS-Aufklärungs-Abteilung 1*, which the previous day had been ordered into the Pressbaum area.

Pressbaum in Austria is not to be mistaken with the German name for the Slovakian capital, Pressburg. Pressbaum and Rekawinkel were both in the Vienna Woods. The Russians reportedly lost three tanks in the attacks. Regardless, the loss of Rekawinkel widened the breakthrough route as the Russians drove onward to the Danube.

Kampfgruppe 12. SS-Panzer-Division Hitlerjugend

A *Kampfgruppe* from *Hitlerjugend,* almost certainly *SS-Kampfgruppe Bremer*, retook the Hohe Lindkogel near Alland after bitter, close-in fighting. The 2,500 foot-high peak was surmounted by the Iron Gate, a lookout tower from which the entire eastern Wienerwald could be seen. It was a key feature to both sides. But alarm units around Alland were attacked by at least a regiment and driven back, leaving the *Hitlerjugend* men atop Hohe Lindkogel exposed in a precarious situation. The Russians were on both flanks and threatening to cut them off by moving south from Alland. Nevertheless, this was the kind of fighting that gave the Germans a chance, small-unit actions in heavily forested and mountainous terrain where the use of mobile forces was limited by the secondary road network. Capturing these positions by assault meant the Russians had to move up steep slopes while under fire, without knowing for certain the strength of the defenders. Even so, along with the *LAH*, both divisions were being stretched further and further apart, with gaps opening between their parts, gaps that left them open to piecemeal destruction.

---

23   Weingartner, James J., *Hitler's Guard, Inside the Führer's Personal SS Force* (New York: Berkley Books, 1990), p. 162.
24   Maier, *Drama*, p. 351.

Another little-known *SS-Kampfgruppe* began to assemble around Wilhelmsdorf, south of Sankt Pölten. Under the command of *SS-Obersturmführer* Jürgen Chemnitz, *SS-Kampfgruppe Chemnitz* was roughly the size of a reinforced panzer company. The infantry was supplied by men from *I./SS-Panzer-Regiment 12* who had no panzers to operate, plus miscellaneous surplus personnel. The panzer component comprised four partly operational Panthers, three recently repaired Mark IVs, four fully operational Mark IVs and, of all things, one Mark IV from *Das Reich*, which apparently was part of another *SS-Kampfgruppe*, under the command of *SS-Hauptsturmführer* Resch. *SS-Kampfgruppe Chemnitz* moved to Ober-Grafendorf, adjacent to Sankt-Pölten on the left. Most of the infantry would later be transferred to *SS-Kampfgruppe Gross*. In the meantime the panzers found the optimal defensive positions and waited.

SS-Kampfgruppe Keitel

Fifteen miles southwest of Wiener Neustadt, Keitel's command had built a series of strongpoints screening the town of Sieding. The only approach to the town for a mechanized military force was from the southeast, through the towns of Ternitz and Sierning, and that's the route the attacking Russians followed. The narrow front concentrated the action, which led to heavy fighting. The German line held for the time being.

6. Armee

Behind the front lines, in Graz, the Nazi civilian and military bureaucracy continued to function at a very high level to support the fighting troops. *Gauleiter* Siegfried Ueberreither sent a steady stream of men to the front, and organized various supply efforts to keep *6. Armee* fighting. *General der Gebirgstruppe* Julius Ringel helped organize the military units and oversaw the fighting of *Kampfgruppe Semmering*.

Graz had a small oil refinery. It didn't produce a lot of fuel, but it did produce some. In the desperate situation confronting Ueberreither's *Gau*, even small quantities made a big difference. Civilians were also put to work reloading spent German rifle ammunition, using captured Russian ammunition to supply the gunpowder and bullets. Whatever food could be spared was sent forward. If Graz fell to the Russians further defense of Styria would be impossible, and both sides knew it.

As for Hermann Balck's command, the more immediate concern was the huge hole ripped in his front north of *Divisionsgruppe Krause*. Having long-since learned to reinforce success, the Twenty-Sixth Army brought up tens of thousands of fresh troops to widen and deepen the breach, perhaps as many as 30,000, and Balck had nothing with which to stop them. Russian reconnaissance patrols appeared in the Upper Lafnitz Valley and town after town fell to the attackers. By nightfall they had pushed as far west as Mönichwald, Waldbach and Sankt Jakob im Wald.

* * *

German intelligence reports began to get hints of Russian reinforcements moving in east of the embattled left flank of *6. Armee*. Ominously, these appeared to be cavalry units of 5th Guards Cavalry Corps commanded by the grizzled veteran Lieutenant-General Sergie Gorškov. Troops on horseback were the ideal type of force to exploit a breakthrough in such mountainous terrain.

SS-Kampfgruppe Schweitzer

Having already lost up to one third of their number, the remaining men of *SS-Kampfgruppe Schweitzer* trudged westward, fighting their way over Hirschenstein and Glashütten, past Schlaining, Alt-Schaining and Unterschützen. The Germans called such a movement a *Kessel*. The literal meaning is an encircled area but it could also means a moving encircled area, which is what *SS-Kampfgruppe Schweitzer* had become. The Russians in front of them were forced out of the way like an air bubble rising to the surface of a lake, but as they moved the Russians fired at them from all sides. A pitched battle at Unterschützen nearly stopped them.

Although sunshine warmed the fields, under the heavy forest canopy the air retained its winter chill. Snow lay in the upper elevations, while sleet and cold rain fell on blustering winds over the slopes. The men of the *Kampfgruppe* were wet, tired, hungry, scared and generally miserable. The teenagers weren't veterans yet and the shock of first combat hadn't worn off. Their morale suffered even more as they watched their comrades die.

As they approached Oberwart the Russian presence grew stronger, with more combat troops and armored vehicles. Veering north of that town they came to a long open area on either side of the Pinka River, a verdant valley called the Pinkatal. It is known for its distinctive wines. Schweitzer's *Kampfgruppe* had no choice but to cross this valley in the face of dug-in Russians on the western side. As they did so Russian fire came in from all directions and ripped into their ranks, while some tanks even attacked into the Germans' left flank. Despite all this, the fleeing Germans managed to destroy several Soviet vehicles and force their way through the positions blocking their escape. As night fell they prepared for one final push the next morning, a last effort to live or die.

* * *

The Russian strategy concerning *Heeresgruppe Süd*'s two southernmost armies had become clear by now. Attacks would continue, especially in *6. Armee*'s area, and if a breakthrough occurred then it would be exploited. But the main purpose of the attacks was to fix the German units in place to deprive them of operational flexibility.

Kampfgruppe Semmering

Around Semmering itself, silence filtered into the Pertl family's cider cellar after days of shooting and explosions, followed by the acrid stench of smoke. The family only survived because of the air shaft cut into their mountain niche. When the shooting had died for a long while they emerged to find their home burned to the foundations. Fifty dead Russians lay scattered among dead horses and the three destroyed guns in the orchard. They had lost everything. Another family found ten Russian corpses and six Germans in their tiny yard.

* * *

The town of Maria Schutz near the eastern end of the Semmering Pass was typically Austrian, with an ornately decorated parish church and ski slopes close by. It was defended by elements of *Landesschützen-Bataillon 581* and was a key position to unlocking the pass on its eastern terminus. On 7 April the Russians attacked after throwing hand grenades and pounding the defenders with mortars, then charging forward firing 50 or 60 automatic weapons, probably sub-machine guns, spraying the German positions to pin them down. Counterattack followed attack, but as usual the Germans had little artillery ammunition to support their men. As the day ended the Russians had taken the town.

* * *

There are 2,689 named mountains in Lower Austria alone. One of those on the northeastern end of the Semmering Pass region was the 2,800 foot-high Kotstein, near the key peak of Kobermannsberg. By 7 April the Russians had already occupied it, but men from the *Gebirgs-Artillerie-Schule Dachstein* fought hard to stop them from keeping it.

The school's batteries set up at the Sanatorium in Breitenstein. This suited the men just fine, since there was a tavern at nearby Kreuzberg that was still operating. The school's officers decided that was an excellent meeting place. The excuse for the trip was scouting out fall-back positions for the artillery batteries, but some of the officers spent the night at a nice inn.[25]

Sperrverband Motschmann

Vorau was not to be spared the ravages of war. On 7 April elements of what had been called *Sperrverband Motschmann* but was essentially *SS-Polizei-Regiment 13*, moved into the little village. Sounds carried in the alpine valleys and any townsfolk and refugees who hadn't yet left heard the echoes of gunfire and artillery coming from nearby Bruck, Mönichwald and Waldbach. The war was getting close.

1. Volksgrenadier-Division

Aufklärungs-Abteilung 54 held an area of small wine-growing villages east of Kohfidisch, east of Tsaterberg. During the afternoon of 7 April heavy Russian attacks hit the exposed battalion, which was built for fast movement, not defense. Fifty men fell in the fighting, either dead or wounded. *Pionier-Batallion 54* also suffered equally heavy losses. Companies throughout the division were bled out, averaging no more than 40-70 men each, putting them between 30-50 percent in strength.[26]

Kampfgruppe 1. Panzer-Division

Withdrawn from the front, the division began moving to Fürstenfeld, east of Graz. It still had no significant armored group but in the mountainous terrain its veterans could help stem the Russian advance without them.

2. Panzerarmee

Russian reorganization of the front continued as 1st Bulgarian Army moved into the area between the Drau and the Mur Rivers. The Germans had been in full retreat for days, but that was finally coming to an end in the rolling hills of southeastern Austria and the Russians wanted to keep the pressure on by keeping in close contact.

---

25   Brettner, *Die Letzten Kämpfe Band I*, p. 109.
26   Brettner, *Die Letzten Kämpfe Band I*, p. 40.

14. *Waffen-Grenadier-Division-der-SS Galizien*

The Russians incessantly broadcast surrender pleas over loudspeakers, hoping the Ukrainians would see the hopelessness of their situation and desert. On the surface this would appear to have been a suicidal decision. Ukrainians were a persecuted minority before the war started. Added to this, Stalin had declared that men who allowed themselves to be taken prisoner were traitors, much less citizens of the USSR who fought against it. Desertion should have been the last thing on their minds.

But this is where *SS-Brigadeführer und General der SS* Freitag's known disdain for his own command had eroded morale to the point where some saw throwing themselves on Stalin's tender mercies as the better choice. It was bad enough to face shortages of everything from socks to food and ammunition, and put up with the racism of your officers even after the division had stood and died at the Battle of Brody the previous year, and saved the situation in Austria within the past week. But to see their exhausted friends shot for any infraction by German, not Ukrainian, officers, was too much for some of them. By twos and threes they slipped out of the German trenches. In the worst case, 30 men were talked into switching sides by two NCOs, and later that night broadcast to their friends in the SS division about how great conditions were in the Red Army. By the end of the war nearly 600 men deserted. The vast majority, however, did not.

* * *

Despite the success of *Galizien* in sealing the breach, *General-der-Kavallerie* Gustav Harteneck knew the precarious position that his corps was in, facing both 6th Guards Rifle Corps and 64th Rifle Corps. Unlike American units, where the word 'cavalry' had evolved into a meaning more in line with 'mobile reconnaissance' than equine, his cavalry divisions still rode horses. On the steppes of Russia, or in the difficult terrain of eastern Austria, this gave them a movement capability far better than standard infantry or motorized units. But men riding horses couldn't carry heavy weapons, so while the divisions were extremely fast and mobile they were inherently low in firepower compared to an infantry division. This made them a poor choice for manning the front lines in static defense, which gave *Galizien* a heavy responsibility as the primary defenders of the corps sector.

Harteneck assumed the Russians would waste no time attacking to regain the ground they'd lost, and he was right. The 10th, 20th and 61st Guards Rifle Divisions led the assault on *Galizien*, with their immediate objective being Trautmanndorf. The nature of the terrain limited armor, artillery and air support, making it more of a straight infantry battle. Regardless, the Russians outnumbered the Ukrainians by some four-to-one, and the Germans were desperately short of ammunition for the heavy weapons it did possess.

On the division's right flank, *Waffen-Grenadier-Regiment-der-SS 29* was driven out of Gleichenberg and Bad Gleichenberg. The high ground known as Gleichenberg Kogel changed hands several times but the Russians were simply too strong. Losing that promontory gave the Russians the advantage of observing movements by the Ukrainians over the entire immediate region.

Usually fighting slackened off with the fall of night, but over the next three days the Russians kept coming regardless of the time of day. Under relentless pressure the Ukrainians adopted a version of how the ancient Roman legions rested the men in the front rank. Front-line companies would be systematically relieved so they could go to the rear to eat something, attend to personal hygiene, clean weapons or sleep.

23. *Panzer-Division*

Although the division was on the move to north of Radkersburg the Russians threatened to move in and cut their route march by invading the Radkersburg area, so once again it was time for a counterattack. *Panzergrenadier-Regiment 128* was reinforced by a Hungarian infantry regiment of dubious quality and two patched-together Panthers. *Panzer-Aufklärung-Abeteilung 23* moved up first and protected the division's assembly area southeast of the city at Zelting, where the early hours of darkness reverberated with the thrum of engines and the clank of tracked vehicles. *Panzergrenadiers* stood around smoking or waiting for orders, and while the newest men wondered what daylight would bring, the veterans just wanted to sleep.

The attack started on time at 6:00 a.m. and initially moved easily over low-lying lands near the Mur River, but then, without warning, heavy fire erupted from strong Russian positions. German losses were heavy with a high percentage of those hit either officers or *Unteroffizieren*, i.e. non-commissioned officers (NCOs). With their leaders falling around them the men hesitated and fell back. The attack was called off and the division retreated to the area west of Vashidegkut, a small village northeast of Radkersburg. Their old positions were taken over by the remnants of *44. Infanterie-Division Hoch und Deutschmeister*,[27] as one of the three groups from that division that had been spread all over Austria.

* * *

The *9. SS-Panzer-Division Hohenstaufen* stopped its westward movement and went over to the defense at Bad Radkersburg on the north bank of the Mur River. They were told to occupy the *Reichsschutzstellung*, something neither *SS-Brigadeführer* Stadler or his men knew anything about, but were excited to hear existed. Permanent defensive positions sounded like a welcome change to men being chased for three weeks. Then they discovered the reality of the so-called *Reichsschutzstellung*. Aside from being rudimentary, the Russians had gotten there ahead of them in many places, leaving the exhausted SS men no choice but to throw them out.

By this point the division's *Panzergrenadier* regiments were down to about one-third of normal strength. Since each regiment had three battalions and it was estimated they had the strength of a single battalion, this puts their probable numbers at about 1,000 men each for the last attack ever launched by the division. Casualties were heavy and many men drowned in the Mur River. At the end of the day the panzer regiment had 15 Panthers and eight Mark IVs battle-worthy.[28]

In the coming weeks *Hohenstaufen* would again be filled up with numbers, but its fighting capabilities wouldn't improve. Men from the *Kriegsmarine*, from the *Luftwaffe* and even from shattered *Heer* units, most of whom had no ground combat training and no motivation for its dirty reality, did nothing to bring the division back to its former performance level.

---

27 Rebentisch, *To the Caucasus*, p. 464.
28 Reynolds, Michael, *Sons of the Reich, II SS Panzerkorps, Normandy, Arnhem, Ardennes, Eastern Front* (Havertown: Casemate, 2002), pp. 296-297.

8

Sunday, 8 April

Heeresgruppe Süd

The Russians focused their air forces on *II SS-Panzerkorps* in Vienna and although few Germans saw them, the *Luftwaffe* put as many aircraft into the air as they possibly could to support their own ground forces.

Heeresgruppe Süd's morning report for 9 April is one of the few documents extant and records the destruction of 39 Russian tanks by *II SS-Panzerkorps* on 8 April.[1] The Army Group also reported the number of Russian tanks destroyed since the start of Operation Spring Awakening on 6 March as 1,264 of all types.[2] A large number of those were American-built Shermans. Even taking into account the inevitable exaggerations the figures indicated huge Russian losses. Remarkably, and quite different from many places where German military morale had collapsed, in Austria the elan of the fighting men remained higher than could be expected given Germany's overall situation.

* * *

Generaloberst Dr Lothar Rendulic's first full day on the job as commander of *Heeresgruppe Süd* found him getting bad news from every quarter. The new commander's reputation was similar to that of *Generalfeldmarschall* Walther Model, namely as a man who could work miracles, aka Hitler's Fireman. Certainly Rendulic looked the part of a Hitler favorite. Square-faced, with close-cropped hair surrounding a high forehead, narrow eyes and Himmleresque rimless eyeglasses, he wore a Hitler mustache over thin lips. As a native Austrian born in Wiener Neustadt in 1887, Hitler hoped he might remedy the situation. His primary mission was to save Vienna but the first thing he learned was how impossible that mission had become. To do that Hitler didn't need a fireman, he needed a miracle worker.

Very well educated, multilingual and refined, Rendulic had proven himself to be a master organizer. In most photographs he appears quite fussy, a man who wants things done his way, like a stern schoolmaster. Rendulic was also another Army general who disliked the *Waffen-SS* and thought little of its commanders, especially Sepp Dietrich. After the war he wrote: "A number of commanding generals of [SS] divisions and corps did not possess any military training worth mentioning, not to speak of the Commander in Chief of the one and only SS-Army."[3]

Known as an ardent Nazi during the war, Rendulic heaped criticism on Hitler after it. During April 1945 he kept up the fight because he believed Goebbels' propaganda that revolutionary *wunderwaffe*, wonder weapons, would soon enter service. Although this makes him sound gullible, he wasn't. The Germans really did have multiple advanced weapons under development and, like most high-ranking officers Rendulic surely had his own sources who verified enough of

---

1   Reynolds, Micheal, *A Soviet Red Army Victory at Vienna*, <https://warfarehistorynetwork.com/daily/wwii/a-soviet-red-army-victory-at-vienna/ accessed>, (Accessed 5 December 2018).

2   Maier, *Drama*, p. 353.

3   Rendulic, *Generaloberst* Dr Lothar, *A Reflection on the causes of German Defeat* <http://www.allworldwars.com/A-Reflection-on-the-Causes-of-the-German-Defeat-by-Rendulic.html>, (Accessed 14 April 2018).

the story to keep him believing the propaganda. Some had already entered service, such as the Messerschmitt ME-262 jet fighter, the Arado 234 jet bomber and the Henschel HS-293 anti-ship guided missile. More were beginning to show up on the battlefield, such as the Heinkel HE-162 jet fighter and the Sperber FG-1250 infrared night-fighting apparatus for panzers.[4] He was a lawyer between the wars and a hard-bitten veteran. During one battle in Russia he stood in the front lines with his men.

He could be a very hard man. As commander of *20. Gebirgsarmee* during the German evacuation of northern Finland the previous autumn, *Unternehmen Birke*, Rendulic's men devastated the Finnish landscape with scorched-earth tactics. The provincial Finnish capital of Rovaniemi was burned to its foundations. For these and war crimes committed in the Balkans, Rendulic in 1948 received a sentence of 25 years in prison from an International Court, although he was pardoned in 1951. Whatever other qualities or defects Rendulic may have had, though, throughout the remainder of the war his command stayed together and stubbornly fought against the Russians.

8. Armee

The first week in April proved to be terrible for *General der Gebirgstruppen* Hans Kreysing's *8. Armee*. Bratislava had fallen after a brief but brutal fight and now Marshal Malinovsky's Second Ukrainian Front threatened to cut his army off from *II SS-Panzerkorps* in Vienna. What could have been formidable defensive positions along the Morava River had been crossed in multiple places, but the danger was greatest in the Marchfeld, the relatively flat region on the north bank of the Danube opposite and adjacent to Vienna. Two powerful Russian armies attacked there relentlessly and in great strength, supported by ground attacks from most of the Red Air Force in the area, and a profligate use of artillery the Germans couldn't hope to match. The Seventh Guards Army attacked on a northern axis through the area, while Major General Alexander Petrushevsky's Forty-Sixth Army was crossing the Danube to attack along the river. Due to the Danube's sharp bend northwest at Vienna, the spearheads of both armies aimed for the same point: Stockerau.

Kreysing was a personally brave officer who'd won the Knight's Cross with Oak Leaves and Swords, so he had no illusions about his situation. With Bratislava's fall and the drive in the Marchfeld, his right flank needed the best units he could give it. Of course, so did every other German commander in *Heeresgruppe Süd*, but Kreysing's situation was doubly dire. Not only was his army reeling backward, it didn't have the inherent terrain advantages that the other three armies in the army group had. What he needed desperately on his right flank was reinforcements, but the new commander of *Heeresgruppe Süd* couldn't conjure soldiers from thin air. All he could do was rob Peter to pay Paul, or, in this case, he sacrificed Vienna to save the men fighting to defend it. If the Russians took the north bank of the Danube *II SS-Panzerkorps* would be wiped out, but the only troops available to stop that from happening were the *Führer-Grenadier-Division* and *SS-Pioneer-Abteilung 3*. This transfer guaranteed that no part of Vienna could be held, but in giving up the city it gave the defenders a chance to escape destruction.

In Kreysing's center the town of Hohenau an der March was still in German hands, but that was about to change. A mixed force of Germans and Hungarians attacked the Russian bridgehead near Hohenau, with heavy losses on both sides. But then, right in the middle of the battle, 80

---

4   To this day the question of whether or not Panther tanks equipped with infrared gear ever entered combat is still debated. What is not debated, but is fact, is that a limited number of Sturmgewehr 44 automatic rifles were equipped with the Zielgerät ZG 1229 Vampir system, a rifle-mounted infrared system, which allowed German snipers to kill during nighttime.

Hungarians defected to the Red Army. This turned the fight from a near-certain German victory to a deadlock that would last for days. Most of the townspeople huddled in the wine cellar of a local inn, only venturing out during the day to take care of farm animals and to gather food. Dodging artillery and mortar explosions, they raided the army food depot at the sugar factory and train station.[5]

The weakest spot was *XXXXIII Armeekorps* on the right flank. At daybreak on 8 April the defense force there was essentially *SS-Kampfgruppe Ameiser*, with *Machinengewehr-Abteilung 117* and the command staff of *Machinengewehr-Abeteilung 118* attached. These were still well to the east near the Danube. Kreysing also had the 4th Battalion, 27th Hungarian Infantry Division, but the Hungarians were underfed, badly armed and demoralized. On *SS-Kampfgruppe Ameiser's* left flank was the veteran but newly downgraded *Kampfgruppe 96. Infanterie-Division*, still with the attached *Kampfgruppe Panzergrenadier-Brigade 92*, a grandiose term for a distinctly weak formation.

Facing these two shrunken German units were elements of three Russian Guards rifle corps, the 10th, 18th and 25th. Kreysing knew his two *Kampfgruppen* could never stop such a force, but Rendulic had nothing to send him. Army Group reserves were bits and pieces of broken and alarm units, none of which could arrive in time to save the situation. Nor could Kreysing redeploy his own forces from elsewhere, as the situation in the Marchfeld wasn't the only crisis he faced. Therefore, there was only one place from which to transfer a unit to stave off disaster; Vienna. And within it couldn't be any of the three heavily engaged panzer divisions of *II SS-Panzerkorps*: it had to be the one full-strength division that gave Bittrich a glimmer of hope for holding any part of Vienna, namely, the *Führer-Grenadier-Division*.

Worse news came when, after heavy fighting, the Germans lost Markthof and opened the door for a Russian advance along the Danube. Fifteen Germans and 22 Russians died in the fighting, and the invaders threw up seven pontoon bridges over the Morava River. Damage to the town was extensive, including the parish church and school. Before long the city would see a clampdown by Russian security forces, as Marshal Malinovsky moved his forward headquarters to Markthof.

* * *

Slowly but surely *8. Armee* was being pushed to the northwest, toward what had once been Czechoslovakia. In the center of *8. Armee's* line, the army-sized Russian Pliyev Group had forced the German front backward by some 50 miles in a week, driving to the outskirts of Břeclav. This indicated clearly that the next target for Second Ukrainian Front was Brno, to the northwest of Břeclav. Standing in their way were the twin *Feldherrnhalle Panzer-Divisionen* and the arriving *25. Panzer-Division*. As discussed earlier, the *Feldherrnhalle* formations probably deployed fewer than 6,000 combat troops between them. Likewise, *25. Panzer-Division* was a veteran division, but weak in infantry.

South of *Panzerkorps Feldherrnhalle* was the Third Hungarian Army. This was the same army that had crumpled under the Russian Vienna Offensive on 16 March, which led to the debacle in Western Hungary. On paper it seemed a formidable force, containing the 27th Székely Infantry Division, 1st Mountain Division, 9th Border Guard Division, 23rd Reserve Division, 2nd Armored Division and the Huszár Division. Except for the 9th Border Guard Division those units were bled out, poorly equipped and demoralized. That one division had just received a large number of replacements and had some combat value, but not much. The Hungarians no longer had a country to fight for and few saw any reason to die in a lost cause.

---

5   Brettner, *Die LetzteKämpfe Band II*, p. 168.

Kreysing's dilemma wasn't simply on his right. The left wing remained echeloned very far forward: *XXIX Armeekorps* stood around Trenčin, some 70 miles east of Břeclav. A breakthrough by the Pliyev Group seemed eminently possible. If that happened, without an immediate withdrawal Kreysing risked having both the *XXIX* and the *LXXII Armeekorps* cut off and destroyed.

Hitler's universal stand fast order made such retreats dangerous for the officer who ordered them, regardless of how highly decorated they might be. Kreysing was a veteran Prussian officer who had been in the Army for 36 years, had done just about everything possible in terms of service and whose personal courage couldn't be questioned. Tall, with a no-nonsense gaze and sagging jowls, he wasn't the sort of man to disobey orders. Neither was he the type to let his men die for no reason. Kreysing withdrew his forces.

Kampfgruppe 211. Infanterie-Division

Like so many veteran German infantry divisions, the *Kampfgruppe 211. Infanterie-Division* had been smashed and refilled on multiple occasions, most recently in December 1944. Its commander, *Generalleutnant* Johann Heinrich Eckhardt, had won the Knight's Cross with Oak Leaves for superior leadership. Like so many German divisional commanders of the time he was a hard man to rattle.

The division's *Grenadier-Regiment 317* established its headquarters at Castle Jedenspeigen, near the town of the same name along the Morava River, a 12th-Century site that was repeatedly damaged over the centuries by war. The other regiment, *Grenadier-Regiment 306,* had been so bled white in earlier fighting that it was absorbed by its sister regiment, although whether it was formally dissolved or not isn't known. The combined regiments defended the area from Jedenspeigen south to Dürnkrut.

* * *

West of the Morara River *Kampfgruppe 101. Jäger-Division* and *Kampfgruppe 96. Infanterie-Division* both engaged in multiple fights to try and repel Russian attacks as they withdrew. As a reaction force, *Kampfgruppe Pipo* was formed from *II./Grenadier-Regiment 284*, the *14. Kompanie* from the same regiment, *Panzerjäger-Abteilung 196* and part of a *Volkssturm* battalion from Krems an der Donau.

Heavy artillery and mortar duels added to the casualty lists as both sides had by now had time to bring their heavier weapons into play, but the Russians weren't hampered by ammunition shortages like the Germans were. This shortage was aggravated when a well-placed Russian shell struck a German artillery ammunition dump, which exploded with a thunderous noise heard for miles. Worse than even that, the crossing of the Danube by the Forty-Sixth Army threatened the rear of *Kampfgruppe 96. Infanterie-Division* and *SS-Kampfgruppe Ameiser.*

On the north bank of the Danube, in the corner of land formed by the junction of the Morava and Danube, Forty-Sixth Army was assembling and regrouping for combat. The SS lodgement at Stopfenreuth was increasingly isolated, but the Russians couldn't move west without first eliminating the *Kampfgruppe*. By nightfall the army had gotten to a line from Marchegg on the north through Groissenbrunn to Loimersdorf, northwest of Stopfenreuth. *SS-Kampfgruppe Ameiser* was spread thin and could only put up limited resistance.

Orth an der Donau was next in the path of Forty-Sixth Army. At 10:00 a.m. a motorized Hungarian artillery battery exchanged fire with a newly positioned Russian battery, as the invaders brought more men across the Danube and attacked the town. By early afternoon it was cleared, with nine German soldiers taken prisoner. They were immediately shot by their captors, probably out of anger that four of their own men had died in the fighting. Within the first days of occupation the town was stripped by its conquerors of every horse, cow, pig, mule, chicken, car, wagon, motorcycle and bicycle that could be found. All weapons had to be turned in. Women between the ages of 14 and 65 were required to work for the Russians, with no exceptions. The town commander had 20 men to ensure their cooperation.

* * *

If *General der Infanterie* von Bünau had any doubts about the consequences for a *Kampfkommandant* who failed to save his city and had the temerity to survive, he need look no further than *Oberst* von Ohlen, *Kampfkommandant* of Bratislava. The Germans had invested a substantial force for the city's defense, yet it fell in three days of heavy fighting. It didn't matter that von Ohlen was power-less to stop the Russian Danube flotilla from landing troops behind his lines to take his men in the rear; all that mattered was the result.

Von Ohlen had been tried by court-martial at Breitstetten by officers of *Kampfgruppe 96. Infanterie-Division* and been found guilty. His service with *Kampfgruppe Ohlen* during the Slovakian Revolt of the previous autumn couldn't save him from the penalty for allegedly surren-dering Bratislava without permission. On 8 April he was executed by firing squad and thrown into an unmarked grave. Only after the war was the body exhumed for proper burial.[6]

Breitstetten itself was defended by elements of both of *Kampfgruppe 96. Infanterie-Division*'s two regiments, *Grenadier-Regiments 283* and *287*, but these two formations were both so depleted by this point that they could no longer defend even the German artillery positions, so the batteries were left to fend for themselves. When the Russians attacked the town the Germans put up their usual stiff resistance, but couldn't hold. They lost 51 men killed in that one fight, to 29 for the Russians. Lost among the dead were three townsfolk.

* * *

The transfer of the *Führer-Grenadier-Division* and *SS-Pioneer-Abeteilung 3* happened quickly once they disengaged in Vienna. Instead of moving up to the now-crumbling front line west of Lassee and Loimersdorf, they took up a line farther back, from Raasdorf to Gross-Enzersdorf, and began to dig in. This would give the shattered units at the front a place behind which to reform.

As the Germans retreated west they encountered the pervasive reek of smoke, and after nightfall dark clouds of it hung low over the Marchfeld. It drifted in from the southwest, over the Danube, and must have smelled familiar to the men who just arrived from Vienna. It came from the fires raging in Austria's once-great capital.

6. SS-Panzerarmee

SS-Oberstgruppenführer Sepp Dietrich probably would have traded places with Kreysing. His army had already been sliced nearly in two, with no less than seven Russian corps between most of *6. SS-Panzerarmee* and *II SS-Panzerkorps*. The capture of Tulln meant that communications and movement now had to go through either Krems an der Donau or Linz, a significant detour.

If Dietrich's army was going to remain intact it had to throw together some force to prevent 5th Guards Tank Corps from driving west along the Danube Valley to Krems. The tactical situation on 8 April showed no significant German forces from Kaumberg to Tulln, a 32-mile gap. If he wanted it enough to divert forces from other sectors, Tolbukhin's dream of advancing to Munich

---

6   Brettner, *Die Letzten Kämpfe Band II*, p. 154. Brettner here lists the place of von Ohlen's execution as Breitensee, but this is in error. Breitstetten was the town then in the zone of defense for *96. Infanterie Division*.

by hugging the south shore of the Danube was within reach. Assuming Stavka would go along, that is.

* * *

But amidst the flood of bad news, for once Sepp Dietrich got some good news; the *710. Infanterie-Division* was on its way to reinforce his shattered army. The intention was to use it in the Sankt Pölten area. The army reported that in the first seven days of April it destroyed 197 tanks.[7]

II SS-Panzerkorps

Kreysing and Dietrich both faced desperate situations, but *SS-Obergruppenführer* Wilhelm Bittrich was staring at the imminent destruction of his entire corps in Vienna. As it was, the loss of Tulln forced the corps' line of communication with *6. SS-Panzerarmee* far to the west. First it ran across to the north bank of the Danube through Floridsdorf, then to Stockerau, before turning northwest to Krems an der Donau, where it would then head southeast to Dietrich's headquarters.

But aside from being far removed from its army, the corps was in increasing danger of being cut off in Vienna. Now it was going to lose the *Führer-Grenadier-Division* to stop the Russians from cutting them off in the Marchfeld. The smart thing would have been to abandon Vienna but Bittrich couldn't do that without violating a *Führer* Order. And even if Rendulic gave permission for such a withdrawal, his remaining forces were too entangled in the city to disengage without risking catastrophe. For better or worse they had to extend their fronts to compensate for the loss of the *Führer-Grenadier-Division,* and then fight it out where they stood.

South of the Danube

Kampfgruppe Volkmann in the Tulln Bridgehead

On 8 April, Volkmann received a *Führerbefehl,* an order from Hitler, to blow up the remaining Tulln bridge over the Danube. Hitler gave Volkmann discretion on timing, but such discretion always came with the threat of execution if the decision was mistimed. Five-hundred-pound bombs were fixed in place, probably by ordnance experts from Langenlebarn air base, who had experience with *Luftwaffe* ordnance.

Just before noon the Russians attacked again at Langenrohr. A deep penetration along the levee on the western side of the town unhinged the defenders. Despite fierce defense, the Russians were far too strong to hold and the Germans retreated to Asparn, closely followed by the pursuing Russians.

Tulln couldn't be held now, not with Russian forces attacking from all directions. One last panzer parked at a key intersection covering both main roads leading to the bridge, giving cover fire to the rearguard. Before leaving the city, a pile of ammunition 15 feet high was blown up.[8]

---

7   Maier, *Drama*, p. 353.
8   Brettner, *Die Letzten Kämpfe Band II*, p. 41.

SS-Kampfgruppe Trabandt II, also known as *SS-Regiment Konopacki*

The exact date this unit arrived in the Tulln area is hard to pin down. Most sources put the date as 9 April, but that seems unlikely when all factors are considered. The likeliest date that the first elements arrived has to be either late on the night of 6 April or early on 7 April.

One of the regiment's three battalions fought in the Tulln bridgehead under *Kampfgruppe Volkmann* and was caught south of the river when the bridges were blown. The evidence points to it having been part of the *I./SS-Kampfgruppe Trabandt II*, commanded by *SS-Hauptsturmführer* Hans Eckert, winner of the Knight's Cross and the Close Combat Badge in Gold. He served as a *Panzerjäger* and infantry officer with *Das Reich* and was wounded eight times.

If further evidence of this unit's identity is needed, from among our sources Georg Maier repeatedly mentions *SS-Kampfgruppe Trabandt* as fighting with *Korps Schultz* and later *Korps von Bünau*. Since *SS-Kampfgruppe Trabandt III,* also known as *SS-Regiment Siegmann*, only crossed south of the Danube around 14-15 April, and *SS-Kampfgruppe Trabandt I* served its entire career in northeast Austria, the orphaned men Maier mentions must have come from *SS-Kampfgruppe Trabandt II*. Complications to this arise because after the fall of Tulln the regiment transferred north with all three battalions accounted for. This makes it likely that part of Eckert's battalion made it across the Danube, and part didn't.

Exactly where this battalion fought is also unknown, but the surviving evidence points to Langenrohr. As previously mentioned, a *Waffen-SS* unit relieved a Hungarian battalion there on 2 April, and the *Waffen-SS* defended that town. Given the probability that some of *I./SS-Kampfgruppe Trabandt II* withdrew west and then south, instead of north over the Tulln bridge, this seems the most likely place for their commitment to battle.

After the elimination of the Tulln bridgehead south of the Danube, the cut-off men of Eckert's battalion retreated to the Sankt Pölten area and wound up in defensive fighting there. In other words, *Abteilung I* was likely cut in two.

The Russians

Second Ukrainian Front continued pouring mechanized forces north across the Danube at Hainberg. Once across they expanded their bridgehead and kept pushing northeast. German intelligence also recognized a buildup in the area of the Carpathian Minor Mountains range, another ominous sign of Russian intentions to intensify their efforts against *8.Armee*.

* * *

One unit that would not be opposing the Russian crossings of the Danube any longer was the Croatian Replacement Regiment. The entire unit, minus the company then fighting in Vienna but including both combat battalions, was ordered west to Haslach in the triangle formed by the Czech, German and Austrian borders. Although they had done nothing wrong, the stigma attached by the suspicion they had been part of *O-5* seems to have tainted them as unreliable. Or perhaps the Croats simply saw no reason to die fighting so far away from home, for a country that wasn't theirs. Whatever the case, and despite their orders, they marched away from the sound of the guns, not toward them, and headed for Croatia.

Vienna

By 8 April the German situation around Vienna had eroded badly and grew worse by the hour. After driving northwest from Baden and capturing Tulln, a powerful column now headed east toward Vienna, hugging the shoreline of the river. Other Red Army units had penetrated the city from the south, east and west, while the situation north of the river had become desperate.

The *Ostbahnhof* had been lost, while the Arsenal and the *Südbahnhof* were lost and then regained in a costly and pointless counterattack, since the recaptured ground had to be given up again shortly. Even worse was the demoralizing news that citizens in the parts of the city already overrun by the Russians had turned on the defenders and materially aided the invaders.[9]

In one of his last diary entries Joseph Goebbels knew exactly where he placed the blame for the disaster in Austria: "I think…the Viennese would have been better kept in check had there been a decent and, above all, energetic political leader at the helm. Von Schirach was not the right man. But how often have I said that and how often has no one listened to me!"[10] Strangely enough, he didn't mention O-5 or the plot to allow the Russians in through the back door. Perhaps he did in later entries, now lost to history.

* * *

It was not just civilian morale that deteriorated with the approach of the Russians. Otto Skorzeny mentioned that soldiers fled with whatever they could carry, a possible result of Tolbukhin's broadcasts. To curtail this, flying courts-martial prowled the streets and hung shirkers, defeatists and suspected deserters throughout the city. Woe unto any man absent from his unit without the proper papers, and sometimes even with the proper papers. Placards looped around their necks or pinned to their coats cursed them in the vilest terms. Nor were these roaming execution squads operating without cause. Throughout history the penalty for desertion has been execution, even in the US Army. In the American Civil War both sides shot deserters, and even during the Second World War American Private Eddie Slovak faced a firing squad for desertion.

That is not to say all those executed in Vienna deserved it, of course. Without a proper court-martial, killing someone for desertion was simply murder, however much a higher authority approved. In late 2014, the city government of Vienna unveiled a memorial to deserters from the *Wehrmacht* at Ballhausplatz, on the eastern edge of the Volksgarten, near both Heldenplatz and Michaelplatz. The simple inscription on the X-shaped monument reads "all alone". Estimates put the number of Austrians who deserted throughout the war at 20,000, with 1,500 being executed. There are no figures available specifically for the Battle of Vienna.

But the identities of three such men are well known. The captured leaders of Operation Radetsky, O-5's plan to turn over Vienna to the Russians, Major Karl Biedermann, Captain Alfred Huth and First Lieutenant Rudolf Raschke, had all been tried in front of a Gestapo court-martial and sentenced to death for high treason. *SS-Standartenführer* Rudolf Mildner[11] ordered *SS-Obersturmführer* Franz Kleedorfer to hang the men from light posts at Floridsdorfer Spitz in the 21st District. This Kleedorfer did, with placards proclaiming they had conspired with the Russians to betray their countrymen. In the warm spring sunshine their bodies bloated as they swung in the breeze. Today in Austria they are celebrated as heroes of the resistance.

---

9   This was not always voluntary, however. The Russians immediately put the Viennese to work supporting their attack by clearing streets or carrying supplies.

10   Trevor-Roper, *The Final Entries*, p. 400.

11   The Gestapo is often reported to have captured the O-5 defendants, which is partly true and is used in this narrative for simplicity's sake. However, the offices of the SD, Sipo and Gestapo had all been closed upon approach of the Russians and combined into one entity, which Mildner commanded.

* * *

As the German perimeter around Vienna became more compressed the fighting within the city grew ever more severe. With the coming of dawn, Russian artillery began firing on German artillery positions in the Prater and the Stadtpark, near the inner city. The Germans fired back and fires broke out again, destroying many factories in the 11th District. With the fire trucks and crews evacuated nothing could be done to fight them. The legendary Ringstrasse, with its priceless architectural and cultural treasures, came directly into the line of fire. The Burgtheater, being used by the Germans as an ammunition dump, was hit and erupted in a huge explosion, followed by many secondary blasts, which destroyed the building completely and left only the facade.

Russian armored cars moved down the Lazarettgasse next to the city hospital, leading local citizens to celebrate having survived the battle. White flags hung from some windows, a potential death penalty offense if the Nazis returned.

24. Flak-Division

When the Russians invaded Austria, one of the strongest German units on paper was the *24. Flak-Division*. With at least 80 heavy batteries, numerous smaller ones, plus fog and searchlight detachments, it was a formidable force. But the division had air defense responsibilities for much of Austria and so was scattered from Steyr to Graz, Vienna to Linz, and Wiener Neustadt. Some units had rushed to the border along the Neuseidlersee where they were smashed, while others were lost along with Wiener Neustadt. The division was being ground up in the fight, but by 7 April it claimed 45 tanks, 18 anti-tank guns and seven aircraft destroyed.[12]

* * *

On the northwestern flank of the perimeter more than 40 Russian tanks pushed through Klosterneuberg and kept going along the banks of the Danube bordering the 19th District. Five tanks were destroyed in the breakthrough but disaster struck for the defenders when the *Luftwaffe* alarm unit defending the Kahlenberg couldn't hold back the Russians. According to some sources they broke and ran, while others say they were overwhelmed. Whichever is true, once that vital mountain was captured the Russians had a perfect perch for directing artillery fire and air strikes, as well as watching German troop movements, through the smoky haze below.[13] There were no reserves to take their place and the Russians were soon moving into the wine-growing village of Grinzing after crossing the Kahlenberg.

Moving in from the west and northwest, often led by German workers acting as guides and informants, by nightfall the Russians had moved through Ottakring and Hernals virtually unopposed. "They reached the Gurtel from Nussdorf to the West Station, effectively Vienna's second line of defense, but they could not break through to Heiliginstadtstrasse south of Nussdorf, where German three inch guns had destroyed several Soviet tanks."[14]

Many of the Radetsky units formed by Szokoll were still in place and Dietrich could not be sure of their loyalty. Rather than relying on units that might bolt and leave loyal forces in the

---

12   Maier, *Drama*, p. 353.
13   Von Bünau, *Combat in Vienna*, p. 17. Von Bünau rated this unnamed *Luftwaffe* unit as having "poor combat efficiency", but no other details are available about who they were or where they came from, nor how they were armed.
14   Weyr, *The Setting of the Pearl*, p. 280. Weyr probably means the 75mm guns that were on either bank of the Danube near Klosterneuberg.

lurch, Dietrich ordered them to withdraw. If nothing else this prevented the sort of switching sides that had occurred with some units of Bulgarians and Rumanians threatened with being overrun. Militarily the loss of those battalions, even with the low combat value of the *Volkssturm*, made a bad situation worse. But aside from the propaganda value of anti-German Austrians fighting for the Russians, counting on units to stand and fight only to have them disintegrate or, worse, switch sides, was a risk Dietrich couldn't take.

* * *

The Russians were also able to push across the Gürtel at Alserstrasse and into the 9th District, threatening the General Hospital. The Russians had found another gap in the defense and there was nothing to bring them up short. Von Bünau considered this the second critical moment in the battle: "The enemy could have occupied the Danube Canal bridges near the Rossauer Barracks easily."[15] But as no battle plan survives contact with the enemy, so does luck play its part in the outcome. A chance engagement stopped the Russians in their tracks. The Red Army units driving east were ambushed by *Führer-Panzergrenadier-Regiment 3*, which was moving across the Alserstrasse to new positions from which to recapture the West Railway Station.

The two forces drove in opposite directions on parallel streets. By sheer good fortune the Germans spotted the advancing Russians first, several streets over on Adler Strasse, and turned to attack, taking them by surprise in their southern flank. The Russians were also confronted by *Kampfgruppe Wessely,* led by retired Austrian *Generalmajor* Marian Wessely. This *Kampfgruppe* was reportedly made up of "an odd crew of children, old men, students, the walking wounded and other Nazi fanatics".[16] Between the two German forces the Russian advance was repulsed. Von Bünau reports that Wessely then gathered whatever alarm units and others he could find and formed them into a makeshift defensive line "running in the general direction Friedensbrücke-University-Rathaus, and thus preserved a certain continuity on this front".[17]

In other words, the German flexibility of command was still working even *in extremis*, meshing a conglomeration of *Volkssturm, Hitlerjugend* and wounded veterans into an effective combat unit.[18] Something similar had happened in Budapest and other battles throughout the Reich, and the Russians themselves had put together units like this during the Battle for Moscow in 1941, although without younger boys. No other country could do so as quickly or effectively as Germany, however, even at the end of the war. The effectiveness of units such as *Kampfgruppe Wessely* varied widely, though, as might be imagined.

The positioning of this *Kampfgruppe* was in the seam between the *Führer-Grenadier-Division* and *Das Reich*, which had crossed behind the *Führer-Grenadier-Division* the day before from its left flank to its right, but was still not completely redeployed. Had this Russian thrust not been stopped it would have driven a deep wedge between the defenders, as von Bünau feared, thereby breaking them apart to be destroyed piecemeal. The gap between Wessely's little group and the Hitler Youth Battalion to the north of Friedensbrücke could not be closed, however. There were not enough men to even form a screen.

* * *

Although at the forefront of the fighting, and despite rumors that he died, Wessely survived the combat and that night ate supper with *Das Reich* commander, *SS-Standartenführer* Rudolf

---

15   Bünau, *Combat in* Vienna, p. 31.
16   Weyr, *The Setting of the Pearl*, p. 280.
17   Wessely was reportedly killed in the area near Mannhardsbrunn, but this was later contradicted.
18   It would seem fair to describe a combat unit as any group of people willing to fight against the enemy. Their effectiveness, of course, is a different matter.

Lehmann. The meal was typical fare eaten during combat: a thick consummé and *Kommissbrot*, dark German-style bread made from rye and whatever other flour was available. German armies had marched into battle eating *Kommissbrot* since the 1500s. During the First World War, when flour of any type was in short supply, sawdust was added to the mix. Lehmann and Wessely ate it the way German soldiers usually did, by dipping their *Kommissbrot* in the consommé and then washing it down with tea, in this case laced with cognac.

Wessely told Lehmann about the plight of eight or 10 Lippizaner stallions quartered nearby, and his fear the Russians would kill them. Sympathetic to the fate of those magnificent animals, Lehmann ordered the division supply officer, *SS-Sturmbannführer* Six, to evacuate them from the city. Accompanied by General Wessely, even as fighting raged a few streets over, the horses were moved to the Krems area.[19]

* * *

Army *Oberst* Ernest Kuhn, the notorious commandant of *Stalag 17B*, knew the time had come to evacuate the camp. The Russians had gotten too close to Krems for comfort so the Americans had to be moved west. Surrounded by armed *Volkssturm* and some officers and camp guards, with two dogs per column, the Americans marched out of the camp in eight columns of 500 men each. Chronically underfed at the camp and already thin and weak, each man was given enough food for five days. They would march for eighteen.

During their ordeal the men would be fed five times, mostly rancid soup and moldy bread. They were allowed to eat any of the dandelions and wild flowers they passed in the fields. Their destination was Braunau am Inn, Hitler's birthplace, 167 miles due west. Before long men began to slip away and disappear. Within a few days of leaving, up to 100 Americans returned to *Stalag 17B*. As awful as it had been, they knew there was shelter there, and the dangers of marching on foot through a combat zone seemed greater than staying at the camp and awaiting the Russians.

2. SS-Panzer-Division Das Reich

Attacks on *Das Reich*'s defensive perimeter began before dawn and continued all day. Penetrations on both flanks threatened it with being cut off. The time to withdraw across the Danube Canal had come.

Führer-Grenadier-Division

With *Das Reich* threatened with encirclement the *Führer-Grenadier-Division* attacked to the west but couldn't break through.

Kampfgruppe 3. SS-Panzer-Division Totenkopf

On the southeastern flank *Totenkopf* continued falling back under heavy attack. Fighting again raged on the grounds of the Arsenal. In an irony of war, two of the Tiger Is that had been repaired at the Arsenal and were picked up one week earlier by men from *Totenkopf* ended up destroyed while protecting it, both in the nearby railway marshalling yards. Now only one of the six Tigers

---

19   Weidinger, *Das Reich*, pp. 377-78.

picked up a week earlier remained in action. Other fights broke out on the grounds of the Army History Museum near the Arsenal, with the Tiger II that had been returned to service the previous day joining the defense there.

Northeast of the Arsenal the crews of the Arenberg Park *Flak* towers fled just before the Russians overran the area, leaving behind a huge dump of ammunition still in the bunkers, as well as food and other supplies. The guns and all technical equipment on the 8th floor were blown up. Although they were of little use at close range, the loss of the deadly 128mm guns for interdicting Russian movements toward Vienna was a devastating blow to the defense. Those guns had wreaked havoc on Russian columns both north and south of the Danube.

As the Russian tide rolled forward even the German commanders were swept before it. On 8 April von Bünau was forced to move from the headquarters from the *Generalakommando Wien* Headquarters to a building he called the XVIII (sic) Corps Deputy Headquarters near the Danube Canal at Number 1 Stubenring.[20] He needed an escape route close at hand, since the danger of being captured by the Russians had become all too real.

* * *

Spearheads of the Russian 912th Self-Propelled Artillery pushed west along the Danube Valley. At Judenau the SU-100s ran into the entrenched Tigers of *Totenkopf's 9./SS-Panzer-Regiment 3* and attacked. The SU-100 mounted a 100mm gun on a T-34/85 chassis to create a dangerous tank destroyer. But sight lines around the little town were excellent, since it was all low-lying farmland, and that favored the Germans with their high-velocity 88mm tank killers.

In many ways the Tiger II was a remarkable waste of time and resources. For the same price the Germans could have built at least triple the number of Panthers. Despite that, the brief fight at Judenau proved the design's value on the battlefield. Both sides would have fought facing each other, since the SU-100 couldn't aim any other way. Its three inches of frontal armor could be penetrated by the Tiger's long-barreled 88 at a range of almost two miles. In theory, at the same range the SU-100's powerful main gun could have penetrated the King Tiger's glacis plate, but most likely would have ricocheted off the sloped armor. And with the Tigers properly sited in good defensive position, hitting it at all proved very difficult.

In the action that followed the Tigers destroyed one SU-100 and knocked out a second, while *Luftwaffe* 88mm guns supporting the panzers wiped out four more, all with no German losses. Despite this Judenau couldn't be held against superior numbers, and the Tigers pulled out toward Tulln in a race to beat the Russians across.

The repair company wasn't so lucky. They were ordered toward Vienna to set up shop in Floridsdorf, moving out of the frying pan into the fire.

* * *

Aside from the three regimental-sized components of *SS-Kampfgruppe-Division Böhmen und Mähren,* other smaller ad-hoc formations were also thrown together and put under the command of that headquarters. Not much is known about their combat history, aside from their origins and existence.

Rudolf Pencz reports on one such unit,[21] *SS-Kampfgruppe Röhwer,* commanded by *SS-Hauptsturmführer* Hans Röhwer, cobbled together from leftover personnel at the

---

20 Von Bünau, *Combat in Vienna*, p. 19. In all probability von Bünau meant the *XVII Wehrkreis* (Military District), not the *XVII Armeekorps*.

21 R.P. is reported to be a legitimate witness to what has been written by Richard Landwehr, but there are those who consider Landwehr himself a questionable source. And yet, Landwehr had access to material that might otherwise remain lost for the very same reasons that some question his written work. The researcher has to

SS-Panzergrenadier Ausbildungsschule Keinschlag 7, near Prague. Röhwer had been a company commander in the most prestigious SS formation of them all, *1. SS-Panzer-Division Leibstandarte Adolf Hitler*, before being badly wounded in 1943. Upon recovery he was assigned as a tactical instructor at the Panzer Grenadier School and wound up leading his students and fellow instructors into battle. "Specifically, it incorporated the Panzer Close Combat Inspectorate Breschan and the Armored Car Training and Replacement Battalion Bukowan. This battle group was outfitted with captured Russian and American armored vehicles."[22] It would make sense that schools for *Panzergrenadiers* and for close-combat training would have examples of enemy vehicles, to explain the strengths and weaknesses of those types and how best to destroy them, and the instructors must surely have known how to drive and use them. What became of this unit isn't currently known; presumably because of its location at Kienschlag it was assigned to *8. Armee*, and it has to be assumed that it saw combat.[23] What is known is that all of the captured vehicles were probably not used because of a lack of ammunition for the foreign guns, although some of them might have been.

South of the Danube

The Russians

Meanwhile south of the Danube, the 38th Guards Rifle Corps and 18th Tank Corps continued moving past Baden to join Sixth Guards Tank Army at the spearhead of the Danube drive, southwest of Tulln. German intelligence picked up a request for fighter cover to block German reconnaissance flights, a sure indicator of an upcoming attack. Sankt Pölten was an obvious target, both for its industrial capacity and the network of roads and railways that converged there. For this objective the Russians had two potential attack routes; first, through Neulengbach and Boheimkirchen, and second, through the valley of the little Perschling River, by way of Kapelln. The problem was how best to use the limited artillery support the Germans still possessed, and the even scarcer reserves, since the two routes made mutual support of defending forces difficult.

I SS-Panzer-Korps

For their part, the Russians spread along the Danube's southern shore heading both east toward Vienna and west toward Krems. They desperately wanted to cross to the north bank into the rear of *8. Armee* but the fall of Tulln left a huge gap where there was no organized resistance south of the Danube. That was a unique opportunity and Tolbukhin seized it.

---

approach such material with grave suspicion, but in the end all that can be done is for him or her to use their best judgment as to whether the material has propagandistic, apologetic or self-serving motives, and whether or not it can be at least partially verified by other sources. In the case of *SS-Kampfgruppe Röhwer*, for example, the author R.P. says nothing about its combat history, but simply that it was brought into existence. No claims are made, there is no opinion given, and there are no apparent underlying motives to have written of such a unit if it did not exist. The conclusion of the objective researcher, therefore, must be that *SS-Kampfgruppe Röhwer* almost surely existed and went into battle using captured enemy equipment.

22   R.P., *Combat Formations of the SS-Kampfgruppe Div. Böhmen-Mähren*, Siegrunen Number 69, Summer 2000, p. 9.
23   R.P., *Combat Formations*, p. 9.

Dietrich's staff frantically worked to organize blocking forces, but only here and there were there even strongpoints. Near Zwentendorf, on the main highway to Sankt Pölten, a battery of 88mm heavy anti-aircraft guns acting in a ground role delayed the Russian advance for a while, even as other westward-moving forces poured through the gap on secondary roads all the way to Würmla. The guns were thus outflanked. That left Sankt Pölten itself under immediate threat. Elsewhere, the eastward thrust by 9th Guards Mechanized Corps brought heavy fighting to Klosterneuberg, on the western outskirts of Vienna.

Korps Schultz

SS-Kampfgruppe Staudinger was informed it would be subordinated to a new corps-level unit organizing in the Sankt Pölten area to try and slow down the Russians' westward advance. Known optimistically as *Korps Schultz*, or sometimes as *Generalkommando Schultz*, it began to attract bits and pieces of regular units, alarm battalions, *Volkssturm*, Hitler Youth and stragglers. It gave Rendulic a higher headquarters to where he could at least direct whatever help he could scrape together.

* * *

Starting on 7 April and even more so on 8 April, the 38th Guards Rifle Corps came into contact with the *Flak* detachments scattered throughout the region, especially those at Moosierbaum. High-velocity rounds caused havoc in the Russian columns as the *Flak* guns filled in for conventional artillery, especially when the 105mm batteries at Asparn and Langenrohr had to be pulled back. On 8 April the triple *Flak* batteries of Michaelhausen were assaulted by Russians at bayonet-point of bayonet. But even though most of the *Flak* guns were fixed and could not be easily moved, they slowed down the Russian advance significantly, particularly the batteries at Moosbierbaum, Barndorf, Oberbierbaum and especially those at the Schusterberg near Tautendorf. Without them it is highly likely the Russians might have turned the left flank of *Korps Schultz* and driven into the rear of *6. Panzerarmee*.[24]

I SS-Panzerkorps

SS-Gruppenführer und Generalleutnant der Waffen SS Hermann Preiss faced a different but equally desperate situation as Wilhelm Bittrich did. Whereas *II SS-Panzerkorps* was compressed into a very small urban area, *I SS-Panzerkorps* stretched on a long front from south of Sankt Pölten around Traisen, northeast through Laaben and Klausen-Leopoldsdorf, southeast through Alland, then south to Berndorf and all the way to Ternitz. The line faced north and northeast until reaching Berndorf, when it then faced east. This was a front of more than 65 miles. To defend this extended perimeter Preiss had the twin SS panzer divisions – the *LAH* and *Hitlerjugend*, although both were reduced to *Kampfgruppen* at this point – the *Kampfgruppe 356. Infanterie-Division* and *SS-Kampfgruppe Keitel*.

It wasn't much.

Working in Priess' favor was the rugged nature of the terrain. The fighting to come would be known as The Battle of the Valleys, because advancing over the high, densely forested mountains

24   Rauchensteiner, *Die Krieg in Österreich*, p. 180.

in the region required control of the valleys for supplies and armored support. But for the next four weeks it would be a desperate game of shifting ever-diminishing forces from one crisis to the next.

Kampfgruppe 12. SS-Panzer-Division Hitlerjugend

Elements of *Hitlerjugend* attacked in the critical area around and between Alland and Raisenmarkt and recaptured high ground in both locations. This kept the tenuous connection with the division's northwestern wing intact and, more importantly, kept eyes on the road network passing through Alland. Five Russians tanks were destroyed in the fighting, in what was less than ideal tank country. The rugged nature of the Vienna Woods is what made possession of the road junctions so important.

Another fight at Klausen-Leopoldsdorf freed a trapped alarm unit but the village was lost. Sitting at the junction of several valleys, it controlled the fastest routes west and north, with steep and forested slopes on either side. Its loss made the Germans' immediate tactical situation more complex and dangerous.

Further south, at Neulengbach, the Germans still held a bridgehead over the Fischa River which the Russians were determined to eliminate. Attacking from three directions on 8 April the defenders barely managed to repulse them, killing more than 150 attackers and destroying six 76.2mm guns.[25]

A strong Russian attack on *Kampfgruppe SS-Panzergrenadier-Regiment 25* south of Rohrbach an der Gölsen was driven back. This represented a deep and critically dangerous penetration on the extreme left flank of *Hitlerjugend*, one that could have turned ugly for the Germans very quickly. Their line held but both sides suffered heavy losses. Far to their east, temporarily attached to the *LAH*, *Kampfgruppe SS-Panzergrenadier-Regiment 26* was also attacked and had to bend on the left to avoid being flanked, thus breaking contact with their sister regiment near Rohrbach. The Russians continued attacking throughout the night.

Kampfgruppe 1. SS-Panzer-Division Leibstandarte Adolf Hitler

The Russians renewed attacks between Pottenstein and Berndorf, using units up to battalion strength. The Germans had few heavy weapons but two Russian tanks were destroyed by *Panzerfauste*. Platoon and company-sized units infiltrated the wooded slopes of the Hohe Wand and the fighting was close and bitter. Other elements engaged in a fight for Grünbach am Schneeberg, about three miles down a lush valley from Puchberg am Schneeberg where another battle was raging for that town.

SS-Kampfgruppe Keitel

SS-Panzerjäger-Abteilung 37, part of *SS-Kampfgruppe Keitel*, was assigned the job of attacking and retaking the main battle lines around Puchberg am Schneeberg, just west of Grünbach am Schneeberg. A separate *Kampfgruppe* was established for the mission. The force included some Austrian Home Guardsmen, an infantry escort platoon, an engineer company, an SS bicycle squadron and a heavy mortar platoon. Its exact composition is lost but in all likelihood this

---

25   Maier, *Drama*, p. 352.

short-lived force, *SS-Kampfgruppe Müller*, probably numbered around two hundred men, perhaps with three or four *Hetzer Jadgpanzer 38s*, a few 80mm *Granatwerfer 34* mortars, some *Panzerfauste* and light machine guns.

Puchberg was like countless towns and villages throughout Styria, a quaint and picturesque settlement in a green valley surrounded by densely treed mountains. Taking the low ground was all well and good, but if the enemy kept any of the surrounding high points they could rain fire down on you. And that's what happened.

Nobody expected them to actually retake their former positions, but against all odds they did. The attack succeeded but with severe casualties on both sides. The Russians responded with murderous artillery and Katyusha fire and, since they weren't hampered by ammunition supply problems like the Germans were, they kept it up all day. The cost for holding newly recaptured Puchberg was losing men on a steady basis to the heavy indirect fire, and the Germans quickly decided the settlement of 2,000 or so wasn't worth the price. *SS-Kampfgruppe Müller* was ordered to pull back to its original starting point. The men who died retaking Puchberg did so in vain.

The town was 52 miles southwest of Vienna. The intense combat in the region clearly showed that the Russians were still probing the German lines in preparation for a breakthrough attack. They might not have the assault forces to rip holes in the German front, especially since the terrain was ideal defensive ground, but if the Russians found gaps they were determined to exploit them. And they were looking.

6. Armee

Like so much of eastern Austria the towns and roads were situated in valleys such as that of the Raab River. Hermann Balck still had his headquarters in Gleisdorf, in the Raab Valley, and the Russians were still driving toward the town.

Because of the relatively static nature of the front in *6. Armee's* area in the coming weeks, the myth would arise that combat there was desultory and light, while nothing could have been further from the truth. Moreover, the front was not static; it only appeared that way from afar, much like the slow grinding Allied offensive in Normandy the previous summer.

During the next three weeks some of the most brutal fighting of the Eastern Front would take place in the mountains and passes of the foothills of the eastern Alps. Russian attacks would be unceasing, and supported by extremely heavy artillery and rocket barrages, but there would be little movement of the front. Counterattacks would follow attacks, and trigger more counter-counterattacks. A captured trench had better be fortified quickly, before the former owners came to take it back. Complicating the situation were more than 200,000 Hungarian refugees who staggered into Styria ahead of *6. Armee,* and filled the interior.

The man in command, *General der Panzertruppe* Hermann Balck, should have the last word on this chapter of the fighting. He wrote his memoirs in 1981 and they were translated into English in 2015, but Balck makes numerous fundamental and inexplicable errors during his description of this period. For example, he said: "I also had to stay tied into the left flank of Army Group Southeast"[26] and "in the center of our front line the newly reconstituted Hungarian Szent László Division…defected to the enemy."[27] He then goes on the speculate that perhaps this is why *IV SS Panzerkorps* disobeyed his orders for what route to take back to Austria, even though that didn't happen, either.

26   Balck, *Order in Chaos*, p. 424.
27   Balck, *Order in Chaos*, p. 425.

None of these three points is accurate or was even his concern. The first makes it sound as if Balck was the commander of *Heeresgruppe Süd* itself. The *2. Panzerarmee* was on Balck's right flank between he and *Heeresgruppe E,* and it was that army's responsibility to stay tied into what Balck mistakenly calls "Army Group Southeast",[28] but was later called *Heeresgruppe F* before being combined with *Heeresgruppe E.* Moreover, by stating that 'he' had to stay tied in, Balck is referring to himself, which could only have been the case if he commanded the army group, or *2. Panzerarmee.*

As for the Szent László Division, while it's true that on 8 April it still belonged to *6. Armee,* on 12 April it was transferred to *XXII Armeekorps* of *2. Panzerarmee.* Even harder to understand is that Balck claims its defection caused him a huge problem, because the division never defected. It remained in the line as one of *2. Panzerarmee'*s best units until the end of the war. Nor did he confuse it with another division, because no division of either army defected. The only possible explanation is that his memory failed him when writing his memoirs and he forgot it was transferred to the adjoining army. As for the remark about the SS, Balck hated the *Waffen-SS* in general, and the *IV SS-Panzerkorps* commander, *SS-Obergruppenführer* Herbert Otto Gille, in particular. He never missed a chance to demean them. But his criticism in this case is unrealistic, as the Russians had already overrun the *IV SS-Panzerkorps'* ordered route of retreat, making it impossible to do anything other than find an alternate route.

* * *

Balck's biggest danger remained the wide gap between his army and *6. SS-Panzerarmee* to the north. All he had to plug that gap were odds and ends, the most important of which was *Kampfgruppe Semmering.* The *117. Jäger-Division* was on the way but hadn't arrived yet, and until it did the Russians had to be held east of the Semmering Pass. If they got through there, Balck's entire left flank might collapse.

As Balck scrambled to find a response to the Russian breakthrough, here and there fragments of German units and *Volkssturm* began to resist the advance, particularly at Reinberg and Riedersberg. But elsewhere their offensive continued without a break. At Vorau the Russians used Stalin Organs against the town itself, leaving it in flames. Other units invaded the Feistritz Valley and moved south through the Pfaffen Sattel to occupy Rettenegg. Several Russian columns came together near Sankt Jakob im Wald at the Eckberg and Ochsenkopf. To all appearances it was a fatal breakthrough from which *6. Armee* and perhaps even *Heeresgruppe Süd* itself could not recover.

SS-Kampfgruppe Keitel

Two units that exemplify the ad-hoc nature of the German defense of Styria are *SS-Kampfgruppe Keitel* and *Kampfgruppe Semmering.* The right wing of the *SS-Kampfgruppe* was on the Gahns and Hochschneeberg, and the boundary with its right-hand neighbor, *Kampfgruppe Semmering,* was the peak known as the Saurüssel. The Gahns towered nearly 4,000 feet high but there weren't enough men to form a continuous line, so once against there was only a screen of strongpoints. At one position five SS men withdrew when 120 Russians approached their position.

The Saürussel had a mixed force from both units, Hitler Youth and a battalion of *Volkssturm* from Gloggnitz subordinated to *SS-Kampfgruppe Keitel.* On other mountains and high points men from the SS, *Volkssturm* and Army were mixed as though in the same units. The Russians forced local farmers to drag their guns up the Gahns, north of Payerbach between *SS-Kampfgruppe Keitel* and *Kampfgruppe Semmering,* using oxen. It was back-breaking work for both man and beast.

---

28   It had been merged with *Heeresgruppe F* shortly before and was now called *Heeresgruppe E.*

Atop the 6,000 feet-tall Schneeberg was yet another *Kampfgruppe*, this time named *SS-Kampfgruppe Kaiserbrunn*. It was commanded by *SS-Obersturmbannführer* Walter Zwickler and contained three *Volkssturm* companies, one each from Gloggnitz, Ternitz and Neunkirchen.

German patrols went out continually to pin down the exact positions of the enemy. One such wandered into a village in search of food, only to be met with a hail of bullets; the Russians got there first. But that didn't slow down the patrols. If anything it accelerated them. Often the strong-points were so far apart that patrols were necessary to ensure the Russians hadn't slipped past into their rear. They also laid minefields between them; at least, they did until the mines ran out.[29]

SS-Kampfgruppe Schweitzer

The worn-out survivors of the *Kampfgruppe* knew they stood within sight of safety. But they couldn't get there without one last, bloody fight. A Russian anti-tank position with two 76.2mm guns was all that stood between the battered survivors of *SS-Obersturmbannführer* Schweitzer's *Kampfgruppe* and breaking through to German-controlled territory. This the bedraggled men overran on the morning of 8 April, inflicting heavy losses on the Russians and destroying both guns, before they reached safety in the vicinity of Markt Allhau and Buchschachen.

Somewhere between 150 and 200 men of the *SS-Ausbildungs-und-Ersatz-Abteilung 11* made it back alive, while perhaps 100 more drifted in over the next few days. No more than 250 of the 800 SS men who went into battle a week before survived. For the rest the distinction between having been killed, wounded or captured almost didn't matter. The fate of captured *Waffen-SS* men was grim.

No figures are recorded for casualties among *Volkssturm-Abteilung 31/191* and the troop from *3. Kavallerie-Division*, but it seems likely they were at least as high of a percentage as that of the SS. Schweitzer's command probably lost in the neighborhood of 800 men in total, including Schweitzer himself, who was badly wounded in the neck while guiding his men through the forest. He was lucky enough to be carried out. His *Kampfgruppe* was disbanded once it reached German lines, having fulfilled its mission better than any could have hoped for.

Near Buchschachen a memorial stands for 21 German soldiers who died in the fields and in the mountains defending Austria from the Russians. For many years rumors persisted that these men were massacred by the Russians, but later investigations concluded these are probably false. It is unknown how many of them were members of *SS-Kampfgruppe Schweitzer*, if any.

Reports have come down that Schweitzer was awarded the Knight's Cross for his actions at Rechnitz on 14 April, in Berlin, by none other than *Brigadeführer und Generalmajor der Waffen-SS* Wilhelm Monkhe, the *Kampfkommandant* of the government sector of the capital. Monkhe and Schweitzer both served in the SS long before it expanded and so they probably knew each other, but that couldn't explain why a severely wounded man would travel to Berlin on the failing rail system. Sepp Dietrich could have done the same thing much closer, and he outranked Monkhe. At any rate, hard evidence for him having actually been awarded this medal does not seem to exist.

Kampfgruppe Semmering

After the loss of Maria Schutz the day before, the German did what they always did: they counter-attacked. This time it was elements from the *Gebirgsjäger Unteroffizier Schule Admont*, who threw

---

29   Brettner, *Die Letzten Kämpfe Band I*, p. 190.

the Russians all the way to the Gostritz Valley more than half a mile to the east. The Germans would keep the town until nearly the end of the war.

* * *

The *SS-Gebirgsjäger-Ausbildungs-und-Ersatz-Bataillon Leoben* established its command post in the Presidential Villa at Breitenstein. Near the Kobermannsberg, at the Kotstein, the men of *Gebirgs Artillerie Schule Dachstein* worried about the *Landesschützen* troops on their left being very weak in numbers and fighting quality. They were augmented by convalescents and walking wounded from hospitals all over the region. However, the SS men of *3.Kompanie/SS-Gebirgsjäger-Ausbildungs-und-Ersatz-Bataillon 13 Leoben* greatly impressed them.

* * *

Complacency has always been fatal in combat situations, but by definition those who are guilty of being complacent don't recognize their inattention, and so it was again on 8 April 1945 near Fröhnitzgraben. A Russian infantry unit strayed too far into a meadow, possibly gathering for an attack. German artillery spotters immediately called in a strike. Two batteries of mountain artillery stationed in the town hit the lolling Russians with a massive barrage, virtually destroying them.

* * *

It became even more urgent to block the breakthrough south of *Kampfgruppe Semmering* when Russian troops moved well past its southern flank. Fearing an attack, a Hungarian *werfer* company near Rettenegg moved into the mountains outside the town. But instead of turning hard right and attacking the Semmering Pass from its western end, the Russians kept moving west and southwest to exploit the massive hole they'd ripped in the German front south of the pass. Unless something could be done quickly, *Kampfgruppe Semmering* was in imminent danger of being cut off from *6. Armee.* But neither *Oberst* Raithel nor *General der Panzertruppe* Balck had any troops to do that.

Sperrverband Motschmann

Not waiting for the Russians to attack them, Motschmann's men struck first. *SS-Polizei-Regiment 13* led the assault and their sudden lunge at Bruck drove the Russians into chaos and captured part of the town. But the Russians regrouped quickly, counterattacked using artillery and armor, and drove the SS men back to their jumping-off points. Before they could launch a second effort, word came that the Russians had erected a *PAK* nest and bunkers. *SS-Hauptsturmführer* Motschmann considered his options and decided to withdraw back to Vorau.

But that didn't last long. A heavy Russian artillery bombardment on Vorau hit the abbey. During the night Motschmann withdrew again, this time into the mountains. Seventy severely wounded men were evacuated to Pöllau in carts pulled by oxen. Other parts of the group are credited with forcing the Russians out of Waldbach and back to Mönichwald.

1. Panzer-Division

The veteran division had begun assembling at Weiz after detaching from the front at Fürstenfeld. One division against three corps wasn't good odds, but it's all Hermann Balck had.

2. Panzerarmee

Large-scale operations against the southern end of *Heeresgruppe Süd*'s front had temporarily stopped. Smaller efforts to undermine the army's flanks continued and intelligence detected movements beyond the Russian lines between the Drau and Pinka Rivers. Fixing attacks in company and battalion strength continued along the line. Ominously, a buildup in the seam of *6.Armee* and *2. Panzerarmee* was detected, and it was here that heavy fighting occurred at the Stradner Kögel, an 1,800 foot promontory that dominated the land around it.

The Russians had been tantalizingly close to grabbing Graz when the counterattack of *14. Waffen-Grenadier-Division der SS Galizien* threw them back, but their strategic objectives hadn't changed. Graz was still the immediate target, so the 61st Guards Rifle Division tried to seize the Stradner Kögel as the jumping-off point for a renewed offensive push.

14. Waffen-Grenadier-Division der SS Galizien

A few miles southeast of Bad Gleichenberg, the key feature was the 1,800 foot-high Stradner Kögel, which dominated the local area. The fight for the mountain had started on 6 April and would last for ten days, during which fighting continued non-stop, often vicious hand-to-hand combat. The 20th Guards Rifle Division was later joined by 61st Guards Rifle Division in seizing the Stradner Kögel, a fight which would draw in new units from both sides.

According to some sources *Waffen-Grenadier-Regiment der SS 31* had only just arrived in the area after a forced march from Slovenia. It had been intended for them to go into reserve so the men could rest after such an exhausting trek, but the situation was too dire for that and they were immediately sent into the fight. The Ukrainians were not yet veterans and, despite fighting hard, they took heavy casualties. Twice the Russians took the mountain and twice Harteneck sent *3. Kavallerie-Division* to retake it.

The first time was on 6 April and the Germans found themselves charging up the slopes in the dark. Somewhere up there a company of Ukrainians held on despite having Russians thick around them, and "in the darkness everyone started fighting everyone else, Germans fought against Russians and, by mistake, against Ukrainians".[30] The inexperienced Ukrainians broke and ran and only calmed down enough to return to battle the next day.

Most of the Ukrainians stood and fought hard, however, despite their commanding general. During the Battle of Brody the previous summer, when *Galizien* was caught in the Russian storm and virtually destroyed, *SS-Brigadeführer und Generalmajor der Waffen SS* Freitag lost his nerve and tried to resign in the middle of the battle. Once again, as the combat at Stradner Kogel grew ever more savage, Freitag tried to hand in his resignation to *General der Kavallerie* Harteneck. The corps commander turned him down cold, but not before reprimanding him in front of the entire headquarters staff. Given their commander's lack of confidence in them, it's no surprise that elements of the division cracked under the extreme Russian pressure.

On 8 April the SS men were again ready for combat and took over the positions on Stradner Kögel from the cavalry. Unceasing Russian mortar barrages had ravaged their ranks and now they needed to regroup, but before the cavalry men could move out a platoon of Russians charged through a hole in the front, blasting away at anything that moved. A follow-on attack never happened because German artillery expended a lot of precious ammunition to break up the

---

30   Melnyk, *To Battle*, p. 254.

assembly of assault troops. The breakthrough group suddenly realized nobody was coming to help and tried to retreat, but were chopped to pieces by machine-gun fire.

23. Panzer-Division

It was a sign of the times. *Panzergrenadier-Regiment 128* was ordered to the area of Jörgen, 10 miles north of Radkersburg and left their billets at Halbenrain very early on the morning of 8 April. Being *Panzergrenadiers* they were supposed to ride when redeployed and did so at the beginning of the trip, but soon enough their trucks and SPWs ran out of fuel, which left them walking like most of the German Army. They relieved elements of *44. Infanterie-Division Hoch und Deutschmeister* in time to repel heavy Russian attacks all afternoon, supported by the artillery regiment. After nightfall the regiment pulled back to match its line with that of *Panzergrenadier-Regiment 126* in the hills east of Hurth.

* * *

Even though the Germans had been expelled from eastern Slovenia, the Russians and their allies, the Slovene irregulars, viewed them just over the Mur River which cut across that land southeast from the Austrian border. The front had momentarily stabilized and the Russians had transferred the Twenty-seventh Army further north for operations against the Raab Valley, but the Fifty-seventh Army stayed behind, and had no intention of letting the Germans dig in. Battle had raged for four days around the 299th Rifle Division's bridgehead at Veržej, but despite their numerical superiority the Russians couldn't expand their holding on the west bank. The armored units which could have broken through the thin German lines had been transferred to the north, where more strategic targets awaited them.

The defenders were from *XXII Gebirgs-Armeekorps*. In addition to *16. SS-Panzergrenadier-Division Reichsführer-SS* and remnants of both *118. Jäger-Division* and *297. Infanterie-Division*, the newly reconstituted Hungarian Szent László Division had finally gone back into the line. Once considered an elite formation, Szent László had been rebuilt from wherever manpower could be found, including a fortress regiment to replace a regiment of Royal Hungarian Air Force personnel that had been destroyed. By combining all four divisions they were finally able to throw the Russian 299th Rifle Division back to the eastern bank of the Mur, inflicting very heavy losses in the process. More than 1,000 Russian troops were killed, wounded or captured.

The war in Slovenia now favored the German defenders in several ways. First, the withdrawal of most Russian armored formations left only a few tank regiments to support the entire front in southeastern Austrian and Slovenia. This left the primary Russian firepower in the hands of the organic artillery for each infantry division, whereas the Germans still had at least one significant armored force in *16. SS-Panzergrenadier-Division Reichsführer-SS*, plus whatever *Jagdpanzer* or *Sturmgeschütz* elements survived in the infantry divisions.

The second significant German advantage in Slovenia was that instead of facing purely Russian units, it was Bulgarians who filled the trenches to their east, and it would be hard to find a less motivated army than the 1st Bulgarian Army for fighting to liberate Slovenia. Bulgaria had never declared war on Russia, and only switched sides at the point of a gun when King Boris was deposed and a communist government was imposed after the Russians invaded after the fall of Rumania. The men fought because the Russians made them fight, whereas the Germans were fighting for their very lives.

But there was no denying the Russian advantage in logistics or in the sympathy of the people living in Slovenia. Perhaps more than anything else the Russians benefitted from the assistance of Tito's Partisan Army, and its Slovene formations in particular.

* * *

A few days before the Soviet bridgehead described earlier had been wiped out, Bulgarian soldiers had entered Čakovec, liberating the Croatian province of Medjimurje and reaching the Drava River to the south of the Mura, thus outflanking the German position there to the south.

9. SS-Panzer-Division Hohenstaufen

Taking up the positions west of the Mur River, the SS men discovered just how poor their defensive positions in the so-called *Reichsschutzstellung* really were. The ground was flat, with few hills even for observation posts. Bad Radkersburg itself lay on the east side of the river and was a trap, but division commander *SS-Brigadeführer* Stadler decided to defend it. He ordered his pioneers to prepare the Mur River bridge for demolition, however, just in case they had to retreat quickly.

118. Jäger-Division

By the strength report of 24 March, the *118. Jäger-Division* had 5,192 men, 20 88mm guns and four *Sturmgeschütze*. Two weeks later it had to have been significantly weaker, since most of that time had been spent in headlong retreat.

Hungarian Szent László Parachute Division

This hard-fighting division was considered the elite division of the *Honved*. Formed in October 1944 from the best personnel of both the Hungarian Army and Air Force it first entered combat in December and suffered very heavy casualties, while inflicting many more in return. Its combat record was outstanding, but it was badly damaged and didn't return to divisional status until the fighting in Austria, after it had been restored by replacements from the 6th, 7th and 8th Hungarian Field Replacement Divisions. By the time it re-entered the front lines in April it was once again combat effective, and fought well until the end of the war, despite Balck's claim that it joined the Russians.

It was a very strong formation. When it surrendered, the best estimate of its remaining strength was 13,000 men. That means it was likely at least 15,000 strong in early April when it returned to action.

71. Infanterie-Division

This veteran division was by this point little more than a reinforced regiment lacking most of its heavy weapons.

9

Monday, 9 April

Heeresgruppe Süd

Rain spread over the region even as temperatures warmed up, but it had no effect on operations, especially in the air. Russian air attacks concentrated on Vienna and the north bank, while the Germans flew in support of *8. Armee*'s right flank and strafed boats in the Danube, as well as attacking ground targets in the Sankt Pölten area. *Luftflotte 4* managed the respectable total of 260 sorties on 9 April, with more than 50 trucks shot up in the area north of the Danube. The air fleet reported 440 total aircraft available on 9 April, with 308 of those in flying condition. Of those, 154 were ground-attack, 62 fighters and the rest either transport or reconnaissance.[1]

Against the American fighter-bomber sweeps now coming from the west, the bomber streams still dropping loads all over Austria and the Red Air Force buzzing over the Red Army like a swarm of angry wasps, *Luftflotte 4* did everything possible to support the men on the ground. Morale remained surprisingly high given the conditions. Even as they were shot out of the sky by overwhelming numbers, the fuel-starved German fliers went down fighting. But while they fought courageously, the outcome was never in doubt.

8. Armee

Kreysing's position grew worse by the hour. He now had Russians to his southwest, south, southeast and east. The only barrier protecting *8. Armee*'s rear area on the west was the Danube River and whatever alarm units could be scraped together to protect the north bank. Aside from Hitler's incessant insistence on standing fast, retreat was also impossible because it would mean the death of the units still fighting in Vienna. But even when the transfer of the *Führer-Grenadier-Division* north of the river was completed, he would still not have enough forces to do more than hold off the Russians for a little longer from overrunning Vienna's districts north of the Danube.

Town after town would fall in the coming weeks, with most being fought over, but with never a hope of actually stopping the Russian juggernaut. Despite Hitler's universal stand-fast order, and despite Kreysing's best efforts, Second Ukrainian Front was bent on destroying *8. Armee* once and for all.

On 9 April Russian spearheads penetrated deep into the army's center at the town of Matzen. The tiny town dated to at least the 12th Century and, like most Austrian settlements, a hillside castle overlooked the homes of the townsfolk. After a brief artillery bombardment the Russians launched a violent attack that overran the town by nightfall. Hand-to-hand fighting raged through the narrow streets, with Russian tanks needed to blast Germans out of fortified houses. When the Germans finally left, 14 civilians lay dead, 80 buildings were totally destroyed and another 200 were heavily damaged. Twelve people committed suicide and the Russians shot all of the horses along with eight more townsfolk. Then came time to plunder whatever had survived the fighting.

---

1   Reynolds, *Men of Steel*, p. 265.

* * *

The fight for Hohenau an der March entered its third day, with the Germans still unable to drive back the Russians after the defection of a Hungarian company the day before. Instead of a direct assault on the German positions, the Russians elected to attack to the south and took Drösing. In response the defenders of Hohenau had to build positions on the south side of town. Machine guns were mounted on the flood levee while the mortars were positioned near the church. The artillery batteries went into fields nearby. Meanwhile, the pioneers blew up the railroad tracks and the signals elements set up field telephones and radio antenna.

Kampfgruppe 211. Infanterie-Division

The division's *Grenadier-Regiments 306* and *317* were so weak that even combined they didn't equal the strength of one regiment. To hold the little town of Dürnkrut, therefore, part of the division's third regiment, *Grenadier-Regiment 365*, came to their aid. Despite their nearly catastrophic losses, the morale of the division remained good and the men were still willing to fight hard.

In a pattern that would be repeated over and over again in the coming weeks, the Russians had been shelling Dürnkrut since the morning of 8 April and the defenders knew an attack was imminent. Ringing church bells that could be heard on the Morava River summoned the *Volkssturm* to take up arms. To the south the Russians had crossed the Morava in strength and pushed hard on a drive through the Marchfeld. At Dürnkrut and points north, however, the Germans kept them pinned down in their bridgeheads.

SS-Kampfgruppe Trabandt III

Three more trainloads of *SS-Kampfgruppe-Division Böhmen und Mähren* brought more of that formation to enter the battlefield as *SS-Kampfgruppe Trabandt III*. Arriving near Absdorf, about 10 miles northwest of Tulln, it consisted of two infantry, one artillery and one pioneer battalion.

SS-Kampfgruppe Ameiser

SS-Kampfgruppe Ameiser, with *Grenadier-Regiment 287* attached, finally retreated from the dangerous pocket they had held in the Stopfenreuth area. The Russians who moved in shot a woman who allegedly threatened them with a pistol, and then raped every girl over the age of 13 and women up to 70. Fully half the Russian soldiers had a sexually transmitted disease, which they passed on to the Germans.[2]

Untersiebenbrunn fell to the Russians, who pursued the *Kampfgruppe* closely. As it became more obvious that Vienna could only be held for a few more days, and as Soviet forces fought their way southeast from the Morava River line, the hard-fighting *Kampfgruppe* retreated into the Markgrafneuseidl vicinity to avoid being surrounded, and to join its parent headquarters in shielding those units of *6. SS-Panzerarmee* fighting in Vienna from a northern attack.

SS-Obersturmbannführer Anton Ameiser had been in tough spots before, most notably the previous year when the first incarnation of *SS-Kampfgruppe Ameiser* had been surrounded in

2   Brettner, *Die Letzten Kämpfe Band II*, p. 150.

Romania and traveled more than 200 miles through Russian-held territory back to the safety of German lines. As a regimental commander in *22. SS-Freiwilligen-Kavallerie-Division Maria Theresa* he'd been surrounded in Budapest and fought through most of the siege, and was flown out on one of the last aircraft to leave the city after being wounded.[3] Despite Hitler's stand-fast order, being surrounded a third time wasn't something he would allow to happen. His *Kampfgruppe* had done all they could. They had held out at Stopfenreuth for three days and slowed the Russian buildup north of the Danube, and only pulled out at the last moment to keep from being destroyed.

* * *

The retreat of *SS-Kampfgruppe Ameiser* was tantamount to removing an obstruction from a clogged spillway. General Kreysing now had more holes to plug in his front than he had troops to fill them, and the situation turned desperate when the Russian Forty-Sixth Army followed close on the heels of *SS-Kampfgruppe Ameiser* along the banks of Danube. Without reinforcements there was a very real danger of the Russians overrunning the retreat route for *II SS-Panzerkorps*. The *25. Panzer-Division* was in transit but even if the front could hold until it arrived, that formation was a shell. During six weeks of fighting in Poland during the Russian offensive in January it suffered 9,000 casualties in just six weeks, although it reportedly had more than 40 operational Panzers.

The new Army Group commander *Generaloberst* Rendulic saw the danger as well and had found only one unit capable of stopping the Russians north of the Danube, the *Führer-Grenadier-Division*. To reinforce it a training formation known as *Panzer-Ausbildungs-Bataillon Donau* had been dissolved and its members divided between the *1. Panzer-Division*, *3. Panzer-Division* and *13. Panzer-Division (Feldherrnhalle 2)*, and the *Führer-Grenadier-Division*. Having no other choice Rendulic had ordered the newly reinforced division back across the Danube and assigned it to *8. Armee*. With it defending Vienna the Russians had pushed the Germans back to the canal. Without it, there was no hope of holding any part of the city.

By nightfall the Forty-Sixth Russian Army had advanced in dangerous leaps toward the west. It held a line from Schönau through Orth an der Donau, Wagram an der Donau, Loimersdorf, and Grossenbrunn to Marchegg. This created a giant bulge on the southern end of the front that closely resembled an aneurysm.

* * *

The Russian wave reached Deutsch-Wagram late in the day, and by 8:00 p.m. shells began raining on the town. The *Volkssturm*, in this case the old men of the town who were unsuitable for any other duty, endured it for a short while and then disintegrated. But the airfield located there could be used as a forward base for the Red Air Force and the Germans were determined to keep it. Both sides prepared for a fight the next day.

Vienna

6. SS-Panzerarmee

As happened in Vienna, fighting continued past sundown on 8 April and lasted most of the night throughout *6. SS-Panzerarmee*'s area. Also, Maier notes that it was about this time that

---

3   Strangely enough, the other cavalry regimental commander from *Maria Theresa*, *SS-Obersturmbannführer* Karl-Heinz Keitel, was also wounded and evacuated late in the siege. Keitel went on to form the other *Kampfgruppe* from *37. SS-Freiwilligen-Kavallerie Division Lützow*, *SS-Kampfgruppe Keitel*.

Heeresgruppe Süd began referring to Dietrich's command as what most of the world now remembers it as being, namely *6. SS-Panzerarmee*.[4]

* * *

In the confusion left by the redeployment of *Das Reich*, the battle group of Guards Captain Loza found a way through on Mariahilfer Strasse, past Schönbrunn Palace toward the Old Town. *Panzerjäger-Ausbildungs-und-Ersatz Abteilung 17*, Antitank Training and Replacement Battalion 17, held this area on *Führer-Grenadier-Division*'s left flank, but this unit probably numbered a few hundred men with some antitank guns. The area they had to defend was huge. Mariahilfer Strasse came to a dead end at Opernring Strasse less than two hundred yards from the Heldenplatz, with the Museum Quarter hard on their left. Loza had slipped right past them with only minor fighting. When his tanks turned left onto Opernring Strasse headed for the Parliament Building, they came under fire from German *PAK-40* 75mm guns on the grounds of the Rathaus, Vienna's city hall. A brief, one-sided duel ensued between the entrenched German guns and the JSU-152s, in which the mammoth 152mm Russian guns[5] blasted the German barricades and silenced the *PAKs*.

With the area temporarily quiet Loza deployed his little force in all-round defense. A few small counterattacks by infantry were driven off. Loza reports that the electricity was on and stayed on until 2:00 a.m. and that the paratroopers used its light to clean out any lingering defenders or scouts.[6] By 11:00 p.m. he reported to his commander that he'd taken the heart of Vienna, the Hofburg, the Heldenplatz and the Museum Quarter. The room where two days earlier *Gauleiter* von Schirach had assured Otto Skorzeny that the Russians would not break through was in Loza's hands.

Now he had to hold it.

* * *

After the previous day's fighting there was no front in Vienna. *Totenkopf* had managed to hold the area around the Arsenal despite repeated Russian assaults, but elsewhere, a hedgehog defense saw many alarm units holding in one spot as Russians moved past them on other streets. *Das Reich* had been surrounded and threatened with destruction. Only immediate counterattacks had saved it.

Sepp Dietrich knew the end was near. North of the city in the Marchfeld, and now on Danube Island itself, the Russians attacked from all directions. This put not only *II SS-Panzerkorps* in danger of being surrounded, but also large elements of *8. Armee*. As he stared at the map late in the afternoon of 9 April, Dietrich knew the time had come to give up the slice of Vienna his men still held onto. The main objective now became keeping his men alive long enough for them to pull behind the Danube Canal.

* * *

Great cities all have their own personalities, their own soul. It's what makes them great. New York, the Big Apple, is known as a sleepless giant that hums with the electricity of commerce. London is the staid capital of a once-mighty empire and bears both the majesty and the scars that come with such a legacy. Paris, the City of Light, evokes images of romance and luxury.

---

4   Maier, *Drama*, p. 353.
5   To put this size gun in perspective, it was the equivalent of the 6 inch guns on the American light cruiser *Brooklyn*.
6   Loza, Dmitriy, translated & edited by Gebhardt, James F., *Commanding the Red Army's Sherman Tanks: The World War II Memoirs of Hero of the Soviet Union Dmitriy Loza* (Lincoln: University of Nebraska Press, 1996), p. 95.

Vienna had always been a uniquely human city, where art and culture were argued about in coffee houses all over the city. The famed Austrian satirist Karl Kraus, who had a venomous love-hate relationship with the city, once wrote that "the streets of Vienna are paved with culture, the streets of other cities with asphalt". Even Adolf Hitler came to Vienna to be an artist.

The streets were always filled with people bustling about on important business. But now Vienna was like one of Dante's circles of Hell, where the only humans abroad on streets swept by gunfire were refugees loaded down with whatever possessions they considered too critical to abandon, looters plundering abandoned stores and warehouses, and sallow-faced men whose unlucky fate was to be a defender of the city. With electricity sporadic at best the nights were lit by the pyres of people's lives, as fires raged out of control. The empty concrete canyons made for hellish avenues of advance and retreat.

On the defenders of Vienna's far right flank pressure was mounting from attacks through Nussdorf, with the aim of crossing the Danube Canal. Already one attempt had been beaten back after nightfall the previous day. Russian spearheads reached the area near the Franz Joseph Station, where *Das Reich* had redeployed to take over the line. In the west savage house-to-house fighting continued south and southeast all along the front. The worst fighting of all occurred at the Arsenal, where the Russians gained only minor advances at the cost of very heavy casualties.

* * *

With the exception of the newly arrived *Führer-Grenadier Division*, by this point the fighting strength of the defending German units was almost gone. *Das Reich* was in the best shape, but only when compared to *Totenkopf* and *6. Panzer-Division*. All three were combing the ranks to find men who could carry a rifle to stick in the front lines. The real tribute to the German command and control structure was not that the divisions were still combat-effective when conditions allowed, but that they held together at all as fighting organizations, considering the enormous losses each had suffered over the previous months.

* * *

As dawn broke on the morning of 9 April, the Russians attacked all along Vienna's defensive perimeter, with four main axes of attack into the inner city.

In some places the defenders held fast and the fighting was severe, in other places alarm and scratch units fought then broke, or ran away at the outset of fighting, and in still others the Russians found gaps in the defense where there were no defenders at all. The Hitler Youth Battalion on the northwest side remained effective even after days of close combat, holding a crucial position for long hours against almost continuous attacks. According to von Bünau:

> The Hitler Youth Battalion had firmly established its all-round defensive position from Nussdorfer Spitz on the Danube Canal, through Grinzinger Allee and Silbergasse, to the Danube Canal north of the Friedensbrücke and the Hohe Warte. In the morning [of 9 April] enemy armored reconnaissance patrols probing this position were turned back. Likewise a later enemy attack launched against the same position from north and northwest was repulsed with high casualties.[7]

The implication for von Bünau was that the Hitler Youth Battalion had lost contact with both flanks and was holding a roughly semi-circular perimeter anchored on the Danube Canal, from the point where the canal detached from the Danube River itself to the main bridge connecting

---

7   Von Bünau, *Combat in Vienna*, pp. 19-20.

Brittgenau and Alsergrund.[8] The battalion had alarm units on either side but these were not field combat forces and this was a very large defensive perimeter for such a hodge-podge of small units to hold, especially since it contained a great many parks and flat areas that gave a clear field of fire for heavy weapons and good traction for tanks. A full brigade would have had trouble defending so much ground. The Hitler Youth tried to make up for a lack of firepower with bravery and enthusiasm, but that could only work for so long. However, the Hitler Youth had something no other German unit had during the Battle of Vienna: reserves. Opposite their positions on the east bank of the Danube Canal, an alarm battalion had been stationed to both support them by defending their rear, and cover them if withdrawal over the canal became necessary.[9]

The popular and beautiful summer bath building at Hohe Warte was shattered in the fighting, the glass and metal structure being ripped open. The Franz Joseph Station fell during the day to a combination of Russian forces advancing from both north and west, which cut the defenders in half. Viennese civilians caught in the fighting cowered in cellars and basements, venturing out only when food and water ran out. Russian and German artillery traded salvos, with Stalin Organs reportedly set up at the intersection of Heiligenstädter Strasse and Grinzingerstrasse firing at German batteries on the north bank of the Danube. Refugees were still in the streets fleeing the onrushing Red Army when the artillery duel started. Horses, cows and other farm animals pulled wagons piled high with their dearest possessions through streets clogged with rubble, but exploding artillery rounds panicked the animals as shell splinters and falling masonry killed animal and human alike, while the blast concussion shook buildings and shattered windows. The Karl Marx Hof had already been damaged by bombing and was further wrecked by the shelling.

As the German perimeter shrank it had the effect of compressing the defenders into a shorter line, but this was counter-balanced by the concentration of the attackers who likewise had a shorter attack front. The fall of the Franz Joseph Station freed up Russian forces to hammer the perimeter held by the Hitler Youth Battalion and the nearby alarm units from the south, while other forces attacked them from the north and west. The Russians were dangerously close to the canal. Initially the youngsters held the line but the pressure was simply too great and it became obvious that the survivors either had to withdraw or die. And so, under cover of darkness, the battle-weary battalion withdrew over the canal in good order and without major casualties.

As mentioned above the Russians tried to cross the Danube Canal at Nussdorf but were driven back. Seeing a chance to avoid an opposed crossing, the opportunistic Russians had closely followed on the heels of the Hitler Youth as they withdrew. They seized a foothold on the Danube Canal lock near Nussdorfer Spitz, on the northern flank of the city, and tried to cross to the narrow island splitting the stream of the Danube River. There were actually two locks, the Nussdorf Weir and the Nussdorf Lock, and it was probably the ornately decorated weir that the Russians tried to cross first. As a gateway to Vienna, the X-strutted bridge had been gilded with columns at either end that were topped with bronze lions, and the steel spars on either side would have given some cover from small-arms fire. Overlooking the lock on the eastern bank was the solid Administration building, which acted as a blockhouse and gave both an excellent field of fire and cover for the defenders, requiring heavy weapons to dislodge them. The assault over the lock was dangerous in the extreme for the German defense. If the Russians could get a foothold on the east bank they could drive south toward the ultimate prize, an intact bridge over the Danube itself.

---

8   During the war the name of the bridge had been changed from the Friedensbrücke, or 'Peace Bridge', to the 'Brittgenauer Brücke'. The name 'Peace Bridge' did not seem in line with the times in 1941 when the name was changed. This should not be confused with the modern-day Brittgenauer Brücke.

9   Von Bünau does not state which alarm battalion this was, but it was likely the *Pionier-Ausbildungs-und-Ersatz-Abteilung 80*, which had been fighting in Klosterneuberg.

The first bridge in their path was the Floridsdorfer. Capturing that bridge in a *coup de main* would threaten to cut off the four divisions still fighting in Vienna: *Das Reich*, the *Führer-Grenadier-Division*, *Totenkopf* and *6. Panzer-Division*. Recognizing the danger, the Germans did what the Germans always did: they counterattacked. But immediate counterattacks could not pry the Russians loose from their tenuous hold on the lock, despite being pressed home with great courage. Men from both sides fell into the canal and the wounded likely drowned.

Even if the Germans could not regain the lock though, neither could the Russians cross over to the island, despite repeated efforts, and they suffered heavy casualties trying to do so. For a brief moment the Russians were stopped. The wolf was at the door but for the time being the Hitler Youth were able to hold the door closed.

* * *

Captain Loza's battle group had been reduced by casualties to a platoon or so of paratroopers and perhaps a dozen Shermans. In an offhand manner he reported negotiating with a restaurant within the sector that was still open to cook meals for 180 men. He names the establishment as the 'Astoria' Restaurant, behind the Hofburg, and claims to have paid for the meal using foreign currency he'd been supplied with. Loza goes on to claim that he toured the Natural History Museum before the Germans made several attacks on his battalion using Panthers and *Panzergrenadiers*, presumably from the *Führer-Grenadier-Division*. The claims match up with the timeline of that division's counterattack in the area, and Loza's story of bars and restaurants continuing service even as fighting swept past on the streets outside mirrors Ernst Barkmann's assertions of the same thing.

Stretched over the large triangular perimeter of the Palace and Museum Quarter his force relied on the firepower of the JSU-152s to fend off small forces of infantry and tanks. But the Germans had no reserves to throw at retaking the area. Every spare man was at the front trying to hold the line against the fierce Russian attacks. The wedge Loza had driven in the defense couldn't be erased.[10]

For his efforts during the war Loza was awarded with Hero of the Soviet Union, the Order of Lenin, the Order of the Red Banner, the Order of Alexander Nevskiy, the Order of the Patriotic War, first and second degree, and two Orders of the Red Star.

* * *

As the Russians advanced through Vienna, every step retraced the footsteps of historical giants. Moving past the working-class districts, the Ring and then the Volksgarten, the men of the Red Army trod ground their commander-in-chief, Joseph Stalin, would have recognized. Indeed, it was in Vienna that the brutal head of the USSR had first signed a letter with the name 'Stalin'. During their advance to and past the Schönbrunn Palace, the Russians had already passed through a space where, in February 1913, Stalin only lived 100 yards from, and where Hitler frequently went for walks and painted. It doesn't seem a stretch to imagine them passing one another while strolling through the zoo. As the Russians passed the burned-out Burgtheater and Volksgarten, they soon came to the elegant Café Central, at the intersection of Herrengasse and Strauchgasse, that in January 1913 had hosted Hitler, Tito, Freud, Trotsky, Lenin and probably Stalin as patrons.

* * *

---

10   Loza, *Commanding*, pp. 99-103.

Fighting had continued throughout the night of 8-9 April, without slackening. By morning on 9 April the defensive situation in Vienna had reached the critical stage, as Dietrich, Bittrich and von Bünau had always known it would. With *Das Reich* effectively surrounded and the Russians closing on the Danube Canal at multiple points, the time had come to start blowing up the bridges, since capturing an intact bridge would have been catastrophic for the Germans. Both the northwest and the northern railroad bridges were ordered blown, chiefly due to the imminent danger of their capture, but also because the engineers charged with destroying them were needed elsewhere.

This did nothing to help the defense of the rest of the city, however, as Russian attacks escalated all along the defensive perimeter. The ferocity of combat on 9 April was even greater than the previous day. Making matters worse, the Russian forces advancing on the north bank of the Danube made progress in the area north of Vienna at Gross Enzersdorf, a direct threat to the rear of the Vienna garrison. This axis of attack was given additional impetus when the two rifle and one mechanized corps of the Forty-Sixth Army began driving northwest in earnest, following on the heels of the outnumbered and retreating *SS-Kampfgruppe Ameiser*.

As mentioned previously, the only troops available to stop them were the men of the *Führer-Grenadier-Division*, who moved southeast from their positions on *Das Reich*'s left flank back across Vienna to the far side of the Danube. As the Hitler Youth Battalion retreated over the canal on the division's left flank, and the *Führer-Grenadier-Division* redeployed on its right, *Das Reich* found both of its flanks up in the air.

II SS-Panzerkorps

The redeployment of the defenders' strongest unit left only the two SS divisions west of the Danube Canal, covering a line that was already too long for three divisions to hold. All units still west of the Danube Canal, chiefly *Das Reich* and *Totenkopf*, as well as *6. Panzer-Division* in the Prater, were running short of effective combatants and struggling to hold off enemy attacks on a suddenly broadened front. The corps reported at least 39 Russian tanks knocked out on 9 April, mostly with *Panzerfauste* at very close quarters, which gives some idea of the ferocity of the fighting.

Throughout the day it became increasingly obvious that defense of Vienna was no longer viable, so ignoring Hitler's orders not to retreat, *SS-Obergruppenführer* Bittrich commanded all of *II SS-Panzerkorps* to cross to the north bank of the Danube Canal during the night of 9-10 April. Such a thing would have been unthinkable even six months before, but once the *Führer*'s bond with his *Waffen-SS* divisions was broken by the cuff band order, there was no repairing it. Their primary loyalty to him shifted to the comrades fighting at their side.

6. Panzer-Division

Since the Russians had already crossed the canal into the Prater, *6. Panzer-Division* had no choice but to hold them back regardless of the cost, which resulted in Vienna's favorite playground seeing some of the bitterest fighting of the campaign. All of the buildings either burned to the ground or were blasted to framework skeletons. Rubble and powdered brick littered the once-pristine avenues. The formerly majestic trees canted at obscene angles on charred trunks. And along with destruction to the infrastructure, the detritus of war lay scattered about in ruined tanks and guns of both sides. A Panzer Mk IV/J with both tracks broken and a destroyed glacis plate lay abandoned across the field from a knocked-out Sherman M4A3/76. The American import showed a penetration hole low on the right side of its turret, probably from a handheld weapon.

At the Gas and Electric Works, *Panzergrenadier-Regiment 114* fought among the generators and smokestacks to delay the Russians and hold down *Totenkopf*'s left flank, but Russian numbers were too much to hold back forever. Attacks continued all day along the division's entire front, supported by heavy Red Air Force ground support. The regiment was forced back to the Erdberger-Mais District on the banks of the Danube, due east of the Arsenal. The area was famous for the four gasometer buildings, world-class examples of industrial architecture that provided the Viennese with gas for cooking and heating.

3. SS-Panzer-Division Totenkopf

The Russians were still trying to push forward through the Arsenal grounds and the South Railway Station, as they had been for days. A slight gain was thrown back by a counterattack from *Totenkopf* with the loss of 5 tanks. The combination of the stout Arsenal building and the nearby South and East Railway Stations had given the defenders multiple fortresses to defend, and open killing grounds in the fire zone in front of the defenses.

The Arsenal had a large parade ground to its east and the Gas and Electric Works to its northeast, while both the railway stations had long open stretches for tracks and sidings. In a way the combat resembled that in Normandy the previous summer. The Americans advanced hedgerow by hedgerow, much like city blocks, and paid an enormous price for every gain. The Germans gave ground slowly but each acre cost them dearly in casualties. *Totenkopf* was in much the same situation, and the battle was decided by the same method. The ground given up by the SS men could be measured in yards, but just as Operation Cobra broke through and outflanked the German defense line in Normandy, Russian advances on either flank in Vienna eventually forced *Totenkopf* backward.

In particular, on 9 April the Russians broke through on *Totenkopf*'s right flank in the area west of the South Railway Station. The defensive stand of the SS division and *6. Panzer-Division* had denied two major traffic arteries to the inner city from use by the Russians, Prinz Eugen Strasse and the Rennweg, which made up the northeastern border of Belvedere Park. But the breakthrough west of *Totenkopf* gave them Wiedner Strasse, which became the famed Kartner Strasse and led straight to St Stephen's Platz.

Führer-Grenadier-Division

The situation north of the Danube was becoming critical, but fighting around the West Railway Station intensified, making it impossible for the *Führer-Grenadier-Division* to withdraw north as quickly as Bittrich needed.

2. SS-Panzer-Division Das Reich

After being surrounded the day before, *Das Reich* fought hard to maintain its right flank. Attacks on the Franz Josef Railway Station were at first repulsed, even when the Russians supported the infantry with 19 tanks.[11] The division found itself in a rough half-circle anchored around the North bridge and extending to the Aspern bridge. The Russian plan to attack along the Danube

---

11 Maier, *Drama*, p. 354.

Canal from both east and west, and thereby cut off both *Das Reich* and *Totenkopf,* was by now obvious. Bittrich asked permission to withdraw the two SS divisions behind the Danube Canal and Sepp Dietrich granted it.

Unlike the Western Allies or the Russians, who covered withdrawals using infantry while the armored vehicles pulled out, the *Waffen-SS* men did the exact opposite. *Das Reich* artillery moved into the streets for a direct-fire role, something unheard of in other armies. The commander of *SS-Artillerie-Regiment 2, SS-Standartenführer* Karl Kreutz, was awarded the Knight's Cross for this action. Once night fell, however, the fighting slackened. The Russians did not try to stop them from pulling out.

The two SS divisions had been caught between the populace, many of whom wanted them to withdraw without fighting, and their *Führer,* who ordered them to die defending the city rather than retreat. In the end, they had resisted until the last possible moment and then withdrew to fight again. *General der Infanterie* von Bünau was the last man to cross over the canal to Danube Island. Within minutes of him crossing the two remaining bridges over the canal blew up and collapsed into the water.

* * *

Ernst Barkmann's Panther wasn't back in service yet, but the emergency situation required all hands to fight. Since the division repair shop had relocated north of the Danube, Barkmann was ordered to take four Panthers and a pioneer platoon and perform a reconnaissance in the direction of Grossenzersdorf. He commanded the little *Kampfgruppe* from an SPW.

The town lay north of the river, 12 miles due east of Vienna's city center in an area near the Danube where heavy Russian pressure threatened to close *II SS-Panzerkorps'* escape route. Even before reaching Grossenzersdorf they met a column of Russians led by disarmed men of the Hungarian regular army, the *Honved.*

The Germans opened fire, and in the ensuing fightfight Barkmann manned an MG-42 mounted on the SPW. The Russian advance was stopped and a hasty defensive line set up, after which Barkmann's group was ordered back into Vienna. Before crossing the *Reichsbrücke,* however, new orders arrived to defend on Danube Island.[12]

Sperrverband Folzmann

With the Russians now on the south bank of the Danube west of Vienna, *8. Armee* had to protect against river crossings into its rear area near Bisamberg. But with every man committed to the front lines trying to hold back Second Ukrainian Front, *General der Gebirgstruppe* Kreysing didn't have many options. According to Maier this mission was accomplished by an obscure blocking formation titled *Sperrverband Folzmann.*

* * *

On the *6. SS-Panzerarmee's* far left flank south of Tulln the Russians reinforced success for a drive west down the Danube Valley. Heavy but indecisive fighting raged all day at Neulengbach as the Russians tried to expand their corridor south of the river, while at the western spearhead of this effort fighting lasted into the night at Moosbierbaum.

---

12   Weidinger, *Das Reich*, p. 380.

Freikorps Adolf Hitler

Late in the war the Head of the National Labor Front, the notorious drunk Robert Ley, proposed the creation of the *Freikorps Adolf Hitler*. The idea was for *Panzerjäger* teams to infiltrate behind Russian lines and attack targets without warning, thus disrupting the rear areas of the Red Army. It was a preposterous idea, but because Ley was still so powerful within the Nazi hierarchy Hitler granted permission to form the unit and 200 men began training at Dollersheim. According to Maier, who was present, Ley showed up at *6. SS-Panzerarmee* headquarters on 9 April to help put his plan into action. But Dietrich told him the war was lost and his plan was ludicrous.[13] Ley disappeared and his men were given to *Heeresgruppe Süd*.

Kampfgruppe Volkmann

At 1:30 a.m. the demolition teams finished wiring the Danube Bridge at Tulln for destruction. After daybreak the sounds of battle could be clearly heard south of the bridge position, but Volkmann wanted to give the rearguard every chance to escape to the north bank of the river.

As the last of the German forces south of the Danube withdrew through Tulln to the north bank, with 5th Guards Tank Corps in hot pursuit, at 7:50 p.m. Volkmann ordered the bridge demolished. But nothing happened. Fearing another Remagen catastrophe,[14] he went to find out why his order wasn't carried out and discovered that a trainload of German troops had raced across at the last second. Five minutes later, the bridge linking the two banks of the river raised high in the air and fell into the river with a huge splash, temporarily ending the threat of Russian forces driving northward into the rear areas of *8. Armee*.[15]

The towns of Langenrohr and Tulln had been heavily damaged in the fighting. At least 19 Germans and 53 Russians died in the fighting there, and three civilians were later shot by the Russians. German artillery shelled Tulln for the remainder of the war to prevent a buildup of materials for a crossing by the Russians, which killed eight more civilians and wounded 15, while minefields account for many more.

Most of *Kampfgruppe Volkmann* remained on the north bank and continued to defend the river crossing…most, but not all. An unknown number of troops from *SS-Kampfgruppe Trabandt 2* couldn't get across the bridge in time and had no other choice than to withdraw to the west, where they came under command of *Korps Schultz*. They would see bitter fighting in the days to come in the region around Sankt Pölten.

Korps Schultz

The corps-level headquarters named *Deutscher Befehlshaber Slowakie*, German Commander Slovakia, formerly attached to *8. Armee*, was transferred to *6. SS-Panzerarmee* and renamed as *Korps Schultz*.[16] At some point after 31 March its commander became *Generalmajor* Paul Schultz, a well-respected veteran who fought in the front lines during the First World War and led a regiment

---

13   Maier, *Drama*, p. 356.
14   On 7 March the Americans had seized the railroad bridge over the Rhine River at Remagen, when American shelling cut the demolition wires. The officers responsible were summarily court-martialed and shot.
15   Brettner, *Die Letzten Kämpfe Band II*, pp. 41-42. Brettner's timeline best matches the actions elsewhere, and is the most recent, but other sources claim the bridge was blown up on 8 April.
16   Sometimes referred to as *Kommando Schultz* or *Schultz Kommando*.

during the Second World War, later becoming the commander of several Army schools. He'd taken over the Slovakian post from *General der Panzertruppe* Alfred Hubicki.

The defense line for his new command ran from Brand-Laaben to Zwentendorf an der Donau, with Russian probing attacks concentrating mainly on the area near Neulengbach and in the valley of the tiny Perschling River, which in places was little more than a ditch and emptied into the Danube. His immediate assessment was that he faced three divisions, but with major attacks coming soon, his independent evaluation was that Sankt Pölten was the obvious next target.[17]

The main terrain feature along this line was the Haspel Forest, a densely wooded area with very steep slopes that was unsuitable for tanks but ideal for infantry infiltration tactics. Located between Neulengbach and Kapelln, the four-mile-long range was the key defensive position on the road to Sankt Pölten. Russian artillery stationed either to the south or north was unable to fire over the mountains to support troops on the opposite side, while German artillery wasn't hampered by that limitation.

The immediate strategy to confront Russian drives on Sankt Pölten was to maintain a flexible forward defense so the meager forces at hand could be directed to wherever the strongest attacks hit the line, while fighting as far east as possible. The closer the fighting came to Sankt Pölten the more the terrain favored the attackers. From Zwentendorf to Atzenbrugg the front-line defense was given to *Panzerjäger-Brigade 2*, which gave an impressive title to a decidedly unimpressive unit. Mostly these were men with *Panzerfauste*, with perhaps a few *Hetzer Jagdpanzers*, some *PAK-40s* and 88mm guns. The part of the front shielding Grabensee had taken over the relatively strong *Panzer-Aufklärungs-Abteilung 1,* the reconnaissance battalion of *1. Panzer-Division*. This unit held the front to Sankt Christophen, with a unit formed from the replacement units of *6. SS-Panzerarmee* and called the *SS-Alarm-Bataillon A* as their right flank neighbor. Finally, another ad-hoc unit named *Alarm-Bataillon C* guarded the line to Brand-Laaben.[18] *Generalmajor* Schultz rated the combat value of his units as low to bad, with the exception of *Panzer-Aufklärungs-Abteilung 1*. Making the situation even worse, both flanks of *Korps Schultz* were up in the air, with no contact in the north with *II SS-Panzerkorps* or in the south with *I SS-Panzerkorps*.

What Schultz did have was a strong heavy artillery component, with adequate stocks of ammunition, making his best defensive tactic to break up Russian attacks in their assembly areas. However, medium-caliber guns, and ammunition, as well as anti-aircraft guns, were both in short supply, so neither air defense nor artillery support during Russian attacks were possible. As if that wasn't bad enough, using his one asset of heavy artillery to interdict imminent attacks required excellent communications with the front-line troops, but both signals men and equipment were in short supply. About the only thing *Generalmajor* Schultz had more of than he needed was Russians.

Over the next few days reinforcements poured into Schultz's corps, but against the veteran 34th Rifle and 18th Tank Corps they weren't nearly enough. His impressive-sounding but thrown-together corps had three reserve infantry battalions, two of them made up of SS men intended as replacements for *6. SS-Panzerarmee*; two battalions from a so-called *Panzerjäger brigade*,[19] so named because the men all carried a *Panzerfaust*; three *Sturmgeschütze* and five artillery battalions; *Panzer-Aufklärungs-Abteilung 3*; and three *Luftwaffe Flak* battalions, possibly of *Flak-Abteilung 653*, which were ordered to assist the corps but didn't actually come under Schultz's command.[20]

17   The National Archives (TNA) M-1035 Fiche 365 B-160 Bünau, General der Infanterie AD Rudolf von *Corps von Buenau 8 Apr – 8 May 1945* (Leavenworth: Historical Division Headquarters United States Army, Europe, 1946), pp. 6-7.

18   Rauchensteiner, *Krieg in Österreich*, p. 179.

19   This may have been the aforementioned *Panzerjäger-Brigade 2*.

20   Reynolds, Michael, *Men of Steel, I SS Panzerkorps, The Ardennes and Eastern Front 1944-45* (New York: Sarpdeon, 1999), p. 263.

This wasn't a very impressive force, but it was better than nothing. Whether or not it could slow down Tolbukhin's rampaging troops was yet to be seen.

Sepp Dietrich gave the corps command of the army's left wing up to the Danube. But with that flank already ruptured Dietrich recognized the near impossibility of what he was asking Schultz to do, namely, stop two veteran Guards armies and one Guards tank corps, so he also gave Schultz command of *Sturmgeschütz-Brigade 261* as an infusion of much-needed armor.

The latter unit had produced one of Germany's greatest panzer aces, Johann Schmidt, with 75 kills. The brigade's vehicles all bore the crest of a red wolf's head on a white background. More interestingly, the German crosses on the side were outlined in red, not white as was usual. Its strength is unknown now, but the surrender of four working vehicles that wound up in the USA after the war gives a hint that it remained a viable fighting force in April 1945.

But the most important reinforcements to arrive during this period were advance elements of the veteran *710. Infanterie-Division*. Although not considered a first-line division, it was under the command of *Generalmajor* Walter Dorn, winner of the Knight's Cross with Oak Leaves and Swords. So far 11 trains filled with the division had arrived and Dorn was given responsibility for defending Sankt Pölten. His men were more rested than most of *Heeresgruppe Süd*. No sooner had their trains pulled into the area before they were sent into an attack west of Hoschstrass that drove back the Russian spearheads and stabilized the right flank of *I SS-Panzerkorps*.

* * *

Pressure mounted on Schultz's corps as it became obvious the Soviets would push down the Danube Valley. The cities, towns and village under immediate threat saw columns of refugees pouring out on the roads leading west, like ants fleeing a flooded nest. In the little town of Kirchstetten, east of Sankt Pölten, famed poet Josef Weinheber heard the approaching guns of the Red Army and decided it was time to die. Weinheber joined the Austrian Nazi Party in 1931 and had been recognized by the Third Reich as a divinely gifted artist who was exempt from service. Alcohol abuse took over his life as the war deteriorated for the Nazis until, with the Russians closing in, he committed suicide with an overdose of morphine. A monument to him in Schiller Park near the Academy of Fine Arts in Vienna has been routinely vandalized over the years because of his association with the Nazis.

* * *

The first attacks from both Russian corps were limited probes looking for the easiest spot for a breakthrough. *Panzerjäger-Brigade 2* was forced to give up Zwentendorf, but the Russians were hot on their heels to gain a bridgehead over the little Persching River. Another push came at Neulengbach, and it began to be obvious that Sankt Pölten was to be outflanked on both the north and south. The Haspel Forest defensive positions became untenable and Schultz had to give them up or lose the defenders and see a huge hole ripped in his lines. The more dangerous realization for the Germans, however, was that it was now obvious the Russian recognized the weakness of the left wing of *6. SS-Panzerarmee*. Atzenbrugg and Grabensee both fell and fighting erupted at Asperhofen.

I SS-Panzerkorps

Around Dreistetten at least three attacks were repulsed to that town's west and northwest and the Russian attack objectives started to become clear. With Russian forces massing to the east of Hohe Wand, meaning 'high wall' in German, their intention to cross the mountain and cut off the Germans around Dreistetten became obvious. The fighting in the area would be so intense that the townsfolk of Maiersdorf, in the valley east of Hohe Wand, would later build a memorial to the dead.

Other attacks at Pottenstein and Schwarzensee were also fought off, despite the Russians being supported by tanks. Fighting continued long after sun-up. Once again casualties were heavy on both sides, with the Russians losing at least two tanks.

Kampfgruppe 1. SS-Panzer-Division Leibstandarte Adolf Hitler

Having run into stout defense in the Berndorf and Pottenstein region, the Russians shifted some of their focus further south to the weaker sections there, while adjusting to losing mobile units to the breakthrough near Vienna. Aside from a few probing attacks the day quietened. This meant the *LAH* had a chance to catch its breath, get some sleep and eat a hot meal. It wouldn't last long.

Kampfgruppe 12. SS-Panzer-Division Hitlerjugend

As previously mentioned several days before *Hitlerjugend* had combed out its ranks from the remnants of *I./Kampfgruppe SS-Panzergrenadier-Regiment 26*, parts of the ambulance company, the medical battalion and even musicians from the divisional band. These men were formed into a *Kampfgruppe* under *SS-Obersturmführer* Möbius and on 9 April were redeployed into the line between Berndorf and Alland. Some of the supply troops for *SS-Panzergrenadier-Regiment 26* plus surplus members of *SS-Flak-Abteilung 12 Hitlerjugend*, men with no guns to serve, were organized into *SS-Kampfgruppe Gross*.

They were inserted into the line beside *SS-Kampfgruppe Möbius* in the Leopoldsdorf-Klausen sector, facing the most dangerous threat to the entire position of *I SS-Panzerkorps*. Supported by the panzer regiment, *SS-Kampfgruppe Gross* surprised the Russians and, as so often happened, the German counterattack drove them back several miles. In the process they relieved a small *Kampfgruppe* that held out all day at Schöpflgitter, a village two miles northwest of the Leopoldsdorf-Klausen line.

Russian attacks had continued on the division's right flank throughout the night. As dawn broke a battalion-sized Russian force moved off toward Altenmarkt an der Triesting from the direction of Steinfeld, due to the east, in a reconnaissance probe accompanied by three tanks. The infantry rode in trucks. Getting to Altenmarkt would have required passing through the German lines between Schwarzensee and Maria Raisenmarkt. The front more or less followed the road connecting the two towns with the main supply route running through Weissenbach an der Triesting.

As it happened the Russians stumbled into an entrenched position of *Kampfgruppe SS-Panzergrenadier-Regiment 25* outside of Schwarzensee. Two tanks immediately went up in flames but the Germans were stretched too thin to hold the town and the garrison pulled back half a mile to the south. But *SS-Gruppenführer* Priess couldn't allow that loss to stand. Without the road leading north through Schwarzensee the entire position north was almost cut off. Therefore, a counterattack was ordered to retake the town at all costs.

The only units available were *SS-Kampfgruppe Taubert*, essentially *Pionier-Bataillon 12*, with some men and SPWs from *III./Panzergrenadier-Abteilung 12* in support. Some of the few remaining panzers also took part. But since this would be near the divisional border with the *LAH*, that division contributed men from the staff of *SS-Panzer-Regiment 1* to help out in the attack. In gathering twilight the men pushed off to regain Schwarzensee.

Like countless towns throughout Austria, Schwarzensee was built in a broad valley surrounded by forested mountains, although calling the tiny settlement a town was tantamount to calling a pony a Clydesdale. It was little more than a Catholic Church with a few houses around it. Nevertheless, its position astride the road from Weissenbach to Alland made it critical. And like all such roads, it ran through a series of valleys. Trying to hold the towns or villages was like being in a shooting gallery where the enemy could occupy surrounding hills to observe their artillery fire, but were largely hidden from the defenders. And the same was true in reverse. Attackers always had the advantage.

The attack took place with *SS-Kampfgruppe Taubert* on the left, or western flank, and the *LAH Kampfgruppe* on the right. In between the two were some men released by *Kampfgruppe-SS-Panzergrenadier-Regiment 25* specifically for the purpose of following in the wake of the attack as a small reserve force. Because of the critical nature of the objective, sufficient artillery ammunition was made available to support the attack and, as discussed above, it was exactly on target. Even in the near-darkness it was possible to direct the fire onto Russian positions. In fact it was so accurate that when the German infantry struck their positions the Russians had no heart left for a determined struggle. Combat raged throughout the night, but by morning on 10 April the smoking rubble of Schwarzensee was once again in German hands.

Kampfgruppe 356. Infanterie-Division

SS-Obersturmführer Hinrich Garbade led a small *Kampfgruppe* in the defense of Hohe Wand. *Kampfgruppe Garbade* contained parts of *Artillerie-Abteilung 501*, possibly men with no guns to serve, and some surplus *Luftwaffe* personnel assigned to *Kampfgruppe 356. Infanterie-Division*. Despite a lack of infantry training the *Kampfgruppe* fought bravely but was outgunned from the start.

The Russian buildup east of the Hohe Wand Mountain finally exploded into an assault that took a Russian battalion to the crest. This was a key loss the Germans couldn't allow to stand. Losing the monstrous mound of tree-covered rock compromised the defense of Grünbach am Schneeberg and Willendorf to the south, and Dreistetten and Markt Piesting to the north. It also made an excellent artillery observation point for further moves to the west. Getting it back was a top priority.

SS-Kampfgruppe Keitel

Larger attacks in company and battalion sizes were beaten back with great difficulty. The lines here remained somewhat fluid, since there weren't enough men to construct a true front line. That led to a style of warfare where strongpoints would be held as long as possible before the defenders withdrew, only to immediately counterattack. To succeed the Russians had to avoid a frontal assault up steep slopes with poor footing, and instead try to come in on the flanks, but if the defenses were mutually supporting that became costly to achieve. And even when Keitel's men succeeded in holding their positions, it cost them in casualties. Little by little his *Kampfgruppe* was bleeding away.

6. Armee

Despite *2. Panzerarmee*'s still critical situation, *General der Artillerie* de Angelis had been ordered to give up the *117. Jäger-Division* and transfer it to *6. Armee*. This transfer had the highest priority. But because of the Russian breakthrough toward Graz early in the month, and the terrible state of the railways, the division had to take a circuitous route to affect the transfer, at least doubling the distance. First, it took trains to Maribor, where they unloaded, made forced marches to Karlsdorf, and then reboarded trains for the last part of the journey.

* * *

Having lost Waldbach the day before to elements of *Sperrverband Motschmann*, after regrouping the Russians took it back again. For his part, Motschmann didn't have enough troops to stop the Russian advance; he could only try to slow them down.

Kampfgruppe Semmering

The *Kampfgruppe*'s front now stretched for a preposterous 22 miles. The Eselstein am Semmering, translated as 'The Donkey Stone', was a peak from which an observer could see most of the Semmering Pass, a panoramic view of Adlitzgräben and Schottenstein all the way to the distant Schneeberg, in the area of *6. SS-Panzerarmee*. The various peaks on the mountain were sharp, white mounds of stone jutting skyward, with huge trees growing in every crevice. Indeed, in places there were so many similar rock formations down the slope they appeared like incisors in the lower jaw of a wolf.

The Russians had captured the prominent landmark and the Germans wanted it back. On 9 April the men of *1./SS-Gebirgsjäger-Ausbildungs-und-Ersatz Bataillon 13 Leoben*, went into the attack. The assault was, in places, up slopes approaching eighty degrees, which was so sheer it put even the defending Russians in danger of falling. Over the course of the month an unknown number of men on both sides did just that, plummeting to serious injury or death because of a crumbling foothold or loose rock.

While heading to the deployment area for the attack, the SS men passed by dead German soldiers lying on the road, including some from their battalion, whom they recognized. As before, the artillery preparation was two shots from each gun, which did little more than alert the Russians of an incoming attack. In response, they fired back with small arms and both mortar and artillery fire that wasn't hampered by a lack of ammunition. In open meadows the Germans made perfect targets, while under the trees the shells bursting in the overhead branches filled the air with wood shrapnel.

The Russian fire was extremely accurate, ripping into the Germans and pinning them to the ground. Cries for medical help came from all over the slope. The order to retreat finally sent the Germans running and sliding back to their starting point. Without proper artillery support, it seemed almost impossible to retake the height, but *Oberst* Raithel hadn't given up yet.[21]

* * *

A battalion-sized Russian attack from the Klamm region hit the convalescents and *Landesschützen* on the left flank of the *Gebirgs-Artillerie-Schule-Bataillon Dachstein*. The fears of the *Gebirgs* artillerists about that flank being unable to hold were borne out when the Russians broke through.

21   Brettner, *Die Letzten Kämpfe Band I*, p. 103.

Some of the battalion's men were fighting as infantry and they were also hit by the attack. Calling in artillery support, the men from the school fought them off, with their defense on the southern slopes of the Kotstein centered around two MG-42 machine guns.

III Panzerkorps
SS-Kampfgruppe Schweitzer

Having fought their way through the surrounding Russians, the exhausted survivors of Schweitzer's command were sent to Hartberg for some badly needed rest. Schweitzer earned the Knight's Cross for his leadership in retaking Rechnitz and delaying the Russian advance long enough for a defense to be erected further west, although there is some debate about who authorized the award.

IV SS Panzerkorps
SS-Brigade Ney

The *IV./SS-Brigade Ney* was attached to *IV SS-Panzerkorps* in the area of St Michael in Salzburg province. A popular ski resort before and after the war, the Gothic Catholic church there has frescoes dating back to the 13th and 14th centuries, as well as the oldest Christian gravestone in the province. The landscape was rugged and picturesque, and easily defensible. Other parts of the brigade were attached to *5. SS-Panzer-Division Wiking* and the *1. Volks-Gebirgs-Division*, and its *III. Abteilung* was still with *Totenkopf*, fighting in Vienna.

Ney's command was unique in one way. Although it had seen heavy and sometimes bitter combat, its strength level had not only remained high, it had actually increased as time went by. Hungarians looking for a source of supply knew that SS units would eat when others might not, since they often had their own depots and warehouses. The dangerous fate facing SS men captured by the Russians was well known, but faded in comparison to the pangs of hunger.

5. SS-Panzer-Division Wiking

The main emphasis of Third Ukrainian Front's attacks may have shifted to Vienna and the Danube, but that didn't mean the rest of the front remained quiet. Graz had been and remained an objective and the main road leading to that city ran through Fürstenfeld. On 9 April a major fight broke out for Hill 385 in the area of that town 67 miles south of Wiener Neustadt. With no reserves to speak of, and only one road to retreat down, the Germans' only choices were to fight, flee or surrender. Surrender probably meant an immediate bullet in the head. Fleeing *might* save the individual at the cost of his comrades, but even conscripted SS men faced a bleak future in a Russian-controlled Austria. With no real alternative, therefore, elements of *Wiking* stood fast despite a lack of heavy weapons, in particular a battalion formed around the survivors of *SS-Panzer-Regiment 5*. The fighting continued for four days.

2. Panzerarmee

Once again the Russians launched local attacks along the front of *2. Panzerarmee* to fix its units in place. In particular they wanted to keep *General der Artillerie* de Angelis from bolstering his left wing, where they still intended to drive on Graz. That didn't stop *23. Panzer-Division* from redeploying to the northwest of Bad Radkersburg, thereby bending the army's front to the north-west to guard against just such an offensive toward Graz. Unfortunately for *9. SS-Panzer-Division Hohenstaufen*, defending the Mur River line in and west of the town of Bad Radkersburg, this uncovered their northern flank.

Meanwhile, other Russian units tried unsuccessfully to drive down the lowlands near the Mur River, while on the line facing southeast a terrible fight broke out in the town of Ljutomer, a few miles south of Veržej. This combat involved Russian units that attacked again and again despite heavy losses, but the Germans retained control.

* * *

Gauleiter Ueberreither was still working night and day in Graz to find warm bodies to send to the front, and on 9 April it was the turn of *23. Panzer-Division* to receive a fresh levy of *Volkssturm*, who were worse than useless for front-line combat. Most of the old men and boys were sent home, although a few were kept for digging secondary defensive positions or, in the case of the children, as rear-echelon messengers.

In the countryside, the Army troops began to face hostility from the local population, and to see the red and white flag of old Austria, the symbol of the resistance movement. Presumably the resistance members weren't foolish enough to present themselves as targets, or to attack the troops directly, since any measures taken against such people would have been deemed justified by the Nazi government. But the troops knew how the locals felt and it didn't help their morale.[22]

14. Waffen-Grenadier-Division der SS Galizien

The Battle for the Stradner Kogel raged into its fourth day with the Ukrainians once again being driven off the top and *3. Kavallerie-Division* once again counterattacking to retake it. Then the Ukrainians rotated back into the front with a spirited attack which drove the Russians back nearly a mile. But before they could entrench in their new positions a deadly artillery and Katyusha barrage tore into their ranks, followed by a strong Russian counterattack. Numerous gaps in the front lines were exploited and the Ukrainians were in danger of disintegrating. The only imme-diate reserve was *Waffen-Pionier-Bataillon der SS 14*, which finally plugged the fractured lines at the cost of severe casualties. Even so, the Russians once again captured the mountain's peak.

The German response was predictable. Yet again *3. Kavallerie-Division* attacked, this time from the south and backed up by Ukrainian contingents, and yet again the Germans retook Stradner Kogel. Viewed from a distance it seemed that nothing had happened in the four days of fighting for the strategic promontory, that the front had been static. Yet the truth was that savage combat and skyrocketing casualty numbers resulted from a stalemate fight neither side was willing to lose.

22   Rebentisch, *To the Caucasus*, p. 466.

10

Tuesday, 10 April

Berlin

In all of the *Wehrmacht*, German panzer inventory totals recorded on this day were 157 Mark IIIs, 468 Mark IVs and *Jagdpanzer* IV/70s and 499 Panthers. On the Eastern Front by itself there were 17 Mark IIIs, 324 Mark IVs and *Jagdpanzer* IV/70s and 446 Panthers, meaning the Western Front was nearly denuded of panzers. No totals are available for other machines, such as the Tiger I or Tiger II, or the *Jagdpanther* and *Jagdtiger*. Nor were all of these machines functional but included panzers in repair.

Mark IIIs had long-since been relegated to training schools as even the most advanced version had been obsolete for two years. The best Mark III version for combat, the L model, only mounted a 50mm gun. When firing a high-velocity tungsten-tipped armor-piercing round it still retained a small value on the battlefield in 1945, but by this point any weapon that functioned was being aimed at Germany's invading enemies. Some of the machines listed weren't even on army rolls but had been returned to their factories for conversion into *Sturmgeschütze IIIs*, the assault gun design mounted on a Mark III chassis.

* * *

Having made his way to Berlin on the failing rail system, Hungarian *SS-Obergruppenführer* Ruszkay was confronted at the SS Main Office with a scheme to dissolve the Hungarian SS divisions and parcel out their men to other *Waffen-SS* divisions in small packets: *25. SS-Waffen-Grenadier-Division der SS Hunyadi* was to be split into 30 detachments, while *26. SS-Waffen-Grenadier-Division der SS Hungaria* would be carved into 40. Ruszkay was finally able to get the order stopped before it was sent, then suddenly found himself being appointed to command *XVII SS-Armeekorps*.

The idea to dissolve the divisions to create replacements for other SS divisions was a much better plan than what actually happened. In the end the Hungarian formations ate a lot of German food and were issued a lot of German weapons, but accomplished nothing in return.

Heeresgruppe Süd
8. Armee

On Kreysing's right flank, the Forty-Sixth Army's two powerful corps, the 10th Guards Rifle Corps and 2nd Guards Mechanized Corps, began to spread out both west and north. As it did so, the litany of captured towns and villages went on. Deutsch-Wagram, Bockfleiss, Gänserndorf, Matzen and Stillfried all fell, some only after bitter fighting, some with no resistance at all.

At Strasshof a German defense force moved in time to guard the airfield, which was not attacked. According to Brettner, however, there was incredibly savage fighting in the area, with 11 Germans killed and the astounding number of 389 Russians supposedly killed in action.[1] For the moment they refrained from attacking the entrenched Germans at the airfield, concentrating instead on the rape and pillage of the town itself. Nine townsfolk died in the fighting and five more committed suicide, at which point there were more Russians in the town than inhabitants.

* * *

Things along the north bank of the Danube had become critical as Forty-Sixth Army charged forward and penetrated north of Lobau, west of Deutsch-Wagram. This penetration was potentially fatal for *II SS-Panzerkorps*. If they were able to drive much further, *6. Panzer-Division* defending in the Prater might be caught in a crossfire from Russian guns both north and south of the Danube. Should that happen their entire position in Vienna would collapse.

Kampfgruppe 101. Jäger-Division

The remnants of the division were still trying to hold the Morava River line on the left flank of *Kampfgruppe 96. Infanterie-Division*, but Russian attacks grew stronger as the front withdrew westward on the right flank of *Kampfgruppe 101. Jäger-Division*. Finally on 10 April a strong Russian push drove them out of Mannersdorf. The Germans retreated under a rain of bombs and artillery shells. During the fights for Angern and Mannersdorf 100 German soldiers were killed and both towns suffered heavy damage. At Gross-Schweinbarth the division lost 14 more men killed.

Along with ammunition and fuel, the Germans were also desperately short of food. One battalion of 647 men received about 88 pounds of meat to divide between them, or about 2 ounces per man, and every second or third day they got a bit of bread.

SS-Kampfgruppe Trabandt I, or SS-Regiment Schultze

A strength return still extant from 10 April gives a good idea of composition of the first regiment-sized *Kampfgruppe* from *SS-Kampfgruppe-Division Böhmen und Mähren*.[2] Serving under him were 50 officers, 508 NCOs and 2,620 enlisted men, for a total ration strength of 3,178. In addition, the *Kampfgruppe* had 23 mortars and a dozen 100mm cannon, along with assorted machines guns, mines and other weapons. The number of *Panzerfauste* isn't known, but as an armored component it did have 12 *Sturmgeschütz IIIs*.[3]

SS-Kampfgruppe Trabandt I had gone into the front lines around Zistersdorf, with orders to hold the oil fields there regardless of the cost. The commander, Knight's Cross winner *SS-Sturmbannführer* Herbert Schultze, was no stranger to combat, having previously commanded the *II./SS-Panzergrenadier-Regiment Der Führer*. Having just turned 31 years old, Schultze was a personally brave and energetic commander who had originally been pulled out of the front lines because he earned the Close Combat Badge in Gold. This meant he'd been in close combat for 50 days, and such men were always pulled back to teach new recruits. At the time he received his

1   Brettner, *Die Letzten Kämpfe Band II*, p. 155. No other source lists this casualty total and it is possibly a misprint, with the real number of Russians killed as 38 or 39.
2   Even today it is impossible to definitively say which *Kampfgruppe* is meant by which name, but the author is confident those listed in this text are most likely the correct ones.
3   Block, Martin, (2003) '*Kampfgruppen* Trabandt, Böhmen und &', KGr. Trabandt or 'Böhmen-Mähren' <https://www.feldgrau.net/forum/viewtopic.php?t=5623>, (Accessed (12 July 2018).

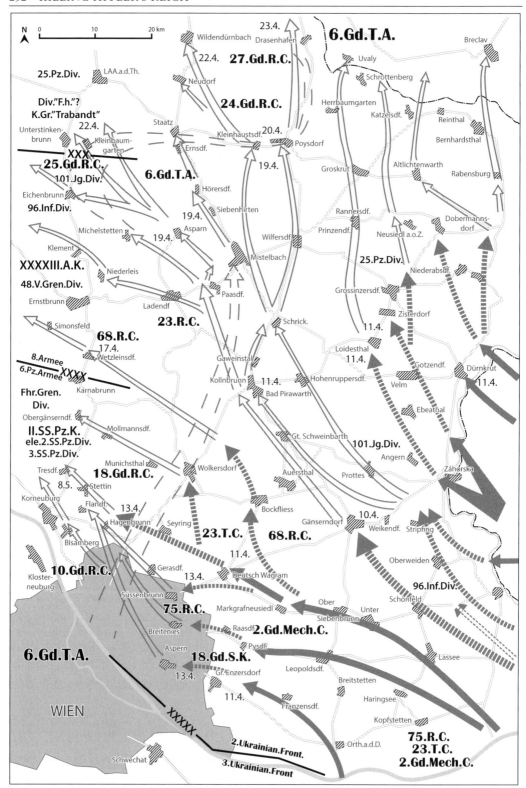

Map 6 German *8. Armee* and defense north of Vienna.

award in late 1943, only 15 other men had gotten it. But in the emergency of the last months of the war, even men such as Schultze received combat commands again.

37. SS-Freiwilligen-Kavallerie-Division Lützow

Pressure continued on all elements of the division, including *SS-Kampfgruppe Ameiser*, forcing it back to the northwest. The headquarters and anti-tank battalion fought in the vicinity of Deutsch-Wagram. With few heavy weapons the mission couldn't be to stop the Russians, but simply to delay them long enough for the units fighting in Vienna to retreat over the Danube. Having barely escaped destruction the day before, *SS-Kampfgruppe Ameiser* counterattacked in conjunction with the *Führer-Grenadier-Division* toward Grosshofen and Aderklaa, but the gains it made couldn't be held for long.

Führer-Grenadier-Division

Having been pinned in place by heavy fighting in Vienna, the division withdrew just in the nick of time. As Russian spearheads reached the northern outskirts of Lobau, the decision to transfer the *Führer-Grenadier-Division* paid immediate dividends. Along with *Lützow* it slammed into the advancing Russians and drove them all the way back to Deutsch-Wagram in heavy fighting. Despite this success the Russians advanced everywhere else, capturing Markgrafneuseidl, part of Deutsch-Wagram, Strassdorf an der Nordbahn, Gänserdorf and Ollersdorf.

Gänserndorf fell with 38 Germans, two Hungarians and 50 Russians killed. The Russians did what they always did and shot eight people, while raping at will. Mannersdorf an der March had not fallen after the first Russian attack on 8 April after a mere 10 men held them off and then blew up the railroad bridge over the river. But on 10 April the Russians came back determined to take the town, which they did after a brief but costly attack. During the next two days the townspeople would be forced to dig graves for 10 Germans and 40 Russians killed in the battle.

The fight at Deutsch-Wagram was particularly brutal. The town was held by an SS unit, probably part of *SS-Kampfgruppe Ameiser*, and the Russians threw everything in their arsenal at wiping out the defenders. While the remaining townspeople cowered in their cellars, praying for deliverance, explosions ripped their little part of the world into glowing chunks of shattered wood and masonry. Heavy artillery, mortars, Katyushas, air attacks, tanks and infantry, the Russians launched an all-out assault. The fighting raged all day, through the night and into the day on 11 April.

Once the fighting died down and the dazed survivors could count their losses, 30 civilians had been killed and 16 more were dead by their own hand. Seventeen buildings had burned to their foundations and 339 houses suffered heavy damage.

Between Deutsch-Wagram and Leopoldsdorf the redeployment of the *Führer-Grenadier-Division* paid immediate dividends when its armored elements slammed head-on into the advancing Russian tanks, precipitating a major tank battle. For once the Germans were back in their element. The terrain was mostly flat, with scattered tree lines but otherwise excellent fields of fire. Even with obsolescent Mark IVs mixed in with the Panthers, *Hetzers* and probably *Sturmgeschütze*, the German fire took a terrible toll on the Russians. Thirteen tanks were knocked out and more than 200 men killed.

Despite their losses the Russian had taken part of the town, and once night fell they plundered their section of Deutsch-Wagram, while the remaining population paid the usual price.[4]

---

4   Brettner, *Die Letzten Kämpfe Band II*. pp. 157-158.

Vienna

Once the last of the Germans were safely north of the canal, von Bünau was relieved of his duties as Battle Commander for Vienna and ordered to *II SS-Panzerkorps* headquarters at the small town of Bisamberg for reassignment. His command had lasted just over a week, but he would not be out of the battle for long.

II SS-Panzerkorps

The air was acrid with smoke from burning buildings and bursting shells, the night alternately dark and impenetrable then lit by the flashes of explosions or the glow from mushrooming fires reflecting from the water of the Danube Canal. Throughout the night men and vehicles from *II SS-Panzerkorps* flowed northeast over the canal while the Russians did virtually nothing to stop them, after which all of the bridges across the canal were detonated and destroyed. Bittrich set up his command post on the northern bank of Danube, near the Reich's Bridge. General von Bünau and his staff were the last defenders to leave, crossing the Aspern Bridge at 3:00 a.m. on 10 April.[5] And so as dawn broke on that morning the heart of Vienna, from the Spanish Riding School to the Museum of Natural History, the glorious Rathaus to St Stephen's Cathedral, even the seat of imperial power, the Hofburg, every world-famous cultural and political landmark that defined the city's unique heritage, all were in Soviet hands.

SS-Kampfgruppe Trabandt II, or *Kampfgruppe Böhmen*, or *SS-Regiment Konopacki*

Under the overall command of *Generalmajor* Volkmann as *Kampfkommandant* for the Tulln region, *SS-Kampfgruppe Trabandt II* continued to arrive over a period of days. As previously mentioned, part of its *I. Abteilung* had been committed to battle in the Tulln bridgehead and was subsequently cut off from the rest of the regiment.

The commander of the regiment was *SS-Obersturmbannführer* Rudolf Konopacki. Konopacki was a combat veteran who had previously commanded a battalion in *4. SS-Panzergrenadier-Division Polizei*. After that he moved on to the *SS-Panzergrenadier Schule* based at Prosecnice-Keinschlag as commander of *Schulegruppe D*. The courses were taught at Netvorice and Neveklov, in the former Czechoslovakia. Beginning in February 1945 this school held a course for training of commanders in *14. Waffen-Grenadier-Division der SS Galizien*.

Similar in size to *SS-Kampfgruppe Trabandt I*, Konopacki's command didn't have the armored component that *SS-Kampfgruppe Trabandt II* did. However, the artillery battalion had 12 150mm cannon. These were used extensively to interdict Russian materiel and equipment buildups across the Danube. It also had eight mortars. Manpower totaled 67 officers, 449 NCOs and 2,144 enlisted men, giving it ration strength of 2,660. These numbers include Eckert's *I. Abteilung*.

The trains carrying the unit to battle unloaded north of Tulln. Once the immediate danger of the Russians crossing the Danube at Tulln had passed, the *SS-Kampfgruppe* took on local security duties until it had been fully assembled. For a hastily thrown-together unit with no cohesion, where the members were mostly young teenagers, it was a priceless time to learn battlefield survival without actually being shot at.

5   Von Bünau, *Combat in Vienna*, p. 22.

Kampfgruppe 6. Panzer-Division

In Leopoldstadt, on the southern end of the Danube Island, the Russians captured the two race-courses, the Trabrennbahn and the Galloppbrenbahn Freudenau, both without a fight. Downgraded to a *Kampfgruppe*, *6. Panzer-Division* wasn't strong enough to defend everywhere and the open spaces of the racing grounds gave no place for defenders to rally behind. The Trabrennbahn was used for harness racing while the Galloppbrenbahn had been opened in 1839 for horse racing, and hosted the annual Austrian Derby. The American bombing campaign had badly damaged them in the months leading up to their capture.

The front in the Prater stabilized at that point and the Russians were unable to break through despite strong attacks. An artillery duel took up much of the rest of the day, which resulted in terrible damage to the Franz Josef Kai, the canalside promenade on the Vienna side, near the inner city. Buildings there burned to the ground and crumbled into the street. Errant shells struck the inner city itself and the Russians set up artillery batteries in St Stephen's Platz.

Kampfgruppe 3. SS-Division Totenkopf

Totenkopf retreated to Leopoldstadt and Zwischenbrücken while *Kampfgruppe 6. Panzer-Division* continued holding in the Prater, where the Russians were already across the canal[6] and pushing back the Germans' left flank. The *Führer-Grenadier-Division* had been withdrawn to the north bank of the Danube to prevent the Russian Forty-Sixth Army from driving behind the three divisions still in Vienna and cutting them off.

For once, however, *Totenkopf* didn't face heavy combat on 10 April. The fight for the Arsenal area and the two railway stations left the division exhausted mentally, physically and logistically. It had been combat as fierce as the worst days in Stalingrad but the horrific casualties affected the Russians too, and as the Russian survivors gingerly closed on the Danube Canal both sides seemed eager to take a break from the fight. That didn't stop their artillery from pounding the SS men, though.

Across the Danube, on the north bank, fighting was also fierce as the Germans defended skillfully and bravely, but futilely. Slowly but surely the Russians slogged their way northwest to threaten the rear of the *II SS-Panzerkorps* units still in Vienna.

2. SS-Panzer-Division Das Reich

The Russian pursuit across the Danube Canal was sluggish, allowing the Germans time to set up a makeshift defensive line based on the waterway. *Das Reich* withdrew into the 20th District of Brittgenau to defend the line of the Danube Canal, with *SS-Panzergrenadier-Regiment Der Führer* on the right and *SS-Panzergrenadier-Regiment Deutschland* on the left. Each regiment kept two battalions up front and the third in reserve.

The battalions of both regiments were listed as 'weak', giving the impression they contained perhaps 300-400 men each, out of an authorized strength of about 1,000. With a constant influx of stragglers, convalescent wounded and incorporation of alarm units, the weak designation also implied a lack of cohesion and experience as veterans died or suffered grievous wounds in combat. One comparison can illustrate the fluctuating nature of the division's roster.

---

6   The Russians began crossing the day before using inflatable boats.

During the withdrawal over the canal the previous night, the commander of *I./Der Führer*, *SS-Hauptsturmführer* Helmut Engelmann, died when his SPW received a direct hit from a Russian tank. The loss of such young and energetic veterans hurt the division far more than simply the loss of one man. As previously mentioned his replacement was *SS-Obersturmbannführer* Hauser, a highly experienced leader but one unknown to his new command.

But also on 10 April, *SS-Sturmbannführer* Helmut Schrieber rejoined *Das Reich* along with the division's *SS-Feldersatz-Bataillon 2*, which would have been a welcome infusion of new men. After being severely wounded the previous year, Schrieber had healed enough to be deployed in the area of the Remagen bridgehead, but sending the newly arrived battalion to join the parent division in the trap of Vienna made no sense, so instead it was deployed in the Sankt Pölten area.

* * *

The division's armored strength for this day was recorded as "15 Panthers, 11 Mark IVs, four *Jagdpanzer* IVs, one *Jagdpanzer* V,[7] and eight *Flakpanzer* IVs".[8]

With dawn the Russians renewed their attacks with a vengeance; they were determined to force a crossing of the narrow canal from the west while continuing to pressure *6. Panzer-Division* from the south. The Germans were now concentrated in a much smaller perimeter behind a narrow but defensible water barrier, but that also meant the concentration of Russian firepower was greater.

After nearly being destroyed the day before, *Das Reich* eliminated the last remnants of the Russian penetration onto the northern tip of Danube Island. The front facing west lined the Danube Canal and the division command post was established near the Floridsdorfer Bridge. No one fooled themselves that the defensive line could hold for long, but Russian attacks supported by tanks were beaten off and for the time being the division's front stabilized.

Hitler Youth Battalion

As night fell the Hitler Youth Battalion was withdrawn across the Danube River and out of the immediate combat zone to Flandorf, near Bisamberg, both to give the boys a rest and to hold them as a reserve. Although young they had fought like demons for four days, and their stand the day before had prevented the Russians from crossing the canal at its northern lock. It was exactly these sorts of teenagers from which *12. SS-Panzer-Division Hitlerjugend* had been formed, which makes that division's impressive combat record more understandable. They had been indoctrinated for 12 years that Adolf Hitler embodied the German ideal, and that it was their duty to defend him and, if necessary, to die for him. This they did with the zeal of idealistic youths.

6. SS-Panzerarmee

Russian attacks continued throughout the night against units holding the front near the Vienna Woods. Marshal Tolbukhin's determination to break through took on the character of a battle of attrition, using his superior numbers and firepower to wear down the mangled SS divisions and

---

7   Also known as a *Jagdpanther*.
8   Reynolds, Maj. Gen. Michael, *The Battle for Vienna: When the Russians Crushed the Nazi Army* <http://nationalinterest.org/blog/the-buzz/the-battle-vienna-when-the-russians-crushed-the-nazi-army-21189?page=show>, (Accessed 23 April 2018).

exhaust them through round-the-clock combat. Sepp Dietrich was in no doubt that such tactics would work.

* * *

Four columns of French and Belgian prisoners left *Stalag 17B* on foot, headed for Auffangelager Weilhartforst, the same place the Americans were going, right outside of Braunau am Inn. Unlike the Americans, however, the French and Belgians were fed every other day with bread and a good soup, and every third day they were allowed to rest.[9]

Korps Schultz, or *Generalkommando Schultz*

If there had ever been any doubt about it, it was now erased: the Russians' immediate objective in attacking west from the Vienna Woods was Sankt Pölten, a town of more than 40,000 citizens 40 miles due west of Vienna and the capital of Lower Austria. In April 1945 its streets were clogged by refugees of all types, from low-level Nazis to peasants with all of their possessions piled high in wagons pulled by farm animals. The ancient city dated back to the 2nd Century AD, when the Romans built the settlement of Aelium Cetium on the Traisen River. Its Benedictine monastery dated to 771 AD. Using armored spearheads the Russians made deep strikes toward the city.

Along with the existing formations of *Korps Schultz*, reinforcements began to arrive in the region to bolster the scattered alarm units backed by *Aufklärung-Abteilung 1, Sturmgeschütz-Brigade 261, Schwere-Heeres-Panzerjäger-Abteilung 653, Aufklärung-Abeteilung 3* and the first men from *710. Infanterie-Division*. Predictably, since they hadn't had a chance to dig in yet, the front gave way quickly to the hardened Russian veterans of 5th Guards Tank Corps supported by 38th Guards Rifle Corps and 18th Tank Corps.

In the previous day's fighting the Germans had barely offered noticeable resistance. On 10 April the Germans threw them back in fluid combat at Grossgraben. Elsewhere, they were only stopped on a line from Ollersbach to Würmla by rushing forward more newly arrived elements from *710. Infanterie-Division* and yet another hurriedly formed alarm unit. Along with local successes against *Alarm-Bataillon C* on the right flank, the Russians made another assault against strongly defended Neulengbach. *Alarm-Bataillon A* fought hard and held the town, but the Russians were simply too strong, and it was foolhardy to think they could hold it another day. Therefore, after nightfall *Generalmajor* Schultz withdrew the surviving 200 men and three panzers from Neulengbach.

Under cover of the Haspelwald the Russians had a chance to regroup. They had been repulsed everywhere during the day's fighting, but nobody expected the defense to hold them for long.

SS-Kampfgruppe Trabandt III, or *SS-Regiment Siegmann,* or *SS-Kampfgruppe Mähren*

On its way to the battlefield was the third regimental-sized *Kampfgruppe* from *SS-Kampfgruppe-Division Böhmen und Mähren*. *SS-Kampfgruppe Trabandt III* had about the same artillery contingent as its two sister regiments, with eight venerable leFH 105mm howitzers and four captured Russian 122mm cannon (leFH stood for *leichte Feldhaubitze*, light field howitzer). Those guns had been built and used by Germany during the First World War. The Treaty of Versailles allowed the Germans to keep a limited number, with others given to countries such as Belgium. When

---

the Germans overran Belgium they recovered many of the guns and put them back into service. Gradually they were taken off the front lines and given to trainting units, only to be returned to combat by units like *SS-Kampfgruppe Trabandt III.*

The regiment only had 12 mortars, with 44 officers, 357 NCOs and 2,631 of lower ranks to total 3,032 men in all. Its commander, *SS-Hauptsturmführer* Erich Siegmann, had extensive front-line experience and had been an instructor of tactics in the SS school.

SS-Kampfgruppe Staudinger

The army's extreme left flank formation, *SS-Kampfgruppe Staudinger,* now subordinated to *Korps Schultz,* had no power to stop the Russians. Consisting of odds and ends and alarm units, the group was driven to the west of Moosbierbaum and Heiligeneich. Dietrich correctly diagnosed this Russian advance down the Danube Valley as the mortal danger that it was. To prevent *6. SS-Panzerarmee's* flank from being turned, it had to bend backwards to form a north-facing front. But to do so it required forces the army didn't have.

Kampfgruppe 12. SS-Panzer-Division Hitlerjugend

After the counterattack of the previous day, *Hitlerjugend* had seven Panzer Mark IVs and one *Jagdpanzer* IV/70 operational on 10 April. Trying to build on the success at Scwarzensee, a *Kampfgruppe* pushed north to recapture Groisbach as a preliminary to attacking Alland. The Russians knew the danger to their spearheads if the main highway leading west through Alland was cut and had no intention of letting that happen. Such disasters were the sort of thing that could get Russian commanders shot.

The German attack took Groisbach just after sunrise and kept moving toward Alland itself, but almost immediately ran into trouble. Three SPWs were hit and knocked out. In a perfect example of German battlefield salvage, however, all three were towed away for repair even though the prime movers were themselves under fire.

Fighting in the forests and mountains had a character that was drastically unlike the open tundra of Russia: claustrophic instead of expansive, with firing ranges often measured in tens of yards instead of thousands, where wood splinters were every bit as dangerous as those made of steel. Moreover, it was sometimes impossible to know where the enemy was.

> "The whole forest was humming with ricochets," said a *Hitlerjugend SS-Untersturmführer.* "In the meantime our machine gun had made it to the front and the Russians fled uphill. Suddenly we heard to our rear…forceful shouts of 'Urrah!' Obviously all the shooting had woken up another nest of Russians."[10]

In the face of bitter resistance the Germans called off their attack toward Alland and dug in near Groisbach. Throughout the day heavy Russian infantry attacks hit the new German positions, but all were repulsed. Ominously, however, the Germans heard loud engine noises coming from behind Russian lines, which indicated a tank attack would soon be rumbling down the road.

On the division's far right flank, *SS-Kampfgruppe Gross* held firm against several attacks, but the position of the division's *Flak* batteries was endangered by the breakthrough near Fahrafeld, in

---

10   Reynolds, *Men of Steel,* p. 264.

the area of the *LAH*. All of the light and most of the heavy *Flak* batteries were transferred to the Laaben area, although one platoon was left behind as a rearguard.[11]

Kampfgruppe 1. SS-Panzer-Division Leibstandarte Adolf Hitler

The division fielded 13 operational Panzer Mark IVs, five Panthers and four *Sturmgeschützen*, with about 46 others in short and long-term repair. If the *Sturmgeschütze* are included in the total this represented operational strength of roughly fifteen percent for the panzer regiment. Counting those tanks in the workshops, however, put the panzer regiment close to 50 percent of authorized strength.

With so few armored vehicles left to service and maintain, hundreds of men were freed up for ground combat. Division commander *SS-Brigadeführer* Otto Kumm recognized this and ordered them organized into infantry companies. The same process happened in all of the panzer divisions as the Germans desperately tried to find men for the front. The rear echelon ranks were combed and combed again to find riflemen.

* * *

After a relatively quiet day on 9 April, all hell broke loose again on 10 April. From Neuseidl to Haidlhof strong infantry attacks hit the Germans, backed by tanks and heavy artillery fire. Penetrations came in a number of places but all were blocked for the moment, with the most dangerous being north of Pottenstein. There, the few remaining panzers supported the division's panzer grenadiers and stopped the Russians just east of Fahrafeld.[12] Another Russian battle group penetrated to the south of that town and forced the movement of the *Hitlerjugend Flak* batteries.

At Schrattenbach, about a mile south of Grünwald am Schneeberg,[13] the German defenders were surrounded and the Russians pushed on to Grünwald itself. The veterans among them had no doubt been surrounded before and didn't panic, but any *Luftwaffe*, *Kriegsmarine* or new conscripts must have been desperate to escape the trap. One can imagine the veteran NCOs giving them a reassuring look and telling them everything would work out fine, just as NCOs have done in every army throughout history, all the while knowing they were in serious trouble.

On the western side of the Schneeberg other assault forces pushed back a weak screening force southeast of Puchberg am Schneeberg. Combined with the loss of the Hohe Wand the day before, these were serious blows to the defense.

Kampfgruppe 356. Infantry-Division

The nature of the fighting on *6. SS-Panzerarmee*'s center and right flank, and along the front of neighboring *6. Armee*, was the same. The foothills of the Alps rose in sometimes sheer, sometimes wooded slopes, bisected by valleys where the villages and homesteads lay, along with the all-important roads. Russian armor made it costly and difficult for the Germans to hold onto these low-lying strongpoints, but that advantage didn't translate to the mountains. To drive the Germans off the high ground the attackers used their superiority in artillery and Katyusha rockets to blast their positions and then send in infantry assaults, usually in company or battalion strength. But that

---

11 Meyer, *The 12th SS*, pp. 472-473.
12 Tiemann, *The Liebstandarte IV/2*, p. 291.
13 Not to be confused with another Grünwald near the Czech border, in *8. Armee*'s zone.

firepower advantage only went so far. Under a dense canopy of oak, beech and fir trees the proper coordination of artillery support was difficult, since the spotters rarely saw their targets. For the defenders, however, the explosion of artillery rounds in the branches overhead filled the air with deadly splinters.

Capturing the high ground, therefore, meant scores of intense, short-range firefights between small squads of men battling in close quarters, sometimes hand-to-hand. Often the opponents heard each other long before they came into sight. It was here that the ubiquitous Russian PPSh-41 sub-machine gun showed its true worth, where a high volume of fire counted for much more than long-range accuracy. The same was true of the German MG-42 machine gun. Its high rate of fire and ease of barrel replacement made it the bane of Russians struggling up slopes deep in rotted leaves and pine needles, often in wet or snowy conditions. For troops of both sides life in the mountains that spring was miserable, even without people shooting at you.

* * *

The loss of the Hohe Wand the previous day threatened to unhinge *6. SS-Panzerarmee*'s right wing so counterattacks were launched to retake it. Fighting on the wooded slope was close and vicious but the Russians managed to hang on. Back-and-forth fighting raged in the whole area. Four Russian tanks were knocked out near Pottenstein and Neuseidl, while other German forces around Berndorf were driven back. Schwarzensee had been lost on 9 April but was recaptured on 10 April, with the destruction of five more Russian tanks. But other attacks succeeded. Dreistetten fell and Oberpiesting after it.

SS-Kampfgruppe Keitel

Large-scale Russian attacks pushed south of Puchberg am Schneeberg, but were finally stopped south-west of that town. With each passing day the defenders were stretched further and further. This penetration was particularly dangerous, however, because it came at the seam between *6. SS-Panzerarmee* and Hermann Balck's *6. Armee*. This was hard on the flank of *Kampfgruppe Semmering*. With each advance the German flanks lengthened even as the men to guard them dwindled.

6. Armee

Fremde Herre Ost, Foreign Armies East, the German intelligence service run by *Generalmajor* Reinhard Gehlen, issued a dire and immediate warning for *6. Armee*, predicting that 5th Guards Cavalry Corps could be expected to attack on the army's left wing. This was a new threat in the already shattered section of the front. According to Maier, reconnaissance indicated at least 700 mounted cavalry in the area south and west of Neunkirchen, along with some armor.[14] Riders on horseback could move faster and farther than infantry, but weren't as hampered in the mountains as tanks and assault guns.

In fact the corps had the 11th, 12th and 63rd Cavalry Divisions, the 57th, 60th, 71st and 150th Guards Tank Regiments, and the 1896th Assault Gun Regiment. The warning from Foreign Armies East was too late. Or, rather, Hermann Balck had no options to act on it. The Russians had already ripped his front to shreds and were about to pour more men into the hole, and there was nothing he could do about it.

---

14   Maier, *Drama*, p. 357.

Kampfgruppe Semmering

Reinforcements arrived in the guise of the *Luftwaffe* crews from *Kampfgeschwader 27*, which had been disbanded on 4 April. Many of the men, not just the *Luftwaffe* crews but all of the alarm units, had been armed with whatever weapons were available, from long French rifles to small Italian carbines with hinged sights that were only accurate within three feet at one hundred yards. Ammunition for these surplus guns was also an issue.

For this reason possession of the battlefield after the shooting stopped was far more important for the Germans than for the Russians. As short as they were on everything needed to fight, the Germans looted Russian bodies for everything they could find, from food and cigarettes to the prized Russian PPSh-41 sub-machine gun, with its 35- or 71-round magazines.

North of Breitenstein fighting continued around Kreuzberg, a small village, where Russian snipers and mortar fire took a heavy toll on the defenders. The terrain was typical of eastern Austria: steep mountains of 1,500 feet or more, sloped meadows surrounded by dense forests of oak, beech, fir, larch and pine, and sudden jagged fields of granite and limestone. Deep ravines and sheer cliffs made moving large numbers of men and supplies difficult at best.

Sometimes the fighting not just around the Semmering Pass but throughout eastern Austria came down to firefights for possession of a large boulder, or a single stand of trees. Against the dramatic background of green peaks standing in spring sunshine was the dirty, personal war fought below the forest canopy.

This was the environment the *Luftwaffe* men found themselves in, fighting off Russian attacks. Their machine guns broke up multiple charges but Russian mortar fire continued to rain on their positions. All told they suffered eight men killed and many more wounded.

1. Volks-Gebirgs-Division

To the division's north was the yawning gap south of *Kampfgruppe Semmering*, but the division's situation was no better to the south. Russian penetrations into the Raab Valley, where there had already been fighting near Feldbach, south of Fürstenfeld, meant that it had to bend its right flank backward, as well as its left flank. This put it in the position of a great arc echeloned far to the east. Because of the thin nature of its main line of resistance the division received orders to straighten its line by withdrawing west. With most of its forward units engaged, the repositioning had to be done as a fighting retreat.

Kampfgruppe 1. Panzer-Division

Although it was only one division, *Kampfgruppe 1. Panzer-Division* began its counterattack northward into the flank of the Twenty-Sixth Army attack. *Panzergrenadier-Regiment 113* made some gains, but this movement had no real effect on the Russian advance. Needing to redeploy and strengthen the attack, the division was withdrawn again and *SS-Polizei-Regiment 13*, of *Sperrverband Motschmann*, again took over securing the area.

Kampfgruppe 3. Panzer-Division

Several days before the Armored Bears had reoccupied Heiligenkreuz without opposition, and advanced part of the division beyond the Reich border. They formed a blocking position to prevent a sudden thrust into Burgenland, and the locals made certain the *Landser* knew how grateful they were for the protection. Unlike most of *Heeresgruppe Süd*, who had short or no rations for days on end, the men of *3. Panzer-Division* were showered with fresh food and more than 30,000 cigarettes. On top of the local largesse, they emptied two abandoned supply trains at Güssing which were stuffed full with chocolate, canned meat and delicacies the men hadn't seen for years. For the first time in memory they slept on full stomachs and gained weight.

Having been outflanked to the north *3. Panzer-Division* had been alerted on 9 April to be ready to move, but that alert was soon cancelled and it was ordered to stay in place. This suited the men and townsfolk just fine.

But the days of wine and roses ended on the morning of 10 April when a heavy Russian artillery barrage slammed into their positions. The veteran *Panzergrenadiers* then heard the sounds they dreaded most: the deep rumble of tank engines followed by the war cry of Russian infantry in the attack. Heavy attacks in regimental strength struck all along the line, including at Heiligenkreuz itself. The overmatched German infantry fought hard, but eventually ran low on ammunition and, without heavy weapons to combat the enemy armor, couldn't hold. Heiligenkreuz fell again and the badly battered *Panzergrenadier-Regiment 394* retreated to Poppendorf.

One of its battalions attempted a counterattack along a narrow mountain road to join up with its parent regiment, but turned back when Russian artillery raked the small column of SPWs. Burning vehicles blocked the road. Eventually it found a roundabout way of getting to Poppendorf, but that only put it in the same danger as the rest of the division. The Russians weren't merely pinning the Germans in place, or bleeding them; the attacks were an attempt to destroy them and break through. Making matters critical, the Russian forces were far stronger than the Germans.

Despite mounting Russian pressure the division avoided encirclement, but attacks kept coming even after dark. The townsfolk knew their protectors couldn't hold out much longer and were torn between wanting the fighting to end and dreading the coming of the Russians.[15]

14. Waffen-Grenadier-Division-der-SS Galizien

The Russian attack on *Galizien* entered its fourth day with neither side backing down from increasing the violence. A key position was Sulz bei Gleisdorf, a prominent hill which dominated the area. Orders were to hold it at all costs, even down to the last man, but under very heavy pressure an *SS-Obersturmführer* disobeyed those orders and withdrew his company.

That unhinged the whole German position and left two companies cut off, also in the vicinity of Sulz. They numbered around 200 men and, to illustrate how strong *Galizien* was compared to other German divisions, one platoon had four NCOs and 40 men. In other words, it was close to full strength. Out of desperation the trapped SS men retreated to the hill, which the Russians hadn't yet occupied, and held it against heavy attacks. It was only when Russian heavy artillery and Katyusha explosions raked the hill that they had to abandon it. It took several days but the survivors made it back to German lines.

Against all preconceived notions of their combat value, the Ukrainians fought stubbornly to hold the line, but in the end all they could do was exact a heavy price for each Russian advance. Trautmanndorf fell once again, despite determined resistance.[16] The disorganized units were driven back to Straden, while *3. Kavallerie-Division* and *4. Kavallerie-Division* tried to organize

---

15   Veterans, *Armored Bears*, p. 285.
16   Melnyk, *To Battle*, p. 252.

a new main line of resistance to shield them while they regrouped. But despite the overwhelming strength of the Russian attack, the Germans held onto the Stradner Kogel for one more day.

9. SS-Panzer-Division Hohenstaufen

Like all of the other SS Panzer divisions *Hohenstauffen* had virtually no armor left. The battered division reported AFV strength of eight Panzer IVs, with only one operational; 15 Panthers, with an unknown number combat ready; seven *Jagdpanzer 38(t) Hetzers*, all under repair; one operational machine of the rarely seen *Jagdpanther* type; and one *Flakpanzer*. It also had seven heavy anti-tank guns, probably 88mm.[17]

2. Panzerarmee

After a quiet night the Russians attacked again with daylight. It was becoming clearer with each day that the Russians would continue attacking the army's right wing to drive a wedge between *Heeresgruppe Süd* and *Heeresgruppe E*.

Starting before dawn heavy artillery and mortar barrages rained down across the army's front, hitting the front lines of *23. Panzer-Division* hard. Then came waves of infantry attacking *Panzergrenadier-Regiment 128*, with both sides absorbing and inflicting heavy casualties in a brutal example of attritional warfare. By noon one company was down to six men still able to fight. The division combed out every man who could carry a rifle and sent them to hold the line, stripping the support companies of any but the most essential personnel.

On the division's left flank *Aufklärungs-Abteilung* of *44. Infanterie-Division Hoch und Deutschmeister* gave way under the heavy attacks, endangering the entire position. The *23. Panzer-Division* counterattacked with all of the troops it could find but to no avail. The division's whole left flank had to bend westward to keep from being enveloped and casualties were extremely heavy. Things were so bad that one of the surgeons picked up a rifle and climbed into a rifle pit along with his medical staff. When the *Feld-Ausbildungs-Bataillon* of *79. Infanterie-Division* showed up as reinforcements late in the afternoon another counterattack was launched, and also failed. But somehow the front line held.

After dark the regiment was finally relieved by elements of *4. Kavallerie-Division* and retired behind the lines to regroup. With no replacements in sight the shrunken companies were consolidated.[18]

17   Nevenkin, *Fire Brigades*, p. 874.
18   Rebentisch, *To the Caucasus*, p. 466.

11

Wednesday, 11 April

Heeresgruppe Süd

The day dawned sunny and warm over eastern Austria, with temperatures near 70 degrees Fahrenheit and not a cloud in the sky. In the years of German conquest this was called *Hitler wetter*, Hitler weather, which ended with the early onset of the Russian season of mud, the 'rasputitsa', in 1941. Now, with the Red Air Force swarming over the battlefield like a nest of angry wasps, it was understandable if the average German rifleman in the front lines cursed the bright spring sunshine. A massive bombing raid hit Korneuberg, since it was the vital artery connecting *II SS-Panzerkorps* and *XXXXIII Armeekorps* to their lines of supply.

What the German troops didn't see was *Luftflotte 4* flying as many sorties as men, machines and gasoline supplies would allow, hitting troop concentrations and tank assemblies in the areas of *6. Armee* and *2. Panzerarmee*. Using the few *Luftwaffe* resources still flying on the central and southern sectors of the front shows how truly critical the situation had become there. With Vienna almost entirely captured, and intense Russian pressure on *8. Armee* in a bid to encircle *II SS-Panzerkorps*, the Germans chose to commit their limited air support elsewhere.

* * *

The army group's supply situation grew worse by the day. Ammunition was running out and gasoline stores were critically low. According to Maier the last supply train had arrived on 5 April.[1] This was a combination of using the limited train transports still available to move units from place to place, and the quantity of supplies being choked off as the Reich was overrun. The *6. SS-Panzerarmee* began to suffer even more as Russian air strikes concentrated on its supply lines.

* * *

Throughout the day fighting remained vicious in places across the army group's entire front, but not in every spot. The initial Russian thrust into Austria had lost momentum and both Marshals Tolbukhin and Malinovsky needed to regroup and reorganize, shifting forces to points of emphasis.

Both armies had turned northwest days earlier, but now had reached the point where the terrain more or less forced a sharper turn in that direction. South of the Danube this was due to the eastern mountains. North of the river it was caused by the river itself. In Vienna, the water's course ran from southeast to northwest. Malinovsky's Forty-Sixth Army, in particular, had no choice except to bend northwest or wind up in the river.

---

1   Maier, *Drama,* p. 358.

8. Armee

General der Gebirgstruppe Kreysing received the ominous intelligence that the Russian Sixth Guards Tank Army was amassing bridge-building and river-crossing supplies southwest of Tulln. The only possible conclusion was that Marshal Tolbukhin intended to cross the Danube into *8. Armee*'s rear, as they were about to do that very day in Vienna. Aside from small local units the only forces in position to oppose such a crossing were the elements of *SS-Kampfgruppe-Division Böhmen und Mähren* which had already arrived. But the severe transport difficulties meant even that unit, which had been formed near Prague, had only partly arrived in the area.

* * *

That was only the beginning of Kreysing's headaches. Second Ukrainian Front was ready to launch its attacks to the west, northwest and north, where it had amassed at least 20 divisions and two tank corps against five weakened German formations. The Pliyev Army in particular was designed as a fast-moving exploitation force. Along with the Fifty-Third Army the Russians attacked in the region of Břeclav on the Thaya River, with their eventual target being Brno.

Kampfgruppe 211. Infanterie-Division

Attacking out of the Morava bridgehead near Dürnkrut and Jedespeigen, the elite 6th Guards Air Landing Division and 72nd Guards Rifle Division struck the badly depleted *Kampfgruppe 211. Infanterie-Division*, penetrated it at multiple points, and drove the survivors backward. The attack was stopped by desperate counterattacks only a few miles south of the oil fields at Zistersdorf.

A similar thrust northeast of Zistersdorf captured Hohenau an der March, as the northern part of a pincers attack on the oil fields by the 141st Rifle Division. An immediate counterattack threw them out again. Further south along the river, Dürnkrut finally fell after four days of bitter fighting where neither side was willing to retreat. The butcher's bill totaled 26 German *Landser* and 12 civilians killed and fully one third of the town destroyed. The fate of the wounded is officially unknown. Before leaving, the German Pioneers destroyed the bridge over the Morava.

After a fight that began on 8 April, the loss of Dürnkrut made holding Jedenspeigen, two miles north along the river, impossible. Once again the toll was terrible, with 39 Germans and 20 Russians killed. Four civilians were shot once the Russians took over, along with two captured Germans who had been in the church bell tower.[2]

SS-Kampfgruppe Ameiser

Just to the northeast of Vienna in Markgrafneuseidl, *SS-Kampfgruppe Ameiser* was released from its attachment to *Kampfgruppe 96. Infanterie-Division* and returned to the command of its parent headquarters, the *37. SS-Freiwilligen-Kavallerie-Division Lützow*. Although still missing its other major combat component, *SS-Kampfgruppe Keitel*, for the first time *Lützow* was functioning together as something of a cohesive whole. For the next seven days this unit would conduct a desperate defense due north of Vienna, in the area of Kreuttal-Hautzendorf. The defense perimeter was slowly being bent backwards to the Danube, leaving an escape corridor for the defenders of Vienna that grew narrower by the day.

---

2 Brettner, *Die Letzten Kämpfe Band II*, p. 161.

SS-Kampfgruppe-Division Böhmen und Mähren

Meanwhile, the components of *SS-Kampfgruppe-Division Böhmen und Mähren* were getting into battle at various spots. The quality of this thrown-together unit was much higher than most other alarm units, because it drew men from the various SS schools scattered through old Czechoslovakia and Austria. Many were officer candidates and tended to be the fittest, smartest and most dedicated of their age group. Percentages are impossible now, but while most were raw recruits, some of the men were veterans. Regardless, young, eager men who were decently armed meant this division rated among the better German units available at the time.

Along with some support elements, the division featured three regiments with the standard SS allotment of three battalions each. *SS-Kampfgruppe Trabandt I*, aka *SS-Regiment Schulze*, had been deployed to the south-southwest of Zistersdorf, screening one of the very last oil fields still in German hands. Hitler had ordered the area held and the SS men did what they could. Fighting in the small villages of Blumenthal, Loidestaal and Gotzendorf, and the surrounding areas, inflicted very high casualties on the *Kampfgruppe*, but it managed to hold the Russians back for almost a week.[3]

SS-Kampfgruppe Trabandt II, another regimental-sized unit commanded by *SS-Obersturmbannführer* Rudolf Konopacki and sometimes referred to as *SS-Regiment Konopacki*, was sent to the area just north of Tulln. Soon enough two of its battalions were performing security duty in and around the town, digging in against the Red Army's 5th Guards Tank Corps poised on the southern bank. The trains carrying its artillery and support elements hadn't arrived yet. The *III./ SS-Kampfgruppe Trabandt II*, not to be confused with *I. Bataillon*, which wound up fighting with *Korps Schultz* south of the river, however, was caught up in the fighting as German units withdrew from Sankt Pölten to the north, eventually making its escape over the Danube bridge still standing at Krems.

All three battalion commanders for *SS-Kampfgruppe Trabandt II* were disabled veterans with extensive combat experience that was invaluable during the chaotic situation of the war's final month, with the *III. Abteilung* commander, *SS-Hauptsturmführer* Herbert Effenberger, having been awarded the German Cross in Gold. Effenberger used a cane and could only move around with difficulty. Despite their injuries, the battalion commanders had all been tactical instructors for a three-month reserve officers' training course, and were pressed into duty in the emergency situation facing the Reich.

* * *

In the early afternoon and with a dense fog hanging on the river, the Russians did what General Kreysing had feared they would do, namely use the Danube flotilla to land behind the defenders on the north bank of the Danube, less than half a mile southeast of the Reich Bridge at Kaisermühlendamm. Although not a large force, this threatened to disrupt the entire defensive position in the Marchfeld area, as its mission was to seize the German bank of the bridge. Throwing in everything available and under cover of a withering barrage from their *Flak* guns the Germans sealed off the landing, but this drew away men who were desperately needed elsewhere.

Meanwhile, the Russian drive to the northwest begin to pick up steam as regimental-sized forces backed by tank battalions smashed through Pysdorf and kept going to take Aderklaa. Second Ukrainian Front's mission to capture Brno became more and more obvious.

---

3   R.P., *Combat Formations of SS-Kampfgruppe Division Böhmen-Mähren: Action in the Austrian Wine Country, April-May, 1945,* (Brookings: Siegrunen 69, Summer 2000), p. 6.

Vienna

II SS-Panzerkorps

Rumors in Vienna were as numerous as the number of Viennese. One that took hold on 11 April was that the SS planned a counterattack over the Augarten Bridge and, like so many other rumors, it began with a kernel of truth. Looking back it's easy now to say this was ludicrous, but it had a basis in fact and shows how such things can grow in the absence of official news.

On 8 April Weidinger writes of a Hitler Youth leader who pressed him to allow his battalion of boys to withdraw from their northern sector of the fighting and counterattack over the Augarten Bridge. At that moment the bridge hadn't yet been blown so this was theoretically possible, but *Das Reich*'s commander quickly quashed the idea.[4] Nevertheless, this was undeniably the origin of this particular rumor.

By 11 April, except for the Floridsdorfer and the Reichsbrücke, the rest of the bridges over the canal lay in the water, although the Augarten Bridge had only been damaged by the demolition charges. Moreover, the SS men had no intention of doing anything except getting out of the city.

Yet rumor still made the rounds. In the hysteria of the moment people believed a counterattack was coming, and that included the Russians. They withdrew all of their guns and troops along the canal in anticipation of the attack, which left a vacuum of authority in the inner city. Looters saw their chance and broke into shops on the Kartnerstrasse and other streets near St Stephen's Platz. And then the fires broke out.

No one knows how they started, but soon fires raged among the city's most cherished landmarks, including St Stephen's Cathedral. As discussed earlier a myth persists that the Allies bombed the inner city on 12 April and the bombs destroyed St Stephen's, but that can be dismissed on the face of it. Even if American unit records didn't prove that the last bombing attack occurred on 30 March, the inner city was under Russian control by then and the Americans would have been bombing their own ally. What really happened is more prosaic. Either the looters set fire to neighborhood shops after they'd stripped them bare, and drifting sparks ignited the cathedral's roof, or the sparks drifted from fires elsewhere in the city.

Regardless of the cause, with no fire companies functioning after von Schirach ordered them all out of the city, and sporadic street fighting still in the area, the flames were soon out of control and began to spread to nearby buildings. Soon enough massive columns of smoke barreled skyward as St Stephen's burned out of control. Massive in scale, the inferno quickly burned through the wooden roof structure, causing it to collapse, which destroyed a large portion of the upper sacristy, the southern Heidenturm,[5] the western windows and the groin vault of the choir. St Stephen's also housed the largest church bell in Austria, the famed 1100 pound *Pummerin*; only the clapper survived.[6] A Walcker organ built in 1886 was a total loss. The pulpit, the tomb of German Emperor Frederick III and various other irreplaceable art masterpieces were saved by protective brick shells that had been erected for that purpose, but the cathedral was gutted.

* * *

Although most combat had come to a halt at sunset the day before, in some places house-to-house fighting continued throughout the night of 10-11 April. It was a nightmare of dark streets and darker shadows cast by flickering flames, muzzle flashes and explosions. Distinguishing friend

---

4   Weidinger, *Das Reich*, p. 377.
5   The Roman Tower, or spire, of the cathedral.
6   Eventually the shards were used in reforging the bell.

from foe in a half-second of glaring light was an instant life-or-death decision of whether to shoot or not. Fatigue slowed reflexes, and as the German numbers thinned the defense turned into small packets of men defending a back alley, or perhaps a solitary panzer firing down a side street.

6. Panzer-Division

Once it became apparent the Germans had no intention of counter-attacking, Fourth Guards Army renewed its assault on the Danube Canal line, and the ferocity of the attacks left no doubt the Russians still intended to destroy *II SS-Panzerkorps* once and for all. The elite Russian 7th Air Landing Division attacked from the area around the Stadlauer Ostbahn Bridge to the northwest, with the obvious intention of yet cutting off *II SS-Panzerkorps*.

* * *

This was the day the Russians put everything they had into the attack. At its widest point Danube Island only measured 689 feet, meaning the concentration of firepower made the fighting particularly brutal. Combat continued in the Prater among the restaurants and arcades. It's likely soldiers of both sides used the Riesenrad for cover, while shells crisscrossed the sky overhead, the Germans shooting from the north bank at Russian batteries to the south that shelled both Danube Island and the north bank.

* * *

Within Vienna the German grasp slipped further as *Das Reich* and *Totenkopf* were squeezed into an ever smaller perimeter with their backs to the Danube. As the Russians fought their way into Brittgenau, at some point they captured the boarding house where Hitler had spent most of the years between 1909 and 1913, the Mannerheim at 27 Meldemannstrasse. The house had been subsidized by the Austrian government for men who were destitute, with other contributions coming from such wealthy families as the Rothschilds and the Gutmanns.[7] Housing up to 544 men, with its own house doctor, the Mannerheim was quite a nice home for men who were down and out, all things considered. It was Spartan but dry and affordable. It is said that Hitler lived there so long he was thought of as one of the old-timers and was allowed to paint in the Reading Room, which allowed him to work indoors even when the weather was bad, a real comfort. Women were not allowed at any time, however, even for a visit.[8] Presumably this did not bother him.

It is likely that Russian infantry ransacked the very room where the *Führer* slept. As reports of the Red Army's progress through Vienna were made known to him during the military briefings, Hitler must surely have been aware that his former home had been lost and it is not unreasonable to assume the depressing effect this must have had on him.

By the end of day the Germans reported another 25 Russians tanks destroyed, along with at least four gunboats from the Danube flotilla.

Kampfgruppe 3. SS-Panzer-Division Totenkopf

The division reported a total strength of 8,393 men of all ranks. Numbers aren't available but if more than 2,000 of those were rifle strength it would be surprising, although by now the idea

---

7   What effect the subsidy of his lifestyle by a Jewish family may have had on the young anti-semite is hard to know.
8   Frank, Walter Smoter, *The Artist*, http://smoter.com/theartis.htm, (Accessed 4 December 2018).

of non-combat elements was becoming obsolete. If the 1 April estimate that *Totenkopf* was at 25 percent strength is true, this would have given a total of around 5,000 men. Following that line of logic, in 10 days of bitter close-quarters combat *Totenkopf*'s strength nearly doubled.

The discrepancy could be due to reunification of scattered elements, addition of replacements and inconsistencies in reporting. What's more likely is that the 1 April number is combat strength. It's probably enough to say the division was exhausted, depleted and lacking in almost everything necessary to keep fighting.

Staging near the Franz Joseph Railway Station, under cover of a smoke screen a Russian attack crossed the Danube Canal in the area of the Augarten Bridge but was driven back by an immediate counterattack. The bridge had collapsed into the canal in a V shape so it was still possible for infantry to scramble across, supported by machine guns and heavy weapons from the south bank.

2. SS-Panzer-Division Das Reich

Ernst Barkmann was again in action on 11 April, this time defending the Danube Canal crossing at the Friedenbrücke with three Panthers and a few *Panzergrenadiers*. Five times the Russians attacked in company strength and five times they were repulsed with heavy losses.

6. SS-Panzerarmee

As the Red Army pushed west past Vienna toward St Polten, the German forces in its path were pushed out of the way to the north, leaving very few defenders to stop the invaders from moving into western Austria. Dietrich's defense plan was smoke and mirrors, throwing whoever and whatever he could into the line to try and slow the invaders down. But unknown to him the Russians had problems of their own.

On a map the way west looked open, but the Russian attack was running out of steam due to supply issues and high losses among the assault units. Everybody involved knew Germany had lost the war and nobody on either side wanted to die in the last days. Only Stalin and Hitler still pushed their forces to fight hard, but since they were the only ones who mattered the killing went on.

* * *

As 11 April wore on it became increasingly obvious that not only was all of Vienna lost, but unless fast action were taken *8. Armee* might also be destroyed. Certainly *II SS-Panzerkorps* faced imminent destruction. Accordingly, Dietrich ordered *6. SS-Panzerarmee* to plan the total withdrawal of Bittrich's corps to the north bank of the Danube, and thence to react to the movements of *8. Armee* so as not to lose contact.

Korps Schultz

If anything illustrated *6. SS-Panzerarmee*'s desperate situation, it was the transfer of *Kampfgruppe 3. Panzer-Division*'s armored reconnaissance battalion away from *6. Armee* and its attachment to *Korps Schultz* on 11 April. The *6. Armee* faced its own dire straits, with both flanks threatened and a weak junction with *2. Panzerarmee* to the south. It had very few armored vehicles and needed every last warm body it could find to man the front lines, so losing an entire reconnaissance battalion represented a major loss. But *6. SS-Panzerarmee* needed them ever more, and so they wound up in the Sankt Pölten area. More reinforcements joined the corps when seven additional trains bearing the *710. Infanterie-Division* arrived, in addition to two Hungarian artillery battalions. Moreover, the various batteries scattered around the region were mostly still operational.

The same reconnaissance that warned *8. Armee* that the Russians were preparing to cross the Danube around Tulln, also reported that the 17th Tank Corps appeared ready to move further west, although whether it would continue to support operations against Sankt Pölten wasn't clear. Platoon and company-sized probes warned of a coming storm. Then the storm broke.

One prominent feature in the area of battle was the Haspelwald, a five-mile-long and two-mile-wide forest near Böheimkirchen, Neulengbach, Kirchstetten, Asperhofen and Würmla. The Russians had captured it a few days before. As their spearheads drove south of the woods and then turned west and northwest, it put the German defenders to the north of it in mortal danger of being outflanked. Those happened to be the first two battalions of *710. Infanterie-Division* to arrive, and when the 18th Tank Corps slammed into them in a frontal assault they had no choice except to retreat or be overrun. In turn, this put the newly arrived *Panzer-Aufklärungs-Abteilung 1* in the dangerous position of losing contact with its right-hand neighbor and possibly being surrounded. Already at half strength, it couldn't stand and fight for long.

German late-war reconnaissance battalions such as the one from *1. Panzer-Division* had a nominal manpower strength of around 1,000. Vehicles included armored cars, SPWs both to transport men and mounting a variety of weapons, *Kübelwagen*, the ubiquitous Volkswagen-manufactured all-purpose vehicle that served as the *Wehrmacht*'s version of a Jeep, motorcycles and perhaps a detachment of *Kettenkräder*, the small tracked all-terrain vehicle. Such a battalion was designed to be fast and flexible, without much firepower to stand and fight pitched battles, but perfect for their role of scouting ahead of fast-moving panzer divisions. So the mission they'd been given by *Korps Schultz* was to do the one thing for which they were ill-suited: stand and fight.

I SS-Panzerkorps

The ferocity of combat across the central and southern sectors of the front showed no signs of slackening, but there wasn't fighting everywhere. Refugees clogged the roads behind the fighting forces and camped in the meadows; not just Austrians, but Hungarians and ethnic Germans from all over the Balkans. Preying on them were deserters and foreign slave workers freed from captivity with no means to survive. Eastern Austria was a hell of death and misery.

Korps Schultz

Somehow, Schultz's corps had cobbled together enough of a defense to stop the initial Russian attempts to capture Sankt Pölten. The fighting front in Vienna had contracted enough to release assault groups for use elsewhere. Having been unable to capture the city on the fly, the Russians paused on 11 April to regroup and began transferring more powerful forces for a drive down the Danube Valley.

In light of this building threat to its left flank, *I SS-Panzerkorps* ordered all three divisions under its command to comb out their artillery, armor and anti-tank battalions for excess personnel to form new alarm battalions. This had been done several times before but battle losses freed up small numbers of men for emergency use. By and large the attack on the German left flank, north of the Haspelwald, had pushed the defenders back with the loss of both Würmla and Murstetten to 38th Guards Rifle Corps. On their right flank, however, the Russians had bogged down in heavy fighting.

SS-Kampfgruppe Peiper

With the desperate need for more units but none available, the *LAH* recreated one of the most infamous *Kampfgruppen* ever formed, *SS-Kampfgruppe Peiper*. During the Ardennes Offensive, known in the west as the Battle of the Bulge, Peiper's *Kampfgruppe* had been the spearhead of the attack. At that time Peiper commanded about 100 Mark IVs and Panthers, along with the Tiger IIs of *SS-Schwere-Panzer-Abteilung 501*.[9] While racing for the bridges over the Meuse River, his objective, men under his command committed a series of massacres, the most infamous of which occurred at Malmedy when troops under his command murdered 84 members of the US 285th Field Artillery Observation Battalion on 17 December 1944. But they didn't kill everybody, and when the survivors spread the word of this atrocity it stiffened American resolve to keep fighting after a series of initial setbacks. Earlier that day several dozen US soldiers guarding a fuel dump were also gunned down. Whether or not Peiper ordered the prisoners to be shot remains a point of debate even today.

Regardless of his involvement, Peiper was a talented and experienced commander who had the respect of his men. On 11 April he was ordered to form *SS-Kampfgruppe Peiper* again. His new *Kampfgruppe* contained *SS-Panzer-Regiment 1*, elements of the artillery regiment from *12. SS-Panzer-Division Hitlerjugend*, *SS-Schwere-Panzer-Abteilung 501* and assorted alarm and *Volkssturm* units.[10]

The *Kampfgruppe* was sent to the corps' vulnerable left flank around the valley of the Traisen River, south of Sankt Pölten. Peiper spread his troops into a number of blocking positions. At Rotheau were a few surviving Panzer Mark IVs from *SS-Schwere-Panzer-Abteilung 501,* along with a handful of Tiger IIs, and men from *SS-Panzer-Regiment 1* fighting as infantry. These were under the command of *SS-Sturmbannführer* Heinz Kling, who up until then had been commanding officer of *SS-Schwere-Panzer-Abteilung 501*. *SS-Kampfgruppe Kling* was subordinated to *SS-Kampfgruppe Peiper*.

Peiper himself commanded a second blocking force in the area from Traisen to Hainfeld, consisting of the *LAH*'s remaining Panthers, and a third group guarded the valley of the Traisen with the *LAHs* Mark IVs.[11] Although much less is known about this incarnation of *SS-Kampfgruppe Peiper* than the previous one, and the scale of the fighting was smaller than in the Ardennes, the ferocity was undiminished.

Kampfgruppe 12. SS-Panzergrenadier-Division Hitlerjugend

Stavka had never shied away from absorbing heavy casualties, or catastrophic casualty levels. But despite this willingness to expend oceans of blood to achieve their objectives, even the Red Army sometimes had to pause, resupply and reorganize the assault formations. So it was on 11 April in *Hitlerjugend*'s area, when the Russians limited activity to patrols and small probes of the SS defenses, all of which were turned back.

Near Laaben the newly arrived *Flak* batteries exchanged fire with Russian artillery. Then the Germans saw something they hadn't seen in weeks, and never expected to see again: a German fighter-bomber. Far off in the distance they spotted a Focke-Wulf FW-190 diving on Russian

---

9   To this day, the exact number of Tiger IIs in the 1944 version of SS-Kampfgruppe Peiper is debated. The battalion had 45 on the rolls, which was full strength, but most were lost or inoperable.
10   Maier, *Drama*, p. 378.
11   Tiemann, *The Leibstandarte IV/2*, p. 292.

positions. And although a single aircraft was relatively meaningless given the enormous scale of the fighting in Austria, it lifted the SS men's morale out of all proportion to its material support. Knowing the outnumbered *Luftwaffe* pilots still flew in the face of overwhelming odds let them know they weren't alone in the struggle to defend Austria.

The division had been expecting attacks on its far left wing near Klausen-Leopoldsdorf and the evidence came during the night that it was near. Engine noises and Russian patrols made it impossible for the exhausted *Panzergrenadiers* to sleep. There would be a fight come the morning.[12]

Kampfgruppe 1. SS-Panzer-Division Leibstandarte Adolf Hitler

Small and medium-sized encounters raged in the division's defensive area, but the division only faced local attacks. More ominously, for the first time the Russians employed heavy-caliber artillery in the area around Pottenstein and Berndorf. The Red Army's 152mm field howitzer was a devastating weapon. Even worse was the 203mm gun. Both could blast a rocky, wooded area with lethal intent, filling the air with splinters of steel, granite and wood. Against houses such as those in Lower Austria and Styria the effect was even more devastating. One hit could destroy a three-storey building and a near miss could collapse walls.

The *LAH*'s remaining artillery batteries tried to suppress this high-explosive rain but ammunition stocks were so low it had no effect. The Russians fired until they got tired of firing. Under this massive bombardment a Russian battle group broke through to Waxeneck, well to the southwest of Pottenstein. This was a dangerous penetration for the Germans, who had nothing to throw them back with.

SS-Kampfgruppe Keitel

Fighting around the Schneeberg flared up again as the Russian 99th Rifle Division renewed efforts to take the mountain. The Germans held it long enough for other worries on the northern flank to distract the Russians. A surprise counterattack by elements of *Kampfgruppe 356. Infanterie-Division* drove them back with such fury that the Germans recaptured the Hohe Wand. This had the effect of stabilizing that region, because no Russian penetration could be sustained without possession of the Hohe Wand. Any advance west through Grünbach and Puchberg was blocked if the Germans held both the Schneeberg and the Hohe Wand.

With attacks toward Puchberg from the east stymied by the loss of the Hohe Wand, the Russians drove on Puchberg from the south and southwest and only fierce defense stopped them short of that town. South of Puchberg, however, they made penetrations into the Piesting Valley. This was the gap area between *6. SS-Panzerarmee* and *6. Armee*. It was definitely the roundabout route for an advance to the west, but the real threat now was that both *SS-Kampfgruppe Keitel* and *Sperrverband Gross* had to bend their flanks at a ninety-degree angle. Otherwise, the entire corps could be outflanked. Combined with the gathering threat on the left flank of *I SS-Panzerkorps*, the plan for a pincer movement across east-central Austria was becoming defined.

12 Meyer, *The 12th SS*, p. 473.

6. Armee
Kampfgruppe Semmering, also known as *Kampfgruppe Raithel*

At some point during this period the designation of *Kampfgruppe Semmering* began to change into *Kampfgruppe Raithel,* after its commander *Oberst* Raithel. That would not be its last designation, however.

Skirmishes and all-out fights took place throughout the region and throughout the month. Scores of battles that cost thousands of lives changed nothing in the larger picture. Earlier in the war positions changed quickly, as armies swept hundreds and thousands of miles back and forth. The front around the Semmering Pass was recorded as 'static' because despite frequent combat, the front lines never changed much. But relating some of those stories gives the reader an idea of what it was like.

* * *

Despite plans for another attack, *Oberst* Raithel reluctantly decided that recapturing the Eselstein with the forces at hand was impossible. He took comfort from knowing that, just as he couldn't drive the Russians out of the high ground north of the valley below, neither could they force him out of the heights on the south side. Plus, in most places his men controlled the low ground of the pass itself. So, despite Russian artillery fire that at times became extremely heavy, he called off further pointless attacks to retake the Donkey Stone. Elsewhere, however, he hoped for better results.

* * *

Towns like Breitenstein changed hands several times during the month. Overlooking Klamm, directly north of Schottwien, was a 3,000 feet-high forested mountain called the Kobermannsberg. After recapturing Breitenstein, the *3./SS-Gebirgsjäger-Ausbildungs-und-Ersatz-Abteilung 13 Leoben* moved toward that peak. They scouted through a no man's land in and around silent Adlitzgraben, where a gypsum mill stood empty and they found an abandoned wagon loaded with useless goods, among other discarded items.

The Germans followed the railway line into Klamm, an area of canyons and waterfalls, which the Russians had occupied. Rising from the side of a mountain there were the spectacular ruins of a 12th-Century castle. It was a terrible environment for attacking, even for men who were ostensibly *Gebirgsjägers*, being cut with deep gorges, fast-flowing streams and waterfalls. Since the SS men were not veterans the attack was badly coordinated. The Germans made the mistake of moving through a cleared space with excellent firing lanes for Russians hiding in the woods, and were cut to pieces. Simultaneously the Russians launched their own attack and the inexperienced Germans were driven back, and although they maintained order they were scattered. As always happened the Russians immediately began building fortifications and a machine-gun nest in the newly won forward areas to stop the inevitable German counterattack. But the Germans struck quickly and silenced it, although some of the Russians survived.

When night fell small groups of Germans were scattered throughout the woods, without contact with each other. Their commander took two men and went looking for his platoon commanders, softly calling their names and hoping he didn't get shot by his own troops. Eventually they circled back to the wounded Russians at the machine gun, who moaned and softly called out "*panje, panje*", although the Germans had no idea what it meant.

From the southeastern slope they could see a long way into Russian-controlled territory, including the Russian artillery set up in Gloggnitz. Every now and then they even lobbed a few shells at the Russian guns themselves, with spotters on the Kobermannsberg. At night the Russians sometimes responded by firing at distant sounds, or by interdicting crossroads.

Occasionally German patrols sparked mortar or artillery fire, or hid from snipers. The Russians kept attacking, but because of their ability to watch all of the enemy movements the German spotters on the Kobermannsberg remained a thorn in the Russians' side. In attack after attack they lost the element of surprise because spotters on the Kobermannsberg saw them and radioed the threatened sector.

III Panzerkorps
1. Volks-Gebirgs-Division

The Russians weren't about to give the division any time to recover. Three rifle divisions with strong armored support kept attacking as the Germans withdrew. As the division pulled out of the Burgau area it blew up all the bridges it could find for twenty miles to slow down the attacking Russians. At times only a single panzer was available to give covering fire. The *III Panzerkorps* gave *Generalleutnant* Wittmann the *Schwere-Panzer-Abteilung 509* for use near Fürstenfeld, on its right flank.

Kampfgruppe 3. Panzer-Division

With *1. Volks-Gebirgs-Division* being slammed to the north *Kampfgruppe 3. Panzer-Division* found itself outflanked on both north and south, and in imminent danger of encirclement. At this stage of the war that would mean total destruction, since no troops were available for use as a relief force. Nevertheless the scattered combat groups held their positions against heavy attacks and even heavier shelling. "The Soviet artillery…was firing at everything that moved. It was only possible to move through the streets of Güssing at eight kilometers an hour."[13]

By 9:00 p.m. the withdrawal order couldn't be delayed any longer and the outlying groups were ordered back. Where discipline held the retreat under fire went well, but the few remaining Hungarian troops ran away, which endangered the German position. Surrounding companies wavered and fled. This led to *II./Panzergrenadier-Regiment 3* being surrounded around midnight. In the dark woods the battalion fought its way west, often without seeing more than muzzle flashes to indicate the path forward. Only in the pre-dawn hours did it break through to German lines.

The very last German soldier had now left Hungarian soil.

2. Panzerarmee

General der Artillerie de Angelis had been keeping a wary eye on his right flank, where the Russian, Bulgarian, Slovenian and Yugoslavian armies were hammering at his units between the Mur and Drava Rivers. But he was also watching events far to his south and southeast, in the area of *Heeresgruppe E*. Much like his fellow army commander to the northwest, Sepp Dietrich, de Angelis now had to begin planning for defensive lines in multiple directions.

---

13   Veterans, *Armored Bears*, p. 285.

14. Waffen-Grenadier-Division der SS Galizien

Caught in the storm of the massive Russian assault, the Stradner Kogel fell to the Russians for the last time on 11 April. It happened that men of the *3. Kavallerie-Division* held it when the final attack drove them off the peak for good. Heavy fighting and breakthroughs all over the area of *I Kavallerie Corps* required numerous counterattacks to keep the front from collapsing, and the Ukrainians now made up much of the counterattacking force. Fighting near Bad Gleichenberg and Straden continued into the next day.

23. Panzer-Division

The *23. Panzer-Division* was pulled back into the area east of Straden, northwest of the battlefield of the previous day. Both of its *Panzergrenadier* regiments manned the front lines, with various parts in reserve. Partisan activities were picking up behind the lines and rear area security required more manpower to safeguard supply dumps and even couriers. In one attack three men were wounded when a truck from the division had hand-grenades hurled its way. Some of the guerillas were deserters, sometimes from more than one army, and whenever such a man was caught he was summarily shot.

By late on 11 April the evacuation of Radkersburg was completed. One of its officers was named *Kampfkommandant* of the town of Mureck, with his defenses facing south as a screen for the division's right flank. Most of the supply trains for *I Kavallerie-Korps* were also moved there to be away from the front. The division had on its immediate left the all-but-destroyed *44. Infanterie-Division Hoch und Deutschmeister,* then *3. Kavallerie-Division* and *4. Kavallerie Division,*[14] and *9. SS-Panzer-Division Hohenstaufen* on its right.

---

14   Rebentisch, *From the Caucuse*, p. 466. Rebentisch here claims that *14. SS-Waffen-Grenadier-Division Galizien (Ukrainische 1)* was on the right flank of *23. Panzer Division*, and that the Ukrainian division was part of the so-called Vlasov Army of two Russian divisions committed to battle in the war's final days. This is incorrect. *Galizien* was formed from Ukrainians, not Russians, and was later designated as the first division of the Ukrainian National Army. Nor was it on the right flank of *23. Panzer-Division*, but had only just sealed a breach in the line further north, on its left flank.

12

Thursday, 12 April

Berlin

Late in the day Joseph Goebbels received word that American President Franklin D. Roosevelt had died. For one brief period it seemed that Hitler's Frederick the Great moment had arrived, that just like the former Prussian king, Germany's *Führer* had stuck it out long enough for the coalition opposing him to fall apart. But within hours it became apparent nothing had changed and the war would go on, and that vast numbers of people would continue dying in a lost cause.

* * *

Five months after he sent Hitler a memo the *Gautleiter* of the Tyrol and Torarlberg, Franz Hofer, finally got a chance to present his idea for the National Redoubt to the only man who mattered, Adolf Hitler. The *Führer* still believed in final victory and therefore saw no point to such an endeavor, but he gave Hofer the go-ahead to make the National Redoubt a reality. Unfortunately for the Germans, the Americans were smashing their way across Bavaria headed for Austria. Nevertheless, *OKW* began issuing orders corresponding to a last stand in Austria.

* * *

The *OKH* issued an order that important communications centers had to be defended to the last man. The signatories were *Generalfeldmarschall* Keitel, *Reichsführer-SS* Himmler and *Reichsleiter* and Head of the Nazi Party Martin Bormann. Death was the punishment for disobedience.

Heeresgruppe Süd

A cold front pushed into northern Austria and the temperature plunged twenty degrees to near 50 degrees Fahrenheit. Clouds early in the day gave way to a low ceiling and rain in the afternoon. The exhausted men of both sides could add wet and cold to their litany of misery. For men stuck at higher elevations this meant sleet and snow.

The bad weather also curtailed air actions. *Luftflotte 4* flew some 90 sorties in support of *8.Armee* during the morning, but whatever effect the loss of air support later in the day might have had on Kreysing's situation, was more than offset by the cessation of Red Air Force attacks.

North of the Danube

8. Armee

Serious danger developed on the army's right wing east of Wolkersdorf. Strong Russian forces broke through and only the deployment of the *Führer-Grenadier-Division* in that area slowed them down. Otherwise, Kreysing had nothing to plug the gap with.

Meanwhile, at Hohenau an der March, the Russians finally launched their attack directly at the town from the south. Both sides hit each other with heavy artillery strikes, but one Russian shell struck the sugar factory and it went up in flames, along with most of the German's food supply. The Russians captured part of the city and fighting continued throughout the night.

XXXXIII Armeekorps
Führer-Grenadier-Division

The most powerful division remaining in *Heeresgruppe Süd* couldn't be everywhere at once. Deployed in the Marchfeld around Grossebersdorf it stopped the direct Russian thrusts toward Korneuberg, although some ground had to be given up. This was the deepest penetration on *8. Armee*'s right flank and the direst threat to *II SS-Panzerkorps*. The *Führer-Grenadier-Division*'s left flank extended well beyond that town, trying to find a friendly unit on the left, but finding none.

On its right flank, at Gross-Enzersdorf, the division was still engaged with Russian armor in an ongoing fight. However, the town was in the outlying *Flak* belt protecting Vienna. This meant that numerous 88mm guns guarded it from fixed concrete positions, as the Russians found out to their loss. Despite strong artillery, mortar and air support, 13 Russian tanks went up in flames under the combined fire of the division's panzers and the *Flak* batteries. For the Red Air Force, attacking entrenched anti-aircraft positions was particularly dangerous.

37. SS-Freiwilligen-Kavallerie-Division Lützow

The division's second regiment, *SS-Kampfgruppe Keitel*, was still fighting in the critical position of holding the right wing of *6. SS-Panzerarmee*. As for the remainder of *Lützow*, it was heavily engaged to the north near the Danube, attached to the *XXXXIII* Army Corps, which by this point had a motley group of units under its command. That corps commanded no intact divisions, having *Kampfgruppen* from the newly arrived *25. Panzer-Division*, the *101. Jäger-Division*[1] and the *Kampfgruppe 96. Infanterie-Division*, *SS-Kampfgruppe Ameiser*,[2] *Grenadier-Brigade 92* (motorized), a *Kampfgruppe* from the remainder of *Lützow*, including the headquarters, with *Grenadier-Regiment 284*, *Panzergrenadier-Ausbildungs-und-Ersatz-Abteilung 82* and some *Volkssturm* attached.

Lützow's headquarters *Kampfgruppe* was fighting in the Russbach-Aspern area, holding the line Aspern-Stadlau-Hirschstetten within the boundary of Vienna's 22nd District, Donaustadt. Austrians revered this area because of the Battle of Aspern-Essling in 1809, when the Austrian Army repelled an attack by Napoleon. In 1858, the installation of a stone lion sculpture in front of St Martin's Church commemorated the Austrian soldiers who fell in the battle. The design of the statue closely resembles the Lion of Lucerne in Switzerland.

Along with *SS-Kampfgruppe Ameiser*, *Lützow* fought stubbornly to hold the area, but the seemingly inexhaustible Russian supply of artillery shells and Katyusha rockets blasted them out of every defensive position. Step by step they were forced to retreat, this time back to the area of Kapellerfeld-Süssenbrunn. With this withdrawal, the Russian Forty-Sixth Army, attacking from the east, closed within six miles of Klosterneuberg, the taking of which would trap *II SS-Panzerkorps*.

---

1   Also known as the *101. Leichte-Infanterie-Division*.
2   Some sources say that *SS-Kampfgruppe Ameiser* had been returned to control of its parent division the day before. Most likely the *Kampfgruppe* was returned and then removed again for independent use.

Alarm-Bataillon 2, Luftkriegsschule 7

After occupying positions on a 900 foot-high ridge north of Stetten, on 9 April the battalion was ordered to march back to Tulln to reinforce the *Alarm-Bataillon 3* which guarded the crossing of the Danube there. Even with the bridge destroyed the danger still existed of the Russians throwing artificial bridges across the river. But once there, new orders came to return to their positions near Stetten. During their march they suffered losses from Russian artillery fire, with at least four dead and 10 wounded.

The ridge position became critical to holding open the bottleneck through which *II SS-Panzerkorps* would have to escape in the next few days. When the battalion arrived back in their old trenches they found the Russians already at the bottom, but no attack came right away. Instead the men had time to clean their guns, eat and expand their rifle pits.

Then the attacks came. And came, and came. Over the next three days the Russians would shell, bomb, strafe and attack the ridge, all without success. The battalion of instructors and cadets held fast, but at the cost of very heavy casualties.

Vienna

O-5

For four days *O-5* had been reconstituting itself and recruiting socialist leaders into its fold. The idea was to present the Russians with a *de facto* local government made up of men with acceptable political beliefs. This pseudo-government would first re-establish law and order in streets that resembled the lawlessness of the early American West, and then obtain the backing of the Soviets to keep maintaining order. A lot of energy was expended on plans and organizations, which in the end showed nothing more than their profound ignorance of how Stalinist Russia worked.

Kampfgruppe 6. Panzer-Division

Fighting throughout the Prater reached a new level of ferocity as the Russians tried to break through. Where once parents had led their children through crowded promenades on a sunny Sunday afternoon, now men darted across open spaces hoping a piece of sizzling hot metal didn't rip into their bodies. Other forces followed the Hauptallee into *Totenkopf*'s left flank near the Northwest Railway Station, but unless *Kampfgruppe 6. Panzer-Division* could be broken the Russians couldn't get through to the Reich's Bridge. For their part, the men of *Kampfgruppe 6. Panzer-Division* stood their ground but paid a huge price in casualties. The Russians lost 15 tanks before midday in savage fighting. *Kampfgruppe 6. Panzer-Division*'s casualties aren't known now, but they had to be ruinous because before nightfall the division had been pushed within half a mile of the Reich's Bridge.

Kampfgruppe 3. SS-Panzer-Division Totenkopf

Blurry photographs taken by members of the *SS-Standarte Kurt Eggers*, the propaganda arm of the *Waffen-SS*, shows men from *Totenkopf* crumpled against walls or lying in alleys, rifles near at hand, sound asleep on the streets of Vienna. The exhaustion of day after day of deadly combat fighting could only be pushed through for so long before the men collapsed. The known widespread use of amphetamines may have kept them on their feet up to that point, but even drugs could only do so much.

Heavy artillery fire lasted all day, augmented by concentrated air strikes despite the weather. Coupled with extreme fatigue, the cumulative effect finally broke *Totenkopf*'s line along Wallenstein Strasse. The SS men retreated into the *Nordwestbahnhof*, Northwest Railway Station, less than half a mile from the Danube. The Russian advance took them over the marshalling yards, where rolling stock provided cover, and though *Totenkopf* stopped them short of the river the situation was critical. When *6. Panzer-Division* was driven backward into their left flank all seemed lost.

2. SS-Panzer-Division Das Reich

During the days of Imperial Rome the Danube River was the boundary between Roman civilization and the barbarian world beyond. South of the river meant that Roman law held sway, while north of the river were the wild lands where the only law was that of the sword. Or so the Romans claimed. The land bordering the Danube was something of a buffer zone between the two competing cultures, including the land now known as Vienna's 20th District, Brittgenau, where *Das Reich* manned defenses along the Danube Canal.

Das Reich had fought tenaciously in the defense of Vienna, but by 12 April most of the battered division had been pushed north of the Danube. Still, as one author puts it: *"II SS-Panzerkorps* delivered a sharp reminder of the tactical expertise of the dwindling number of veteran Panzer crews as the formation withdrew on the 12th – a single Panther of *Das Reich*, commanded by *Leutnant* Arno Giesen, knocked out 14 T-34s and JS-2s whilst holding one of the Danube bridges."[3]

The above quote is instructive for more than one reason, however. The bridge was the Floridsdorfer, the date this happened was 13 April, not 12 April, and the author repeats a common mistake in the identity of this tank ace. Arno Giesen is, in reality, *SS-Obersturmführer* Arnold Friesen, who used a *nom-de-guerre* in the postwar years to avoid any problems that might have arisen from his service in the *Waffen-SS* during the Second World War. Given that the entire SS was declared a criminal organization, both the *Allegemeine-SS* and the *Waffen-SS*, his caution is understandable. Merely being in the *Waffen-SS* was to invite suspicion and prosecution, especially for veterans with impressive war records. Some men, such as Otto Weidinger, were held captive for six years for supposed war crimes, only to be found not guilty after a trial.

This natural tendency to self-preservation has lead to some confusion, however, since Arnold Friesen was one of the top tank commanders of all time, finishing the war credited with 111 kills.[4] Given the lack of records surrounding late-war German actions it is surprising more such mistakes are not found. Nevertheless, a number of SS veterans using false names have led to confusion and the inability of historians to verify sources. Giesen/Friesen shares the fog of anonymity with a panzer commander mentioned several times by John Toland in relation to his account of *Unternehmen Frühlingserwachen*, a man supposedly named Fritz Hagen but who doesn't appear on the rolls of *Das Reich*, and there are numerous other examples. Nor does Arno Giesen/Arnold Friesen have anything in common with Bruno Friesen, a tank gunner in *7 Panzer-Division, 25.*

---

3   Porter, David, *Order of Battle, The Red Army in WWII* (London: Amber Books, 2009), p. 175.
4   Mansoor, First Lieutenant Peter R., 'The Defense of the Vienna Bridgehead' *Armor: The Magazine of Mobile Warfare*, January-February 1986 Vol XCV No. 1, (Fort Knox: US Army Armor Center, 1986), pp. 26-28. The name Arno Giesen was used by then Lieutenant Mansoor in his article "The Defense of the Vienna Bridgehead" in the January-February 1986 issue of *Armor* magazine. The article was based on interviews Mansoor conducted with Friesen and the name change was intentional on Mansoor's part, at the request of his interview subject. Later historians, however, using the article as a source, repeated the name change without comment.

Panzer-Regiment, who has written his own account of his wartime exploits, aside from a similar name. Arno Giesen's real name, Arnold Friesen, is used here.

Friesen's story shows that in modern war, in battles involving tens or hundreds of thousands of troops, swarms of tanks and aircraft, with the movement of armies as inexorable as flood-tides, even amidst such martial materiel might, there is still the chance for one man, or one small group of men, to influence events out of all proportion to their numbers. In one sense the German Army was built on that principle, a system known as the strategic corporal. At its core, this carries the chain of command all the way down from a unit's commanding officer to its lowest-ranking members, so that if only two men of equal rank were left in a unit, they would still know who was in charge. And so it was with Arnold Friesen and the crew of Panther 227 on 12 and 13 April 1945.

The story begins on 12 April when, also inside the perimeter and back in his Panther, was Knights' Cross winner *SS-Oberscharführer* Ernst Barkmann, another one of the great tank aces of the war for either side. Barkmann's path to the perimeter had been more circuitous than most. As related earlier in this narrative, during the retreat from Hungary Barkmann's Panther company had been separated from the battalion and made it back to Austria by attaching itself to *1. SS-Panzer-Division Leibstandarte Adolf Hitler.* Then, after being newly reunited with *Das Reich,* his Panther had broken down. The Panther battalion's repair company had moved to Floridsdorf and Barkmann had to drive a *Bergepanzer,* a specially designed recovery panzer, through the streets of Vienna guided by a Hitler Youth sitting beside him on the turret. Never quite sure where the Russians were, with the boy's help Barkmann towed his broken Panther safely to Floridsdorf.

While awaiting the return of his Panther Barkmann led his small *Kampfgruppe* east of the 22nd District of Donaustadt, the one mentioned that contained three Panthers and his command SPW, before coming back into Vienna to help repel several Russian assaults. With his tank again operational, he drove back into the fight and found himself supporting the *Panzergrenadiers* in the perimeter on Danube Island, in Brittgenau. The actions of both he and Friesen on those two days in April are not disputed, in the main, but sources differ on exactly what happened and when.

* * *

The story of the fighting at the Floridsdorf Bridge shows how many details remain in conflict even today, nearly 70 years after the fact. The fog of history makes it difficult to decipher exact occurrences, as conflicting accounts blur historical facts. While some things are not in dispute, others are and probably always will be. Based on late evidence from Dr Mansoor about the article he wrote in 1986: 'Indeed, the following incredible story of Panther 227 in the Vienna Bridgehead may be apocryphal after all; at this late time no one can say for certain anymore. But if it is, then let it stand as an example of how the men of Das Reich viewed their defensive mission in Vienna.'

The once-beautiful capital of Austria had become a tumbled hell of broken buildings that slid into the streets like melting wax, hissing and sizzling and turning historic cityscapes into ash and cinders. As dawn sunlight filtered through the smoke palls rising over Vienna on 12 April, the Russians hammered the Germans on Danube Island with relentless artillery barrages. The only upside for the defenders was that the proximity of their enemies made air strikes too risky. Instead the Red Air Force prowled other skies.

Das Reich had mostly withdrawn north of the river by 12 April, while infantry supported by some panzers occupied a bridgehead south of the Danube in the form of a semi-circular perimeter connected to the north shore by one bridge, the Floridsdorfer, just downstream from the point where the Danube Canal branches off from the river. During the day relentless assaults by 20th Guards Rifle and 1st Guards Mechanized Corps drove the SS men back from the line of the canal despite ferocious defense.

On their left flank was another bridgehead occupied by *Totenkopf*. That division was nearly surrounded. The men had their backs to the Danube, and like *Das Reich* they also had one bridge connecting them to safety on the north bank, the *Reichsbrücke*. To their left *6. Panzer-Division* still held out against waves of attacks, even when the Russians committed 25 tanks to support the infantry.

Only in those small strips of Brittgenau and Leopoldstadt did the Third Reich still hold sway in Vienna. At its widest point the German foothold on Danube Island didn't exceed 500 feet. The rest of the former Habsburg capital south of the Danube was lost to the Red Army, from the Prater to the Ringstrasse and north to the Kahlenberg.

* * *

By the morning of 12 April *Das Reich* was depleted from weeks of hard fighting with no time to rest or repair equipment, no replacement vehicles and few replacement men. Most of the division's remaining armor had been pulled out of Vienna by then. Notwithstanding that any panzers still south of the river would be cut off if the Floridsdorfer Bridge were seized by the Soviets, the Germans had suffered heavy losses of their remaining panzers during the urban warfare of the previous week, where rubble and buildings gave individual soldiers with anti-tank weapons plenty of opportunity to attack a panzer. *SS-Panzer-Regiment 2* had gone into *laagers* around Stammersdorf, some three miles north of the Danube. The division's few remaining panzers were literally irreplaceable. Even damaged ones that could not be salvaged could be scavenged for parts. Those within the perimeter were simply buying time as the only force that could hold at bay the Soviet tanks streaming through the city.

Holding the bridgehead wasn't possible for long, and everybody knew it. Yet abandoning the south bank and pulling back north of the Danube was not an option for a variety of reasons. Aside from the unrealistic orders coming from *OKH*, if the bridgehead defense collapsed it would put the entire German position north of the river in jeopardy, especially if the Russians captured a bridge intact. In essence, the troops on the southern side were risking their own destruction to buy time for their comrades on the northern bank to form a defense against the Soviet forces pushing west through the *Marchfeld* and beyond the Little Carpathians

Aside from the obvious threat of a forced crossing of the Danube into the rear of the German units still fighting north of the river, direct enfilade fire into the German right flank would also make that position untenable. The Russians knew all of this and attacked the bridgehead perimeter relentlessly but carefully. They badly wanted at least one bridge over the Danube seized intact and all of the rest were already in the water.

Reports of SS survivors say the Russians were aided by the Viennese themselves. The activities of O-5 and comments by Goebbels in his diary make the idea of civilians actively fighting the *Waffen-SS* at least feasible. It's difficult to say for certain if these were isolated cases or a mass movement. The fog of war has given way to the fog of time.

Das Reich's perimeter had the Danube as its northern boundary. Along the river there was a narrow strip of parkland with trees and shrubs, a promenade. Just up from that was the river road, the Handelskai, which ran from Brittgenau south-east, paralleling the water for more than 8 miles to Leopoldstadt. Further inland from the park and across the Handelskai were waterfront buildings and side streets running north-south. Just west of the bridge was a large rectangular plaza, Pater Abel Platz, which was surrounded by large buildings. Originally named Friedrich Engels Platz, and changed back after the war, it was renamed in 1934 after a famous anti-Semitic priest, Father Abel, whose extreme right-wing political views foreshadowed and, possibly, influenced Hitler's. Father Abel was well-known in Vienna during Hitler's years there. As a nominal Catholic it seems almost guaranteed that Hitler was aware of his preaching against Jews and communists, and it is not much of a stretch to see Father Abel's influence in *Mein Kampf*.

One block further west of Pater Abel Platz was the Brigitte Kapelle, the Chapel of St Brigitte, after which the 20th District was named. Built in 1650, the small octagonal chapel had been heavily damaged in an earlier bombing raid, the windows having been blown out and the roof ripped open. The *II SS-Panzerkorps* had been using it as a morgue for some time. About 400 yards west of the chapel the Danube Canal flowed in a southeastern arc from the main river course to form the long, narrow Danube Island.

Facing the Germans was armor from the 5th Guards Tank Corps, equipped with T-34/85s and JS-II heavy tanks. Unlike the vulnerable Shermans they'd been facing, the Russians had brought in the heavy stuff. Russian attack plans were straight-forward enough. The streets leading into Pater Abel Platz, and thereafter to the bridge itself, were clogged with rubble and largely impassable, except for the river road, the Handelskai. This was protected further south by *Totenkopf.*

With no large buildings flanking the Handelskai little rubble had accumulated there. Tanks would have a hard time moving down the blocked side-streets and would have to be slow and cautious, leaving them vulnerable to anti-tank fire, but not close to the river. Russian infantry worked slowly forward, battling *Panzergrenadiers* in the ruins, especially from each side near the waterfront. The priority for the Russians above all others was taking the Floridsdorfer Bridge intact and an attack down the relatively clear Handelskai offered the best chance for that.

Within the German defenses the situation was approaching desperate. More than anything on that April morning, the defenders of the perimeter needed food and ammunition, but getting supplies over the river in daylight bordered on suicide. Because the Russians had seized the Kahlenberg, the mountain to the northwest, the bridge was under direct Soviet artillery observation, directing both direct and indirect fire. The mountain had been a critical strategic point for decades. When the Polish King Sobieski saved Vienna in 1683, his artillery on the Kahlenberg ripped up the Turks before his cavalry charge broke them.

But if crossing in daytime involved deadly dangers, waiting until night was only marginally less dangerous. The bridge was damaged and had a large hole near the center. Neither option offered much hope for success, but the few panzers left in Vienna were particularly short of main gun ammunition.

On the north flank of the perimeter was a lone Panzer Mark IV from the *6./SS-Panzer-Regiment 2*, in position just north of the bridge, in the parkland near the river and using the vegetation for cover. A few Panthers were scattered about the perimeter. Without immediate resupply the bridgehead would have to be evacuated, regardless of whether defenses were ready on the northern bank, or whether the wounded could be safely evacuated.

The bridge was in a vicious cross-fire, with most of it coming from the southern bank. On the northern side and somewhat down-river the Soviets were well east-southeast of the bridge. On the southern side they were south, west and northwest of the bridge. Added to the artillery on the Kahlenburg this meant fire came in from all direction. Only to the north and north-northwest did the Germans still hold a corridor.

There was no good choice for crossing the bridge, then, but once darkness fell the threat of Soviet fire abated somewhat and that seemed the preferable option, even though the bridge was badly damaged and men or vehicles could easily fall into the Danube below, or drive into the large bomb crater at the center of the bridge. The only solution was for a tank to take the risk and run the gauntlet, and darkness seemed to give the only chance.

Early in the afternoon of 12 April the commander of *SS-Panzer-Regiment 2*, *SS-Standartenführer* Enseling, gathered his tank crews and asked for volunteers to take a panzer over the bridge with supplies. Close by was a battery of *Hummels* that still had ammunition and were hammering away with their 155mm guns in support of the perimeter. Enseling had to scream over the noise to be heard.

By all accounts Enseling was irritated and disappointed when nobody jumped at the chance to undertake a suicide mission, and told the assembled crews that their comrades needed them and there would be volunteers. In the end, Arnold Friesen's 44-year-old driver nudged the 19-year-old tank commander, and Friesen raised his hand. Friesen had 97 confirmed kills by this point, having joined the division before Kursk and fought in every major engagement since, so bravery was not the issue. Staying alive was. However, once he had been volunteered there was no turning back. Friesen moved forward cautiously to mentally map out his route, and while reconnoitering the bridge he ran into a *Luftwaffe* officer commanding a battery of 88mm guns who said: "Not for a million marks would I drive across that bridge! Only the *Waffen-SS* could be so crazy!"[5]

But Friesen had a mission and he had no choice but to carry it out and try to help his comrades. How much could you cram in a Panzer Mark V Panther in an emergency? According to Mansoor: "The Panther was loaded with 92 rounds of 75-mm main gun ammunition, ten cases of machine gun ammunition, five insulated containers of hot food, and cigarettes and two bottles of cognac for good measure."[6] The tank also towed an ammunition trailer with another 50 rounds of main gun ammunition. A Panther towing a trailer over a damaged bridge with a bomb crater in the center in total darkness was incredibly dangerous, but doing so in broad daylight with anti-tank and artillery fire coming from all directions, when one hit on the trailer would mean that the whole bridge might blow up, was insane. Friesen had no choice except to wait until dark.

The division artillery fired off precious ammunition from both its *Wespe* and *Hummel* batteries to pin down any Soviet fire. Crazy or not, Friesen led his tank over the bridge in total darkness and somehow managed to avoid both the bomb crater and the river below, largely due to the skill and calmness of his driver. Despite the darkness, one source says that aimed anti-tank fire missed and small-arms fire rattled off the tank's armor. Once on the southern side and into the open space of Pater Abel Platz, Soviet artillery rounds splattered the area, some as close as 20 meters from the tank. Friesen followed a guide into a side street and parked on the front lines, where he felt immensely safer with buildings on either side. All quietened down quickly along the front, as the Russians did not usually like urban fighting at night.

Down the street was the Panther of none other than *SS-Oberscharführer* Ernst Barkmann, who had 82 kills. Oddly enough, Friesen and Barkmann had never met each other despite being in the same regiment and being two of Germany's top panzer aces. But the tale of exactly what happened next is fuzzy, and shows some of the problems inherent in researching this last part of the war.

According to Franz Kurowski, during the day of 12 April Barkmann tried to lead three Panthers over the bridge to the regimental command post, but a panicked German NCO mistook his tank for a T-34 and fired at it with a *Panzerfaust*, hitting the turret and showering the crew with shell splinters and knocking out their communications.[7]

It seems almost certain that Barkmann was heading from the northern side into the perimeter to shore up the defense, sometime during daylight on 12 April, although sources differ even on this. When communications in the tank were knocked out, Barkmann had to shout driving instructions to the loader or gunner, who then had to relay them to the driver. This clumsy arrangement would lead to the panzer's destruction in the near future. In the meantime, however, it seems that Barkmann's tank remained in the perimeter for the rest of the day of 12 April and that as night fell he was resupplied by Friesen.[8]

5   Mansoor, *The Defense*, p. 28.
6   Mansoor, *The Defense*, p. 28.
7   Kurowski, Franz, *Panzer Aces III* (Mechanicsburg: Stackpole, 2010), pp. 17-18.
8   In the article in *Armor Magazine*, Friesen says that the Panther he resupplied, which he names as Barkmann's, was soon destroyed by an urban guerilla, using a *Panzerfaust* or something like it. Given the confusion that likely reigned in the German defenses at the time, this may or may not verify that he spoke with Barkmann,

According to Friesen, he distributed the rations and ammunition to Barkmann when his Panther was down to five rounds of main gun ammunition. Apparently while this was going on, from out of the darkness a Russian tank showed up and roared down the street before the Germans could destroy it, causing chaos but no damage, and then vanishing again, after which everything calmed down.[9] The Germans took cover for the night, with Friesen and his tank hunkering down in the perimeter to get some sleep.

* * *

At 11:15 p.m. *SS-Obergruppenführer* Bittrich ordered *General der Infanterie* von Bünau back into Vienna to take command of the bridgehead and to hold it at all costs. Michael Reynolds described this as "a convenient move".[10] Von Bünau immediately dispatched staff officers to contact the three panzer divisions and assess their strength and situation; as expected, all three were far worse off than they had been two days before in terms of strength, while the tactical situation was disastrous. Von Bünau then crossed back over the Danube to oversee the finale of the bloody drama that was the Battle for Vienna.

Kampfgruppe 3. SS-Panzer-Division Totenkopf

As midnight approached the remaining elements of *6. Panzer-Division* and *Totenkopf* withdrew over the Reich's Bridge to the north bank of the Danube. Even as Bittrich sent von Bünau back across the Danube to take command of the defense in Brittgenau, two-thirds of his defensive force was heading the other way across the river, meaning the men of *Das Reich* would wake in the morning to find their left flank open and undefended.

But to make matters even worse, for some reason the Reich's Bridge wasn't blown up and the Russians seized it intact. They couldn't storm it under fire as anti-tank guns and 37mm *Flak* cannon covered its long expanse, but the Germans on the north bank were also under pressure from the other Russian forces advancing on the Danube's north shore.

25. and 26. Waffen-Grenadier-Divisionen der SS Hunyadi and Hungaria

In the area of Grafenwöhr in Germany, Hungarian *Generalmajor* von Grassy had taken command of the three nomad Hungarian SS divisions, *25. Waffen-Grenadier-Division der SS Hunyadi* and *26. Waffen-Grenadier-Division der SS Hungaria*, and the partly formed 1st Hungarian *Honvéd* Division 'Kossuth'. None of those units was anywhere close to fully armed and both of the *Waffen-SS* divisions

since the latter's tank actually was struck by a *Panzerfaust*. Supposedly it was fired by a panicked German NCO, but there were also reports floating around that other Panthers had been destroyed by urban guerillas fighting with the Soviets. The scenario used in the narrative seems the most likely, but the episode is also indicative of the fog of war that even today surrounds events during this last phase of the war, including Friesen's entire story, for which he was the only source.

9   Another source says this Panther was NOT Barkmann's, it was a different Panther and that Friesen conferred with the tank's commander but a Soviet soldier with a bazooka crept to a nearby house in the confusion caused by the Russian tank, and hit it with an AT round, and that the Panther blew up, killing its crew. The Panzergrenadiers then went through the surrounding buildings shooting anyone they found in retaliation. The other account is included because it fits the overall timeline better, but at this distance in time there is no way to be 100 percent certain which is correct, or if either is correct.

10   Reynolds, *The Battle for Vienna*, <http://nationalinterest.org/blog/the-buzz/the-battle-vienna-when-the-russians-crushed-the-nazi-army-21189?page=show>, (Accessed 23 April 2018).

had just fled the Neuhammer area having suffered losses from the battle group they supplied to act as a rearguard. By some reports Grassy combined these divisions while at Grafenwöhr.[11]

Agreements signed with the Szálasi government had promised that Hungarian troops would not be used against the Western Allies unless they invaded Hungary. By 12 April, however, the Szálasi government had no Hungary left to govern or defend, and so the point was moot. There would be no reason for the Hungarians to fight the Western Allies, which would make it all the more shocking when a few of them did exactly that.

But all agreements were forgotten as *Generalfeldmarschall* Kesselring, commanding all German forces in the West, ordered them into battle regardless of agreements or how unprepared they might be for combat. Somehow, though, this order was not enforced, or was ignored, because soon Grassy was leading the homeless Hungarians south to Austria. They would eventually wind up due south at Atterlee.

Korps Schultz

Fremde Heeres Ost, Foreign Armies East, the intelligence service of the German Army, predicted that after the capture of Sankt Pölten the 18th Tank Corps would have to rest and regroup for a few days before continuing the attack to the west and north. That was cold comfort for anyone in *Korps Schultz*, as the intensity of the Russian attacks showed no signs of diminishing. The only places where the German front had not buckled were where *Generalmajor* Schultz had veteran troops to put into the line, such as *710. Infanterie-Division, Panzer-Aufklärungs-Abteilung 1* and *Panzer-Aufklärungs-Abteilung 3*.

So far the Russians had two corps attacking Sankt Pölten, the 18th Tank and 38th Rifle Corps, but more units were on the way from Third Ukrainian Front's central and southern sectors. Sheer firepower might have overwhelmed the thin German front lines, and earlier in the war that's what the Russians would have done. But the Red Army had learned a lot about warfare since 1941. And so, southeast of Sankt Pölten, the Russians used trickery to outflank the thin German defensive line.

Taking advantage of the hedge-hog defensive setup necessitated by a lack of troops, the Russians used the night of 11-12 April to sneak into the rear of the German front line. At daybreak they attacked from west to east and dislodged the German front lines, which only rallied near Hochgschaid. This penetration threatened to crumple the right flank of *Korps Schultz*.

That desperate moment called for an equally desperate measure. Schultz ordered every officer in his headquarters who could walk to the Traisen River, with orders to stop any fleeing troops and have them dig in on the higher western bank. He'd already sent engineer troops there to construct defenses, but with no reserves his only choice was to rally the broken formations running for their lives. Using pistols, threats, curses and shame, the officers calmed the terrified men and had them burrow into the dirt and, little by little, a line began to form.

But even as the right flank bent and crumpled the corps' left flank was again pushed backward in the area between Ollersback and Würmla. An intense artillery bombardment preceded an attack by fresh forces. The Russian assault ran out of steam after gobbling up a few more miles, but the front line still had holes. One such was closed by part of *Panzer-Aufklärungs-Abteilung 3*, but there were many others and the situation remained critical.

* * *

---

11   In all likelihood, this refers to the order to dissolve the divisions to supply manpower for other formations, rather than a decision to combine them into one.

Generalmajor Schultz had waited as long as he could, and therefore on the evening of 12 April, he ordered all troops in the Perschling-Seelackenbach sector to withdraw and only to maintain a bridgehead at Boheimkirchen. The new strongpoints of the defense would be Kapelln and Boheimkirchen. To assist in rapidly building new fortifications, two *Baubatillone*, construction battalions, from *Pionier-Regiment z.b.V. 548* were committed to the job.

6. SS-Panzerarmee

On 12 April 1945 *SS-Kampfgruppe Keitel* was officially included in the Army War Registry as part of *1 SS-Panzerkorps*, along with *Kampfgruppe 1. SS-Panzer Division Leibstandarte Adolf Hitler*, *Kampfgruppe 12 SS-Panzer-Division* and *Kampfgruppe 356. Infanterie-Division*.

I SS-Panzerkorps

As the days unwound it became increasingly clear that the Russian strategy in the area was to force *6. SS-Panzerarmee* back by driving into its rear areas, which in turn would affect the *6. Armee* position south of the Semmering Pass. Carrying out this plan meant continuing to attack *I SS-Panzerkorps* to slice up the corps and destroy it.

Kampfgruppe 12. SS-Panzer-Division Hitlerjugend

The division's extreme left flank was being hammered around Brand-Laaben. This area acted as a choke point for further Russian advances along the Danube Valley and they were determined to capture it quickly. *SS-Kampfgruppe Gross* defended the area, with the addition of a few state-of-the-art *Jagdpanthers* and *Jagdpanzer IV/70s* from the *Schwere-Panzerjäger-Abteilung 560*. Given a few panzers from *Hitlerjugend*, and with most of the battalion fighting as infantry, this group was known as *Kampfgruppe Goldammer*.

Late in the day the desperate situation in *Korps Schultz's* area on the corps' left flank was recognized as the greatest threat to the corps, so the commander of *Schwere-Panzerjäger-Abteilung 560*, Major Goldammer, was ordered to withdraw and lead his *Kampfgruppe* to reinforce the threatened sector around Sankt Pölten. The *Hitlerjugend* panzers were probably detached first and returned to their parent regiment.

Taking its place was the weak *SS-Kampfgruppe von Reitzenstein*. *SS-Hauptsturmführer* Reitzenstein didn't even get to keep the communications equipment already at the *Kampfgruppe* headquarters atop the Kogelhof, two miles southwest of Laaben. He got to keep two *Kübelwagen*, but only had one driver. His personnel had no heavy weapons and were spread thin. Most were artillery gunners with no guns to serve, plus some *Luftwaffe* men and a few grenadiers. Von Reitzenstein inspected his new command and came away convinced that, with the equivalent of a few companies of men, some *Flak* cannon, a handful of SPWs and light machine guns, in the event of a fight the little *Kampfgruppe* could do little except act as a picket force to keep division headquarters informed. Only late in the day did he receive some reinforcements in the form of panzer men without machines from the *I./Panzer-Regiment 12*. They had been separated from the division in Hungary, and then took a circuitous route that included a detour through Vienna before finally being directed to join von Reitzenstein.[12]

---

12   Meyer, *The 12th SS*, pp. 475-476.

The *Kampfgruppe* came into existence like most such units did. With little transport, and limited fuel for what transport existed, and supplies nearly as bad, the surplus men from the companies mentioned above were commanded by *SS-Hauptsturmführer* Gerd von Reitzenstein,[13] a company commander in *SS-Aufklärung-Abteilung 12* and a well-respected officer. Assembled at Hainfeld, a picturesque town of some 3,800 citizens in the Gölsental Valley, the men were driven in some of the few remaining trucks to Kaumberg, a few miles to the east. They unloaded in Kaumberg and ate their first hot meal within memory, then were given cold rations and spent the night in the hamlet before moving off north into the mountains east of Sankt Corona am Schöpfl the next morning.

Its first introduction to combat was harrowing. One small road led northeast to Klausen-Leopoldsdorf and the *Kampfgruppe* deployed on the southern side of the road, while on the northern side was a *Luftwaffe* unit deployed as infantry. None of the men of either unit had combat experience or entrenching tools, and most had no training in ground fighting. The only cover was fallen trees and natural depressions in the soil.

Soon enough the Russians attacked the *Luftwaffe* unit and it disintegrated immediately, the men running away without looking back. *SS-Kampfgruppe Reitzenstein* had to send half of its men to hold the *Luftwaffe* positions. The fighting was vicious and Russian snipers took a terrible toll, and as casualties mounted the SS men had no choice but to withdraw or be overrun. They could not hold Sankt Corona and built a position to the southwest, from which they could hear the screams of women being raped throughout the night.

Unexpectedly, reinforcements from *Hitlerjugend* showed up the following morning in the form of men from *SS-Panzer Regiment 12* reorganized to fight as infantry, possibly *SS-Kampfgruppe Gross*, so that when the Russians attacked they were driven off with heavy losses. Situated on the edge of a forest on a steep hill, with a cleared meadow below, the field of fire was excellent. But the Russians were characteristically stubborn and eventually broke into the SS positions. After savage hand-to-hand combat the Russians were thrown back, although losses on both sides were extremely heavy. Fighting went on for days. When another attack seemed likely to break through, from nowhere a still-functioning Wirblewind showed up like a Guardian Angel; the vortex of fire from its four 20mm anti-aircraft guns broke the Russian attacks yet again. Eventually, outnumbered, outgunned and in danger of being outflanked, *SS-Kampfgruppe Reitzenstein* was forced to retreat, leaving behind so many dead they were interred in a mass grave near Sankt Corona.

East of this fighting another Russian assault broke through along the road from Schwarzensee to Fahrafeld. The attack was preceded by the customary Russian saturation barrage, ranging from medium-caliber mortars to 152mm heavy guns. With the aid of more *Flak* batteries the Germans stopped them short of Fahrafeld. Close-range fighting continued all through the night, including some hand-to-hand combat in the German fortifications.

* * *

Once again German defenders found themselves under attack at Groisbach and in this case the attack worked, with the effect being opening the breakthrough channel to the Danube Valley even wider. Overwhelmed and thrown back, the Germans withdrew to the high ground southwest of the town. This was not because of ground attacks, however. The maelstrom created by Russian artillery and air strikes was so severe that the defenders took heavy casualties simply from the bombardment. Staying would have risked them being wiped out where they stood. But the Russians could not advance into the town because the *Flak* batteries mowed down anybody and anything that approached it.

---

13   Von Reitzenstein was implicated in the murder of 156 Canadian soldiers the previous year in Normandy, but was never brought to trial.

But fighting for the day was just getting started. *SS-Kampfgruppe Bremer* attacked with support from a few panzers down the road from the Nöstach-Dörfl area. A prominent mountain overlooking the road from the east was captured but quickly lost again to a Russian counterattack. They were brought to a stop short of Dörfl, and reports came through of many tanks and heavy artillery pieces in the town. The Russians then launched their own attack to the southeast from the area south of Klausen-Leopoldsdorf, with the intention of outflanking *SS-Kampfgruppe Bremer* on the west.

Confused patrolling and fighting took place all afternoon in the wooded mountains west of the Nöstach-Groisbach road. German reconnaissance groups met Russian infantry in a series of short, violent firefights. The nature of the terrain, coupled with the depleted state of the German infantry units, meant that Russian infiltrators often slipped past to attack from the rear, or to ambush supply columns. The division reorganized some of its defenses to combat the situation and laid numerous minefields.

Along the crucial Weissenbach-Raisenmarkt road the Russians attacked at dusk and drove the Germans back, before continuing through to Schwarzensee which the Germans evacuated. Once German artillery zeroed in on them, however, the Russians withdrew.

This left *Hitlerjugend* to defend a 16-mile front by itself, with the *crisis du jour* being at Laaben. Elements of the *Flak* battalion were then redeployed from around Berndorf and attached to *SS-Kampfgruppe Gross*. Without reinforcements, *SS-Oberführer* Hugo Kraas had no choice but to play a shell game of redeploying his ever-diminishing forces in reaction to the most dangerous threat of the moment.

Kampfgruppe 1. SS-Panzer-Division Leibstandarte Adolf Hitler

To the north the Russian breakthrough between Fahrafeld and Berndorf the day before could only be halted with maximum effort a mile northwest of Pöllau. At first thought to be minor, the size of this thrust was actually in brigade strength, which overwhelmed the German defenses and was part of a major effort to break through on either side of Alland. Driving southwest in this break-through threatened *Hitlerjugend* being flanked to the east, and the *LAH* to the west.

As the *LAH* fought in central Austria west of Weiner Neustadt, the *II./SS-Panzer-Regiment 1*, bereft of tanks and being used to reinforce other units, was converted into a strictly infantry role. *Wiking*'s tank regiment had already suffered the same fate. So as the premier SS armored division put its highly trained tank crews and mechanics into the line as cannon fodder, Sepp Dietrich would one day shake his head and wonder where it had all gone wrong, but there was no time for that now.

* * *

Six companies of men from *SS-Panzer-Regiment 1* fighting as infantry counterattacked the break-through near Waxeneck and stopped the Russian thrust. They had been trying for days to block the way west along the Triesting Valley between Pottenstein and Berndorf. They still had a few Mark IVs that hadn't been attached to *SS-Kampfgruppe Peiper*, along with some *Sturmgeschütze* and *Jagdpanzers*, but many had dry fuel tanks. No ammunition or fuel had made it to the front for days, but then came one of those bizarre coincidences that sometimes happen in war. By sheer luck an NCO driving down a bad road in the fog came upon a lone sentry guarding two full tanker trucks. The man asked if the NCO knew anybody who needed fuel. Such a precious find bordered on the miraculous, since it was enough gasoline to fill up all the empty tanks.[14]

---

14 Tiemann, *The Leibstandarte IV/2*, p. 293.

Kampfgruppe Koch

The battalion of *Fahnenjunkern*, *Volkssturm* and discharged medical patients was the only protection on the left flank of *Kampfgruppe 356. Infanterie-Division*. With intelligence that Russian attacks were coming, three Mark IV panzers from a *Waffen-SS* unit, probably *SS-Panzer-Regiment 1*, reinforced them and brought word of a new *Führerbefehl* that was identical to every *Führerbefehl* that came before, namely, that each man would fight and die where he stood. There was to be no retreat.

It wasn't long before massive Russian attacks slammed into the *Kampfgruppe* in the area around the village of Mothmannsdorf, with the intention of turning the left flank of *Kampfgruppe 356. Infanterie-Division* and seizing the Hohe Wand from the west. Although resisting with all of their might the Germans weren't strong enough to stop the Russians; all they could do was give ground slowly and extract the highest possible price in Russian blood.

Kampfgruppe 356. Infanterie-Division

Fighting again raged in the Schneeberg area. Most of the Hohe Wand remained in German hands, with *Kampfgruppe 356. Infanterie-Division* defending the north side and *SS-Kampfgruppe Keitel* defending in the south, where their energetic defense stopped Russian attacks at Puchberg, Waldegg and Wopfing.

6. Armee

Things on *General der Panzertruppe* Hermann Balck's left flank were going from bad to worse. The largely undefended areas led to deep and dangerous penetrations that he didn't have the reserves to stop. Bruck an der Mur had fallen a few days before, as had other towns and villages in the region. This was a dangerously deep penetration in any area where no forces blocked their way west.

The *III Panzerkorps* had been virtually split in two. Southwest of Pinggau, Friedberg fell, as did Sankt Lorenzen am Wechsel. Spearheads penetrated to the Lafnitz Valley and forced *1. Volksgrenadier-Division* to pull back.

Kampfgruppe Semmering

On the northern edge of the Semmering area, the *3./SS-Gebirgsjäger-Ausbildungs-und-Ersatz-Bataillon 13 Leoben* had been cut up and scattered during an attack late the previous day. In the process they had knocked out a Russian machine-gun nest, and now, after regrouping, wanted to go out and get it for themselves, but the Russians hiding in the nearby forest laid down a withering fire and drove them back. After nightfall, however, a single *SS-Untersturmführer* crept out with a few men under cover of darkness and brought it back without the Russians knowing it. Following these heroics the company was pulled out of the line for a few days of rest.

Sperrverband Motschmann

SS-Hauptsturmführer Motschmann had led his blocking formation with elan, but his sector was the most endangered on the entire *6. Armee* front. Nor were *Sperrverbande*, blocking formations, meant to be a long-term organization, so on 12 April his command was absorbed by *Divisionsgruppe Krause*.

Divisionsgruppe Krause

When ordered to form a *Divisionsgruppe* to fight the dangerous breakthrough at the front, *Generalleutnant* Krause established his command post at Vorau. With the opening of the Russian offensive against *6. Armee*'s center, Krause was instructed to block the Lafnitz valley to the north and he personally briefed *General der Panzertruppe* Hermann Breith on his plans. For the purposes of his mission, an *SS-Kampfgruppe* had already arrived in the area below Vorau the day before with two battalions, one artillery battery and strength of about 1,000 men. Many of them were older *Volksdeutsche* from Croatia, but while physically fit they had no combat experience.

Krause's formation had responsibility for the valley of the Lafnitz south of Mönichwald-Vorau, and was echeloned to the northwest on *1. Volksgrenadier Division*'s left flank. Intelligence reports indicated the Russians had fortified the high ground to the north, and motorized units were reinforcing them. Breith therefore ordered Krause to counterattack west of Bruck the following day, with the intention of cutting off the Russian spearheads. It was imperative that the attack succeed. Simultaneously, he was expected to secure the northern flank from the attacks that had started from the Twenty-Sixth Army in the east.

With the mounting ferocity of the assaults on *1. Volks-Gebirgs-Division*, Krause was obliged to return the three battalions of mountain troops to their parent division, which is why he was given *Sperrverband Motschmann*.

1. Volks-Gebirgs-Division

According to Stavka's order to launch the Graz offensive no later than 12 April, the Twenty-Sixth Army renewed its offensive against *III Panzerkorps*. Pressure on the division came on both flanks and its center. Some elements hit *Kampfgruppe Semmering*, now coming to be known as *Kampfgruppe Raithel*, others drove into the void defended by the remnants of *Sperrverbande Motschmann*, while the strongest elements hit *Generalleutnant* Wittmann's mountaineers. This time they concentrated on the division's weakened right flank. With no time to erect new defenses it retreated all the way to the eastern heights above the valley of the Lafnitz. Pushing off from Grosspetersdorf, Sankt Michael im Burgenland and Güssing, in places they drove the Germans back 20 miles and more.

* * *

The citizens of Fürstenfeld had been watching the fighting to their east with unease, but so far the authorities had allowed them to go about their daily routines. That all changed with the success of the Russian offensive against *1. Volks-Gebirgs-Division*. On 12 April a mandatory evacuation order sent 3,000 people out of the city to the west, adding to the ocean of refugees already flooding the countryside.

* * *

The town of Kukmirn fell without a fight as the Germans retreated into the hills near the Zellenberg, the beautiful mountain that overlooked Güssing Castle. Numerous trenches and bunkers had already been dug there and when the Russian infantry attacked, they were repulsed. Some of the Russians filtered around the back, where the *Gebirgsjägers* themselves dug trenches, but attacks there also failed, despite the profligate use of artillery and self-propelled assault guns. During the night the two sides exchanged heavy rifle and machine-gun fire.[15]

---

15   Brettner, *Die Letzten Kämpfe Band I*, p. 41.

Kampfgruppe 3. Panzer-Division

As the division to their north withdrew, so did the Armored Bears, taking up positions at Kaltenbrunn and the mountain just to its south. The little town of gingerbread chalets was built into the side of a gentle slope, whose grass was that bright shade of green only seen in early spring. Soon enough, however, the green carpet spewed clumps of black soil as Russian mortars and artillery raked the German entrenchments. By dusk the advance spearheads reached the town and were met by the *Volkssturm*. The old men and boys stood their ground and tried to protect their homes but it was hopeless. They were overrun with very heavy casualties, many of them dying in what was literally their front yard.

The division again pulled back, this time to Dietersdorf. Morale had plummeted since the halcyon days at Heiligenkreuz when the locals plied them with food and cigarettes. Now, instead of giving them bread and cheese, they were met with patriotic slogans pasted to the walls of buildings: "*Panzerfaust und deutscher Landsers sind starker als rote Panzer,*" (the *Panzerfaust* and the *Landser* are stronger than Red tanks).[16] A bottle of schnapps and a cigarette would have been much more appreciated. In the event the division had to pull back yet again, this time to Altenmarkt.

2. Panzerarmee

At the center of the army's front, *23. Panzer-Division* was hit with day-long attacks in company strength, with heavy artillery and mortar support, but none were strong enough to break through. In repelling the assaults, the Germans inflicted heavy casualties on the attackers. But on their left it was a different story. The weak elements of *44. Infanterie-Division Hoch und Deutschmeister* disintegrated under a strong attack. A few remnants attached themselves to the panzer division but otherwise there was nothing left of them. A reserve company was brought forward to screen that broken flank but not to counterattack: there wasn't strength for that. And so another hole had been ripped in the line.

The Russians were finally ready to renew their push to separate *Heeresgruppe Süd* from *Heeresgruppe E*. In good weather on the southern end of the front strong attacks drove against the Mur River line. Further south the Russians had pushed across the river and began to attack northeast, into the space between the Mur and the Drava.

---

16   Veterans, *Armored Bears*, p. 285.

13

Friday, 13 April

Heeresgruppe Süd

After the brief cooling of the day before, the weather again turned warm and sunny. This boded ill for the Germans and gave the Red Army a chance to rain bombs and bullets on the last defenders of Vienna. *Luftflotte 4* flew in response and the outnumbered *Luftwaffe* struck the Russians hard, but compared to the hell on Earth around the Floridsdorfer Bridge it was a pin prick. Fortunately for the Germans, the Russians' aim was as terrible as usual. What the swarms of IL-2 Sturmoviks' rain of bombs and bullets on Vienna managed to accomplish was mostly to blow up more buildings and fill the air with more smoke and brick dust.

Throughout the army group's area the ammunition shortage had become critical. High-value targets were often passed up because nobody had artillery shells to engage them. The Germans were running out of everything, including Germans.

But rumors ran rife in the city. One of the more plausible ones said that the former *Gauleiter*, Baldur von Schirach, had taken up arms to defend his *Gau* and been killed in the final days. Garnishments to the initial rumor said that opposition forces had hung his body from the Floridsdorfer Bridge. The plausibility comes from von Schirach's undoubted courage under fire early in the war. He was still a *Wehrmacht Leutnant*, after all, and while the Viennese had joked about him being the first into the air raid shelter, one thing von Schirach was not was a coward. But neither did he seek out danger if he could avoid it.

After fleeing Vienna he showed up at *6. SS-Panzerarmee* headquarters. Probably wanting to get rid of him, Dietrich put von Schirach to work as a liaison to his outlying corps and division commanders.

North of the Danube

8. Armee

The fight for Hohenau an der March flared up again around dawn and the Russians pushed into the center of town, but a German counterattack backed by three Tiger IIs drove the Russians back to their starting positions on the southern edge of town. Hohenau had an unusual number of ponds and lakes that were used for cooling at the sugar factory, and these limited the avenues of approach the Russians could take. After this defeat fighting died down for the day as the Russians regrouped.

* * *

Large-scale attacks hammered the Aspern area in a desperate attempt to cut off *II SS-Panzerkorps* before it could withdraw across the Danube, but none of the attacks gained much ground. Moreover, by this point most of the corps was across the Danube on the north bank anyway.

To the northwest, however, a much more dangerous situation threatened both *II SS-Panzerkorps* and *XXXXIII Armeekorps*. After elements of the *Führer-Grenadier-Division* helped stop them the day before, a large armored force drove southwest from the Grossebersdorf area, shoving the Germans all the way back to Hagenbrunn, a mere four miles from Korneuberg. And, if that wasn't threatening enough, during the night part of the Russian 34th Guards Rifle Division crossed the Danube under cover of an artillery and mortar barrage. Starting from the southern shoreline near Kritzendorf, they landed west of Korneuberg and formed a bridgehead.

Just like the previous year in the Falaise Gap, and the previous month around Lake Balaton, the Germans now found themselves having to withdraw through a narrow corridor being shelled from all sides and under heavy air attack. Korneuberg was especially hard-hit. The city had already endured days of Russian bombing from the Red Air Force, but on 13 April it reached a crescendo as advance Russian infantry units fought their way northward out of the bridgehead over the Danube, on Korneuberg's south side.

* * *

At Gross-Enzersdorf, during the night and under cover of a staggering mortar barrage, Russian snipers infiltrated the town. At daybreak they began taking a heavy toll on the defenders, and with the Russian penetration to the north the Germans in the town found themselves at the far end of a shrinking sack.

As for the Russian Forty-Sixth Army, it committed four divisions to the continuing attack toward the west, hitting both the *Führer-Grenadier-Division* and *37. SS-Freiwilligen-Kavallerie-Division Lützow*. Despite a German willingness to stand and die, the Russians simply had too much firepower to be stopped for long.

37. SS-Freiwilligen-Kavallerie-Division Lützow

Lützow returned *Grenadier-Regiment 284* to its parent formation, the *Kampfgruppe 96. Infanterie-Division*, giving up its primary infantry component. Following this, the remaining elements launched an ill-advised counterattack toward Aspern. It is unknown now who ordered the attack, or why, since German salvation lay to the west, not the east. Regardless of where the order came from, however, *Lützow*'s assault failed, with heavy casualties.

Vienna

6. SS-Panzerarmee
II SS-Panzerkorps

By the morning of 13 April most of the corps was over the Danube to the north side, and looking forward to a well-earned period of rest and regrouping. But with Russian spearheads within four miles of Korneuberg they were in more danger than ever of being trapped. Fatigue, lack of ammunition and fuel, and depleted numbers didn't matter now; the only thing that did was escaping through a narrow neck that led through Korneuberg.

Map 7 *6. Armee, 2. Panzerarmee* and the defense of Central and South Austria.

Kampfgruppe 6. Panzer-Division

When the survivors of the division withdrew over the Reich's Bridge the night before they were but a remnant of what they had been just ten days before. Hundreds of their comrades lay dead in the ruins of the city. The burned-out hulks of the division's armor littered the battlefield and, like most of its panzers, *Kampfgruppe 6. Panzer-Division* was virtually destroyed.

Kampfgruppe 3. SS-Panzer-Division Totenkopf

The failure to blow up the Reich's Bridge gave the Russians the chance they needed to cross the Danube into *XXXXIII Armeekorps'* rear areas on the north bank. To prevent that, the Germans covered it using anti-tank guns that could have been put to better use elsewhere.

Totenkopf's 9./SS-Panzer-Regiment 3 increased its working panzer total to 3 Tigers, as a Tiger II under repair joined the two Tiger Is and all three were joined by the last two operational Panthers. The division's Panzer Regiment should have numbered more than 120 machines, counting the *9. Kompanie*, but had been reduced to a mere five. This little force was dubbed *SS-Kampfgruppe Neff.*

According to author Ian Wood, another force, *SS-Kampfgruppe Langanke*, was attached to *Totenkopf* on 13 April, presumably because of the chaotic situation in the Vienna area. If Wood is correct this unit was powerful and contained most of *Das Reich's* remaining armor. Named after the commander of *2./I./SS-Panzer-Regiment 2*, Knights' Cross winner *SS-Obersturmführer* Fritz Langanke, the *Kampfgruppe* had 13 Panthers, nine Mark IVs, three Tiger IIs and even four *Bergepanthers*.[1] Having three different panzer types wasn't unusual at this stage of the war, and it's possible this *Kampfgruppe* was a combination of panzers from *Schwere-SS-Panzer-Abteilung 503* and *Das Reich.*

Concentrating all of the two panzer divisions' armor made sense, if that is in fact what happened. This increased its fighting power in accord with the *Wehrmacht's* doctrine of using panzers as a whole instead of parceling them out and gave the Germans' desperate situation north of the Danube a mobile striking force to keep the escape lanes open to the northwest. But this arrangement didn't last long, as *SS-Kampfgruppe Neff* ended the war with its five panzers but no *SS-Kampfgruppe Langanke*. It also contradicts the following story.

Regardless of the composition of *SS-Kampfgruppe Langanke*, one member of the *2./SS-Panzer-Regiment 2* didn't join either *Totenkopf* or *SS-Kampfgruppe Langanke*, because Arnold Friesen and Panther 227 had spent the night in the Brittgenau perimeter.

2. SS-Panzer-Division Das Reich

In Vienna, the end was near. No less than three Russian Guards corps had lined up to attack one badly depleted *Panzergrenadier* regiment, *SS-Panzergrenadier-Regiment Der Führer*: 9th Guards Tank Corps attacked on the northern flank, 9th Guards Mechanized Corps in the center and 39th Guards Rifle Corps in the south. Arnold Friesen's story might, or might not, be authentic. In

---

1   Wood, *Tigers*, p. 244. The *Bergepanther* was a battlefield recovery vehicle based on a Panther's chassis, except with a large winch and cable system in place of the turret. It should be noted that Wood's account of *Kampfgruppe Langanke* is unsupported by other sources.

relating it here the author believes it is probably true, but in any case is representative of the situation in the bridgehead on 13 April.

At 4:00 a.m. *General der Infanterie* von Bünau, who had been given the dubious honor of commanding the Vienna bridgehead, realized the extent of the mess he'd inherited. During a meeting with *Das Reich*'s commander, *SS-Standartenführer* Rudolf Lehmann, he immediately recognized the horrific conditions extant in *Das Reich*'s sector and the hopelessness of the situation. Yet a message from *OKW* on 13 April, countersigned by *Generalfeldmarschall* Keitel, *Reichsführer-SS* Himmler and *Reichsleiter* Bormann, made it clear that any thought of retreat was out of the question: "Cities are located at important traffic junctions. They must therefore be defended and held to the utmost...all *Kampfkommandanten* are personally responsible to ensure that these orders are obeyed. If they behave contrary to their soldierly duties, then they will be...sentenced to death."[2] This meant that von Bünau's family was in danger if he ordered an evacuation, which is probably why Bittrich gave the responsibility for defending the last toehold back to him.

For the exhausted SS men still holding the perimeter around the Floridsdorf Bridge, the situation was dire. It was obvious they couldn't hold off the Russians much longer. As dawn approached and Russian attacks began for the day, *Das Reich*'s tenuous hold on the last small slice of the city south of the Danube would be under continuous Soviet assault. And then von Bünau discovered the worst of it: *Totenkopf* was no longer on *Das Reich*'s left flank. Without informing anyone from *Das Reich*, during the night both *6. Panzer-Division* and *Totenkopf* withdrew across the *Reichsbrücke*, the Reich Bridge, and did so in such haste that it wasn't destroyed as it should have been. The Russians had their bridge over the Danube, although traversing it was impossible due to no less than six 37mm *Flak* cannon and multiple 88mm guns covering its span.

And so, instead of a near-suicidal charge over the *Reichsbrücke*, 1st Guards Mechanized Corps wasted no time in attacking the vacated space around the Northwest Train Station. The loss of this key urban feature was particularly devastating, as the layout of the marshalling yards and station meant the Russians would have had to attack down a long, open area toward the main terminal building, much like castles and forts had cleared areas adjacent to their walls to provide a clear field of fire. It was a killing zone similar to that held by *Totenkopf* around the *Südbahnhof* and Arsenal during the previous week.

Now, from the very last man of regiment *Der Führer* on the left flank all the way to the Danube, there was nothing to keep the Russians from grabbing the Floridsdorfer Bridge too. *Der Führer* was already spread thin. The perimeter was held by its already depleted battalions, remnants hastily cobbled together with a few panzers in support. They totaled no more than a thousand men and covering hundreds of yards of new front wasn't possible, so von Bünau had no choice but to pull back from the line of the canal they had successfully defended for two days, and into a perimeter some seven hundred yards long that secured the left flank. He didn't fool himself that the new positions could be defended for long, though.

Throughout the day heavy artillery and mortar fire rained down on the defenders, filling the air with shell splinters and causing scores of casualties. The less seriously wounded who could walk formed a steady stream heading to Floridsdorf over the bridge, darting this way and that to avoid incoming fire. Stretcher cases piled up under the bridge supports where, to show support for the men in the perimeter, not only the three command staffs of *Der Führer*'s battalions but also the regimental staff and the division commander all stayed behind to direct the defense. This was in addition to *General der Infanterie* von Bünau, who refused to take cover and exposed himself to Russian fire: "One got the impression that he was finished with life and hoped to die from the

2   Weidinger, *Das Reich*, p. 385.

enemy fire as he saw no other way out."[3] Compounding the problems of holding the perimeter was the deafening noise level created by constant explosions, gunfire, low-flying aircraft, tank engines and shouting. Firing back from the German side were the division's remaining artillery with an orphan Army *Flak* battery of 88mm guns that had asked to be attached to *Das Reich.* The range was so close that shells screaming over the defenders' heads landed mere yards in front of their positions. This cacophony made even the transmittal of the simplest orders difficult. Men standing beside each other had to yell to be heard.

The perimeter shrank during the day as the Russians pressed hard to wipe out the SS men. At one point the line shrank below 200 yards and only immediate counterattacks managed to expand it again. Both Lehmann and von Bünau knew that if their men were not withdrawn north of the Danube soon they were lost, and the last moment for that withdrawal was drawing perilously close. This created a conflict, since von Bünau's very life was at stake if he withdrew, while Lehmann had no intention of sacrificing his men for no purpose. Yet both men knew that 13 April had to be their final day in Brittgenau if they were going to survive.

Now that the Russians had captured a bridge, though, a withdrawal during daylight would draw the concentrated fire of every Red Army gun that could be brought to bear. Such a storm of both direct and indirect fire would spatter the area with bullets and shell splinters that nothing could live through. And so there was no choice but to somehow hang on for one more day… if they could. In the meantime, von Bünau sent his operations officer to find Sepp Dietrich and request permission to withdraw to the north bank. Dietrich agreed.

* * *

In the pre-dawn darkness, made worse by the drifting clouds of ash and smoke, *SS-Oberscharführer* Ernst Barkmann's damaged Panther drove into a deep shell crater near the approaches to the bridge and couldn't be salvaged. The clumsy communication system forced on the crew by the previous day's damage had, in the end, proven fatal to their panzer. Instead of driving instructions being given instantly over the tank's communications system, they were relayed by shouting, and in the hazy darkness that proved too slow to avoid the crater. With no prime-movers in the perimeter, and none of those unarmored vehicles able to cross the bridge under fire, the Germans could not pull the stricken Panther from its grave. One well-placed shot from a *Panzerfaust* destroyed the damaged panzer once and for all, while Barkmann and his crew picked up weapons to fight as infantry.

Arnold Friesen and the crew of Panther 227 were awakened at 4:00 a.m. and ordered to report to the bridgehead command post, where both the *Das Reich* commander Lehmann and *General der Infanterie* von Bünau gave them new orders. The divisional headquarters for *Das Reich* had been moved to the north bank of the Danube, but the forward post was still inside the perimeter. According to Mansoor, Friesen and his men were told that during the night "guerillas destroyed four tanks".[4] Regardless of whether or not this was true, with the other tanks gone Friesen's Panther would have to take their place.

SS-Sturmbannführer Schmidt was in tactical charge of the defense and ordered Friesen's tank to cover the river road, the Handelskai, on the east side. Running beside the Danube, the Handelskai was broad and fairly straight, with trolley tracks and trees on its landward side, affording open fields of fire in both directions. The other roads were all wired with explosives, choked with rubble

3   Weidinger, *Das Reich*, p. 387.
4   Barkmann is said to have been leading three Panthers over the bridge when his tank was struck by a *Panzerfaust*, yet there is no further mention of these tanks being in the perimeter. This could provide evidence that such tanks were destroyed during the night, just as was reported. Or perhaps this was confused with Boska's attempt to reinforce the bridgehead during the afternoon of the next day.

and covered by *Panzergrenadiers* armed with anti-tank weapons, but because of its wide, straight construction, the Handelskai was difficult to block. Nevertheless, concrete dragon's teeth and steel railway rails had been scavenged and put up as barricades, and these at least might slow down attacking armor.

The two available tanks could hide behind those, one on either of the perimeter's flanks. The less-threatened western road would be covered by the lone Mark IV that was the last operable machine from *6./SS-Panzer-Regiment 2*. Protecting the more vulnerable eastern flank would be Friesen's mission.[5] Also blocking the Handelskai was a battery of two 75mm *PAK-40* anti-tank guns set up behind sandbags, with a few *Panzergrenadiers* for support. Friesen used the foliage in the riverfront park for cover and waited, with the Danube on his left.

Around 8:00 a.m. the Russians began attacking the eastern flank that Friesen was guarding. Their plan was to drive straight down the Handelskai, dodging the steel rails to seize the bridge in a *coup de main*, thus cutting off the entire perimeter and seizing the bridge intact. Under the bridge supports, the most severely wounded SS men were being sheltered until they could be evacuated by night. In Russian hands their fate would be sealed. The mission for Friesen and his Panther was to prevent that regardless of the cost.

The day's action began with a lone T-34 probing down the road to gauge the strength of the German defenses. It was quickly destroyed by a shot to its rear hull and exploded in a storm of shrapnel. As the morning went on four more tanks popped out of side roads and were quickly dealt with in their exposed flanks. A jeep full of drunken Russians came down the road until the Panther's machine guns riddled them. Russian infantry kept creeping forward, building to building, and Friesen's panzer was hit by several rifle grenades, which did no damage. Not willing to risk a lucky hit, Friesen used his main gun and machine guns to collapse the buildings and drive off or kill the infantry inside. By this time, seizing the bridge by a *coup de main* was an obvious failure.

Air raids by IL-2s began in the early afternoon and continued throughout the day, doing as much damage to the Russians as the Germans. The planes dropped their payloads seemingly at random from level flight. Sometime around 2:00 p.m. Friesen was told that a Stalin tank was parked on a side road some 75 meters from the Handelskai. It turned out to be a JS-II from the 5th Guards Tank Corps, the heaviest Russian tank to see action on the Eastern Front.[6] Reconnoitering through the smashed concrete and glass clogging the streets, Friesen found the tank with an infantry squad perched on top, oblivious of anything more than enjoying the spoils of war. Going back to his tank, he carefully planned his attack and practiced it with his crew. As German infantry fired their weapons to drown out the sound of the Panther moving, Friesen moved into position, his gunner fired one round and hit the Stalin forward and just below the turret ring. The Stalin exploded before three *Panzerfauste* from the infantry hit it again, one after another, while machine-gun fire raked up and down the street. The Russians were wiped out.

As the afternoon wore on the Russians brought up an anti-tank gun to try and force the river road, but Panther 227 destroyed that as well as three more T-34s that showed up. A round from the anti-tank gun glanced off the Panther's glacis plate, doing no damage but scaring Friesen's crew. A non-penetrating round slamming into a tank was a loud and shocking reminder that just outside their armored skin a dangerous enemy wanted their blood. Life and death was a matter of millimeters, in this case millimeters of steel armor. Around 4:00 p.m. four more T-34s came roaring down the road, trying to force their way through with speed and surprise. At a range of

---

5   There were also two 75-mm *PAK-40* guns to support the tanks, but their effect on the fighting is unknown.

6   To this day there are some sources who insist that the JS-III tank was used during the war, and specifically in the Battle of Vienna, but this author was unable to verify this.

300 yards Friesen ordered "feuer!" The panzer's high-velocity 75mm round struck the first T-34's turret and knocked it askew. The four tanks swerved into side roads, exposing their flanks, and three were hit and destroyed before they could escape. By this point the Handelskai was littered with flaming tanks and dead Russians.

Later in the afternoon the Russians managed to set up an anti-tank gun and fired one round at Friesen's panzer, but the shell glanced off its glacis plate. In return it was destroyed, possibly by the Germans' *PAK 40s*. At some point during the fighting Panther 227's turret had become jammed: whether from battle damage or some other reason Friesen didn't know. He ordered the tank moved into an underground garage as night drew near. Friesen and his radioman, *SS-Unterscharführer* Gunter Rau, grabbed *Panzerfauste* and spread out to guard the tank while it was being repaired.

* * *

Confusion in the defense was further aggravated when the commander of *Das Reich*, *SS-Standartenführer* Rudolf Lehmann, was wounded by a shell splinter in the early afternoon and had to be evacuated to the north bank of the Danube. Division commanders didn't usually put themselves in the front lines, but there could be no denying the effect on the common soldier when the man in charge risked his own life fighting beside them. Likewise, *General der Infanterie* von Bünau stalked among the defenders with a stick grenade stuck in his belt, smoking and offering words of encouragement. Such gestures couldn't entirely make up for a lack of numbers and munitions, but they helped. Before leaving, Lehmann issued orders to *Der Führer*'s commander, *SS-Obersturmbannführer* Otto Weidinger, to evacuate the bridgehead after dark, which directly contradicted von Bünau's determination to go down fighting to the last. Seeing no other choice, von Bünau sent a second courier to find Sepp Dietrich and ask for further orders.

As the day's fighting had worn on, the Germans tried to send Friesen some help. Twenty-four-year-old *SS-Obersturmführer* Karl-Heinz Boska, commanding officer of *6./SS-Panzer-Regiment 2*, was ordered by wounded division commander Lehmann to round up his tanks on the northern side of the bridge and lead them into the dwindling bridgehead. According to Kurowski, Lehmann was still in the perimeter and gave the order for Boska's attack to Ernst Barkmann and his crew, who were fighting on foot, to carry across the bridge.[7] Barkmann backs up this version of events. During daylight any movement on the bridge drew a hail of fire, from both sides of the Danube. Barkmann and his men reportedly dodged among the spans and supports while crossing the bridge, with the river swirling far below, and miraculously nobody was hit.[8]

This is yet another example of the confusion surrounding the entire campaign. In Boska's case other sources indicate that he was given the order directly from Lehmann, but with Lehmann still in the perimeter and Boska on the opposite side of the river, this seems unlikely, unless Lehmann had already crossed the river after being wounded.[9] Regardless of how he was told, Boska was not a man to shrink from a hard mission. Boska had won the Knight's Cross more than a year before, in December 1943 and was a hardened veteran of countless fights, not a man to be easily daunted; but he was a man who knew a suicide mission when he saw one, and recrossing the bridge in daylight, in tanks, bordered on suicide.

---

7   This indicates that the German commander either was not in radio communication with his division across the river, which seems highly improbable, or that the Russians were listening and he did not want to give them warning that Boska would be leading tanks back across the river.

8   Kurowski, *Panzer Aces III*, p. 18.

9   Lehmann was hit by a shell splinter in the knee. Photographs also show him with his arm in a sling standing beside the Floridsdorfer Bridge on 13 April. Despite the danger, he was evacuated across the bridge by two field policemen who carried a rifle as he sat on it.

Some sources have stated that Boska protested the mission face-to-face with Lehmann, basing his misgivings on the narrowness of the bridge and its inability to support the weight of his Panthers in its damaged state, that the Russians had the bridge under direct fire, and that the necessary slowness of their crossing would make them perfect targets for the eager Soviet gunners. These sources state that Lehmann was having none of it, however, and that he rejected Boska's argument because without reinforcement the perimeter could not hold out until nightfall and this made the risk worthwhile. It was then up to Boska to figure out how to accomplish what appeared to be a one-way mission without getting everybody involved killed, himself included.

The problem with this scenario is that according to most sources, Lehmann was on one side of the Danube and Boska was on the other, and it directly contradicts Kurowski's claim that Ernst Barkmann carried Lehmann's order across the bridge to Boska. If, however, one substitutes Barkmann for Lehmann in Boska's account – that is, Boska argued with the man who actually delivered the orders, Barkmann, and not the man who gave the orders, Lehmann – then the scenario makes sense. Barkmann was the messenger and the scene seems more likely by seeing Boska protesting his mission to a fellow tank commander, rather than the division commander. Whichever is the actual case, though, Boska was left trying to figure out how to get across the river without getting killed.

The only vehicles Boska had to choose from were assorted remnants. The situation made the lighter Panzer IVs and the one remaining *Jagdpanther* unsuitable, the first being too lightly armored to survive the heavy anti-tank fire they would inevitably draw, while the second was too large and heavy for the damaged bridge. The only option was to use Panthers. Boska stated that he could not possibly force his men to undertake such a dangerous mission without him, so he left his own command *Jagdpanther*, took over the Panther and crew of *SS-Obersturmführer* Wahlmann and selected two other Panthers to support him.[10]

The three panzers moved forward together and halted short of the bridge. Boska and the two other vehicle commanders went forward to carry out a final reconnaissance of the bridge before attempting to cross. The only crossing plan that made sense was for each tank to wait until the one in front was halfway across before starting, with the third following by the same margin. Boska felt that it was likely the first Panther would be destroyed on the bridge and gave the order that in this event, the other two vehicles were to abandon the attempt to cross and withdraw. He also told the others that his tank would be in the lead.

Boska's Panther crept slowly onto the damaged bridge and made it to the large hole in the centre without incident, at which point the second tank, commanded by Ludwig van Hecke, moved onto the approaches of the bridge. Once Boska had passed the centre of the bridge he ordered his driver to speed up and head for cover. Roaring off the bridge into Pater Abel Platz, the Panther found itself the target of a storm of Soviet fire which ripped into the hull and penetrated, killing both the driver and the radio operator. The Panther caught fire immediately and Boska and the two surviving crewmen scrambled away from the flaming tank before the main gun ammunition began to explode.[11] Falling awkwardly, Boska broke his right foot and only made it to safety with the help of his two subordinates. The destroyed panzer burned for hours, but Boska and his crew were able to escape across the Danube once darkness fell. Seeing the destruction of their leader, the

10   Kurowski, *Panzer Aces III*, p. 18. Kurowski says that Boska was ordered to lead all of his Panthers back into the bridgehead, and that total was five, not three.

11   Kurowski, *Panzer Aces III*, p. 18. Once again Kurowski differs on exactly what happened, saying that Boska's crew was killed and he was badly wounded, with the maintenance sergeant of *6./SS-Panzer-Regiment 2* commandeering a motorcycle with sidecar, then racing across the bridge to pick up the wounded Boska before returning to the north shore, all the while dodging Soviet fire.

remaining Panthers followed Boska's order and abandoned the attempt to get across the bridge. No further attempts were made.

Barkmann stated that all three Panthers were destroyed and that a different tank commander was the man rescued from the middle of the bridge.[12] The weight of evidence seems to support the first version.

All efforts to reinforce the bridgehead had failed because the Soviet noose had been drawn too tight. The last sliver of Vienna was slipping away. Attacks continued in remorseless house-to-house fighting. As the perimeter shrank around the bridge the Red Army captured the Brigitte Kapelle just west of Abel Pater Platz. As the Germans had done, they began bringing their dead and wounded there, and are said to have executed wounded SS men they found there.

* * *

By 4:00 p.m. von Bünau's representative had returned with orders from Dietrich to withdraw at nightfall. Now the *Kampfkommandant* had the orders he needed to protect his family and agreed to the withdrawal. Ambulances were assembled near the north end of the bridge and the wounded were laid on blankets so they could be carried across. But as evening approached the Russians launched one final assault in an effort to wipe out the Germans. By now the lines of the SS had been thinned to the point where they couldn't hold, until a final barrage from German artillery broke the back of the Russian attacks.

As full darkness settled in around 7:00 p.m. the evacuation of the bridgehead began. As men approached the bridge they were assigned in groups of four to carry a wounded man across the river. Only then did the *Panzergrenadiers* still manning the perimeter begin to pull out. Small groups of *Panzergrenadiers* and some SPWs withdrew over the bridge, careful to avoid the hole in the center. No fire came to interrupt the movements until around 8:30 p.m., when tanks could be heard approaching the bridge.

By this time the perimeter had largely been emptied and only the rearguard remained. The only weapons to oppose these tanks were *Panzerfauste,* since Panther 227 still sheltered in its underground hiding spot while the crew worked to repair the jammed turret. With Russian tanks on the prowl Friesen feared the bridge might be blown before he and his men could evacuate. For the *Waffen-SS*, capture by Russians was virtually a death sentence. Once assured the bridge would not be blown before they could get across, Friesen and his radio operator, 20-year-old *SS-Scharführer* Günther Rau, went hunting with their *Panzerfauste*. Four T-34s had formed a circle in Pater Abel Platz and stopped in the dark, but without infantry support.

No doubt the flames and smoke made for a hellish scene of dancing shadows amid the ruins as Friesen and Rau darted through the darkness toward the Russians. As if sensing danger, the Russians started their tanks and began moving back to their own lines, but it was too late. Friesen destroyed two of the tanks at close range and Rau clipped one but didn't stop it. The two surviving T-34s accelerated into the darkness. For the day Friesen's score stood at 13 tanks and one anti-tank gun destroyed.

By the time Friesen and Rau made their way back to the underground garage the turret had been fixed. The destruction of the two T-34s had checked any further Russian advances and during the lull the Germans accelerated their pull-out. The infantry had built a wall of sandbags, and in the best tradition of the *Waffen-SS* Friesen pulled his tank behind it to act as rearguard. He was still nervous that the bridge might be blown before he and his crew could get across, but he was again assured that would not happen. The night quietened, and although the Russians must have

---

12   Weidinger, *Das Reich*, p. 387.

heard the troops and vehicles crossing the bridge, they didn't interfere. At 10:30 p.m. the Mark IV made it out,[13] closely followed by Friesen, who kept his turret pointed to the rear.

By 11:15 p.m. it was over. In 1938 *I./SS-Panzergrenadier-Regiment Der Führer* had been formed in Vienna right after the *Anschluss*. The battalion's first commander was Wilhelm Bittrich, now commanding *II SS-Panzerkorps*. Seven years after its inception the battalion left the city of its birth for the last time.

Vienna had fallen.

* * *

SS-Obersturmbannführer Rudolf Enseling, commander of *Das Reich*'s panzer regiment, told Friesen he should be awarded the Knight's Cross, although he never was. And even if the award had been authorized it was no sure thing that it would actually have been given, since even Germans whose decorations were officially approved didn't always receive them before the war ended. For example, the commander of *SS-Panzergrenadier-Regiment Der Führer*, *SS-Obersturmbannführer* Otto Weidinger, only found out that he was given the Swords to his Knight's Cross in 1951. The commendation had been approved on 6 May 1945, but in the confusion of the final days it was never awarded and he was never told.

* * *

After the battle, von Bünau openly wondered why the Russians didn't finish off the bridgehead when they had the chance. "I have no idea why the Russians did not hit us harder. They could easily have eliminated the forces at the bridgehead and could probably have taken the Floridsdorf Bridge…undamaged."[14]

* * *

At the close of day Tolbukhin and Malinovsky could report to Stavka they had fulfilled their primary mission of capturing Vienna according to the timetable they'd been given. It hadn't been easy and they accomplished this despite fierce resistance every step of the way, as evidenced by the heavy casualties their armies had suffered.

Maier quotes Russian sources as claiming 47,000 Germans taken prisoner, along with 633 tanks and 1,093 guns.[15] This is absurd on the face of it, particularly the tank figure. But while the Russians had inflicted very heavy losses on the defenders, what they hadn't done was destroy *II SS-Panzerkorps*.

Unfortunately reliable figures aren't available and probably never will be. No one knows how many alarm and *Volkssturm* battalions, training units, Hitler Youth companies, stragglers, conscripts, *Kampfgruppen* and men press-ganged into service without even an entry in their *Soldbuch* died an anonymous death in the cauldron of Vienna.

I SS-Panzerkorps
Korps Schultz

The overall situation in the corps' sector south of the Danube appeared no less dire. The Russian 18th Tank Corps had renewed its attack toward Sankt Pölten and a few penetrations were sealed

---

13   Some sources claim it had been destroyed in the fighting.
14   Maier, *Drama*, p. 377.
15   Maier, *Drama*, p. 360.

off with immediate counterattacks, although the Russian attacks had taken on a new scale and scope. East of those fights another series of attacks in the Kasten region were also stopped. Elsewhere though, seven miles northeast of Sankt Pölten, major attacks pushed forward behind 30 tanks and broke through, driving to the town of Böheimkirchen. Immediate counterattacks by *Panzer-Aufklärungs-Abteilung 1*, *Infanterie-Regiment 730* and a battery of small-caliber *Flak* guns slowed down the advance but couldn't stop it entirely. The nearby town of Kirchstetten, however, was retaken. Both towns of Kapelln and Böheimkirchen suffered heavy Russian assaults, but the Germans held them at great cost. Neither was captured by the Soviet attackers despite the use of tanks, artillery and aircraft, especially in the northern assault group, where they lost 10 tanks to German fire.

Further north, in the Danube Valley another Russian armored attack group with 30 more tanks and self-propelled artillery ripped open the German front and drove through Trasdorf and captured Sitzenberg. This put the Russian spearheads within 13 miles of the Danube bridges at Krems. To counter this wave of Russian armor, the only reinforcements the corps received were half a battalion of infantry from *710. Infanterie-Division*. The 105th Guards Rifle Division, part of 38th Guards Rifle Corps, reached the Traisen River at Sankt Andra an der Taisen. They wasted no time pushing patrols over a footbridge to Herzogenburg on the western side.

Alarm-Bataillone A, *B* and *C* performed as might be expected against combat-hardened Russian troops. The first two never got into position, while *Alarm-Bataillon C* was crushed in the fighting. The alarm battalions had barely slowed them down.

Kampfgruppe 12. SS-Panzer-Division Hitlerjugend

A definitive strength return for this day put *Hitlerjugend* at 7,731 men. Michael Reynolds speculates this had to be only the combat elements,[16] so the true number would probably be closer to 12,000 to 13,000.

Like a rubber band that is stretched too tight, on 13 April *Hitlerjugend*'s front line broke under a massive Russian assault. Sankt Corona am Schöpfl fell to this powerful Russian thrust, endangering not only the division's left flank but the whole position of *I SS-Panzerkorps*. The supply jugular for both SS panzer divisions, *Kampfgruppe 356. Infanterie-Division* and *SS-Kampfgruppe Keitel*, ran through the Gölsen Valley, a mere three miles south of Sankt Corona. If the Russians cut that road the entire German position in eastern Austria would be endangered.

SS-Brigadeführer Hugo Kraas had done all he could with the forces at hand, but protecting 16 miles with his depleted division, especially with its dearth of heavy weapons, was asking for the impossible. More breakthroughs could be expected. In response corps commander Hermann Preiss ordered *SS-Kampfgruppe Peiper* to take over the defense of Brand-Laaben. This shortened *Hitlerjugend*'s front and freed up troops for use elsewhere, which had been necessitated by the loss of *Kampfgruppe Grossamer*.

In the mountainous area northeast of Laaben bei Neulengbach the Russians assembled a large attack force and moved northwest, west and southwest early in the morning. The defenders of Laaben suffered under a massive rocket bombardment by Katyusha launchers and retreated to Forsthof, a settlement to the northeast that was little more than a farmstead. Heavy attacks around Groisbach were stopped only by committing every last man to the defense.

That proved successful also at Hinterholz, where *Flak* elements chewed up a Russian assault, but it wasn't enough at Oberkühlberg, north of Alland, where the Russians broke through elements of

SS-Kampfgruppe Gross. Contact with the *Kampfgruppe* was lost. And as had been obvious for days, the overstretched *Hitlerjugend* could not defend its long front successfully. Even accounting for the assistance of *SS-Kampfgruppe Peiper*, it wasn't strong enough.

The news in *Hitlerjugend's* center was better. Around Alland company-sized attacks pushed back the defenders initially, but the Germans stiffened and stopped the Russians in their tracks. On the right flank, however, the larger attacks to their south had resulted in the breakthrough to Waxeneck and Kraas had no resources to launch a counterattack. With danger on both flanks, if the *LAH* couldn't bring the situation under control *Hitlerjugend* would be forced to retreat again, or face being surrounded.

In the black of night the Russians launched a new attack, this time toward Schwarzensee. Taken by surprise, the defenders were overwhelmed and the Russians captured the town, endangering the entire position of both *Hitlerjugend* and the left flank of the *LAH*.

Kampfgruppe 1. SS-Panzer-Division Leibstandarte Adolf Hitler

The division listed its strength on hand as 10,552 but, like *Hitlerjugend*, didn't say if this was rifle or ration strength. In the case of *LAH* this was probably ration strength, that is to say all members of the division.

SS-Brigadeführer Otto Kumm knew that if he couldn't seal the Russian penetration at Waxeneck then the entire position of *I SS-Panzerkorps* was compromised. Yet he had no reserves to commit, so once again men had to be shifted from one hotspot to another. This time it was the remnants of *II./SS-Panzer-Regiment 1*.

Once upon a time, such redeployment would have meant climbing aboard trucks for transport to the assembly area near Weissenbach an der Triesting. But those days were long gone. Aside from the general lack of fuel, trucks were also in short supply, so the battalion spent the entire day marching over mountain trails into position and the attack didn't start until 4:30 p.m. Four companies had been assembled and, while exact numbers aren't available, a good estimate would be 200-300 men.

An attack that late in the day surprised the Russians, as the Germans moved through the rough, mountainous terrain to attack. A few precious artillery rounds were used in support and Pöllau was recaptured with only light resistance. The garrison fled, but in fleeing they warned the defenders of nearby Steinhof that a counterattack was underway. Outside the little mountain village of Steinhof the Red Army did what it had always done with newly captured territory; they fortified it. A *Pakfront* with three 76mm guns, guarded by a lot of machine guns, stopped the Germans short of the village. Try as they might, without heavy weapons there was no breaking the Russian defense before night fell.

Elsewhere, *SS-Panzergrenadier-Regiment 2* took the last step before actually disbanding when it dissolved the supply elements, leaving only a few men to distribute the bare essentials. By doing this the combat element was increased, but such a situation could only last so long. Someone had to procure the food, fuel, ammunition and other necessities, and then distribute them to the men at the front, otherwise the fighting units had to detail their own men to do those tasks.[17]

Pushing southeast, late in the day the forward elements of the *Kampfgruppe* met the panzer men of *II./SS-Panzer-Regiment 1* in the mountains southwest of Berndorf. Tenuous though it might be, the *LAH* once again had a contiguous front.

---

17 Tiemann, *The Leibstandarte IV/2*, p. 295.

Kampfgruppe 356. Infanterie-Division

In the region around the Hohe Wand, the Germans finally ran out of men to hold onto the mountain's crest. Once that peak fell the Russians pursued the survivors to the southwest, west and northwest. It wasn't quite a breakthrough, but given the gap between the right flank of *Kampfgruppe 356. Infanterie-Division* and *6. Armee* it had the potential for disaster.

SS-Kampfgruppe Keitel

Assault groups of 30-80 men hit the *Kampfgruppe* throughout the day but made no inroads. The rough terrain made deploying larger groups difficult, both to control and to supply. Coordination of attacks was also lacking.

6. Armee

Despite all efforts *6. Armee* and *6. SS-Panzerarmee* hadn't yet joined their fronts when the Russians renewed their assault on Hermann Balck's command using the 5th Guards Cavalry Corps, as the German intelligence service had forecast, along with two rifle corps. The brunt of the blow fell on *III Panzerkorps* in the vicinity of the Lafnitz Valley, and the Russians immediately penetrated the front lines using armor.

The 5th Guards Cavalry Corps was commanded by the aggressive and veteran Major General S.I. Gorshkov. He was not an officer to underestimate. In typical Soviet fashion he put accomplishment of the mission ahead of all other considerations, including losses, because Russian generals who expended their men's lives in pursuit of their assigned tasks were less likely to be punished for failure.

Balck's comments about this attack in his memoirs are typical of the work: "Along the left flank where the *6. SS-Panzerarmee* had not established a tie-in with us, five Russian divisions facing only minor resistance marched toward Graz through a gaping hole between Pinkafeld and the Semmering Pass."[18] At no point in his account of the fighting in Austria was anything ever his fault, although in truth he conducted the best defensive campaign possible with his limited resources. He blamed the *Waffen-SS* even though *6. SS-Panzerarmee* had no more resources than he did, but also gave an accurate picture of events. The truth is that neither Dietrich's army nor Balck's had enough men, panzers, food, fuel, ammunition or air cover to do more than make the Russians pay a high price for capturing Austria. Nobody was to blame except Adolf Hitler.

* * *

Balck and his staff couldn't figure out Marshal Tolbukhin's ultimate purpose in this new offensive. Either it was an attempt to take *Kampfgruppe Semmering* from behind to open the pass, an encircling movement to the south meeting a second pincer coming through the Raab Valley to destroy *III Panzerkorps*, or a straight push west to sever *6. Armee* from the rest of *Heeresgruppe Süd*. All were possible and all made sense, but the Russians gave no indication of which direction they would go.

---

18   Balck, *Order in Chaos*, p. 426.

What Balck did know was that if the Russians really wanted to split his army in two, they could do it. He had nothing to stop them. But one more thing he didn't know was that the Russians were about to stop themselves.

The Russians

There was a good reason the Germans couldn't figure out the Russians' intentions, because the Russians didn't know themselves. One leading theory is that they would drive as far as Fischbach and then halt without driving into territory that would later become the British zone of occupation. After all, why spend blood to capture territory you planned to hand over to your allies?

But there are several reasons why this might not be true. Stalin had growing paranoia over the possibility of an Anglo-German alliance. Ample evidence for this will be given later in the narrative timeline, but the further west his forces got before the war ended, the more bargaining power he had after the war. His actions in the conquered territories of Austria also make it clear that he wanted the country in his sphere of influence; that is, with a pro-Soviet socialist government. The machinations already underway in Vienna make this quite clear, as did the installation of pro-Soviets later on in Graz, Sankt Pölten and elsewhere.

However, other fronts had higher priority for the use of troops. Second Ukrainian Front, in particular, had a lot of territory to conquer in Czechoslovakia. That country had been a democratic republic before the war and Stalin had no intention of allowing that to happen again, so Marshal Malinovsky had to beat the Americans to the punch. To that end, Tolbukhin at Third Ukrainian Front was ordered to transfer Sixth Guards Tank Army to Second Ukrainian Front, and to withdraw Ninth Army into reserve for deployment into Czechoslovakia, too.

The loss of these two armies greatly relieved the pressure on *6. SS-Panzerarmee*'s center and right flank, although fighting still raged in both places as fiercely as ever for the rest of the war. As for *6. Armee*, this limited Tolbukhin's ability to reinforce his successes, such as Twenty-Sixth Army was then creating, or to continue reinforcing success. The effect of losing those armies would be felt very soon.

* * *

Twenty-Sixth Army's offensive kicked into high gear as 30th Rifle Corps attacked on the northwest toward the Hochwechsel, 5th Guards Cavalry Corps in the center aiming for Fischbach and 135th Rifle Corps pinning down *Divisionsgruppe Krause* and *1. Volks-Gebirgs-Division* on the Russian left. The fresh 11th Guards Cavalry Division headed northwest from its jumping-off point west of Freidberg supported by strong armored forces, while 36th Rifle Division was assigned the capture of the Hochwechsel and Waldbach, and both 68th and 155th Rifle Divisions moved southwest toward Vorau, Puchegg and Schachen.

Kampfgruppe Semmering

The Russian breakthrough to the south put the *Kampfgruppe* in a precarious position. If it held its ground then it would have to strengthen the defensive line facing south to prevent being taken in the flank. But that would require drawing off forces from defending the pass itself. *Oberst* Raithel was like other German commanders with too few resources and too many gaps in their defenses; they could only move men from crisis to crisis and hope for the best.

* * *

In order to limit Raithel's options and possibly break through on their own, the Russians around the Semmering Pass never stopped attacking. The fight at the Kobermannsberg and Klamm never let up, with Russians attacking nearly every day at least once, and sometimes twice. Night attacks were common, and during storms and bad weather they redoubled their efforts, since it was impossible to hear them coming through the forest. The *SS-Gebirgsjägers* defending the area never broke and repelled all attacks, despite their inexperience and poor armaments. Gradually they captured Russian weapons to replace the antiquated and inferior ones they'd been issued.

Whenever the attacks looked like they might break through, the Germans would fire a few precious *Panzerfauste*, which though intended to penetrate armor also caused great damage to infantry. This was especially true in heavy woods, where one round might topple a huge tree or fill the air with splinters. This usually had the effect of stopping the Russian charge in its tracks. German losses mostly came from mortar and artillery fire, or in counterattacks, but even so late in the war fresh replacements kept filling up the *3./SS-Gebirgsjäger-Ausbildungs-und-Ersatz-Bataillon 13 Leoben*.

The company fought all over the area, including next to the *Luftwaffe* men of *Kampfgeschader 27 Boelcke*. During one particularly strong attack a *Luftwaffe* platoon broke and ran, but the SS company commander stopped them with his reserve platoon and distributed them in his own front lines. The implication seemed clear enough; run again and we'll shoot you in the back. After bringing up more men, and a short but very accurate artillery bombardment, the SS attacked and retook the lost *Luftwaffe* positions. By the end of the war the surviving *Luftwaffe* men had developed into very good soldiers, despite having no formal ground combat training.[19]

Despite getting no positive results, the Russians kept attacking, day after day, and their men kept dying on the same killing fields. They didn't stop until the war ended.

* * *

On the Harterkogel the little-known *SS-Kampfgruppe Schoffer*, formed from elements of *SS-Freiwilligen-Panzergrenadier-Ausbildungs-und-Ersatz-Abteilung 11 Nordland*, received the order to withdraw from the Harterkogel, and was transferred to Rettenegg. As they passed through the Pfaffensattel the SS men greeted the *Luftwaffe* men stationed in the pass, which seemed to summarize the defense of Styria. A fragment of an SS division serving in another country and formed around foreign volunteers, interacted with men who'd been trained to keep aircraft in the air and fighting, but who were now trying to figure out how to use rifles and machine guns.

The *Luftwaffe* unit defending the area was composed of Hungarian ME-210 and ME-410 pilots, since both aircraft and fuel supplies were virtually gone. The unit also had Germans who had been flight instructors and maintenance personnel. Along with their duties patrolling the area, the SS men had also taught the Hungarians about ground combat, from tactics to how to load and clean their weapons. The *Luftwaffe* unit had been stationed at the Semmering Pass starting on 1 April, with an original strength of 116 men. Then they'd been shifted to block the road through the Pfaffensattel, less than a mile from the front lines.

III Panzerkorps

The four Russian corps involved in the offensive that broke through north of *Divisionsgruppe Krause* included the 30th and 135th Rifle Corps, 1st Guards Mechanized Corps and the newly

19   Brettner, *Die Letzten Kämpfe Band I*, p. 108.

arrived 5th Guards Cavalry Corps. As mentioned previously, the latter corps had three cavalry divisions, two of which were Guards, and the valleys of Styria were like highways for cavalry forces.

Striking at both *1. Volks-Gebirgs-Division* and the vulnerable area in the seam between *Kampfgruppe Semmering* and *Divisionsgruppe Krause*, they quickly broke into the Lafnitz Valley north of *Divisionsgruppe Krause*, headed for Sankt Kathrein am Hauenstien, with rifle divisions following. One depleted *Jäger* division wasn't much to stop them, but it's all Hermann Balck had. By the end of 13 April, Hermann Breith at *III Panzerkorps* had to be wondering if he could hold his northern flank, or if he was about to be enveloped.

Those major Russian forces attacked the weak corps east of Ratten and broke through without much trouble. This was north of the area of *Divisionsgruppe Krause* where the Germans had little more than the pickets of what used to be *Sperrverband Motschmann*. This offensive threatened to cut *III Panzerkorps* in two, with *Kampfgruppe Raithel* to the north and the rest of the corps to the south. It became obvious now that to the northeast the Russians planned to move through Sankt Kathrein am Offenegg to attack the forces blocking the Semmering Pass from the rear. The situation became so critical that many artillery batteries ran completely out of ammunition, leading *Generaloberst* Rendulic at *Heeresgruppe Süd* headquarters to authorize the flying in of four tons of ammunition.

Divisionsgruppe Krause

SS-Hauptsturmführer Motschmann showed up at the headquarters of his new commander at 9:00 a.m. at the head of a strong battalion of SS and immediately went into the attack toward Lafnitz in response to the newest Russian offensive.

The fortified line Krause had established between Oberwart and Markt Allhau felt the full brunt of the attacks, but despite extremely violent fighting his line held. That couldn't last too long, however, since his left flank was up in the air, and the Russians had already broken through.

Meanwhile, his attack to the northwest pushed off at mid-morning, led by *SS-Hauptsturmführer* Motschmann with a strong battalion formed from the best troops of his defunct blocking group, mostly the men of *SS-Polizei Regiment 13*. Russian attacks elsewhere required the detachment of men for use to fend those off, weakening the main assault.

Motschmann's target was the village of Lafnitz, the namesake settlement for the river. As they approached the town he ran right into the advancing Russian offensive. Devastating rifle, machine-gun and artillery fire hit them from Lafnitz itself, and from the forests on either side. Russian armor drove toward them down the Lafnitz Valley and Motschmann's men didn't have any heavy weapons to fight them off. His attack group took terrible losses. Therefore, despite reports that Mönichwald was under threat Motschmann had no choice but to retreat.[20] Had he continued in the face of the Russian onslaught it's likely his entire force would have been wiped out.

Wenigzell fell in the afternoon after a short, brutal fight, where Russian mortars started fires that destroyed much of the town. Mönichwald, Sankt Jakob im Walde and Waldbach all fell for the second time. Russian cavalry regiments spread out in several directions, moving faster than the Germans could. Nor did they stop at the fall of night. One cavalry group pushed on through the night and rode into Fischbach at 3:00 a.m. on 14 April. A few shots were fired by the *Volkssturm* before they fled, leaving the town in Russian hands.

---

20   Brettner, *Die Letzten Kämpfe Band I*, pp. 29-31.

For the Germans this breakthrough could have been disastrous. In one day the Russian spearheads had penetrated 30 miles from their starting point, virtually cutting *6. Armee* in two. Fortunately for Hermann Balck, help was already on hand.

Throughout the area towns and villages were overrun. At Sankt Jakob many buildings were destroyed and some women who had stayed behind were attacked. The local pastor fled. Ratten saw ferocious fighting. Russian mortar fire hit the church and school, and 17 buildings burned to the ground. Ten people died and three more were taken prisoner. Ten more buildings collapsed. Bitter hand-to-hand fighting left 41 German, one Hungarian and 12 Russian soldiers dead. Fortunately for the women and girls they had been evacuated five days earlier.

117. Jäger-Division

The veteran division had been smashed and rebuilt several times but went into action as one of *6. Armee*'s more powerful units. Like the US Cavalry riding to the rescue in a Hollywood western, the *117. Jäger-Division* showed up in the area of Sankt Katharein an der Laming just in the nick of time. The elements began marching for Mürzzuschlag, northwest of Rettenegg, to prepare for a counterattack. Because of the haphazard fashion in which it had been transported, however, the division would take some time to assemble and organize before it could go back into action.

1. Volks-Gebirgs-Division

The attacks of the previous day continued, pinning the mountain division in place as Russian armor broke through to the north. As the day broke the division occupied a line east of Wirterberg, through Neudau and down to Furstenfeld, with the Lafnitz Valley at their backs. Back-and-forth fighting kept the Germans pinned in place but didn't move the line.

At the Zellenberg Russian bombardments were followed by heavy attacks as the Russians charged up the slopes. Casualties on both sides mounted. When the fighting died down 11 civilians were dead, along with 60 German soldiers either killed or wounded.

IV SS-Panzerkorps

Once again a Russian penetration south of Fürstenfeld called for an immediate counterattack, and once again *SS-Obergruppenführer* Otto Gille cast about for men to carry it out. The bottom of a barrel can only be scraped so many times, after all. Like so many commanders before him had done, he chose the Armored Bears.

Kampfgruppe 3. Panzer-Division

In response to Gille's need for attacks to relieve the pressure around Fürstenfeld, the *I./ Panzergrenadier-Regiment 3* counterattacked using all available SPWs. It failed miserably and the weak battalion absorbed losses it couldn't sustain. Successful German attacks now needed the element of surprise, since the first sight of an attacking soldier attracted a blizzard of mortar, artillery, Katyusha and machine-gun fire.

I Kavallerie-Korps
14. Waffen-Grenadier-Division-der-SS Galizien

On the fourth day of violent attacks from the area of Trautmannsdorf in east Styria, supported by the relentless pounding of Russian artillery, the Ukrainian SS division was on the verge of having its right flank give way. Casualties had been heavy on both sides and *General der Kavallerie* Harteneck saw no alternative except to commit *3. Kavallerie-Division* to the fight, and, a few days later, *SS-Panzer-Aufklärungs-Abteilung 16*, from *16. SS-Panzergrenadier-Division Reichsführer-SS*. Between them they stopped the Russian attack before it could break through.

At Gleichenberg Castle, however, the fighting went on. When Bad Gleichenberg fell three days earlier, the elements of *Waffen-Grenadier-Regiment-der-SS 29* that had been driven out retreated to Castle Hill, a 1,250 foot-high mountain overlooking the town. Atop the peak was the formidable Gleichenberg Castle, and the Ukrainians were determined not to give it up without a fight.

By 13 April the Russians had been assaulting it for three days. The mountain had sheer wooded slopes leading up to what had once been a fairy-tale structure with lots of delicate arches. But anything can be destroyed if enough force is applied. Artillery bombardments were so heavy they damaged stone walls more than six feet thick, but the Ukrainians would not retreat. Finally the Russians managed to surround the hill and cut off the men still defending the promontory, hoping the trapped enemy would surrender. They didn't. They just kept on fighting, until two days later when food and ammunition were almost gone. Then, and only then, did the garrison break out along a narrow path cleared by a relief force.

The past two weeks' fighting had left *Galizien* damaged and disorganized. It was finally pulled back to regroup and incorporate replacements from *SS-Feld-Ersatz-Bataillon 14*. During the recent combat more than 1,600 men from the division fell dead, wounded or captured, not including deserters.

Subordination of the division was switched from *2. Panzerarmee* to *6. Armee*. On its left flank now stood *5. SS-Panzer-Division Wiking* and on the right *4. Kavallerie-Division*. *SS-Brigadeführer und Generalmajor der Waffen-SS* Freitag learned that the disarming of his division was cancelled once and for all. Not only that, 4,000 surplus *Luftwaffe* men destined for *10. Fallschirmjäger-Division* would now be sent to *Galizien*.

Freitag saw an opportunity to Germanize his division using those men. He either wanted to replace Ukrainians with the *Luftwaffe* officers and NCOs, or to form a 100 percent German battalion in each regiment. As it turned out, though, none of the new men had any infantry training or weapons, and their number only totaled 2,500. Reluctantly Freitag ordered them to undergo an extended period of basic training.

2. Panzerarmee

The army's left wing had been under increasing pressure from tank-supported infantry forces aimed at capturing Radkersburg. Such a penetration threatened to irreparably rupture the center front of *2. Panzerarmee*, with disastrous results for both *Heeresgruppe Süd and Heeresgruppe E*. The blow fell hardest on *23. Panzer-Division* in and north of Radkersburg. After the disintegration of the *Kampfgruppe* from *44. Infanterie-Division* on 12 April, the Russians wanted to expand the breakthrough by attacking the units to either side. The shattered parts of *44. Infanterie-Division* had fallen back on an elevated position called Hill 336 and parts of *Panzergrenadier-Regiment 128* dug in beside it. The rest of the panzer division fell back to eliminate bulges in the line.

By this point *23. Panzer-Division* was forced to do what the other panzer divisions had done, namely, use surplus panzer crews, mechanics and armorers as replacements for the lost

Panzergrenadiers. Doing so was an admission that no replacement panzers would be coming, since training a panzer driver, for example, took months of intense and specialized instructions. Using such highly specialized men as cannon fodder was a last, desperate way to keep men in the trenches.

Hill 336 became the focal point of fighting for the next four days, and drew *4. Kavallerie-Division* into the struggle. The Russians captured it multiple times and the Germans recaptured it every time in a grisly game of 'king of the hill'. Artillery from both sides raked the slopes, depending on who had possession at any given moment.

* * *

On 13 April the Bulgarian First Army began attacking *2. Panzerarmee*'s Drau River line. General de Angelis now found both flanks in danger of envelopment and isolation from neighboring armies. The only bright spot was the arrival of the combat-ready elements of the *10. Fallschirmjäger-Division.*

14

Saturday, 14 April

Heeresgruppe Süd

The news of Franklin's Roosevelt's death filtered down to the troops in the days afterward. As so often happens within military forces, the Americans called it 'scuttlebutt', but in Germany rumors ran rife that they would soon join the Western Allies in fighting Russia. On the surface of it more than 70 years later this seems absurd. But desperate people believe what gives them hope, and sometimes even not-so-desperate people.

One man who gave these wild fantasies credence was Josef Stalin. Just as Eisenhower fell victim to the propaganda about a National Redoubt and adjusted his military strategy accordingly, Stalin would also change Third Ukrainian Front's priorities in the coming weeks based on those rumors.

* * *

When the sun rose on 14 April, it was like that moment after a long illness finally claims a family member. The relatives all knew it was coming and thought they were prepared, until they realized they would never see their loved one again. And so it was with the fall of Vienna, the cultural capital of Eastern Europe. After the exhaustive effort to keep the Russians out, Sepp Dietrich and Rudolf von Bünau could have been forgiven for wanting to take a deep breath.

But the danger was far from over. The Russians attacked everywhere along the army group's front. If anything, the fighting intensified, especially as Second Ukrainian Front swung to the northwest against the center and left wing of *8. Armee*. Despite rain moving into the region the Red Air Force pounded Kreysing's command, while *Luftflotte 4* put forth a maximum-effort 270 sorties in the same area.

* * *

Technically Floridsdorf was Vienna's 21st District, but if the *Waffen-SS* men who escaped over the Floridsdorfer Bridge expected succor there they were rudely shocked. Like many other Viennese, the people of Floridsdorf just wanted the war to end. Many houses had signs denying entrance to members of the German *Wehrmacht*, which again shows how far morale had fallen.

North of the Danube

8. Armee

Just as it seemed *8. Armee*'s situation couldn't get worse, it did. With German attacks on the bridging equipment assembled on the south bank of the Danube, 31st Guards Rifle Corps fooled them by executing a crossing between Bisamberg and Klosterneuberg. They advanced and captured Korneuberg from the south, restricting both *II SS-Panzerkorps* and *XXXXIII Armeekorps'* escape corridor even further. The bottleneck through which the escaping units had to pass narrowed to a few miles. More and more it began to resemble the Falaise Gap, or the start of the Russian Vienna offensive a month earlier.

In addition, the main Russian force closing in for the kill in the north was 2nd Guards Mechanized Corps of Forty-Sixth Army, which attacked toward Enzersdorf. In support of this main effort 10th Guards Rifle Corps launched holding attacks on 2nd Guards Corps' left flank, toward the 22nd District, Donaustadt.

The topography of the new battlefield in the 21st District of Floridsdorf was dominated by Bisamberg, a mountain nearly 1,200 feet high and surrounded by foothills. What passed for roads often were nothing more than dirt footpaths or rutted forest tracks. Far more rural in nature than Vienna itself, the first settlements date back to before 4,000 BC. Many taverns sold their own homegrown and homemade wine, made from grapes cultivated in their own vineyards.

* * *

The one place the Russians did not attack was straight across the Danube at Vienna. The rearguards left to cover the Reich Bridge and other crossing points could not have contained a determined effort supported by the Russian Danube flotilla. Had this occurred the pocket would have collapsed and most of *II SS-Panzerkorps* would have been destroyed. But the fierce German defense had taken a heavy toll, so heavy that the exhausted Russian forces in Vienna couldn't follow them across the river in strength. The one time they'd tried it during the battle the attackers had been wiped out, and they weren't eager to repeat that failure.

* * *

To the east, Hohenau an der March had been under attack off and on for a week. The previous day the Russians lost heavily in their attack, and on the 14th were determined not to be thrown back again. First they hit the town with a heavy artillery attack that lasted all morning but suddenly stopped, followed by machine-gun and mortar fire. This time they used overwhelming force in a major attack, broke through the German defense, and pushed them back to the railway line. The Germans rallied there and tried to build a line of resistance, but by late afternoon it was over. Hohenau had finally been taken. The defenders retreated in the direction of Hausbrunn and Rabensburg.

The Russians dragged the townsfolk from the wine cellar and plundered the town. The women and girls suffered the usual fate. The casualty list was long, with 105 German soldiers and 30 civilians being killed. German prisoners were shot. Fifty houses were destroyed, along with the sugar factory. All of the German food supplies went up in flames.

* * *

Kampfgruppe 211. Volks-Grenadier-Division, Kampfgruppe 48. Volks-Grenadier-Division and SS-Kampfgruppe Trabandt I, aka *SS-Regiment Schulze*

The first regiment from *SS-Kampfgruppe-Division Böhmen und Mähren*, along with *Kampfgruppe 211. Volks-Grenadier-Division* and one under-strength regiment from *Kampfgruppe 48. Volks-Grenadier-Division*, found itself under heavy attack in the far northeastern corner of Austria at Zistersdorf, where the Germans desperately tried to hold onto one of the last sources of natural oil in the Reich.[1] Those fields have been largely forgotten or their value underestimated by historians. After oil was first discovered there in 1934 the oil-pumping infrastructure grew so that by 1944

---

1   Contrary to popular belief, the Germans had oil fields in Germany itself, around Hanover. They were small and their production facilities had been hammered by Allied air raids, but they existed.

the wells around Zistersdorf produced a significant 1.2 million tons of crude. That fell off in 1945, of course, but even with the disruptions caused by the war they still produced 500,000 tons. The damage caused by the fighting wasn't fully repaired until 1949, when production again passed 1 million tons.[2] In modern times Austria is the second-largest oil-producing nation of Western Europe. By comparison the Nagykanitza oil fields in Hungary produced less than 1 million tons in 1944 but Hitler supposedly changed the course of the war to try and protect those. The orders for the defenders were quite clear. A message from Hitler stated that:

> The city should be held according to the *Führer* command issued on April 13 to the commander of the *211. Volksgrenadier-Division* in Zistersdorf: Zistersdorf is declared a fortress, its oil facilities must never fall into enemy hands. The Fortress Zistersdorf must be held to the last man. The commander is *Generalleutnant* Eckhart.[3]

Generalleutnant Johann-Heinrich Eckhart was the commanding officer of *Kampfgruppe 211. Volks-Grenadier-Division*, winner of the Knight's Cross with Oak Leaves. Many of the men defending Zistersdorf were from the *Wienvertiel*, the area of northeast Austria north of the Danube. On 14 April the Germans kept control of the town for a while, but the fighting was heavy and costly to both sides. Most of Second Ukrainian Front's air power spent the day ravaging the Germans in the pocket north of Vienna and couldn't support attacks on the oil fields.

On either side of the town elements of the 4th Guards Air Landing Division and the 409th Rifle Division drove toward the oil fields. These were already threatened to the north by the 6th Guards Air Landing Division and the 93rd Guards Rifle Division. As time went by the defenders of Zistersdorf became the hardened end of a long, narrow corridor.

Outflanked and threatened with being encircled, the defenders on the northern flank withdrew to a line running from Hobersdorf to Dobermannsdorf. Even this three-mile retreat wasn't enough, however, and nobody thought the new main line of resistance could hold for long. Many of Zistersdorf's residents had fled, but not all, and 25 either died in the fighting, committed suicide or were killed by the Soviets. Like in all German territory overrun by the Red Army, women and young girls were raped for many weeks to come.

II SS-Panzerkorps

Vienna may have fallen but *II SS-Panzerkorps* was in more danger than ever. The immediate concern was blocking Russian forces trying to pursue them across the Danube from Vienna. There had already been covering forces on the north bank to guard the bridges, but when General von Bünau left Vienna during the night he took over command of those forces and reinforced them, especially those guarding the only span still standing, the *Reichsbrücke*.

It's hard to say now why that bridge had not been destroyed. Some said army engineers failed to properly rig the span for demolition. The SS men blamed von Bünau who, acting as Battle Commander Vienna, wanted the bridge to remain standing for a potential counterattack back into that city. A Russian crossing would have been potentially disastrous, which von Bünau now understood. However, with the fall of Vienna he had become superfluous and so his command of

2   Kreuzberger, Dr Hans, 'Oil in Austria', Annals of Public and Cooperative Economics, 1961, <https://onlinelibrary.wiley.com/doi/abs/10.1111/j.1467-8292.1961.tb00004.x> (Accessed 15 June 2018).
3   Brettner, *Die Letzten Kämpfe, Band I*, p. 171.

the covering forces was brief. Later on 14 April he was relieved of his duties and ordered back to *II SS-Panzerkorps* headquarters for reassignment.[4]

Regardless of who was in command, the German situation on the north bank was precarious. After having barely avoided entrapment in Vienna, *II SS-Panzerkorps* again faced imminent destruction. It was the Falaise Gap in summer of 1944 all over again, when *12. SS-Panzer-Division Hitlerjugend* stood and died to hold open a narrow escape corridor for the rest of the Germans trapped in Normandy. Or the escape from Hungary the previous month, when *9. SS-Panzer-Division Hohenstaufen* held off the Russians as the rest of *6. SS-Panzerarmee* poured through a bottleneck to safety. And now, yet again, superior enemy forces threatened to close the trap and it was the *Führer-Grenadier-Division*'s turn to hold in place and absorb casualties while *II SS-Panzerkorps, 37. Freiwilligen-Kavallerie-Division Lützow,* the Hitler Youth battalion, 27th Hungarian Division, various alarm units and fragments of units all poured through a gap that narrowed to as little as one-and-a-half miles wide.

According to von Bünau the German positions "ran approximately along the line Stadlau [Donaustadt]-Kagran-Leopoldau-Stammersdorf-Hagelbrunn, and to the north thereof".[5] Essentially there was an oblong pocket through which the shattered units that had just escaped from Vienna were trying to withdraw, a pocket that in places narrowed to within three miles of the Danube and the Russians firing from the south bank. To the west, south and east the Russians were pressing hard to close the pocket and it was all the Germans could do to maintain the defense. Then *II SS-Panzerkorps* had a nasty surprise when, during the day of 14 April, the Russians crossed the Danube north of Klosterneuberg and drove on Königsbrunn, threatening to cut off the entire corps, with a secondary thrust in the direction of Gerasdorf. This was the last of the critical moments that von Bünau identified in the Battle for Vienna, because further Russian success on the next day in driving east could have completely surrounded *II SS-Panzerkorps* and meant its total annihilation. In mere hours, the entire German position north of the Danube suddenly became untenable.

Once again the flexibility of the German system saved the day. The closest unit to the new threat was *SS-Panzer-Aufklärungs-Abteilung 2*. The commander, *SS-Sturmbannführer* Ernst-August Krag, organized an immediate counterattack using the battalion's *2. Kompanie*, with two attached Tiger IIs, a platoon of SPWs mounted with cannons and a few army personnel. Weidinger reports that an unknown general was present when Krag organized the little *Kampfgruppe*, and it seems probable that this was von Bünau.[6]

The *Kampfgruppe* ran into Russian spearheads outside Bisamberg and drove them back a few hundred yards. Orders to drive the Russians back into the Danube proved unrealistic, but the speed of the German attack stopped the Russian advance in its tracks. A reinforced company wasn't much of a defense against a determined assault, but it didn't have to be. All they needed to do was buy a few more hours.

* * *

The best unit in *II SS-Panzerkorps* was the *Führer-Grenadier-Division* defending the Lobau floodplain along the Danube's north bank opposite Simmering and Schwechat, just south of Gross-Enzersdorf. The swampy, densely forested area is nicknamed 'the jungle of the Viennese' and was excellent defensive ground. The flat terrain just to the north of the Lobau, beginning near

---

4   The cynical view of this is that once a scapegoat for the fall of Vienna was no longer needed, neither was von Bünau.

5   Von Bünau, *Combat in Vienna*, p. 26.

6   Weidinger, *Das Reich*, p. 392.

the medieval town of Gross-Enzersdorf, was good tank country, however, putting pressure on the division's left flank as the Russians tried to drive to the Danube from the north and cut off *II SS-Panzerkorps* before it could withdraw. The fighting was intense and prolonged, and the division was heavily engaged. Worse, the *Führer-Grenadier-Division*'s place at the southernmost end of the pocket meant that even if it could disengage from the fighting there it was in no position to counterattack the new threat near Königsbrunn. On 14 April the *Feldersatz-Bataillon-Brandenburg*, which had been formed in southern Austria and never operated with its parent division, was assigned to the *Führer-Grenadier-Division*.[7] But even with priority they didn't arrive until 17 April. By then it was far too late for them to participate in a counterattack.

Nor were there other formations suitable to counterattack in the meantime, as the German units were either exhausted remnants, such as *6. Panzer-Division* or *Kampfgruppe 3. SS-Panzer-Division Totenkopf*, hastily thrown-together *Kampfgruppen* or newly formed units such as *37. SS-Freiwilligen-Kavallerie-Division Lützow*, which did not even control most of its components. None of the available units had significant attack potential.

37. SS-Freiwilligen-Kavallerie-Division Lützow

The staff of *Lützow*, along with a heavy battery from *SS-Artillerie-Abteilung 37*, were part of a *Kampfgruppe* near Floridsdorf, where artillery blocking positions were built after a move from the Hollabrunn-Horn area north of Krems. This would have put it in the immediate vicinity of the breakthrough. *SS-Kampfgruppe Ameiser* was depleted by this point, but these losses were partially offset when *Panzergrenadier-Brigade 92* was detached from *Kampfgruppe 96. Infanterie-Division* and given to *Lützow*. That unit had been destroyed in Belgrade the previous October, but rebuilt starting in January 1945. Other small packets of *Lützow* were in action along the withdrawal routes out of the trap north of Vienna.

One such fragment tried to hold back 18th Guards Rifle Corps and 2nd Guards Mechanized Corps' attacks on Stammersdorf and Hagenbrunn, but it was overwhelmed. The SS men put up what resistance they could but it wasn't enough. Next to fall were Hagenbrunn and Wolkersdorf.

* * *

On 14 April, however, the situation was critical and no reorganization of forces would help. Given the danger of being cut off from the north, *II SS-Panzerkorps* did the only thing it could do: run. One last chance remained. The Russians spent most of 14 April getting organized for the final push to cut off *XXXXIII Corps* and *II SS-Panzerkorps*. The race was on to get out of the nearly closed pocket before morning on 15 April, when Russian attacks would begin anew. If the two corps were not completely out of the pocket then whatever elements were still strung out trying to withdraw would make easy targets for Russian ground-attack aircraft, artillery and rampaging tank columns, just like at Falaise. It would be a slaughter.

Under cover of darkness, therefore, both corps began a withdrawal to new positions along the line Leobendorf-Tresdorf-Manhartsbrunn, all north of Korneuburg. The *II SS-Panzerkorps* command post was first moved to Ober-Rohrbach and then to Unter-Sierndorf. The retreat was as orderly as possible given the circumstances, but it was understood that once daylight came any

---

7   Nevenkin, *Fire Brigades*, p. 621. According to Nevenkin, the battalion joined its parent division in 1944, but was reportedly reformed in February 1945. It is this reincarnation with is supposed to have been absorbed by the *Führer-Grenadier-Division*, which itself began as an outgrowth of *Panzerkorps Grossdeutschland*, as did *Brandenburg*.

units still in the pocket would probably be destroyed. The route was winding, as the most direct roads could not be used due to the possibility of Russian interdiction. Haste was the watchword and consequently materiel losses were very high, with a great many precious artillery pieces left behind, as well as large quantities of supplies. Nevertheless, despite the difficulties when morning came the new line was established, with a much narrower front to cover than had previously been the case. Not all of *Das Reich* had gotten out by daybreak, however, as traffic jams on the one rutted dirt road out of the sack delayed them.

With the establishment of the new front *General der Infanterie* von Bünau became redundant and was released from service to *II SS-Panzerkorps* during the evening. His responsibilities to Vienna were over; his new assignment would come through the next day. Having been unable to save the doomed city, he later reflected on what had been accomplished: "[T]he battle of Vienna was regrettable from a human point of view, however, it tied down very strong Russian forces, and made the establishment of a new front line south of the Danube possible. It also made possible… the evacuation of some 9,000 wounded from the battle area and their removal westward."[8]

2. SS-Panzer-Division Das Reich

For the third time in eight months the men of *Das Reich* had to run a narrow gauntlet between enemy pincers to escape total destruction. They could have been forgiven if any of them wondered who the hell kept getting them into those situations. Making things more difficult, the division's commander, *SS-Standartenführer* Lehmann, had to relinquish command because of the wound suffered the day before. The commander of the artillery regiment, *SS-Standartenführer* Karl Kreutz, took over from Lehmann.

As it withdrew, *SS-Panzergrenadier-Regiment Deutschland* had to do so under constant mortar fire, while *SS-Panzergrenadier-Regiment Der Führer* was repeatedly attacked and suffered significant losses. The dirty and exhausted survivors finally stumbled into the new main line of resistance and passed through the lines of the *Führer-Grenadier-Division* and *Kampfgruppe Volkmann*.

* * *

Bisamberg fell after a short fight, but the town remained within range of German artillery until the final days. Since the main road to the new front lines ran through the village of Bisamberg, a steady rain of shells fell like a never-ending storm as the Germans fired at Russian supply columns. Fifteen people eventually died under the barrage.

* * *

It was Korneuberg's turn to become a battleground city, a state which would last for the next three weeks. Throughout the morning German columns withdrew through the northern part of the city, heading west. Gunfire could be heard clearly throughout the city, and by afternoon the first Russians hunted house by house on the south side, looking for German soldiers.

To stop further advances out of Korneuberg the Germans shifted forces to the area west of the city. A *Kampfgruppe* of *Panzergrenadiers*, along with an unknown SS battalion from Tulln, possibly from *SS-Kampfgruppe Trabandt II*, and another group from the *SS-Unterführer-Schule Radolfzell*, moved into the line. And although the distance to the Tulln area north of the river was a mere 17 miles, the line would hold until the end of the war.

---

8   Von Bünau, *Combat in Vienna*, p. 32.

As the Russians moved through Korneuberg there was one last German unit to try and evacuate. The *24. Flak-Division* scrambled to hitch up its remaining guns and to get out while it could. With the trap closing around it the last elements pulled out minutes before it would have been too late.

Vienna

After the battle it was always the same, be it Stalingrad, Warsaw, Königsberg, Budapest or the former capital of Austria: a desperate search for a way to survive amid the glowing ruins of war. With no authority in place and the triumphant Red Army raping and looting at will, while holding the power of instant death over the newly conquered populace, citizens used to their government making all decisions for them suddenly were thrust into an individual battle for survival. This meant an immediate inventory of the dead, an assessment of imminent danger and a means to keep on living.

As Vienna began its first full day under Soviet rule both the Danube River and Canal were clogged with the flotsam of broken bridges and modern war. Explosions could be heard from the fighting on the north bank and German artillery rounds still fell on northeastern Vienna, so the city was not done suffering just yet. Smoke sifted upward through the ruins and the Viennese people nervously began to poke their heads above ground to see who was alive and what the future might hold. Citizens were still too wary to venture far in their search for food, but that reluctance would pass soon enough.

A rising stench replaced the sweet smells of spring. For months Vienna had been unable to collect and dispose of trash owing to fuel shortages and appropriation of specialized vehicles for war-related purposes. The only option had been to throw refuse on the ever-increasing piles of rubbish heaped all over the city. Added to the reek of decaying garbage were the smells of ash, gunpowder and the unburied bodies of soldiers and civilians alike that had already begun to decompose in the warm weather: 10,400 Viennese had been killed during the fighting and almost none had been buried yet on 14 April, except those under fallen buildings. The cemeteries and hospitals were choked with corpses. Dead soldiers of both sides lay strewn throughout the city. Most of the dead would be hastily buried before disease could sweep over the city, in whatever plot of ground could be found. With no transport available, corpses were buried in parks, vacant lots, backyards, anywhere and everywhere. A mass grave in the Zentralfriedhof was filled with the bodies of some 200 Russian officers and 1,800 common soldiers and NCOs, evidence of how fierce the German resistance had been. According to the official Soviet statistics, the final figure for Russian losses capturing Vienna would top 17,000, which for once doesn't seem exaggerated.

Fires blazed out of control in many places. Von Schirach's order for the evacuation of the fire-fighters magnified the extent of the damage many times over. "The substance of economy had been destroyed, the traffic and transport system wrecked; the population had been stripped of all food and fuel stores and the city of all power supplies."[9] Shell craters holed the streets as tram cables sagged overhead. The food situation was so bad that even Stalin felt impelled to react, in May authorizing 1,000 tons of peas to be distributed to the Viennese.

During the hours of darkness the only illumination came from the flickering fires. There was no artificial lighting save candles. Vienna needed what all 20th-Century cities needed to function properly – power – and Vienna had none. The city was completely without gas, electric power or water. The main gas line was damaged in more than 2,400 places and the gas distribution system had suffered heavy damage as *Totenkopf* tried to hold the area of the Municipal Gasworks during

---

9   Riemer, Hans, *This Pearl Vienna* (Vienna: Jugend und Volk, 1946), p. V.

the fight for the Arsenal and *Südbahnhof*. Further damage came in *6. Panzer-Division*'s fight in the area of the gas storage tanks. Nor did the electric infrastructure fare any better:

> 60 percent of the buildings and machinery of the Municipal Electricity Works were damaged or destroyed, the coal supplies were exhausted, the connections to the water-power works were broken off in hundreds of places, 570 cable supports had been knocked down, 6,000 isolators wrecked, 5,700 transformation stations were out of commission, and the cable lines in the city were damaged in 15,000 places. Vienna was without electric current.[10]

Nothing could move in or out of the city because the transportation system was virtually non-existent. Aside from roads that were either cratered or blocked with rubble, and railway lines that were ripped up or broken, there were no means of movement even had the damage to the roads and railways not been severe. Motorized transport had completely disappeared, either destroyed in the fighting or, more likely, driven off by those who were able to evacuate the city. There were very few cars or trucks left in Vienna. One source reports only 40 light trucks in the entire city, and a mere 11 out of a fleet of more than 1,600 vehicles belonging to the Municipality of Vienna. For the time being this was irrelevant, however, since there was no fuel even if more vehicles had been available.

The Viennese had made extensive use of their sophisticated rail system but the extreme damage to trams, cars, tracks, stations, repair depots and iron supports, not to mention the electricity that ran the trams, meant that the system would not be back in service for months at the soonest. Perhaps worst of all, 146 bridges had been destroyed, including every bridge over the Danube Canal and all but one, the *Reichsbrücke,* over the Danube itself. People improvised as best they could but there was not much to work with. Railway hand-cars that could follow the rail lines were pressed into service to move heavy loads, but for the most part transportation had been pushed back to more primitive means. Pushcarts and muscle power were the primary means of moving objects, and people walked wherever they went. Shovels were worth their weight in gold. In the meantime, distribution of vital supplies such as food would be totally dependent on the largesse of the conquering Russians.

Damage was scattered throughout Vienna but certain districts were hurt more than others. Leopoldstadt, Simmering, Brittgenau and Meidling all suffered very badly because the ground fighting there was more severe than other places. More than 20 percent of the housing within the city was either partially or totally destroyed; 110,000 flats were uninhabitable.[11] Virtually every cultural or historic landmark was either badly damaged or destroyed, and damage within The Ring was heavy and in places catastrophic. No art form meant more to the Viennese than opera, and no icon represented opera in Vienna more than the State Opera House; it had "the biggest stage and the best acoustics".[12] Between the Allied bombers and the street fighting, the elegant building was almost a total loss; performances, however, resumed within months at other houses. The Vienna Philharmonic lost most of its instruments. Across from the State Opera, the Heinrichshof was a burned-out shell; just behind it to the north north-east, Tegetthofstrasse and Neue-Markt were choked with the rubble of destroyed buildings sliding into the street. Worst of all, however, was the destruction of the exquisite The Well of Raphael Donner. This fountain represented the essence of Vienna's charm and grace and its loss was a heavy blow to the Viennese, but the broken pieces of The Well were preserved and this allowed it to be reconstructed in the postwar years; other pieces of Vienna's heritage were lost forever.

---

10   Riemer, *This Pearl Vienna*, p. 59.
11   This includes housing destroyed by bombing attacks from the Allied air forces.
12   Riemer, *This Pearl*, p. 18.

20 memorial statues and wells, among them statues of Lessing, Popper-Lynkeus, Otto Wagner, Dr Julius Ofner and many beautiful wells, landmarks of Vienna such as The Moses Well on the Franziskanerplatz, the Leopolds Well on the Graben, the Tilgner Well of the Resselpark, the Gänsemädchen (goose-girl) on the Rahlstiege were carried away to be melted down. Neither plaster casts nor models have been left of them.[13]

This was not the entire list of losses; the Donau Woman in the Stadtpark, for example, was also destroyed. Some monuments of special importance that were too large to move had been bricked over to protect them, such as the Prinz Eugen at the Heldenplatz and the Pestsäule on Graben. On Kärntnerstrasse the famous hotel Grand Duke Charles was a skeleton and the popular coffee house Fenstergucker was roofless and shattered. The Burgtheater also suffered disastrous damage; the interior was gutted, a burned-out wreck that was a complete loss.[14]

Perhaps no single building represented the religious soul of Vienna more than St Stephen's Cathedral which, as previously described, while not completely destroyed, was left a roofless, shattered shell filled with rubble and ash. Here again von Schirach's order stripping the city of its firefighters left no way to limit fire damage; fires could burn until there was no fuel left to burn, including those that consumed St Stephen's. Businesses in the surrounding Stephensplatz mostly still stood, but the windows were gone and facades all damaged.

Nor was St Stephen's the only church damaged during the battle. Vienna's oldest church,[15] the Ruprechtskirche, near the Danube Canal, suffered heavy roof damage. The church is dedicated to Saint Ruprecht of Salzburg, patron saint of the Viennese salt merchants, and while its origins are obscured by the shadows of the Dark Ages, it was probably founded in the late 8th or early 9th Century. It stands in the oldest part of Vienna, the Roman settlement of Vindobona. Surviving more than ten centuries of warfare, it was struck by shells during the fight for the city. The 13th-Century Salvator Church was spattered with shells splinters and bullet holes, the roof was mostly smashed and the overall damage was very heavy. The Neulerchenfeld Church, in the 16th District Ottakring, was almost completely destroyed by the bomb hit suffered on 1 January 1945. Also damaged to varying degrees were the church of the Franciscan Monastery, the church on the Leopoldsberg and the church on the Margaretengürtel.

The University of Vienna was heavily damaged, with the Zoological Institute and Institute of Law, Chemical Institute and the lecture room of the Anatomical Institute being particularly hard hit. It would take months after the war for the university to reopen on a reduced scale of teaching, even with the eager help of the students in making repairs. The Academy of Arts did not escape damage, with one whole section caved in. Secondary schools scattered throughout the city suffered varying degrees of damage as well. According to Riemer, of 411 school buildings in Vienna, 50 were totally destroyed and a mere 46 came through the battle unscathed.[16]

The government district was targeted by the Allied bombing campaign and suffered accordingly, including the beautiful Parliament building, which was very badly damaged; the peristyle and club rooms were shattered and other sections were completely destroyed. Likewise the Hofburg was extensively damaged, including the ironic destruction of the balcony from which Hitler addressed the throngs crowding the Heldenplatz after the *Anschluss* in March 1938. The headquarters for *Wehrkreiskommando XVII* in the old Ministry of War building suffered heavy interior damage, while the Seat of the Kreisleitung on the Schwarzenbergplatz lost all of its roof

13   Riemer, *This Pearl*, p. 33.
14   Riemer attributes the extreme fire damage to a supply of 'sticky bombs' stored in the Temple of Muses that ignited and became an inferno.
15   There are some who dispute this claim.
16   Riemer, *This Pearl*, p. 52.

and top floor, and consequently was a total loss. Particularly distressing to the citizenry was the extensive damage done to Friedrich Schmidt's Gothic masterpiece, the Rathaus, or City Hall. Astride the Ringstrasse just across Rathauspark from the Burg Theater, the surrounding area was a favorite gathering place for festivals and markets. The fairy-tale quality of the building, with its central tower and dual spires on either flank, is best reflected by the Rathausmann, a ten foot-tall statue of an armored knight bearing a lance that tops the central tower and was created by master smith Alexander Nehr after a design by Franz Gastell. The central building's roof was completely gone while jagged timbers and broken masonry clogged the interior.

These had all been impressive structures that reflected upon Austria's glorious past, but not all of the destruction was regretted by the Viennese. When the headquarters of the Gestapo in the Hotel Metropole on Morzinplatz, 31-33 Franz Josef Kai at the base of the Ring near the Salztorbrücke over the Danube Canal, was smashed flat by Allied bombs, nobody was sorry and the hotel was never rebuilt, becoming instead a memorial for those who were tortured and died within its confines.

Nothing was spared the hard hand of war, not even the historic palaces from the Imperial years when the Habsburgs ruled the land. Schönbrunn Palace suffered worst. Between the Allied bombings and the ground combat the palace was very badly damaged, with one end of the Gloriette smashed flat. Much worse, however, was the fate of the much-loved Zoo, which was virtually destroyed and most of the animals killed.

The magnificent Belvedere Palace was not damaged too badly, but the nearby Schwarzenberg Palace was smashed on one side with more damage near the entrance. The Palffy Palace in Augustinerstrasse was a complete wreck; Lichtenstein Palace took a bomb hit that caved in the roof and filled the staircase with piles of rubble and debris.

The lush greenery of the horse chestnut trees once lent a fairytale charm to the Prater, especially in early spring, but the wounds inflicted on Vienna's delightful amusement park during 6. *Panzer-Division*'s stiff defense were terrible. Despite its depleted status the veteran panzer division fought stubbornly to hold the left flank; the Russians had desperately fought to cave in that flank and drive down the Danube, capturing bridges and cutting off *II SS-Panzerkorps*. The 6. *Panzer-Division* prevented this, but the consequences were the near total destruction of the area. The world-famous Reisenrad,[17] built for the Golden Jubilee of Emperor Franz Josef I in 1897, with its delicate struts and spacious gondolas,[18] stood like a giant scorched skeleton over Vienna's denuded playground; the gondolas were all lost to fire. Trees were splintered and toppled. Buildings were flattened throughout the park and craters made movement through the heaps of debris treacherous. The famous Zirkus Busch, opened in 1892, was nothing but a shell. Heaps of rubble blocked the entrance. The roof was mostly gone, while the windows were shattered and the walls were pock-marked by shell splinters and bullets. The mill-stream was nothing more than a collection of huge, blackened gears scattered on the ground, and the pirate ship hung forlornly from its supports over a field of rubble. "A warped hoarding marks the place where the wonder-world of the Grottenbahn once revealed itself to wide-eyed children. Burnt-out machinery is a reminder of the unique building of the *Hochshaubahn* [Switchback]."[19]

As happened everywhere the Red Army appeared, the first wave of Russians were more interested in fast loot, such as watches, than alcohol or women; they soon moved on in pursuit of the Germans.[20] The second wave, however, were not hardened and well-disciplined combat veterans,

---

17   German for 'giant wheel'.
18   Prior to the Second World War the Reisenrad had 30 gondolas, but when rebuilt after the war that number was halved to 15.
19   Riemer, *This Pearl*, p. 70.
20   The Russians did not just rape and pillage in the Reich or its allies, but also in 'liberated' countries such as Poland.

and it was not long before widespread rape and murder were the order of the day. Any female was fair game, from the very young to the very old, the pregnant, the infirm, all of them. The only thing that seemed to discourage the rapists was the specter of disease, which lead to an infinite variety of disguises simulating every malady from smallpox to syphilis. Sometimes it worked, sometimes not.

As 14 April ended the war began to move further from Vienna's immediate vicinity, leaving it exposed to its fate like a receding tide uncovering a shipwreck. And like a shipwreck, the scavengers were prowling the ruins in search of anything edible.

II SS-Panzerkorps

The Battle of Vienna may have ended but the battle for survival raged on. Although the Floridsdorfer Bridge had been blown up, the Russians still made major efforts to cross both there and over the *Reichsbrücke*. *Das Reich* and *6. Panzer-Division* both fought against those attempts and turned them back. At daybreak, six miles northeast of there in the Süssenbrunn area, large Russian attacks tried to break through into the escape corridor still being held open for *II SS-Panzerkorps* and *XXXXIII Armeekorps*. They failed at great costs to the defenders, who stood exactly as *9. SS-Panzer-Division Hohenstaufen* had done the previous month around Lake Balaton. Northwest of Hagenbrunn and Stammersdorf, however, the Russians broke through. Less than three miles separated the Russian bridgeheads over the Danube near Bisamberg and the spearheads of those advances, and if they closed the Germans would be trapped.

Then, as if Bittrich didn't have enough to worry about, Dietrich made him responsible for the defense of Krems an der Donau, 40 miles to the west. Fortunately, Dietrich intended to send the shattered *Das Reich* into the bridgehead on the south bank of the Danube below Krems to regroup, so this made sense. First, of course, *Das Reich* had to survive.

South of the Danube

Korps Schultz

Using every means at his disposal *Generalmajor* Schultz had cobbled together the semblance of a contiguous front from Krems to the area southwest of Sankt Pölten near Obergrafendorf. Stragglers motivated to fight again or stopped at the point of a gun had been spread into the trenches. Broken units without orders found a place to stop and fight. Backed by arriving reinforcements, Schultz had created a defense using smoke, mirrors and energy. It was a remarkable military achievement, but against the powerful Russian formations it remained to be seen if it would hold.

The answer came soon enough. The defense in the Danube Valley began to give way on 14 April when Russian infantry crossed the Traisen River around Herzobenburg, only a handful of miles south of the Danube. Heavy tank and artillery support overwhelmed the outnumbered defenders. Immediate counterattacks sealed off but couldn't eliminate the bridgehead. Krems on der Donau now found itself a front-line city in imminent danger of being attacked.

After being frustrated for days when trying to capture Kapelln and Böheimkirchen, on the morning of 14 April the Russians finally cleared both towns of Germans. *Generalmajor* Schultz had no real choice but to pull back west of the Traisen, although heavy fighting continued around Kapelln and Böheimkirchen. German artillery proved especially effective in holding back the Russians moving out of Sankt Pölten to the west and northwest, but they were losing men and using up ammunition at an alarming rate, and even this position was undermined by the capture of bridges over the Traisen River at both Spratzern and at Sankt Pölten.

Even more ominous, Foreign Armies East warned that after the fall of Vienna the Sixth Guards Tank Army could be assumed to redeploy into the Sankt Pölten vicinity, with the long-term target being Linz. This was particularly dangerous because the bridgeheads the Russians pushed over the Traisen River could only be contained, not eliminated, despite desperate German attacks from all directions. Once those were defeated, and with their hold over the Traisen secured, the Russians split into two armored battle groups. One moved north to capture Herzogenburg from the west, while the other drove on Sankt Pölten.

At the same time another Russian force attacked Sankt Pölten from the Böheimkirchen area and overran the last defenders. They made it all the way to Phyra, near Sankt Pölten's city limits. Russian patrols then moved west into the woods south of Reichersdorf in preparation for further advances. In the nick of time *Korps Schultz* got some badly needed reinforcements, in the form of *710. Infanterie-Division*'s artillery regiment. Heavy weapons were always welcome, but ammunition remained rationed.

I SS-Panzerkorps
SS-Kampfgruppe Peiper

A four-mile gap in the German lines extended from the right flank of *Korps Schultz* at Obergrafendorf, to the positions of *SS-Kampfgruppe Kling* at Wilhelmsburg. From there, another gap existed between Obergrafendorf and Michelback, where *SS-Kampfgruppe Peiper* had a defensive line to Brand.

The loss of Sankt Corona am Schöpfl left Pieper's position to the northwest at Brand-Laaben dangerously exposed, like a finger of German territory thrust into the side of the Russian advance along the Danube Valley. Therefore, he either had to withdraw, which was unacceptable, or counterattack, which is what happened.

The force selected to launch this crucial counterattack was the small *Kampfgruppe* formed under the command of the highly decorated *SS-Hauptsturmführer* Gerd Freiherr von Reitzenstein, consisting of men of the divisional artillery regiment with no guns to serve, one platoon from the division escort company, two *panzergrenadier* companies and some attached *Luftwaffe* men. The only armored vehicles were a few SPWs, with no heavy weapons. To the shock of all involved, Russian and German alike, not only did this little force retake all of the ground lost the day before, including Sankt Corona, but did so without suffering any casualties.[21]

Kampfgruppe 12. SS-Panzer-Division Hitlerjugend

On Peiper's immediate right flank was *SS-Kampfgruppe Gross* of *Hitlerjugend*, holding nearby Laaben. Yet another *Kampfgruppe*, *SS-Kampfgruppe von Ribbentrop*, held east from Laaben on *SS-Kampfgruppe Gross*'s right flank. The commander, *SS-Hauptsturmführer* Rudolf von Ribbentrop, was the Knight's Cross and German Cross in Gold-winning son of Foreign Minister Joachim von Ribbentrop.

Heavy attacks once again slammed into *Hitlerjugend* all across its front. South of Groisbach *SS-Kampfgruppe Bremer* had to fall back under battalion-sized attacks and infiltrators, with its right wing west of Pankrazi, a tiny settlement northwest of Dörfl. A breakthrough was sealed off

21   Reynolds, *Men of Steel*, p. 267.

with two SPWs and a *Jagdpanzer IV/70*, another indication of how hollow the German formations were with such paltry armored support.

SS-Kampfgruppe von Reitzenstein held newly recaptured Sankt Corona. Near Alland was *SS-Kampfgruppe Bremer*, consisting of the remnants of the division's reconnaissance battalion and SPW battalion of *Kampfgruppe SS-Panzergrenadier-Regiment 26*. The rest of *SS-Panzergrenadier-Regiments 25* and *26* held the front between Schwarzenbach and Weissenbach.

After capturing Schwarzensee five miles south of Alland, Russian probes cut the Neuhaus to Nöstach road two miles to the west, leaving the German forces around Neuhaus in a precarious position. Counterattacks temporarily stabilized the front but didn't restore the situation. And in the area north of Sankt Corona further Russian gains were made to the southwest and counterattacks failed to push them back. Another Russian drive south started near the Schöpfl, a 2,900 foot mountain, and captured the high ground south of Sankt Corona am Schöpfl along the road from Hainfeld to Nöstach. This increased the pressure on the division's left flank even more. At least one panzer was destroyed during the day's fighting.

* * *

This area had once contained the famous tourist attraction called the *Seegrotte*. This lake nearly 200 feet below the surface had in reality been a flooded gypsum mine. During the war pumps emptied the old shafts to allow for production of the brand-new Heinkel HE-162 Salamander jet fighter, sometimes called the *Volksjäger*, the People's Fighter. The concept for this revolutionary weapon had been to build a deadly new fighter from non-essential materials, but one that was easy enough to fly that it required only a short training course. Some people naively thought Hitler Youth trained on gliders might be able to pilot it.

The plane is usually referred to as a failure because it didn't meet its design criteria, and that much is true. A novice pilot could never have successfully flown the aircraft. But the design was brilliant, as the Allies discovered after the war. The HE-162 really was a *wunderwaffe*, a wonder weapon, and, in the hands of an experienced pilot, its performance was leaps and bounds ahead of anything the Allies had on the drawing board.

The factory was part of what is sometimes called the Second Ruhr, the underground complex of small factories spread through southern Germany, Silesia and Austria, which had become necessary when the huge above-ground factories were bombed into rubble by the Allied strategic bombing campaign. The capture of this factory would give the Russians access to Germany's latest aviation technology.

Kampfgruppe 1. SS-Panzer-Division Leibstandarte Adolf Hitler

The *LAH* defensive front started southeast of Weissenbach and ran west of Berndorf, before turning south at a ninety-degree angle to the Piesting River. On the division's far right flank, heavy Russian attacks in the direction of Pöllau,[22] about two miles due west of Berndorf, turned into a massacre of the attackers. Spearheads moved into the forests west of the town but were soon cut off by a counterattack. The attack elements of *LAH* that had combined the day before first surrounded them, and then hunted them down in the thickly forested hills. The scattered Russians fought hard and inflicted heavy casualties, but were eventually wiped out.

One mile southwest of Pöllau, other elements of the combined battle group renewed the attack on Steinhof, and the nearby Steinberg. This sort of combat was terrifying for the men involved,

---

22   Not to be confused with the municipality of Pöllau, in the district of Hartberg-Fürstenfeld, in Styria.

as the account of one participant makes clear. A high spot in Russian hands dominated the surrounding area and had to be recaptured: "There was a steep, rocky cliff in front of us, then the storm broke over our heads. Machine guns and machine-pistols hammered relentlessly, hand grenades detonated around us…our attack stalled in the Russian fire."[23] Only a surprise night attack allowed the Germans to seize the hill.

The penetration to Waxeneck, that had looked so promising for the Russians just a few days before, had been defeated. Once again the Germans had rallied to turn back a Russian breakthrough, but they were fast running out of men and munitions to keep up the fight.

SS-Kampfgruppe Koch

The Russians had been pounding the thrown-together defenders north of the Hohe Wand for days, and pushed them back far enough to threaten the Dreistetten-Markt Piesting road. The loss of that link would seriously threaten the entire German position along the Piesting Valley and, in turn, the defensive line facing the Vienna Woods. Panzer and infantry reinforcements were promised, but none came and the road was cut.

Fortunately for the civilians, Dreistetten had already been evacuated. The original three SS Mark IV panzers were still with the *Kampfgruppe* and it had long-since dissolved its command post so the staff could fight on the front lines, but it didn't matter. Under a steady rain of mortar rounds the Russians attacked with relentless ferocity and a seemingly endless supply of ammunition. Losses mounted and there seemed no way out.

Kampfgruppe 356. Infanterie-Division

The ongoing combat throughout the eastern mountains belies accounts that the Russians stopped attacking there in early April. After losing the Hohe Wand the day before, and seeing Russian columns spread out in all directions, a counterattack by elements of *Kampfgruppe 356. Infanterie-Division* on 14 April once again regained the mountain's crest. The see-saw nature of the fighting exhausted both sides. By now the forest floor atop the 3,700 foot-high peak was littered with discarded equipment, smashed tree limbs and broken boles. Shell craters buried into the thick humus, while shell splinters scarred the trees.

A few miles to the south, the division fought off Russian attacks between Puchberg am Schneeberg and Grünwald am Schneeberg, although some Russians had infiltrated gaps in the line south of Grünwald.

SS-Kampfgruppe Keitel

SS-Kampfgruppe Keitel saw hard defensive fighting in Gruenbach, Klaus and Puchberg, after which it was ordered back to a new line in the mountains that ran Heutberg-Kloster-Taler to Gscheid-Sparbachter Huette on the Schneeberg to Singerin-Nasswald. Some part of the *Kampfgruppe* was in the Schwarzau area and the Pernitz Mountains at the end of April, and finally wound up around St Aegyd. As April proceeded various parts of the still-forming division were used in various *Kampfgruppe*. The final order received from the *SS-Hauptamt* directed *Lützow* to the Sisak area for

---

23   Tiemann, *The Leibstandarte IV/2*, p. 296.

equipping and refitting, but due to the collapsing war situation this was not possible. Toward the latter part of April, *Lützow* headquarters was relieved of its *Kampfgruppe* duties north of Vienna and took charge of the remaining undeployed elements of the division

6. Armee

For all his shifting of blame and bitterness toward the *Waffen-SS*, the discovery of plans for the offensive in a Russian command car gave Hermann Balck a clear understanding of Russian objectives in their offensive against his left flank: "The Russian plan was to thrust through Hatzendorf, Fürstenfeld, Burgau, Hartberg, Riegersburg, Ilz, Gross Steinbach, and Hartberg, effectively encircling *6. Armee*." Worse, he notes that some of the front-line units were showing signs of disintegration.[24]

Kampfgruppe Raithel

After the failed attempt to seize Klamm, the *3./SS-Gebirgsjäger-Ausbildungs-und-Ersatz-Bataillon 13 Leoben* never tried to take it again, its losses had been heavy, and the Russians still had an excellent field of fire on all of the possible avenues of attack. Instead it stood on the defensive for the rest of the war.

Unlike many German units, food came every day between 3:00 and 4:00 a.m. whether the Russians were shooting at them or not. One of the company cooks led a train of pack animals forward with food strapped to their backs. After unloading his precious cargo he stayed long enough to exchange gossip before moving back to the rear. It was another example of how men adapt to the conditions of combat, seeking regularity and consistency in an otherwise insane world of chaos.

III Panzerkorps

Russian attacks increased along *6. Armee*'s left flank and center. The area south of *Kampfgruppe Semmering* in the Semmering Pass, and north of *Divisionsgruppe Krause*, continued to be the flashpoint of danger. Elements of the four Russian corps attacking there were strong enough to open the Semmering Pass by hitting *Kampfgruppe Semmering* from behind, continue driving west toward Leoben, and also flank *Divisionsgruppe Krause* on the north and roll up *III Panzerkorps*' entire line.

SS-Kampfgruppe Schweitzer

Having rested from the ordeal of the fight for Rechnitz, Schweitzer's command went back into the line, with *Kampfgruppe Raithel*.

---

24   Balck, *Order in Chaos*, p. 426.

117. Jäger-Division

The division established its command post at Mürzzuschlag and built defenses around the town, while also assembling to strike the unsuspecting Russians. An immediate liaison was established with *Kampfgruppe Raithel*, whose commander, *Oberst* Raithel, must have been relieved to have a German division protecting his exposed right flank and rear. And at that moment, despite the failing state of the German railways, and it taking more than a week to travel less than 100 miles as the crow flies, Soviet intelligence had no warning of a German division assembling to attack on their flank.

Divisionsgruppe Krause

Strong Russian attacks from the area southwest of Mönichwald made fast progress during the morning and captured Vorau in the afternoon. *SS-Polizei-Regiment 13* suffered terrible losses and was driven back to Puchegg, which the Russians tried and failed to capture on the fly. While the SS were pinned down fighting at Vorau, other Russian forces followed those that had crossed the Lafnitz near Mönichwald the day before, reinforcing their success.

Early that morning the Russians had captured Wenigzell. At Birkfeld, German reinforcements arrived in the form of an armored car platoon, an SS replacement battalion with about 150 men and an Army replacement artillery battalion with two batteries, presumably of 105mm howitzers. The SS men were sent three miles northeast to secure Meisenbach bei Birkfeld, thereby blocking the fastest road to Wenigzell. Unfortunately for the Germans, the SS commanding officer and the two battery commanders were killed when they went forward to scout positions for the guns.

At Neustift an der Lafnitz the Russians attacked from across the river and a bloody fight ensued. It lasted all day and into the next, with the Germans stubbornly holding onto the town, but at midday on 15 April they withdrew to Grafendorf bei Hartberg. That's when the women and girls who hadn't left fell victim to the Russians.

1. Volks-Gebirgs-Division

As pressure mounted on the division's flanks, parts of its center were still defending far to the east around the Zellenberg. Only in the morning of 14 April did Russian attacks hit Limbach am Burgenland. Eleven houses went up in flames. The fall of Limbach would leave the men on the Zellenberg virtually surrounded.

On 14 April the division was given use of the orphaned *I./Panzer-Regiment 24*, the Panther battalion of *24. Panzer-Division*. The battalion had been sent to Hungary in January to help in the *Konrad* attacks aimed at the relief of Budapest, and never returned to its parent division. By mid-April it had six Panthers operational, and three *PAK-40* anti-tank guns. Under the 1944 Table of Organization for a panzer division, the battalion could have up to 73 Panthers and 86 Mark IVs, not counting specialized panzers such as *Befehlpanzers*, command tanks.

IV SS-Panzerkorps
Kampfgruppe 3. Panzer-Division

The relentless Russian attacks continued on 14 April as the ever-shrinking division tried to maintain its lines. It even became difficult to set up clearing stations for the wounded, as Russian spearheads often showed up without warning. At Rudersdorf the wounded were evacuated out of the town just ahead of the Russians. The reconnaissance company fought long enough to allow their injured comrades to escape because, even though they weren't *Waffen-SS*, the men of the army knew that few wounded ever survived being taken prisoner.

2. Panzerarmee

If there had been any doubt about plans to separate *2. Panzerarmee* from *Heeresgruppe E* they were dispelled on 14 April. Strong attacks hit both the Drava and Mur River lines, as well as the Fürstenfeld area. Although no penetrations got through the defenses it forced the army to expend ammunition and fuel that couldn't be replaced, with the promises of more attacks to come.

In particular the fighting in the southeastern line around the village of Kog was a last effort by the Russians to break through before being relieved by Bulgarian divisions. For almost a week fighting had flared here and there, along with heavy artillery duels, but nothing decisive had been achieved by either side. Nor was it on 14 April, despite heavy casualties.

15

Sunday, 15 April

Reliable strength and casualty figures for both Second and Third Ukrainian Fronts are available for the period 16 March–15 April 1945. For that month, the rate of Russian losses in those two fronts, if calculated on a daily average, nearly equaled those sustained during the Berlin Offensive.

The Vienna offensive began on 16 March. The following two weeks saw the Russians first break through the German front lines and then pursue them across western Hungary. The character of that combat had the Germans turning to fight their pursuers, standing until they were almost surrounded and then withdrawing at the last moment. The rate of casualties escalated once the fighting entered Austria.

On 16 March Marshal Tolbukhin's Third Ukrainian Front commanded 42 rifle divisions, four airborne divisions, three cavalry divisions, three independent tank corps, two independent mechanized corps, one mechanized brigade and one self-propelled artillery brigade. Total manpower was 536,700 men. The number killed in action or missing was 32,846, with a further 106,969 wounded or sick, making a total of 139,815 casualties. Average daily losses were a staggering 4,510 men.

Only the left wing of Marshal Malinovsky's Second Ukrainian Front battled against *Heeresgruppe Süd*. The rest of it fought through old Czechoslovakia against *Heeresgruppe Mitte*. The parts facing *Heeresgruppe Süd* included Forty-Sixth Army and 2nd Guards Mechanized Corps, as well as part of Fifth Air Army. Forty-Sixth Army was quite powerful by Soviets standards, and the total for just these formations was 101,500 men. Killed or missing were 5,815 men, with 22,310 sick or wounded for a total of 28,125 and a daily average of 910 casualties.

Lastly, fighting on the southern end of the area against *2. Panzerarmee* was the Bulgarian First Army, with a listed strength of six divisions and 100,900 men. The Bulgarians weren't involved because they despised Nazism or loved Bolshevism. Bulgaria had not declared war on the Soviet Union, but when Romania fell that didn't stop the Red Army from overrunning the country and deposing King Boris. Stalin had never been shy about attacking smaller countries like Poland, Finland or the Baltic States, and so Bulgaria became communist whether it wanted to or not.

The men of First Bulgarian Army paid a heavy price for Stalin's unquenchable thirst for power, as 2,698 Bulgarians died or went missing and 7,107 became ill or were wounded, for a total of 9,805 casualties. The average daily rate of loss was 316.

The total manpower committed to the Vienna Offensive was 745,600. When all of these losses are totaled, in that single month the campaign cost 41,359 men killed or missing and 136,386 sick or wounded, for total casualties of 177,745. The daily average of casualties was 5,733.[1]

In just one month, a staggering 23.83 percent of the men in those formations because casualties. If the support services are taken out and only the combat forces considered, the figure goes up dramatically, since men in supply, artillery batteries, mechanics and medical detachments didn't routinely face danger from the Germans.

---

1   Krivosheev, Colonel General G.F., editor, *Soviet Casualties and Combat Losses in the Twentieth Century* (London: Greenhill Books, 1997), p. 157.

Heeresgruppe Süd

The newly appointed commander of *XVII Waffen-Armeekorps-der-SS (Ungarishes)*, *SS-Obergruppenführer* Ruszkay, finally arrived in the Alpine Lakes region of Austria where the two Hungarian SS divisions that made up the corps were encamped along with various smaller formations. *SS-Oberführer* Laszlo Deak assumed the duties of running the corps headquarters. In the paranoid atmosphere of mid-April, and with Ruszkay refusing to commit the Hungarian SS divisions in battle against the Americans, the German high command had to send *Feldgendarme* units – to watch over their erstwhile allies.

* * *

The first issue of a newspaper printed by Third Ukrainian Front, intended for the Austrian populace and titled the *Österreichische Zeitung*, declared: "The liberation of Austria is happening in several directions. All German attempts to hold suitable defensive positions have failed again and again...of particular importance is the capture of Zistersdorf, Germany's last oil reserve."[2] It's worth nothing that countless histories since the war have declared that the Hungarian fields were Germany's last source of natural oil, but as shown earlier Hitler knew the production of the Austrian fields down to the last barrel, and so did the Russians. And that production was higher in Zistersdorf during 1944 than at Nagykanizsa.

* * *

Heeresgruppe Süd's front was a mess: *8. Armee*'s left wing was echeloned far forward, while strong Russian forces kept up the pressure on its center. The right flank held on by smoke and mirrors. The Russian crossing of the Danube around Korneuberg had been slowed down by using all available forces, and further west more crossings threatened at Tulln. By far the biggest danger, however, was the sack that parts of both *II SS-Panzerkorps* and *XXXXIII Armeekorps* found themselves in north of Vienna. With only a narrow neck through which to escape, 15 April became all about getting out of the trap. Even as they marched north the Russians attacked with mortar, artillery and air strikes, inflicting losses without the Germans being able to fight back.

The *6. SS-Panzerarmee* faced even greater danger. Technically, Dietrich still counted *II SS-Panzerkorps* as part of his command, but his responsibilities now stretched from Bittrich's corps in desperate trouble north of the Danube, to isolated *SS-Kampfgruppe Keitel* thrust far forward on the right flank and with their own right flank up in the air. Attacks along the army's entire front required emergency measures all up and down the line, with the gravest threat south of the Danube facing *Korps Schultz* in the Danube Valley, as the Russians assembled a large tank force there. Dietrich's two best divisions, the *LAH* and *Hitlerjugend*, had long since become so weak they'd been reduced to cannibalizing their own specialist members for front-line duty. Neither *Kampfgruppe 356.Infanterie-Division* nor *710. Infanterie-Division* had ever been considered front-line units, although out of necessity both had been pressed into combat duties, and now the former was a remnant. *Kampfgruppe 356. Infanterie-Division* had been heavily mauled throughout 1945, with no real reinforcement. Nor did Dietrich have a significant force of operational panzers or *Sturmgeschütze*, along with food, fuel, ammunition and everything else a modern mechanized force needs to stay in the field.

---

2   Vavra, Dr Elisabeth and Rossiwall, Theo, *Kriegsschauplatz NÖ 8 / 10 Die letzten Tage: 18. April – 24. April 1945*, Museum Niederösterreich, 2016 <https://www.museumnoe.at/de/das-museum/blog/18-april-24-april-1945>, (Accessed 22 July 2018).

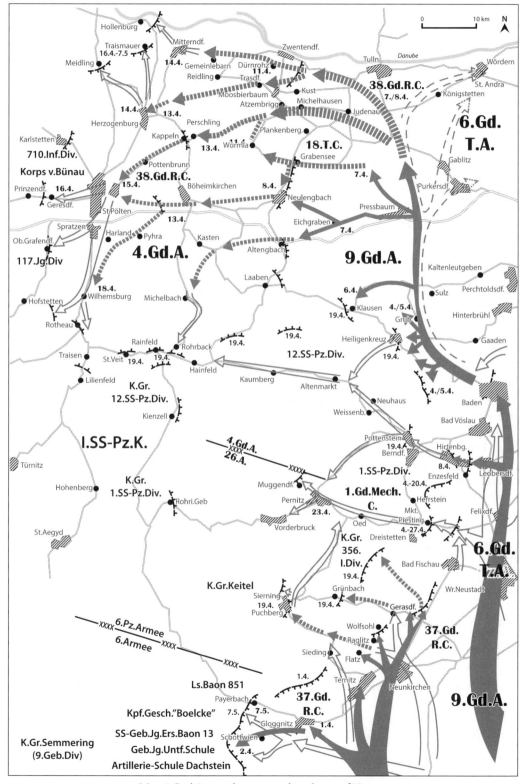

Map 8 Red Army advances south and west of Vienna.

Hermann Balck's *6. Armee* faced similar peril, although in better defensive terrain. Balck also had the energies and expertise of both *Gauleiter* Ueberreither and General Ringel to find men to man the front lines. He also had the *1. Volksgrenadier-Division* holding in the center and the battered but veteran *IV SS-Panzerkorps* on the right. Even so, both of his flanks were once again endangered and his army endured constant attack on its entire front, with particular pressure on the junction with *2. Panzerarmee*.

As for *General der Artillerie* de Angelis' *2. Panzerarmee*, it held a defensive line on the Drau River and another one further west on the Mur. The Russians maintained steady attacks on the army's center to tie down forces, with heavier attacks coming on the left to try and separate *2. Panzerarmee* from *6. Armee*, and even stronger ones on the right to isolate *Heeresgruppe E* in the Balkans.

Viewed from above, Second and Third Ukrainian Fronts had taken a decidedly northwestern turn. Some prongs of the offensive continued driving due west, especially down the Danube Valley, but a great number of formations headed for Brunn and further into Czechoslovakia. It was much like a flash flood down a dry river that suddenly encounters a huge boulder blocking the stream bed.

For commanders at all levels, from Lothar Rendulic on down, reserves were hard to come by, while replacements and reinforcements were in even shorter supply. All they could do was shift men from one place to another to meet whichever crisis demanded attention at the moment.

Rumors swirled at the time to explain why the Russians didn't just punch through the fragile German lines and drive as far as they wanted. One popular one said that the Russians hesitated because they feared the Americans and British turning on them and joining the Germans. It was even said that British agents had been secretly encouraging the Germans to keep fighting until they could arrive to help. As will be seen later, although the rumors were simple fantasies, the Russians weren't so sure.

Other schools of thought were that the Russians had reached the limits of their postwar occupation zones and saw no reason to waste men's lives trying to capture territory they would have to give back.

The truth was more prosaic. Russian losses since 16 March had been terrible. Just in the period from 11-15 April, *6. SS-Panzerarmee* claimed to have destroyed 80 Russian tanks and assault guns. Russian losses in manpower, trucks, artillery, aircraft, etc. had also been ruinous. In fact the Germans had hurt them too badly for the Russians to continue an all-out offensive everywhere.

Sixth Guards Tank Army, in particular, had sustained very heavy casualties and needed rest and replenishment. It was pulled out of the line and transferred north, to help Second Ukrainian Front in the coming Prague Offensive. But more narrowly focused attacks could and did continue, partly to carve out new territory as far to the west as possible, and partly because the men fighting south of the Vienna Woods and Sankt Pölten were the despised *Waffen-SS*. The scale of the fighting diminished somewhat, but the ferocity intensified.

North of the Danube

8. Armee

The odds against the Germans were daunting: "The *8. Deutsche Armee* with its 7 abused divisions now faced 8 Russian armies."[3]

By this point the boundary between *Heeresgruppe Mitte* and *Heeresgruppe Süd* had been redrawn so that *8. Armee* lost the two endangered corps on its left flank, the *XXIX* and *LXXII Armeekorps*.

---

3   Brettner, *Die Letzten Kämpfe Band II*, p. 165.

This simplified Kreysing's situation, although at that point in the war nothing could solve the countless problems still facing his army.

* * *

The powerful Russian Forty-Sixth Army had overrun the Marchfeld and taken Korneuberg in a pincer movement coordinated with elements of Third Ukrainian Front that crossed the Danube around Klosterneuberg. But that's where *II SS-Panzerkorps* had retreated after the fall of Vienna and now, with the German main line of resistance straightened out, the defenses were thicker and tougher. Therefore, instead of trying to blast their way through, and in accord with an overall shift in priority away from *8. Armee* and toward *Heeresgruppe Mitte,* the main emphasis of the Russian attacks veered due north toward Mistelbach.

This new attack route paralleled the German front line, and maneuvering in the face of the enemy showed how contemptuous the Russian high command was of *8. Armee*'s ability to launch a counterattack. The first immediate goal was to capture the oil fields at Zistersdorf. The Russians claimed to have already captured them, but that wasn't true.

* * *

Korneuberg suffered the same fate as all other cities and towns captured by the Red Army. The townsfolk were put to work digging graves for the dead as the city was looted of anything and everything worth taking. Food was especially wanted, while 70 percent of the girls and women were raped and 117 civilians died.[4]

II SS-Panzerkorps

The corps executed a fighting withdrawal to the west throughout the day and night. But unlike Allied tactics the previous year, when Canadian forces stopped short of closing the gap at Falaise, heavy Russian attacks from the bridgehead around Bisamberg showed they had no intention of making the same mistake: *II SS-Panzerkorps* had already escaped them once the previous month in Hungary and Marshal Tolbukhin was determined it wouldn't happen again. Using large numbers of tanks the Russians drove west to capture Bisamberg itself, and in doing so disrupted the evacuation numerous times. Despite their best efforts, however, while the Russians threatened to close the noose around all German units still in the sack north of Vienna, they never quite managed to do it.

6. Panzer-Division

A strength return for 15 April shows the battered division with nine Panzer IVs, four of which were combat ready; 16 Panthers, with eight operational; two *Jagdpanzer IV/70s*, both of which were ready; one *Bergepanther*, operational; no *Flakpanzers* left at all; and six heavy antitank guns, probably 88mm. Manpower totals are unavailable, but on 1 April the division reported losses in the previous month of nearly 3,300 men, with only 902 replacements, so its ration strength before Vienna was likely around 12,000. After the vicious fighting during the first two weeks of April it likely had somewhere between 8,000 and 9,000 men, perhaps even fewer.[5]

---

4   Brettner, *Die Letzten Kämpfe Band II*, p. 164.
5   Nevenkin, *Fire Brigades*, p. 200.

As the situation on *8. Armee*'s left flank began to deteriorate, *6. Panzer-Division* was alerted that it would be detached from *II SS-Panzerkorps* and sent northeast to shore up the defenses there. But moving a division even such a relatively short distance required a tremendous amount of organization. If some or all of the division would be using rail transport that had to be arranged for, and this was no easy task on a failing Reich railway system. Elements using roads needed instructions on which routes to take and, in a situation where refugees and broken units clogged many of the main roads, guards had to first clear the route and then keep it clear. Food and fuel had to be attained and supply depots set up at the new location.

In short, any movements of units in a supply situation such as faced *Heeresgruppe Süd* in the second half of April 1945 was a grave decision that carried serious consequences regardless of what decision was made. In *6. Panzer-Division*'s case, however, there was no real choice. *General der Artillerie* Kreysing only had three options: move the division, withdraw the left flank and hope it didn't disintegrate, or watch the Russians break through and destroy *8. Armee*.

Kampfgruppe 2. SS-Panzer-Division Das Reich

After daybreak the marching columns of the divisional remnants passed the new main line of resistance, taking casualties up until the final minute. Once safely behind German lines, the pieces of *Das Reich* were *hors de combat*. Exhausted from the Battle for Vienna and the narrow escape from entrapment north of the Danube, Dietrich ordered *Das Reich* to use the Krems bridge and cross back over to the south bank and regroup in places south and west of that town.

But not all of *Das Reich* made it out. The *I./SS-Panzer-Artillerie-Regiment 2* got cut off by Russian spearheads and were trapped. Knowing their fate, the artillerists had the surviving *Hummel* self-propelled artillery guns fire over open sights, and supported by specialist troops acting as infantry, they blasted their way through to safety. Losses were heavy but most of the battalion got out. The *IV./SS-Panzer-Artillerie-Regiment 2* wasn't so lucky. Blocked on the narrow roads by traffic jams and stalled vehicles, the *IV. Abteilung* was strung out and overrun by the Russians a mile short of the new German lines. Some of the men escaped on foot without their guns, while at least half were killed or captured, and for the SS capture meant almost certain death.

In the days to come *Das Reich* would receive yet another infusion of manpower. They would again be untrained non-volunteers, including a group of Fire Protection Police from Dresden.[6] Once the remaining veterans had rested and healed for a few days, the imperative became training the new replacements, repairing equipment and scrounging whatever they could to increase combat power. In terms of the armored fighting vehicles that gave *Das Reich* its designation as a panzer division, however, no new machines would be forthcoming.

Vienna

The Soviets reported losses between Second and Third Ukrainian Fronts of 38,661 dead in the month from 16 March to 15 April 1945, with 129,729 wounded. Tank and assault gun losses were given as 603, guns as 764 and combat aircraft as 614. Numbers from Soviet sources must always be taken with a grain of salt, but even if the numbers of close to 170,000 casualties in a month

---

6   This is a literal translation of their official title, *Feuerschutzpolizei*. These were firefighters and technically part of the *Ordnungspolizei*, the Order Police.

were exaggerated, half that number would still equal the same casualty total that America suffered in the Battle of the Bulge.

On the German side the figures totaled more than 19,000 dead, at least that many wounded and tens of thousands more taken prisoner. Put in perspective, that's roughly the same number of killed as the Americans suffered in the Battle of the Bulge. Nor does that number count casualties suffered in *Unternehmen Frülingserwachen*, which would add thousands more killed, wounded and missing.

* * *

In prostrate Vienna, brutal vignettes were being played out as the Red Army took its revenge. At the small Brigitta Kapelle in the 20th District two *Waffen-SS* men left behind were reportedly shot in front of the altar. Prisoners roamed the city after the jails and prisons had been emptied. Some of the newly freed people were political prisoners, but many were criminals set free in a city in chaos. Organized gangs of criminals systematically looted foodstuffs armed with weapons picked up off the streets. Estimates also put the number of refugee Hungarians in the city as 100,000. With no ruling authority and no timetable for restoring services, Vienna remained a very dangerous city.

The Russians had no time or men to spare solving the problems of the conquered city, save a few engineer units that threw emergency footbridges over the canal and river. The damage from the 52 Allied bombing raids and the urban fighting was severe, food distribution was non-existent[7] and while Weiner Neustadt suffered a much higher percentage of buildings and homes destroyed, in terms of sheer numbers Vienna was by far the most heavily damaged.

The University of Vienna had not escaped the destruction. The first bombs struck the campus in September 1944, and by 15 April fully 30 percent of its buildings were destroyed, with 65 percent of the roofs gone.[8] The beloved zoo on the grounds of Schönbrunn Palace was an almost total loss. Public transportation was mostly destroyed, rubble clogged the streets, and gas electrical services weren't fully restored until the end of April.[9]

The damage to Vienna didn't come to an end with the fall of the city, especially the damage to the Viennese themselves. In the days to come the Russians would take machinery of every conceivable shape, size and function, to be shipped back to the Soviet Union. Herds of people were rounded up off the streets and shipped to Siberia, never to be heard from again. But the women suffered most of all. Rape was epidemic, as it was everywhere the Red Army set foot, with venereal disease rates skyrocketing in the months after the war's end.

* * *

Like moles exposed to sunlight, the Viennese emerged from their shelters and tried to understand their new reality. Everywhere they looked were horse-drawn carts and trucks loaded with booty, everything from bathtubs to radios and record players. Livestock roped to the wagons plodded along behind them, leaving their waste in the streets. Even destroyed cars had been looted of their engines and tires.

As the Russian combat formations pursued the retreating Germans, Vienna became a lawless wasteland where gangs of liberated workers picked up automatic weapons and went looking for vengeance. The Russians didn't care what happened to the Viennese as long as the gangs stayed out of their way; nor were roving gangs the only thing to fear, as the Russians preyed on the

---

7   A British study on Vienna's food situation in 1945 illustrates just how dire things were.
8   An historical tour of the University of Vienna, *Archiv der Universität Wien*, <http://www.univie.ac.at/archiv/tour/19.htm>, (Accessed 12 April 2012).
9   Lucas, James, *Last Days of the Third Reich, The Collapse of Nazi Germany, May, 1945* (New York: William Morrow and Company, 1986), p. 96.

citizens themselves. Rape was epidemic and anyone who interfered was shot. Women who fought back were shot. People suspected of ties to the Nazis were shot, even if they were innocent. Men wearing glasses were shot. Sometimes the Russians shot people for no reason other than they spoke German. For the Viennese, surviving the first few days of peace was every bit as dangerous as surviving the last days of war.

With no fire department, burning buildings crumbled into ashes that floated on the breezes and left an acrid pall over the city. The air tasted like charcoal. Scattered body parts littered the sidewalk. A pair of legs in German Army Pants lay in the rubble with no sign of the rest of the body. The head of a Russian solder sat upright near a shattered column, the tongue sticking out as if the man bit down in pain while being decapitated. Food distribution was non-existent. As hoarded supplies ran out people became desperate, and dead horses were quickly carved up for their meat.

6. SS-Panzerarmee
II SS-Panzerkorps
Kampfgruppe 3. SS-Panzer-Division Totenkopf

The division had one Panther operational with a handful of other panzers in repair. When it transferred to Hungary in late December 1944, *Totenkopf*'s panzer regiment was down to 20 percent strength, meaning no more than 40 panzer-types. Three-and-a-half months later almost all of them were burnt-out hulks scattered throughout western Hungary and Vienna.

South of the Danube

Korps von Bünau, formerly Korps Schultz

After being released from the service of *II SS-Panzerkorps*, General von Bünau was given a new mission, to command the defense of the sector near Sankt Pölten, but the staff that had served him throughout the previous two weeks was not to accompany him and was dissolved at its headquarters near Roselfeld. His new and reduced staff would be housed at the ancient Schloss Schallaburg some three miles from Melk. The magnificent castle dated back some 900 years but had been updated several times and stood as a cultural icon near the Wachau Valley in the Mostvertiel, rising above the surrounding area like a watchful sentinel of Austria's bygone Imperial greatness.

During the night of 15 April the Russians reached Sankt Pölten; they also climbed the high ground south of the city, making any remaining German positions east of the Traisen River indefensible.

SS-Kampfgruppe Trabandt III, or SS-Regiment Siegmann

Some 50 miles west of Vienna the Russian spearheads approached Krems, the strategic town at the confluence of the Krems and Danube Rivers. Graves on the site dating back some 27,000 years showed just how important the joining of those two rivers had always been to control of the region. Unable to cross the Danube near Tulln, and stymied by the quick reaction of *II SS-Panzerkorps* from expanding its bridgehead on the north bank near Korneuberg, securing Krems would have given the Russians an anchor on which to move north into Czechoslovakia, or west following the course of the Danube to seize more of Austria before the Americans could cut them off. With no reserves near Krems, *SS-Kampfgruppe Trabandt III*, commanded by *SS-Sturmbannführer* Erich

Siegmann, was rushed to the hilly area near Krustetten, south and southeast of Krems, straight from their assembly areas. The *Kampfgruppe* was attached to *Korps von Bünau* and started moving into position on 14 April.[10] Right away they were engaged in fierce defensive fighting.

The regiment was deployed near Öberwöbling with the boundary line between the *I. Abeteilung* and *II. Abteilung* being near Kuffern, although most of the town lay in the *I. Abteilung*'s zone. The front lines of the bridgehead ran from Oberwöbling through Niederwöbling and included the small towns of Kuffern, Nussdorf and Wetterkreuz, near Hollenburg, with the left flank anchored on the Danube. Siegmann was a talented commander, being a former tactical instructor at the SS Leader's School in Prague.[11]

Meanwhile, an *SS-Feldersatz-Bataillon* organized for *Das Reich* had been fully reconstituted with new recruits and a full complement of weapons, and, since the division itself had been pulled out of the line for rest and regrouping, a weak battalion's worth of men ready for combat was sent to join *SS-Kampfgruppe-Division Böhmen und Mähren*, and wound up assigned to *SS-Kampfgruppe Trabandt III*. This formation wasn't the official *Feldersatz-Bataillon 2 Das Reich*, however, nor did it have a known *Kampfgruppe* title. It was simply a group of men who had been trained to join *Das Reich* who were sent to join Siegmann's regiment. *SS-Feldersatz-Bataillon 2* continued functioning as normal to supply replacements for the parent division.

On 15 April a Russian attack overran all of Kuffern, overwhelming the new and unnamed *Kampfgruppe*. After taking Kuffern the Russians continued attacking to the west but couldn't penetrate the German defenses further. Siegmann's newly formed regiment stopped them.

Korps Schultz

Having ripped open the front north of Sankt Pölten the day before, the Russians finally took the town itself and sent the defenders fleeing, but not without a bitter fight. The Germans put up a tenacious defense but were outgunned and prised out of their strongpoints one by one. Finally the defense broke.

Tolbukhin's Third Ukrainian Front now had a reinforced Sixth Guards Tank Army blasting its way down the Danube Valley, with 17th Tank Corps and both brigades of 9th Guards Mechanized Corps attached. The Germans also confirmed that 5th Guards Tank Corps was being pulled out of Vienna and assembled in open areas west of that city.

On 15 April no less than three mobile brigades drove south of Sankt Pölten, two of them tanks and one mechanized. Outflanked now on both sides, with substantial Russian bridgeheads over the Traisen River in both places, attacks from north, south and east dislodged defenders and sent them reeling backwards. General Schultz used every available officer to halt his demoralized forces and rally them into a counterattack. By this quick action they threw the Russians back to the northwest of Sankt Pölten and managed to cobble together a shaky defensive line, but retaking the lost town was out of the question. The Russians had crossed the Traisen in force and meant to stay there.

Good news came in the Obergrafendorf area, where Schultz's corps closed the gap with *SS-Kampfgruppe Peiper*. The line wasn't strong but at least strongpoints could alert them to danger.

10   Von Bünau's corps did not actually become active until late on 15 or 16 April.
11   R.P., *Siegrunen 69*, pp.7-8.

SS-Kampfgruppe Peiper

Russian patrols to reconnoiter *SS-Kampfgruppe Kling*'s position south of Sankt Pölten were driven back or wiped out. Then Peiper ordered Kling to counterattack from the area around Wilhelsmburg into the left flank of the Russian advance south of Sankt Pölten, before the Russians had time to dig in. Kling inflicted heavy casualties and drove them back more than two miles, recapturing Sankt Georgen am Steinfelde in the process. But just as elements of *Korps Schultz* had failed to recapture Sankt Pölten itself, or to close the breach in the front, so the SS men also failed to complete their victory. The Germans simply didn't have the firepower to fight so much Russian armor; the attack ran out of steam before inflicting a serious defeat, and they had to go over to the defensive. For a moment the Russian advance had stalled, but the threat to *6. SS-Panzerarmee*'s rear areas, not to mention the Danube Valley, remained dire.

The Russians then targeted Wilhelmsburg and went on the attack themselves, setting off a two-day battle for the town. Wilhelmsburg was a southern suburb of Sankt Pölten, with a population of around 5,000. Like many Austrian settlements Wilhelmsburg's urban area hugged the bank of the local river, in this case the western bank of the Traisen. At its widest point the town was no more than 2,000 feet in width, but close to two miles in length.

The initial assault was thrown back. The SS men fought with a tenacity that most German formations no longer exhibited, so victory on the first day of fighting went to Kling.

Kampfgruppe 12. SS-Panzer-Division Hitlerjugend

After savage attacks the day before the Russians had to pause to regroup, giving the division a much-needed respite. There were a few probing attacks on *SS-Kampfgruppe Bremer* and *SS-Panzergrenadier-Regiment 26*, but nothing terribly strong. Reconnaissance patrols showed Nöstach clear of Russians, although a prominent nearby hill was crawling with them. *SS-Panzergrenadier-Regiment 25* attacked the hill and recaptured it, securing the area, but Katyusha fire immediately saturated the mountain, causing heavy casualties.

Kampfgruppe 1. SS-Panzer-Division Leibstandarte Adolf Hitler

Having attacked the day before and retaken substantial ground in the region west of Berndorf and Pottenstein, *LAH* spent the day mopping up the Russians it had previously surrounded. Once finished doing that, further attacks by an ad-hoc *Kampfgruppe* retook the old front lines and both towns.[12] German casualties were moderate, although the attrition of NCOs and junior officers continued at a disproportionate pace.

Kampfgruppe Koch

The survivors of the *Kampfgruppe*, mostly the remaining *Fahnenjunkern* and wounded veterans, discovered that the three SS Panzer Mark IVs had been ordered to leave Dreistetten and break through to Markt Piesting. The *Kampfgruppe* commander, *Hauptmann* Koch, tried to get the order rescinded or delayed, but to no avail.

---

12   Tiemann, *The Leibstandarte IV/2*, p. 297.

The *SS-Oberscharführer* in charge of the SS panzers had got on well with the men of the *Kampfgruppe* and they had established a soldierly bond. Without warning, a heavy Russian bombardment from artillery, mortars and anti-tank guns hit the area. *Hauptmann* Koch had been saying goodbye to the panzer crews when a shell splinter struck him over the left eye.

Even as explosions rocked the area around him, the *SS-Oberscharführer* bound the captain's wounds and helped him inside the panzer. Then, with the road cut to Markt Piesting, he took a serpentine course toward the Piesting Valley, determined to blast his way through any roadblocks to get the injured officer to an aid station. Even semi-conscious inside the steel hull, Koch could hear the panzer being hit with splinters and blast waves. He also heard the roar of its cannon, but eventually they made it through safely.

The remnants of his *Kampfgruppe* had been ordered to retreat through the dense forests to the area around Oberpiesting and Waldegg. But Koch's ordeal wasn't over. He woke up in a field hospital with his wound stitched closed and a bandage on his head. The doctor told him to lie still, and that within an hour he and the other wounded would be captured by the Russians. Koch said to hell with that, crawled out of bed and walked in the direction of Waldegg, determined to hook up with a group still fighting. Soon enough he found himself among a mass of German troops all retreating toward Waldegg, including wounded *Fahnenjunkern* from his own *Kampfgruppe*. After contacting the command post of a local regiment, he was given a small number of men, totaling between 30 and 60, around which to form a new *Kampfgruppe*, with between 30 and 60 men.

SS-Kampfgruppe Keitel

Fighting around Puchberg continued unabated. *SS-Kampfgruppe Keitel*'s artillery component had never been adequate, and with few heavy weapons the SS men couldn't interdict Russian assembly areas. In turn, this meant they had to rely on close-quarters combat to stop Russian tanks and assault guns. What they needed were a few dozen 88s. The reality was that their only defenses against armor were hand-held weapons such as the *Panzerfaust* or Tellermines.[13] Without the ability to destroy Russian armor at a distance, the Germans had to trade blood for steel.

Nor did they have the ammunition supply needed for effective counter-battery fire, which consumed shells at a prodigious rate. The heavy ammunition they did have was needed to break up attacks or support counterattacks. This gave the Russian artillery and rocket batteries free rein to pound the German positions.

Among the trees and boulders on the high ground this wasn't so critical. Combat there usually involved squads or platoons fighting at close range. If the Russians took a German position, the defenders knew they had to counterattack immediately. The Russians could dig new rifle pits and trenches remarkably fast, which meant driving them out would cost that much more blood.

But there was only so much blood to give. Keitel's command had 2,000 men when it entered combat, a paltry number to defend such a broad and rugged area, and losses greatly reduced it. Yet his position on *6. SS-Panzerarmee*'s far right flank was critical. Therefore, on 15 April the *LAH* had to parcel out another component, the *SS-Werfer-Bataillon 501*, for attachment to *SS-Kampfgruppe Keitel*. Despite the acute ammunition shortage this would at least give that fast-dwindling formation some long-range killing ability.

The defense of Puchberg depended on the capture of some hills to the southeast. Otherwise, Russian artillery observers could maintain a steady and accurate fire on all German movements in the area. But a counterattack to retake the area failed.

---

13   The Tellermine came in many different models, but most were round and triggered by a pressure plate.

6. *Armee*

Accounts of the fighting in Austria tend to focus solely on Vienna. James J. Weingartner's comment typifies how this combat is classified in most histories: "By the middle of April, pressure along most of the front of *Heeresgruppe Süd* had eased, as the major weight of the Russian offensive moved north of the Danube."[14]

The implication is of a quiet front with occasional skirmishing. The Russians' heavy and mobile units were indeed driving northwest into Czechoslovakia, but that didn't mean the front in east-central Austria was quiet. In fact, as has already been shown, the fighting on 6. *Armee*'s front was vicious, prolonged and costly to both sides. James Lucas described it as follows:

> The troops stayed isolated in the mountains, devoid of any comfort. There were few cigarettes, little alcohol, no women, the food was poor and spring in the high country is a time of unending rain and freezing fog… Hell is not necessarily a place where souls are roasted; it can be a bare mountaintop in wartime.[15]

III Panzerkorps

At Sankt Kathrein am Hauenstien a fierce battle broke out at the intersection of the road to Ratten over the Alpl, and Sankt Kathrein itself came under heavy artillery fire. Late in the evening a 2,000-man Russian strike group set out west to take Fischbach-Schanz im Mürztal.[16] The breakthrough was now deep and potentially fatal to the entire German position in east-central Austria.

Kampfgruppe Raithel

Rettenegg's turn came at 10:00 a.m. when 36th Guards Rifle Division, of 30th Guards Rifle Corps, attacked the town. The small defense force, probably *Volkssturm* with support from the Hungarian *werfer* battery in the nearby hills, were no match for the veteran Guardsmen.

1. Volks-Grenadier-Division

After two days the division had no choice except to retreat across the valley of the Lafnitz River south of Stegersbach. The front line now ran through the northern edge of empty Fürstenfeld, but only briefly. Fürstenfeld couldn't be held either, and in the afternoon the Russians occupied it.

The Germans immediately brought it under artillery fire, having pre-registered the batteries. During the fight for the town and subsequent bombardment, 241 men died, 37 houses were totally destroyed and ten more damaged. In the entire Fürstenfeld district, which included the valley of the Lafnitz River, 947 soldiers of both sides died, along with five civilians, and 53 were missing.[17]

---

14   Weingartner, James J., *Hitler's Guard, Inside the Führer's Personal SS Force* (New York: Berkley Books, 1990), p. 162.

15   Lucas, *Last 100 Days*, p. 106.

16   Brettner, *Die Letzten Kämpfe Band I*, p. 35.

17   Brettner, *Die Letzten Kämpfe Band II*, p. 16.

Kampfgruppe 1. Panzer-Division

The division reported one Mark IV and two Panthers operational. In its report on 1 April the division listed 39 Panthers in total, with most of them in repair, but on the 15th that total number was down to seven, meaning only five were with the workshop company. It's unknown what happened to the missing 32 Panthers, but in all likelihood the workshop sites were overrun and, without enough heavy transport available, the machines under repair were destroyed.

Regardless of its condition, the division was sent northwest to the Styrian town of Ilz. Numerous castles in the area made it seem like an idyllic fantasy realm of soaring mountains splashed with the colors of spring. And for years that's exactly what it had been, the perfect postcard for the beauty of Austria. But now war had come to shatter that reality. *Kampfgruppe 1. Panzer-Division* was there to lead a counterattack against the dangerous bulge punched into the front by the Russian Twenty-Sixth Army.

Kampfgruppe 3. Panzer-Division

Castle Kalsdorf, near the beautiful little town of Ilz, had long been known for its cultivated lands and well-kept fields. Built in the 1600s, it had once been owned by Count Georg-Ernst of Erbach-Wildenstein, a German prince. Its stately architecture matched the majesty of the surrounding countryside.

On the morning of 15 April the command staff of *3. Panzer-Division* pulled up to the front doors and set up the divisional headquarters inside. There was no time to lose in deploying the remaining divisional groups, as the Russians were even then closing in on Fürstenfeld, a few miles to the east. They had already taken the high ground in the Lafnitz Valley east of Fürstenfeld, and spearheads that passed south of that town were closing in on Ilz. The fight was on.

> Heavy rounds from howitzers and rockets rained down on the pretty city. A hurricane of fire…drove its citizenry into the deepest hiding places…in between the breaks in the firing, the rattling of tracked-vehicle movement could be heard. The Russians were coming.[18]

Despite fierce resistance, including the local *Volkssturm*, the Germans were thrown back to Fürstenfeld itself. There were just too many Russian tanks and infantry, too much firepower, to resist for long. Every house and every street corner saw bitter firefights and countless counterattacks by half a dozen men or fewer. Houses changed hands multiple times. The citizens who hadn't fled got in the line of fire, hampering the defenders, sometimes trying to drive them away from their house. Treasured crockery shattered under machine-gun bullets and irreplaceable windows crashed in jagged shards. Everywhere the Germans fought they were driven back, regardless of Russian losses.

One company made a stand at the freight yards but was surrounded and destroyed. Even so, the remaining defenders continued the fight long past the point of exhaustion. If sheer human will could overcome bullets they were determined to prevail. But in the end the bullets won, as they always do. After vicious combat that lasted all the day, the last German vehicle pulled out to the southwest, still firing at the Russians. It was a captured T-34.

---

18   Veterans, *Armored Bears*, p. 286.

The loss of Fürstenfeld was a serious blow to the continued defense of Styria. Situated as it was in the Lafnitz Valley, it commanded that waterway and opened the door for a drive on Graz.

14. Waffen-Grenadier-Division der SS Galizien

Despite everything, the German logistics and replacement systems still functioned, even if in a haphazard and often bizarre fashion. In the middle of the month *Galizien*, with all of the other formations that desperately needed replacements, including the shattered SS divisions of *II SS-Panzerkorps*, was given 2,500 surplus *Luftwaffe* personnel. Most of them were mechanics or technicians, a few were pilots, but none had any infantry training whatsoever and were completely useless in ground combat. Fortunately for them they were never used to fight. Some were put to work as mechanics or radio operators, some were sent for training and the rest were shuttled about. The division commander, *SS-Brigadeführer und General der Waffen-SS* Freitag, was delighted to receive so many Germans, regardless of their worth, since his disdain for the Ukrainians under his command was well known. The Ukrainians, on the other hand, were as distrustful of these Germans as they were any others. The bigger question, of course, is how these Germans wound up in a foreign division in the first place, when so many German divisions were bled white, and when Hitler was obviously so distrustful of eastern troops. Perhaps they were sent there as stiffeners, to increase the fighting morale of the Ukrainians. Or perhaps the SS Main Office simply assigned the men to the nearest unit so they would not be snatched up by needier units during transport elsewhere. Whatever the reason, a division that was already enormous got even bigger.

* * *

Meanwhile Freitag and his chief of staff, Army Major Wolf-Dietrich Heike, were at their desks eating a late supper when word came of a strong assault on Gleichenberg Castle. Reserves were immediately thrown into the fray. As the situation cleared, it became obvious that heavy Russian barrages drove the Ukrainians out of their positions around the hill on which the castle was built, but not from the castle itself.

A counterattack was planned using *Grenadiers* and flame-throwers, with a battery of 150mm howitzers in support. The guns were limited to firing just 60 shells in total. In the darkness the German counterattack soon led to hand-to-hand combat, but by 2:45 a.m. on 16 April the break-through had been sealed off.[19]

Kampfgruppe 3. Panzer-Division

One of the three nucleus panzer divisions of the *Wehrmacht* reported three Panthers, one *Jagdpanzer IV/70*, one *Sturmgeschütz III*, one *Sturmhaubitz 42*,[20] two *Jagdpanzer 38(t) Hetzers*, one *Panzerbeobachtungswagen*, an artillery observation panzer used along with mobile artillery batteries, such as *Wespes* or *Hummels*, and six heavy *Flak* guns, as combat ready on 15 April. And like its sister division *Kampfgruppe 1. Panzer-Division*, *Kampfgruppe 3. Panzer-Division* had also

---

19   Heike, Wolf-Dietrich, *The Ukrainian Division 'Galica', 1943-1945* (Toronto: The Shevchenko Scientific Society, 1988), pp. 124-126.

20   The *StuH* was essentially a *Sturmgeschütz III* with a howitzer as its main gun instead of the usual cannon. This made it more effective against infantry.

sent its reconnaissance battalion north to join *Korps von Bünau*. Neither division would get them back.

* * *

As 15 April faded into the chronicles of history the Germans might have been forgiven for thinking the Russian thirst for vengeance had been slaked with the fall of Vienna, but in fact Stalin and Stavka still had big plans for the remaining weeks of the war. And in the west, Patton's Third Army captured Nuremberg. Casting his eyes toward Germany, Lothar Rendulic began planning for a new defense line facing west.

16

Monday, 16 April

Berlin

With the opening of the final Soviet offensive on Berlin, Hitler and the *OKH*'s attention to *Heeresgruppe Süd* and *Heeresgruppe Mitte* gave way to more pressing concerns as Marshal Georgi Zhukov's First Belorussian Front smashed into *Heeresgruppe Vistula*'s defenses along the Oder River. Besides Berlin itself, the heart of the German General Staff and the largest communications complex in all of Europe, at Zossen, was in the direct path of the Red Army advance. Staff officers were far more concerned with their own immediate danger of being overrun at their desks than in some remote command that could not influence the outcome of the only battle that really mattered to them now: the fight for Berlin.

But Hitler never forgot his homeland. In his Order of the Day issued to *Heeresgruppe Vistula*, Hitler only mentioned two cities by name, Berlin and Vienna: "If every soldier on the Eastern Front does his duty in these coming days and weeks, the last assault from Asia will be broken, just as the invasion by our enemy in the west will fail in spite of everything, Berlin will remain German, Vienna will be German once more and Europe will never be Russian."[1]

So, even as the final assault had begun and the eyes of the entire world were focused on Berlin and the broken old man directing its defense from a dank air raid bunker under the Reich Chancellery, some part of Hitler's mind was on lost Vienna.

Heeresgruppe Süd

The spring weather had turned warm and sunny. Flowers bloomed on Alpine meadows and green buds adorned the trees. Such conditions would have made for a perfect day during any other year, but in 1945 it allowed the Red Air Force to strafe and bomb at will. As for *Luftflotte 4*, the air fleet's remaining airfields were circled by American fighter aircraft waiting for targets to show themselves or take to the air. Despite this, the *Luftwaffe* managed to fly 180 sorties against Russian buildups near Tulln and Sankt Pölten. More and more they took to flying at night.

* * *

As the final battle for the capital of the Reich erupted on the banks of the Oder, in Austria the Red Army kept pushing forward against weakening resistance. By 16 April the front was far to the west, south of Linz, where Gerersdorf was in Russian hands. Sankt Pölten had been lost after heavy fighting and a huge bulge had been pushed into central Austria. The Germans had no meaningful reserves to throw into the breach, but the weeks of fighting had left the Russians tired, heavy losses had depleted their already under-strength formations and their supply lines grew ever longer. The Russian juggernaut was losing its momentum.

---

1   Strassner, *European Volunteers*, p. 331.

The Russian assault on Austria resembled a rushing river that is partially blocked by a large stone. If the water cannot go through or over the stone, or dislodge it, then it rushes around it. But it never stops eating away at the surface of the stone and eventually, if the process lasts long enough, the river will wash away even the largest boulder.

So it was in the battle for Austria. Ever since encountering stiff resistance in the south and center of the battle area, in the foothills of the Alps the Russian advance had taken a decidedly northwestern turn. Malinovsky's dream of driving down the Danube Valley to Munich faded in the face of stiffening German resistance. Nevertheless, the Russians continued attacking until the very end of the war, putting paid to the idea that Austria became a tranquil backwater. In fact the opposite was true. It remained a killing ground more reminiscent of the First World War than the Second World War, where Russian advances were measured in meters and one successful attack might result in a dozen counterattacks.

As a reflection of how savage the fighting in Austria had been, the *Heeresgruppe* reported that on 14 and 15 April 70 Russian tanks had been destroyed, including 47 in the battles around Sankt Pölten.[2] These German figures are likely too high, and a large number of damaged tanks were undoubtedly put back into service, but if such losses were sustained over the entire month it would mean no less than 1,000 Russian tanks and assault guns knocked out.

North of the Danube

8. Armee

While in the pocket north of Vienna, the German defensive lines had been very long. As soon as the pocket evaporated that was no longer the case. This drastically shortened the area to be defended and allowed General Kreysing's patchwork units to form a true front line again. Russian assaults couldn't penetrate the new lines and in places the Germans had recovered enough to launch counterattacks.

Kampfgruppe 101. Jäger-Division

The next strategic objectives for Second Ukrainian Front were Brno, Brunn in German, in old Czechoslovakia, and the oil fields at Zistersdorf. To take the first meant first having to take the second. But Zistersdorf was fortified, so capturing it would require attacking from multiple directions, and two key towns guarding its western flank were Wilfersdorf and Mistelbach.

The terrain south of both towns was mostly flat agricultural land. With such long sight lines heavy weapons took on an all new importance, as did any defensible feature, such as the town of Schrick, five miles southeast of Mistelbach. The town's main distinction was being astride the *Reichsstrasse* from Vienna to Poysdorf. Beyond that one main highway, Schrick only had two other north-south streets. It was no more than a mile long and perhaps 1,000 feet wide. Like any such settlement there were some outlying structures.

The *101. Jäger-Division* had responsibility for defending that section of the front. Both sides recognized that Schrick was a key position and for days both the *Luftwaffe* and the Red Air Force had pounded targets in and around the town. Heavy defensive fighting followed as neither side was willing to accept defeat, and as such battles often do that combat drew in more troops, in

---

2   Maier, *Drama,* p. 365.

this case elements of *25. Panzer-Division*. As might be expected the casualties were heavy, with 46 German and 60 Russian soldiers killed, along with four townsfolk. Schrick itself was virtually destroyed, with 71 buildings smashed flat and 158 more damaged.

The infantry was too exhausted and scattered to offer much more resistance, so a new battle line was formed around *Artillerie-Regiment 196*, from *Kampfgruppe 96. Infanterie-Division*, reinforced by a battalion from the *Schwere-Artillerie-Regiment 25* and a heavy *Flak* battery, probably of 88mm guns. They were ordered to set up a so-called Artillery Main Line in space around the Höhen Grossussbach-Hornsburg, a dominating height. Instead of being well back from the front line, this line of artillery would be on the front line, firing over open sights. The positions were sighted so as to be mutually supporting, with ammunition supplies close at hand and well protected. Any non-essential personnel would wield a rifle or machine gun and fill in the gaps.[3]

* * *

The *6. Panzer-Division* repulsed Russian probes and launched an attack that recaptured Seebarn and Mannhartsbrunn, moving the front to the east almost into the path of the redeploying units moving to attack Mistelbach. *Kampfgruppe 96. Infanterie-Division* also repulsed all Russian attacks around Mollmannsdorf and Gaweinnstal. Other towns, such as Nieverfellabrunn, Obergänserndorf, Hautzendorf and Trainfeld, all fell, but only after ferocious fighting.[4] *Kampfgruppe 101. Jäger-Division* successfully fought off attacks on Höbersbrunn and Schrick, but lost Palterndorf to the Russian 93rd Guards Rifle Division.

In the Stetten area German outposts were pushed back to Tresdorf, which was only a minor loss of ground. As early as 13 April the Russians had bombed the area, aiming for the *Panzerwerkestätte*, the tank repair facility established there by an SS platoon, probably from *Das Reich*. Once the panzers left, refugees from Vienna moved in, including policemen. It wasn't until 14 April that the Russians made their first probes toward Stetten itself, in the form of five tanks with infantry. Three were destroyed by anti-tank fire and the remaining two pulled back to safety.

But the SS men holding the town knew the Russians would be back and in strength. Holding Stetten had been necessary to shield withdrawing units, but during the night of 14-15 April they pulled out, too. But even though the Germans had abandoned the city, there was an eerie calm on 15 April because the Russians didn't move in immediately. Only on the morning of 16 April did they finally occupy the town.

They found a devastated town with at least 70 dead. In one house they found a German soldier who'd been beheaded by an explosion.

* * *

In Mistelbach itself the *Gauleiter* of Lower Austria, and *SS-Obergruppenführer* Dr Hugo Jury, arrived in the town and began ordering it to prepare for battle. Jury was an Austrian Nazi even before the *Anschluss* and was trusted by both Hitler and the Party. As an Austrian he had tried hard to improve conditions for workers and was rabidly anti-Viennese, considering the city a bad influence. And, unlike so many Nazi leaders, Jury actually practiced what he preached. After leaving the Mistelbach area he formed his own small *Kampfgruppe*, armed only with rifles and *Panzerfauste*, and fought the invaders at Jaidhof.

---

3   Brettner, *Die Letzten Kämpfe Band II*, p. 170.
4   Brettner, *Die Letzten Kämpfe Band II*, p. 169.

Before that, however, he was busy organizing the defense of his *Gau*. He ordered all administrative offices, firemen and their equipment to evacuate to Laa an der Thaya. German tanks moved into the town and set up defensive positions. At 10:00 p.m. the *Volkssturm* was called out, but most of the men were drunk and hard to assemble. The battalion commander patiently gave them some time to sober up, until he learned that the local Party officials had almost drunk themselves unconscious, at which point he dismissed the men and told them to go home.

SS-Kampfgruppe Trabandt II, or SS-Regiment Konopacki

Russian pressure on *8. Armee*'s center, combined with *Kampfgruppe Volkmann*'s successful defense of the Tulln sector on the Danube's north bank, allowed for the transfer of most of the *Kampfgruppe*'s two remaining battalions to the Poysdorf area. A few small components appear to have stayed in the Krems area, perhaps remnants of the battalion that had gone south to fight with *6. SS-Panzerarmee*.

North of the Danube

6. SS-Panzerarmee
Führer-Grenadier-Division

West-northwest of Korneuberg, the Danube lowlands proved a significant barrier to Russian armor. They followed the river's course as far as Krems, which is why Tulln was so important to the attackers, because even though the bridge had already been blown up, the roads running through the city led north through the lowlands.

But for the Russians north of the river, the only way west involved driving the Germans back from their newly formed defensive line and the *Führer-Grenadier-Division* anchored the right flank. Throughout the day of 16 April the Russians attacked to the northwest from Korneuberg in battalion and regimental strength, backed by armor. In heavy fighting the Germans gave ground, up to two miles in places, but the Russians couldn't break through.

There is a story that sometime in mid-April, the *6./SS-Panzer-Regiment 1* was attached to the division. The men were said to no longer have panzers and were sent to flesh out the division's depleted infantry regiment. Why they would have been sent north, when their parent division was desperately short of infantry, isn't known, and the story is unlikely to be true.

Kampfgruppe Volkmann

Luftwaffe Generalmajor Volkmann learned of a Russian buildup on the Danube west of his position, in the area east of Hollenburg, a few miles east of Krems. Worse, reconnaissance identified Russian assembly areas at Zwentendorf, seven miles west of Tulln. And not far to the northeast, heavy fighting at Stockerau and points north of that town threatened his position from the east.

South of the Danube

The Russians

With the capture of Sankt Pölten, Marshal Tolbukhin had fulfilled the conditions for ending his offensive to the west as laid out by Stavka. The limit of the Russian advance was to be the Traisen River. But he was given one bit of hope for continuing the offensive. It was permitted to attack where the German resistance was obviously weak. Lastly, Ninth Guards Army was ordered to go into reserve in the Vienna Woods.

Korps von Bünau

During the day, the command of *Korps Schultz* was formally and officially transferred to the former *Kampfkommandant Wien*, *General der Infanterie* von Bünau, and from that moment became known as *Korps von Bünau*. He established his headquarters at Schallaburg Castle three miles from Melk. It was in excellent repair and rose from the surrounding forest like a fairy-tale castle built in the Italian Renaissance style, complete with terra cotta mosaics of gods and mythical creatures. The white and red-trimmed central tower stood out against the pale blue skies of spring. Two 98 foot-long dragons sat on either side of the main gate. Ornamental trees and blooming flowers completed the picture of an idyllic spot to rest, which was completely out of character for the hard-working von Bünau.

Even as the Russians were slowing their advance, the Germans were desperate to reverse the situation caused by the loss of Sankt Pölten, but any counter-measures would have to succeed quickly. There simply weren't enough men or supplies for prolonged attacks or to fill the gaps in the front line. Remarkably, German air support from *Schlachgeschwader 10* and the Hungarian *Jagdgeschwader 101* repeatedly struck Russian march columns and artillery positions, and contributed heavily to the success of *Korps von Bünau* in preventing a full-blown breakthrough along the Danube.[5]

In the Krems bridgehead due north of Sankt Pölten, the newly arrived *SS-Kampfgruppe Trabandt III* launched a counterattack to recapture the small town of Kuffern. The previous day the men trained for *Das Reich* but not actually part of the division had been thrown out of Kuffern with heavy losses. The counterattack by the fresh men of *SS-Kampfgruppe Trabandt III* was successful, which led to the discovery of the bodies of 97 wounded SS men who had been left behind the previous day, allegedly murdered.[6] The Russians reacted quickly with counterattacks of their own but couldn't wipe out the German bridgehead.

Von Bünau's new command had a strong artillery component and a company of *Sturmgeschützen*, numbering as many as 16 machines. Moreover, it also had the *1.* and *3. Aufklärungs-Abteilungen* attached, although the former was at 60 percent of strength and the latter only at 50 percent. Reconnaissance battalions depended on various types of armored cars to perform their missions, and their tactical mobility gave von Bünau a rapid reaction force with some firepower. However, their depleted state meant that between them they equaled about one full-strength battalion.

5   Ruachensteiner, *Die Krieg in Österreich*, p. 182.
6   Landwehr, *Siegrunen 38*, p. 32.

710. Infanterie-Division

After serving with *6. SS-Panzerarmee* in Hungary, the *710. Infanterie-Division* was a welcome reinforcement, even if it was a third-rate division. Formed from older men as a small static division to be used for coast defense, it nevertheless had seen a considerable amount of fighting in replacing better-equipped divisions at the front. Seven more trains carrying components of the *710. Infanterie-Division* showed up on 16 April near Sankt Pölten.

It wasn't a minute too soon. After probing the division's entire front the Russians found several gaps and moved through them. From Herzogenburg on the west bank of the Traisen River, Russian forces moved west and northwest to Wöbling. This breakthrough was dangerous as it closed within six miles of Krems, but after heavy fighting Wöbling was retaken.

After nightfall even larger Russian groups, up to regimental strength and with strong tank support, pushed southwest from the Sankt Pölten area and drove to Gattmannsdorf. Counterattacks proved futile. This drive stretched the *710. Infanterie-Division*'s thin defenses even further and, unless the drive could somehow be stopped, threatened all of *I SS-Panzerkorps*' left flank with being turned.

Other Russian units pushed due west from Sankt Pölten. Ambach was lost and multiple counterattacks failed to retake it. Orbitzberg fell but an immediate counterattack retook it, only to have the Russians capture it a second time late in the afternoon.[7]

I SS-Panzerkorps
SS-Kampfgruppe Peiper

Due South of Sankt Pölten was the historic town of Sankt Georgen am Steinfelde. Roman and pre-Roman graves indicated the lush flatland had been occupied since at least the 2nd Century BC. Nearby armaments factories attracted air attacks that left Sankt Georgen badly damaged, and when the town fell to the Russians most of the remaining houses had been destroyed in the fighting. Using the little town as a staging area, the Russians launched new attacks to the south, toward Wilhelmsburg.

As on the previous day *SS-Kampfgruppe Kling* repulsed this newest Russian effort, but after regrouping they came on again, backed by armor and made in regimental strength, and pushed into the northern half of the town. The Germans knocked out at least four Sherman tanks and one SU-100 – eleven tanks in total were reported destroyed – but immediate counterattacks failed to restore the previous position. The Russians were determined to keep what they'd won. Skirmishing went on throughout the night.

Kampfgruppe 12. SS-Panzer-Division Hitlerjugend

The relative peace of the previous day didn't last.

On the division's western flank, its left, battalion-sized Russian attacks broke through between Obergrödl and Wöllersdorf, the mountainous country south of Forsthof. The terrain was heavily forested and, in places, sheer rock walls. There were no roads so the combat was between infantry forces. Artillery strikes were limited by the numerous mountains, but where it was possible to use

7   Maier, *Drama*, p. 364.

them the effects were multiplied by the overhead canopy. Shells bursting in the treetops sent deadly wood splinters raining downward. Mortars had the same effect and were easier to transport.

Next to fall was the Schöpfl hill, the key to Sankt Corona am Schöpfl hill. The danger from this breakthrough was now too great to ignore. If the Russians could hold the terrain between the highways, instead of their attacks sticking strictly to the roadways, then the division's entire position might crumble. Once again the redoubtable *SS-Hauptsturmführer* von Reitzenstein assembled an assault team from his *Kampfgruppe* at Sankt Corona and counterattacked. Once again his relative handful of men achieved the near-impossible and retook Schöpfl Hill. There weren't enough Germans to destroy the now cut-off Russians, but they were forced to retreat.

More heavy attacks struck *Hitlerjugend*'s lines around Nöstach in battalion strength, but were driven back. With snow-capped mountains as a backdrop, the little town seemed more like a place to relax for the weekend than to fight a battle. Elsewhere the Russians took Keinberg and Gadenweith, entering the Triesting Valley and making it almost into Weissenbach an der Triesting.[8] Loss of that town would cut the main supply road for all units further east, including the *LAH*.

The attacks came between Neuhaus, a tiny settlement half a mile north of Weissenbach, and a low hill one mile to the northeast. Stretched into little more than a blocking line, the Germans couldn't hold and the Russians quickly broke through. Only on a promontory known as the Dernberg Hill did the defense hold out, despite being essentially surrounded. That was *SS-Kampfgruppe Möbius*, and by hanging on instead of retreating, the SS men prevented a much larger breakthrough.

Heading south the Russians approached the eastern entrance to Weissenbach, but once again an immediate German response saved the situation. A thrown-together *Kampfgruppe* from *SS-Panzergrenadier-Regiment 26* closed the breakthrough gap and cut off the battalion-sized Russian force near Weissenbach. Realizing their situation, the Russians tried to set up a defense but they were overwhelmed.

The fighting was confused and units became mixed up in the dense woods. North of Pankrazi *SS-Kampfgruppe Bremer* showed why the *Waffen-SS* was still feared by their enemies on the battlefield. A battalion of Russian infantry attacked their positions on a hill, with support from mortars and machine guns situated on another nearby hill. During the ensuing firefight German artillery supported the defense with a few well-placed rounds, which pinned down the attackers. A squad of five or six men with two machine guns climbed into a single SPW and attacked the Russian gun positions on the opposite promontory. Taken completely by surprise, the Russians fled and the Germans took the hill, which put the assault battalion in a cross-fire. After absorbing high losses the battalion scattered and ran. Three SS men died in the fighting.[9] By the end of the day *Hitlerjugend* still held the line, but mounting losses and diminishing fuel and ammunition supplies didn't forebode well for the immediate future.

Kampfgruppe 1. SS-Panzer-Division Leibstandarte Adolf Hitler

Battalion-sized attacks in the Pankrazi area drove *LAH* back before counterattacks stopped the Russian momentum. Around Steinhof the Russians counterattacked to retake the town amid a constant mortar barrage. Casualties among the German rifle platoons reached 50 percent and more, flooding the aid stations with wounded.

---

8   Tiemann, *The Leibstandarte IV/2*, p. 298.
9   Meyer, *The 12th SS*, p. 481.

Russian attacks in the rugged mountains a mile or so southeast of Wollersdorf were driven back with heavy losses. The fighting took place where there were no roads, only game and hiking trails. Mortars and artillery were of limited use since fall of shot was hard to pinpoint, although explosions in the crowns of the trees rained deadly wood splinters onto anyone below. But in the claustrophobic confines of the rugged forests of Central Austria, tanks were useless and an MG-42 machine gun flanked by a platoon of infantry could hold a strongpoint against many times their number.

In the valley leading to Wollersdorf, however, the Russians pushed within a mile of the village, and held their gains despite immediate counterattacks. Worse for the Germans, 13 miles to the northwest, at Farhafeld near Weissenbach an der Triesting, a battalion-sized Russian force supported by tanks had moved west without interference.

Kampfgruppe 356. Infanterie-Division

The Germans controlled most of the area, but not all of it. The day before the *Kampfgruppe 356. Infanterie-Division* attacked to seize the rest of the mountain, but failed. On 16 April it launched more assaults and recaptured several strongpoints on the northern side of the mountain. The five mile-long ridge had more than 200 caves in which defenders of both sides waited to ambush the enemy. With the south wall being nearly sheer and the slopes densely studded with trees, it made for a murderous battlefield since all combat was at short range.

SS-Kampfgruppe Keitel

SS-Obersturmbannführer Keitel's regimental-sized *Kampfgruppe* had fought throughout the month in rough country on *6. SS-Panzerarmee*'s right flank. In the heavily forested hills it continued defending the line of Nasswald-Hütberg. Casualties had been heavy from the day it first entered combat. The fighting had depleted the *Kampfgruppe* so badly, in fact, that only strongpoints could be formed. On 16 April the Russians launched multiple attacks to break through once and for all, but *SS-Kampfgruppe Keitel* held once more. Indeed, the fighting was so fierce and the group's defense so steadfast that it was mentioned in *6. SS-Panzerarmee*'s War Bulletin for the day.[10]

6. Armee

The Russian offensive on the army's left flank slowed down after the huge gains of the day before. Although he'd been planning a counterattack of his own for days, *General der Panzertruppe* Hermann Balck had to judge the possibility of making successful counterattacks against the wisdom of pulling back and regrouping. Given the overall weakness of *6. Armee* the penetration to Fischbach had not been unexpected, but knowing disaster is possible and dealing with it once it happens are two quite different things. Given his standing orders not to retreat, in the end Balck launched what counterattacks he could.

He explained his decision in typical Balck fashion: "This situation required tough, decisive, and most importantly fast action…Only the attack would be effective here. We scraped up everything

---

10   Afiero, Massimilliano, *37. SS-Freiwilligen-Kavallerie-Division Lützow* <*http://www.maxafiero.it/37div.htm*>, (Accessed 7 May 2018).

we could muster. It was high risk, of course, but we had to accept risk somewhere else." Balck went on to say that by 16 April a superior German force had been assembled to deal with the crisis.[11]

The plan was laid out as a classic pincers attack, with spearheads coming from north, east and west. Part of *Kampfgruppe Raithel* would strike from the north from the area around Pfaffen and the Fiestritz Saddle, a critical mountain pass between the Wechsel and the Stuhleck, a towering peak in the Fischbach Alps. From the west would come the *117. Jäger-Division*, and finally from the east *Kampfgruppe 1. Panzer-Division* would attack, with *II./Gebirgsjäger-Regiment 98* attached, both of them moving north-northeast.

Kampfgruppe Raithel

For days the Russian artillery had pounded the German front lines along the east-facing border of *Kampfgruppe Raithel*. One platoon in the Feistritzsattel lost three men on 15 April and seven more on 16 April. In the following days the artillery fire slackened off somewhat, but a rain of mortar shells took its place. The only defense against this bombardment was huddling as deep in a rifle pit or bunker as possible and praying it didn't take a direct hit. Aside from skirmishes between patrols, however, the Russians launched no major attacks in the Trattenbach area.

117. Jäger-Division

At 2:00 a.m. the division moved through Sankt Kathrein on the orders of *6. Armee* as part of the three-pronged counterattack. Their immediate objective was the recapture of Waldbach, on the southern end of the Wechsel Mountains. This prominent terrain feature might become a nearly impregnable defensive position if the Germans could get it back.

The division command staff moved with the forward units, keeping close to the spearheads. The plan called for *Jäger-Regiment 737* and *Jäger-Regiment 749* to attack on separate tracks through the rugged terrain. The first objective was Ratten. Thus began a remarkable counterattack that proved German military competence could still deal heavy defeats on an unprepared enemy.

III Panzerkorps
Kampfgruppe 1. Panzer-Division

The counterattack to retake the Pöllau area began with *Kampfgruppe 1. Panzer-Division* participating. The battle would be more than a week of grinding combat. Such as it was the panzer regiment didn't participate, but instead went north to be attached to the *Führer-Grenadier-Division*, although five panzers reportedly participated. Likewise, one of the werfer brigades operating as infantry supported the attack.

Kampfgruppe 1. Panzer-Division attacked over a broad front, from Birkfeld to Pöllau and Vorau, with one battalion from *Gebirgsjäger-Regiment 98* attached. The rapid capture of Vorau cut the road to the west through which the Russian supplies flowed. This was a critical success that put all of the Russian units to the west in immediate danger of running out of fuel and ammunition. At Meisenbach bie Birkfeld the *Gebirgsjägers* engaged the 236th Rifle Division in close combat atop the mountains around the town.

---

11   Balck, *Order in Chaos,* p. 426.

1. Volks-Gebirgs-Division

The badly battered *Gebirgs-Pionier-Battailon 54* was withdrawn from the division's left wing and sent to the right to regroup while staying in reserve.

Kampfgruppe 3. Panzer-Division

Once upon a time *3. Panzer-Division* had raced across the Russian steppes all the way to the Caucasus, not far from the Turkish border. Along the way it gained battle honors to rival those of the other two original panzer divisions, *1. SS-Panzer-Division* and *2. SS-Panzer-Division*. On 16 April, dawn broke on a ruined division with two working Panthers, four anti-tank guns that still had their prime movers, twelve artillery tubes and two mortars. Both of its *Panzergrenadier* regiments were classified as weak, with probably less than fifty percent in manpower and much less in motorized transport. Companies that should have had 100 men or more often had 20, and most of those were the fresh, inexperienced faces of men not trained for ground combat. Veterans were obvious from their drawn gray features. Having established a strong position at Altenmarkt, the division awaited the next attack. They knew the Russians were getting close again.

2. Panzerarmee

General der Artillerie de Angelis had to be shocked that his cobbled-together front line had held as long as it had. The loss of *117. Jäger-Division* left him desperately short of troops, but the reality of the situation was that, from the standpoint of essential factories, refineries, rail junctions and supply points, *2. Panzerarmee* defended the least essential parts of Austria and Slovenia. And so, despite being attacked on almost every foot of its front line, de Angelis' army could expect no reinforcements, very little in the way of supplies and nothing more from *Heeresgruppe Süd* commander Rendulic than his best wishes.

23. Panzer-Division

On the division's far left flank, where it had been supporting *4. Kavallerie-Division* and the shattered remnants of *Kampfgruppe 44. Infanterie-Division Hoch und Deutschmeister* in the fight for Hill 336, *23. Panzer-Division* was itself hit with a vicious assault on another promontory in its main line of defense, Hill 332. The hill was lost, and then immediately regained by a counterattack. Just like Hill 336, the fight for Hill 332 would go on for days.

Meanwhile, as the division fought for its life in southeast Austria, it was ordered to send a contingent north to Sankt Valentin, site of the famed *Nibelungenwerke*. Something nobody expected to happen, had happened; *23. Panzer-Division* was being issued factory-fresh Panthers. Why the panzers weren't being given to any of the divisions already fighting in close proximity to the factory wasn't explained, and the division commander, *Generalleutnant* Joseph von Radowitz, wasn't going to ask. He sent the men north and crossed his fingers they weren't shot as deserters, or that the panzers weren't given to another formation before his men got there.[12]

---

12   Rebentisch, *To the Caucasus*, p. 466.

9. SS-Panzer-Division Hohenstaufen

Regardless of the desperate situation facing *2. Panzerarmee*, General de Angelis was about to lose his only SS panzer division, although by this time it was more like an infantry division than one centered around panzers. The badly battered *Hohenstaufen* received news that it would be pulled out of the line near Radkersburg in preparation for a northward move to Amstetten. There it would rejoin *6. SS-Panzerarmee* and establish a defensive front facing west, against the rapidly advancing Americans.

SS-Bau-Bataillon 9

Members of this little-known unit had been defending Radkersburg along with their SS brethren from *Hohenstaufen*. After the bridge had been blown to stop the Russians from using it to cross the Mur River, the battalion crossed to the south bank using rubber rafts. It had suffered heavy losses during the fighting. What happened to it next isn't known, but it seems probable that it was absorbed by *Hohenstaufen*.[13]

---

13 Landwehr, *Siegrunen 55*, p. 63.

17

Tuesday, 17 April

Heeresgruppe Süd

Once again the gorgeous spring weather favored the Russians, with temperatures approaching 70 degrees Fahrenheit and only high, thin clouds to interrupt the sunshine. Consequently both sides flew north of the Danube, where Second Ukrainian Front was hammering the Germans in an attempt to break through to Brno. *Luftflotte 4* could only muster 70 sorties. Losses combined with lack of fuel had leeched its combat power, but prowling American fighters also kept many planes in their protective revetments. The Americans jumped on any target that showed itself.

The Russians

The Germans must have wondered whether the Russian manpower pool was truly inexhaustible. Their own ranks were thinner than a threadbare suit but the Russians just kept coming. Marshals Malinovsky and Tolbukhin knew the chimera of their own strength.

Both Second and Third Ukrainian Fronts were badly damaged by a solid month of heavy combat. Tank losses had been particularly heavy in the close confines of Vienna and in the fighting in the Danube Valley. Supplies that had initially been lagging due to the speed of advance across western Hungary had caught up, so fuel and ammunition were not a problem.

For the last two weeks of war, attacks on *6. SS-Panzerarmee*, *6. Armee* and *2. Panzerarmee* never stopped, but future commitment of armored forces had to be focused on the biggest strategic objectives, such as Zistersdorf and Brno. The front in Styria and eastern Carinthia had devolved into constant mountain warfare of the most brutal kind, but north of Vienna the mobile forces still had a chance to break through. Therefore, the northwestern thrust of the offensive intensified. Tolbukhin looked for a way to cross the Danube to the north while Malinovsky concentrated on capturing Zistersdorf through a pincer attack. This latter concentration would involve renewed attack by Sixth Guards Tank Army and would pay immediate dividends.

North of the Danube

8. Armee

In the Austrian wine country near Zistersdorf, *Kampfgruppe 211. Volksgrenadier-Division*, *SS-Kampfgruppe Trabandt I* and the other German units screening the last small oil fields near Zistersdorf were finally forced to retreat to the northwest, in the direction of the Czech border near Laa an der Thaya. Not even the last-minute intercession of *6. Panzer-Division* into the Russian flanking forces could save the situation. Combat had been fierce and German losses were high as they had held the line for nearly a week, but eventually the superior firepower of the Red Army's elite 4th Guards Air-Landing Division and the 409th Rifle Division proved decisive. The Germans continued fighting during their retreat, because the Russians closely pursued them. Just capturing Zistersdorf wasn't enough; the Russians wanted to trap the entire defensive force. The retreat didn't end until it had reached Kettlasbrunn.

But they still weren't out of danger. Two more Guards divisions were attacking on a northerly axis, the 6th Guards Air Landing Division and 93rd Guards Rifle Division. The Germans tried to make a stand along the line Hobersdorf to Palterndorf-Dobermannsdorf, but the Russians were too fast and that line also gave way.

The men and boys of *SS-Kampfgruppe Trabandt II* had only just dug a shallow line of rifle pits when a hail of fire from infantry weapons sliced into their ranks. The terrified men crouched, crawled and ran to Hobersdorf, where a Russian anti-tank gun had targeted the church tower but, despite multiple hits, it didn't fall. On one street sat four Tiger IIs. Once inside the town they made hasty defensive arrangements. When the young SS men took up their positions, some of the townsfolk must have known the Russians were close behind and shared food with them. It wasn't long before Russian mortars started pounding the German positions and the Tigers withdrew.

* * *

The hungover men of the Mistelbach *Volkssturm* battalion were once again mustered to the Boys' School, where they were ordered to march to Laa an der Thaya. The majority of them trudged off toward that city, but most turned back without getting halfway there. Some never left and simply went home again, presumably with headaches from the night before.

But war was on Mistelbach's doorstep whether its local defense force was ready or not. The air raid signal blared three times, which meant it was time to flee or take cover. Those who wanted to evacuate gathered at the main railway station for a train to Laa an der Thaya. Everyone else headed for their cellars.

Mortar shells started landing in the town and wounded townsfolk flooded the hospital. The citizens of Mistelbach couldn't help but notice the exhausted state of the retreating German troops, although a large number of panzers gathered near the cemetery in Hüttendorf.

Those panzers had to have been part of *25. Panzer-Division*. Southwest of the city were *Kampfgruppe 101. Jäger-Division* and *25. Panzer-Division*, both of which were part of *Panzerkorps Feldherrnhalle*. The battle for the city was about to begin, and it would be violent in the extreme.[1]

* * *

The town of Zistersdorf suffered the fate that all others did. Six townsfolk died and damage was extensive, including to the City Hall, which lost its roof and top floor. As for the *Führerbefehl* declaring Zistersdorf a fortress and committing the commander of *Kampfgruppe 211. Volksgrenadier-Division* to personally hold the oil fields to the last man, timing may have been everything. *Generalleutnant* Eckhart might have held his position just long enough to avoid a firing squad. The opening on the previous day of Marshals Zhukov and Koniev's assaults on Berlin directed Hitler's attention away from other fronts to the defense of the capital. Had he lost Zistersdorf on 15 April, Eckhart might well have been one more executed German officer who couldn't achieve the impossible.

* * *

Along the north bank of the Danube at Krems-Hollenburg, an attempted Russian crossing was defeated by elements of the *Kriegsmarine*'s *Danubeflotille 2* based at Krems. Starting east of Tulln and extending west, the north bank of the Danube was marshy lowlands with few crossing points. The Russians tried to cross at the first strip of solid ground that wouldn't limit movement once

1   Brettner, *Die Letzten Kämpfe Band II*, p. 175.

across the river, and so the attempt had been obvious. Moreover, the Germans had been bombing, strafing and shelling the materiel buildup in preparation for a crossing for days.

6. Panzer-Division

The fighting around Schrick escalated as neither side would acknowledge defeat. General Kreysing knew that the *Kampfgruppe 101. Jäger-Division* was a spent force, even reinforced by the artillery regiment from *Kampfgruppe 96. Infanterie-Division* and several other battalions. The only way the Germans had so far stopped a major breakthrough was by committing the artillery guns and their crews to the front lines, exposing them to small-arms fire. Therefore he ordered the *Führer-Grenadier-Division* to extend its front and *Totenkopf* to go back into the line, thereby allowing *6. Panzer-Division* to move north, where the mounting threat to the Zistersdorf oil fields required an all-out defensive effort.

After racing north the division went straight into action in the Zistersdorf area. Russian attacks had escalated and the fighting was catastrophic. The Germans only gave ground to avoid being completely wiped out, but held onto territory at the cost of oceans of blood. As for the attackers, the Russian troops wanted to survive the war as much, or more, than any other soldiers. Every time they saw a comrade mangled or killed, their anger and resentment against the Germans only increased. Why did they keep fighting? Didn't they realize they'd lost the war? Mercy had always been in short supply on the Eastern Front, but now it was almost non-existent.

Against an enemy who outnumbered them as much as four-to-one, and who outgunned them in every category up to ten-to-one, fueled by hatred that had boiled for four years until it became all-consuming, all the German courage in the world was useless.

* * *

On the division's far right flank was the little town of Harmannsdorf, one of the key positions in the new German line of resistance. The town was about three miles northeast of Korneuberg and was defended by the *Panzergrenadier-Regiment 114*. The regiment had seen the worst of the fighting in Vienna, particularly in the Prater and near the Gas Works. It had gone into the line straight from that combat and on 17 April was slammed by heavy Russian attacks. The depleted and exhausted regiment disintegrated under the assault.

The German response was a counterattack to retake Harmannsdorf by elements of the *Führer-Grenadier-Division* and a left-behind element from *Das Reich*.[2] The Russians were forced out but the Germans suffered heavy losses on the day. Fifty men died and many more were wounded. Only 12 Russians could be confirmed dead, but the line had been restored and would not be ruptured for the rest of the war.

---

2   Brettner, *Die Letzten Kämpfe Band II*, p. 171. Brettner here identifies the *Waffen-SS* element involved as the *SS-Begleit-Bataillon Reichsführer-SS*. In other words, Himmler's personal escort battalion. But in fact there were at least three such battalions, one of which fought in the Battle of Berlin, perhaps attached to *38. SS-Grenadier-Division Nibelungen*; a second battalion developed into the *16. SS-Panzergrenadier-Division Reichsführer-SS* and a third battalion was attached to *Reichsführer-SS*. If Brettner is correct, then it would have to be the third of these incarnations that had been attached to *Das Reich* at some point.

II SS-Panzerkorps

Even without *Das Reich* in the line, for three days the corps had stood firm against heavy Russian attacks, which continued all day on 17 April. Assaults on Leobendorf failed, but tank-supported attacks at Seebarn and Tresdorf drove outlying listening posts backward. Elsewhere, at Tulln, Höflein and Korneuberg, concentrations of Russian vehicles were shelled with artillery.[3]

Alarm-Bataillon 2, Luftkriegsshcule 7

Having been chewed up defending the high ridge north of Stetten, the battalion was first withdrawn for two days of rest before being sent to defend a place familiar to all of them; the emergency landing field at Wolfpassing. One of the surviving cadets wrote in his diary: "Never would I have thought that I would be used as an infantryman to defend this place."[4]

The author could not have meant Zeiselmauer-Wolfpassing, in the Tulln district. While this would have made sense as the emergency landing field used by cadets at Langenlebarn, it had long since been overrun. The other Wolfpassing, also south of the Danube, was much further west, to the southwest of Melk near Amstetten. By now the Russians were threatening Krems and Amstetten would be next, so this is most likely where the battalion was redeployed.

Kampfgruppe Volkmann

Volkmann's *Kampfgruppe* was reinforced by the arrival of four trains carrying more of *SS-Kampfgruppe Trabandt II* into the area north of Tulln. The rest of the *Kampfgruppe* had been ordered to move north to Poysdorf and it is presumed that these newly arrived elements either joined the transfer or followed soon after.

Although *SS-Kampfgruppe-Division Böhmen und Mähren* only existed for five weeks, all three of its regiment-sized *Kampfgruppen* fought well in battle. The combination of inexperienced but highly motivated troops led by combat veterans went a long way toward making up for the lack of heavy weapons, inadequate supplies and enemy control of the skies. Unfortunately for the *Wehrmacht*, such rank and file had become the exception instead of the norm.

South of the Danube

2. SS-Panzer-Division Das Reich

Das Reich crossed the Krems Bridge over the Danube and assembled between Krems and Melk in preparation for a counterattack at Sankt Pölten. The battered division had only been away from combat for two days and wasn't ready for any offensive movements yet. Fortunately for them the attack was cancelled.

---

3   Maier, *Drama*, p. 365.
4   Prigl, *Die Geschichte des Fliegerhorstes Langenlebarn von 1936 bis 2000*, <http://www.gotech.at/lale2/langenlebarn_2.html>, (Accessed 7 October 2018).

6. SS-Panzerarmee

By this point both sides had a pretty good idea of their enemy's strengths and weaknesses. The Russians knew the Germans had no significant reserves and, if they kept attacking long enough, eventually the German front lines would collapse. Their attacks to the south from the Sankt Pölten area were meant not only to widen and secure the Danube Valley corridor, but also to threaten the rear of *Hitlerjugend, Kampfgruppe 356. Infanterie-Division* and *SS-Kampfgruppe Keitel*. None of these units had enough men for rear area security, so threats from the flank could only be countered by a retreat. In turn this would endanger *6. Armee*'s rear.

SS-Oberstgruppenführer Dietrich was trying to rectify his lack of reserves by withdrawing units to regroup and refit behind the lines. What neither side knew was how much longer the German front could remain intact.

* * *

At the village of Raxendorf, north of the Danube and a few miles southwest of Mühldorf, the bedraggled column of Americans trudging away from *Stalag 17B* was stopped by men reportedly of the *Sturmabteilung*, the Brown-Shirted SA. Three officers and 40 guards were arrested for desertion and turned over to the Gestapo for trial.[5]

Korps von Bünau

By 1945 Red Army night operations had matured into well-planned and aggressive alternatives to far more costly daytime attacks. Indeed, as the US Army concluded after the war: "[T]he Russians conducted night operations more often and on a larger scale than any of the other combatants in the Second World War."[6] Russian daytime attacks on Wilhelmsburg, 8 miles south of Sankt Pölten, had so far ended in bloody defeat, so on the night of 16-17 April they tried something different. A night attack took the Germans completely by surprise and the Russians captured the town.

At dawn the Germans did what the Germans always did; they counterattacked. From the north *Korps von Bünau* attacked, and *SS-Kampfgruppe Peiper* did the same from the south. Together the two-pronged attack drove the Russians out and recaptured the town. The burned-out hulks of eleven Russian tanks littered the streets.

On Bünau's left flank, Russian attacks southwest of Krems aimed to capture Mount Statz and use that 2,400 foot mountain as an anchor and observation point for attacks to capture the wooded area near Hollenburg, on the Danube. The Germans nearly lost the peak in bloody fighting, but the men of *SS-Kampfgruppe Trabandt III* showed up at the last possible moment and drove the Russians back. That *Kampfgruppe* was very well equipped and its combat value was high, with good morale, the type of regiment-sized unit that had become scarce in recent months. Its third battalion was an exception, however, rated very low in all regards. Nevertheless, the combat debut of the *Kampfgruppe* was a spectacular success. The loss of another hill north of Kuffern could have turned fatal for the defense of Krems, since it overlooked the entire German defensive area below.

* * *

5   Doubledee, *Stalag XVII B The Final Days* <http://www.stalag17b.com/final_days.html> (Accessed 27 July 2018). The assertion this was done by the SA seems odd, since this was not the usual job of members of the SA. It seems more likely it was a unit of the SS.

6   Sasso, Major Claude R., *Soviet Night Operations in World War II* (Fort Leavenworth: Combat Studies Institute, 1982), <https://usacac.army.mil/cac2/cgsc/carl/download/csipubs/sasso.pdf> (Accessed 7 October 2018).

General von Bünau had visitors at his headquarters on 17 April, in the persons of his army commander, *SS-Oberstgruppenführer* Dietrich, and his new army group commander, *Generaloberst* Lothar Rendulic. They no doubt listened to reports coming in as company-sized Russian probes to the southwest and west of Sankt Pölten were turned back from Gerasdorf and Vollerndorf. Ominously for von Bünau's corps, however, reconnaissance showed roads in and around Sankt Pölten jammed with Red Army vehicles moving west and south. It didn't seem to matter how many tanks or assault guns or trucks they destroyed, the Russians always seemed to have more.

The terrain now favored a Russian advance on the corps' right flank, where gently rolling hills and small stands of trees made for good tank country, whereas on the left a defense forest up to the Danube made armored movement slow and tedious. The road network also ran through the southern sector.

Von Bünau's right flank ran for thirty miles along the Pielach River, while on the left the front ran through the ring of hills surrounding Krems an der Donau. "For the most part this ring was admirably suited for defense, but was too large for the small defense force available." Worse, every time the Russians took a hilltop they stared down at Krems and could direct artillery fire onto targets below.[7]

On the plus side, seven more trains carrying the *710. Infanterie-Division* unloaded west of Sankt Pölten, exactly where they were needed most. But they weren't in time to stop a new Russian attack to the southeast from the area of Fahrafeld, which captured an important hill.

* * *

The *I SS-Panzerkorps* two right flank formations, *Kampfgruppe 356. Infanterie-Division* and *SS-Kampfgruppe Keitel* both endured attacks to their front and noted strong Russian armored columns moving west from Heiligenkreuz toward Alland.

SS-Kampfgruppe Peiper

Against all odds, *SS-Kampfgruppe Kling* recaptured the northern half of Wilhelmsburg in the morning and then had to defend it against more attacks all day long. The town itself was bisected by the Traisen River, with high ground on either side that dominated the valley below. Fields of fire at ground level tended to be restricted, making control of higher ground even more important. This gave German infantry the chance to use hand-held weapons against the Russian armor. The town itself had become a flaming ruin.

After taking back Wilhelmsburg, Kling spent the rest of the day leading his men in the hunt for hidden Russians and then wiping them out. Eleven burning tanks and dozens of bodies littered the battlefield, but the stubborn Russian assaults once again captured the town's northern half before nightfall. When full darkness came, and only flames licking through ruined homes lit the night, the front lines in some places were no further away than across the street. Another Russian attack during the night took all of the *Kampfgruppe*'s strength to repel, and even then the Russians retook parts of the northern town. No rations came up for the exhausted defenders, who huddled cold and miserable in the shadows, not daring to sleep because skirmishing continued until morning.

The nearby Schöpfl Mountain also saw renewed fighting. Several times Peiper's men were thrown off the crest before immediate counterattacks retook it. Close combat went on all day, sometimes hand-to-hand, and seldom beyond hand-grenade range. The density of the forest wouldn't allow

---

7   Von Bünau, General der Infanterie Rudolf, *Corps von Buenau 8 April–8 May, 1945* (Leavenworth: Historical Division Headquarters United States Army, Europe, 1946), p. 15.

for anything else. One side would fight their way to the summit and eject the enemy, who would retreat down the slopes, regroup and counterattack. When the sun finally set and the fighting died down, the Germans retained control, but 800 men from both sides lay dead, with thousands more wounded.[8]

Battalions of Russian infantry supported by tanks drove through German defenses south and southwest of Wald, then turned into the rear of the defenders near Perschenegg in a small-scale example of what they were trying to do to all of *I SS-Panzerkorps*.

Kampfgruppe 12. SS-Panzer-Division Hitlerjugend

With the road through the Triesting Valley once again in German hands, *Hitlerjugend* withdrew from Neuhaus so that the entire defense line from Pottenstein to Neuhaus could be defended by the *LAH*. Along most of the division's line the day was quiet, as the Russians regrouped after suffering severe losses the day before.

But it was not calm everywhere. Attacks in company strength took place along the boundary with *SS-Kampfgruppe Peiper*, on the division's line north of Sankt Corona am Schöpfl, in the area near the Schöpfl hill that saw the Russian breakthrough of the previous day, and at Sankt Corona itself. Once again *SS-Hauptsturmführer* von Reitzenstein was the master of the situation. His motley assemblage of mostly ill-trained men fought off all attacks on the town.

At Schöpfl hill it was a different story. Russians cut-off the day before attacked from the south, but they were repulsed by the small force of Germans holding the heights. Then stronger attacks came in from north and east, and when they heard the sounds of battle the Russians to the south also launched another attack. The combination was too much for what was probably no more than a platoon of German defenders and they were forced to withdraw.

Yet again, however, von Reitzenstein accomplished the near impossible. It's tempting to say that he was keeping the Russians at bay using smoke and mirrors, but in truth it was tactical expertise combined with determination and courage. With no reserves and his lines thinned by creating the tiny *Kampfgruppe* that took and held the Schöpfl the day before, and with attacks hitting his lines at Sankt Corona, he once again took men from those positions to form yet another small *Kampfgruppe*. This second force, which couldn't have numbered more than 100 men, attacked Schöpfl hill just as happened on 16 April, and with the same result. The Russians were driven off the summit and the breakthrough gap was once again plugged.

Southwest of Schöpfl hill and south of Brand, *SS-Kampfgruppe Gross* held a 2,600 foot-tall peak called the Wittenbachberg. Russians who had broken through there on 14 April had since been trapped but not eliminated, and represented a latent danger. With no other choice except to clear the woods, the former supply and artillery men plunged into the rough country and wiped out the remaining Russians in a series of short, bitter firefights.

Kampfgruppe 1.SS-Panzer-Division Leibstandarte Adolf Hitler

The division had to extend its line to Neuhaus because of the withdrawal of the *Hitlerjugend* men who had occupied it. Such movements rarely went unnoticed by the enemy and, after the vicious back-and-forth combat of the previous few days, neither side was entirely sure where the forces of the other were.

---

8   Tiemann, *The Leibstandarte IV/2*, p. 299.

Viewed on a map nothing seemed to change on 17 April in the *LAH*'s region, but in fact the day was filled with constant small-scale fighting. The Russians probed the German positions with groups from patrol-sized, six or eight men, to company-sized, looking for weak spots. As they encountered the entrenched Germans, firefights broke out all through the forests and mountains. In their turn the Germans also sent out patrols to find out where the Russians were. Such patrols could march for hours up and down the steep slopes, with snow still under the forest canopy and a chill which seeped into a man's bones, and never encounter a Russian. Or it could stumble on a well-camouflaged machine-gun nest and get ambushed. The need to be constantly alert, searching the shadows and listening for the slightest crunch of a boot underfoot, led to physical and nervous exhaustion.

Newly recaptured Steinhof was fortified while new bunkers were built in the woods surrounding the town. Mortars killed more men during the Second World War than direct fire, and the Russians used their ammunition advantage to saturate the area. The only proof against a mortar blast was a sturdy structure, and in the case of a direct hit even that might not be enough.

In the trenches east of Neuhaus, Tiemann quotes a *SS-Hauptsturmführer* from the divisional security company who gives a rare report on how many men remained in his platoon: five officers and 22 men.[9] That's roughly half-strength or maybe a little more. Since a company might have three such platoons, and a battalion three or more companies, it helps to understand how many men were in the line, and how many had been lost.

Later in the day the Russians launched an attack near Weissenbach, which was repulsed.

SS-Kampfgruppe Keitel

Both *Kampfgruppe 356. Infanterie-Division* and *SS-Kampfgruppe Keitel* defeated attacks on the Hohe Wand, with the former division holding its north side and the *SS-Kampfgruppe* holding the south. Here and there the Russians still had some fortified positions on the lower slopes in the north.

6. Armee

The oddly named *1. Ungarische-SS-Schi-Bataillon*, now three battalions strong, was training at the Mountain Warfare School in the Seetaler Alps when, under emergency circumstances, it was rushed to the area of Sankt Margarethen an der Raab in the Weiz district, just east of Graz. There it was placed under command of *IV SS-Panzerkorps* and attached to *5. SS-Panzer-Division Wiking*, which was in dire need of infantry support. Around this time the battalion lost roughly half of one company supporting a *Kampfgruppe* composed of Hungarian paratroopers from the Svent Laszlo Parachute Division, *Group Ghyczy*. The *Kampfgruppe* itself was then assigned to the *1. Ungarische-SS-Schi-Bataillon* for the duration.

* * *

By this time in the war most Hungarian soldiers just wanted to survive and go home, but as shown above there were still those who found a reason to fight and die battling Bolshevism. Hermann Balck's insistence that the Szent László Division had defected, however, is in direct conflict with this evidence: "There was a danger that the newly forming Hungarian First Army would follow

---

9   Tiemann, *The Leibstandarte IV/2*, p. 299.

the example of the Saint László Division and cut off our line of retreat. I ordered the immediate disarmament of all Hungarian units in Styria."[10]

Once again Balck misremembered events. The Hungarian First Army had existed for many years, and was then fighting with *Heeresgruppe Mitte* and, as previously stated, the Svent László Division never defected. Moreover, although it was true that many Hungarians had quit the war, others continued fighting in the *6. Armee* sector until the bitter end, with their weapons.

Kampfgruppe Semmering

Desertion was a major problem for both sides during the war, but in 1945 it was particularly so for the Germans. Even *Waffen-SS* men sometimes deserted. On 17 April two SS men who had been caught deserting in civilian clothes were hung, not by the Gestapo, or the *Feldgendarmerie* or even the special Flying Courts Martial set up behind the lines to execute men abroad without orders. The two men were executed by their own company, although which company of the numerous ones fighting in the area isn't known.[11]

* * *

A strong Russian attack drove the men of *Fliegerhorstkompanie E 218/VII* backward off the Sonnwendstein, with heavy losses among their officers. But despite their lack of training the *Luftwaffe* men fought well, and retreated to their second line of defense in good order. There, along with the *Gebirgsjägers* from *Gebirgs-Regiment 134*, they stopped the Russian advance. Several men earned the Iron Cross for bravery.

* * *

The Germans had lost Rettenegg two days before, but they hadn't forgotten about it. In the quiet chill during the dark of night, 10 volunteers crept back into the town. They overwhelmed a sentry and captured a machine-gun post in the center of the town, and then opened fire on any Russian they could see. Surprised Russians spilled into the street, but the Germans weren't suicidal. With the damage done they retreated back to the safety of their own lines.[12]

Kampfgruppe 1. Panzer-Division

Moving north and northwest, the division encountered a landscape largely empty of military forces, either Russian or German, but after capturing Puchegg and Schachen they were stopped. On the eastern flank of the attack they retook Siebersdorf and Wagendorf.

The Russians weren't ready to give the Germans back all the ground their recent offensive had won. An attack on the western flank, aimed at Birkfeld, threatened to hit *117. Jäger-Division* in the flank, or even drive south toward Graz. At Birkfeld the only German defenses were a few *Volkssturm* and a battery of *Luftwaffe* 88mm cannon. The town was about to be recaptured when the timely arrival of the division's *Begleit Kompanie*, "escort company", with three Panzer IVs, blasted the Russians and turned back the attack. Elsewhere they found a few police armored cars

10   Balck, *Order in Chaos*, p. 426.
11   Brettner, *Die Letzten Kämpfe Band I*, p. 109.
12   Brettner, *Die Letzten Kämpfe Band I*, p. 118.

engaged in a firefight with Russian infantry and drove them off, too. The division then spent the rest of the day and night reorganizing for a push toward Strallegg.

1. Volks-Gebirgs-Division

Increasing their attacks against the front of General Wittmann's division, strong Russian attacks hit the II./*Gebirgsjäger-Regiment 98* on the right flank. Because of the violence of the Russian attacks, and the declining fighting power of the division, precautions were taken to scout the back roads west of the Lafntiz Valley in case the main roads were cut by a breakthrough.

IV SS-Panzerkorps

While *Wiking* regrouped near Graz, three NCOs were awarded the Knight's Cross for taking command of their units after the commanding officers were killed.

Kampfgruppe 3. Panzer-Division

Russian attacks on the division's lines around Altenmarkt came as expected. Supported by tanks and an artillery bombardment the infantry charged forward shouting "Urrah, urrah!" But strangely, the assault wasn't as strong as feared. Stadtbergen, on the far left flank, was lost, but the line held less than half a mile beyond that town.

During all of this local *Volkssturm* helped clear minefields, lug supplies to the front and collect unexploded ordnance. Some also acted as messengers. Two stories illustrate the combat of those days. In the first one, a few remaining SPWs used the terrain to outflank two Russian anti-tank guns and wiped them out. In the other a lone *Landser* who knew the area intimately grabbed two *Panzerfauste* and crept off into the woods after dark. A Russian battalion had commandeered an inn for its headquarters, and parked two T-34s and a self-propelled gun outside. If there were any guards they weren't vigilant. The man crept up to a window from where he could see the headquarters staff, raised a *Panzerfaust* and pressed the firing trigger. The explosion wiped out men, papers, radio gear, records, everything necessary to run an infantry battalion. Wheeling, he then fired the other *Panzerfaust* into the self-propelled gun at close range. The resulting explosion was so massive that it caught one of the T-34s on fire and it, too, exploded. The intrepid soldier won the Iron Cross, First Class.[13]

2. Panzerarmee

Near Judenberg, in the relatively peaceful center of Austria, *SS-Obersturmbannführer* Hans Dorr, former commander of *SS-Panzergrenadier-Regiment 9 Germania*, died from the wounds he sustained on 21 January during *Unternehmen Konrad III*. He had survived 15 previous wounds, but the 16th proved fatal mere weeks before the war ended.

Dorr embodied the very essence of the veteran SS man, the soul of the divisions in which he served. In appearance he could have been the image off a recruiting poster, with a strong,

---

13   Veterans, *From the Caucasus*, p. 287.

square jaw, high cheekbones and an intensity of gaze that reflected his inner dynamism. Heinrich Himmler could not have commissioned artwork more perfectly suited to illustrate a *Waffen-SS* officer. Dorr joined the SS in 1933 and had been awarded the Knight's Cross with Oak Leaves and Swords for battlefield bravery. He had worked his way up from the lowest ranks to command a regiment. It is worth noting that, while the divisions in which he served, most notably *Das Reich* and *Wiking,* committed war crimes, Dorr himself was never personally accused of participation. From a German standpoint, men with such experience were irreplaceable. The Russians understandably saw it otherwise.

14. Waffen-Grenadier-Division der SS

Generalleutnant Pavlo Shandruk had spent his entire life fighting for an independent Ukraine, first in the army of the Ukrainian National Republic and then in the Polish Army, when part of the Ukraine was claimed by Poland. When that country fell to the Germans he was at first made a prisoner of war, and then underwent *Gestapo* interrogation before working in a menial job until February 1945. He was then approached to lead the Ukrainian National Committee, a Nazi-sponsored organization dedicated to the idea of a free Ukraine aligned with Germany. Along with accepting that post he became leader of the Ukrainian National Army, which did not exist at that time.

Shandruk had no way of knowing that Hitler had forbade any such movement until the Nazis had irrevocably lost the Ukraine, at which point it cost them nothing to pretend they supported Shandruk's mission. The lynchpin of the planned 200,000-plus man army was *Galizien*, which is why he had traveled ten days on the failing railway system to reach Völkermarkt, 12 miles east of Klagenfurt in the division's area of operations.

When Shandruk met with *SS-Brigadeführer und Generalmajor der Waffen-SS* Freitag he ordered the division to remove their SS insignia and to affix the new symbols of the Ukrainian National Army. New caps were given out to replace those with the familiar Death's Head skull and crossbones. He interviewed NCOs, officers and men while getting to know the unit.

None of it mattered. Regardless of what the men wore, or what they were called or what army they fought in, the end was in sight. But that didn't stop Shandruk from expending a lot of energy repackaging them.

23. Panzer-Division

The division was involved across its front, from the fight for Hills 336 and 332 on its left flank, to the overflow from the battle near Radkersburg on its right. Its pull back a few days before exposed the northern flank of *9. SS-Panzer-Division Hohenstaufen*, but there had been no choice with the heavy combat on the left flank, and its insatiable hunger for troops. Late in the afternoon Hill 332 was again captured by the Russians, and retaken in yet another counterattack by *4. Kavallerie-Division*. Probes and patrols also continued across the region, but no large-scale attacks north of Radkersburg.

* * *

Hohenstaufen had defended Radkersburg for more than a week. The Russians could have been forgiven for not risking attacks in what was daily becoming more evident as the last weeks of the war, especially in a backwater part of the front like extreme southeastern Austria and Slovenia. Indeed, if queried most people in the West probably couldn't have said exactly where Slovenia was, and the Russians were now moving into the acknowledged British zone of occupation after the war. There was no real reason to keep attacking into Austria.

And yet that's exactly what they did. The Slovenes had designs on southern parts of Austria, so their willingness to fight and die for territory was understandable. They wanted the land, and agreements made at Yalta be damned. The Bulgarians attacked because they were forced to attack, but the Russians were playing a different game than mere conquest. As subsequent events would make clear, they wanted to instill in Austria a government friendly to the Soviet Union, to extend the limits of their influence to southern Germany and the Swiss border. Churchill had already foreseen this move and tried to convince Roosevelt of its legitimacy, but the dying American president was too enamored of Stalin to take the threat seriously. Fortunately for Churchill and Austria, Eisenhower had made a peremptory decision to change Allied policy that just happened to thwart any such plans.

* * *

Otto Skorzeny would have been proud of the Russian infiltration tactics used against Bad Radkersburg on 17 April. Assault groups wearing German uniforms crept into the city through the sewer system and engaged the men of *Hohenstaufen* in fierce combat. Distracted by this attack from within, the SS-men could not contain follow-up Russian attacks from outside the city and soon urban combat raged from one end of town to the other. However, with their northern flank unsupported the Germans were trapped against the river with only one way out, namely, a retreat over the Mur to the southwest, back into Slovenia.

The division's pioneers blew the river bridge just in time, as the Russians were already mounting a crossing, but not all of *Hohenstaufen* was on the west bank. Most of *SS-Ausbildungs-Abeteilung 9* was stranded on the east bank, and had to cross under fire in rubber boats, leaving behind any bulky equipment.

* * *

Far to the south the war was coming to its inevitable conclusion in Croatia, as the front lines gave way before Tito's Yugoslavian Partisan Army. *Heeresgruppe E* began its long retreat toward Austria, and *General der Artillerie* de Angelis immediately realized the repercussions that would have on his own army and began making preparations for his own withdrawal to the west.

18

Wednesday, 18 April

Anticipating that Germany would soon be cut in half, *Reichsführer-SS* Heinrich Himmler named Ernst Kaltenbrunner as *Oberbefehlshaber* of all *Wehrmacht* forces remaining in the south. At first glance this is confusing, because Hitler named Kesselring and Dönitz as supreme commanders in a divided Reich. At this point such overlapping authority no longer mattered, as there was nothing militarily that Germany could do to affect the situation. Kesselring dutifully set up his headquarters at Strub, very close to Berschtesgaden.

Kaltenbrunner worked as though his position had some actual meaning, but in truth it meant little. The Reich was daily being gobbled up on both fronts by the advancing enemy forces and nothing could be done to stop it. His main task seemed to be reorganizing the intelligence services for a shadowy independent Austrian government he intended to set up, the so-called Project Herzog. There is divided opinion whether this was Hitler's idea or not, with the timing apparently spawned by the Allies' refusal to recognize the puppet Soviet government established in Vienna.

Author Glenn B. Infield states that the idea for an independent Austria was given to Skorzeny by Hitler, and was even given a code name, *5K Immergruen*.[1] The idea was to set up a puppet government seemingly in revolt against the Third Reich and join the Allies in a fight against the Russians. In the end it didn't matter where the idea came from; it was all madness. The Americans had no intention of allying with any German government against the Russians. At this point all the American high command wanted was to end the war as fast as possible, with as few casualties as possible, so the veteran divisions could be shipped to the Pacific and the coming invasion of Japan. But for the Germans, holding onto the hope of an Allied-Russian split allowed them to think that maybe, just maybe, if they held on long enough, there was a way to escape retribution after all.

The man himself probably knew better anyway. Playing cards in a cabin later in the month, Kaltenbrunner told Adolf Eichmann: "It's all a lot of crap…the game is up."[2] In that he was right; both men would die at the end of a rope.

Heeresgruppe Süd

Luftflotte 4 had a hard time putting aircraft in the air. Aside from a shortage of planes and pilots, and dried-up fuel supplies, clouds of American fighters waited to jump on anything that tried to take off. Even reconnaissance flights became nearly suicide missions.

---

1   Infield, *Skorzeny*, p. 112.
2   Toland, *The Last 100 Days*, p. 639.

8. Armee

General der Gebirgstruppe Kreysing met with the *Kampfkommandant* for Stockerau, *Generalleutnant* Kullmer, and the commander of *Kampfgruppe 96. Infanterie-Division, Generalmajor* Harrendorf, to discuss the situation with the troops at the front. They pointed out to Kreysing that the men were close to their breaking point, with insufficient sleep, food, fuel, ammunition, or indeed any of the vital necessities for continuing to fight. Kreysing was sympathetic but explained there was nothing he could do. He had no reserves to pull units out of the line for a rest, and supplies only came intermittently now, if they came at all.[3]

* * *

Russian attacks along the army's center and left flank penetrated the thin front lines in a west-northwesterly direction. Second Ukrainian Front's next objective was Brno and, beyond that, into the southern flank of *Heeresgruppe Mitte*. Heavy fighting raged on its right flank at Korneuberg, but for the time being the Germans held the city. The citizens of Wilfersdorf, five miles south of Poysdorf, those who hadn't fled, cowered under any cover they could find as Russian artillery rained shells on them for three straight days. The bombardment wrecked at least a third of the town. It is interesting to note what one regimental commander said in his order of the day about continuing the fight, even though the situation seemed hopeless:

> We have only one task: to hold our position…this must be drummed into every soldier… nowhere else does he have it as good as here with his regiment, and his company. Here he has firm camaraderie, here he has a home.[4]

There was no appeal to their oath of allegiance to Hitler, or guilt if they didn't defend their women and children, or even threats of death if they fled, just an appeal to stay with your comrades-in-arms, and the implication they will do everything in their power to shelter you.

SS-Kampfgruppe Lenk

SS-Kampfgruppe Lenk, half of the *1. Ungarische SS-Sturm-Regiment*, was absorbed on 18 April into the *1. Ungarisches SS-Schi-Bataillon*, which was at this point more of a reinforced regiment, or even a brigade, with three battalions and ration strength of approximately 3,000 men. Lenk's men were incorporated into the unit's *I Bataillon*, giving them the perplexing address of *I Bataillon, 1. Ungarisches SS-Schi-Bataillon*; they were the first battalion of the first ski battalion. *SS-Kampfgruppe Lenk* had also picked up the name *SS-Waffen-Schi-Bataillon 26*, although its strength was way beyond that of a battalion.

37. SS-Freiwilligen-Kavallerie-Division Lützow

The headquarters *Kampfgruppe* of *37. SS-Freiwilligen-Kavallerie-Division Lützow* was withdrawn from combat and sent to the area of Pisek-Tabor to continue the process of forming the division,

---

3   Brettner, *Die Letzten Kämpfe Band II*, p. 172.
4   Vavra and Rossiwall, Die letzten Tage: 18 April – 24 April 1945, <https://www.museumnoe.at/de/das-museum/blog/18-april-24-april-1945>, (Accessed 22 July 2018).

along with its associated specialty formations. However, neither one of its cavalry regiments, fighting as *SS-Kampfgruppe Ameiser* and *SS-Kampfgruppe Keitel*, went with it. During its time in combat the division's headquarters had commanded various attached units, including the Vienna Hitler Youth Battalion that was a so-called anti-tank brigade, as well as some Hungarian *Honved* units, but not its own cavalry regiments, except for one brief period. Commanding *SS-Kampfgruppe Ameiser*, which seems to have retained that name even when under command of its parent headquarters, the division had fought to defend the escape corridor for *Das Reich* and the other defenders of Vienna in the Kreuttal-Hautzendorf area since 11 April. On 18 April, however, it was pulled out of the line, leaving *SS-Kampfgruppe Ameiser* behind to pull back through Znaim and wind up in the Freistadt area next to *Kampfgruppe 96. Infanterie-Division*.

SS-Kampfgruppe Trabandt I, or SS-Regiment Schultze

The *Kampfgruppe* settled into Laa an der Thaya. That town was located at a critical road and waterway junction on the border with old Czechoslovakia, and was the next tactical objective of Second Ukrainian Front.

SS-Kampfgruppe Trabandt 2, aka SS-Regiment Konopacki

Situated north of the Danube, the Wienviertel has always been a fertile and desirable region of Austria. During Imperial Roman times the Romans were plagued by incursions of the Germanic tribes into Pannonia, and the Emperor Augustus briefly sponsored an excursion north of the Danube by his step-son, Tiberius. The rich land allowed the native tribes to grow large and fierce, making them a significant threat to Rome. In the late second century, the Emperor Marcus Aurelius tried to establish the new Roman province of Marcomannia by conquering the area of what is now Lower Austria and parts of Slovakia between 174 and 180 AD. His successors gave up the idea of maintaining a Roman colony north of the Danube, but Rome's influence continually increased in the following centuries anyway.

All manner of wines were grown there,[5] including sparkling wines around Poysdorf, but agriculture and vineyards were not on the minds of the combatants in April 1945, although numerous instances of wine cellar plundering occurred on both sides. Where the terrain was flat it gave the defenders no advantage, but there were rolling hills, too, around which to build a defense.

In that far northeastern corner of Austria, the *III./SS-Kampfgruppe Trabandt II*[6] had been pushed to the area just north-northwest of the small town of Altlichtenwarth, 36 miles northeast of Vienna near the Slovak border.

That regiment had been in the area when both *XXXXIII Armeekorps* and *Panzerkorps Feldherrnhalle* had been pushed further north under the Russian assault, and the *Kampfgruppe* had been pulled back to the area near *Kampfgruppe 357. Infanterie-Division*. Ever since entering the line on 11 April it had seen fierce fighting and had taken heavy casualties. Once in the vicinity of Poysdorf-Altlichtenwarth, *SS-Kampfgruppe Trabandt II* was resupplied and readied for more combat.

---

5   And still are.
6   It is not clear whether part of this battalion, or one of the regiment's other two battalions, had part of its number caught south of the Danube to fight there with *Korps Schultz* and *Korps von Bünau*.

The regiment was subordinated to the virtually destroyed *44. Infanterie-Division Hoch und Deutschmeister*, or whatever part of *I./SS-Kampfgruppe Trabandt II* hadn't remained south of the Danube. *I./SS-Kampfgruppe Trabandt II* and *II./SS-Kampfgruppe Trabandt II* were first incorporated into the main defense line around Poysdorf, and some part of the *III. Bataillon* joined an attack to retake high ground around Herrnbaumgarten, just northeast of Poysdorf. The attack was successful and the Germans held those positions for the remainder of the war. At least part of *I./SS-Kampfgruppe Trabandt II* likely saw action with *Kampfgruppe Volkmann* and probably *Korps von Bünau*, so the elements involved at Herrnbaumgarten must have been from men who stayed with the regiment.

Russian artillery spotters on the hills just north of Altlichtenwarth had unobstructed views into German-held territory, meaning the Germans either had to retake the hills and town, or retreat further out of Russian artillery range. Having just pulled out of Altlichtenwarth that morning, it seemed rash to spend lives retaking it, but something had to be done to eliminate the artillery spotters. The decision was made to attack and retake Altlichtenwarth.[7]

The *III./SS-Kampfgruppe Trabandt II* was attached to a larger *Kampfgruppe* led by Knight's Cross winner *Hauptmann* Otto Hafner for the attack on Altlichtenwarth. Hafner won the award in September 1943 and had served with the notorious *SS-Sturmbrigade Dirlewanger*, a *Waffen-SS* unit formed from criminals and military men from various branches of service who were discipline problems, although Hafner's service had been with the Army. After this he had been assigned to *Feldersatz-Bataillon 357*, which was in the line not far from Altlichtenwarth. Hafner was an experienced and successful leader, but when he saw the quality of the troops assigned to him, he was appalled.

Many of the young boys who made up the soldiers of *III./Kampfgruppe Trabandt II* were from the Austrian wine country and eager to participate in an attack to retake Altlichtenwarth, but veteran *Waffen-SS* men might have had trouble believing those teenagers were also SS; they were the last scrapings of the German manpower pool. Most wore ill-fitting uniforms and did not have the strength of grown men. Helmets that were too large swiveled on their heads. Hafner knew immediately that the young men were not ready for combat and was upset at having to order them into battle, where many would surely die. It was not part of his sense of duty to command children and the situation made him sick, but he had no choice except to attack.

Two of *III. Bataillon*'s companies took part in the assault, with the *11./III. Abteilung* being in the initial attack and *10./III. Abteilung* held in reserve. There were no heavy weapons available for support, not even mortars, only a few machine guns, and while the Russians were caught by surprise they fought back tenaciously. On the right, the SS men were supported by a *Wehrmacht* company in the assault on the hills just north of the town. Fighting was fierce and the *11. Kompanie* suffered ruinous casualties, including the company commander. Even in the vineyards, where there was some cover, losses were high. By noon, however, despite house-to-house fighting, Altlichtenwarth was back in German hands, and after that the rail line was captured. The Russians were driven into the woods just south of the town.

To their horror, the Germans found numerous abused women scattered throughout the town, some dead, some still alive. The atrocities were so bad that "even the older soldiers were shocked by the scenes of these barbarous acts".[8] By this point the Russians had been raping and pillaging their way across German territory for some time, and Goebbels' propaganda machine had not had

---

7   Schulze-Wegener, Dr Guntram, Editor in chief, 'Blut, Ehre und Tod', *Der Landser number 2854* (2012), p. 22. Sources differ on precisely when this counterattack took place. Some say it was the night of 19 April, but the best sources all agree on 18 April. The essential details are not in dispute.

8   R.P., *Siegrunen 69*, p. 8. Some might consider the source unreliable. It is used here because the Russians are known to have raped women en masse as they moved across Europe, and the weight of evidence supports such an assertion as made here.

to conjure up false images of Soviet brutality to frighten the German populace into stiff resistance; reality itself was worse than anything he could create. Refugees brought with them lurid stories of Russian brutality. Still, for many Germans the threat remained an abstraction until the Red Army actually overran their homes, and the young recruits of *SS-Kampfgruppe Trabandt II* fell into this category. Hearing horror stories about Russian abuses, or seeing newsreel footage from briefly liberated cities such as Lauban, verified that the threat was real, but there was no way to prepare for the shock brought about by the gruesome reality of seeing such sights for yourself. Appalled by what they had seen, the liberators of Altlichtenwarth dug in to defend their newly liberated prize, but were only able to hold it for two days until being forced to retreat again.[9]

Damage to the town left it essentially in ruins. The local cemetery has the remains of 59 German soldiers and 27 Russians buried there. Civilian deaths exceeded 74. Fifty buildings were totally destroyed and 40 more badly damaged. Most of the surviving inhabitants had fled after the German counterattack, leaving only 50 or so people behind. After the Red Army retook the town, these people were forced to work at nearby Rabensburg doing farm and house chores.[10]

* * *

At Hobersdorf the Russians had kept the Germans awake all night with intermittent machine-gun and mortar fire. With daybreak they attacked with renewed intentions of capturing the town. The Germans had no heavy weapons beyond some *Panzerfauste* but were well equipped with machine guns. House-to-house fighting was bad enough, but terrified farm animals scurried around the town underfoot, including baby geese. During breaks in the action the men passed around wine bottles.

The fighting lasted all day, with breaks long enough to smoke a cigarette followed by hellish close combat. By afternoon at least 200 Russians had pressed into the town and the Germans knew they had to hang on until nightfall, or they'd be cut to pieces withdrawing in daylight. Outnumbered at least five to one, they managed to hold part of the town, but only with a maximum effort. Among each other the Germans called it "*kleine* Stalingrad", which had become slang for particularly horrific urban combat. Under cover of night the survivors of the company, 23 men, loaded the wounded into horse-drawn wagons and retreated into the shadows.

* * *

To the west, at Mistelbach, only the rumble of three Tiger IIs passing through the nearby fields broke the stillness of the night. It was the deep breath before the war cry of battle. Around 4:00 a.m. the quiet was shattered by German artillery firing from a nearby ridge to cover the retreat from Zistersdorf, and it wasn't long before Russian counter-battery strikes landed among the German guns. Battle was joined.

At 6:00 a.m. the cannons' roar increased in volume. Salvoes from Katyushas, known universally to the German civilians as *Stalinsorgen*, Stalin Organs, blasted the town. Russian infantry launched attacks against the outlying defenses to the east and southeast. Despite fierce resistance, by 9:00 a.m. the Russian spearheads were in the vineyards to the northeast, and soon thereafter the bridge over the Zaya River blew up in their face.

Half an hour later they let Mistelbach itself feel their wrath, with low-flying ground-attack aircraft bombing and strafing at will, plus artillery and even rocket fire from Katyushas filling the air with rocks and splinters. One house collapsed on a group of soldiers whose defensive position

9   R.P., *Siegrunen 69*, pp. 8-10. This version of events is backed up by Reserve Captain Otto Hafner, the *Kampfgruppe* commander, in his manuscript TransDanube Diary, under the date of 18 April 1945.

10   https://austria-forum.org/af/AustriaWiki/Altlichtenwarth (Accessed 25 July 2018).

was inside. Russian ground troops followed almost as soon as the explosions died down, with tanks in support, and the dazed Germans found it impossible to fight back. By 10:00 a.m. tanks and trucks filled with Russian troops were through and headed through the fields and roads to Wilfersdorf, two miles to the northeast. Other spearheads turned southwest, toward Paasdorf.

The Germans did finally fight back. At the main square they knocked out several Russian tanks with the ubiquitous *Panzerfauste*. Combat then grew heavy until about 4:00 p.m., when it slackened off and the Russians began a house-to-house search for any surviving German soldiers. Once they'd cleared the town of any remaining resistance, the search was on for anything that could be looted. Watches were especially popular.

A backlog of Russian columns moving through the town drew German artillery fire, which was answered by Russian batteries. After a while that slackened off, too. The brief but vicious fight had cost the lives on 70 Russian soldiers, and 18 citizens of Mistelbach. Fifty buildings were totally destroyed and 100 more damaged. All of the local bridges were gone. Perhaps worst of all, the injured and sick Germans were expelled from the hospital and forced to move to City Hall so the Russians could claim it for themselves.[11]

Late in the day fresh Russian forces moved into the city, as Sixth Guards Army prepared for the follow-on attack toward Laa an der Thaya and, beyond that town, Brno.

II SS-Panzerkorps

Ominously, the corps detected Russian preparations to cross the Danube in its rear area, despite the marshy ground on the north bank. If the Russians managed it Kreysing knew his army's entire position would be hopelessly outflanked. The *Führer-Grenadier-Division* repelled attacks on Tresdorf and Mollmannsdorf.

6. Panzer-Division

Still defending near the Danube as part of *6. SS-Panzerarmee*, the critical situation on *8. Armee*'s left flank needed reserves to close multiple breaches, but there weren't any. With no other choice, Kreysing once again sent *6. Panzer-Division* to rescue the situation.

3. SS-Panzer-Division Totenkopf

The division occupied a line from Stockerau to Stettendorf am Wagram. *III./SS-Panzer-Artillerie-Regiment 3* located its batteries on the grounds of the sugar factory, which was the town's largest employer. From there they were able to fire on the Russian tank assembly points in Korneuberg, breaking up potential attacks. Part of *SS-Panzergrenadier-Regiment 6 Theodor Eicke* was subordinated to *Kampfgruppe Volkmann* to protect the Danube shoreline. The *14. Kompanie* remnants were sent to secure the shoreline south of Stockerau.

SS-Panzergrenadier-Regiment 5 Thule had relocated to the area of Krems an der Danube, and by mistake the radios for *Theodor Eicke* went with them. This left the scattered elements of that regiment in the Stockerau area with no other way to pass orders than by messengers.

---

11   Brettner, *Die Letzten Kämpfe Band II*, p. 175.

South of the Danube

Mattsee, Austria

Leader of the Hungarian Government of National Unity and the Arrow Cross Party, Ferenc Szálasi, married his long-time mistress Gisella Lutz, in a Catholic ceremony at the Parish Church in Mattsee. At some point around this time German diplomat Kurt Haller offered a plane to fly Szálasi to safety in Spain, but he declined, noting that: "if I am guilty I accept it." As a wedding gift the priest presented the newlyweds with a copy of *Mein Kampf*.[12]

The Russians

One of the basic requirements for high command in any army is the ability to read a map, and Marshal Malinovsky could do it as well as anyone. The Russians didn't have exact knowledge of where the Allied spearheads were, but Malinovsky didn't need it to know that time was running out on the war. Consequently, Third Ukrainian Front launched a maximum effort all along the line. Some of the assaults were intended to break through while others were made to pin the German units in place. Combat on 18 April was some of the heaviest of the entire campaign.

6. SS-Panzerarmee

One primary responsibility for an army staff is determining the enemy's future operations. By 18 April Sepp Dietrich's staff had a pretty good idea of Marshal Tolbukhin's strategic plan. The German defense in the Danube Valley had stiffened considerably, but while that remained the best avenue of advance for his massed armored forces, off in the distance both the Germans and the Russians could see the Americans riding into view.

As the Operations Officer for *6. SS-Panzerarmee*, *SS-Obersturmbannführer* Georg Maier was an eyewitness to many of the incidents he relates in *Drama Between Budapest and Vienna*. Clues to their intentions had been coming in for days and the conclusion drawn by *6. SS-Panzerarmee* was that the Russians had turned powerful forces to the south and southwest, aiming for Sankt Viet an der Gölsen. The purpose behind this move was to cut off *6. SS-Panzerarmee* elements echeloned far to the east.[13]

* * *

As Second Ukrainian Front's offensive against *8. Armee* gained momentum, *6. SS-Panzerarmee* took over part of *XXXXIII Armeekorps'* sector to lessen *General der Artillerie* Kreysing's area of responsibility. This extended Sepp Dietrich's zone well north of the Danube, but made it more critical than ever to keep the Krems Bridge.

---

12   Detre, Gyula László, *History First Hand* (Lakitelek: Antológia, 2007), p. 35. Some sources claim the ceremony took place on 29 April 1945, the same day as Adolf Hitler and Eva Braun were married. However, Detre commanded Szálasi's bodyguard battalion and attended the wedding, so his testimony is used here.
13   Maier, *Drama*, p. 366.

Schwere-Panzer-Abteilung 509

Having fought during *Unternehmen Frühlingserwachen* in March, *Schwere-Panzer-Abteilung 509* had come out of the fighting with only five out of 45 machines operational. One story has it that on 13 March, 16 of the battalion's Tiger IIs attacked a line of Russian SU-152s entrenched behind a minefield and every Tiger wound up damaged or destroyed. But in doing so they wiped out all 24 of the SU-152s. Given kill ratios by *SS-Schwere-Panzer-Abteilung 501* during that same period, when on 20 March one Tiger II is documented to have destroyed 15 Russian tanks, and on 21 March one Tiger II in company with two Panthers destroyed another 17 Russian machines, the report about the Tigers of *Schwere-Panzer-Abteilung 509* seems quite plausible.[14]

On 5 April the battalion received five Tiger IIs from *SS-Schwere-Panzer-Abteilung 501*, bringing their total to 18. The 6. *SS-Panzerarmee* received news on 18 April that the battalion had begun to arrive at Amstetten, directly in the path of any Soviet units driving west down the Danube Valley.

Korps von Bünau

More components of *710. Infantry Division* detrained west of Sankt Pölten. The piecemeal arrival of this division perfectly illustrates the damaged state of the remaining German rail network. Relentless bombing of bridges and marshalling yards, combined with incessant attacks by Allied aircraft in Western Europe and in Germany, had taken a terrible toll on German locomotives and rolling stock.

When a division was moved by rail it required a certain number of trains:

> German military trains were smaller [than Russian trains] at 90 axles long with a gross weight of 850 tonnes and a net cargo load of 450 tonnes in a series of standardized military trains (I Type: 26 flatcars, 28 goods vans, one brake van carrying 350 men, 20 vehicles, and 70 horses) so that an *Infanterie* Division could be carried by 70 trains or a Panzer Division in 90.[15]

As this implies, moving units by rail had always been a highly complex calculation based on the capacity of the track over which the train would pass, necessary speed, available bridges and a thousand other variables. By mid April 1945, when the network itself was in a shambles but pressure on the available trains was higher than ever, the efficiency of using what few trains were left dropped dramatically. The situation wasn't helped by the conflict of authority that arose in who would run the rail network. In combat areas that had long since been done by the *Wehrmacht*, who had no expertise for this and refused to ask for help from those who did.

An under-strength infantry division with far fewer vehicles or guns, such as *710. Infanterie-Division*, might still require 30 or 40 trains to move the whole unit. Someone had to calculate this and then make arrangements for whatever trains were available in the region to come pick up the unit. Other facts also came into play, such as priority and something the Germans called tempo. This was how many trains had been devoted to movement of a given unit. In the halcyon years of conquest a division might move at a tempo of 60 or 70, meaning 60 or 70 trains had been devoted

14   Wilbeck, Major Christopher W., *Swinging the Sledgehammer: The Combat Effectiveness of German Heavy Tank Battalions in World War II* (Lucknow Books, 2014), p. 79.

15   H. G. W. Davie, 'The Influence of Railways on Military Operations in the Russo-German War 1941-1945', (The Journal of Slavic Military Studies, 30:2, 321-346, 2017), DOI: <10.1080/13518046.2017.1308120> (Accessed 30 July, 2018).

to moving it, which meant it would arrive faster than if the tempo were 20 or 30. But in April 1945, tempos could fall as low as two or three.

Aside from the combat elements, a division had numerous specialized parts. Cooks, supply troops, mechanics, signals and radio personnel, command staff, the medical staff, veterinarians and horse handlers; German divisions required a far larger supporting force than did Russian divisions. And by this late in the war a second-rate division such as *710. Infanterie-Division* moved either by train or horse power.

The image of the mechanized German Army had never been accurate. Even at the launch of *Unternehmen Barbarossa*, Operation Barbarossa, the infantry divisions marched across the border dependent on horses to haul everything from supplies to artillery batteries. In April 1945, with vehicles and fuel supplies dwindling, infantry divisions were more dependent than ever on their animals. And when moving by rail the horses required a lot of rolling stock.

So when three trains arrived, such as happened on 18 April, it only represented about 10 percent or less of the total division. Earlier in the war the division probably would have all arrived within a day or two, but in April 1945 it could take up to two weeks. When committed to battle piecemeal and straight off a train, such as happened throughout *Heeresgruppe Süd*, the men would often be part of a *Kampfgruppe* where they didn't know the officers or other parts of the group, or had no idea of the immediate combat situation. Was the commanding officer competent? Was ammunition available? What about air and artillery support? Would they be fed any time soon? All of these things and more ran through the minds of men newly dumped into the middle of a battle. Unit cohesion became a luxury in the final weeks of the war.

SS-Kampfgruppe Trabandt III, or SS-Regiment Siegmann

No late-war unit is more problematic to decipher an accurate history of than *SS-Kampfgruppe-Division Böhmen und Mähren*. Georg Maier states that on 18 April "a *Kampfgruppe Siegmann* was formed from *Kampfgruppe Trabandt III* and *Heeres Panzerjäger Brigade 2*", He positioned this unit on the left flank of *Korps von Bünau*.[16] Von Bünau himself refers to this unit as "*SS-Regiment Maehren*".[17] It's hard now to know with 100 percent certainty what components made up this unit, but some probabilities can be deduced.

What he called *Kampfgruppe Trabandt III* was almost certainly the men of *SS-Kampfgruppe II* that had been cut off south of the Danube with the fall of Tulln. The actual *SS-Kampfgruppe Trabandt III* arrived south of Krems on 15 April, and it was also known as *SS-Regiment Siegmann*. Maier appears to have understandably confused these poorly documented units, but it seems straightforward that what he is referring to is the actual *SS-Kampfgruppe Trabandt III* and was also known as *SS-Regiment Siegmann*, with the orphaned battalion from *SS-Kampfgruppe Trabandt II* attached.

The identity of *Heeres* [Army] *Panzerjäger Brigade 2* is more problematic. A few sources connect a unit with this designation to *Panzerjäger Brigade Oberschlesien*, which was formed to defend Upper Silesia. Driven back, it was later surrounded in Czechoslovakia but broke out and made it to Bavaria. On the surface it seems possible this was the mystery unit, but by all accounts this brigade never came close to the area in question.

But another *Panzerjäger* formation makes for a much better match. *SS-Kampfgruppe Donau*, known better as *SS-Panzerjäger-Regiment Oberdonau*, was formed in April in the area of Linz,

16   Maier, *Drama*, p. 366.
17   Von Bünau, *Corps von Buenau*, p. 18.

Steyr and Amstetten, from camp guards at Mauthausen, unassigned and surplus men of the *Waffen-SS* and some Hitler Youth. Release of the camp guards became possible when the orphaned Vienna Fire Department[18] showed up at Mauthausen on 13 April and was ordered to take over some of the guard duties. It does seem that the regiment was attached to *SS-Kampfgruppe Trabandt III* instead of being integrated, because some sources indicate it remained subordinate to the local battle commander, *Generalmajor* Paul Wagner, under the name *SS-Panzerjäger-Regiment Donau*. Once it became operational this unit served mostly north of the Danube against the Americans.

* * *

If *General der Infanterie* von Bünau thought the pressure on him would be eased after the fall of Vienna, he was wrong. Russian intentions seemed to be concentrated on destroying his rag-tag collection of units. Their immediate attention focused on the strategic town of Ober-Grafendorf, five miles southwest of Sankt Pölten. They had driven north and south of the town, but like a boulder in the middle of a stream their advance couldn't flow until the road network passing the town had been captured. Attack after attack struck the German defenses. Despite everything they held the town, which was more than could be said of Ambach, a mere five miles south of Krems. Russian attacks continued through the night.

SS-Kampfgruppe Peiper

This was not the sort of fighting that could be controlled by a higher headquarters. If Erwin Rommel and Erich von Manstein both showed up to control the battle it would have made no difference. Strategy had no part here. Operational-level plans made no difference. This was a war fought by captains, lieutenants and the men they led, not by generals. All such high-ranking officers could do was try to feed men and supplies into the front lines. As one *SS-Oberscharführer* from *SS-Kampfgruppe Peiper* put it: "It was a war of battle groups, a shaky affair."[19]

The nature of the fighting in the mountains followed a similar pattern throughout the region. The Russians would saturate a position with artillery, rocket and mortar fire, perhaps also with air support, and then attack. Any trenches, bunkers or rifle pits they captured would have to immediately be counterattacked by the Germans. Otherwise, the Russians would dig in and have to be dug back out, usually with prohibitively high casualties to the Germans.

Many men were new to ground combat and only discovered how quickly death could find them when it was too late. Even simple acts they normally did without thinking, such as standing up, could provide an alert sniper with the perfect target. In the front lines there was no such thing as relaxing, not even for a moment.

In the valleys the Germans had to use their anti-tank guns judiciously, leaving their most effective defense against armored attack as the *Panzerfaust* and *Panzerschreck*. Most towns were located in valleys, which gave the advantage to the Russians, since artillery spotting was better and tanks could be used en masse. But advancing only through the valleys without securing the surrounding mountains left the spearheads open to being cut off and destroyed piecemeal. And so along the entire German front a gigantic grinding battle continued day after day, as the Russians wore down the Germans by trading blood for blood, and lives for lives.

* * *

---

18   The reader is reminded that *Gauleiter* von Schirach ordered them out of Vienna on 7 April.
19   Tiemann, *The Leibstandarte IV/2*, p. 301.

Marshal Malinovsky was determined that Third Ukrainian Front was going to smash the Germans in eastern Austria and in the Danube Valley to beat the Americans into Passau at the very least, if not further west. In order to speed things up, therefore, the Russians committed an entire tank corps against the left flank of *I SS-Panzerkorps*. Ten miles southeast of Sankt Pölten, in the area of *SS-Kampfgruppe Peiper*, the Russians supported an attack against Michelbach with no less than 38 tanks. Fighting was heavy but in the end the Germans couldn't fight against such numbers. The Army Group reported 15 tanks and assault guns destroyed on 18 April, with Peiper's command accounting for most of them.[20]

* * *

The town of Schwarzenbach an der Pielach, located 28 miles southwest of Sankt Pölten, was barely larger than a village. Like so many similar Austrian towns it lay in a valley, with most of the buildings erected along the highway, making it long and narrow. Lush, dense forest marched up steep mountains slopes on all sides.

Russian attacks toward the town made such a deep penetration it threatened the entire position of *I SS-Panzerkorps*, placing the Russians due west of the most forward-echeloned German units. An immediate counterattack drove them back. But instead of another assault, the Russians elected to stop driving toward Schwarzenbach and change direction, heading southeast. Their strategy of forcing *I SS-Panzerkorps* to retreat by driving into their rear areas couldn't have been more obvious.

After three bloody days trying to capture Wilhelmsburg, the Russians changed tactics. Instead of attacking *SS-Kampfgruppe Kling* directly through the flaming ruins of the town, they opted for a pincer attack. Due south of Sankt Pölten the newly arrived *Luftwaffe* men of *Fallschirmjäger-Regiment 30* faced at least a battalion of Russian tanks attacking south on both sides of Wilhemsburg. The Russians crushed the paratroopers on the flanks and surrounded Kling's command.

Having sacrificed so much to hang onto the town Kling now had to fight his way out, and he didn't waste time thinking about it. The *SS-Hauptsturmführer* led his men in a successful breakout attack before the ring around the town could be tightened, and they re-formed at Rotheau.[21] One of the precious remaining Tiger IIs crashed from a bridge during the escape and was lost.

This latest Russian thrust opened a dangerous gap with *Korps von Bünau*, and every available man was thrown into counterattacks to try and close it. But as these attacks left the Germans scrambling to respond, another attack at Michelbach broke through and left a Russian tank battalion driving toward Sankt Veit an der Gölsen.[22] Should the town fall it would cut the main supply line to both the *LAH* and *Hitlerjugend*. But then the Russians changed direction to due east, thereby threatening the rear areas of the SS units fighting at Brand and Laaben.

Peiper had no choice and counterattacked into the Russian flank. After heavy fighting the Russians withdrew, leaving 15 armored fighting vehicles burning on the battlefield.

10. Fallschirmjäger-Division

By this point in the war the term *Fallschirmjäger*, or paratrooper, was strictly an honorary one. The Germans no longer jump-trained the *Fallschirmjägers*, who fought as ordinary infantry. Manpower

---

20   Maier, *Drama*, pp. 366-367.
21   The exact date of Kling's breakout remains in dispute. Some sources put the date on 18 April, others 19 April and still others on 20 April.
22   Like so many towns in Austria, Sankt Veit an der Gölsen shared a name with another town in *I. SS-Panzerkorps'* area, Sankt Veit an der Triesting. The full names of both towns will be used henceforth to help the reader distinguish between the two.

for the division came from surplus *Luftwaffe* personnel, including pilots, crews and ground crews from *Kampfgeschwader 101*, which had been disbanded in October 1944. As the *Luftwaffe* continued to shrink from losses and lack of fuel, jobless men were handed a rifle and pointed to the front. In existing formations they usually had at least some veterans around them, but in formations like *10. Fallschirmjäger-Division* there were only their equally untrained *Luftwaffe* comrades. The extravagant waste of manpower that began with the *Luftwaffe* Field Divisions therefore lasted until the final day of the war.

In compensation for losing the depleted but veteran *6. Panzer-Division*, *6. SS-Panzerarmee* was given this untried, untrained division. But regardless of its value, the first two battalions arrived in the area west of the Traisen, exactly where the Russians' next attacks were expected.

2. SS-Panzer-Division Das Reich

After a few days of rest, and with new men filling out the ranks, all three battalions of *SS-Panzergrenadier-Regiment Der Führer* went back into the line near Gansbach, west of Krems. Aside from giving the new replacements a taste of life in a combat zone, this blocked any Russian breakthroughs short of the Danube where it bent south to the southwest of Krems.

I SS-Panzerkorps

Pressure on the corps' left flank continued between Wilhemsburg and Pottenstein, as the Russians showed no intention of slowing their attacks. In one way the fighting resembled that of the previous summer in Normandy. The Germans occupied excellent defensive ground but were outnumbered and badly outgunned, while their enemy seemed content to win a battle of attrition. And while *I SS-Panzerkorps* now occupied mountainous terrain instead of hedgerows, the actual shooting was mostly done at shorter ranges because of limited sight lines.

Kampfgruppe 12. SS-Panzer-Division Hitlerjugend

SS-Panzergrenadier-Regiment 26 shifted from the division's right flank to Sankt Corona am Schöpfl in response to the strong Russian effort to break through the seam between *SS-Kampfgruppe Peiper* and *Korps von Bünau*, on the far left flank of *I SS-Panzerkorps*. Before that happened, however, the Russians launched attacks on both Sankt Corona and the Schöpfl hill, supported by artillery. By now von Reitzenstein's *Kampfgruppe* was nearly bled out by casualties. They held onto the town until the *Panzergrenadiers* got there, but not so the Schöpfl hill, which again fell to the Russians. That meant the town was once again threatened with attacks from the east and south, and the loss of Sankt Corona would endanger the division's entire front. Something had to be done.

Near Sankt Pölten *SS-Kampfgruppe Chemntiz* engaged the first tentative spearheads. On the extreme northwest flank of the division *SS-Kampfgruppe von Ribbentrop* held firm against medium-strength attacks. Further southeast, a strong Russian attack supported by 38 tanks overran Michelbach and continued driving beyond the town.

As Lothar Rendulic began thinking of ways to counter the onrushing American attack from the west it became increasingly obvious that only by pulling units out of the line could he build a western-facing defense. *Das Reich* seemed like a perfect choice for this mission, as did *Hitlerjugend*, but somehow the front had to first be stabilized.

On the far right flank *SS-Kampfgruppe Bremer* withstood tank attacks with infantry support that broke into the German front lines and deteriorated into hand-to-hand fighting. A few *Panzerjägers* from the army showed up and knocked out two T-34s. Fighting continued until after dark.[23]

6. Armee

The long-awaited counterattack planned by *General der Panzertruppe* Hermann Balck against the hole ripped in his left front started in earnest on 18 April. The Russians had poured through the gap in huge numbers and Balck's response involved two under-strength divisions that were reinforced by whatever troops could be scraped together.

No less an eyewitness than *Oberst* Raithel himself gave Balck all the credit after the war. According to him Balck "stubbornly" waited two or three days to launch the attack, until the Russians were over-extended and spread out. Then he struck. Raithel claimed that Balck cleared up the breakthrough in two days,[24] but that wasn't accurate, which taints his testimony that everything that followed was part of Balck's plan. But whether it was or it wasn't, the Germans were about to do what they did best.

Kampfgruppe Raithel

Near the Sonnwendstein, the survivors of *Fliegerhostkompanie E 218/VII* expected another Russian attack like the one that had driven them back the day before. Instead, what they got was an earth-quaking bombardment interspersed by strafing runs and air strikes using fragmentation bombs. The *Luftwaffe* men, who had spent most of their war keeping German aircraft in the air and dealing out punishment to the Russians, now got a dose of their own medicine. Despite pounding the defenders relentlessly, the Russians ceased attacking in the area due to their extraordinarily high losses. Instead they began improving their own field fortifications.[25]

117. Jäger-Division

In response to the Russian offensive against *III Panzerkorps*, the newly arrived *117. Jäger-Division* was finally in position to counter-attack. Just as few German units were in the area, neither were there many Russians. The five divisions that had broken through five days earlier had dispersed throughout the countryside to wreak as much havoc as possible. The commander of *117. Jäger-Division*, *Generalmajor* Hans Kreppel, was a career army officer who had fought throughout the war and won the German Cross in Gold. The coming battles would be fought with limited intelligence, too few supplies, exhausted troops and in difficult terrain. Kreppel would acquit himself well.

The Russians were laagered in Ratten, which they had captured on 13 April during their offensive, and as has been seen, they had captured many of the towns, villages and high points west and southwest of that town. Kreppel's attack plan called for *Jäger-Regiment 749* to attack the town from the northwest, and *Jäger-Regiment 737* from the northeast. This area was held by the 68th

---

23   Meyer, *The 12th SS*, p. 485.
24   Brettner, *Die Letzten Kampfe Band I*, p. 118.
25   Brettner, *Die Letzten Kämpfe Band I*, p. 113.

Guards Rifle Division. Kreppel's intention was to arrest any further forward movement by the Russians and to secure the huge area of wilderness with no other organized German resistance. Initial resistance had been stiff, despite complete surprise, but the Germans quickly broke through at Ratten and headed east. After the attack succeeded the two regiments split up to take different routes for a meeting at Waldbach.

The distance to Waldbach wasn't far, only about ten road miles, but this was rough territory. *Jäger-Regiment 749* made excellent progress, getting more than halfway from Ratten to Sankt Jacob im Walde before nightfall and stopping on the Ochsenkopf. Progress was slowed by Russian resistance and bursts of heavy fighting. Its sister regiment had a much longer route through very difficult terrain and lagged more than a day behind.

Kampfgruppe 3. Panzer-Division

After the brutal defensive fighting of the past three days the division expected more of the same on 18 April, but the attacks never came. It might have seemed as if Russian manpower and materiel was inexhaustible, but in fact the attackers had suffered severe losses and needed to regroup. Both sides were exhausted.

The division used the next few days to repair uniforms, clean weapons and reorganize. Three Knight's Crosses were handed out, along with a number of German Crosses in Gold. Many of the local populace who had been driven out of their homes built lean-tos and shacks in the fields among the livestock.

14. Waffen-Grenadier-Division der SS

Like *Kampfgruppe 3. Panzer-Division, Galizien* expected fresh attacks, but the day passed with nothing more than harassing fire. By now the division defended the line from Feldbach on the left to Gleichenberg on the right, with artillery support evenly divided among the front-line units. Ammunition supplies had become critical, with some men having no grenades, no *Panzerfauste*, none of the equipment necessary to fight with. Stocks of bullets were limited to what the men carried on their persons.

Russian attacks didn't stop altogether; they kept coming in until the end of the war, but they grew progressively weaker as time went on. Artillery and mortar fire never ceased. The Ukrainians spent their days improving their positions and doing everything they could to chase away boredom. Late in April an attack broke through Russian lines and captured a large number of weapons, took prisoners and left 68 dead Russians behind.[26]

---

26   Melnyk, *To Battle*, pp. 259-260.

19

Thursday, 19 April

Berlin

At 6:00 p.m. Berlin time, as Russian artillery shells raked the capital's eastern suburbs with shrapnel, a single aircraft touched down at Tempelhof airport. Inside was a representative from the World Jewish Congress, who was driven through bomb-ravaged Berlin in an SS staff car to the estate of Felix Kersten, the masseuse and confidant for *Reichsführer-SS* Heinrich Himmler. With the end in sight, Hitler's most loyal paladin had been duped into believing that the Allies wanted Germany to join them in a war against the Russians, but only if he spared the remaining Jews in the extermination camps. Himmler is famously said to have wondered on Hitler's birthday whether to shake Eisenhower's hand or give him the Nazi salute. The source for his delusion now seems clear.

This had a direct impact on the fighting in Austria because of the inordinately large number of *Waffen-SS* units in *Heeresgruppe Süd*. No less than 13 *Waffen-SS* divisions were part of its order of battle on 19 April, not counting *Kampfgruppe SS-Division Böhmen und Mähren*, or *17. SS-Panzergrenadier-Division Götz von Berlichingen*, which was still in Germany but would soon wind up in Austria, or *7. SS-Freiwilligen-Gebirgs-Division Prinz Eugen*, part of *Heeresgruppe E* that was in Slovenia. Yet instead of doing everything he could to support his men as they fought for their lives, the most powerful patron of those formations was trying to find a way to save his own skin.

* * *

Weather in Austria remained warm, with passing clouds and occasional rainstorms. The Red Air Force flew most of their sorties against *6. SS-Panzerarmee* and *8. Armee*, particularly in the Mistelbach area. The headquarters of *Kampfgruppe 211. Volksgrenadier-Division* watched those Russian air strikes from the ruins of Castle Falkenstein, high on a hill north of the battle area, as the Red Air Force hammered their new positions in the vineyards near Poysdorf. The *Luftwaffe* managed a few sorties in return, also near Mistelbach.

The Russians were pressing forward in the area, with 9th Guards Mechanized Corps and 31st Guards Mechanized Brigade four miles northwest of Mistelbach in Hörersdorf, on the road to Laa an der Thaya; 30th Guards Mechanized Brigade was north of Mistelbach and moving toward Poysdorf. This was a mass of fast-moving armor spreading out in pursuit of the shattered left wing of *Panzerkorps Feldherrnhalle*. If they could hit hard enough, fast enough, a decisive breakthrough was in the offing. But the Germans weren't ready to quit. The corps commander, *General der Panzertruppe* Ulrich Kleeman, was a highly respected veteran panzer tactician. His resources were few and his units both depleted and exhausted, but he was determined to stop the Russian advance. This set the stage for the last great tank battle of the Second World War.

* * *

Four miles to the east at Waltersdorf bei Staatz, the townsfolk had been strongly urged to evacuate to the west before the Russians arrived, but only one family took the advice. The local *Volkssturm* was ordered to move through Laa an der Thaya to Auspitz, although most of them deserted and returned home later, and most of the foreign farm workers from the east – Poles, Ukrainians, Russians – had also been moved.

Soldiers of the *25. Panzer-Division* pulled out after putting up token resistance. There were only two panzers to defend the town, which made it a suicide missions. As it was, eight Germans were killed to only three Russians. A close pursuit brought them to the gates of Frättingdorf, driving through the German rearguards to join the movement toward Staatz.

* * *

The gateway to Laa an der Thaya was the town of Staatz, where two major highways came together about seven miles to the southeast. The highway leading into Staatz from the south passed through Ernsdorf bei Staatz, one mile from the larger town. Desperate to stop the burgeoning Russian offensive toward Laa, every last man was put to work building tank traps and barricades, some of which used heavy oak logs buried deep into the dark soil to form strongpoints.

Later in the day a Russian tank battalion showed up west of the town with between 30 and 40 tanks, but they directed most of their fire north toward Staatz. As dusk drew near four tanks moved cautiously toward Ernsdorf. Three stopped just inside the town while one moved forward. Unwilling to risk a fight at night, the Russians stayed in place and set up watches. A nervous quiet settled on the town.

* * *

At Staatz itself the Red Air Force gave the townsfolk a taste of what was coming. The *6. Panzer-Division* had set up its command post there on 15 April but a devastating air attack on the 19th was only a foretaste of what the Russians had in mind. The bombing was terrible and 38 townsfolk were killed. The command headquarters for the division, however, had been set up in the ruins of Castle Staatz, high on a hill overlooking the town.

* * *

The 9th Guards Mechanized Corps wasted no time capturing Aspern an der Zaya straight from their road march to the town. A brief firefight drove out the German defenders and left five civilians dead.

But not everything went the Russians' way. At Wilfersdorf they ran into the few remaining Tiger IIs of *Schwere SS-Panzer-Abteilung 503*, which were attached to *SS-Kampfgruppe Trabandt II*. The town lay on the banks of the Zaya River, which in places was a formidable waterway and in others little more than a ditch. The Guardsmen wasted no time attacking and were repulsed with 60 men killed in a bloody check on their advance. Two civilians were killed and one of the precious Tigers went up in flames.

37. SS Freiwilligen-Kavallerie-Division Lützow

On 19 April 1945 the bulk of the *37. SS-Freiwilligen-Kavallerie-Division Lützow* marched through Pisek-Tabor and Zwettl to join the left wing of *6. SS-Panzerarmee*, still with orders to continue assembling the division. Around this time the divisional headquarters was informed that Hitler had formally bestowed upon the unit its honorific title of *Lützow*.

At this far remove in time and attitude, it may be difficult to understand the impact this would have had on the division. It was just a name, something you could stitch on your sleeve, completely meaningless in the larger sense. This is true, but also misses the point.

By this time parts of the *37. SS-Freiwilligen-Kavallerie-Division Lützow* had been fighting for more than a month, oftentimes in desperate straits against overwhelming forces, parceled out to various larger units like orphans. For the teens filling out its ranks this must have been both grueling and shocking. Like all German units everywhere, food would have been short, ammunition and fuel supplies uncertain; there would have been times when units to either side could not be found, or Russians were in the rear. This scene was repeated all over the Hungarian, Austrian and Czech battlefields. In the midst of such hopeless chaos, for the *Führer* of the Reich to stop and recognize your unit, in effect, you personally, by allowing you to wear an honorific title on your uniform, would have had a great effect on morale, at least for the young. It was evidence that you were not forgotten. The combat veterans would probably have shrugged and asked for American cigarettes or chocolate instead.

6. SS-Panzerarmee

As if Sepp Dietrich needed more to worry about than holding back the Russians attacking his front, he now had the nightmare of defending against the Americans, who were advancing fast through southern Germany. The day before their spearheads had emerged from the Black Forest.

His intelligence officers estimated that the army had destroyed 42 Russian tanks and assault guns in the past three days, 24 of them by *SS-Kampfgruppe Peiper* in the area south of Sankt Pölten near Wilhelmsburg. That the Russians could still afford such losses told him everything he needed to know about the relative strength of his enemy.

North of the Danube

II SS-Panzerkorps

Russian attacks slackened off against the corps, but their columns could be clearly seen moving north with lots of tanks and assault guns. The implication was clear, namely that Malinovsky's Second Ukrainian Front was shifting the weight of its offensive further north to drive into old Czecholslovakia.

2. SS-Panzer-Division Das Reich

The remnants of the German war machine began to disintegrate, and there is no better example than *Das Reich*'s fate in the last three weeks of the war. It wasn't the military that lost cohesion, although desertions increased with each passing day. But the penalty for being away from your unit was both swift and brutal, and flying courts martial roamed the rear areas looking for just such men. Especially among regular army or *Waffen-SS* units, however, most of the men had long-since given up fighting for the Fatherland. Their motivation for continuing the fight was because they didn't want to abandon their brothers in arms. Instead it was the apparatus of government and the chain of command that began to fall apart.

After having moved into the line around Gansbach the previous day, the men of *SS-Panzergrenadier-Regiment Der Führer* were replaced in those positions by *SS-Panzer-Grenadier Regiment Deutschland*. The intention was for *Deutschland* to form the core of a *Kampfgruppe* to retake Sankt Pölten. It was reinforced with elements of the Reconnaissance Battalion, the I Battalion of Artillery, one Pioneer company and a battery of *Sturmgeschütze*. The group spent 19 April preparing for the assault.

Kampfgruppe 3. SS-Panzer-Division Totenkopf

The shifting of units further north necessitated *Totenkopf* to take over defense of the Danube from Stockerau to Krems. Along with this shuffling, *Kampfgruppe Volkmann* was sent to the *Führer-Grenadier-Division* to replace *6. Panzer-Division*, which had shifted even further into northern Austria. *Generaloberst* Rendulic had no more reserves to fill in the breaches, although the expected arrival of the *Schwere-Panzer-Abteilung* was at hand. After detraining near Melk it was immediately sent on a road march to join *8. Armee.*

Once *Totenkopf* arrived in Stockerau, however, life improved dramatically for the survivors of the previous months of combat. Most Nazi officials had already left the city, and the officers moved into their quarters. For the rank and file it was like they had moved into a fairy tale. "The rats have left the sinking ship. It [the coming battle] is all foreshadowed by the best food and drinks, it's like living in the land of plenty."[1]

As for the rest of the army group, all Rendulic could do was move units where they were needed most, but with fuel running low and trains under attack from both east and west, even that could only be done in the direst of circumstances.

South of the Danube

The Russians

After a maximum effort the previous day, Marshal Tolbukhin fed new units into the fight to increase the pressure on *I SS-Panzerkorps*. The German defense was already stretched to the limit and Tolbukhin did everything he could to shatter it once and for all. The effort showed immediate results as the German front threatened to cave in completely. The scale and intensity of combat reached heights rarely seen on the Eastern Front.

Korps von Bünau

A new Russian corps moved into the line west of Sankt Pölten, further proof that Tolbukhin had no intention of stopping his attack down the Danube Valley. *General der Infanterie* von Bünau once again spent the day touring the headquarters of the units under his command. Assaults along his front were mostly repelled, although German counterattacks had mixed results.

After nightfall, the Russians finally took Schwarzenbach. They'd gotten close the day before, were driven back by a counterattack, and took the town on 19 April. The dagger-like thrust endangered the entire German position east of von Bünau's corps.

* * *

All 31 trains transporting *710. Infanterie-Division* had now arrived and *Fallschirmjäger-Regiment 30* of *10. Fallschirmjäger-Division* had too. *General der Infanterie* von Bünau immediately committed them to the front lines to contain the Russian breakthrough southwest of Sankt Pölten, and while they weren't crack troops by any stretch of the imagination, they were much better than alarm units and untrained troops. Moreover, the German line was beginning to thicken.

---

1 Brettner, *Die Letzten Kämpfe Band II*, p. 176.

I SS-Panzerkorps

The corps' position was daily becoming more untenable. The far right flank had quietened some-what, but in the center constant holding attacks pinned the defenders facing east even as dire threats developed to the northwest. Russian spearheads south of Mittelbach turned east, for the key positions between Rohrbach an der Gölsen and Laaben bei Neulengbach. As became more evident with each day's casualty totals, the Russians were winning the war of attrition and the Germans' ability to hold out was on the wane. By 19 April the front was in danger of disintegration.

SS-Kampfgruppe Peiper

The seam between *Korps von Bünau* and *SS-Kampfgruppe Peiper* had already been split open and the Russians weren't slow to take advantage. All along the front they advanced as far as they could as fast as they could, and the only tactics the Germans had was to react and counterattack quickly. But being heavily outnumbered and outgunned, this meant a steady drain of losses in men and materiel that the Germans couldn't replace.

The biggest Russian threat remained cutting the Gölsen road, which ran in the river valley through Sankt Veit an der Gölsen and Hainfeld. If there was one thing the Germans simply couldn't afford to lose it was that road, so they committed every last man to keeping it open.

New Russian attacks pushed off from the areas south of Michelbach and Stössing, heading east-southeast. These were stopped at blocking positions near Stollberg with heavy Russian losses in men, anti-tank guns and vehicles.[2] But new attacks from Wilhelmsburg reached the outskirts of Rotheau, only being stopped there by a desperation counterattack. *SS-Kampfgruppe Kling* held, but it was a close-run thing. Both sides took heavy casualties and, while the Russians didn't have a limitless supply of manpower, on the German side the situation was far more acute. Kling was running out of men.

For several days fighting had raged for a hilltop named Hill 779. The Germans had shed a lot of blood keeping it and the Russians had shed even more trying to seize it. Now, even after multiple successful counterattacks on that key mountain position northwest of Rohrbach an der Gölsen, the Germans had to give it up because they couldn't stop the Russian advance on their flanks. However, a direct attack toward Rohrbach by six Russian assault guns was repelled with the loss of two of them.

Halfway between Rohrbach on the east and Traisen on the west, Sankt Viet an der Gölsen had already been lost the day before. But counterattacks on 19 April by *SS-Kampfgruppe Peiper* recaptured the town, which dated back to at least the 11th Century. Peiper had been reinforced by *SS-Kampfgruppe Sternebeck* and *SS-Kampfgruppe Hansen* from the division's right flank, and it was these men who enabled Peiper to regain Sankt Veit an der Gölsen.

The Germans spent the rest of the day hunting down Russian infiltrators and survivors. They would not lose the town again until withdrawing on the night of 7-8 May. As an indication of how terrible the combat had been, the local cemetery has 51 named and 144 unnamed graves of German soldiers killed defending the area, along with 37 civilians. Twelve concentration camp inmates who were shot are also interred there.[3]

2   Maier, *Drama*, p. 367.
3   Baumgartner, Bernhard, 'Gedenktage-Kirchenführer mit Kleiner Chronik u.a. 1945, 2009', <http://wandertipp. at/bernhardbaumgartner/2009/10/31/gedenktage-kirchenfuhrer-mit-kleiner-chronik-u-a-1945/>, (Accessed 22 July 2018).

Nearby Hainfeld also fell and was recaptured immediately by attacks from both east and west. To the north, however, the news was worse as the Russians took Brand, Laaben and Sankt Corona am Schöpfl.

Kampfgruppe 12. SS-Panzer-Division Hitlerjugend

SS-Kampfgruppe von Reitzenstein and *SS-Panzergrenadier-Regiment 26* had lost so many men, not to mention irreplaceable veterans, that when fresh Russian assaults hit them at Schöpfl hill and Sankt Corona they were unable to hold. The Russians first took high ground called Point 648 in vicious fighting. When the Germans finally gave up that height the Russians took the town in a rush. Nor was there anything left to counterattack with.

Schöpfl hill also fell to a strong attack, changing hands for at least the third time and, also for at least the third time, a counterattack made up for small numbers by the violence and immediacy of the response, once again taking the hill back. Nevertheless, the formation was now exhausted and nearly depleted too far to fight. Their main mission now became to guard the supply artery along the valley of the Gölsen River, and points further east.

Kampfgruppe 1. SS-Panzer-Division Leibstandarte Adolf Hitler

Once again Russian attacks hit the division's left flank in the Neuhaus area, south of Schwarzensee. Confused fighting over the area sucked in the last of the operable panzers and the remaining *Flak* batteries. In many cases the Russians infiltrated past the hedge-hog German positions without knowing it, so that both sides stumbled into surprised fire-fights.

Backed by smaller-caliber *Flak* cannon, a counterattack at dusk drove the Russians back toward Fahrafeld before the Germans turned east. Fighting lasted into the night, when the only light came from explosions and muzzle flashes. At one point in the forest the Germans saw one of those bizarre sights that happen in combat, even if it seems like something from a nightmare.

> We found two Russian horse-drawn vehicles in the forest not far from our command post. On one vehicle lay the corpses of fallen Russians. The Red Army soldiers must have been taken by surprise at our attack and the horse and wagon simply kept going in headlong flight.[4]

6. Armee
Kampfgruppe Raithel

Members of the *Nebelwerfer,* shortened in 1942 to simply *Werfer,* platoon of *5./SS-Gebirgsjäger-Ausbildungs-und-Ersatz-Bataillon 13 Leoben* were lucky enough to be billeted in a farmhouse near the Kreuzberg. One day 50 women and children arrived and were also housed around the farmstead, under any available roof. They were refugees from Klamm and Schottwien who had been evacuated. The SS men were glad to have a moment of tranquility among the horrors of war. They played with the children and made them little presents.

The *Werfers* themselves were positioned on the Kobermannsberg where, despite limited ammunition and the inherent inaccuracy of their weapons, they played havoc with the Russians. Time

---

4   Tiemann, *The Leibstandarte Adolf Hitler IV/2*, p. 303.

after time the Russians attacked their positions during the night or at dawn, positions which were difficult to hit with artillery. Time after time they closed within hand-grenade range and even to hand-to-hand combat, and time after time the Germans drove them back.

117. Jäger-Division

Gebirgsjäger-Division 749 continued its march over the Ochsenkopf, a mountain west of Kaltenegg, toward Waldbach. Heavy resistance in the rugged country slowed their progress to a crawl. Losses among the regiment's officers were especially heavy. To the south, the Russians pulled out of Fischbach to avoid being cut off by the division's attack.

20

Friday, 20 April

Kirchheim unter Teck, Germany

Hitler's 56th and final birthday was to be the occasion for the launch of the first three manned and armed *Bachem Ba-349 Natters*, one of the *Führer*'s vaunted *wunderwaffe* and the world's first vertical takeoff manned aircraft, or its first surface-to-air missile, depending on the configuration. It was a more advanced version of an idea that began the year before with the piloted V-1 rocket. The potential for this weapon was unlimited, although by 20 April 1945, it was a year too late to affect the war situation.

Since the *Natter* took off like a *V-1* rocket it needed no airfield, only a small concrete pad and steel launch tower. Maximum speed topped 600 miles per hour and in many ways it resembled the Messerschmidt ME-163 rocket fighter, even using the same engine and fuel. Although a quantum leap forward in aviation technology, the aircraft was very dangerous to fly. Much like the ME-163, the operational plan for its use called for the pilot to zoom past the bomber formation, at which point the *Natters'* fuel would run out. Nosing downward, the rockets carried in its nosecone would be fired like a torpedo spread into the bomber stream and the aircraft would then glide back to Earth, with various parts having their own parachutes, including the pilot. Its one previous manned flight had ended in the death of Lothar Sieber, the pilot. Still, time was running out and desperate measures were called for.

Unfortunately for the Germans, American tanks rolled into the idyllic city of Kirchheim unter Teck, at the confluence of the rivers Lindach and Lauter. The city was very close to the *Natter* launch pads located in a small nearby wood, so that with the appearance of Americans the historic flights were cancelled at the last instant. The Germans pulled out quickly to avoid letting the revolutionary weapons fall into Allied hands, and were never again able to plan a launch for their *wunderwaffe*.

* * *

Division of the Reich hadn't occurred yet, but Hitler anticipated it and split the command of the armed forces by naming *Generalfeldmarshall* Kesselring as *Oberbefehlshaber Süd* and *Grossadmiral* Dönitz as *Oberbefehlshaber Nord*. The command staff of the *OKW* immediately began the move to Berchtesgaden, which would become its base of operations under the direction of *General der Gebirgstruppe* August Winter. In Eisenhower's mind this only reinforced his belief in the National Redoubt, despite mounting evidence to the contrary. All the forces of the Reich seemed to be heading there, unless he could cut them off first.

Whether or not Hitler ever intended to go south is still debated by historians in the 21st Century. As much as Hitler's intentions can be deciphered, he seems to have been of two minds. The only place in the world he ever seemed to find peace was at the Berghof, so the natural desire to go there seems to have nagged at his will. Even on this last birthday he is known to have asked Reichminister of Armaments Albert Speer his thoughts about going south. Certainly his generals advised this.

Joseph Goebbels argued otherwise. He knew, as did Hitler, that the National Redoubt didn't exist, so if Berlin fell the war was lost anyway. If that was the case the *Führer* might as well die surrounded by his enemies rather than hiding in his bedroom at home. And perhaps the legend of Custer's Last Stand played a part in his decision. During his service in the First World War, one of the officers in Hitler's regiment was a *Leutnant* Keogh, who was the grandnephew of a troop leader in George Armstrong Custer's 7th Cavalry Regiment. That officer died at the Battle of the Little Bighorn. Keogh was an Irish Republican who trained in America before the war, joined the British Army and became a POW, then joined the Germans to advance the Republican cause. He even claimed to have ridden the only survivor of Custer's massacred regiment, the horse named Comanche. Of course, Comanche died the same year that Keogh was born, but the anecdote makes it clear he liked to spin stories. It seems reasonable to envisage the grizzled veteran of three armies whiling away cold nights in the trench by entertaining his comrades with tall tales.

Anyway, Keogh claimed to have comforted Hitler as he lay on a stretcher after being wounded in 1916. Later, after the war, Keogh commanded troops in a *Freikorps* in Munich and once broke up a riot where up to 200 men were beating two others to death in a gym. One of those he saved was Adolf Hitler.[1] So the notion that the doomed *Führer* remembered the courageous image of Custer fighting to the last while surrounded by enemies, and saw himself in the same light, must be considered as being at least possible.

Heeresgruppe Süd

Warm and sunny weather continued as a tranquil contrast to the mayhem and chaos spreading over Austria. The supply situation grew increasingly acute. Fuel had been scarce for a long time but now heavy ammunition stocks had also been exhausted. Artillery, *Nebelwerfers* and *Flak* guns were all limited to whatever stocks they had to hand.

* * *

The Army Group's ration strength on 20 April was 766,095 men and 149,310 horses.[2] This is a force of approximately the same size as had been assembled for the defense of Berlin in *Heeresgruppe Vistula*. Four days later, however, in a note prepared for *SS-Obergruppenführer* Karl-Hermann Frank, its strength was put at 618,000 men and 128,000 horses. For his part, *Generaloberst* Rendulic estimated his army group at 800,000 men.

8. Armee

General der Gebirgstruppe Kreysing had been shuffling his units to meet the increasing pressure from both Second Ukrainian Front and Forty-Sixth Army from Third Ukrainian Front. In army reserve was *Sturmgeschütze Brigade 325* and *Sturmartillerie Brigade 239*. The latter was armed with the *Sturmhaubtize 42G*, the successor model to the *Sturmgeschütz III*.

His task had been made much easier when the two most northerly corps of his army were transferred to control of *Heeresgruppe Mitte*. The headquarters for *Panzerkorps Feldherrnhalle* had now moved entirely out of Austria into old Czechoslovakia at the town of Jaroslavice, although many

1   Historywithatwist, 'Adolf Hitler and the Battle of the Bighorn', (2014), <https://historywithatwist.wordpress. com/2014/06/23/adolf-hitler-and-the-battle-of-little-bighorn/>, (Accessed 30 July 2018).
2   Rauchensteiner, *Krieg in Österreich*, p. 326.

of its men still fought on the Austrian side of the border. In corps reserve was *Schwere-Panzerjäger-Abteilung 662.*

On 20 April Freysing's front lined up as follows. *Panzerkorps Feldherrnhalle* held the far left flank up to the border with *Heeresgruppe Mitte. Panzer-Division Feldherrnhalle 1* held down the far left position, and beside it stood *Panzer-Division Feldherrnhalle 2* with one regiment from *44. Infanterie-Division Hoch und Deutschmeister* attached.

In reserve behind the two *Feldherrnhalle* divisions, Rauchensteiner lists a certain *Panzerjäger-Brigade Wilke* in the vicinity of Znojmo in old Czechoslovakia.[3] At that time Znojmo was near two highways leading northeast and northwest, giving the so-called brigade fast access to the front in case of a breakthrough.

This brigade isn't found in *Wehrmacht* records under that name, but it can only have been the *Panzerjäger* battalion from *19. Panzer-Division*, which was stationed on the right flank of *Heeresgruppe Mitte* adjoining *8. Armee.* One platoon of that battalion was led by Knight's Cross winner Lieutenant Giselher Wilke, who bore a passing resemblance to American actor Edward G. Robinson. Wilke had won the Knight's Cross during the Soviet winter offensive in Poland and learned on 14 April that it had been approved. On 20 April the commander of *19. Panzer-Division*, *Generalmajor* Hans Källner, presented Wilke with his award.

Next to *Feldherrnhalle 2* were *Kampfgruppe 211. Volksgrenadier-Division* with one regiment from *48. Volks-Grenadier-Division* attached; *357. Infanterie-Division* and *SS-Kampfgruppe Trabandt II.* These were echeloned forward as far east as Reinthal, with the shoulder of that bulge running through Herrnbaumgarten to Poysdorf. In reserve behind was *SS-Kampfgruppe Trabandt I* at Laa an der Thaya.

The *8. Armee's* other corps was *XXXXIII Armeekorps*, which had *25. Panzer-Division* in the line around Ungerndorf. This division was without *Panzerjäger-Abteilung 87*, which was at the Grafenwöhr training grounds. It had been brought up to 100 percent strength in manpower, but only 30 percent in materiel and 25 percent in motorized vehicles. It had received no new armor, and this important component of the division would never rejoin its parent, nor would *Schwere-Flak-Artillerie-Abteilung 279*, which also had been brought up to full strength in men, and nearly full strength in materiel and vehicles.[4]

To the right of *25. Panzer-Division* was the newly transferred *6. Panzer-Division*, then *Kampfgruppe 101. Jäger-Division* and *Kampfgruppe 96. Infanterie-Division*, with *Grenadier-Brigade 92* attached. The latter had been *Grenadier-Regiment 92* until being designated a brigade in January 1945.

Second Ukrainian Front

The sharp northwesterly flow of the Russian offensive carried the Pliyev Cavalry Group and 4th Guards Cavalry Corps into the front of *Heeresgruppe Mitte,* although part of their attack front overlapped that defended by *Panzerkorps Feldherrnhalle.* Listing the Front's corps facing *8. Armee* from north to south, first came Sixth Guards Army, commanded by twice Hero of the Soviet Union Colonel General Andrei Kravchenko. The other army was Seventh Guards Army, commanded by Colonel General Andrei Shumilov. Between them these two armies contained five corps: 5th Guards Tank Corps, 9th Guards Mechanized Corps, and 24th, 25th and 27th Guards Rifle Corps. In reserve was the Rumanian First Army. This strong attack group concentrated its

---

assault between Michelstetten and Herrnbaumgarten, with Laa an der Thaya as the immediate objective. This put part of the *Kampfgruppe 101. Jäger-Division*, along with *6. Panzer-Division* and *25. Panzer Division*, squarely in the crosshairs of the attack.

And that attack was coming.

* * *

Between Wilfersdorf and Poysdorf the Russians overran the little village of Bullendorf, killing 25 German soldiers and three civilians, while only losing six of their own men. Instead of pursuing the broken German formations, however, the Russians stopped for the usual orgy of plunder, drink and rape, thus allowing the Germans time to regroup. Also as usual, the SS defenders blew up the Zaya bridges during their retreat.

* * *

Hitler's birthday marked the last major tank fight of the war. Second Ukrainian Front's offensive toward Brno picked up steam, overrunning no less than 33 villages on 20 April, including Fallbach, five miles south-southeast of Laa an der Thaya. Combat then moved to Ungerndorf, just north of Fallbach in the area near Staatz, where an armored battle broke out between elements of both *6. Panzer-Division* and *25. Panzer-Division*, and tanks of 5th Guards Tank Corps. The difference in priority between Second and Third Ukrainian Fronts is evidenced by 5th Guards Tank Corps having been armed with Russian tanks, mostly T-34/85s, and not the more vulnerable American Shermans.

Spread over a fairly wide area, the encounter wasn't one large grouping of tanks versus another, but a series of smaller engagements that were part of the whole Russian thrust toward Laa. The geography of this area made it ideal tank country. Cultivated fields with little more than undulations in the landscape gave the attackers the advantage of engaging targets at much longer distances. Worse for the defenders, artillery spotting made the fall of shells much more accurate and air support had clear targets. But for once the Germans had effective weapons to counter the masses of Russian tanks, and the few veterans still in the German ranks reminded the Russians of just how formidable the German Army once had been. While the fighting raged for much of the day, when night fell the Russians had suffered terrible losses of 70 tanks.[5] German losses are reported at between two and four panzers. The battlefield was littered with burning Russian tanks. Such losses couldn't be sustained for long, even by the Red Army.

* * *

The four Russian tanks that spent the night at Ernsdorf bei Spaatz cranked up their engines at dawn and crept further into the town. The main German defense position was in a field northeast of the village on the road to Enzersdorf bei Spaatz. Well dug-in was a tiny *Kampfgruppe* from 6. *Panzer-Division*, with one panzer (probably a Panther), one *PAK-40* 75mm anti-tank gun, one *Sturmgeschütz* and 11 men, which was typical of the thinly spread German defenses in the entire region. The position was well chosen and even better camouflaged.

It was over in seconds. When the Germans opened fire they immediately destroyed three of the four Russian tanks, including one parked next to the local department store, which went up in flames. One German fell to the Russian's return fire. For the rest of the day more Russian

---

5   Brettner, *Die Letzten Kämpfe Band II*, p. 178. The war diary for *Heeresgruppe Süd* entry for 21 April is quoted at length by Brettner, and it puts a figure of 41 destroyed tanks on the previous day's fighting. However, that was written the morning following the fighting, with communications and estimates being incomplete. The higher figure more closely matches the probable total based on later estimates.

tanks tried to move past the blocking position, or to destroy it, but like attacks across the region the efforts were uncoordinated and ineffective. Before the day ended as many as 15 knocked-out Russian tanks lay smoking on the battlefield, to the Germans' one.

* * *

At nearby Wildendürnbach 50 houses were hit by bombs from Fifth Air Army during ground-support attacks, an indication of how active the Russians were in the air. On the southern fringe of the fighting at Ungerndorf, *6. Panzer-Division*'s *Panzergrenadier* regiment held its ground despite a wave of Russian armor. It was a critical position and the Germans knew it, since a breakthrough couldn't be sealed off.

Around the tiny hamlet of Loosdorf, just south of Laa an der Thaya, the *Panzerjäger* company from *SS-Kampfgruppe Trabandt I* went into action with *Panzergrenadier-Regiment 114*. The regiment committed three *Panzergrenadier* and one heavy weapons companies, while the SS men brought their six *Hetzer Jagdpanzers* to the fight. Loosdorf changed hands several times as the Germans were thrown out, counterattacked, and were thrown out again. The SS *Hetzers* destroyed six or eight T-34s. Finally, late in the afternoon, the fighting died down and the Germans again held the village.

The battalion commander, *SS-Hauptmann* Persch, called an officers' meeting to discuss their situation. Supplies were ordered for the next day and defense plans laid out. As the meeting broke up and the officers left, a Russian artillery strike hit and killed two SS men. Many others were wounded, including Persch. Surviving the day's battles meant nothing; a man could die at any time without warning.[6]

* * *

One mile west of Poysdorf was the village of Kleinhadersdorf, which was defended by small elements of both *Schwere SS-Panzer-Abteilung 503* and *SS-Kampfgruppe Trabandt II*. Coming on the road toward Poysdorf from Mistelbach, the Russians tried to capture the village on the fly using tanks alone, but the Tiger IIs feasted on the Sherman tanks rumbling toward them over open country. Even the improved armor of later Sherman models was useless against the high-velocity 88mm main gun of a Tiger II, which could penetrate the American tank at effectively any realistic distance. If the Tiger could see the Sherman, the Sherman was in serious trouble. And unlike the diesel engine of a T-34/85, the Sherman's engine ran on gasoline, which meant they caught fire easily. At Kleinhadersdorf 13 burning Shermans clogged the fields around the village.

But the Russians kept coming. They outnumbered the Germans so badly that despite horrific losses they took the village and all but wiped out the small SS force. The Tigers withdrew and took the surviving infantry with them.[7]

* * *

Poysdorf was lightly defended by an under-strength platoon, probably from *SS-Kampfgruppe Trabandt II*, with a mortar, a few machine guns, snipers and 20 or so other men. At 9:00 a.m. eight Russian tanks clanked down the road from the west, without opening fire. For their part the Germans didn't shoot, either, since they had no heavy weapons anyway. The Russians drove through the town to the Poybach River on the eastern outskirts, and then back the way they came.

6   Jordan, Franz, *April 1945 – Die Kämpfe im nordöstlichen Niederösterreich, Österreichischer* (Militärverlag: Salzburg, 2003), p. 298.
7   Brettner, *Die Letzten Kämpfe Band II*, p. 178.

An hour-and-a-half later two small battalions of Russian infantry headed across the fields toward Poysdorf. Nearing the town, they met and demanded of a civilian, "where are the German soldiers?" The Russians then moved in cautiously, setting up their artillery near the town's train station. Most of the people had done the smart thing and descended into their cellars, but even so when the shooting started 12 died in the fighting. After the battle, the old men in the town were forced to bury 20 German and five Russian soldiers killed in the brief battle, along with 17 towns-folk who were executed. This time, the usual plundering included the apothecary store. Around nightfall the leading Russian elements moved out to the north, but ran up against German strong-points near Herrenbaumgartner.[8]

* * *

Ungernsdorf, a mile north of Fallbach, was the next Russian target, but there the Russians got a nasty surprise. Waiting for them were Tigers IIs from *Schwere SS-Panzer-Abteilung 503* and Panthers from *6. Panzer-Division*. In heavy fighting the Russians destroyed four German tanks, but lost 20 of their own. The drive on Laa was stopped in its tracks.

* * *

After recapturing Altlichtenwarth two days before, *SS-Kampfgruppe Trabandt II* and the other German forces in the area were ordered to join the general retreat to the northwest, into the Protectorate of Bohemia and Moravia, the old Czechoslovakia, after which their division was named. Whether or not they were reluctant to abandon the locals to their fate after discovering the horrors heaped upon the populace the first time the Russians overran the town, there was really no choice unless the soldiers wanted to die themselves; the Red Army was moving past them on both flanks and if they held their position they would have shortly been cut off. Fortunately the residents made their decision easier by fleeing when the town was recaptured.

Vienna

For more than a week O-5 had busied themselves putting together the framework of its govern-ment while in communication with the two other significant political groups in the city, the socialists and the communists. What was needed was a leader. That man arrived on the 20th in the identity of former Austrian Socialist Chancellor Karl Renner, who was hand-picked by Stalin to head the postwar government. Renner was a cranky 74-year-old whose appointment by Stalin fulfilled all of Churchill's fears about the Soviet leader's duplicity.

But Renner wasn't universally liked even by members of his own government. During the *Anschluss* he'd called for a 'yes' vote and many of his political enemies would never forgive him for it. In particular Viktor Matejka, who was in charge of cultural affairs after the war, hated Renner for what he considered his betrayal of Austria. And as time went by the Russians themselves began to doubt the wisdom of their choice, as Renner could be intransigent. He was an Austrian first and a socialist second, and that wasn't what they'd had in mind.

8   Brettner, *Die Letzten Kämpfe Band II*, p. 178.

6. SS-Panzerarmee

SS-Oberstgruppenführer Sepp Dietrich now commanded three corps: *II SS-Panzerkorps* north of the Danube, *Korps von Bünau* south of it and *I SS-Panzerkorps* echeloned forward with its headquarters around Pernitz. Viewed on a map, the deep thrust west down the south bank of the Danube resembled a dagger pointed at the heart of the army. The Russians held the south bank within a few miles of Krems, but the north was in German hands west of Korneuberg, a distance of about 36 miles. The Russians had few suitable crossing points because of the wetlands north of the Danube and the Germans didn't have the forces to cross the river and counterattack south into the rear of Ninth Guards Army. Neither did *I SS-Panzerkorps* have forces to attack north to cut off the Russian spearheads.

This situation meant that the further Ninth Guards Army's spearheads drove west, the more protection they needed. To ease this draining of forces from the main point of attack, Fourth Guards Army had been hammering away at *I SS-Panzerkorps* on both the northern and eastern fronts and would continue to do so.

Meanwhile, because of the pressure on *8. Armee,* Dietrich's army had been ordered to extend its front further north, with the dividing line between the two armies running from Naglern west to Grub with a slight northwest angle from there. Facing them was the powerful Forty-Sixth Army on the north bank of the Danube. South of the river was the sector of Third Ukrainian Front. The two armies facing Dietrich were Fourth Guards Army, whose commander was Lieutenant General Nikanor Zakhvatayev, and Ninth Guards Army, under the command of Hero of the Soviet Union Colonel General Vasily Glagolev.

II SS-Panzerkorps

The corps had responsibility for the front from Naglern down to the Danube at Korneuberg, a distance of 13 miles. The terrain there was mostly flat farmland and vineyards, with a few crags and forested areas. On this front *SS-Obergruppenführer* Wilhelm Bittrich had the *Führer-Grenadier-Division, Kampfgruppe 3. SS-Panzer-Division Totenkopf* and *Kampfgruppe Volkmann*. *Grenadier-Regiment 130* was the only remnant left of *45. Volks-Grenadier-Division*, an understrength unit that had been torn to shreds during the fighting in Silesia. Its last commander was *Generalmajor* Erich Hassenstein, who soon would be given the hopeless task of defending Passau. In the meantime, this last component of his former command was renamed *45. Divisionsgruppe* and attached to the *Führer-Grenadier-Division* for the duration of the war.

No attacks came on 20 April as Russian efforts hammered away further to the north, but the division noticed a lot of scouting activities along their front. This indicated detailed planning by the Russians for a new attack.

In corps reserve was *Sturmgeschütz-Brigade 325*. Ominously, the defenders could see timber being cut south of the Danube and being used to build fortifications at what they believed would be the points where the Russians would try to cross. Combined with the increased reconnaissance activity, *II SS-Panzerkorps* had to anticipate a two-pronged attack, one against its eastward-facing front to pin down *Führer-Grenadier-Division* and its attached units, and the other to cross the Danube to cut them off from the west.

The Russians

Facing *II SS-Panzerkorps* was the Russian Forty-Sixth Army under the command of Hero of the Soviet Union Lieutenant General Alexander Petrushevsky, and five corps, consisting of 20th Guards, 31st Guards, 68th Rifle, 2nd Guards Mechanized and 23rd Tank Corps. Reorganizing and in reserve was 4th Guards Mechanized Corps at Bratlislava. The front line ran from Leobendorf, through Tresdorf to Rückersdorf and Obergänserndorf.

South of the Danube

Once the Gestapo had tried and convicted the men herding the Americans from *Stalag 17B* west, who had been arrested in the 'Raxenburg Incident', an SS unit swooped down on the camp and took over administration.

Korps von Bünau

General der Infanterie von Bünau's corps now defended the front from the Danube east of Krems, through Prinzersdorf to Rotheau. A survey of the former Battle Commander of Vienna's mixed bag of units on 20 April included *SS-Kampfgruppe Trabandt III*, with the Hungarian 88th Artillery Battalion attached. That battalion had three batteries equipped with 80mm mortars. Also part of the corps was *Kampfgruppe Kommandant Krems*, probably miscellaneous officers in the Krems area and *Volkssturm*, with some Hitler Youth, and the previously mentioned *Schwere-Panzerjäger-Brigade 2*. That so-called brigade was essentially men mounted on bicycles carrying a *Panzerfaust*, or perhaps a *Panzerschreck*, the German anti-tank weapon that inspired the American bazooka. In the case of this particular unit one company was motorized, probably using Volkswagens and a *Kübelwagen* or two.

Von Bünau's strongest unit was the *710. Infanterie-Division*, which had never in its history been considered a first-rate formation but which the general rated as being effective for mobile defense. For a few days during this period *Das Reich* was attached to *Korps von Bünau* as it recovered from the Vienna battle.

Panzer-Aufklärungs-Abteilung 1 and *Panzer-Aufklärungs-Abteilung 3* were still separated from their parent divisions, which were fighting on the army group's far right flank. *Panzer-Aufklärungs-Abteilung 1* was at about 60 percent strength while its companion might have been as strong as half strength. Together they formed about one full-strength battalion.

The veteran *Volks-Artillerie-Korps 403* provided firepower, with one light field howitzer battalion, two heavy field howitzer battalions, one 170mm cannon battery, one 210mm *Nebelwerfer* battalion and one battalion of 88mm guns. *Artillerie-Brigade 959*[9] added two light and one heavy howitzer battalions, a mixed battalion with one 100mm cannon battery and two heavy batteries probably armed with 150mm guns, to von Bünau's strongest asset, his artillery. In a postwar interview von Bünau rated its combat value as "quite good".[10] Attached to the brigade after 11 April was 103rd Hungarian Artillery Battalion, armed with three batteries of 210mm *Nebelwerfers*. It may be assumed that neither of these units was anywhere close to full strength. Also, like all German

---

9   Some sources list this unit as part of Arko 3. It may have been reassigned during the course of the fighting.
10   Von Bünau, *Corps von Buenau*, p. 29.

rocket and artillery units during this period, ammunition stocks were low and the batteries could only provide sporadic support in the most important situations.

Sturmgeschütz-Brigade 261, aka *Sturmartillerie-Brigade 261,* had three battalions with eight *Sturmgeschütze* each, probably *StuG. 42Hs.* This battalion-sized unit had a long combat record and had anywhere from 10-16 machines operational at any given moment. *Schwere-Panzerjäger-Abteilung 653* had the distinction of being one of the few *Wehrmacht* units equipped with the largest German armored vehicle to go into production during the war, the *Jagdtiger.* Built on a Tiger II chassis this behemoth mounted a specially adapted version of the deadly 128mm *Flak* cannon. Prone to mechanical problems and with its huge gun in a fixed mounting, the *Jagdtiger* had its drawbacks. But when face-to-face with the enemy there were few tanks that could fight it and survive. Unfortunately for the Germans, only about 80 were ever produced. The number of operational *Jagdtigers* in the battalion is unknown.

Luftwaffe Flaksturm-Regiment 4 had one light and two heavy batteries, which were more or less up to full strength except for some of their transport vehicles. Von Bünau even commanded two gunboats of *Donauflottille 2,* Danube Flotilla 2, armed with 88mm and smaller guns.

Two SS alarm battalions armed only with hand weapons and some *Volkssturm* battalions fleshed out the order of battle for battalion-sized units and larger. In addition to these, a few smaller units were also attached to the corps, both infantry and artillery, mostly of company size or even smaller.

A corps reserve was scraped together from stragglers, convalescents and selected men who had proven themselves in battle. The idea was to have one quick-reaction force that could be counted on for a counterattack, and it received the name *Korps-Sturmbataillon.* Because of its designated mission von Bünau equipped it with enough trucks for its whole complement of men, and the necessary fuel so there would be no delay if they were needed in an emergency situation. They never were.

* * *

Fighting for the hill near Kuffern overlooking Krems an der Donau entered its fourth day, as the Germans simply couldn't allow the Russians to keep it. Through sheer enthusiasm and determination, the men gathered from SS schools into *SS-Kampfgruppe Trabandt III* finally recaptured the height on 20 April. With that, serious Russian efforts to take Krems came to an end, even if the Germans didn't know it at the time.

I SS-Panzerkorps

Parts of the newly formed *10. Fallschirmjäger-Division* were on hand with more elements in transit. Although its title sounds impressive, the men of that division didn't even have basic infantry training, except as taught in *Luftwaffe* schools. They were pilots, mechanics, fuel truck drivers, air crew, staff officers and miscellaneous personnel. The division's combat value was minimal, and it was a microcosm of a fatal flaw within Hitler's *Wehrmacht.*

A vital component of Hitler's method of wielding and staying in power was for each of his paladins to guard their fiefdoms with jealous rage. For example, the *Waffen-SS* could be commanded by an Army Officer for tactical purposes, that is, on the battlefield. But a *Waffen-SS* unit was something separate and apart from the Army. It was the armed wing of the Nazi Party and was the de facto fourth branch of the *Wehrmacht.* As *Reichsführer-SS,* Heinrich Himmler had no issues incorporating men from other branches into the *Waffen-SS,* but never allowed an SS man to be transferred to the Army, *Luftwaffe* or *Kriegsmarine.*

The same jealousy was true of *Reichsmarschall* Hermann Göring. As far back as 1942 it became apparent that the *Luftwaffe* had hundreds of thousands of excess personnel, and the question of what to do with those healthy young men sparked vicious arguments. The Army wanted to use them to make good the losses suffered up to that point in Operation Barbarossa by using them as replacements for depleted divisions. It was estimated those 200,000 or so men could bring 40 infantry divisions back up to full strength.

Göring would have none of it. He had long dreamed of having his own *Luftwaffe* ground force, in addition to the famed *7. Flieger-Division*, soon to be renamed the *1. Fallschirmjäger-Division*. In 1943, therefore, the *Hermann Göring Panzer-Division* would be formed, with a second armored division, this time a parachute panzer division, being formed in 1944. These were then combined to create the *Hermann Göring Panzerkorps*.

Such division of effort crippled the German war effort, and in 1942 the enmity between Göring and the Army led to using those 200,000 men not to rebuild the Army divisions, but to create 18 *Luftwaffe* field divisions. The *Reichsmarshall* had gained Hitler's approval of this counter-productive scheme by declaring that he didn't want the men's "fine National Socialist attitudes"[11] polluted by the Army. It should also be noted that Hitler preferred new divisions to maintaining old ones, because that increased the illusion of strength. As things turned out the *Luftwaffe* field divisions proved close to useless on the battlefield, but for Göring that was preferable to allowing the Army to have them.

Another example of Göring's personal intransigence costing the *Wehrmacht* dearly occurred during the Battle of Velikiye Luki in the winter of 1942-1943. The Russians had surrounded the city and its garrison much like they had done at Stalingrad. German forces trying to break through ground their way forward until a single battalion actually made it into the city, but was too weak to hold open a corridor for other units to enter. Meanwhile, less than 30 miles away was the famous veteran *1. Fallschirmjäger-Division*, which was rested, fully equipped and at full strength. It would have won the battle for the Germans without question, except Göring blocked its use because he didn't think the objective worth the lives of his men. And so the city's garrison and the battle were lost.

Two years later the same mistakes were being made. The men who made up *10. Fallschirmjäger-Division* could have fleshed out any of the depleted German divisions in the area. Putting untrained men with combat veterans at least assured they could lean on the knowledge of their comrades when battle came, and in quiet moments basic training could be taught. But while surplus *Luftwaffe* men had long since been used for that purpose, whenever possible Göring still created new and ineffective divisions, and Hitler let him, because they looked good on a map.

As it was, *10. Fallschirmjäger-Division* was especially hard-hit by infiltration tactics in the mountains and heavily forested area south of Sankt Pölten. It held on in terrible fighting, but casualties were heavy.

SS-Kampfgruppe Peiper

Under a continuing assault the German front wavered. All along the left flank of *I SS-Panzerkorps* the Russians launched attack after attack in an attempt to break through, beginning before dawn and continuing into the night. To speak of a German front anywhere in *I SS-Panzerkorps'* area at this point would be misleading. Instead, defenders grouped in fortified positions that were ideally within range for mutual support. Towns and villages became strongpoints and the control of roads was critical to the Russian advance, since hauling supplies cross-country in such rugged topography was impractical, if not impossible.

---

11   Mitcham, Samuel R., *Hitler's Legions, German Army Order of Battle World War II* (London: Leo Cooper, 1985).

On the paratroopers' right flank was *SS-Kampfgruppe Peiper* in the St Veit an der Gölsen and Hainfeld area. The Russians immediately pressed their attacks on Hainfeld. Despite fierce fighting Peiper's men lost Hainfeld again and it was occupied by Russians from the 17th Tank Corps, probably at least one company from the 106th Rifle Division, supported by armor. This was a critical loss. Without that road supplies would have to detour many miles to the south, so Peiper sent those same panzers back into the attack.

As the Germans always did, Peiper counterattacked without delay and recaptured the town yet again.[12] Vicious close-quarters street fighting again erupted in the town. Smoke lowered visibility and burned the eyes of men from both sides.

A new *Kampfgruppe* formed from the *LAH*'s *SS-Panzergrenadier-Regiment 2*, *SS-Kampfgruppe Siebken*, arrived on Hainfeld's eastern edge as the battle raged. The men jumped straight from their trucks into battle as Russian riflemen charged at them across open fields. A *Flakpanzer IV Wirblewind* chopped up their ranks like Confederates in Pickett's Charge at Gettysburg, while a Panther from Peiper's *Kampfgruppe* stood in the town square firing round after round. This wasn't the last time that a *Wirblewind* intervened to stop a Russian advance, and it seems highly likely it was the same vehicle in every case. If so, the crewmen of that *Flakpanzer* are the unsung heroes among the *Waffen-SS* defenders.

The Russians kept coming regardless of how much firepower the Germans turned on them. Fighting became house-to-house, and then within the same house. Individual rooms changed hands many times, back and forth, until the interior walls of some homes began to collapse from all of the battle damage.[13]

At the height of the battle Peiper was called to take an urgent phone call from none other than Adolf Hitler himself. Amid the chaotic situation around Berlin, and the gathering of his paladins to wish him a Happy Birthday, the *Führer* had called to congratulate Peiper on his promotion to *Standartenführer*, the equivalent of a full colonel in the Army.[14] The reader may properly wonder if Hitler heard the gunfire of Peiper's *Kampfgruppe* over the phone connection, or if Peiper heard Russian artillery shells rattling the *Führerbunker*.

The Russians threw everything they had at Hainfeld but this time the Germans held it, thus keeping the supply road open to the east. The Russians had lost the town yet again, this time at the cost of scores of dead. But they weren't about to give up yet.

* * *

Hainfeld wasn't the only bitter fighting of the day, though. After the fall of Schwarzenbach *SS-Kampfgruppe Peiper*'s left flank faced west-northwest to keep the Russians from driving behind Sankt Viet and further east, into the back of *Hitlerjugend* and the *LAH*. Peiper's defensive line could only be extended so far, even if it was only outposts, as he simply didn't have the manpower to stretch it too far. That created the imminent danger of being outflanked.

One of Peiper's battle groups fighting south of Sankt Viet an der Gölsen was driven backward to the southwest, while others fought and lost Rohrbach an der Gölsen. To rescue wounded men being treated at the forward aid station, Peiper personally led his few remaining panzers into Rohrbach to cover their withdrawal.[15] Everyone knew what happened to wounded SS men captured by the Russians, or thought they did, and Peiper wasn't going to let that happen to his men. The Russians responded with a heavy mortar barrage, and then they attacked to try

12   Maier, *Drama*, p. 368.
13   Reynold, *Men of Steel*, p. 271.
14   Parker, *Hitler's Warrior*, p. 122.
15   Tiemann, *The Leibstandarate IV/2*, p. 304.

and prevent the withdrawal. Hand-to-hand combat raged throughout the town, which was left a flaming ruin, but the wounded were evacuated before the Russians captured it.

Kampfgruppe 12. SS-Panzer-Division Hitlerjugend

Immediately to Peiper's right, around Sankt Corona am Schöpfl, *Hitlerjugend* once again endured heavy attacks on its left flank from enemy spearheads moving east instead of south to join the attack on Hainfeld. The re-capture of Schöpfl hill the night before was nullified by an early morning Russian attack on Sankt Corona, which both captured the town and the high ground to its north, Hill 648. The unflappable *SS-Hauptsturmführer* von Reitzenstein wasted no time retaking Hill 648 and, when reports showed that Sankt Corona had few Russians in it, he took back the town as well.

To their right a Russian push toward Altenmarkt an der Triesting was stopped by two SPWs and a handful of infantry. Small to medium attacks hit the division in multiple spots, forcing a constant realignment of units. More and more the Russian objective of cutting the supply artery leading east became obvious.

Late in the day a Russian assault broke through *SS-Kampfgruppe Gross* and drove on Klammhöhe. Although stopped short of the town by German blocking positions, *SS-Brigadeführer* Kraas had to wonder whether it was still worth holding the Sankt Corona and Schöpfl hill areas. Neither *SS-Kampfgruppe von Reizenstein* nor *Panzergrenadier-Regiment 26* had enough strength left to hold against determined assaults, so here too, the German front was in danger of shattering under the renewed Russian attacks. Sankt Corona had already been lost multiple times but *SS-Kampfgruppe von Reizenstein* had suffered very heavy casualties to date. And while they still held the Schöpfl, with Klammhöhe threatened the danger of being cut off from the southwest loomed all too real. *SS-Kampfgruppe Gross* was under attack at Kaumberg, astride the vital road from Hainfeld to Altenmarkt, so *Hitlerjugend* commander Kraas finally decided to pull his men in the Schöpfl region back to Kaumberg to reinforce Gross. The defenders had achieved near miracles in holding as long as they had, and paid dearly for their determination, but in the end it was all for naught. Dead *Landser* filled the local graveyards.

As night deepened the situation was unclear and highly unstable. Kraas didn't know where all of his own units were, much less those of the enemy. He sent multiple scouting patrols into the dark woods along his front line to clarify matters, but which only partly did so.

Kampfgruppe 1. SS-Panzer-Division Leibstandarte Adolf Hitler

From around Alland the front turned sharply south, where the *LAH* guarded *Hitlerjugend*'s right rear in the vicinity of Raisenmarkt all the way down to Pernitz, near the corps headquarters. Fresh attacks hit both Altenmarkt an der Triesting and Berndorf, but in places the SS held firm and repelled the attackers.

Kampfgruppe 356. Infanterie-Division

Moving south from there was *Kampfgruppe 356. Infanterie-Division* defending the northern Hohe Wand region. Strength levels by this point are unknown due to lost records, but the division had been crushed fighting at Székesfehérvár a month before. Never having been considered a first-rate division, and therefore being lower in priority for replacements, as well as having fought in Italy for the previous six months, it was probably no larger than a reinforced regiment.

SS-Kampfgruppe Keitel

On the corps' far right flank was the battered *SS-Kampfgruppe Keitel* south of the Hohe Wand. Keitel's original strength had been about 2,000 men, and while the *Kampfgruppe* had likely absorbed some stragglers and blocking forces, it couldn't have come close to replacing losses. By the end of the war the regimental-sized *Kampfgruppe* would be virtually destroyed.

The Russians

Facing *SS-Obergruppenführer* Hermann Preiss's collection of depleted and burned-out units was another part of Ninth Guards Army. The main force in contact with *I SS-Panzerkorps* was 37th Guards Rifle Corps, deploying three rifle divisions, the 98th, 99th and 103rd Guards. But in reserve around Vienna and ready to either exploit a breakthrough against the SS or move north of the Danube was Fourth Guards Army, commanded by the veteran winner of the Order of Lenin, Lieutenant General Nikanor Zakhvatayev. Having fought for the Czar's army in the First World War, and winning numerous medals for his skill, the fact that he attained high rank after the purges of 1937-1938 says much about his ability to command. Fourth Guards Army had two corps, 20th and 21st Guards Rifle Corps. It also had three assault gun regiments attached at army level.

* * *

Some sources say that on 20 April *Rumänische SS-Regiment 2* of the proposed Rumanian SS division was ordered to re-form itself as a tank destroyer unit, turning in its guns for anti-tank weapons. Whether or not this actually happened is not known for certain. The men for this planned formation came from the Rumanian 4th Infantry Division, which had been refitting in German-held territory when their nation defected to the Russians. Some members of Romania's fascist Iron Guard who eluded Russian capture were also incorporated. The men of the first so-called regiment, which had four companies and was the size of an average battalion, fought on the Oder Front with *III SS-Panzerkorps*. Like so many other units defending Berlin it was utterly destroyed.

The *Rumänische SS-Regiment 2* fared better. With no weapons available to form a combat unit, the troops organized into field construction battalions for building fortifications. By late in the month one such battalion was near Lilienfeld and another near Sankt Aegyd. They were likely formed from two existing grenadier regiments.

As for the highly motivated Rumanian *SS-Hauptsturmführer* Emilian, who by this time had arrived back in Austria from his training class in northwestern Germany, he was first assigned to the staff of *6. SS-Panzerarmee* and then sent on to *I SS-Panzerkorps* near Sankt Aegyd. Once there he was told, in essence, that he should stand by and wait for orders. The Rumanian battalion in the vicinity seems to have been doing little but cutting down trees, which may well have been fine with the men but seems to have rankled Emilian. Late in the month he ran into Sepp Dietrich during a staff conference. Richard Landwehr describes the encounter as follows:

> Amazingly, Dietrich immediately recognized the Rumanian SS officer and asked him if they had met before.
> Emilian replied: 'Yes, *Oberstgruppenführer*. I had the honor of meeting and talking with you while serving with the staff of the *170th Infantry Division* during the battle for the Sea of Azov, although I was wearing a Rumanian uniform.'
> 'Son of a gun. That's right!' replied Dietrich. 'You were that Maximilian of the Rumanian Cavalry…?'

'Emilian, *Oberstgruppenführer.*'

'So it is. I remember you completely now. What are you doing here?'

'Practically nothing, *Oberstgruppenführer.*'

Dietrich was sympathetic to Emilian's desire to get into combat and ordered him to form an alarm unit out of whatever drifters and stragglers he could find. Emilian immediately did just that, rounding up six officers from the Rumanian construction battalion and setting about finding men to fill out his unit. Eventually he found some Dutchmen, convalescent *Waffen-SS* wounded, a few *Luftwaffe* stragglers from the *10. Fallschirmjäger-Division*, some grenadiers of a replacement unit from Weiner Neustadt, a smattering of Danes, French, a Russian and a Swede. Even after Hitler's death was announced Emilian kept trying to organize his unit. In early May they moved near Lilienfeld trying to find more men, but the war was winding down and men were looking for a way out, not a way to stay in.[16]

* * *

Along with the Rumanians, the *Bulgarisch Waffen-SS-Grenadier-Regiment 1* was also ordered re-formed as a tank destroyer unit. Stationed for training at Dollersheim, the regiment was really little more than an average-strength battalion. In many ways the formation of the Bulgarian unit mirrored the Rumanians, but its numbers were never more than about 500. Unlike the Rumanians there were no large Bulgarian formations in German territory from which to draw manpower. The only action the unit saw was when some 20 or so of its members deserted from Dollersheim and were tracked down by other Bulgarians, a fight during which 10 or 12 men were killed. The remainder of the men surrendered to the Americans in western Austria, although a few Bulgarians are known to have fought with Skorzeny's *Jagdverbande Südost*.

South of the Danube

2. SS-Panzer-Division Das Reich

The *Kampfgruppe* assembled around *SS-Panzergrenadier-Regiment Deutschland* to recapture Sankt Pölten suddenly found the operation cancelled. Instead, the men and all of their equipment were loaded onto transports and driven 125 miles west to Passau, on the German-Austrian border. Their new mission was to hold the crossings of the Inn and Danube against the rapidly advancing Americans. Operating away from the parent headquarters had happened many times before, but this was the last time. The remainder of *Das Reich* planned to follow in short order, but before they could begin moving to join the *Deutschland Kampfgruppe* new orders came for the bulk of the division to move north to the Dresden area. Never again would the once-elite division operate together as a whole.

Meanwhile, *SS-Panzergrenadier-Regiment Der Führer* stayed behind and absorbed 620 untrained replacements, which inflated its rifle strength but did nothing to increase combat power.[17]

* * *

16   Landwehr, Richard, *Romanian Volunteers of the Waffen-SS, 1944-45* (Brookings: Siegrunen, 1991), pp. 115-117.

17   Weidinger, *Das Reich*, p. 396.

In the sector of *Hitlerjugend* the town of Brand-Laaben fell after breakthroughs on either side that led to the garrison being enveloped. The loss increased the pressure on the units holding out further east, as the Russians pushed further into their rear areas.

Next in the eastern-facing front came *General der Panzertruppe* Hermann Balck's *6. Armee*, whose front ran from northwest of Gloggnitz to Edelsbach bei Feldbach. The northernmost of his two corps was *III Panzerkorps*, with *Schwere-Panzer-Abteilung 509* attached, and then followed the unit whose commander Balck despised, *IV SS-Panzerkorps*, led by *SS-Obergruppenführer* Herbert Otto Gille. Gille's personal bravery couldn't be questioned, as by this point he'd won the Knight's Cross with Oak Leaves, Swords and Diamonds, but the outright hatred between the two men, and their Chiefs of Staff, too, continued to affect operations.

On Balck's far left flank adjoining *SS-Kampfgruppe Keitel* stood the remarkable *Kampfgruppe Raithel*, although this positioning is misleading. The two *Kampfgruppen* rarely had contact with one another and only outposts in the no man's land between them.

Divisionsgruppe Krause

Generalleutnant Krause had performed his duty as emergency front-line commander beautifully. His *divisionsgruppe* had done everything humanly possible to shield Styria from Russian invasion. On Hitler's birthday his command was dissolved and the troops given to other formations.

As for Krause himself, he was needed back in his original post as *Korück* of *6. Armee*; that is, the rear area commander. Unlike in the occupied territories, such duties in the home country imposed some limitations on the commander's authority. Krause was responsible for keeping the men in line, traffic control and training anti-tank squads to deal with Russian tanks that broke through the front lines.[18] The constant flood of refugees moving into and out of the region didn't make his job any easier.

117. Jäger-Division

Two days before the division had attacked through Ratten and crushed the Russian garrison there, before encountering stiff Russian resistance on the road to Waldbach. As it closed in on the town the Russian garrison fought ever harder, so instead of moving on *Jäger-Regiment 749* elected to form a defensive position on the Hochwechsel, a large, high mountain north of the town, and wait for *Jäger-Regiment 737* to come up from the south. But *Jäger-Regiment 737* had also encountered hard-fighting Russians.

Time was of the essence, however, so both regiments went back to the attack and inched their way forward in the worst conceivable conditions. The terrain was heavily forested and cut with ravines, confusing those who were unfamiliar with the area. Bringing up supplies on the narrow pathways that doubled as roads proved extremely difficult. Ammunition, in particular, ran low. Fighting forward through even the smallest blocking positions required a lot of time and progress was slow.

* * *

On their right was *Kampfgruppe 1. Panzer-Division*, still with a mountain infantry regiment from *1. Volks-Gebirgs-Division* attached. Another attached unit was *SS-Polizie-Regiment 13*, the former

---

18   Brettner, *Die Letzten Kämpfe Band I*, p. 54.

Sperrverband-Motschmann which had been fighting partisans in Slovenia until March. The SS in its unit designation was strictly honorary, as the regiment was not part of the *Waffen-SS*. Its designed duties had been rear area security but in the emergency of April 1945 it was every man to the front.

On 20 April, troops from *Kampfgruppe 1. Panzer-Division* counterattacked to recapture Birkfeld, a small town in the valley of the Feistritz River. The Russians who took the town fought hard to keep it, as this marked the deepest penetration so far of *6. Armee*'s entire front. The Russian 155th Rifle Division had 236th Rifle Division on its right flank, and between them they probed and pushed to find holes in the porous German defenses. A series of mountain roads came together at Birkfeld and if the Germans could recapture it, further Russian advances would be difficult to supply.

Next came *Arko 3*, a collection of alarm units and *Volkssturm* led by the most capable high-ranking officer available. Holding the center of *6. Armee*'s front was *1. Volk-Gebirgs-Division*, minus the regiment attached to *Kampfgruppe 1. Panzer-Division*. The Russians had been hammering away at the army's flanks but in the coming weeks *1. Volks-Gebirgs-Division* would feel their enemy's full force as the Russians desperately tried to break through before the war ended.

Kampfgruppe 3. Panzer-Division was to their right, followed by the army's right flank unit, *Kampfgruppe 5. SS-Panzer-Division Wiking*, with *1. Ungarische SS-Schi-Abteilung* attached. Fortunately for the men of *Wiking*, the Hungarian SS battalion was larger than even a regiment as it took in vagabond Hungarian soldiers with nowhere else to go.

The Russians

Balck's army faced two very powerful armies, the Twenty-Sixth and the Twenty-Seventh. Between them these two had no less than nine corps attacking into Styria. The commander of Twenty-Sixth Army was the veteran Lieutenant General Lev Skvirsky, who had fought the Germans from day one of Barbarossa, while Twenty-Seventh Army's commander was Hero of the Soviet Union Colonel General S.G. Trofimenko. Putting so many corps into two non-Guards armies was highly unusual.

Battering away at Balck's far left flank in the vicinity of *Kampfgruppe Raithel* was 1st Guards Mechanized Corps with no less than four mechanized Guards brigades, one Guards tank brigade, four Guards tank regiments and a Guards assault gun regiment, not to mention a rifle division at the front and 5th Guards Cavalry Corps behind them as an exploitation force.

Immediately south of these was 135th Rifle Corps, which had four rifle divisions attacking *117. Jäger-Division* and *Kampfgruppe 1. Panzer-Division*; 135th Rifle Corps also had a rifle division in reserve. The 104th Rifle Corps fielded three divisions attacking *1. Volks-Gebirgs-Division*, with a Guards rifle division in reserve. Finally, Twenty-Sixth Army had 75th Rifle Corps held in reserve.

In the area of the Twenty-Seventh Army, 35th Guards Rifle Corps deployed four rifle divisions and two assault gun regiments against *Kampfgruppe 3. Panzer-Division* in the Fürstenfeld sector. To that corps' south was 37th Rifle Corps with three more divisions in the line south of Fürstenfeld, facing *Kampfgruppe 5. SS-Panzer-Division Wiking*. The army's final corps was 33rd Rifle Corps, with two rifle divisions and an assault gun regiment opposite *14. Waffen-Grenadier-Division-der-SS Galizien*, near Feldbach.

2. Panzerarmee

Genderal der Artillerie de Angelis' army had, by this point, been largely denuded of any mobile units that could be taken. That it still had one SS panzer, one panzer and one SS panzer grenadier division owed more to the state of transport and the difficulty in disengaging contact with the enemy than anything else.

The army still had three corps. From north to south they were *1 Kavallerie-Korps, XXII Gebirgs-Armeekorps* and *LXVIII Armeekorps*, which was echeloned dangerously to the east about 25 miles so as to maintain the junction with *Heeresgruppe E*. This meant *LXVIII Armeekorps* had a long northern flank the other two corps didn't have.

The *I Kavallerie-Korps* had the over-strength *14. Waffen-Grenadier-Division-der-SS Galizien* on its left flank. The corps boundary started at Feldbach, then ran through Petersdorf and to the northwest. Although the division had already suffered heavy casualties, when the month started its ranks were full and its replacement battalion overflowed with 8,000 men. Although Hitler and many of his generals viewed this division with skepticism, including its own commanding officer, the Ukrainians who filled its ranks fought well throughout the campaign.

South of the Ukrainians was *3. Kavallerie-Division* followed by the relatively powerful *16. SS-Panzergrenadier-Division Reichsführer-SS*, holding the front around Grabersdorf. The commander of Himmler's namesake division was one of the most highly decorated men in Nazi Germany, Otto Baum, who had won the Knight's Cross with Oak Leaves, Diamonds and Swords. Because of Himmler's patronage the division often received priority of supply and weapons.

Next came *4. Kavallerie-Division* with the depleted but veteran *Kampfgruppe 23. Panzer-Division* on the corps' right flank near the Slovenian border. The past few days had been quiet for the panzer division, but on 20 April the far right flank was pushed by a surprise attack on *Panzergrenadier-Regiment 126*, but the situation was quickly restored. Sometime around now the division was reinforced by two armored trains that moved along tracks a mile behind the front.

In corps reserve was *Kampfgruppe von Rudno*, commanded by *Oberstleutnant* Günther von Rudno, winner of the Knight's Cross. The exact composition of von Rudno's formation is unknown, but probably had motorized infantry elements left over from an earlier formation, *Sturmbrigade von Rudno*. It was likely odds and ends of broken formations, with a mix of whatever vehicles could be found.

Defending Radkersburg and northeast Slovenia was *XXII Gebirgs-Armeekorps*, with *Kampfgruppe 9. SS-Panzer-Division Hohenstaufen* to the left, with *297. Infanterie-Division* in transport and the elite Hungarian parachute division *Svent Lazlo* on the right flank near the Slovenian village of Veržej.

Defending the far right flank of both *2. Panzerarmee* and *Heeresgruppe Süd* was *LXVIII Armeekorps*, with three divisions in the line: *118. Jäger-Division, 13. SS-Freiwilligen-Gebirgs-Division Handschar* and finally *71. Infanterie-Division*. This corps had the critical duty of maintaining contact with *Heeresgruppe E*. As was becoming increasingly apparent, the time for *Heeresgruppe E* to withdraw from the Balkans was drawing near and it was up to *LXVIII Armeekorps* to shield its northern flank during the retreat.

Unfortunately for *General der Gebirgstruppe* Rudolf Konrad, his one SS division was considered the worst of them all, both by their contemporaries and by historians after the war. The idea behind *Handschar* had been to recruit Bosnian and Croatian Muslims, inculcate them with a hatred of communism and Judaism, and then turn them loose to fight partisans in the Balkans. One of Himmler's pet projects, the division received numerous incentives that were unavailable to other SS units, including Imams and special religious considerations. The *Reichsführer-SS* considered Islam to be the perfect religion for soldiers.

Unfortunately for him their service wasn't worth the effort of keeping them in the field. In 1944 they mutinied and killed some of their officers. During their service in the Balkans they often preferred slaughtering Christian civilians to performing their duties. For a German division in April 1945, *Handschar* was impressively strong, but its German leadership was mediocre and the officers themselves arrogant toward the remaining Muslims.

The Russians

The *2. Panzerarmee* faced two armies from Third Ukrainian Front, the 57th on the north and 1st Bulgarian south to the junction with *Heeresgruppe E*. The 57th Army had three corps, the 6th Guards Rifle Corps, with two divisions, a mechanized Guards brigade and a tank regiment, facing *3. Kavallerie-Division* and *16. SS-Panzergrenadier-Division Reichsführer-SS* in the area around Ebersdorf. The army's second corps was 64th Rifle Corps, deploying two Guards rifle and one ordinary rifle division against *4. Kavallerie-Division* and *Kampfgruppe 3. Panzer-Division* near Radkersburg. This was where the front swept dramatically eastward.

The Fifty-Seventh Army's last corps was 133rd Rifle Corps, with three rifle divisions spread over a broad front from Radkersburg to Hotiza, a distance of about 20 miles.

The army on Third Ukrainian Front's far right was the Bulgarian First Army, with one corps facing *2. Panzerarmee*. Its commander was Lieutenant General Vladimir Stoychev. He was a well-traveled anti-monarchist who enthusiastically joined the pro-Soviet Fatherland Front after Bulgaria switched sides in September 1944.

His army wasn't quite as enthusiastic. Only 3rd Corps faced the front of *2. Panzerarmee*, with three rifle divisions. The rank and file had already suffered heavy casualties fighting their way through the Balkans and Hungary. In mid-March the army numbered just over 100,000 men, but by 15 April it had suffered 9,805 casualties.[19] Their service was compulsory, and the introduction of political commissars was necessary because they had all grown up under the monarchy of King Boris. Morale was low and they were so ill-equipped that in March the Russians gave them dozens of T-34/85 tanks, plus hundreds of aircraft, guns, trucks and 30,000 small arms. After that infusion of materiel they at least had the capability of fighting, but they still only did so under threat of draconian punishment.

---

19   Krivosheev, *Soviet Casualties*, p. 157.

21

Saturday, 21 April

The weather over most of the battlefield remained perfect, with a high of 70 degrees Fahrenheit, until a cold front moved through in late afternoon and brought with it much colder temperatures and rain. The Red Air Force now flew almost unopposed, hitting targets across the Wienvertiel, Marchfeld, Korneuberg and Amstetten.

Heeresgruppe Süd

Even as Russian soldiers rummaged through the German High Command headquarters at Zossen, the *Wehrmacht* Daily Report found a way to praise *Heeresgruppe Süd* for holding the line against heavy Russian attacks, and for destroying numerous Russian tanks.[1] Meanwhile, in the Danube River itself, German divers laid mines to hamper the Russian Danube Flotilla.

North of the Danube

8. Armee

Despite ruinous casualties the previous day, the tempo and intensity of attacks increased against *8. Armee*'s center, particularly in the area of *25.* and *6. Panzer-Divisionen*. It had been obvious for days that the next objective for both Second Ukrainian Front and Forty-Sixth Army from Third Ukrainian Front was Brno. Holding attacks against *8. Armee*'s flanks restricted Kreysing's ability to shift units to respond to the new point of concentration, as attacks in company and battalion strength hit the main line of resistance from north of Korneuberg to Karnabrunn. Marshal Tolbukhin knew that time was running out for him to take the city he'd been ordered to capture, and even the prospect of more heavy losses was no deterrent to accomplishing the mission he'd been given by Stavka. For him it was now or never.

Kreysing now knew for certain that Tolbukhin's immediate target was Laa an der Thaya, and after that it would be Brno. Knowing this, however, was pointless if he couldn't organize a stronger defense. *Panzerkorps Feldherrnhalle* had inflicted terrible losses in the previous day's fighting, but in doing so the corps' already depleted units also suffered heavily. Worse, they were scattered and disorganized. Top priority was given to shoring up the defenses on either side of Laa, but in truth there wasn't much he could do.

North of Poysdorf and west of Herrenbaumgarten the front was particularly vulnerable, although as of yet the army's connection with *Heeresgruppe Mitte* wasn't threatened. But the front was porous elsewhere, too. Between Ameis and Enzersdorf bei Staatz at around dawn 20 Russian tanks loaded with infantry slipped past the German positions unnoticed and sped north. First they surprised the

---

1   Maier, *Drama*, p. 368.

command post of *Panzer-Division Feldherrnhalle 2* in the village of Kottingneuseidl and rolled over it, and then did the same thing to the headquarters and motor pool of *Kampfgruppe 211. Volks-Grenadier Division* in Wildendürnbach. This was the first news that either *8. Armee* or *Panzerkorps Feldherrnhalle* had of a rampaging Russian tank force within five miles of the Thaya River northeast of Laa.

The remaining German armor had been distributed along the strongpoints of the front, but now they were needed to seal the breakthrough. Small groups of Tiger IIs and *Hetzers* sped toward Wildendürnbach from several directions. The Russians had caused tremendous damage but no follow-on forces were in their wake to solidify the hole they'd torn in the German defenses, and their commander must have sensed the Germans closing in on him. His battle group turned and sped east to make their escape, but it was too late. The German panzers cornered them and completely wiped them out. Once again, uncoordinated Russian attacks had squandered an initial success and allowed fast German counterattacks to seal the front. Even in the last weeks of the war German professionalism continued to give them a battlefield edge.

In stopping the breakthrough Kreysing had to use every last resource he had, including both *SS-Kampfgruppe Trabandt I* and *SS-Kampfgruppe Trabandt II*, plus parts of every division and battalion anywhere close to the area of battle. The *8. Armee* put every last man and machine it had left into the fight, and it paid off. By the time it was over Sixth Guards Tank Army had been so badly mauled that it was withdrawn from the front and transferred further north for the drive on Brno. The Russians wouldn't stop trying to capture Laa an der Thaya, but they'd got as close as they were going to get.

Showing the aggressiveness that most German panzer commanders had shown throughout the war, *General der Panzertruppe* Kleeman ordered *Grenadier-Regiment 317* to cross back over the Thaya River to build a substantial bridgehead at Ottenthal. That force even managed to put a few knocked-out Russian tanks back into service.[2]

Two of the German vehicles that saved the day from what should have been a disastrous Russian breakthrough were at opposite ends of the design spectrum. One was the Tiger II and the other was the humble but plentiful *Hetzer*. In late April 1945 the *Schwere-Panzer-Abteilung 503* only had a handful of machines left in working order and yet they dominated the battlefield south of Laa. The *Hetzers* filled in the gaps and prevented the cumbersome Tiger IIs from being outflanked.

II SS-Panzerkorps
Führer-Grenadier-Division

The patrols and reconnaissance thrusts of the previous day materialized in attacks of battalion strength, as could have been expected. These came north of Korneuberg and were repulsed every-where, but quite obviously seemed to be probes looking for weak points.

SS-Brigade Ney

The choices facing Hungarians in the SS were stark; keep fighting for a lost cause, surrender and face certain execution, or desert and take your chances. German SS captured by the Russians had little chance of survival, but for the Hungarians it was even worse. If the Russians didn't shoot them, their own countrymen would certainly hang them. Desertion meant hiding in the hills and forests and scrounging for food while avoiding detection. So the vast majority stayed in the ranks

---

2   Brettner, *Die Letzten Kämpfe Band II*, p. 178.

and hoped for the best. However, their commander walked a fine line between fighting alongside other formations of the *Waffen-SS* and not allowing his unit to be attached to any of them. *Ney* fought as an allied but separate and distinct brigade.

The *III. Abteilung* had a combat strength of 710 men and was attached to *I SS-Panzerkorps*, holding the sector due west of Wiener Neustadt. "Other parts of the unit were deployed in support of *XXXXIII Armeekorps* of the *8. Armee*."[3] The other two battalions had been attached to *III Panzerkorps*. The brigade, therefore, had been split among three different armies.

Although widely scattered, Ney's entire brigade listed strength on this day of 4,211 men, with bayonet strength of 3,100, an extraordinary total for the times. Also on its rolls were 21 75mm *PAK-40* anti-tank guns, seven *Liechte Panzerspähwagen* light armored cars, 11 trucks, nine automobiles, 53 other vehicles and 141 horses. It was, in fact, larger than some divisions.[4]

The brigade's expanded roster is hard to understand. Where did all of the new men come from? Presumably there were numerous Hungarian *Volksdeutsche* driven from their homeland, or former *Honved* men looking for a home. In the swirling chaos of the day attachment to a *Waffen-SS* unit meant attachment to a supply chain, or, in other words, food and shelter and the safety of your comrades. Regardless of how poor the supply links might be, on paper they still existed, and if your comrades ate, then you ate. To men whose country had been overrun, whose army no longer had a government to serve, the chance to latch on to a functioning military unit would have been a powerful inducement to join.

* * *

The citizens of the village of Raxenberg looked on as the three officers from *Stalag 17B* who had been convicted of desertion by the Gestapo were hanged in the town square. Placards hung around their necks proclaimed they were traitors and deserters who wanted to join the Red Army. The bodies stayed up for several days.[5]

South of the Danube

6. SS-Panzerarmee
2. SS-Panzer-Division Das Reich

SS-Panzergrenadier-Regiment Der Führer didn't follow its sister regiment, *Deutschland*, to Passau, nor did it accompany the rest of *Das Reich* north. Instead it deployed to the southwest of Sankt Pölten. The intent had been to launch a reconnaissance in force but that was called off. The resources to recapture and hold territory no longer existed and would only result in unnecessary losses.

Korps von Bünau

General der Infanterie von Bünau spent the day traveling to the headquarters of the units he commanded, but his mind was elsewhere. His family lived in Stuttgart and that city was now encircled. Although distracted, his corps of motley odds and ends managed to retake Oberwöbling.

3   Pencz, Rudolf, 'The Story of the Hungarian SS Volunteer Brigade "Ney"' (Brookings: Landwehr, 2004), Siegrunen Volume XIII, No. 2, Whole Number 76, Fall 2004, p. 23.

4   *Hungarian Formations of the Waffen-SS and Sondertruppen der Reichsführung-SS*, <http://www.hunyadi.co.uk/page7.php>, (Accessed 19 June 2018).

5   *Stalag XVIIB The Final Days*, <http://www.stalag17b.com/final_days.html>, (Accessed 27 July 2018).

I SS-Panzerkorps

The Russian maximum-attack effort against Hermann Preiss' corps entered its fourth day with increasing ferocity. Each day brought the Americans closer to western Austria, and while the rank and file of the Red Army might have been content to wait for the end of the war, the ranking officers were not. More specifically, Marshal Tolbukhin wasn't.

10. Fallschirmjäger-Division

The *Luftwaffe* men retook Eschenau, south of Rotheau. It was a small but important victory. By throwing the Russians back it stopped the momentum of their southward move to cut off *I SS-Panzerkorps*, even if only briefly, and forced them to draw forces away from the attack on *SS-Kampfgruppe Peiper*.

SS-Kampfgruppe Peiper

In Peiper's sector the Russians attempted to follow up the previous day's bloody fighting around Hainfeld by attacking the town yet again. The stench of decaying bodies, scorched metal and burned wood from the houses and shops lining the town's streets filled the morning air. And like so many times before, the Russians seized Hainfeld yet again. Then, like clockwork, Peiper ordered a counterattack using the remaining panzers of *SS-Kampfgruppe Sternebeck*, but this time the Russians were ready. The Germans fought their way back into the town but couldn't retake it entirely.[6] Realizing it was hopeless, Peiper called off the effort and ordered his men to retreat into the surrounding hills.[7]

To the west the combat swirled in a series of attacks, counterattacks and counter-counterattacks. Russian infantry backed by armor attacked from the Eschenau area down the Gölsen Valley road in an attempt to sever the road from Hainfeld to Traisen, but were stopped short of Sankt Viet an der Gölsen. But as they did this *SS-Kampfgruppe Kling*, which had been regrouping at Rotheau, drove south and recaptured Eschenau. By the end of the day neither side could be quite certain where the other was.

Kampfgruppe 12. SS-Panzer-Division Hitlerjugend

In *Hitlerjugend*'s sector the Russians continued grinding south. A large group of Russian troops were spotted assembling for an attack on the road between Beringer and Pankrazi, but a heavy German artillery bombardment was so on target and so effective that it stopped the attack before it started. All attacks on the far right sector were driven back.

Elsewhere, however, things didn't work out so well for the Germans. *SS-Kampfgruppe Reitzenstein* couldn't hold at Sankt Corona am Schöpfl, even with support from the seemingly ubiquitous

---

6   Reynolds, *Men of Steel*, p. 274. Michael Reynolds says this happened on 22 April.
7   Landwehr, Richard, *Waffen-SS Miscellany*, Siegrunen 80, 2014. Richard Landwehr writes of a *Kampfgruppe* from the SS Motor Vehicle Technical School Vienna that fought in the battles around Hainfeld, but all that is known for certain about the commander is that he was an *SS-Hauptsturmführer*. This matches the description of the *Kampfgruppe* supposedly ordered into existence by *SS-Obergruppenführer* Steiner. The fate of these men is also unknown, or how they escaped the ring around Vienna to join *I SS-Panzerkorps*.

Flakpanzer IV, and three miles south of there the town of Kaumberg was the next to suffer. House-to-house fighting during the day left 23 homes and the local railway facilities destroyed.

The loss of Kaumberg cut the main road leading west, effectively severing *SS-Kampfgruppe Peiper* from the rest of the corps. Communications and supplies would have to travel over primitive secondary roads through no man's land south of Kaumberg, with no guarantee there wasn't a Russian ambush hiding in the dense woods. This left the division fighting in several directions at once.

SS-Kampfgruppe Möbius continued fighting in the mountainous forests east of Sankt Corona am Schöpfl and north of Hainfeld. By 21 April Möbius' *Kampfgruppe* had Russians on all sides except the east, and heavy attacks made it clear the Russians wanted to wipe it out. Only a long fighting retreat over broken country saved any of them.[8] The cemetery at Sankt Corona has the graves of 121 unknown Germans who died in the fighting. Their identities aren't known because the Russians routinely stripped German dead of their identity tags.

* * *

Around 3:00 a.m. *SS-Kampfgruppe Gross* attacked the high ground outside of Klammhöhe to alleviate the threat to the town, but was repulsed by a Russian *Pakfront*, which was essentially a wall of anti-tank guns in bunkers. Since the hill couldn't be retaken, *SS-Kampfgruppe von Ribbentrop* formed a blocking line south of it which ran to the west. *SS-Kampfgruppe Hauschild*, to the southeast, launched a counterattack north of Kaumberg to stop the Russian drive on the main east-west supply road. Commanded by *SS-Hauptsturmführer* Karl Hauschild, the *Kampfgruppe* was comprised of *II./SS-Panzergrenadier-Regiment 26*, of which he was the commanding officer. *SS-Kampfgruppe Möbius* also took part. Although initially successful with *SS-Kampfgruppe Möbius* leading the way, the attack soon ground to a halt in the face of heavy Russian fire. After capturing a Russian rocket-firing position the *SS-Obersturmführer* led his men in an attack on a truck column but was killed. Having already taken heavy casualties the Germans tried to retreat and were cut to pieces. Very few men survived. The Russians reportedly took the dead Germans' pay books and identity disks so they would forever be unknown in their graves.

Hauschild's *Kampfgruppe* had a small armored group in support, two *Sturmgeschütze* and four SPWs. They made initial progress but ran into fierce resistance and became pinned down. A blown bridge stopped the armor. Scouting groups then found the main Russian thrust heading towards Kaumberg and established a blocking position half a mile north of the town. They didn't have to wait long for a fight.

At 2:00 p.m. Russians outflanked *SS-Kampfgruppe Hauschild* and took Kaumberg, although their infantry suffered heavy casualties from German machine-gun fire. The *Kampfgruppe* shifted position and set up a new line east of the town, now with a solitary *Jagdpanzer* added to its support. But when new Russian forces attacked from the east, behind the *Kampfgruppe*, it disintegrated in the cross-fire. The men fled to nearby Faschingbauer to regroup. North of Kaumberg more Russians came down the road from Sankt Corona toward Klein-Mariazell. The whole German position along the road was becoming unwound.

The loss of Kaumberg made the situation of *Hitlerjugend* and the *LAH* desperate, since the only supply routes now ran far to the south. If a withdrawal became necessary, the roads would be jammed and the route circuitous. That made its immediate recapture vital. After failing that morning further north, *SS-Kampfgruppe Gross* was ordered to retake Kaumberg that afternoon.

---

8   Reynolds, *Men of Steel*, p. 271. Reynolds says Möbius died in the fighting on 21 April, but actually *Hauptsturmführer* Rolf Möbius survived the war and went on to write a monograph for the US Army on heavy armor operations.

The *Kampfgruppe* had a few panzers in support but was blocked by a blown bridge west of town. This led to an ugly incident where Gross was blamed for the failed attack and replaced by *SS-Hauptsturmführer* von Ribbentrop. Even in the dying days of the Third Reich, in the *Waffen-SS* failure remained an orphan.

* * *

Russian attacks were just as strong moving south from Schwarzansee and Neuhaus, with their main objective being Weissenbach an der Triesting. The capture of that town would cut off the entire division from its headquarters via the Altermarkt-Pernitz road, which was the only one left after the road through Hainberg was interdicted by the loss of that town. *SS-Panzergrenadier-Regiment 25* withdrew under extreme pressure to the west of Altenmarkt, while *SS-Kampfgruppe Bremer* endured a half-day bombardment from artillery and Katyusha rocket launchers, followed by a heavy attack that drove them back to Nöstach.

SS-Panzergrenadier-Regiment 26 pulled back south of the Hainberg road, while *SS-Kampfgruppe Gross* pulled back through Hainberg, which had momentarily been retaken. As the division pulled back it left *SS-Kampfgruppe von Reitzenstein* isolated southeast of Sankt Corona, so it, too, was ordered to join the rest of the division in positions south of the road.[9]

Kampfgruppe 1. SS-Panzer-Division Leibstandarte Adolf Hitler

Attacks by 37th Guards Rifle Corps continued from Berndorf to Alland as the Russians stepped up the pressure. Accompanied by armored support, the direction of the attacks was southwest to exploit the gap with *Hitlerjugend*. Nor were these small-scale attacks; regimental-sized forces moved through Grillenberg, two miles south of Berndorf, on the road to Hernstein. The size of the penetrating Russian units was too great to be thrown back, so all the Germans could hope to do was limit the damage. On the division's left flank, after the bloody fighting near Neuhaus the Russians sent out patrols to scout the German positions, but most were destroyed or turned back.

6. Armee
Kampfgruppe Raithel

German forces in the town of Trattenbach had endured day after day of artillery and mortar barrages. Men fell dead and wounded with no chance to defend themselves, but on 21 April the Germans did something about it. After a ten-minute strike by German artillery, they attacked in battalion strength toward the Feistritzsattel and drove the Russians out of their positions in heavy hand-to-hand fighting. It gave them a respite from the incessant enemy fire, but the cost was terrible. In one company eight men died and 23 more were wounded, which more or less equaled an entire platoon.[10]

Despite the necessity for such attacks, and the occasional success, south of Semmering Pass the Russians had gradually advanced from the Feistritzsattel to the Harterkogel. Now, having taken possession of the latter mountain, which was more than 4,500 feet high, they had the dominating peak in the area as well as a massive manpower and firepower advantage.

---

9   Meyer, *The 12th SS*, pp. 488-489.
10   Brettner, *Die Letzten Kämpfe Band I*, p. 117.

117. Jäger-Division

Just northwest of Waldbach, the *Jäger-Regiment 749* was hit with a violent Russian attack coming from the direction of the town. Russian attacks continued throughout the day, sticking the regiment in defensive mode in the high country west of Waldbach. The fighting was bitter but eventually the Russians were repulsed. An exhibit commemorating the combat of those days, and the ones yet to come, was erected after the war.

South of this combat, *Jäger-Regiment 737* fought its way forward against stubborn resistance but finally got across the Kreuzberg, west of Waldbach. The country was so rough the two regiments often lost radio contact with each other.[11]

1. Volks-Gebirgs-Division

Heavy defensive fighting raged in and east of Neudau, where massive Russian artillery strikes hit the *I./Gebirgsjager-Regiment 99*. Because of ammunition shortages the German batteries couldn't respond, so the men had no choice but to sink low in their trenches and pray for survival. By commitment of all available forces, including a company taken from the *II./Gebirgsjäger-Regiment 99*, the front was barely held. Nine civilians died in the fighting. At least one woman was captured by the Russians, gang-raped and then killed.

The fighting on this one day was so terrible that the division suffered more than 200 casualties in that area alone. Between all three battalions of *Gebirgsjäger-Regiment 99*, the regimental command staff, *Gebirgs-Pionier-Battailon 54* and a few Hungarians still fighting with the division, 164 men, 13 *Unteroffizieren* (NCOs) and 2 officers were killed, and 67 more of all ranks wounded.[12]

1. Panzer-Division

For added punch what was left of *I./Panzer-Regiment 24* was attached to *1. Panzer-Division*. On 21 April that was three Panthers, less than a platoon.

The division's counterattack reached Strallegg, smashing into the Russians at the railway station and in the village itself, and it recaptured the village in heavy fighting that saw 21 homes and farms destroyed. The local residents hid in their cellars as combat swirled in the streets and fields above them, while Ukrainian refugees took cover wherever they could. Part of the *Kampfgruppe* that took the village set up a defense behind a stone wall. An immediate Russian counterattack supported by T-34 tanks sparked a tank fight with the German Panzer Mark IVs, and the Russians were thrown back.

Casualties on both sides were very heavy. After the battle Strallegg became a munitions depot, with 30 trucks and 66 horse-drawn wagons assembling there.[13] The spearheads of the division turned northeast and during the night met a battalion from *117. Jäger Division* high in the mountains.

It was a seminal moment. With the joining of the two divisions, that part of the hole ripped in the German front had been sealed shut.

---

11   Brettner, *Die Letzten Kämpfe Band I*, p. 51.
12   Brettner, *Die Letzten Kämpfe Band I*, p. 43.
13   Brettner, *Die Letzten Kämpfe Band I*, p. 35.

The Americans

General Alexander Patch's US Seventh Army approached Austria with orders to drive down the eastern side of the National Redoubt, thereby cutting it off from the German units fighting against the Russians. American intelligence fully expected tens of thousands of well-armed and well-trained SS men to fall back to heavily fortified defenses from which they could hold out for months, if not years. Knowing this, the combat forces expected fanatical resistance.

Sometimes they got it, from diehards or Hitler Youth, but most of the time they were met by women waving anything white, with bed sheets hung from windows to signify surrender. Casualties were light although not non-existent. Moreover, in the days to come the Americans not only intermixed with the shattered units of *Heeresgruppe Süd*, they also encountered elements of the two Germany armies they had driven out of Germany into Austria, the *1. Armee* and the *19. Armee*, both part of *Heeresgruppe G*.

The American experience in Austria would prove very different from that of the Russians. Some German units still fought stubbornly against the Western Allies, but more and more these were SS units, not regular Army ones, most of which hemorrhaged deserters on a daily basis. To the east, however, there was a much greater willingness among the front-line troops to risk their lives to stop the Russians.

22

Sunday, 22 April

Berlin

With Russian medium-range artillery pounding the government quarter, Adolf Hitler was informed that his order for *SS-Obergruppenführer* Felix Steiner to attack with part of his *11. SS-Panzerarmee* and cut off the First Belorussian Front then attacking Berlin could not be carried out. The *Führer* flew into a rage and declared the war was lost. He said he'd stay in Berlin and shoot himself, if it came to that.

Among his officers word spread quickly of Hitler's breakdown. Among the men fighting and bleeding in the trenches, if they heard about it, the sentiment was probably closer to "what took you so bloody long to figure that out?"

Heeresgruppe Süd

The cold that passed into Austria late on 21 April brought snow to the higher elevations and rain over most of the area, particularly in the Marchfeld. In areas south of the Danube, particularly the mountains, sleet made footing treacherous. The weather slowed both the Russian advance and the German retreat.

North of the Danube

Despite the weather the inexorable Russian advance continued. Marshal Malinovsky pushed Second Ukrainian Front hard to break through. During the day more towns and villages fell to the Red Army. The citizens of Altruppensdorf, Neudorf, Staatz, Ottenthal, Steinebrunn and many others found themselves under Russian control. Goebbels' propaganda machine hadn't had to exaggerate the rapacious behavior of the Russians once they overran a German town or city. And while Stalin had told them they came to Austria as liberators, not conquerors, that gave little comfort to those caught up in the reality of war. Whatever horrors might befall them next, however, the one inescapable fact was that so far, they'd made it. They'd lived through the fighting, and now they had to live through the peace.

But while Malinovsky's men ground forward day after day, the German defense continued to fight back. Instead of breaking, as by all rights they should have, he found them as stubborn as ever. His counterpart, *Generaloberst* Lothar Rendulic, juggled what few assets he still possessed to prevent a breakthrough from happening. It was inevitable, though, and both men knew it.

8. Armee

For days the Red Air Force had bombed and strafed at will in places like Wildendürnbach, five miles northeast of Laa an der Thaya near the Czech border. Civilians died and German traffic was disrupted. Already in Korneuberg some 117 people had been killed in recent air attacks.

In the center of the front the Russians reached Enzersdorf am Thale. Like every village and town in Austria, Enzersdorf had a Catholic Church. During the fighting it was hit at least 54 times. Other penetrations came west of Ernstbrunn in the area of *Kampfgruppe 96. Infanterie-Division* and around Eichenbrunn in the sector of *Kampfgruppe 101. Jäger-Division*. The most dangerous one reached to the key town of Laa an der Thaya, which was a lynchpin of the German defense.

Despite desperate resistance by the Germans, Second Ukrainian Front's offensive gained momentum. *Heeresgruppe Süd* reported that *8. Armee* destroyed 52 Russian tanks the previous day, many by the men of *Panzergrenadier-Regiment Feldherrnhalle 1* using *Panzerfauste*.[1]

* * *

Despite mauling the attacking Russians, around midnight on 21 April the survivors of the tiny *Kampfgruppe* near Ernsdorf bei Staatz finally had to withdraw toward Staatz. Thereafter, Ernsdorf fell to the Russians about 10:00 a.m. Aside from the 15 tanks they'd lost to the small German blocking position beyond the town, another 10 Russians from the infantry had been killed and were buried by the townsfolk as hard-eyed Russians forced them to dig at gunpoint.

* * *

With word of the fighting near the southern outskirts of Staatz, headquarters and medical personnel of *6. Panzer-Division* evacuated Castle Staatz. The mountain on which it stood had been under direct mortar and artillery fire for two days in an attempt to knock out the anti-tank guns dug-in on its slopes and the mortars on the reverse slope. A few panzers defended the southern outskirts.

Throughout the afternoon and night of 20 April, retreating German soldiers had told the people of Staatz what they could expect when the Red Army arrived. Like invading armies throughout history, the Russians wanted food, drink, valuable goods that were easily transported, and women. Alerted to their imminent fate, the townsfolk hid the essentials of life, including clothing, shoes and jewelry. Food such as sugar, fat, canned meat and grain they sealed in milk cans.

The southern horizon glowed red from fires burning 20 miles to the southeast at the oil wells around Zistersdorf. Having done all they could to secure their possessions ahead of the fighting, the townsfolk took shelter in their basements.

When the Russians finally attacked on 22 April it was the same story as happened over the entire area. German mortars hit them before they ever left Ernsdorf, one mile south, and from the moment the tanks showed themselves they were under heavy fire. Russian artillery intervened to cover them, but the German fire didn't slow down. Throughout the day the two sides blasted away, and when it was over eight Russian tanks had been destroyed. One T-34 with a dead driver had collided with and run over the carcass of a second T-34. A third had its turret blown off when the ammunition inside cooked off, with an explosion so severe the sides bulged. Trucks littered the highway from Ernsdorf like so much road kill.

Despite these losses there were just too many Russians and the Germans were forced to give up the town. Before leaving they blew up viaducts, bridges and anything else that might slow down the invaders. Once the Russians moved in it was the same story as in every other Austrian town, only worse. One woman raped by 12 men died, while in perhaps the most egregious gang-rape

---

1   Maier, *Drama*, p. 369.

of the Austrian campaign 36 men reportedly assaulted one woman in the train station at nearby Frättingsdorf.[2]

Alarm-Bataillon 2, Luftkriegsschule 7

The battalion had shown their mettle in combat by defending with zeal, but by 22 April their losses amounted to 75 percent of their original strength. This likely meant the battalion had suffered between 200 and 300 casualties in ten days.

South of the Danube

6. SS-Panzerarmee
I SS-Panzerkorps

By 22 April Preiss' corps was a shrunken, depleted and exhausted force. Even combining both SS divisions wouldn't have equaled the combat power of more than a brigade, and a brigade without much armor at that. What's more, the ranks had been filled by men with little or no ground combat training, putting even more pressure on the surviving veterans.

The Russians knew all of this. Throughout the *I SS-Panzerkorps* sector the 'War of the Valleys' continued at an ever-increasing pace. The fighting escalated as the Russians funneled more and more men into attacks on the corps' front south of the road from Hainfeld to the east. Rather than awaiting the end of the war, they were determined to crush the SS once and for all.

There was no good military reason to expect the Germans not to crack. They were heavily outnumbered, outgunned by an order of magnitude, had few panzers, little food and less ammunition. Rather than a defensive line they had a string of mutually supporting bunkers and machine-gun nests. By all rights they should have collapsed. That they didn't fall apart despite some of the heaviest attacks of the war can be attributed first to the unique *esprit de corps* of the *Waffen-SS*. As Michael Reynolds put it: "Well trained soldiers, led by commanders they respected, were able to reach levels of military performance to which modern armies can only hope to aspire."[3] The second reason they held on despite everything was the fate awaiting them if they fell into Russian hands.

SS-Kampfgruppe Peiper

The withdrawal planned the previous day to positions south of the road from Traisen to Hainfeld began in Peiper's region. The survivors of Peiper's *Kampfgruppe* were running out food, fuel, ammunition and, most importantly, the strength to resist. One man reportedly died of hunger.

Whatever the difficulties, the retreat had to be orderly and planned, because there were no reserves to seal a major breakthrough. Under continuous attack along the Gölsen Valley road, the SS men counterattacked whenever a gain was made. Peiper's own command post came under direct attack. Fighting went back and forth on a broad front all day on 22 April, but when night fell the road had been cut in numerous places. After all of the bloodshed keeping the road through Hainfeld open, the Germans finally gave it up in a hail of mortar fire. The plan had been to give

---

2   Brettner, *Die Letzten Kämpfe Band II*, p. 184.
3   Reynolds, *Men of Steel*, p. 273.

up the road anyway, but this loss endangered the entire corps since it threatened the rear of all forces fighting to the east.

Kampfgruppe 12. SS-Panzer-Division Hitlerjugend

It must have seemed a relief when the Russians occupied their little town for what seemed like the last time, and the citizens of Hainfeld probably wanted nothing more than for the fighting to end. But its loss seriously endangered the left flank of *Hitlerjugend* by cutting the Gölsen Valley road, and *I SS-Panzerkorps* commander *SS-Gruppenführer und Generalleutnant der SS* Hermann Priess ordered it retaken again.

The day must have seemed like a never-ending nightmare to the few cowering residents who hadn't fled to the countryside. Combining infantry from the *SS-Panzergrenadier-Regiment 2* and elements of *SS-Kampfgruppe Peiper*, the group attacked Hainfeld from the south and once more threw the Russians out, except for a handful of snipers who took a steady toll on the Germans. This time, however, the Russians assembled mortars and anti-tank guns on a hill overlooking the smoldering ruins and poured fire down on the SS men. The *Kampfgruppe* had three panzers, but the ammunition shortage made it unprofitable to engage in a long-range duel where the precious panzers might be damaged or destroyed.

Ralf Tiemann quotes a story about two Army men who'd become separated from their unit with an MG-42 and wound up part of the *Kampfgruppe* in Hainfeld. Sited in the corner of a house overlooking a field, they helped defeat a Russian attack. But a Russian anti-tank gun hit their position and both were killed. In the course of the surrender a few weeks later their names were lost to eternity.[4]

Counterattack followed counterattack as the town changed hands several more times. Adding to the misery of the battle was a pouring rain that left everyone soaked and clouded visibility. Finally, with every building either flattened or on fire, the Germans withdrew half a mile south. Two *Sturmgeschütze*, four SPWs and a 75mm gun had been lost in addition to numerous infantry. The final few German infantry had been holed up in the last house on the south side of town, and only fled out of the back door when the Russians came through the front. Automatic weapons fire followed them as they ran like hell for the safety of the woods, and just when it seemed like they would all get away safely the last German to die in defense of Hainfeld was cut down on the edge of the tree line. He'd been a father of five.[5]

The Russians regrouped and then attacked those positions, driving them even further back. More attacks hit the area near Altenmarkt as the Russians captured the town. As so often happened they shot the parish priest and, just to add to the townsfolk's misery, the Germans blew up the bridge leading to Hafnersberg. Neuhaus was lost for the last time, as was Thenneberg, with the Germans destroying bridge after bridge in their wake.

SS-Kampfgruppe Bremer had no choice but to retreat to Weissenbach and give up Nöstach. It was either that or be surrounded, but the Russians didn't let them go easily, following close on their heels and trying to take Weissenbach on the fly, but being driven back. Other units moving into the line south of the road were *SS-Kampfgruppe Minow*, *SS-Kampfgruppe von Ribbentrop* and *SS-Kampfgruppe Taubert*. One of the new key positions became the town of Ramsau, three miles southeast of Hainfeld, where the only road in the area ran southward from Hainfeld. Another was the Hocheck, an area of heavily wooded hills northwest of Furth.

---

4   Tiemann, *The Leibstandarte IV/2*, p. 307.
5   Tiemann, *The Leibstandarte IV/2*, p. 310.

Hitlerjugend was pulling back but the Germans were having trouble retreating fast enough to stay ahead of the Russian advance. Right after the division command post moved to Furth an der Triesting, a counterattack was needed to drive back Russian spearheads that had penetrated within two miles of that crucial town into the Hocheck. Through Furth ran the one road still supplying the division; its capture would be catastrophic for both *Hitlerjugend* and the *LAH* on their right flank.

Combat for the day didn't end with nightfall. Crossing the road east of Kaumberg, strong Russian patrols moved off in a southwesterly direction until they found the positions of *SS-Kampfgruppe von Reitzenstein*. They were driven back. But other Russian patrols found gaps in the German lines.

Kampfgruppe 1. SS-Panzer-Division Leibstandarte Adolf Hitler

As they had all along the front, the Russians stepped up their attacks yet again. They were determined to cut the Triesting Valley road as they had the Gölsen Valley one in *SS-Kampfgruppe Peiper*'s sector. Under heavy artillery fire the Germans retreated south to a line Grabenweg-Fahrafeld, but this couldn't hold long and Grabenweg fell to a surprise attack. A large first aid station couldn't be evacuated and the attending physician was reportedly shot.[6]

For two weeks the battle had raged for the little town of Altenmarkt an der Triesting, due east of Kaumberg, and the nearby village of Weissenbach an der Triesting. Both were typical Austrian settlements, with homes and storefronts crowding the road, surrounded by farms and mountains. At Weissenbach a plaque commemorates the 25 German and 14 Russian soldiers, and the eight civilians, who died during the fighting for the town.

Decades after the war had ended the mass grave of eight Russian soldiers was discovered near Altenmarkt, on the slope of a nearby ridge called the Pankraziburg. Searchers found three badges that marked them as Guards among the decomposed remains. Eighty soldiers who died in the fighting were buried at the local cemetery. When the Russians finally captured the town they were furious at their heavy losses. The village priest, Father Leopold Weishaupt, was shot in his church by the Russians.

The SS still held the tiny settlement of Altenmarkt-Thenneberg, north of the main town, but now the garrison found themselves surrounded on three sides. With no other choice they pulled out.

Kampfgruppe 356. Infanterie-Division

The fight for the Hohe Wand had proven to be as brutal as anywhere on the entire front. The defending Germans were like most of the units holding the line, that is to say a mixture of men whose only commonality was that they could hold a rifle and pull a trigger. During the night of 22-23 April the last 100 men still defending the high plateau of the Hohe Wand were ordered to move west along with most of the army. They were a combination of *Waffen-SS*, *Fahnenjunkern* from the *Kriegsschule Wiener Neustadt* and the *Kampfgruppe 356. Infanterie-Division*.

---

6   Tiemann, *The Leibstandarte IV/2*, p. 306.

SS-Kampfgruppe Keitel

The fight for Puchberg am Schneeberg had dragged on for weeks. Like most Austrian towns the local Catholic Church was more than just a place for worship, it was the social and cultural center of town, not to mention an important meeting place. All of the parish births and deaths were registered there, and so far Puchberg's church had escaped destruction. Of late Gothic design, its history could be traced at least to the year 1069 AD, but on 22 April it became the latest casualty of the fighting. Something started a great fire and it burned to the ground. This loss proved so traumatic that a large and elaborate painting now commemorates that day, with the burning church in the center with long flames licking the sky.

* * *

After heavy artillery preparation, the Russian troops in the area of Höflein attacked with two battalions towards Grünbach. Fighting alongside the SS men were some of the survivors of the *Kriegsschule Wiener Neustadt*. Supported by armor, the Russians renewed the fight and at least one T-34 took a direct hit from a *Panzerfaust*. When they ran out of ammunition, one German platoon grabbed Russians weapons and turned them on their former owners, as so many of their countrymen had already done. The firefight escalated into combat so fierce that in one German company, only seven men out of 53 survived it unhurt.

Despite that fierce defense the German troops were pushed back to the line Hochschneeberg-Schober after heavy defensive fighting around Puchberg. One Russian platoon of 25 or 30 men was completely wiped out, but others broke through. It had taken three weeks but the Russians had finally captured the key to the Schneeberg.[7]

After most German troops left during the night, the first Russians tried to fight their way past the north side of the Schneeberg. The German troops occupied positions at the Hochschneeberg, Sparbacher Hutte and several other prominent points. With the help of local civilians (partisans armed by the Russians), Soviet reconnaissance troops tried to move behind them.[8]

* * *

Townsfolk of Rohr im Gebirge got physical evidence of the approaching front as early as mid-March, when a contingent of *Osttruppen*, Russians fighting in German uniforms, passed through the town.[9] Who they were remains a mystery. But they were soon followed by an avalanche of refugees moving west along the main road through the mountains, which passed through Rohr im Gebirge. Between 2,000 and 3,000 people per day trudged along the road. Refugees, foreign civilians, prisoners of war, Frenchmen, Belgians, Dutch, Danes, Polish, Italians and Hungarians, they all came in never-ending columns of people desperate to escape the oncoming Red Army.

The local church did what it could, even allowing people to shelter inside overnight and to sleep in the pews, and the townspeople sometimes invited the refugees into their own homes. But food was scarce. Sometimes this meant there was little for anybody, and sometimes it led to fights. Many people used a 25 gallon washtub to boil thin soups, but this was too small for the huge numbers of hungry people and often 8 or 10 batches had to be cooked.

7   Brettner, *Die Letzten Kämpfe Band I*, p. 193.
8   Brettner, *Die Letzten Kämpfe Band I*, p. 195.
9   Brettner calls these men Vlasov soldiers. General Vasilly Vlasov was a captured Russian general who formed two divisions from Russian POWs to fight for the Germans under the banner of the *Waffen-SS*. Whoever they were, they were not from Vlasov's unit.

As the fighting progressed and the front crept closer, *SS-Kampfgruppe Keitel* moved into the area, along with other *Waffen-SS* units retreating over the Rohr Sattel. This could have resulted in the massacre of 16 Hungarian Jews who had taken refuge in Rohr and slept in a building near the town, but they were hidden by the townsfolk. Unfortunately for 10 Russian refugees, the SS men found them and shot them on the spot. They also confiscated 63 head of cattle, five horses, three pigs and 26 sheep over protests from the farmers who owned them.[10]

6. Armee
117. Jäger-Division

Around the village of Waldbach the *Jäger-Regiment 749* attack made progress against stout resistance in that most dangerous section of the front. Having beaten back repeated Russian attacks the day before, the division's other regiment had finally come into the area south of Waldbach. But the Russians had ten T-34 tanks in Waldbach and the regiment had no weapons capable of dealing with them, except for *Panzerfauste* which required getting dangerously close to the target to use. With Russian infantry protecting their T-34s, that was nearly impossible. The Germans had no choice except to await the arrival of *Sturmgeschütz-Brigade 303*.[11] Between them, the two regiments recaptured the village.

1. Volks-Gebirgs-Division

German units attacked the Russians on the outskirts of Rettenegg and drove them back into the town. These were probably advance elements of *II./Gebirgsjäger-Regiment 98*, which was advancing toward the town and captured it the following morning. Although the Russian breakthrough had already been sealed, retaking Rettenegg solidified the front.

Kampfgruppe 1. Panzer-Division

With the Russians retreating to the east, during the night part of the division took off in pursuit, trying to catch them before they could organize to make a stand. A small *Kampfgruppe* with panzers and supported by fire from the remaining self-propelled guns, *Wespe*,[12] made it all the way to Wenigzell by morning. Heavy hand-to-hand fighting raged for hours as the Germans drove the Russians back to the edge of town.

The Russians weren't losing Wenigzell without a fight, however, and a counterattack hit the Germans as they entered the eastern edge of the town. A Mark IV panzer took a direct hit from the huge 122mm main gun of a dug-in JS-II heavy tank. The tank had been built to counter the German Tiger I and was a match even for the Tiger II, whereas the Mark IV had been Germany's heavy tank six years earlier. It was still effective on the battlefield, but no match for newer weapons systems like the JS-II.

10   Brettner, *Die Letzten Kämpfe Band I*, p. 196.
11   Brettner, *Die Letzten Kämpfe Band I*, p. 57.
12   Literally, 'wasps'. The *Wespe* was a self-propelled artillery howitzer mounting a 105mm gun on the reliable Panzer II chassis. The other main SP vehicle used by the *Wehrmacht* was the *Hummel*, 'bumblebee', which mounted a 150mm howitzer on the larger Panzer III/IV chassis. Both guns proved highly successful in combat.

Nevertheless, the crippled panzer hit three more Russian tanks and disabled them, bringing the counterattack to a standstill.[13] The cost to the town was heavy, with more than 20 civilians killed, at least 50 farms wrecked and numerous buildings in the town burned out or damaged, including the parish church.

For the Germans, however, the spoils were excellent. Twenty abandoned Russian tanks were captured.[14] Nothing more is known for certain, but it seems likely that some of them wound up as *Beutepanzers*.[15]

1. Volks-Gebirgs-Division

Still fighting in the Lafnitz Valley, the division launched a counterattack toward Stegersbach. Panzers moved in the direction of Burgau to support the attack, but their fuel was so limited that once there they had to turn back. After penetrating the front lines the attack was stopped, with 29 German soldiers killed in the attempt. Russian losses are unknown, but 12 civilians died, and 72 women and girls reported being raped.[16]

---

13   Brettner, *Die Letzten Kämpfe Band I*, p. 52.

14   *Die Kämpfe im Bezirk Oberwart*, <http://members.aon.at/dbundsch/kaempfeStyria.html>, (Accessed 25 September 2018).

15   Literally 'looted armor'; captured enemy vehicles put into service for the Germans. Both sides did this sort of thing. The American 83rd Infantry Division was nicknamed the 'Rag-tag Circus' because it had so many German vehicles.

16   Brettner, *Die Letzten Kämpfe Band I*, p. 42.

23

Monday, 23 April

Near Magdeburg, Germany

In the early morning light the German *Generalleutnant* cut a trim figure in a well-tailored and neatly pressed uniform. Rising on his left was a well-kept brick home and to his right a wrought iron fence with flame-tipped finials. The two men who flanked him were members of his staff and vital to his work as the official military radio commentator for the *Wehrmacht*. His broadcasts were known and trusted by countless millions of people on both sides. His name was Kurt Dittmar.

Dittmar had crossed the Elbe River just after dawn to surrender and was immediately whisked away by US Army Intelligence officers. Only one thing concerned them, details about the National Redoubt. How many men were there? How many tanks? Where was Hitler's headquarters? Where was Göring's?

Being thoroughly confused, Dittmar asked what they meant, but all they did was press for answers. He kept repeating himself with the answer they didn't believe, that a National Redoubt didn't exist, it was simply a hoax, a fantasy, a figment of Goebbels' imagination. What's more, he told his captors that Hitler was still in Berlin. The Americans assumed he had already gone south.

Only now, far too late to affect operations, did Eisenhower begin to realize the truth. The National Redoubt didn't exist. It never had. It had all been a gigantic *ruse de guerre*, a trick of war. He and his intelligence services had been duped.

* * *

Cold and stormy weather continued over most of Austria. Not only did this bog down ground movement but also curtailed air operations.

* * *

Not all *Waffen-SS* soldiers wound up dead or vilified. Born in the Sudetenland, 20-year-old Rudi Franzel of *Hitlerjugend* was captured on 23 April and eventually sent to England as a POW. In the war's aftermath Franzel was billeted to pick potatoes at Gosford POW camp near Aberlady in Scotland. He eventually married Betty Young after they met at a farm in East Lothian, and he settled down to become a Scotsman, living a long, full life.[1] But he was one of the few.

---

1 'A wartime romance that risked the wrath of families', (*The Scotsman*, 6 November 2008), <https://www. scotsman.com/news/a-wartime-romance-that-risked-the-wrath-of-families-1-1278292>, (Accessed 23 July 2018).

North of the Danube

8. Armee

Unlike Russia, where paved roads were few and far between, the Austrian transport network featured an extensive network of hard-surfaced roads and highways. During periods of bad weather, such as had settled down over the region, it greatly helped movement behind the lines. Refugees could keep moving, the German military could redeploy and defenders could concentrate their heavy weapons on places where armor could approach.

Combined with bad weather, the heavy Russian losses took their toll. Attacks continued as Second Ukrainian Front ground its way forward. Deep penetrations had been made toward Laa an der Thaya but an all-out breakthrough had been thwarted, and the offensive began to lose momentum. The focus of the offensive shifted west, toward the forests around Ernstbrunn, as the Russians sought for a weak spot. This was a strategic mistake if Laa was still the target.

To speak of a German front line would be to exaggerate their defenses. With a shortage of artillery, mortars and ammunition, the surviving panzers, *Jagdpanzers* and *Sturmgeschütze* were scattered among the strongpoints that comprised a main line of resistance. Moving the area of the fighting to the west brought different German forces to combat the Russian attacks that were in better shape than those south and east of Laa.

But the German Army remained the German Army, and its tactical doctrines hadn't changed. With the slowing of the Russian offensive, the depleted units of *Panzerkorps Feldherrnhalle* did what the Germany Army always did, they counterattacked.

* * *

Kampfgruppe 6. Panzer-Division launched their attack with the idea of recapturing the distant Zistersdorf oil fields, with the two battered battalions of *SS-Kampfgruppe Trabandt II* attached. Russian resistance was fierce, but the Germans made initial progress until ordered to break off the attack and move north. This was in response to a fresh Russian attack on the bridgehead *Grenadier-Regiment 317* held over the Thaya River, which ultimately had to be abandoned.

SS-Kampfgruppe Trabandt I, or SS-Regiment Schulze

Starting in 1935, Czechoslovakia built a belt of fortifications known as the Beneš Line, named for President Beneš. Many of the large blockhouses had heavy weapons, with smaller pillboxes defending them against infantry. As it turned out the Czechs never had the chance to use the bunkers, but in 1945 the Germans did as the Red Army moved into old Czechoslovakia. With the Russians exerting heavy pressure on Eighth Army's center, *SS-Kampfgruppe Trabandt I* moved from Poysdorf into the old pillboxes and trenches of the Beneš Line around Hrušovany nad Jevišovkou, ten miles north of Laa an der Thaya.

II SS-Panzerkorps

For days the Red Air Force hammered at the important town of Obergänserndorf, eight miles north of Korneuberg. Seventy structures burned to the ground under the aerial assault. That area of the Marchfeld was flat, with few natural defensive positions, and Obergänserndorf had no other towns within miles. Both sides recognized its value.

Holding the line in this area were the *Führer-Grenadier-Division, Kampfgruppe Volkmann* and the headquarters company of *Totenkopf*. After heavy fighting the Russians captured the town, but it was like a heavyweight boxer throwing punches in the 11th round; they still carried power but there were fewer of them.

Further north, in the sector of the *Kampfgruppe 101. Jäger-Division*, troops from both 5th Guards Tank Corps and 9th Guards Mechanized Corps seized Michelstetten after an intense three-day battle that left the town 70 percent destroyed.[2]

South of the Danube

2. SS-Panzer-Division Das Reich

SS-Panzergrenadier-Regiment Deutschland must have felt they had been sent on holiday by their transfer to Passau to await the Americans. Not only had the Americans not yet arrived, with the Red Army ninety miles to their rear, but on a railroad siding they found the personal train of none other than *Reichsführer-SS* Heinrich Himmler. Without the slightest hesitation they helped themselves. Onboard they found delicacies unseen in Germany for years and thought nothing about adding them to their own meager food supplies.[3] During this period, *Das Reich* was detached from *II SS-Panzerkorps* and attached to *Korps von Bünau*.

* * *

SS-Panzergrenadier-Regiment Der Führer moved into Central Austria at the town of Sankt Margarethen im Lungau. Warm spring sunshine on the grass-covered mountains must have made them also feel as if they'd hit the jackpot. With the war winding down, it looked like the SS men would finish the war in peace and quiet, but that was not to be.

* * *

In the third week of April – at least one source says it was the 23 April – the vagabond Hungarian government of Ferenc Szálasi met in Salzbug with the command staff of the newly formed *XVII Waffen-SS Armeekorps*, the headquarters that controlled the two bloated Hungarian SS divisions.[4] Between them these formations boasted in the neighborhood of 40,000 men, but the troops were only armed with some 5,000 rifles. Had those 40,000 men ever become operational, been given sufficient weapons or committed to fight the Red Army, they might have been of some use. The rearguard defense some of them put up while defending the training grounds in Silesia proved they could fight. However, that was never done.

The irony of Szálasi's conference was that Hungary was now fully occupied by Soviets; if anything, Szálasi headed a government-in-exile.[5] He lived in protected luxury at nearby Gasthof Seewirt, overlooking the Mattsee in the village of the same name. Szálasi was said to have received visitors in the inn's dining room and insisted on rigid formality, as befitting his status as head

---

2   Vavra and Rossiwall, *The Letzten Tage*, <https://www.museumnoe.at/de/das-museum/blog/18-april-24-april-1945>, (Accessed 23 July 2018).

3   Weidinger, *Das Reich*, p. 397.

4   Szálasi stayed in nearby Mattsee, north of Salzburg, at the Gasthof Seewirt.

5   At this meeting there must have been Karoly Beregfy, aged 56, a confirmed supporter of the Arrow Cross party. He was the last Commander-in-Chief of the Hungarian Army, as well as Chief of the General Staff and Minister of Defense. After the war he was tried for treason by the new Hungarian government and executed on 12 March 1946.

of a nation allied to Germany. Never mind that said nation had been overrun by the enemy. Reportedly he arrived in Salzburg with 200 men and his own private train, at a time when rolling stock was in desperately short supply throughout the Reich.

On the surface, the purpose of the meeting was to establish the combat-readiness of *XVII Waffen-SS Armeekorps*, but the true reason was essentially to figure out what to do now that the war was lost. Returning to Hungary was suicidal with the Soviets in control. Nor did fighting against the rapidly advancing Allies seem like a good idea. The Hungarians hoped not to anger the Americans so that once they surrendered they could ask for, and get, political asylum, rather than be returned to their home country. They would fight the Russians if they had to, but the likelihood of the Russians making it that far was no longer very good. They do not seem to have been given orders by the High Command during this period, and it seems unlikely they would have obeyed them anyway. Fighting the Americans would have ruined their hopes for sanctuary and fighting the Russians would have meant moving far to the east. In neither case were the divisions armed for such combat. As matters stood, they were 40,000 mouths to feed and supply that added nothing to the military capacity of the collapsing Reich.

The best chance of arranging surrender to the Americans, it was decided, was to move the troops from southern Germany into Austria. This they did over the next week or so, until they finally wound up in the area of Attersee. Other scattered Hungarian units, such as *SS-Brigade Ney*, were directed to join their countrymen there. Soon enough tens of thousands of Hungarians were billeted in that Alpine region as spring bloomed all around them. The season of renewal was at hand; their hopes of asylum in the West were not to be fulfilled, however.

I SS-Panzerkorps

Corps commander *SS-Gruppenführer und Generalleutnant der Waffen SS* Hermann Priess was not a man given to hasty decisions. His personal bravery was never in question and his quiet, contemplative personality belied a preference for rapid and aggressive action. Army leaders as diverse as the brutal Nazi *Generalfeldmarschall* Ferdinand Schörner and the model for the German general staff system, *Generaloberst* Otto Wöhler, sung Priess' praises. He was a first-class combat leader.

But even such a man as Priess couldn't work miracles. With *I SS-Panzerkorps* under continuous Russian assault along the entire line, the time had come for the inevitable retreat. Heavy losses could no longer be made good by combing out rear area services, and dangerous gaps had opened along its entire front. The corps had held the line for as long as possible, at least partly to give refugees the best chance to escape to the west, but the time had come to withdraw or die.

This was something the remaining SS veterans knew how to do all too well, having done it countless times during the two previous years. Battle groups held key points, towns, road junctions or high ground overlooking a road until the last moment and then retreated. Other rearguards would set up behind them and in their turn hold up the Russians while the first group moved back through their lines. And so on. It took nerves, skill and experience to know the difference between withdrawing too soon and too late.

The Russians realized what all the movements meant. It was the culmination of all the fighting they'd done for the past fortnight, to force *I SS-Panzerkorps* out of its eastern positions, and they stepped up the scale of their attacks. If they could strike the retreating Germans during a road march, it would allow little chance for defense. It was their chance to destroy the SS divisions once and for all.

SS-Kampfgruppe Peiper

Before the fighting started less than 4,000 residents lived in the birthplace of the modern Social Democratic Party of Austria, Hainfeld. Then, after the vicious struggle for neighboring Rohrbach, Hainfeld had been the next town to suffer the ravages of war. The town had changed hands at least four times over the previous week, and perhaps as many as twelve times. By the time troops of the Russian 18th Tank Corps captured the old Roman market town for good, 62 buildings had been destroyed along with 14 farmsteads. Devastation ruined the countryside. Only Wiener Neustadt suffered a higher percentage of structures destroyed.

The *Kampfgruppe* had become separated into two parts, *Obersturmführer* Sternebeck's small group of Panzer IVs five miles south of Rohrbach an der Gölsen, and Peiper's mostly infantry group in the valley of the Traisen River. Sternebeck's panzer group had to turn and fight many times in a narrow valley, and Russian infantry almost overran them. North of Lilienfeld the Russians broke through at multiple points, cutting the *Kampfgruppe* into several smaller battle groups. They finally dug in on the hills overlooking Lilienfeld.

Kampfgruppe 12. SS-Panzer-Division Hitlerjugend

As the general withdrawal began, somebody had to stand their ground so the others could get away, and *Hitlerjugend* got the call. But there weren't enough forces for a static defense. Since the available men couldn't be everywhere at once, and the Russians closely pursued the withdrawing units, the only solution was counterattacks along the line from south of Thenneberg, southeast of Kaumberg and east of Hainfeld. The purpose of the attacks wasn't to retake territory but only to force the Russians to deploy and defend until the retreat was completed. Once all of *Hitlerjugend* pulled out it was intended for use on the Enns River, against the rapidly advancing Americans.

* * *

The Battle of Berndorf claimed a high-ranking victim on 23 April. The commander of the Russian 99th Guards Rifle Division, Major General I.I. Blazhevich, ordered his command post transferred to a newly captured hill overlooking the town. It had been a heavily fortified German defense position, sewn thick with mines, but Blazhevich was too impatient to wait for it to be completely cleared. While looking over the German trenches and bunkers, surrounded by his officers, he stepped on a mine and was killed.[6]

* * *

One large Russian reconnaissance force from the previous night waited for dawn at the foot of Hocheck Mountain, northwest of Furth an der Triesting, where *SS-Kampfgruppe Taubert* held the high ground. At first light they attacked up the slopes to capture the crucial peak by surprise, but hand grenades, *Panzerfauste* and machine guns drove them back with heavy losses.

From atop the mountain observers saw heavy Russian traffic on the road a few miles to the north. German artillery interdicted the traffic with their fire directed from the mountain. To the west, *SS-Kampfgruppe Minow* pulled back to a mountain south of the Hainfeld-Kaumberg road, but made the mistake of setting up their defensive positions on the north side, facing the Russians. It didn't take long before artillery and Katyusha rounds sprayed shrapnel into the ranks, followed by

---

6   Maslov, Alexander A., *Fallen Soviet Generals: Soviet General Officers Killed in Battle, 1941-1945* (Abingdon: Routledge Press, 1998), p. 28.

direct fire from 76mm guns and then machine guns. Along with another *SS-Kampfgruppe*, this one a company-sized unit commanded by *SS-Hauptsturmführer* Götz Grossjohann, *SS-Kampfgruppe Minow* had no choice except to retreat to Ramsau.

South of Altenmarkt the blocking forces didn't retreat, but should have. Attacked from both flanks and from the town itself, the company or so of Germans was, as Hubert Meyer put it, "massacred, approximately twenty men were able to retreat to the south". Taking advantage of this sudden gap ripped in the line, the Russians kept moving south. Simultaneously other attacks hit the few German forces left on the Altenmarkt-Weissenbach road at Tasshof.

SS-Panzergrenadier-Regiment 25, long-since reduced to nothing more than a *Kampfgruppe*, stayed in positions along the road long enough for the *LAH* to withdraw according to plan, after which it joined *SS-Kampfgruppe Taubert* around Hocheck Mountain. There was no sanctuary to be found from Russian artillery barrages, which hit all along the line for most of the day, including the town of Furth itself. As the day wore on it became more and more obvious that the Russian objective was Pernitz, the key transit point for the withdrawal of the *LAH*. Scouting patrols sent west and north from Furth showed Russian positions far advanced around the tiny settlement of Harras and dug in for defense, so that counterattacks would fail. This put the Russians due west of Furth. With Furth now under threat, the division moved its command post again, this time to Riegelhof, half a mile from Muggendorf. The road to get there was little more than a rutted dirt track, made worse by a heavy snowstorm.

Nightfall brought no relief and now it was Ramsau's turn on the firing line. *SS-Kampfgruppe Grossjohann* fell back to the town cemetery, where they took cover behind a high stone wall. Two company-sized attacks came at them in the dark but, aided by *Flak* cannon, they cut the Russians down and sent them backward. The next morning they counted 25 bodies in front of their position.[7]

Kampfgruppe 1. SS-Panzer-Division Leibstandarte Adolf Hitler

Yard by yard, 37th Guards Rifle Corps ground its way forward against the right flank of *I SS-Panzerkorps*, and no town faced harder fighting than Pottenstein. Situated a few miles southwest of Baden, the town faced the breakthrough channel south of Vienna through which much of Third Ukrainian Front had passed.

If the German front line was thought of as a dam, then the Russian penetration in early April could be seen as a hole broken in the face of the dam. Around the edges of the hole, the face of the dam still held back water, forcing it to flow only through the hole. But little by little the water ate away at those edges to enlarge the hole. In this analogy, Pottenstein would be the edge in contact with the water, and on 23 April it finally got swept away.

The cost of the fight was terrible. The Germans lost between 140 and 150 men, mostly from the *LAH*. Sixty-nine civilians died out of a population of less than 3,000 people, while 50 houses, the courtyard and a textile factory burned down.[8]

The withdrawing Germans passed through Weissenbach and then Furth an der Triesting.[9] After darkness fell the *Flak* batteries followed them as Russian artillery shells burst all around them. Taking casualties the whole way, they eventually got out of range and were trucked to the west.

---

7   Meyer, *The 12th SS*, pp. 491-492.
8   Vavra and Rossiwall, *The Letzten Tage*, <https://www.museumnoe.at/de/das-museum/blog/18-april-24-april-1945> (Accessed 21 August 2018).
9   Tiemann quotes *SS-Oberscharführer* Heinrich Nebel, commander of the *12./SS-Panzergrenadier-Regiment 1*, that the battle group moved through Hainfeld to Furth an der Traisen. This is obviously incorrect, Hainfeld

SS-Brigadeführer Kumm's division command post in Weiseenbach nearly waited too long to head west. With the road through Hainfeld now cut the only options were mountain paths that couldn't accommodate the vehicles, so Kumm sent the pioneers to widen what were essentially footpaths and game trails for the wheeled transport. That took time, time they didn't have, but luckily the Russians didn't attack as they were strung out in marching columns. First moving through Furth an der Triesting, their path next took them over the back roads through Steinwandgraben and Muggendorf to Pernitz.[10]

One strongpoint held until the last moment was Berndorf. The little town had an offshoot Krupp factory that produced fine dinnerware adorned with Nazi decorative patterns, including for Klessheim Castle in western Austria, where state dinners were often held. Arthur Krupp had a villa nearby that was ransacked. Remnants of the *SS-Panzer-Regiment 1* held on under an intense bombardment until surrounded on three sides, before finally withdrawing during the night. With Russians to the north, east and south, the only escape route first led west through Furth an der Triesting and then south to Pernitz, the same route taken by Kumm's headquarters. As mentioned above, these weren't roads; they were temporary cuts through the forests. But despite traffic jams, blockages and crowding, they all made it through.

Like nearby Pottenstein, Berndorf had been a front-line town for weeks. Hundreds of men died fighting for it. One cemetery filled with Russian war dead underwent renovation in 2017 and now remembers the fallen with towering stone monuments laid out in neat rows.

SS-Kampfgruppe Keitel

Schneebergdörfl, Losenheim and Sonnleiten were all occupied by Russian troops after *SS-Kampfgruppe Keitel* withdrew. Yet again Austrian partisans guided the Red Army men through the dense forests in an attempt to capture the north side of the Schneeberg. The Germans had already pulled back and left only rearguards. The Russians responded by moving up their artillery and mortars.

Kampfgruppe Koch

The one-time commander of the *Kampfgruppe* built around the *Fahnenjunkern* of the *Kriegsschule Wiener Neustadt* received an order for all surviving officer cadets to be immediately sent marching toward Grafenberg. This included the wounded and all officers up to the rank of *Hauptmann*.[11]

117. Jäger-Division

The headquarters of the division moved into the area near Rohr im Gebirge, while the division itself deployed in the surrounding forests. It didn't take long for the Russians to close on their front. The Russians had spread their artillery over a wide area while the Germans put their remaining tubes in Rohr, but the dwindling ammunition supply severely limited their ability to support

---

had already fallen and Furth an der Traisen didn't exist. Furth bei Göttweig is a possibility, as this is near Krems an der Donau and the mouth of the Traisen River. But Furth an der Triesting makes the most sense, since this town was three miles west of Weissenbach.

10   Tiemann, *The Leibstandarte IV/2*, p. 309.
11   Brettner, *Die Letzten Kämpfe Band I*, p. 166.

operations. For example, one battery of three 150mm cannon could have provided critical fire support to help break up Russian attacks or troop concentrations, but there were only five rounds for all three guns.[12]

6. Armee

Even at this late stage of the war *Luftflotte 4* still flew reconnaissance missions. One such flight showed Russian units moving down the valley of the Lafnitz, trying to infiltrate the seam between the right flank of the units attacking north toward Mönichwald and the left flank of *1. Volks-Gebirgs-Division* arrayed further south behind the Lafnitz Valley.

Kampfgruppe Raithel

At the Feistritzsattel the Germans launched another attack to drive the Russians back again. Aside from solidifying their defensive position they also wanted to capture the positions from which the Russian artillery and mortars kept pounding them. Like the attack two days before, it succeeded, but at terrible cost. One platoon began the attack with 31 men and only 13 came back. With only two weeks left in the war, the German military still functioned, even at the smallest level. The platoon's losses were made up by the influx of 18 new men from the battalion's reserve company, who brought two machine guns with them.[13]

1. Volks-Gebirgs-Division

Attached to *II./Gebirgsjäger-Regiment 99* was the *II./Panzergrenadier-Regiment 1*. The *Gebirgsjäger* battalion had 453 men, 28 machine guns, three medium-caliber mortars and one 20mm *Flak* cannon. The panzer battalion only added 160 men that had been combed out of the repair, supply and artillery elements that had no more heavy weapons to service. They only had seven machine guns, two mortars and an anti-tank gun, but most of them were at least combat veterans.

The Germans expected an attack in the vicinity of Neudau but the day passed in relative peace. Then around midnight the night erupted with Russians screaming their characteristic battle cry "Urrah! Urrah!" Except this time the voices sounded different because it was an all-female Russian combat unit doing the shouting and fighting. That attack was defeated, but at 3:00 a.m. it happened again, with the same result. Despite fighting for their lives in the middle of the night, the Germans made wisecracks and jokes about being attacked by women.[14]

Kampfgruppe 1. Panzer-Division

A patrol scouting ahead of the main force discovered the Russian positions in Vorau and set fire to the quarters of the Russian officers in the town. In their fury, the Russians mistook their own

---

12   Brettner, *Die Letzten Kämpfe Band I*, p. 196.
13   Brettner, *Die Letzten Kämpfe Band I*, p. 114.
14   Brettner, *Die Letzten Kämpfe Band I*, p. 47.

troops withdrawing from Wenigzell and Waldbach for Germans and fired a Katyusha barrage into them, further ravaging the already battered group.[15]

Having successfully scouted the Russian positions, at 4:15 a.m. a brief artillery strike proved unusually effective, followed by an attack on the town. Fighting was typically heavy, but by noon the town was back in German hands.

When the Germans rolled back into Vorau they were met by large crowds of people shouting and dancing with joy. The *1. Panzer Division* didn't stop with the recapture of Vorau, however, and pushed on toward Reinberg, which forced the Russians back to Rohrbach. In Vorau and along the trail of the fighting, hundreds of bodies and weapons littered the battlefield.

Kampfgruppe 3. Panzer-Division

As the counterattack to the north sliced into the Russian flank, it had relieved pressure on the Armored Bears. A Russian attack was expected on 23 April but never came. Mortar and artillery barrages came as they had been during the previous days, there were patrol skirmishes in no man's land and Russian loudspeakers blasted the night with pleas for the Germans to surrender, but nothing more.

Life in the front lines was still dangerous. Russian snipers never rested, mortar rounds came in at odd times and without warning, and Russian patrols came close looking for prisoners. But behind the lines it was a different story. Some of the wounded had time to heal and the men had time to sleep. Officers even had to think of ways to combat boredom. Considering the nature of the past six weeks' fighting, nobody complained.

9. SS-Panzer-Division Hohenstaufen

As the chain of command started breaking down, confusing and desperate orders began getting issued to the field units. With the arrival of the Americans on Austria's border imminent, *Hohenstaufen* was ordered to be detached from *2. Panzerarmee* and sent north to Amstetten. But this wouldn't be the only transfer order the division received.

---

15   Brettner, *Die Letzten Kämpfe Band I*, p. 54.

24

Tuesday, 24 April

Nasty weather continued over the region, with unusually cold temperatures, heavy rain and snow in the mountains. Both sides were exhausted but there was no let up in the fighting.

In an order from Hitler, command authority of the *Wehrmacht* was officially divided between Grand Admiral Dönitz in the north and *Generalfeldmarschall* Kesselring in the south. This meant that while Hitler remained the ultimate authority, *Generaloberst* Rendulic now reported to Kesselring as his immediate superior. Himmler's edict that Ernst Kaltenbrunner take over command in the south meant that he now reported to Kesselring, at least in theory.

* * *

In a decision that probably went unnoticed by the miserable *Landser* manning the front lines, whose immediate concerns involved staying alive and maybe finding something to eat, *Heeresgruppe Süd* was renamed *Heeresgruppe Ostmark*.

North of the Danube

8. Armee

The Russians ramped up their attacks in Ernstbrunner Waldes, the oak forest between Ernstbrunn and Hollabrunn, and renewed their tank attacks to the northwest of Enzersdorf bei Staatz, but all of them were repulsed. Along with these armored attacks, other infantry attacks in company and battalion strength hit various points on the German front. Those, too, were driven back.

Then, during the night, *General der Gebirgstruppe* Kreysing lost much of his remaining army. As the Russians tightened their noose on Berlin, Kreysing was ordered to transfer *6. Panzer-Division*, *SS-Kampfgruppe Trabandt II* and part of *25. Panzer-Division* to Ferdinand Schörner's *Heeresgruppe Mitte*. Hitler and his advisers were frantically trying to find a way to break the ring of steel that had closed around the capital and drafted orders to strengthen Schörner so he could attack from the south and save them. It was far too late for that, of course, and before long the *Generalfeldmarschall* would also be encircled east of Prague.

The unit that had to extend to cover their part of the front was the regiment of *44. Reichs-Grenadier-Division Hoch und Deutschmeister*, which was a burned-out shell. Indeed, it was so depleted that it doesn't even appear on most orders of battle from this period, in any of the armies its parts fought in. But as happened several times in the past, it was filled back up with 5,000 fresh replacements and sent into the line between Laa an der Thaya and Hollabrunn.

Kampfgruppe 211. Volksgrenadier-Division, SS-Kampfgruppe Trabandt I

Still hanging onto Zistersdorf despite the loss of the nearby oil fields, the defenders had to endure a massive bombardment on 24 April, which left the Town Hall in flames and the streets clogged with rubble. Then the Russians moved in on their left flank, attacking with tanks, but those were probing attacks and were driven back. Other attacks south and northeast of Laa an der Thaya were also repulsed.

Well to the northwest, however, repeated Russian attacks in battalion strength broke through west of Nový Přerov, further jeopardizing the finger of German-held territory around Zistersdorf. Smaller attacks between Drnholec and Brod nod Dyjí were thrown back. It is probable the defenders were the elements of *SS-Kampfgruppe Trabandt I* not involved in the fighting near Achlichtenwarth.

25. Panzer-Division

Despite orders to send the two panzer divisions to *Heeresgruppe Mitte*, that couldn't be done until they disengaged from the front and Fifth Guards Tank Corps didn't slow down its tempo of operations to allow that to happen. The tank fight south of Laa an der Thaya continued throughout 24 April, despite the bad weather. Along with *6. Panzer-Division*, *25. Panzer-Division* fought them to a standstill. The *Wehrmacht* evening report claimed 52 Russian tanks destroyed, which is almost certainly exaggerated.[1] Nevertheless it shows the intensity of the combat on this last day before the division was transferred to the north.

Kampfgruppe 96. Infanterie-Division

With Russian attacks having moved west, the division became involved in the forest fighting between Ernstbrunn and Hollabrunn. Although short of ammunition, its artillery component still had some shells for its remaining guns. The bigger problem was fuel. With no hope of ever getting more gasoline, they began converting to having horses once again pull the guns. Later in the day a group of replacements arrived from *Wehrkreis XVII*, the Vienna Military District. As for the men of the rank and file, they paid close attention to the American spearheads then closing in on Passau.[2]

6. SS-Panzerarmee

Rear area security has always been a vital component of modern warfare. Road traffic behind the lines had to be managed properly to allow for the free flow of men and supplies, both to and from the front, and doing so was as much art as science. Railroads had to be kept in repair and guarded from sabotage. Fuel depots needed to be established along the routes of movement. Priorities needed to be decided for which unit had the first right of passage. And above all, non-combat units had to be safe from ambush. This had been especially true in Russia but was also true in Austria, even though it was part of the Reich.

The problem for *Heeresgruppe Ostmark* was that most of the armed, and organized, rear area security forces had already been sent to the front lines. The few remaining troops were awash in an ocean of refugees, broken military formations, stragglers, deserters, escaped foreign slave laborers

---

1   Vavra and Rossiwall, *The Letzten Tage*, <https://www.museumnoe.at/de/das-museum/blog/18-april-24-april-1945>, (Accessed 23 July 2018).
2   Brettner, *Die Letzten Kämpfe Band II*, pp. 184-185.

and redeploying units. Outlying farmsteads were at risk of being ravaged by people desperate for food and shelter.

Korps von Bünau

The multiple layers of command of the *Wehrmacht*, combined with the chaos in collapsing Berlin and the fog of war that had settled over the high command at Berschtesgaden, meant that conflicting, obsolete and ridiculous orders could be expected from that moment forward.

After having *2. SS-Panzer-Division Das Reich* assigned to von Bünau's corps the previous day, on 24 April it was taken away again. Von Bünau had intended to deploy it north of the Danube above Passau, against the Americans, but that wasn't going to happen now. Then he was going to use it in an attack with the mission of regaining the line of the Traisen River, but that was called off, too. And the intention of the new order was for it to be assigned to *Heeresgruppe G* in southern Germany, but that never happened, either. The officers involved all tried to disentangle the various authorities claiming the right to make dispositions. From *Führerbefehle*, *Führer* orders, *Gauleiters*, the *Oberbefehlshaber Süd* Kesselring, the area commander Kaltenbrunner, various local Nazi Party functionaries, *Heeresgruppe Ostmark* commander Rendulic, the various army commanders Kreysing, Dietrich, Balck and de Angelis, corps commanders, divisional commanders and on down the chain of command, conflicting orders sent men and units all over the map in an effort to obey often ridiculous instructions from an overlapping command structure that had devolved into a mess.

It wasn't only the chain of command that was in shambles, either. Even the most basic functions of military operations were no longer being performed, namely, systematic reconnaissance that commanders could count on. And so it was that with the Americans racing toward him from the west, *General der Infanterie* von Bünau sent long-range patrols north of the Danube as far as Waidhofen an der Thaya, nearly fifty miles from Krems. Other patrols went west to Budweis, Grein and Freistadt.[3] The last thing the general needed was a US task force showing up unexpectedly in his rear.

I SS-Panzerkorps

As *I SS-Panzerkorps* pulled back the clogged roads complicated its movements. Panic broke out in places as refugees realized what the sudden appearance of SS units moving west meant. If the Germans were gone the Russians couldn't be far behind. For many that was good news, until the Russians actually arrived.

Fourth Guards Army had been hammering away at the corps' defensive line along the southern edge of the Vienna Wood for nearly three weeks. Every day they had gained more ground, and just like the grinding war in Normandy the Germans had traded blood for time. And, just like in Normandy, there came a day when there was no more blood to trade and the retreat was on. That day had come on 23 April, and as 24 April dawned the pace accelerated.

For the *LAH*, *Hitlerjugend* and all of their attached units the withdrawal route first led through Gutenstein, southwest of Pernitz. The only significant highway for so much traffic led due west from the little town of 1,700 citizens, and through a mountain feature called the Rohr Saddle. This high mountain pass led through the Gutenstein Alps at a height of 2,835 feet and featured a

---

3   Von Bünau, *Corps von Buenau*, p. 23.

dangerous switchback road. The maximum grade was 84 degrees. The final objective was the area around the Kalte Kuchl, another mountain pass three miles west of Rohr im Gebirge.

Only three main roads led west from *I SS-Panzerkorps'* defense area in eastern Austria. One passed through Hainfeld and Sankt Viet an der Gölsen and was already in Russian hands. This highway turned south and was blocked south of Lilienfeld. The only other option beside the road that passed through Gutenstein was the one through Terz, 25 miles southwest of the Kalte Kuchl. This area would be defended by *Kampfgruppe 356. Infanterie-Division* and *SS-Kampfgruppe Keitel.*

The terrain on either side of the main highway through the Kalte Kuchl was steep, rugged and heavily wooded. Any army advancing west would have to take that road, or advance cross-country, which was nearly impossible for wheeled vehicles and armor. This made it the ideal position to defend.

SS-Kampfgruppe Peiper

Ever since losing Hainfeld, the *Kampfgruppe* that had fought for the town had conducted a fighting retreat south through the mountains until it finally came to Kleinzell, four miles southwest of Hainfeld. The little town became famous after the war because every Saturday at noon the bell of the local parish church tolls as a reminder of the wailing of air raid sirens. One of the young people born there wrote a book based on her memories titled *Through Innocent Eyes: The Chosen Girls of the Hitler Youth.*

At Kleinzell the SS men turned to fight. Any further retreat would bring them close to the route of retreat for the rest of *I SS-Panzerkorps* and would collapse the corps' left flank. The Russians knew this too, and launched heavy attacks down the narrow route leading into the town, but were repulsed in bloody fighting.

Kampfgruppe 12. SS-Panzer-Division Hitlerjugend

The Russian plan to drive south and either cut off *I SS-Panzerkorps* or force its forward-echeloned units to withdraw had finally begun to work. While the rest of *I SS-Panzerkorps* withdrew west, somebody had to stand and hold back the pursuing Russians on the northern shoulder, and *Hitlerjugend* was selected. When the Russians closed on their positions heavy fighting broke out, but everywhere the SS men held the line.

In some places the withdrawal order almost came too late. On the extreme left flank of *Hitlerjugend*, the combined losses of Pottenstein, Weissenbach an der Triesting and Altenmarkt an der Triesting had left the defenders of Alland isolated and surrounded on three sides. Much like Pottenstein, Alland had been on the front lines since 6 April.

Pottery shards dated to the Stone Age had been found in the area, and the building of the first church came in the 8th Century AD. At the nearby Imperial Mayerling Hunting Lodge on 30 January 1889, Crown Prince Rudolf and his lover, Baroness Mary Vetsera, apparently died in a murder-suicide. Dire consequences for the Austro-Hungarian Empire ended in its disastrous involvement in the First World War.

There is a diabolical association of that date with Austrian history. Aside from the loss of the popular Crown Prince, which led to Archduke Franz Ferdinand being named heir to the Habsburg throne, 80 days after Rudolf's death an Austrian child was born who would grow up to lead his homeland into the devastating maelstrom currently ripping it apart; Adolf Hitler. And Hitler would become Chancellor of Germany on 30 January 1933. Firmly in his mind then was the eventual *Anschluss,* the joining of the two German-speaking nations of Germany and Austria.

Emperor Franz Joseph turned the hunting lodge into a Carmelite Monastery in Rudolf's memory. After the *Anschluss,* the Nazis expelled the nuns and turned the monastery into a forced labor camp to aid in the extension of the *Reichsautobahn* highway system into Austria. Only after the war were the nuns allowed to move back.

The Church of Saints George and Margareta, and the local school, both burned down in the fighting in 1945, along with 41 other buildings. The Germans had already withdrawn from their position at the Lung Sanatorium and abandoned two panzers that were out of fuel. The citizens of Alland hid from the Russians in an abandoned mine tunnel near Groisbach and in the Arnstein Cave, a mile south of the town at the foot of the castle rock at Raisenmarkt. Once word came for the rearguard to pull out, the remaining SS men blew the bridges over the Schwechat River, as ordered, and headed west.

Blowing up bridges and wrecking roads to prevent the enemy from pursuing a retreating foe were a basic tenet of warfare. Armies had done this for as long as armies had existed. It was not unique to the *Wehrmacht.* The Russians themselves had coined the term 'scorched Earth' during their retreat from the Germans in 1941 and 1942. But while it was nothing new to wreck infrastructure in the wake of withdrawal, for local townsfolk caught in the whirlpool of war it was a life-altering catastrophe. After years of life under the stern and often cruel authoritarianism of the Nazis, and with the coming of the brutal exploitation of the Red Army, the people of Alland now had no bridge to cross the river that many depended on for their livelihood.

* * *

Russian attacks fell heaviest on the most vulnerable spot in the division's line, the mountainous terrain south of the Hainfeld-Altenmarkt road. *SS-Kampfgruppe Minow* held Ramsau despite heavy attacks, but it was forced to withdraw closer to the town. Russian forces passed to their east without interference, however, since Minow's *Kampfgruppe* had no contact with their neighbor to the east, *SS-Kampfgruppe von Reitzenstein.*

The German defense was spread so thin that *SS-Kampfgruppe von Reitzenstein* had no contact with the flank defenders on either side, leaving it in the dangerous position of being like a rock in the ocean. Infiltrators could pass on either side and they wouldn't have known it. The yawning gap between von Reitzenstein's men and *SS-Kampfgruppe Taubert,* still holding Hocheck Mountain to their east, worried division commander *SS-Oberführer* Hugo Kraas more than did anything else. The divisional *Begleitkompanie,* the company responsible for the security of the division's headquarters, had already been committed to battle and every non-essential man was in a *Kampfgruppe.* Kraas had no more men to even form blocking positions.

He had withdrawn the division headquarters just in time. In the dim light of early morning strong Russian attacks hit *SS-Kampfgruppe Hauschild* around Furth an der Triesting. After a brief but violent fight the town fell but, as always, the Germans mounted a counterattack. This time it was the *Begleitkompanie* supported by two SPWs with triple 20mm cannon that fought to retake Furth.[4] By mid-morning hand-to-hand fighting raged in the middle of town and the Germans appeared on the verge of taking it, but then fresh Russian troops turned the tide back in their favor. By 11:00 a.m it was over. The remnants of the *Begleitkompanie* retreated south through the dense woods to rejoin the headquarters at Riegelhof.

---

4   The Germans did not manufacture a vehicle with a triple 20mm cannon array, but in the face of incessant air attacks on both fronts the men built their own field-modified vehicles to fill the need for mobile air defense. A single 20mm cannon was only marginally effective against low-flying Russian aircraft like the Ilyushin IL-2, but three of them firing in unison could be effective. Against infantry such a storm of fire proved devastating. It could even immobilize tanks by tearing up their treads, although that would have required great courage and even greater luck.

SS-Hauptsturmführer von Reitzenstein didn't need intelligence reports to tell him that his situation had become untenable. From the high ground west of Hocheck Mountain his observers saw strong Russian columns moving south toward the Furth area, while on his left a Russian reconnaissance force at least a battalion in strength passed south without resistance. Unless he acted quickly his *Kampfgruppe* would be surrounded. Russian patrols had already started probing his lines for weak spots, and while so far they had all been repulsed, sooner or later they would find one.

But he didn't retreat. Instead, he set his defense to an all-around one, with a blocking line south of Marienthal. Contact with division headquarters had been lost and until it was regained, or the position was in imminent danger of falling, von Reitzenstein would hold his ground. One has to wonder whether the disgrace of *SS-Obersturmführer* Gross had anything to do with his decision. An SS man was never punished for obeying orders.[5]

Kampfgruppe 1. SS-Panzer-Division Leibstandarte Adolf Hitler

The part of the panzer regiment that had pulled out of Berndorf the previous afternoon arrived near dawn at Pernitz, after marching all night. But if they expected a moment's peace they were disappointed. Russian guns had the town under fire so the survivors climbed aboard trucks and were driven all the way to Hölle, eight miles south of Rohrbach an der Gölsen. For the moment nobody was shooting at them and the exhausted men could rest, but conditions were far from comfortable. "The company's night camp was a barn with tree branches as straw. It was bitterly cold!"[6]

The garrison of Pottenstein spent the night on a farm west of the mysterious town of Furth, almost surely Furth an der Triesting. Early on 24 April a surprise attack by overwhelming numbers drove them back in disarray. The Russians were closing in when once again out of nowhere a *Flakpanzer IV Wirbelwind* showed up to decimate the infantry running over the fields. Nothing mounted on a tank chassis could chew up a charging horde of riflemen like quadruple-mounted rapid-fire 20mm cannon. This was at least the third time this had happened, all in the same small region of the front, so this must surely be the same *Flakpanzer* as the first two times. When the Russians tried to set up an anti-tank gun to deal with it, the *Flakpanzer* shot that to pieces, too. Then the Germans withdrew further and were eventually picked up by trucks.[7]

Once through the Rohr Saddle the division command post redeployed to Rohr am Gebirge, which was only a few miles south of *SS-Kampfgruppe Peiper*'s battle group at Kleinzell led by *SS-Obersturmführer* Sternebeck. The withdrawal shortened the front by many miles, thus freeing up men to thicken the line.

6. Armee

The Russians withdrew the thoroughly mauled Twenty-Sixth Army and inserted the fresh Twenty-Seventh Army into the area on the left flank of *6. Armee*. The changeover gave the counterattacking Germans a chance to take advantage of the inevitable confusion.

---

5   Meyer, *The 12th SS*, p. 493.
6   Tiemann, *The Leibstandarte IV/2*, p. 308.
7   Tiemann, *The Leibstandarte IV/2*, p. 308.

The *117. Jäger-Division* had been under-strength when it transferred from *2. Panzerarmee*, and suffered heavy casualties once it went back into action. The *1. Panzer-Division* was officially designated as a *Kampfgruppe* before the counterattack, although it had long been at *Kampfgruppe* strength. *Kampfgruppe Raithel* was never able to apply much offensive pressure from the north to help draw off Russian reinforcements. Considering the limited forces available, the German counterattack against Twenty-Sixth Army had achieved remarkable success.

But the loss of *117. Jäger-Division* meant that any future attacks would be made against much stronger Russian resistance, since they no longer had to worry about attacks from the west.

117. Jäger-Division

The *117. Jäger-Division* began its attack on Mönichwald, meeting with tough Russian resistance. After retaking the town, during the evening it turned it over to elements of *1. Volks-Gebirgs-Division*, as the exhausted and depleted *Jäger-Division* was ordered north to join Sepp Dietrich's *6. SS-Panzerarmee*, its third army in the last three weeks. The fighting over the previous week had been as vicious as any during the war. Testimony to the violence was that during the counterattack that started at Ratten, the division lost 850 men killed, wounded or missing.

The withdrawal west of the forward-echeloned elements of *I SS-Panzerkorps* put even more pressure on *6. Armee's* left flank. North of *Kampfgruppe Raithel*, therefore, Hermann Balck's extreme left flank was exposed with the only significant force to screen it being the badly depleted *SS-Kampfgruppe Keitel*, which had never been stronger than a regiment anyway.

Balck had to pull his army back to match Dietrich's move, but he still had to protect Graz which meant that he had to stay echeloned further east and far to the south. The gap between his command and Sepp Dietrich's had never really been closed, it was just that the Russians never exploited it as they could have. But with the Hohe Wand in their possession and probably fewer than 1,000 men left in *SS-Kampfgruppe Keitel*, the chance to outflank *Kampfgruppe Raithel* on the north was very real.

There were no good options available to solve this problem. The only possible solution was to shift a unit from *6. Armee* to the north and subordinate it to *I SS-Panzerkorps*, so the *117. Jäger-Division* was ordered to march north from the Hochwechsel to the area of the Rohrer Sattel. In turn, however, that shifted the problem of *Kampfgruppe Raithel's* flank from the north to the south, leaving a gap of more than 30 miles between it and its nearest neighbor, *Arko 3*. That was even more dangerous than the hole in the front that *117. Jäger-Division* had filled, because it was much closer to Graz, the army's main support base.

But again, Balck had no uncommitted units to send. The only thing he or *III Armeekorps* commander *General der Panzertruppe* Hermann Breith could do was to split the already badly damaged *1. Volks-Gebirgs-Division* and send the bulk of it to replace *117. Jäger-Division*, along with a few elements of *1. Panzer-Division* and what was left of *SS-Polizei-Regiment 13*. The rest of *1. Volks-Gebirgs-Division* stayed behind south of *Arko 3* around Wörth, to support the bulk of *Kampfgruppe 1. Panzer-Division*.

If the front had been as quiet as portrayed in some accounts this wouldn't have been dangerous. But in fact the Russians had no intention of allowing the Germans to withdraw quietly into that night. Nor were the Germans done fighting, either.

Kampfgruppe 1. Panzer-Division

At Neustift an der Lafntiz, which the Russians had overrun on 15 April and subsequently ran amok raping the women and girls, a German counterattack hit the garrison supported by *Sturmgeschütz* IIIs and at least one *Hetzer*. Fighting went on all day, all night and into the 25th, when the Germans finally drove the Russians out of the town and back to Rohrbach. During the war six civilians had died and 23 buildings burned down.[8]

* * *

Having slept for one night without the terror of being attacked by Russians in their homes, the remaining townsfolk of Vorau must have prayed it was permanent. Having discovered what life was like under the Red Army, a few doubtless took that second chance to flee west. For those who stayed their relief proved to be short-lived.

Infuriated by the previous day's friendly-fire incident, the Russians punished Vorau with a heavy air raid that lasted more than an hour. The town was left in flames. Then an artillery bombardment smashed more houses and buildings for the rest of the day.

Vorau was famous for its 12th-Century abbey, a magnificent structure on a high hill. The church and library were of world-class splendor. One of the oldest books in the library dated to 1150 AD. The abbey was specifically targeted and burned to the ground, although miraculously the church, sacristy and library remained undamaged.

* * *

Reconnaissance reports of Russian activity in the Lafnitz Valley led the advance elements of *1. Panzer-Division* to veer east from Vorau and take back Kleinschlag and Eichberg, on the road to both Rohrbach an der Lafnitz and the town of Lafnitz itself. The Russians withdrew under heavy German pressure. The devastation was particularly widespread, with 80 buildings destroyed and 13 civilians found dead.

Elsewhere the service company of *I./Panzer-Regiment 24* worked miracles and brought the battalion's operational strength up to three Panthers, four Mark IVs, one *PAK-40* and even a T-34 *Beutepanzer*. The T-34 was a model 1943, with the redesigned hexagonal turret and twin cupolas, which the Germans nicknamed 'Mickey Mouse' because of how it looked with the two turret hatches open.

1. Volks-Gebirgs-Division

The withdrawal of *117. Jäger-Division* not only nullified the effectiveness of any future counterattacks on *6. Armee*'s left flank, but also left a gaping hole at a critical point in the front. American spearheads were almost at the Austrian border and the thoughts of German commanders had turned to defending their western flank. Any westward thrust by the advance units of Twenty-Sixth Army not only threatened to cut *Heeresgruppe Ostmark* in half, but a southern turn could surround *6. Armee* entirely.

Faced with this dire situation Balck did the only thing he could: he ordered *1. Volks-Gebirgs-Division* to move northwest and take over the defense of the Wechsel area from *117. Jäger-Division*. By necessity he had to move part of *Kampfgruppe 1. Panzer-Division* south to take over part of the

---

8   Brettner, *Die Letzten Kämpfe Band I*, p. 34.

front, with *Arko 3* filling in the rest. Simultaneously he had to withdraw westward to straighten out his lines.

Even this didn't completely fill in the gaps. Between *Kampfgruppe Raithel* and the new positions of *1. Volks-Gebirgs-Division*, there was still an undefended gap leading west through the area of the Feistritzsattel and the Pfaffensattel. The Germans could only afford to screen the region. Any determined assault would have broken through easily.

Kampfgruppe 3. Panzer-Division

One virtually unknown and overlooked aspect of the war in Austria was the anti-Nazi partisan effort behind German lines. Once into the Reich itself the men had believed that the local population, at least, would be friendly and in many cases that's what happened, but not every time. Resistance radio broadcasts urged the people to rise up and harass the German military units in any way possible. This often involved ambushing unguarded supply columns and isolated farms often found themselves attacked by roaming gangs looking for food and loot.

Adding to this burgeoning threat were Russians who had broken through and been cut off, German deserters, shot-down enemy pilots and freed prisoners. By 24 April it had become such a concern that *Generaloberst* Rendulic ordered the creation of anti-partisan units to patrol *6. Armee*'s highways and back roads. The composition of this detail shows how bankrupt the German war effort had become. Led by a *Leutnant*, it had three NCOs, ten soldiers and bicycles for mobility.[9]

---

9   Veterans, *From the Caucasus*, p. 289.

25

Wednesday, 25 April

Berlin

After his collapse on 22 April and subsequent declaration that the war was lost, Hitler had since regained some of his energy. Suddenly, with Berlin surrounded and Russian spearheads closing in on the heart of the city, he took a renewed interest in *Heeresgruppe Ostmark*. He spotted the orders for *2. SS-Panzer-Division Das Reich* to defend Passau and countermanded them, then also countermanded the orders for it to join *Heeresgruppe G*. One can almost picture the *Führer* behind his little table in the crowded chamber in the *Führerbunker*, bending over a situation map with his magnifying glass, micro-managing units whose reports to him depended on a radio antenna held aloft by a balloon. Then he saw a small bridgehead north of Sankt Viet an der Gölsen that *SS-Kampfgruppe Peiper* still held. He ordered that given up to free units for use by *8. Armee*, but the subsequent withdrawal did no such thing. Remarkably, though, a *Führerbefehl* was still a *Führerbefehl* and carried the force of law that few people dared to disobey, even then. *Das Reich* would discover this, much to their misery.

* * *

Having regained interest in the south, one of the last *Führer* briefings for which records exist explain his decision not to conduct a final defense there: "I am the *Führer* as long as I can really lead. I can't lead by setting myself on a mountain somewhere…This so-called southern fortress is not self-sufficient. That is an illusion."[1] Goebbels had long advised him that losing Berlin would be the end, and only by staying to defend Berlin could Hitler achieve either victory or everlasting glory. It probably didn't help that both men knew that the National Redoubt was a hoax.

* * *

Warm spring temperatures and sunny skies returned to the region, which opened the skies to both Russian and American aircraft. Aside from ground attacks by the Red Air Force, mostly against *8. Armee*, the US Fifteenth Air Force bombed Linz for the 23rd time during the war, concentrating on the railroad marshalling yards. Three hundred and sixty civilians died under the rain of steel. Strike photos taken the next day look like a moonscape of blasted earth and craters.

Heeresgruppe Ostmark

Russian progress toward Brno was accelerating as Second Ukrainian Front sliced northwest into the area of *Heeresgruppe Mitte*. But this was no longer the concern of *8. Armee* or *Heeresgruppe Süd*. What was of immediate concern to *Generaloberst* Rendulic was the battle around Berlin, since the repercussions had already cost him units he couldn't afford to lose. When Zhukov and Koniev's

---

1   Heiber & Glantz, *Hitler and His Generals*, pp. 722-723.

troops surrounded the capital, it seems to have finally dawned on Hitler that his situation was dire. Whether from a true belief that if he died the Third Reich died, or simple narcissism, *der Führer* began ordering units all over his shrinking domain to come to his aid. Many of them would come from *Heeresgruppe Süd*.

SS-Kampfgruppe Trabandt I, or SS-Regiment Schulze

After taking heavy casualties in the first two weeks of its life, the regiment was attached to another Army unit in desperate need of fresh blood, this time the *Kampfgruppe 101. Jäger-Division*. It moved into the line between the *25. Panzer-Division* and *Kampfgruppe 211. Volksgrenadier-Division*.

6. Panzer-Division

Throughout its long history, *6. Panzer-Division* had moved from hotspot to hotspot, sometimes to exploit a breakthrough, more often to launch desperate counterattacks or plug a hole in the front. And as had happened so many times before, on 25 April the division moved one final time in response to a crisis. As the Russians began their drive on Brno, *6. Panzer-Division* had been ordered into the fray and had helped fight 5th Guards Tank Corps to a standstill in the previous three days. Burnt-out tanks and assault guns littered the battlefield south of Laa an der Thaya. Now the division was moved again, this time to the west of Brno in response to Hitler's orders for it to join *Heeresgruppe Mitte*. The men would surrender to the Americans in western Czechoslovakia on 9 May, but that would only last a day before they were handed over to the Russians.

Stockerau

This city's strategic position had always made it an objective of Second Ukrainian Front's assault on *8. Armee*. Situated two miles from the Danube, the land to its south was too marshy in places and heavily forested to support anything more than light infantry operations, although it was in range of Russian artillery south of the Danube.

As the front line moved closer during the first half of April, the Monastery of Sankt Kolomann became a hospital for wounded soldiers. Businesses and factories had shut down and life became one long search for food, with a two-pound loaf of bread requiring hours of standing in line. Assuming the store still accepted ration cards, which some no longer did. Life moved underground wherever there was a cellar to hide in. Russian bombs hit the church and vicarage.

On 24 April artillery fire increased, both from across the Danube and German counter-battery fire. The next day was a day of air raids: first, low-level strafing attacks followed later by heavier ground-attack bombing raids, and finally three waves of bombers hitting the artillery positions north of the city. Stockerau's *Volkssturm* had already been mustered and moved into the Marchfeld to fight, but now returned to defend their homes.[2]

---

2   Brettner, *Die Letzten Kämpfe Band II*, p. 170.

Linz

Keeping the Americans out of the area of Upper Austria south of the Danube was critical to the continued existence of *Heeresgruppe Ostmark*. All of their remaining supply sources lay within that area. So, with the American 11th Armored Division pressing hard toward Passau, the time had come to organize a defense for Linz, and this thankless task fell to Knight's Cross winner *Generalmajor* Alfred Kuzmany. Kuzmany had the *Flak* batteries scattered around Linz to start with. To this were added some infantry battalions without heavy weapons support to block the main highways leading to the bridge over the Danube. These quite possibly contained some of the SS men from Mauthausen. Behind them were a Reich Labor Service battalion, a few pioneers and some unarmed *Volkssturm*. As weak as these forces were, however, there were no plans to send Kuzmany reinforcements. Threats elsewhere took priority.

South of the Danube

A hallmark of liberation by Russians was the quick installation of a pro-Soviet government, even in nations where they had vowed to allow free elections. The Karl Renner government in Vienna was one example. Another came in Sankt Pölten, where Gunter Benedikt was appointed Mayor by the Russians. He immediately ordered the destruction of anything related to National Socialism. Banners, badges, armbands, photos, pamphlets, statuary, journals; it all had to be gone by 30 April.

On 16 May he gave up the post in favor of the Commander of the Auxiliary Police Department of the Red Army in Sankt Pölten, Franz Käfer. Käfer had been a member of the Social Democratic Party until it was banned in 1934, and later was imprisoned at Buchenwald. Demonstrably anti-Nazi sentiments had gone from being potentially fatal to qualifying someone for political office.

2. SS-Panzer-Division Das Reich

After a few refreshing days in Sankt Margarethen im Lungau, *SS-Panzergrenadier-Regiment Der Führer* received new orders to boards trains and join their sister regiment *Deutschland* in defending Passau. Although this promised more combat, the regiment would again be facing Americans, not Russians. Capture by the Americans didn't mean automatic execution, as it often did with the Russians.

According to the commander of *Heeresgruppe Ostmark*, *Generaloberst* Dr Lothar Rendulic, *Das Reich* had been completely restored to a full-strength 1945 panzer division. That is, not the 19,000-plus men and more than 150 panzers, assaults guns and *Jagdpanzers* of its previous incarnation, but rather the new guidelines limiting panzer divisions to one armored battalion. Rendulic claims *Das Reich* had 65 panzers,[3] and was actually over-strength, which made it a formidable force again. Where all of the machines supposedly came from isn't known.

---

3   Newton, *German Battle Tactics*, pp. 227-228.

Korps von Bünau

After days of nothing more than patrols, the corps was again hit with strong attacks on positions east of Obergrafendorf, but repulsed them all. By now there had been time to construct a strong defensive line which the Russians couldn't break without a major effort. The situation grew dangerous when contact was lost with *I SS-Panzerkorps* on its immediate right, though; *12. SS-Panzer-Division Hitlerjugend* would take up that position eventually, securing the junction between von Bünau's and Priess's two corps, but not for a few days yet. Until then they were on their own, and the Russians were making headway beyond von Bünau's far right flank where *SS-Kampfgruppe Peiper* had given up ground without a fight to establish a straighter front.

I SS-Panzerkorps
SS-Kampfgruppe Peiper

Having put some space between themselves and the attacking Russians, the Germans began construction of a new defensive line. Cold weather and packed snow hampered movement in the mountains south of the Traisen-Hainfeld road, and made the digging of trenches and building of bunkers difficult.

The former defenders of Hainfeld, along with the panzer *Kampfgruppe* led by *SS-Obersturmführer* Sternebeck, formed a rearguard in the mountain passes around Kleinzell. It was a continuation of the miserable style of combat men of both sides had to endure during that long month of fighting in Austria. Slopes of more than sixty degrees made simple walking difficult, particularly when weighed down by the equipment of war. Countless caves, boulders, rock faces and dense stands of trees gave opportunities for ambush at every turn. Shadows under the forest canopy gave a contrasting background for blinding sunlight reflected off the deep-packed snow.

In places Germans and Russians occupied adjoining mountains and took shots at each other across the space between them. The claustrophobic world under the tree branches often hid the combatants from one another until they stumbled into the enemy. Firefights broke out without warning, especially during the nights. The Russians had the advantage in numbers and firepower, and their mortars took an especially heavy toll, but wherever they attacked across a meadow, the Germans made them pay. Fighting ebbed and flowed throughout the day on 25 April, with sometimes a patrol running into the enemy and exchanging skirmishing fire, and other times attacks or counterattacks coming in platoon or company strength. Most of the combat came in the Halbach Valley around Kleinzell.

Kampfgruppe 1. SS-Panzer-Division Leibstandarte Adolf Hitler

With Peiper's command now on the division's left flank, the remnants of the *LAH* were effectively one unit again. With Peiper's men defending a north-northwesterly line, the remainder of the division dug in facing east to the north of the Rohr Saddle and connected with Peiper's right flank. The remaining *Flak* batteries built defensive positions near Traisenbeck, south of Kleinzell, to engage ground targets. By this time that amounted to four 88mm cannon, one of which had just been repaired, and some 37mm guns. For large attacks on assembly area was needed, and whenever such a gathering took place in sight of German artillery observers they were taken under fire by the 88mm guns to break up the attack before it began. Sometimes it worked, sometimes it didn't.[4]

---

4   Tiemann, *The Leibstandarte IV/2*, p. 311.

Kampfgruppe 12. SS-Panzer-Division Hitlerjugend

After blocking the pursuing Russians, *Hitlerjugend* was still east of the *LAH*'s main line of resistance from Ramsau southeast to the area around Furth an der Triesting. This north-facing line was held by *SS-Panzergrenadier-Regiment 25* with *SS-Kampfgruppe von Reitzenstein* now attached. The division entrenched along that line for the night, but it was a temporary expedient. Russian patrols and small groups skirmished with German outposts but there was no time to organize a major attack. But the relative calm would only last so long. Reconnaissance patrols and direct visual observation all showed strong Russian forces continuing to deploy to the south and southwest. *Hitlerjugend* still had a long way to go to be safe within German lines.

At Ramsau, *SS-Kampfgruppe Grossjohann* not only repelled small Russian attacks but regained some lost positions by a timely counterattack. Small elements of *Hitlerjugend* had helped defend Berndorf for two-and-a-half weeks by 25 April. The town itself was a wreck, with 350 homes damaged or gutted and more than 100 citizens dead, but the ground fighting was only the latest scar left by the war.

The Krupp family had a factory in Berndorf that once employed 6,000 people. After the *Anschluss* it became part of the larger Krupp manufacturing conglomerate. Like flies drawn to fresh meat, this factory attracted the attention of the American strategic bombing campaign. But even the bomb damage wasn't the worst of it. In 1944 the Triesting River flooded the town, causing terrible damage. Before nightfall the SS evacuated the town, leaving scores of their comrades buried in the Lower Austrian soil.

SS-Kampfgruppe Keitel

For nearly two weeks combat had raged on and around the Hohe Wand, a mere 13 miles due west of Wiener Neustadt. With the fall of Pottenstein, Weissenbach an der Triesting and Altenmarkt an der Triesting, the Hohe Wand became the most easterly position still held by *I SS-Panzerkorps*. The defenders had lost the crest of the mountain more than once, only to regain it every time with rapid counterattacks. Aiding *SS-Kampfgruppe Keitel* were local *Volkssturm*, who knew the area very well, and the surviving cadets of the Wiener Neustadt War Academy.

None of the defenders knew that far to the northwest, near Torgau on the Elbe River, the American spearheads had met the Russians and cut the Third Reich in two. The land bridge to the man they had sworn to die for, Adolf Hitler, had been cut. They only knew that their position atop the Hohe Wand had become untenable. Through rain, snow, shot and shell they'd held out as long as they could, but along with *Kampfgruppe 356. Infanterie-Division*, the time had finally come to withdraw in the direction of Miesenbach. Hundreds of their comrades could not follow, having died defending the mountain. Nor could hundreds more Russians pursue them, having fallen assaulting it.

6. Armee

A small *Kampfgruppe* from *Arko 3* teamed up with the *I. Battailon/24. Panzer-Regiment*[5] to retake Rohrbach an der Lafnitz and Reinberg. After the fighting was over the only thing left standing

---

5   The battalion's parent division was in *OKH* reserve in northern Germany. This last battalion was left behind when the division transferred from Slovakia to the north.

in Reinberg was the church. Similar levels of damage ravaged towns and villages throughout the region. No fewer than 68 Germans and even a few Hungarians were killed in action. Russian losses are unknown.

* * *

Throughout the region towns faced with Russian occupation reacted in different ways. At Miesenbach, about five miles southeast of Pernitz, a dozen or so *Hitlerjugend* under the command of a 19-year-old SS man fought back with rifles and hand grenades, to no avail. At Birkfeld the people in the town heard fighting in the mountains above the town and later found three dead German soldiers.

Deserters roamed the region. Sometimes they preyed upon the refugees and populace, but in many cases the townsfolk hid them. By this point the morale of the home front had collapsed and become raw desperation. There was a general feeling that Russian conquest was inevitable, so the only thing resistance could accomplish was to destroy their homes and farms.

Kampfgruppe 5. SS-Panzer-Division Wiking

Despite Germany's prostrate condition, the pending joining of Allied and Russian forces to cut the Reich in two, the destroyed state of the transport system, millions of casualties and millions more prisoners of war, and an Allied bombing campaign that had laid waste to German industry, and caused massive damage to its economy, the German war machine still functioned. The *5. SS-Panzer-Division Wiking* was a formation of ghosts in mid-April, a panzer division with no panzers, few vehicles of any type and only skeletons of its component formations; its panzer regiment had even been converted to infantry. But even now the division was being rebuilt and replenished:

> A heavy replacement stream was still coming. Intensive training was carried out at the end of April; various training courses, instructions in hand-to-hand combat, etc. Discipline was outstanding. Replacements also reached the artillery regiment from its replacement garrison as well as new guns and prime movers!... The German war machinery appeared simply inexhaustible.[6]

So much new artillery equipment and personnel poured in that a new battery was formed around Graz; had these been available two months earlier things might have gone quite differently around Stuhlweissenberg.

But as *Wiking* was being rebuilt *Totenkopf* found itself almost bereft of heavy weapons and combat personnel, reporting strength on 25 April of 8,743 of all ranks. "In just about seven weeks, the formation had lost a full 50 percent of its personnel."[7] And like *Wiking*, missing most of its armor, *Totenkopf*'s panzer regiment had been reorganized to fight on foot.

---

6   Strassner, *European Volunteers*, p. 331.
7   Michaelis, *Panzer Divisions*, p. 165.

14. Waffen-Grenadier-Division der SS Galizen, or 1. Ukrainische Division der Ukrainischen National Armee

Generalleutnant Shadruck received permission to rename *Galizien* as the 1st Division of the Ukrainian National Army. The Germans could see no downside to allowing this, as it continued the myth of a pan-European anti-communist crusade and encouraged the Ukrainians in the *Wehrmacht* to fight all the harder. But it was all smoke and mirrors, as no practical changes came from the edict. *SS-Brigadeführer und Generalmajor der Waffen-SS* Freitag remained as commander of the division, and most of the German officers and NCOs stayed in place in its units. For the rest of the war Shadruck continued expending a lot of energy and issuing detailed orders, including those to remove anti-Ukrainian Germans from the division's rolls, few of which were implemented. It was all too little, too late.

The Americans

Across all of western and northwestern Austria, civilians and *Landser* alike knew the Western Allies were getting close, and the vast majority of both felt they couldn't get there soon enough. Despite Dittmar's declaration that the National Redoubt, the *Alpenfestung*, was a myth, the French First Army and the US Third and Seventh Armies were bearing down on the border in what they believed was a race against time.

26

Thursday, 26 April

Berlin

On 26 April, Hitler personally awarded Artur Axmann the Golden Cross of the German Order in recognition of the role played by the Hitler Youth in the defense of Germany. Meanwhile, the defense of Berlin had failed and Hitler finally realized it. He radioed to *Grossadmiral* Dönitz that the Battle of Berlin would decide Germany's fate and all possible forces should be sent there to relieve the city.

The plan, such as it was, involved *Heeresgruppe Ostmark* sending all available units to reinforce the left wing of *Heeresgruppe Mitte*, which was the closest intact formation to the capital. The order was made as if enough rolling stock could be gathered in Austria in time, and enough units could be disengaged in time, and enough fuel scrounged to move those units to the railheads in time. None of it made any sense from a logistical standpoint.

But the ruptured chain of command and fantasy orders didn't stop there. At 2:30 a.m. the high command in Berschtesgaden, the *Führungsstab Süd*, ordered *2. SS-Panzer-Division Das Reich* to move with all possible haste to Bischofswerder, a town north of Berlin already under Russian control. This order ignored the fact that the Reich had been cut in two at Torgau, so confused officers could only wonder what they should do. This began a short-lived tug of war over the veteran division.

Half an hour later new orders arrived, this time from Hitler himself. *Das Reich* was ordered to Iglau, Jihlava in Czech, a city in the center of old Czechoslovakia. This was in accord with the order to strengthen the left wing of *Generalfeldmarschall* Schörner's *Heeresgruppe Mitte*.

That wasn't the end of it, however. *Generalfeldmarschall* Kesselring conferred with Schörner and decided to keep *Das Reich* moving toward Passau, but by the time these orders were issued it was too late for most of the division except *SS-Panzergrenadier-Regiment Deutschland*. The rest had already boarded trains bound to various points.

The end would come with *Das Reich* scattered all the way from Dresden to Prague and back to Krems, a fractured division torn apart by fractured orders. At the very time the Germans most needed their best fighting forces concentrated, the oldest *Waffen-SS* division was ripped into pieces not by enemy action, but by German bureaucratic meddling. As for *Generaloberst* Dr Rendulic's immediate reaction to Hitler's orders to denude his forces, he mostly ignored them. *Heeresgruppe Ostmark* had enough problems without creating more. But Hitler and the generals still at Army Headquarters in Berlin weren't finished demanding quite yet.[1]

* * *

The SS men occupying *Stalag 17B* looked up on the morning of 26 April to see a column of POWs appear. These were the men from *Stalag 17A*, who had evacuated that camp weeks earlier. No

---

1   Maier, *Drama*, p. 370.

doubt the dismal surroundings looked better than they really were. After so many nights spent out in the open, at least there was a roof overhead.

* * *

Meanwhile, the Americans who had marched out of *Stalag 17B* on 26 April trudged into their final destination at Auffanglager Weilhartforst, near Braunau am Inn, but if they'd expected food, water or accommodations of any kind, they were rudely surprised. The site had nothing to offer, not even shelter. With no German guards caring what they did anymore, the men started felling trees to build their own huts. The next day the columns of French and Belgians would join them.

* * *

With manpower for the front lines exhausted, the men of *Sturmpanzer-Abteilung 219* finally got orders to join combat formations involved in the fighting. The Third company was attached to *Schwere-Panzer-Abteilung Feldherrnhalle*, while the rest of the battalion was shipped without heavy weapons to Waidhofen an der Ybbs to join *Jagdpanzer-Brigade Trumpa*, defending the area southwest of Melk. This obscure formation was apparently commanded by *Hauptmann* Heinz Trumpa, former commander of *5./Panzergrenadier-Regiment 130*, from *Panzer Lehr Division*, from which the original *Panzer-Division Feldherrnhalle* drew its initial cadre of men.

* * *

With less than two weeks left in the war, the front had more or less stabilized along the position it would hold until the Germans frantically began withdrawing to surrender to the Americans. The commitment of *6. SS-Panzerarmee* to Austria meant that most of that country was still in German hands, even if Vienna had been lost. But where would *Heeresgruppe Ostmark* have been at this point if *6. SS-Panzerarmee* had not been sent to Hungary for Spring Awakening, but instead had followed Guderian's recommendations to bring it north to defend Berlin? The *I SS-Panzerkorps* and *II SS-Panzerkorps* would be gone, and the other units would have had to extend their fronts to make up this enormous gap.

They could not have done it; not and stop the Red Army anywhere close to its final lines, even if no additional Russian forces had been committed. One glance at the front line on 26 April will show that. So the question then becomes how far the Red Army would have got without *6. SS-Panzerarmee* there to fill the gaps? Such speculation is always fraught with uncertainty and opinion, but it is quite likely that Austria could have fallen in its entirety, or with perhaps only the westernmost parts in American or British hands.

And if this had happened, then what? Would Stalin have honored his pledge for Austria to fall into the Western Allies' sphere of influence? Maybe, maybe not. Given how many other promises Stalin broke, there is no guarantee that he would have kept this one, or that he would not have demanded additional payment to keep it, perhaps in the form of ceding parts of Italy or Austria to the new communist-dominated Yugoslavia.

On 26 April *Heeresgruppe Ostmark* disposed of its forces as follows: from the northern boundary with *Heeresgruppe Mitte*, in the area of Pohorelice, in old Czechoslovakia, the front ran south to slightly southwest in the direction of Laa an der Thaya; this was the defensive responsibility of *8. Armee*. Kreysing's army headquarters had *Sturm-Artillerie-Brigade 239* attached under Army command, along with the two remaining subordinated corps. *Panzerkorps Feldherrnhalle* was the northernmost corps, with the following units attached: *Schwere-Panzerjäger-Brigade 662*, *Schwere-Panzer-Abteilung 509* and *Sturmpanzer-Abteilung 219*, which was one of only four battalions composed of *Brummbärs*, 150mm infantry support guns mounted in a square steel superstructure on top of a Panzer IV chassis. Exactly how many operational machines the battalion had is unknown. A maximum 313 of the vehicles were built during the war.

The corps headquarters seems to have been located in the area just northwest of Bozice. Under its command were *Kampfgruppe 357. Infanterie-Division* with *Jäger-Regiment 28* from *8. Jäger-Division* and *SS-Kampfgruppe Trabandt II* attached. These were in the vicinity of the small towns of Drnholec and Hrusovany, just over the Czech border north of Laa an der Thaya. To the south of *Kampfgruppe 357. Infanterie-Division*, down to the Austrian border, was a *Kampfgruppe* from *211. Volksgrenadier-Division*,[2] and *Grenadier-Regiment 126* from the rump *48. Volks-Grenadier Division*.[3] *Panzerkorps Felldherrnhalle*'s boundary ended at the Austrian border and gave way to *XXXXIII Armeekorps*.

The *XXXXIII Armeekorps* boundary picked up at the Austrian border and extended south, with the corps headquarters located near Mitter Graben. It appears that all of its units were deployed forward, with no reserves: *25. Panzer-Division* was holding Laa an der Thaya on the northern, or left, flank, and just to the south was *Panzer-Division-Feldherrnhalle 2*. Subordinated to it was the recently rebuilt regiment of *44. Infanterie-Division Hoch und Deutschmeister* and *SS-Kampfgruppe Trabandt I*.

The front bowed sharply southwest at that point, south of the area of *Feldherrnhalle 2*, from Strunsdorf to Oberstinkenbrunn, where the *Kampfgruppe 101. Jäger-Division* held the front with no attached units. Just south was *Kampfgruppe Grenadier-Brigade (mot.) 92* and *Kampfgruppe 96. Infanterie-Division*, holding around Ezenrsdorf. From there the front went southeast to *Kampfgruppe 48. Volks-Grenadier* on the corps' southern flank, where it joined the boundary of *II SS-Panzerkorps* around Ernstbrunn. This is where the gap would have begun had *6. SS-Panzerarmee* not been on hand, with the exception of a few smaller units such as the *Kampfgruppe* from *Totenkopf*. That is to say, had the *6. SS-Panzerarmee* not been attached to *Heeresgruppe Süd*, and had no other reinforcements been sent to Austria, then deleting all the subsequent *I* and *II SS-Panzerkorps* units will give an idea of what would have been available to hold back the Red Army.

The *II SS-Panzerkorps* headquarters was situated just south of Hollabrunn, astride the highway leading from Vienna up to Ceske Budojovice and then on to the Strakonice area. To the corps' eastern front was the *Führer-Grenadier-Division*. Next in line came *Kampfgruppe Volkmann* near Stockerau. From Stockerau the front bent almost directly west all the way to Krems an der Donau, held by *Totenkopf*, then crossed the Danube and headed east into the area held by *Korps von Bünau*, thereby forming a large bulge along the Danube.

Korps von Bünau and the headquarters of *6. SS-Panzerarmee* were directly to the Soviets' west, with the headquarters of *Heeresgruppe Süd* itself in the same vicinity. South of *6. SS-Panzerarmee* headquarters was *I SS-Panzerkorps*, tied to von Bünau's left flank. *SS-Panzer-Regiment 12* was on the left flank southwest and south of Sankt Pölten, with the rest of the division transferring in over the next few days. Just east of the *Hitlerjugend* was the hastily formed *10. Fallschirmjäger-Division*. Along with the *Fallschirmjägers*, in the area around St Veit an der Golsen, were some *Flak* units, including part of *Flak-Regiment 133*. Somewhat to the southeast were the advance elements of *12. SS-Panzer-Division Hitlerjugend*, probably in nothing more than *Kampfgruppe* strength, and *SS-Kampfgruppe* Peiper. Then came the *I SS-Panzerkorps* headquarters itself, with *Volks-Artillerie-Korps 403* attached, near Sankt Aegyd am Neuwalde. Also close by was *117 Jäger-Division*, fresh

---

2   In Siegrunen 69, Pencz gives a chronology that means *Kampfgruppe Trabant II* was *SS-Regiment Konopacki*, since it was this unit that was attached to *357. Infanterie-Division*. However, he also puts the *Kampfgruppe* north of Laa an der Thaya as *SS-Regiment Schulze*, which was *Trabandt I*, not *Trabandt II*. He then places the *Trabandt Kampfgruppe*, whichever one it was, to the right of *Kampfgruppe 211. Volks-Grenadier-Division*, not to the left, as Rauchensteiner says.

3   The *48. Infanterie-Division* was destroyed on the Western Front in November 1944, but ordered rebuilt as a Volksgrenadier-Division. That process was never completed but the combat-ready elements were sent into combat with *Grenadier-Regiment 126*.

from its successful counterattacks in the *6. Armee* area. *Kampfgruppe 356. Infanterie-Division* and *SS-Kampfgruppe Keitel* still held the area down to the boundary with Balck's *6. Armee*, which ran from Pottsebath to the west-northwest.

2. SS-Panzer-Division Das Reich

The men of *SS-Panzergrenadier-Regiment Der Führer* entrained for the short move to Passau where they would again operate beside *SS-Panzergrenadier-Regiment Deutschland*. The regimental staff took a motor convoy through Erdsdorf and Melk, planning on rejoining their command at Passau. On the way, however, the staff lost communications with the trains hauling the men and equipment. When they finally arrived in the area they were told that a *Führerbefehl* had diverted the trains north. As the regimental commander, Weidinger claims to have been told this "when reporting to *LXXXIV Armee-Korps* directly south of Passau".[4]

Weidinger was mistaken. *LXXXIV Armeekorps* was destroyed the previous August in France, but his statement has led to the corps being mistaken in a number of extant histories. In fact, the corps directly south of Passau was *Korps Bork*, commanded by *Generalleutnant* Max Bork, who wrote a detailed postwar essay titled *Comments on Russian Roads and Railways*. Bork had been nominated for the Knight's Cross on 14 April 1945, and his nomination was received in Berlin, but the end of the war prevented all the paperwork being filled out. Nevertheless, he is generally recognized as having won the award.[5]

The trains carrying *Der Führer* were believed to have been diverted to the area near Budweis, in old Czechoslovakia, to be used in the defense of Brno. But then Weidinger discovered that a General Staff officer cited the *Führerbefehl* and sent them north toward Dresden. Officers who protested they wanted orders from their regimental commander were threatened with being shot for disobeying an order from Hitler himself. Weidinger raged against this blatant breach of the chain of command but the point quickly became moot. All of *Das Reich* was ordered to the Dresden area, although *Deutschland* held in place until relieved by an Army unit. To their great good fortune the regiment would never follow their comrades in the rest of the division.[6]

The men of *Deutschland*, meanwhile, set up a blocking position nine miles west of Passau, no doubt believing their sister regiment would soon be at their side again. On 26 April they made first contact with the Americans. Fighting was brief but heavy. At the end of the day the SS still held out.

Korps Bork, Western Austria

487. Ausbildungs-und-Ersatz-Division

As the primary formation under *Korps Bork*, the *487. Ausbildungs-und-Ersatz-Division* fielded two regiments of mostly raw recruits with personal weapons. The officers and NCOs were likely veterans who, for one reason or another, had been rejected for front-line service. All of the men

---

4   Weidinger, *Das Reich*, p. 398.
5   Maclean, Major French L., *The Unknown Generals – German Corps Commanders of World War II* (West Point: The US Military Academy, 1974). Adding to the confusion of the identity of this corps, it reportedly had 3 commanders after Bork, beginning on 15 April. <http://www.dtic.mil/dtic/tr/fulltext/u2/a198043.pdf>, (Accessed 20 June 2018).
6   Weidinger, *Das Reich*, p. 398.

knew the Americans were coming and had time to prepare their defenses. What is unknown is how many of them wanted to fight. The military commander of the Oberdonau *Gau*, the area north of the Danube and west of Linz, was the commander of *487. Ausbildungs-und-Ersatz-Division*, *Generalmajor* Paul Wagner.

I SS-Panzerkorps

As *10. Fallschirmjäger-Division* boarded trains bound for the north flank of *Heeresgruppe Mitte*, and *Hitlerjugend* moved to take their place in the line, *6. SS-Panzerarmee* desperately needed more troops to hold its far right flank. Therefore, *Generaloberst* Rendulic ordered *117. Jäger-Division* transferred to the area south of *SS-Kampfgruppe Keitel* and attached to Dietrich's command.

Kampfgruppe 1. SS-Panzer-Division Leibstandarte Adolf Hitler

With their new defensive positions completed, the SS men experienced only skirmishes with enemy patrols during the day. Their swift withdrawal had left the Russians in need of regrouping and reconnaissance, and bought the Germans a period of much-needed rest. The remnants of *SS-Panzer-Artillerie Regiment 1* established itself in Hohenberg, four miles to the northwest of the Kalte Kuchl, from where it could support most of the front-line positions.

Kampfgruppe 12. SS-Panzer-Division Hitlerjugend

At long last orders came relieving the exhausted SS men. After acting as the rearguard for the *LAH* it was *Hitlerjugend*'s turn to withdraw to the main line of resistance. Beginning in the morning and continuing throughout the night, it moved from the exposed positions east of the *LAH* and headed west to relieve *10. Fallschirmjäger-Division* in their positions west of the Traisen River around Rabenstein.

The wet, mud-spattered *Waffen-SS Landser* trudged to their collection points up and down steep crags and slippery trails. Once there the men had a chance to eat a fast meal and grab a smoke before mounting trucks for the drive west. If anyone complained about the brief period of rest, nobody recorded it.

6. Armee

Near Mönichwald the supreme moment of danger for the Germans came before dawn. As the last elements of *117. Jäger-Division* pulled out of the front lines for the transfer north, there was an inevitable moment when the defenses were unmanned and in confusion as their replacements took over. A strong Russian attack would have sliced right through them with disastrous results for the defenders. But nothing happened. The Russians remained blissfully unaware of the changeover.

Mönichwald was a key position, situated as it was on the southern end of the Wechsel Mountains, with the Hochwechsel, the highest peak in the short chain, at the northern end. By holding those the Germans blocked almost any advance to the west. But with the *117. Jäger-Division* heading north to replace the soon-to-be-transferred *10. Fallschirmjäger-Division*, further attacks had to be curtailed as *1. Volks-Gebirgs-Division* took over for the missing *Jäger-Division*.

The initial changeover left dangerous gaps between the battalions of *Gebirgsjäger-Regiment 99*. Fortunately for the Germans the Russians were slow to exploit this. Because of the lack of Russian response, the regiment immediately attacked Russians occupying the Hochwechsel, with the attack coming from the south and southwest. This was rugged mountain territory, precisely the sort of environment the *Gebirgsjägers* had been specially trained and equipped to fight in. The Russians were taken by surprise and thrown off the dominating peak with heavy losses.

1. Volks-Gebirgs-Division

Generalmajor Hans Kreppl, the commander of *1. Volks-Gebirgs-Division*, received warning that his division would be moving northwest, but Kreppl knew his men were spent after weeks of constant combat and especially after the bitter fighting in the Waldbach area. He needed them refreshed if they were going to keep fighting in their new positions, so as much as possible he used 26 and 27 April as days of rest.

Kampfgruppe 5. SS-Panzer-Division Wiking

A steady flow of replacements poured into *Wiking*, although the fitness of the men varied wildly. Nevertheless, "intensive training was carried out at the end of April: various training courses, instruction in hand-to-hand combat, etc".[7] And in what must have seemed a near miracle, new artillery pieces and prime movers were supplied, as well as crews for the new pieces. So many men and guns came in that a brand new battery was established for the regiment. What didn't show up, however, were panzers. Nevertheless, if combat resumed *Wiking* was much better prepared to fight.

* * *

Around 2,000 BC a group of people settled on land at the confluence of two rivers, where fish and plentiful game assured their food supply and dense forests gave them an ample supply of home-building materials. Some 1,700 years later a tribe of Celts moved into the same area and became miners. The Romans came in 15 BC when Emperor Augustus Caesar was at the height of his reign. Under Emperor Claudius the area acquired the name Aguntum as part of the new Roman province of Noricum.

Over time the two rivers came to be called the Drava and the Isel. The surrounding mountains became the Hohe Tauen range, the region was called the Tyrol and the settlement turned into the town of Lienz.

The citizens of Lienz must have watched the approach of Allied armies with hope and trepidation. Nobody wanted to be overrun by the Red Army, but the town was situated in the south Tyrol barely 10 miles from the Italian border. The closest enemy army wasn't the Russians, the Americans, or even the French; it was Field Marshal Montgomery's old command, the British Eighth Army.

Just after noon on 26 April, a bright spring day, they heard a sound never heard in the skies over Lienz before; the drone of American heavy bombers. Aircraft from at least two bomb groups dumped their loads on the railroad marshalling yards, obliterating them along with 16 percent of the town. After almost six years of war one of the most isolated and idyllic places in Europe learned at first-hand the horrors of war.

---

7   Strasser, *European Volunteers*, p. 331.

9. SS-Panzer-Division Hohenstaufen

In retrospect it seems unbelievable, but when *Hohenstaufen* received orders to move north, ostensibly to participate in the drive to relieve Berlin, it was once again at full authorized strength of 18,500 men, and perhaps even over-strength. Regardless of their defects as front-line soldiers – some of the men were sixty years old – the division actually resembled a true SS panzer division. Every vehicle that could be repaired had been, uniforms were patched and cleaned, the men were rested…in short, *Hohenstaufen* was combat-ready again; at least, as combat-ready as possible in those final chaotic days.

The Americans

General Dwight Eisenhower was still so concerned about the National Redoubt that he committed all or part of three armies to overrunning Austria before the imaginary defense fortifications could be occupied by the retreating *Wehrmacht*. These were under the overall command of Sixth Army Group, Lieutenant General Jacob Devers commanding. For the Czecho-Austrian operations Devers was given Lieutenant General George Patton's Third Army. Part of that force was assigned the mission of capturing Salzburg. The capture of Innsbruck was given to the 7th US Army, commanded by Lieutenant General Alexander Patch. The far western Austrian province of Voralsberg fell under the mission of the First French Army, commanded by *Général d' Armeé* Jean de Lattre de Tassigny.

A strong mixed task force from the 11th Armored Division crossed the Austria border headed for Linz. Springtime weather at the lower elevations did not follow them into the high mountains, where the narrow roads couldn't support the heavy tracked vehicles and trucks, and rain, sleet and snow pelted them. Armed resistance wasn't strong even when it was encountered, but the weather was a different story. *Heeresgruppe Süd* now officially faced war on three fronts.

* * *

The previous day found American and Russian units meeting near Torgau, in Central Germany, thus cutting the Reich in two. Despite this, Dwight Eisenhower still worried about the chimera of the National Redoubt. Redoubt: "The strong possibility still existed that fanatical Nazis would attempt to establish themselves in the National Redoubt."[8]

---

8   Eisenhower, *Crusade in Europe*, p. 415.

27

Friday, 27 April

Berlin

Once again *Generaloberst* Rendulic received orders to "ruthlessly weaken the right wing and center to release forces for the reinforcement of the left wing of the *8. Armee* at Brünn [Brno]".[1] From a military standpoint this not only risked *Heeresgruppe Ostmark* being outflanked and destroyed, it also risked *Heeresgruppe E* being cut off if the Russians could push west as far as Klagenfurt. The British were charging hard through northern Italy and Tito's partisan army was hot on the heels of *Heeresgruppe E*. All of that to rescue a man more than five hundred miles away, with the enemy only a thousand yards from his underground bunker. Even if Rendulic had wanted to save his *Führer* it was far too late.

* * *

In the very last *Führer* situation conference for which records still exist, Hitler shows how important the Austrian oil fields had always been to Germany: "The two oil field areas in Austria provided us with a total of 120,000 tons. That could be increased to 180,000 tons."[2]

Numerous histories have listed the justification for *Unternehmen Frühlingserwachen* as being an active defense of the last natural oil fields in German possession, those at Nagykanisza. This has always been in error, as previous discussions and the above quote makes clear. The Hungarian fields were important, but they weren't the last source of oil, or even the largest remaining source.

As for Zistersdorf, the defenders did everything humanly possible to keep them, staying at their posts long after it made no military sense.

Vienna

In Soviet-occupied Vienna, the former Austrian Socialist Chancellor Karl Renner finished putting a cabinet together to fulfill Winston Churchill's biggest fear, establishing a pro-Soviet puppet government under Stalin's control. The same thing had already happened in Poland, Czechoslovakia, Rumania, Bulgaria, Hungary, the Baltic States and was in the process of happening in Yugoslavia. The loss of Austria would make the defense of Western Europe in a future war all but impossible. Churchill immediately declined to recognize Renner's government. Much to his relief, so did the United States. But in Stalin's eyes possession was nine-tenths of the law, so the race was on to capture as much of Austria as possible before the hourglass of war ran out.

On 27 April Renner met with Marshal Tolbukhin, who, in the name of the Soviet Union, immediately recognized him as the legitimate Austrian Chancellor and his cabinet as the legitimate

---

1   Maier, *Drama*, p. 370.
2   Heiber & Glantz, *Hitler and His Generals*, p. 733.

government. Renner took the opportunity to nullify the *Anschluss* and reinstate the constitution of 1920. The Austrians declared it to be Independence Day.

But in his first speech Renner sounded more like a nationalist than a communist dupe. Instead of blasting the Nazis he mostly let loose on the Austrian Fascists and assured his listeners they would have no part in his government. He also prohibited Nazis; but not all Nazis, only the bigwigs. The little guys who only went along because they had to would be cut a break. The speech shocked the two living men who dictated the fate of millions at Yalta, namely Churchill and Stalin, but for entirely different reasons. If Stalin had been expecting a puppet he got something entirely different.

6. SS-Panzerarmee

Lothar Rendulic's headquarters received a new *Führerbefehl* to be enacted immediately. *Heeresgruppe Ostmark* was ordered to reconnoiter and prepare to establish a National Redoubt! At the very end of the war, with the Russians within sight of his bunker, Hitler decided it was time to think about fortifying the Alps. This was like ordering a fence built around a herd of stampeding horses.

Rendulic's reaction isn't known, but that of Sepp Dietrich is. When an *Oberstleutnant* phoned the headquarters of *6. SS-Panzerarmee* wanting to cooperate on this fantastic project, "we listened to him in a friendly way – and only shook our heads. The headquarters of *6. [SS] Panzer Army* did nothing."[3]

I SS-Panzerkorps

Any hope that Marshal Tolbukhin might have achieved all of his goals in east-central Austria were dashed when fighting erupted along the corps' entire line. The end of the war was plain for all to see, and while the relatively static nature of the front has since inspired the idea that once Vienna fell the fighting in Austria slackened off, those who lived through it know better. Combat remained as fierce as ever in the high mountains. Men continued dying by the hundreds and thousands.

10. Fallschirmjäger-Division

The *6. SS-Panzerarmee* was ordered to send the paratroopers north to *Heeresgruppe Mitte* with the highest priority. Hitler's fantasy of relieving Berlin continued to damage his field armies. The division would still be in transport when Hitler put the barrel of his Walther PPK against his temple and pulled the trigger.

12. SS-Panzer-Division Hitlerjugend

Replacing the *10. Fallschirmjäger-Division* was *Hitlerjugend*, which had begun the process of transferring to west of the Traisen River the day before. This was an especially dangerous moment for all of the corps, since the paratroopers withdrew before the *Hitlerjugend* men were in place. Fortunately for the Germans, the Russians didn't launch what could have been a devastating attack. For a brief period the sector remained quiet.

---

3   Maier, *Drama*, p. 370.

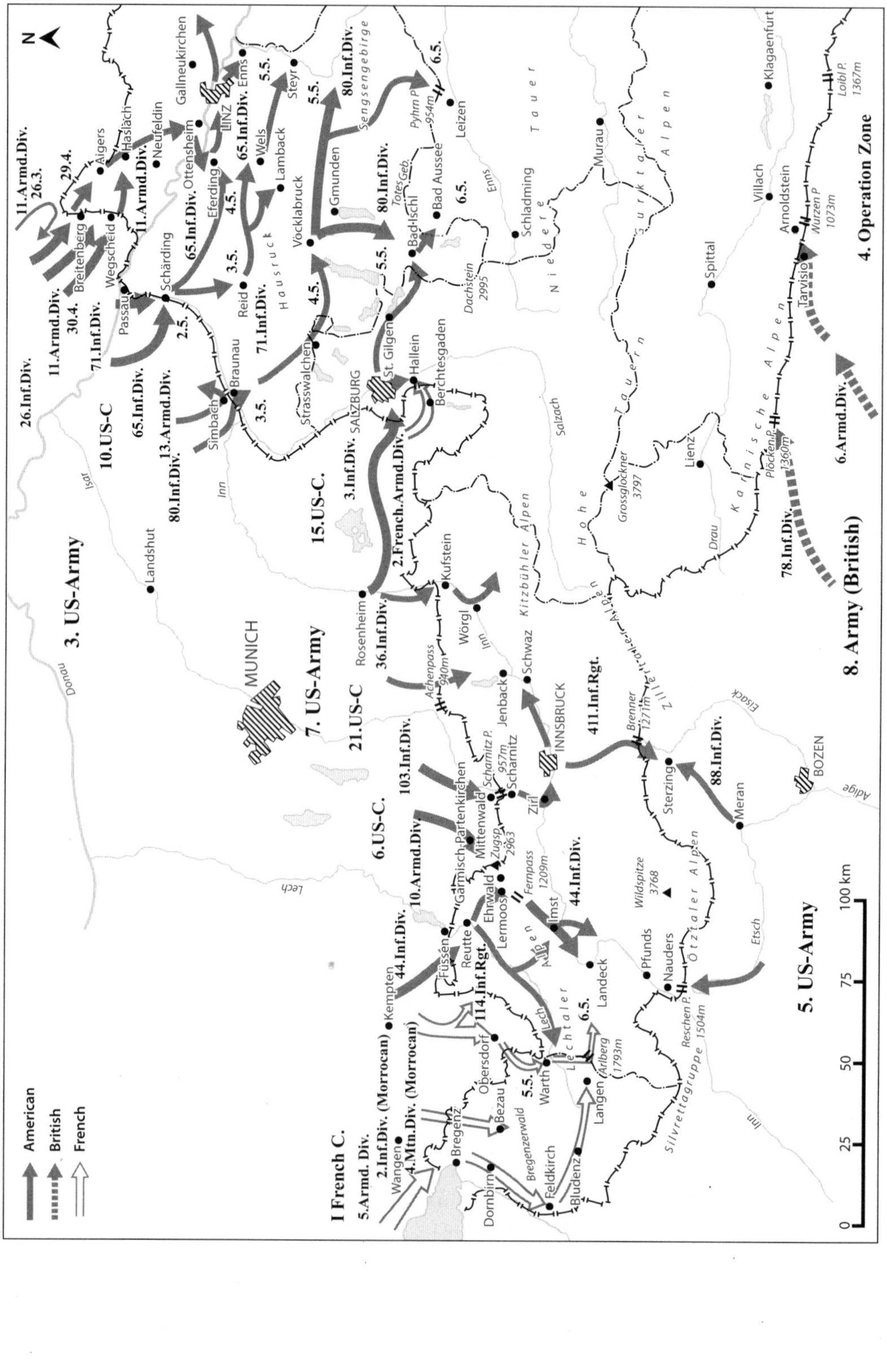

Map 9 American, British and French advances into South and West Austria.

Most of the division's *Kampfgruppen* were dissolved and the men returned to their parent units, although a few remained in existence, such as *SS-Kampfgruppe Grossjohann*. Patrols were sent out to scout the new positions and noted a few Russian movements, including one breakthrough toward Tradigist on 28 April. The *Fallschirmjägers* wiped that out with a counterattack before finally leaving the area.

What is truly amazing about this period is that once *Hitlerjugend* arrived on the corps' left flank it began to receive replacements. With the war virtually over men were still being funneled into the *Waffen-SS* divisions. Some were the division's own wounded who wanted to end the war with their brothers-in-arms, but most were the now-usual untrained men from various other *Wehrmacht* branches. Basic ground-combat training began immediately. For the veterans it was a chance to repair equipment, sleep and maybe take a bath.

SS-Kampfgruppe Peiper

Although effectively part of the *LAH* again, Peiper still held his independent command on the left flank in the Rotheau area. Exact numbers are impossible now to estimate, but the German line was thin. Even the precious few panzers had to be exposed at the front of the defense, often without infantry support, and without much ammunition. The Russians came, but not in strength, instead turning to infiltration tactics. Sometimes these worked but usually not, leaving the Germans in possession of the roads, without possession of which no advance could be sustained for long. But if this seems like the fighting had died down, that was only true of the scale. The nasty war in the mountains kept going between small groups in dozens of firefights all through the day.

Kampfgruppe 1. SS-Panzer-Division Leibstandarte Adolf Hitler

After a lull the day before the Russians closed up to the new German main line of resistance across its entire front and launched immediate attacks. One mile southwest of Kleinzell a company from the division's panzer regiment had dug in on a mountain called the Hochstaff. Intense mortar fire drove them back without need of an infantry attack.

Elsewhere the four or five remaining panzers were held back as a reserve. The rugged country gave few opportunities for using panzers anyway, but with inadequate infantry support and ammunition limited to whatever was on hand, the risk of using them in the front lines was deemed too great. The shortage of *Panzergrenadiers* had become so acute that the remainder of the supply company was added to the security company as an extra platoon, with 6 officers and 35 men.[4]

Kampfgruppe 356. Infanterie-Division

The fall of the towns along *I SS-Panzerkorps'* eastern flank had a domino effect on all of those to the south, and on 27 April it was Markt Piesting's turn. For more than three weeks *Kampfgruppe 356. Infanterie-Division* held the town against all assaults, but the loss of Pottenstein outflanked the defenders to the north and left only Berndorf protecting that flank. It was defended by the *Kampfgruppe 12. SS-Panzer-Division Hitlerjugend*, but they too were on the brink of being surrounded.

---

4 Tiemann, *The Leibstandarte IV/2*, p. 312.

Both towns now stood echeloned far forward at the end of a narrowing strip of land, and the time had come to withdraw. During the battle for Markt Piesting 16 civilians had died, more than 40 houses had been destroyed or damaged and two bridges demolished. The old Seiser Mill, built in the 19th Century, also saw heavy damage from the fighting, as did the ruins of the 12th-Century castle at Starhemberg. High up on a mountain, the Germans used it as an observation point and the Russians countered with day after day of artillery fire to drive them out.

* * *

Meanwhile, at Enns, Ernst Kaltenbrunner met with *Generaloberst* Rendulic about supply problems. Details of the meeting are unknown, but by this point there wasn't much left to say. If you didn't already have something on hand, it wasn't likely that you were going to get it. Sometime around 27 or 28 April, in a desperate bid to find a way to set up his independent Austrian government, Kaltenbrunner later told interrogators that he met with *Generalfeldmarschall* Kesselring and *Generalleutnant* August Winter across the border at Königssee in southern Germany. Winter was the ranking officer at *Führungsstab Süd*, High Command South. By this point, however, there wasn't much left to organize and nothing came of the meeting.[5]

A curious postscript to this day was that Himmler telegraphed Kaltenbrunner demanding to know what tasks Bormann had given him and why he was performing them. Himmler had long feared his number two man, but Hitler trusted Kaltenbrunner and the two men had a close relationship. If Kaltenbrunner replied to Himmler's queries those answers have been lost, and soon thereafter Himmler had other things to worry about anyway. The next night Hitler learned of his secret negotiations with the Allies, stripped him of all Party titles and authority, and ordered his arrest.

Volks-Werfer-Brigade 19

OKH ordered the dissolution of *Volks-Werfer-Brigaden 17* and *19*, with both folded into a reformed *Volks-Werfer-Regiment 19*. The *Oberkommando des Heeres*, High Command of the Army, was essentially Hitler himself as Commander in Chief of the Army. His decisions went through the Chief of the General Staff, General of Infantry Hans Krebs, and were then disseminated to whatever parts of the Army to which it applied. The mechanisms and personnel to distribute and carry out these orders were located in a sprawling complex at Zossen.

But by this time the Germans had lost Zossen, the purpose-built command center and largest communications complex in Europe. It was located twenty miles south of Berlin. That means that with the Russians closing in on the Reichstag, and artillery shaking concrete dust out of the roof of the *Führerbunker* onto his maps, Hitler found time to worry about what was essentially a trivial matter, and had the order transmitted via the bunker switchboard which was connected to the outside world by an antenna held aloft by a balloon.

6. Armee

The dangerous bulge in the German lines south of the Semmering Pass had been reduced thanks to the multi-pronged counterattacks, which had made excellent progress. But with the offensive's primary assault force, *117. Jäger-Division*, no longer available, further attacks had to be called off.

Kampfgruppe Raithel

During the night of 27-28 April the men of *Luftwaffeneinheit ABK-Z* attacked the Harterkogel, with fire support by an 88mm *Flak* gun that still had ammunition. This was the mixed company of Hungarian fliers with German and Hungarian ground crew and German officers. Against all odds the attack succeeded and the Russians retreated back to the Feistritzsattel. The *Luftwaffe* Company lost four men wounded and four more missing, including three Hungarians.

This attack stabilized the German front and deprived the Russians of their highest point in the area. Someone gave the company a 20mm *Flak* gun, which they mounted on the nearby Kleine Pfaffen, a smaller mountain, and one of the Hungarians operated it. This helped when a Russian counterattack hit their southern flank, killing one man before it was driven off. By good fortune, a folder with upcoming Russian plans was left on the battlefield.

The Russians continued their attacks in the area until the end of the war. But more constant even than those assaults was the incessant mortar fire, which never let up.

1. Volks-Grenadier-Division

Because of the transfer of *117. Jäger-Division*, most of the division had moved approximately 40 miles north from the area of Fürstenfeld and now held a defensive line based on the Hochwechsel. *Generalmajor* Kreppl hadn't forgotten how tired his men were and gave them every chance to rest, but torrential rains made life miserable for everyone. And once they arrived at their new positions field fortifications had to be built, rifle trenches dug and fields of fire cleared. Digging on steep slopes in heavy rain was especially miserable.

The division was now so far north it was subordinated to *I SS-Panzerkorps*. Beginning at the 5,200 feet-high Schöberlriegel on the north, the division's front ran south to the area of Mönichwald. The highest point was the area known as the Hochwechsel, part of the Wechsel mountain range. Although not part of the Alps themselves, they were part of what is called the Pre-Alps. The slopes were mostly covered in dense forest, with clear meadows here and there, the ideal killing fields.

The division's redeployment caught the Russians by surprise. The *Jägers'* withdrawal and *Gebirgsjäger* takeover left them scrambling for a response, giving the new defenders at least a 24-hour respite before the first Russian units closed on them.

Atop the Hochwechsel a bicycle and a *Pionier* platoon waited on regular mountain troops to take over, but in the meantime they hunted down individual Russians who had stayed behind when their units retreated. Late in the afternoon elements of *III./Gebirgsjäger-Regiment 99* took over just in time to smash the first Russian counterattacks, inflicting heavy losses. Other enemy columns heading southwest from Gloggnitz and through the mountains to Ratten were stopped cold by the *Gebirgsjägers* blocking the road.

2. Panzerarmee

Desperation jumped out from the order received by the army at 7:45 p.m. to immediately bring *9. SS-Panzer-Division Hohenstaufen* up to full strength using replacements. Once that was done, the division was to be transferred to *Heeresgruppe Mitte* with the highest priority, even more than food or ammunition.

28

Saturday, 28 April

Berlin

Der treu Heinrich, 'loyal Heinrich', Hitler's most trustworthy paladin, had secretly been negotiating Germany's surrender with the Allies through the Deputy Chief of the Swedish Red Cross, Count Folke Bernadotte. On 28 April the BBC broadcast news of the negotiations.

Hitler went berserk. He stripped Himmler of all offices, threw him out of the Nazi Party and ordered his arrest. This had no practical effect, since his SS guards kept Himmler safe and the *Waffen-SS* had problems of their own. When *Grossadmiral* Dönitz formed his government after Hitler's death, Himmler was told there was no place for him.

Heeresgruppe Ostmark
8. Armee

The Russian offensive toward Brno made progress as the Germans ran out of artillery and tank ammunition, not to mention fuel and men. Although not part of his defensive concern, *General der Gebirgstruppe* Kreysing had to worry about his army's denuded left flank. Fighting along his entire front had become desultory, as even patrols who encountered the enemy were reticent to engage in a firefight.

* * *

Within two days Adolf Hitler would be dead; within two weeks, the war itself would be over. On the southern end of the Russian front the great rush forward of Second and Third Ukrainian Fronts had run its course, sputtering out as burned-out assault units ran out of men, supplies and time. Yet despite there being little reason to continue attacking, continue the Russians did, both suffering and inflicting heavy casualties. And on 28 April they mortally wounded the greatest tank ace who ever lived.

* * *

Kurt Knispel had survived nearly four years of war, the last two as a member of *Schwere-Panzer-Abteilung 503*, one of the fire brigades that were counted on to spearhead a breakthrough or plug a hole in the front, and throughout every battle he had been the most deadly warrior on the field. By 28 April Knispel had 168 confirmed kills, including a T-34 destroyed at the unbelievable range of 3,000 meters. First in a Tiger I and then in a Tiger II, Knispel played havoc with both the Russians and with the Nazis; he wore his hair much longer than regulations allowed and even sported a beard. He won every award the Germans could offer, from the Iron Cross First Class to the Tank Assault Badge in Gold, except for the Knight's Cross; while nominated for the Knight's Cross on four occasions, Knispel's cavalier attitude toward both his superiors and military honors kept him from ever receiving the award. His utter disregard for Army rules even saw him go so far as to assault a superior officer who was mistreating Russian POWs, a grave offense in any army, and only his stellar service record kept him out of a military prison or penal battalion. In one action his Tiger reportedly took 24 hits without being destroyed.

There are two predominant theories about the date and manner of his death. The first story comes from one of Knispel's fellow soldiers in the *Schwere-Panzer-Abteilung 503*. On 28 April, Knispel and his unit were defending the small town of Vrbovec in old Czechoslovakia, less than two miles south of Znojmo near the Austrian border and about 47 miles north-northwest of Vienna. Knispel's tank reportedly took a penetrating hit and he was severely wounded in the stomach. Taken to a nearby field hospital in Vrbovecu, he died the next day, the same day that Hitler and Eva Braun were married in the dank corridor of the *Führerbunker*.

The other version comes from the diary of *Hauptmann* von Diest-Körbera, commander of *Schwere-Panzer-Abteilung 503* which states: "On 30 April 1945 between Nová Ves and Vlasatice we knocked off several Russian attack(s) and destroyed 10 Russian tanks. Unfortunately we lost 2 *Königstigers* with their commanders – Feldwebel Knispel and Feldwebel Skoda."[1] As the Russians launched an assault to capture Vrbovec, the two commanders were killed fending off the attack. What seems possible, if not probable, is that the date when the two Tigers were lost was actually 29 April, not 28 April; that Knispel died the next day, 30 April, and in the confusion of the last days of fighting the dates were mixed up in accounts. He was 23 years old.

The mass grave where Knispel's body was found is shaded now by an apple orchard. Knispel was the only *Wehrmacht* non-commissioned officer ever mentioned in an army communiqué and for years the exact place of his burial was unknown. In the spring of 2013, however, the news broke that his body had been found and identified near Vrbovec, both by the tattoo on his neck, something else of which his superiors disapproved, and by his metallic identification tag. His remains were exhumed for reburial in the German section of the Military Graveyard in Brno. Knispel's legacy shows that even in the German *Heer* of the Third Reich, where draconian punishments routinely awaited those who did not follow orders and individualism was virtually a criminal offense, men of high character could and did fight for their country in the most honorable traditions of military warfare, while simultaneously irritating the hell out of the Nazis.

I SS-Panzerkorps

Postwar depictions of German soldiers as robotic fanatics who would rather die than surrender were as inaccurate as those portraying all Russian soldiers as bloodthirsty communist rapists. There were some of those in both armies, it's true, but for the most part the war was fought by men who would rather have been anywhere except in combat.

The premier *Waffen-SS* divisions had cultivated an *esprit de corps* to rival or exceed that of any other military in the world. But the vast majority of the men who fleshed out those divisions when they were formed had long since fallen, as had their replacements, and the next generation, and the one after that. The depleted ranks in late April 1945 had been filled out by conscripts who'd had no choice but to join the *Waffen-SS*, and that ate at the core of what is most important to combat troops, namely trust in your comrades.

The front lines of *I SS-Panzerkorps* were not a series of adjoining trenches with dugouts, breastworks and firing pits. Indeed, the words 'front lines' are misleading, as there weren't enough men left for that sort of defense. Instead, there were camouflaged bunkers made from logs, branches

1   Jan S. (2013), 'Kurt Knispel, a tank ace with 168-195 kills found in CZ', <http://www.warrelics.eu/forum/battlefield-archaeology/kurt-knispel-a-tank-ace-with-168-195-kills-found-in-cz-289019/>, (Accessed 25 April 2013).

and leaves. In the valleys the defenders built roadblocks from whatever was nearby, or fortified towns through which the road might pass. A typical bunker might have five or eight men in rifle pits and an MG-42 machine gun behind some thick logs. Within eyesight there was perhaps another such position so they could be mutually supporting. In between was open country. The best description for this type of defense was not front lines, but main line of resistance.

In prior times the sight of German soldiers who were personally unknown to the men manning the main line of resistance would have been a welcome sight. In the elite world of the *Waffen-SS*, any SS man was your comrade, regardless whether you knew him or not. But those days were over. Now suspicion fell on anyone who wasn't part of your squad or platoon: "Comradeship, trust, obedience and even loyalty only existed where people knew each other…if no one believed in 'final victory', one only felt safe 'at home' within his own group."[2] Among those men who did know each other, however, the bond had never been tighter.

12. SS-Panzer-Division Hitlerjugend

For the first time since 4 March, the day before *Hitlerjugend* moved up to the start line for *Unternehmen Frühlingserwachen*, the SS men woke up without facing imminent combat. German casualties had been terrible in the previous seven weeks, but the Russians had suffered even worse and could no longer attack everywhere at once. So as the Americans closed in from the west, and the Russians hammered the *LAH* to the east, the men of *Hitlerjugend* reveled in a rare day of relative quiet.

Kampfgruppe 1. SS-Panzer-Division Leibstandarte Adolf Hitler

The catastrophic scale of casualties in the previous seven weeks left the division so short of manpower that many strongpoints were isolated, without another German position anywhere close. Therefore, communications with the command post were essential. This duty fell on the *Nachrichten-Abteilung-SS Leibstandarte Adolf Hitler*, *LAH*'s signals battalion, which in German parlance was the part of the division charged with maintaining internal communication links. And this usually meant running telephone cables, since radio signals could be intercepted.

Such cables were often cut during combat, either intentionally by the enemy or by mortar, artillery or rocket explosions. Repairing those breaks under fire was critical for commanding officers to control the battle. When a position wasn't within sight of other defenders it became even more crucial for it to be in constant contact with headquarters. If it was overrun and nobody knew it, the entire defensive position could be destroyed.

And yet the *LAH*'s signals battalion had been combed out for manpower just like the other non-combat units, such as supply or security. Maintaining vital communications became an exhausting and never-ending job, which was complicated by the scarcity of cables, handsets and other vital equipment.

* * *

Along the entire German front lines, from *6. SS-Panzerarmee* through *6. Armee* to *2. Panzerarmee*, the conditions were similar. With the end of the war now in sight the ferocity of the fighting all along the German front increased to levels rarely seen during the entire Russo-German war. The

---

2   Tiemann, *The Leibstandarte IV/2*, p. 314.

scale of mortar, Katyusha and artillery fire, already some of the worst of the war, increased even more. Russian attacks bordered on suicidal at times, charging through rifle and automatic weapons fire and frequently getting into the German positions, which led to hand-to-hand fighting. Instead of decreasing as the war wound down, the flow of blood increased.

Nor did the spring weather have much effect in the mountains, where winter lingered. Fresh snow and sleet occasionally fell on the old packed snow; other times it was rain. A thick carpet of rotting branches and leaves retained moisture and kept everything wet. Freezing nighttime temperatures made sleeping difficult.

Few hard numbers are now available to define the pace of casualties, but extrapolation from what we have is possible. As mentioned above, on the previous day, with no supplies coming in, the supply company formed a platoon to join the security company at the main line of resistance. Its original strength had been six officers and 35 men, but after the fighting on 27 April that had fallen to four officers and 23 men. Two officers and 12 men had therefore died, been wounded or captured on 27 April, one-third of the platoon's original number.

Heavy attacks struck their positions on 28 April. Fighting came down to fists, knives, rocks and kicks. The Russians were finally driven off, leaving a carpet of dead and dying on the mountain slope, but the platoon's casualties totaled three killed, two missing and 17 wounded. Forty-one men marched into battle the day before, and twenty-four hours later only one officer and four men remained unhurt.

After the shooting stopped the wounded then had to be evacuated down steep, icy and rock-strewn slopes so they could be taken to the nearest aid station. With so few men left, that meant instead of medical personnel coming to get those injured, some of the survivors had to stay watchful in the bunkers and trenches while others had to try and carry the wounded to safety. They had to do this while exhausted, sleep-deprived and hungry. The scenario repeated itself over and over again.[3]

6. Armee

If General Eisenhower had been hoaxed by Goebbels' propaganda into changing the entire strategic thrust of the Allied armies, the Russians believed a different set of lies as deeply as Ike had. Everywhere along the entire front line, in the zones occupied by the Red Army, the population was put to work digging defensive fortifications. The belief that the Western Allies would soon join with Nazi Germany in a war against the USSR had found fertile soil in Stalin's paranoid mind, and he was determined to hang onto every bit of ground that his armies had won. This also goes a long way in explaining why Third Ukrainian Front kept attacking until the very end of the war.

Along with digging trenches and anti-tank ditches, loudspeaker trucks assailed the Germans with pleas not to "dash madly into a new war. Come over to the Red Army!"[4] The same rumors were rife throughout the region among civilians, and this reinforced the Russian belief. Indeed, Sepp Dietrich considered the potential of these broadcasts so dangerous that a pamphlet was issued throughout 6. SS-Panzerarmee urging his men to stand fast and not be swayed by false promises.

3   Tiemann, *The Leibstandarte IV/2*, p. 313.
4   Tiemann, *The Leibstandarte IV/2*, p. 314.

1. Volks-Gebirgs-Division

In the center of the *6. Armee* front ferocious combat raged atop the Hochwechsel. The summit was mostly bare, with trees on the lower slopes, giving whoever possessed it clear fields of fire in all directions. The Russians recaptured it during the day, but that night it changed hands again as the Germans took it back, capturing eight 76mm *PAKs* in the process. Even better, they took huge amounts of ammunition for the guns, which greatly augmented the firepower of *Gebirgsjager-Regiment 99*.[5]

Kampfgruppe 3. Panzer-Division

The rear-area security details formed on 24 April by all units of the army came together for a joint operation. Sweeping through the area where the latest partisan activity had been reported, they picked up fourteen escaped British prisoners-of-war and, ominously, one member of *Panzergrenadier-Regiment 394* who had deserted.

Desertion had become a serious problem in every unit along the front, despite roadblocks from the SS and the *Feldgendarmerie*, the Field Police. There was only one punishment for men caught behind the lines without specific orders: immediate execution. Deserting comrades in battle was not only breaking the oath all soldiers took to Hitler, it was a betrayal of men they'd fought beside, sometimes for years. Among veterans there was no greater crime. Despite this, and despite knowing their fate if caught, desertions continued to rise as the war went on.

2. Panzerarmee
9. SS-Panzer-Division Hohenstaufen

For other units, including *9. SS-Panzer-Division Hohenstaufen*, the past fortnight had been relatively peaceful.. Flush with new members because of Hitler's order for it to be rebuilt with top priority, the division had not only received replacements yet again but became something of a collection point for broken *Wehrmacht* units and stragglers. It was once again over-strength, despite the horrific losses suffered in Hungary. On 28 April it received orders to move to Amstetten, some 110 miles away from its position at Radkersburg. It had been filled up based on an order from Hitler, and was supposed to be sent with all possible speed to the northern flank of *Heeresgruppe Mitte* for use in the relief of Berlin, but never got out of Austria.

* * *

German observers noticed that something strange began to happen on Third Ukrainian Front's left flank. The Russians impressed the local population into beginning construction of a 12 mile-deep defensive belt behind their lines. No one knew why, because the Germans were in no position to attack, but then word spread of the Russian harangues and leaflets telling the Germans not to join the Western Allies, and the men put two and two together. It could only have meant there was truth to the rumors of them joining the Americans and British in a war against the Russians![6]

---

5   Brettner, *Die Letzten Kämpfe*, p. 58.
6   Vavra and Rossiwall, *Die Letzten Tage, 25 April – 1 Mai, 1945*, <https://www.museumnoe.at/de/das-museum/blog/25-april-1-mai-1945> (Accessed 23 July 2018).

Obviously Stalin considered the joining of the Western Allies with the Germans a real possibility, and means that Churchill's top secret Operation Unthinkable probably wasn't the only contingency drawn up in case of war between the Soviet Union and its erstwhile friends. It appears that Stalin wasn't taking any chances either.

The Americans

In their forest camp on the banks of the Inn River, the group of American, French and Belgian POWs from *Stalag 17B* received Canadian Red Cross packages, one for every five men. Few guards were left. Those that remained were most likely glad to have a non-combat duty and a reason to wait for the Americans to show up. As the executions at Raxenberg showed, nobody was safe as long as the Gestapo or SS could still get their hands on you.

* * *

In western Austria, the Tyrolean lake country between Vils and the German border town of Pfronten was a kaleidoscope of greens in every tint and hue imaginable, contrasted by fields that were splashed with white, red and yellow flowers like bold abstract brushstrokes. The view from peaks around the little towns showed the nearby Weissensee shimmering in the spring sunshine. An observer there would have noted the incredible blue tint of the water as it reflected the clear sky overhead. And if he or she had been observant enough, they might have seen the columns of American vehicles of the 103rd Infantry Division pouring into Austria.

29

Sunday, 29 April

Berlin

During the First World War, Adolf Hitler did something that was very unusual for enlisted men; he won the Iron Cross First Class for bravery. That medal may have been the most important item he owned. He only wore three items on his uniform coat: his Nazi Party pen, wound badge and Iron Cross. In 1945, as Russian shells blasted the Reich Chancellery building and the explosions echoed through the *Führerbunker*, he donned that beloved medal before marrying Eva Braun. She was delighted at finally becoming *Frau* Hitler, but for him taking a wife was an admission that it was all over. The war was lost and, with the Russians only a few hundred yards away, the time had come to die.

After dictating his will and political testament, he spent his last night asking for the exact location of *General der Panzertruppe* Walther Wenck's *12. Armee* and of *Kampfgruppe Steiner*. The Russians' next target was the Reichstag, with units of the Red Army closing in from all directions. Steiner's attack had never been possible. Wenck's army made great progress toward the capital, getting so far as Postdam before being stopped. Wenck then informed *Generalfeldmarschall* Keitel that his army couldn't continue the relief attack toward Berlin, and Keitel gave him permission to call it off. And so while Hitler was still in the bunker his last questions went unanswered, because nobody was coming to his rescue.

* * *

In one of the final official acts of his life, Hitler named *Gauleiter* of the Tyrol and Vorarlberg, Franz Hofer, as *Reichverteidigungskommissar der Alpenfestung*, Reich Defense Commissar for the Alpine Fortress, aka the National Redoubt. Hofer was instructed to turn Innsbruck into the capital of the fortress complex Eisenhower had feared for so long. Six months after he'd submitted his idea, the *Führer* had given him the green light. But Hitler only had hours to live and Hofer only four days before being captured by an OSS agent, so beyond pleasing the *Gauleiter* immensely this edict had no practical effect.

Caserta, Italy

Operation Sunrise, the surrender of all German forces in Italy, was about to come to fruition. After months of secret negotiations, and without Hitler's permission, German plenipotentiaries *Oberst* Viktor von Schweinitz and *SS-Sturmbannführer* Eugen Wenner signed the surrender of all forces under the command of the *Oberbefehlhaber Südwest, Generaloberst* Heinrich von Vietinghoff. Included in the surrender was *Heeresgruppe C*, nearly a million men in northern Italy. The surrender would take effect on 2 May. Nobody knew about this in advance, and this left the entire southern flank of *Heeresgruppe Ostmark* open, with the rear of *2. Panzerarmee* threatened immediately.

Many high-ranking Nazis had their fingers in the Sunrise pie, including Ernst Kaltenbrunner's deputy *SS-Sturmbannführer* Wilhelm Höttl as well as Kaltenbrunner himself, and *Gauleiter* Franz

Hofer of the Tyrol and Vorarlberg. *Generalfeldmarschall* Albert Kesselring, von Vietinghoff's direct superior, was aware of the negotiations but not directly part of them, preferring to play both sides in case the whole thing blew up. The point man was *SS-Obergruppenführer* Karl Wolff.

SS-Panzergrenadier-Regiment Deutschland

By the end of April only *SS-Panzergrenadier-Regiment Deutschland* remained under *Heeresgruppe Süd*'s command, with the rest of *2. SS-Panzer-Division Das Reich* having moved north for a counterattack to relieve Berlin. The regiment had remained at Passau for more than a week, and still held its blocking position west of the city. On 29 April orders arrived to move into Eferding, because American forces were moving in east of Passau on the north bank of the Danube. The SS men were ordered to stop them.

Replacing the *Waffen-SS* at the blocking position were some *Volkssturm* and Hitler Youth. The American 65th Infantry Division recognized this and attacked immediately, throwing the newcomers back into Passau. Those defeated and demoralized old men and boys now became its primary defenders. North of the city it was protected by 150 or so Hitler Youth and a few stragglers from *SS-Panzerjäger-Regiment Oberdonau*.

487. Ausbildungs-und-Ersatz-Division

The *487. Ausbildungs-und-Ersatz-Division* now took over defense of Passau. Commanded by *Generalmajor* Gustav Wagner, not to be confused with *SS-Oberscharführer* Gustav Wagner of Sobibór death camp infamy, the division had been established in 1942 at Linz, to recruit and train men from northern Austria for the Army. Wagner won the Knight's Cross in 1941 and had an excellent reputation. However, his command lacked heavy weapons and took on the defense of a wide area. South of the Danube it dug in on the east bank of the Inn River from Braunau to Passau.

The division's right flank north of the Danube had held a line up to Breitenberg, but that line had been driven backward by the US 11th Armored Division until by 2 May its front line extended from Neufelden through Haslach an der Mühl to Aigen im Mühlkreis. This left the part of the division south of the Danube with an open right flank all the way from Passau to Aschach an der Donau, a distance of 36 miles. The only thing preventing the Americans from attacking the Germans holding the line of the Inn River from behind was the Danube itself.

* * *

To the north Patton's Third Army prepared for battle in Austria. The 11th Armored Division moved toward the border north of Passau along several axes of advance, and its 21st Armored Infantry Battalion reached the area before Breitenberg and dismounted in preparation for an attack on Passau. The Americans had been told that the *Waffen-SS* formed a strong defensive line there, but were unaware that *Deutschland* pulled out during the day, so strong reconnaissance groups were sent to probe the German defenses. Two actions on the outskirts of the city illustrate the disparity in combat effectiveness of the opposing forces at this time.

One of the battalion's patrols came across a dug-in German company. Using bayonets and hand grenades they crushed the Germans, killing 25 and making 100 more prisoners, with apparently no American casualties. In the second incident, elsewhere another patrol group faced one of the few Mark IVs still operational near Kringell, close to Passau on the north but over the border in Germany. At 2,000 yards range a brand-new American M-26 Pershing used its powerful 90mm cannon to destroy the German panzer. The war ended before it could have any real effect on the fighting, but that incident clearly indicates the yawning gap between the obsolescent Mark IV and the newest American tanks.[1]

Regardless of where the panzer came from, the Germans had to be either a *Volkssturm* unit whose identity is lost to history, or from the *487. Ausbildungs-und-Ersatz-Division*.

6. SS-Panzerarmee

Reconnaissance patrols were sent west past Eferding to find the American spearheads. If they made contact, Sepp Dietrich ordered his units to withdraw without a fight.

Korps von Bünau

The German war machine still functioned, after a fashion, but growing disorganization generated bizarre events. One example came on 29 April when six factory-fresh Tiger IIs joined *Korps von Bünau* as an independent company with no unit designation. Despite there being heavy panzer battalions equipped with Tiger IIs in the immediate vicinity, the machines were given to the closest headquarters that would take them. One can visualize a company representative for the *Nibelungenwerke* handing a clipboard to one of von Bünau's officers acknowledging receipt of the panzers, and sighing in relief after the transaction was finished. Now they were somebody else's problem.

Kampfgruppe 12. SS-Panzer-Division Hitlerjugend

Despite the withdrawal of the *Fallschirmjägers* and the insertion of the *Hitlerjugend* men, the Russians didn't attack during the period of changeover, when there had been a certain amount of confusion that always followed such a switch. The Russians had observation posts watching most of the German line, but did nothing to take advantage of the situation. It was an opportunity lost for the Russians, as most of the *10. Fallschirmjäger-Division* wasn't officially relieved until late on 29 April.

SS-Panzergrenadier-Regiment 25 deployed on the right flank near Eschenau, one mile west of Traisen. *SS-Kampfgruppe Grossjohann* set up on their right in the direction of Eschenau to the southeast. The rest of the division moved in to the left of the *Panzergrenadiers*, and even long-detached *SS-Kampfgruppe Chemnitz*, which had been fighting near Ober-Grabendorf for nearly two weeks, was ordered to rejoin *SS-Panzer-Regiment 12*.

Regardless of the depleted ranks being filled by new conscripts, and the increased cohesion that came from re-assembling the scattered elements of the division's component units, the combat power of a division short on everything needed to fight a modern war was barely increased. It helped to rest, but empty bellies made that hard. It helped boost the men's morale to see familiar faces, but weakened it at the realization of all the faces they would never see again. Cleaning weapons only mattered if there was ammunition for them once they were cleaned. Repairing panzers was useless if they had no fuel. If it came to one final fight then *Hitlerjugend* would do its best, but with everything it didn't have, that wouldn't count for much.

---

1   The 11th Armored Division Legacy Group, '21st Armored Infantry Battalion (AIB)', (11th Armored Division Association), <http://www.11tharmoreddivision.com/history/21st_AIB.html>, (Accessed 22 June 2018).

Kampfgruppe 1. SS-Panzer-Division Leibstandarte Adolf Hitler

After the terrible combat of the day before, on 29 April fighting was restricted to aggressive Russian patrols and harassing mortar fire. The troops' biggest enemy was the cold and snow, which seemed more like winter than spring. With inadequate food to replace the calories burned up by fighting, digging and shivering, the men grew thinner by the day. Along the entire front the German defenders were reaching the limits of human endurance.

The line still had a bulge where it veered east around Ratheau. In order to shorten this and free up troops, preparations were made to withdraw the forward elements even more. Most of the remaining mobile units not part of *SS-Kampfgruppe Peiper* withdrew to the area near Schwarzenbach an der Pielach, including the panzer regiment, *Panzergrenadiers* in SPWs and the *Flak* batteries. This left the strongpoints on the main line of resistance more isolated than ever.

One situation that improved because of the division's redeployment was the ammunition supply. For some time it had first been sailed down the Danube on barges and then offloaded at Melk, where it would normally have been trucked to the division's supply dumps behind the front lines. But the scarcity of trucks and, even more so, fuel eliminated that option. Instead, it was loaded on horse-drawn wagons for the long trip to *Hitlerjugend*. One of Augustus' legions two millennia in the past would have recognized that method of supply. With the division's redeployment the trip to the front was much shorter.[2]

6. Armee
1. Volks-Gebirgs-Division

Positions atop the Hochwechsel were unlike many others in Austria in that the higher slopes were bare, not forested. Positions were built out of piled stones and even boulders. Where logs were felled to build a shelter the men could sleep in, high stones walls protected them from mortar and artillery splinters.

Fighting on the high slopes of both the Hochwechsel and the Gipfel, in the Wechsel Mountains, both peaks once again changed hands as the Russians took them back in heavy hand-to-hand fighting that raged all over the slopes. But this time the Germans didn't have enough men left for another counterattack. Indeed, gaps showed up between the battalions of *Gebirgsjäger-Regiment 99* and the first priority was plugging those, even as they fought off heavy Russian follow-on attacks. The regiment's *11. Kompanie* and *13. Kompanie*, in particular, suffered horrific losses in the fighting.

Simultaneously, more Russian attacks hit Mönichwald on the south end of the Wechsel Mountains. There the *III./Gebirgsjäger-Regiment 98,* supported by a squadron of *Sturmgeschütze*, defended the town against heavy attacks all day and into the night. The Russians never broke through.[3]

---

2   Meyer, *The 12th SS*, p. 497.
3   Brettner, *Die Letzten Kämpfe Band I*, p. 58.

The Americans and the French

The Allied invasion of western Austria proceeded along three main axes of attack. Lieutenant General Jean de Lattre de Tassigny's French First Army moved into the Vorarlberg and Lieutenant General Alexander Patch's Seventh Army drove toward Innsbruck, while Lieutenant General George S. Patton's Third Army made for Linz.

In Berlin Hitler's first military conference of the day reported the grim news that Russian spearheads had closed within a few hundred yards of the *Führerbunker*. The last grains of sand in Hitler's personal hourglass were falling to the bottom. Despite this imminent personal danger, Hitler knew the French 5th Armored Division had crossed into Austria.

After rampaging through the nation that had caused the French people five years of misery and despair, the French entered a nation they were officially told was friendly. Proper conduct and fair treatment of the population were the order of the day. And at first their welcome was warm. Nobody shot at them; they encountered no opposition. The locals looked at them with hopeful skepticism and wanted no more of war; at least for the most part.

The French 5th Armored Division spearheaded the French First Army's mission to drive south from Lake Constance and cut off all German forces defending the far western province of Voralsberg. Like the drive through southern Germany, resistance was sporadic and largely confined to isolated *Volkssturm* with small arms and a *Panzerfaust* or two; dangerous to the invaders only if the defenders had the motivation to stand and die, which few did.

But few isn't none, as the French soon discovered. On the far northwestern border with Germany, hugging the shoreline of Lake Constance, are the two small Austrian towns of Lochau and Bregenz. In 1945 they were connected by a narrow road along the lake's shoreline. And while the National Redoubt was almost entirely a myth, one of the only places that defenses had been erected was Bregenz. So as the French set off into Austria they found this roadway mined and covered by batteries of deadly 88mm guns.

Expecting no opposition, the French columns drove down what is now called the Bregenzer Strasse. Mines halted their advance and then the anti-tank guns stationed in Bregenz opened up. Shells ripped into the column and French casualties were heavy. Infuriated at seeing his men killed and wounded in the final days of the war, the French commander gave the Germans an ultimatum: surrender immediately or see Bregenz destroyed.

Emissaries from the Austrian resistance, along with medical staff, begged the French not to bombard the town. More than 3,000 wounded had been evacuated there and most of them would surely be killed, but the division commander refused to negotiate. He made it clear that he didn't care how many Germans died, but he would not risk his men in costly assaults. Talks went on for days. According to James Lucas, a 'stand or die' order from the *Führerbunker* ensured there would not be a peaceful ending to the situation.[4]

Heeresgruppe C

German units withdrawing north were chased and harassed as the Allies kept up the fight despite the Germans having already signed the surrender document. After six years of war, the British weren't taking any chances.

---

4   Lucas, *Last*, p. 201.

30

Monday, 30 April

Berlin

The time had come. For three years Hitler had watched the front lines roll inexorably backward toward Berlin. At one time in early December 1941, the closest Russian units had been 1,100 miles from the capital of the Reich, and large stretches of deep water separated *Festung Europa* from the Western Allies. Now, as fighting raged at Königsplatz and in the Tiergarten, and the Reichstag was the last fortified building between Hitler and the vengeful Russians, the front line was less than 600 yards away. One strong push and they could overrun the area of the *Führerbunker*, in the garden of the New Reich Chancellery. So for the one-time 'Master of Europe', the *Gröfaz*, the greatest warlord of all time, the time had come to die.

* * *

Hours after Hitler's death, 20-year-old Georg Hauner was discovered at his parent's home in Braunau am Inn, Hitler's hometown. Hauner was a deserter who'd been home on leave but never returned to his unit, and there was only one penalty for desertion: death. A court martial was called at the insistence of an *SS-Obersturmbannführer* and also by the Court Officer of the *Braunauer-Ersatz-Bataillon*, also known as *II./487 Ausbildungs-und-Ersatz-Division*, who was appointed chairman of the jury.

But in a shocking twist Hauner was not found guilty. Instead, his case was remanded to the division court of the *487. Ausbildungs-und-Ersatz-Division*, which was tantamount to an acquittal since the Americans were almost in Braunau. Clearly his fellow townsfolk didn't want him killed, but the unnamed *SS-Obersturmbannführer* wouldn't hear of it and dissolved the court martial. He then formed one of his own, which condemned Hauner to death within minutes. The SS officer then personally shot Hauner and had him buried where he fell.

But the grotesque events of Hitler's death day weren't over yet for his hometown. For the first and last time in the war, bombs fell on Braunau am Inn. Late at night a stick of bombs overshot the railway station and destroyed an air raid shelter, wiping out an entire family. A man injured in the attack died two days later. It was almost as if the town itself was being punished for producing the *Führer*, and for not stopping Hauner's execution.

Oberbefehlshaber Süd

Gauleiter Franz Hofer of the Tyrol and Vorarlberg knew all about *Unternehmen Sonnenaufgang*, Operation Sunrise, the surrender of German *Heeresgruppe C*, and had no intention of keeping quiet. The previous November he had sent a memorandum to Hitler regarding the construction of the National Redoubt, an incident that American intelligence used as evidence to prove the redoubt's existence. Even now, with enemies closing in on all sides, Hofer believed the existing German forces could hold out for months, or even years, in the Alps.

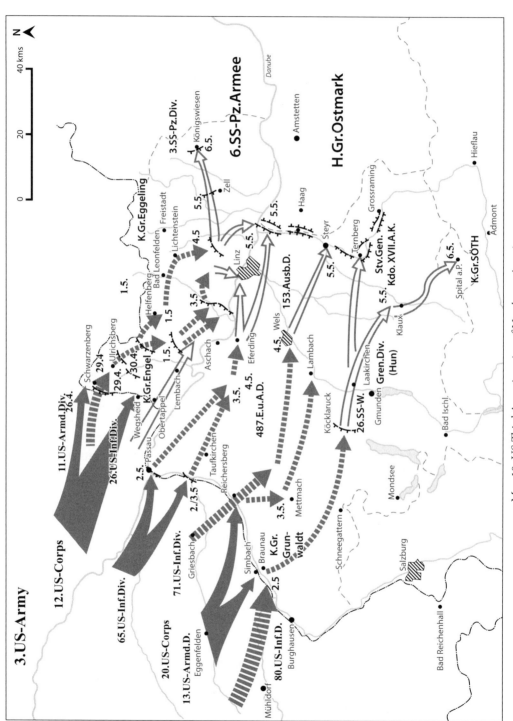

Map 10 US Third Army invasion of Northwest Austria.

Then he called *Generalfeldmarschall* Kesselring to discuss it. Kesselring knew he was walking a tightrope between allowing the plan to go forward and being shot for treason, so he pretended to be furious and phoned *Generaloberst* von Vietinghoff to relieve him of command. The two men argued for four hours until Kesselring finally reappointed him. In the meantime, squabbling between the Germans led to misunderstandings with the Americans, and that led to Italian partisan leaders who wanted their pound of flesh getting into the act, which in its turn led to on again, off again fighting.

But at this point the Allied armies weren't wasting time on niceties. The British Eighth Army was at the gates of Austria east of Trieste, near Udine and Verona, and the Germans either had to sign on the dotted line or see their armies ripped to shreds. The Germans signed.

8. Armee

While military officers, party bureaucrats, police and intelligence agents and various hangers-on all scrambled to find a way to avoid the consequences of their actions, the men at the front continued to fight and die. In the area of *8. Armee,* the defense of Brno had stiffened until the Russians suspended attacks due to excessively high casualties.

* * *

Throughout far southeastern Germany and western Austria the invaders were mostly welcomed, even by the *Waffen-SS*, but not always. As the Americans neared the railway station at Brno, *Kampfgruppe* from *25. Waffen-Grenadier-Division der SS Hunyadi* attacked and destroyed several Shermans, despite orders from their own high command not to do so. For the Americans it only reinforced the idea that everybody in the *Waffen-SS* was crazy.

To the east, at Stockerau, the exodus began. The city had been in the front lines for weeks by now and some of the townsfolk had slept in cellars for a month. Food was scarce, nobody had work to do anymore and life had devolved into nothing more than cowering and trembling under the endless shelling.

And now it was time to go.

As *8. Armee* prepared to pull out, with hordes of refugees that would follow in their footsteps, men between 15 and 60, plus women younger than 50, were ordered to evacuate along the *Au,* the flat wooded meadow near the bank of the Danube opposite the village of Greifensteiner. Even before the Nazis had left the area new underground political parties were being formed: three in the previous week. Everyone had known the end was near for weeks, but somehow it kept not ending.

Like so many places throughout the rump of the Reich, civil disobedience was the order of the day. There were many places in Stockerau where citizens helped *Wehrmacht* men shed their uniforms and slip into civilian clothes. Even military officers helped in the effort, despite the danger of doing so. The only Nazi to be feared now was the one pointing a gun at you, and there weren't many of those left.

Korps von Bünau

A surprise counterattack retook Ambach, south of Krems. This was probably carried out by *SS-Kampfgruppe-Trabandt III*, and reminded the Russians that the Germans could still be deadly.

* * *

Somewhere around this time *SS-Brigade Ney* was re-formed in eastern Styria, with its scattered elements coming back together and a total strength of some 4,921 men. Their armament was adequate, but just as with most units in the *Wehrmacht* they were missing some weapons and supplies. Any notion that the fighting had wound down in the closing days of the war is dispelled by the casualty figures for the brigade during those final weeks from the middle of April to the beginning of May: "472 killed, 32 missing and numerous wounded."[1]

* * *

With Berlin drowning in the Russian flood, the SS Main Office transferred control of *XVII Waffen-Armeekorps der SS (Ungarische)* to the Hungarian Defense Ministry, a ministry in a government without a country, commanding troops they ordered not to fight.

* * *

The *6. Panzer-Division* had fought from the first day of the war until the end was in plain sight. On 30 April, even as Adolf Hitler said goodbye to his staff and carried out his suicide in the *Führerbunker*, the division staff labored at doing a monthly report listing casualties and condition of personnel and equipment. Because of this effort we now know that in the course of its service from 27 November 1942, until that fateful April day, the division lost a total of 34,926 men killed, wounded, missing or sick.[2] In other words, more than 200 percent of its men became casualties in just two-and-a-half years of combat.

SS-Panzergrenadier-Regiment Deutschland

Deutschland pulled out of Passau and redeployed to Eferding, although three companies probably stayed behind at Passau. With the US 11th Armored Division moving on the north bank of the Danube, the river crossings at Eferding became critical to the defense and the only reliable unit available was *Deutschland*. The third oldest city in Austria was the home of Hitler's friend from his youth, August Kubizek, but aside from shipping docks nearby on the Danube, the little town's main value was the bridge spanning the river. *Deutschland* now had enemies coming from the west, north, east and, if you count the British crossing into Austria from Italy, from the south.

But in the confusion of the war's final days, nobody knew who might shot at whom. *Deutschland* no sooner moved into the Eferding area than it captured a company of Americans. Instead of sending them to a POW camp, however, the Germans took their weapons, released them and pointed to the west.[3]

487. Ausbildungs-und-Ersatz-Division

Although the *487. Ausbildungs-und-Ersatz-Division* could offer no more than minimal resistance to a full-strength American armored division, the 21st Armored Infantry Battalion of 11th Armored moved southeast to Oberkappel to outflank *487. Ausbildungs-und-Ersatz-Division*'s defensive line and encountered nothing more than Hungarian *Honved* troops wanting to surrender.

1   Pencz, *Siegrunen 76*, p. 23.
2   Scheibert, Horst, *Bildband der 6. Panzer Division* (Bad Nauheim: Hans-Henning Podzun, 1958), p. 44.
3   Weidinger, *Das Reich*, p. 400.

I SS-Panzerkorps
12. SS-Panzer-Division Hitlerjugend

The puzzled SS men watched as their enemies spent most of the day digging in and fortifying their positions. As they had been doing for days, loudspeakers continued blaring admonitions not to join in a new war, and that men who gave themselves up would be well treated by the Red Army. Aside from being puzzled why the Russians held off attacking, most of the Germans first wondered what the barrage of loudspeaker harangues meant, and they scoffed at the notion of the Russians doing anything except shooting them out of hand if they surrendered. But as long as they weren't being shot at, the men of *Hitlerjugend* were content to let the Russians continue with whatever it was they were doing.

Late in the day they found out the reason for the Russians' odd behavior. A patrol had grabbed a Russian prisoner who "gave the astounding reply: We will be awaiting the Americans in these positions."[4] *Korps von Bünau* had reported the same incredible news, and added that whole forests were being cut down and the local Austrians forced to build bunkers and fortifications all along the Russian front lines. The rank and file reacted with hope, but *SS-Brigadeführer* Hugo Kraas and his staff didn't believe any of it.

But all of that was beyond the influence of men at the front, and the war continued. Kraas ordered an attack on a prominent height that overlooked his positions, but reconnaissance showed it to be heavily fortified. An assault would likely fail with heavy casualties, so he called it off. Another large patrol to the southeast toward Lilienfeld happened upon a Russian assembly, which they surprised and shot up with very heavy Russian casualties.

Kampfgruppe 1. SS-Panzer-Division Leibstandarte Adolf Hitler

Throughout the day skirmishes and small-scale attacks broke out along the front from the Traisen to Kleinzell, and south to beyond the Kalte Kochl. The miserable men of *SS-Kampfgruppe Peiper* and the *LAH* did receive some relief from the constant worry of imminent death by the arrival of a few supplies. The men felt better after a meal but nothing could be done about their fatigue.

It was worse at night because they were isolated in the darkness. Even under clear skies moonlight only dappled the forest floor and communication with the nearest friendly strongpoint could only be done on foot. Infiltrators could be very quite in patches of snow, so alertness meant staying alive, but dog-tired men can only stay awake for so long.

On the division's far left flank, the men of *SS-Kampfgruppe Peiper* woke up to find a mass of Russian armor and infantry in a valley west of Wilhelmsburg. The crew of a surviving Panzer IV surprised a T-34 with a shot in the side of its turret, and then engaged the infantry in what promised to be a one-sided fight. At the last moment a messenger rode up with the order to withdraw and assemble south of Traisen before moving on to Markl. Another Mark IV and one Panther also arrived there and a new defense line was established.[5]

Unlike the recently filled-up *Hitlerjugend*, the *LAH* typified the skeletal condition of the German divisions by this time, with regiments the size of weak battalions, battalions the size of companies and companies the size of platoons. Hunger and fatigue dragged at their limbs and sapped their energy. Ammunition of all kinds had become precious, even for small arms. They kept fighting

---

4   Meter, *The 12th SS*, p. 495
5   Tiemann, *The Leibstandarte IV/2*, p. 316.

because there was nothing else they could do. Despite the reassuring promises on the loudspeakers, the Russian Army had come seeking revenge on all Germans, male and female, and the *Waffen-SS* in particular. Some men did surrender, but most of those still standing fought on to the bitter end.

37. SS-Freiwilligen-Kavallerie-Division Lützow

With the Americans pouring into Austria from the west and northwest, the division was ordered to move west to Sankt Aegidi, on the Danube due east of Passau. Not only did this plug a defensive hole, but put the SS men facing the Americans for when the time came to surrender. *SS-Standartenführer* Karl Gesele still didn't command either of his cavalry regiments, however.

SS-Kampfgruppe Keitel

The command post for the *Kampfgruppe* had moved to Schwarzau am Gebirge. One of the two cavalry regiments for *Lützow* was reduced by this point to the strength of an average battalion. The booming thunder of heavy artillery could be heard by the remnants of *SS-Kampfgruppe Keitel* positioned in the mountains south of the Rohr Saddle, down to Schwarzau.

A variety of armor was used in the Schwarzau area. Most were the usual *Jagdpanzer IV/70s* and *Sturmgeschütz IVs*, but not all. At least one strange, unidentified vehicle took part in the fighting. It was tracked like a tank, with five road wheels and a suspension bar between the second and fourth wheel, a front sprocket and rear idler wheel. The superstructure was fixed, not a turret, and it had both a driver's and gunner's visor, with a machine gun on the right side of the sloped superstructure. It was about the size of a Panzer Mark I and did not appear to be field-modified. Its combat value must have been nil, but in the desperate days of April 1945, the Germans pressed every possible weapon into service.

6. Armee

In the conquered areas of Pinggau-Friedberg every shop, house or apartment had been totally plundered, with almost everything taken, whether the Russian troops could use it or not. Horses, mules, pigs and especially chickens virtually disappeared from the landscape. It was estimated that 90 percent of all chickens were taken by the invaders.[6]

1. Volks-Gebirgs-Division

The *Wehrmacht* report for the day stated that the front in Lower Austria had stabilized, but this would have been news to the men of the *1. Volks-Gebirgs-Division*, and the *Gebirgsjäger-Regiment 99* in particular. Still standing fast at the center of *6. Armee*'s front, the regiment was pounded by more than 4,000 artillery rounds on 30 April alone. That was at least two or three rounds for every man in the regiment's trenches.

---

6   Brettner, *Pinka*, p. 43.

2. Panzerarmee

The stabilization of the front couldn't continue forever. To the army's south, Tito's Yugoslavian Army, along with the Russians, Slovenes and Bulgarians, was pushing hard for the Adriatic coast at Trieste. *Heeresgruppe E* resisted where it could, but the war was obviously winding down and all German commanders were considering withdrawal plans.

The *23. Panzer-Division* inserted the bled-out *I./Panzergrenadier-Regiment 128* into the line at Hill 336, replacing *Reither-Regiment 41* from *4. Kavallerie-Division*.[7] Every so often the *II. Abteilung* relieved its sister, but major action had died away to patrolling for prisoners, dodging the occasional mortar round and a vicious sniper war from both sides. An exposed head all too often caught a bullet. And despite everything, German morale remained inexplicably good.

The Americans and French

Western Austria's border was open and the Western Allies began to pour through. The state of Vorarlberg had a few strongpoints from the efforts of *Gauleiter* Hofer to construct an *Alpenfestung*, but no organized defensive line. But diehards at Bregenz weren't going to be captured that easily.

* * *

The US 11th Armored Division moved southeast to the Danube and crossed over into Austria. At Oberkappel they encountered hordes of Hungarian troops who wanted nothing more than to surrender. Their sheer numbers delayed the division's advance. Once on the move again the spearheads came to Lembach im Mühlkreis, where a blown bridge stopped them until the engineers built a way to cross. Once that was done they continued rumbling down the north bank of the Danube. In most of the towns they captured the Americans were cheered as liberators; most, but not all.

Before they rolled into Oberkappel, however, at Wegscheid, on the German-Austrian border, it was a different story. The Germans put up a stiff fight for the town and it wasn't until 11:00 p.m. that the Americans considered it cleared of the enemy. The Americans lost one man killed, 10 wounded and five Shermans knocked out, but the defenders were slaughtered, losing 74 killed and 84 taken prisoner.[8]

---

7   Rebentisch, *From the Caucasus*, P. 467.
8   The 11th Armored Division Legacy Group, '55th Armored Infantry Battalion (AIB)', <http://www.11tharmoreddivision.com/history/55th_AIB.html> (Accessed 16 November 2018).

31

Tuesday, 1 May

Broadcasting in English, Radio Bremen alerted the world of an important announcement soon to come at 9:00 p.m., but that time came and went. For the next ninety minutes all German stations still controlled by the Reich played Richard Wagner's solemn *Tannhäuser*, then a piano concerto by Carl Maria von Weber, followed by Wagner's *Götterdämmerung*, *Rheingold* and the slow section of Anton Bruckner's 7th Symphony. This long period of music set a grim mood with the audience, which was interrupted frequently by frantic shouts of an important news bulletin that would soon be coming from the German Government. Ever since 30 January 1933 the words German Government been replaced by Reich Government, so this alone clued listeners that something important could be expected.

Without warning, at 10:25 p.m. the music stopped. Trumpets and drums ratcheted up the tension. After a brief moment of silence, an announcer read the bulletin:

> It is reported from *Der Führer*'s headquarters that our *Führer* Adolf Hitler, fighting to the last breath against Bolshevism, fell for Germany this afternoon in his operational headquarters in the Reich Chancellery. On April 30 *Der Führer* appointed Grand Admiral Dönitz his successor. The grand admiral and successor of *Der Führer* now speaks to the German people.[1]

After praising Hitler, Dönitz asked for all Germans to maintain order and discipline, and to continue the struggle for the sole purpose of saving as many Germans as possible from the Russians. He promised to do all he could to preserve life, especially for the women and children.

* * *

Throughout the Reich men reacted to the news of Hitler's death in different ways. Some saw it as a release from their oath and therefore that it removed the stigma from surrender. Others had long since given up fighting for Hitler anyway, and only fought on because their comrades did. Many commanders reminded their troops that while the oath had been to Hitler himself, it had also been made to the German Reich, which still existed and therefore the oath was still in force. Whatever other effect the news may have had, it signaled to everyone that the war's final days were at hand.

* * *

Refusing to swear an oath of allegiance to Ferenc Szálasi, *Obergruppenführer* Jeno Ruszkay was removed as Inspector of Hungarian Troops, a completely meaningless demotion. By this point the last thing the Hungarians were thinking about was fighting; they were simply planning on the best way to surrender while avoiding combat if at all possible.

---

1   'Adolf Hitler: Doenitz announces Hitler's Death (May 1, 1945)', (Jewish Virtual Library), <https://www. jewishvirtuallibrary.org/doenitz-announces-hitler-s-death-may-1945>, (Accessed 25 June 2018).

Heeresgruppe Ostmark

Despite spring being nearly half over in its march toward summer, in many places across Austria the weather remained cold and wet. German survivors all referred to the conditions as 'wintery', although it was much worse at the higher altitudes. It's also likely that food deprivation meant their bodies couldn't produce enough heat to combat the chilly temperatures, so that conditions felt worse than they really were.

* * *

For the men still fighting and dying on the front lines, Hitler's death was the moment when any lingering fantasies that the war could still be won evaporated. In the back of their minds even the most fanatical men knew it would take a miracle not to lose the war, but even as their world collapsed around them some held out hope that the *Führer* could work a miracle. Now the *Führer* was dead.

But with his death came a new hope that the war could finally end. While Hitler lived the Allies had made it clear that only unconditional surrender would be accepted, and Hitler had made it clear that was out of the question.

Reactions varied among the men of *Heeresgruppe Ostmark*. Some despaired, but most didn't have much reaction at all. They were too tired and hungry to care, and if Hitler's death hurried the end of the war that was fine with them.

Rumors ran rampant through the ranks. Some were true and some weren't. Word spread that the Enns River was the demarcation line between the Americans and the Russians, and also that surrender would be made to whoever you'd fought last. Many spoke of an imminent ceasefire, and others pointed to the Russians' work digging defensive positions as evidence of an impending alliance between Germany and the Western Allies.

On one thing most of the men could agree, namely that *Grossadmiral* Dönitz's call to hold fast in the east so that as many people as possible could reach the safety of American lines was an honorable mission, one worth fighting for to the last. And so, even as any unneeded equipment was destroyed and plans were made for a retreat to the west, the war continued with undiminished fury.

North of the Danube

Eidenberg was a small town in Upper Austria, about five miles northwest of Linz. Throughout April various military elements had passed through, including a *Luftwaffe* headquarters that stayed for two weeks, burned their papers and uniforms, and left town in civilian clothes. On 1 May a company of 160 *Waffen-SS* moved in to defend the town from the oncoming Americans. Their unit is unknown, but *SS-Panzerjäger-Regiment Oberdonau* seems a likely candidate. When news of Hitler's death spread through the company the men hung their heads, but perked up when informed that *Grossadmiral* Dönitz ordered the war to continue. They were ready to keep fighting.

The SS men quartered themselves in a barn and hotel. To supplement their rations they hunted in the local woods and killed a deer, which became the meat for a stew. The inhabitants knew what having armed troops in their town would mean when the Americans finally showed up, but there was nothing they could do about it. The elementary school called off classes in the face of the imminent danger, and many people went into hiding.[2]

---

2   'Um Jugend und Leben Betrogen, Das bedrückende Schicksal von drei deutschen Teenagern im Mühlviertel zu Ende des zweiten Weltkriegs', (Oberösterreichische Zeitgeschichte), <http://www.ooezeitgeschichte.at/Zeitgeschichte/umJugend_u_Leben_betrogen_2.html>, (Accessed 20 July 2018).

* * *

The news of Hitler's death came to Stockerau via a mourning banner strung from a local government building around 11:00 p.m., and it was greeted with the same mix of despair, joy, fear, desperation, excitement, relief and anger as it was everywhere else in the shrunken Reich. As if to accompany the *Führer*'s spirit, a court-martial at the courthouse sentenced a deserter to death and he was hung in a local *platz* with the placard declaring him a coward. But this had the opposite effect of what was intended, as even more men stripped off the uniforms and made for the marshy meadows along the banks of the Danube. A whole group of deserters was in hiding there, and while the remaining Nazis might have liked to get their hands on them, most people with guns had other things to think about.[3]

South of the Danube

At a field hospital in Bad Aussee, the wound suffered by another *Waffen-SS* veteran on 9 March near Székesfehérvár had turned gangrenous. On the first day of May it claimed the life of the former commander of *2. SS-Panzer-Division Das Reich*, and one of the highest-ranking German generals killed in action, *SS-Gruppenführer und Generalleutnant der SS* Werner Ostendorff. With a backdrop of snow-capped mountains, the fisherman's dream Traun River splashing nearby and spring flowers blooming in the Austrian sunshine, the fairy-tale setting of the Salzkammergut was in sharp contrast to the hideous, painful death suffered by Himmler's one-time chief of staff.[4]

6. SS-Panzerarmee
Korps von Bünau

Despite their division having officially been written off more than a month before, a few members of the short-lived *232. Reserve-Panzer-Division* were still in the line south of Sankt Pölten as members of *Korps von Bünau*.

12. SS-Panzer-Division Hitlerjugend

The quiet of the previous few days continued. The damage inflicted on 30 April to the Russian assembly near Lilienfeld did not lead to a retaliatory attack, which must have seemed odd to some of the veteran SS men. By now the NCOs and company officers were conducting daily training exercises to combat boredom and keep the men's minds off the lack of food, as much as to get new recruits trained before the next battle. Only late in the night did *Grossadmiral* Dönitz's broadcast of Hitler's death send shockwaves through the ranks.

Although most of the old veterans were long-since dead or too seriously wounded to fight again, a few were still with *Hitlerjugend*, men who had personally met the *Führer*, had shaken his hand and looked into his eyes. For them it was solid evidence that everything they had fought for was in vain.

---

3   Brettner, *Die Letzten Kämpfe Band II*, p. 170.
4   Sources disagree on the exact date of Ostendorff's death. Some put it on 1 May, others 4 May and still others on 5 May.

1. SS-Panzer-Division Leibstandarte Adolf Hitler

But if *Hitlerjugend* was enjoying a peaceful respite, in the area of *SS-Kampfgruppe Peiper* Russian attacks continued unabated. What panzers remained, probably no more than four Mark IVs and two Panthers, acted as reserves or a counterattack force, but the expenditure of scarce fuel and ammunition limited their use to only the most dangerous situations.

6. Armee
1. Volks-Gebirgs-Division

The ordeal of *Gebirgsjäger-Regiment 99* continued as the Russians launched incessant attacks along its front, supported by an artillery bombardment even worse than the 4,000 shells recorded the previous day. It was a maximum effort to break through once and for all and the Germans couldn't respond since there was no more artillery ammunition. Shivering in their wet trenches, with food and small-arms ammunition scarce, the *Gebirgsjägers* nevertheless held their positions against all attacks.

The French and Americans

Since 29 April the Austrian resistance leaders near Bregenz had begged the commander of the French 5th Armored Division not to bombard the town to overcome the German defenses there, but on 1 May their time ran out. Before the next French attack Bregenz was targeted by waves of fighter-bombers, heavy bombers and artillery fire. This time when the French attacked resistance had been smashed and they rolled into the ruined town, where at least 72 homes had been destroyed. Six years of war had left the picturesque Alpine town on the shores of beautiful Lake Constance untouched, like a delicate flower growing in a junkyard, and in a few hours that had all been erased. Bregenz burned.

* * *

In many places the Austrians resisted the French simply because they were French, since France was a traditional enemy. Americans, on the other hand, were viewed as generous and well supplied. Wherever possible, Austrian partisans slowed the French to allow the Americans time to arrive in their vicinity first, without realizing that the Allies had already delineated their zones of occupation.

* * *

During their advance through southern Germany the Americans had grown used to encountering hard knots of fanatical resistance, wedged into large swaths of territory where the population was only too happy to surrender. During the capture of Munich, for example, the Americans encountered little resistance except for the remaining SS men headquartered in the city, who had hunkered down in the ruins of police headquarters and fought to the last man.

The day before, 30 April, had been warm and sunny in the birthplace of Nazism. For most of the time the biggest resistance met by the Americans was the rubble and ruins from years of bombing by the Allied strategic bombing campaign. Crowds of Germans surrounded the American spearheads, mostly women, very young children and very old men. Near the famous Marienplatz they found the local police lined up and waiting to surrender, with their weapons inventoried and tagged.

And yet unrepaired battle damage still shows that bitter fighting did occur in some sections of the city. The building at 1 Schellingstrasse, where it dead-ends into Ludwigstrasse, retains a lower wall with the heavy damage it received during the fighting as a testament to what happened on 30 April 1945.

As the US Seventh Army headed into Austria, then, this is what the soldiers had come to expect: rapid advance through a populace tired of war and ready to surrender, with sudden outbursts of violence. Once inside Austria the hope had been that partisan groups would deliver cities into Allied hands without a fight, as O-5 tried to do with Vienna. But while anti-German partisan groups were active in north and central Austria, they were never able to significantly influence the course of the fighting.

Korps Bork

North of the Danube, *Ersatz-Regiment 587* of *487. Ausbildungs-und-Ersatz-Division* had been driven back from its line anchored at Breitenberg, first to Haslach an der Mühl and then from hastily prepared positions on the Mühl River. Already demoralized by the hopelessness of the war situation, the regiment began to disintegrate.

* * *

Generalmajor Erich Hassenstein spent most of the war teaching in specialized military schools and commanding training organizations. He'd been ordered to take command of the defense of Passau with whatever men he could scrape together, and finally arrived in the city on 1 May. Immediately upon arriving he was confronted with a demand for surrender from the Americans on the city's western edge. Most of his forces were either *Volkssturm* or Hitler Youth, but even so Hassenstein flatly refused to wave the white flag.

Hassenstein wrote a letter to the citizens of Passau that was printed in the local newspaper, the *Donauzeitung*, on 30 April: "All cowardly traitors will be put to death! Long live Germany! Long live the *Führer*!"[5] Unfortunately for him, the first thing the Americans did when entering Passau's western suburb of Hal was to tell the people of Hitler's death. The people had no inclination to fight a hopeless battle anyway, but with Hitler gone the last shred of loyalty to the Third Reich went with him. When a few dozen Hitler Youth gave up without a fight, Hassenstein headed for the nearby Neuburg Forest.

SS-Panzergrenadier-Regiment Deutschland

With no higher headquarters to give them orders, the regiment's commander officer, *SS-Obersturmbannführer* Günther-Eberhard Wiscileny, younger brother of war criminal and Nuremberg witness Dieter Wiscileny, appealed to the *Gauleiter* of Upper Danube for orders. August Eigruber declined to give any, stating: "I am not a sergeant to issue military orders."[6]

Still unsure what he was supposed to do, Wiscileny contacted *Generalmajor* Wagner, who had become Battle Commander of Linz. Wagner told him to hold in place, which was singularly unhelpful. The SS commander wanted to know what he was supposed to do and nobody could tell him.

SS-Kampfgruppe Keitel

As April turned to May, the badly damaged regiment occupied a line of strongpoints from the Rohr Saddle to Schwarzau im Gebirge, resulting in a main line of resistance at least five miles long.

---

5   Rosmus, Anna Elisabeth, *Out of Passau: Leaving a City Hitler called Home* (New York: Open Road Media, 2014), p. 2.
6   Weidinger, *Das Reich*, p. 400.

Given the swindling number of men in Keitel's *Kampfgruppe*, this could be nothing more than isolated bunkers within sight of each other wherever possible.

The Americans and French

Forty-two centuries before 1945, in approximately 2,200 BC, the third largest mountain collapse in the history of the eastern Alps filled a neighboring pass to a height of more than 1,000 feet. A number of lakes also formed due to this massive rock slide. The pass created was surrounded by soaring peaks of bare, snow-covered rock. Much later, people would name it the Fern Pass.

Entering this ancient avenue between the mountains was the US 44th Infantry Division, approaching from the northeast. Freezing rain pelted deep snow drifts piled atop rock slides and craters, making making passage difficult. Even worse for the Americans, a 300-man battalion from *47. Volks-Grenadier-Division* blocked the twisting roadway. The situation exactly replicated that facing the Persians at Thermopylae in 480 BC, with 300 Spartans defending a narrow pass against many times their number of invaders. There was never a question of whether the attackers in either case would break through. The only uncertainty was how long it would take and how much it would cost.

The commander of the 44th Infantry Division, Major General William F. Dean, decided not to take any chances. He sent a reinforced company out as a flanking force on a forty-mile march to come at the Fern Pass from the southwest. Their trek took them along a glorified game trail and, as things worked out, was completely unnecessary.

* * *

The US 13th Armored Division of XX Army Corps closed on the Austrian border at Braunau am Inn, Hitler's hometown, and south of Passau. An American armored division in 1945 was a formidable sight. Their arrival across from the latter city is what caused most of General Hassenstein's defenders to think better of trying to resist. Engineers immediately began fording the Inn River in three places.

* * *

A series of redrawn unit boundaries and reassignment of objectives marked the first step in the next phase of the war. With more than a week left before Germany's surrender, America's highest-level commanders began drawing down combat forces for transfer to the Pacific. Men who fought their way across France, Belgium and Germany were earmarked to lead the assault against the Japanese home islands.

* * *

Elements of XX US Army Corps closed on the Inn River at various points, but the only bridges they found standing were at Tittmoning and Burghausen. At Schärding, eight miles south of Passau, they faced 200 *Waffen-SS* men, possibly from *SS-Panzerjäger-Regiment Oberdonau*, along with 500 *Volkssturm* and 300 men from the Labor Service. Seven 20mm *Flak* batteries might have made for an effective defense, but had no ammunition. Although this force could have made crossing the Inn River difficult, when the first American Sherman tanks opened fire the defenders fled in panic.[7]

---

7   Vavra and Rossiwall, *Die letzten Tage: 25. April – 1. Mai 1945*, <https://www.museumnoe.at/de/das-museum/blog/25-april-1-mai-1945>, (Accessed 24 July 2018).

* * *

At Kramerschag the 55th Armored Infantry Battalion of 11th Armored Division, part of Patton's US Third Army, crossed the Austrian border and drove to Peilstein im Mülviertel. The town of about 1,500 people was built on the side of a gently sloped hill. In normal times it was a tranquil bucolic place. But on 1 May a German roadblock met the western invaders and, in a bitter fire-fight, left four Americans dead and eight wounded.

* * *

Many of the Hungarians who surrendered appeared to the Americans to be first-class soldiers, well-groomed, sharp and disciplined, but with absolutely no desire for a fight. They marched into American captivity in perfect columns, some with their violins tucked under their arms, all with caps tilted at a rakish angle. Women and children tagged along behind them in what seemed more like a parade than a military surrender. Not even a heavy spring snowstorm could dampen what the Hungarians clearly saw as a happy occasion.

* * *

At Braunau am Inn the air raid sirens wailed at noon, but it wasn't to warn of bombers. Rather, it signaled the approach of the Americans. Without warning a tremendous explosion shook the town. The blast wave damaged roofs and shattered windows. Debris rained on the neighborhood closest to the river.

This was no doing of the Americans, however. It was the bridge over the Inn being expertly demolished so that only a short span still stood, and it was only in December 1946 that it became serviceable again. American engineers worked all night under generator-supplied floodlights to build a pontoon bridge in the fast current, which illustrates how completely US firepower dominated the battlefield at this point. With no knowledge of what awaited them in the town, the Americans were confident enough in their firepower to shine bright lights on themselves.

In apparent anger at being denied use of the bridge, or so it seemed to some of the citizens, two American shells immediately struck the church steeple, stopping the town's clock mounted there at precisely 12:45 p.m. Other shells hit the town and then, almost in defiance, charges on the railroad bridge detonated and sent it crashing into the water.

Sparks swirled in the spring air and started fires. Shell splinters mowed down several civilians. Power went out. In desperation the residents tried to attach a white flag to the *Rathaus*, the Town Hall, but it failed.

6. Armee

The surrender of *Heeresgruppe G* left *6. Armee* isolated and with no protection to the west. If the Americans or British moved fast enough they could cut off the army's retreat routes, so Hermann Balck sent *Generalmajor* Wilhelm Söth, former commander of *Kampfgruppe 3. Panzer-Division*, to block the Pyhrn Pass, Pötschen Pass and the valley of the Enns River near Radstadt. To accomplish this he received miscellaneous troops amounting to a reinforced regiment or so, perhaps 3,000 men with no heavy weapons. At best they were a *Sperrverband*.

Söth's men couldn't have been too upset at moving west, especially since Hermann Balck's army was down to enough ammunition for only two days of hard fighting, and the food and fuel situations were even worse.

9. Gebirgs-Division (Ost), formerly Kampfgruppe Raithel

No German formation of the Second World War had a more bizarre origin than did *9. Gebirgs-Division (Ost)*. To this day the existence of this division is questioned in some sources. On 1 May *Oberst* Raithel, the commander of *Kampfgruppe Raithel*, addressed his men in an order of the day to inform them he had been named the commander of a brand new division, the *9. Gebirgsjäger-Division*. Authorization for this change had been requested by *6. Armee* on 25 April but approval came slowly because of the chaotic state of the Army High Command. Raithel goes on to tell his men that it might be a mistake because there is already a division by that name in the north; however, a renaming would not be done at that point.[8]

And so came into being one of the strangest divisions in the *Wehrmacht* order of battle. Raithel's *Kampfgruppe* had grown to the size of a division, functioned like a division and had defended the front of a corps, but it also contained men from every conceivable part of the *Wehrmacht*: from the *Heer*, *Luftwaffe*, *Wehrkreis*, *Waffen-SS* and even some Hungarians. Somehow, in less than a month, *Oberst* Raithel had shaped an amorphous mass of humanity into an effective division-sized formation, and its new designation only acknowledged what was already fact. When established it had a strength of 10,400 men of all ranks: *9. Gebirgs-Division (Ost)*, formerly *Kampfgruppe Raithel*, formerly *Kampfgruppe Semmering*, had fought its way into existence.

At the same time, the fragment of *OKW* still functioning authorized *XX Gebirgskorps* in Norway to redesignate *Divisionsgruppe Kräutler, Division zur besonderen Verwendung 140*, Special Purpose Division 140, as *9. Gebirgs-Division*. Arrived at independently, the decision forced the two *Gebirgsdivisionen* to append the modifiers of *Nord* and *Ost* to the unit designations.

Regardless of what his command was called, however, *Oberst* Raithel saw ominous signs that the Russians were preparing a new assault to crush it, as sometime around the beginning of May the Russian 1st Battalion of the 9th Armored Brigade of 1st Mechanized Corps arrived near Semmering. The battalion's parent regiment had 56 American Sherman tanks and had been in the thick of the fighting for Vienna. Its next mission was the capture of Graz, and to get there it had to capture the Semmering Pass to secure its northern flank.

* * *

Near Rettenegg a German patrol heard approaching voices speaking a Slavic language, interspersed with German, hidden by a bend in the forest trail. Melting into the underbrush they set up an ambush, only to see men in the uniforms of a German *Polizei* unit. It turns out the Germans were from Saxony while the men were Estonians and Latvians.[9] Another patrol escorting an *Oberleutnant* on an inspection of Russian positions near the Feistritzwald had a different experience; none of them returned.

* * *

The remaining members of *Luftwaffeneinheit ABK Z* were, after a month in combat, veterans. But like any other veteran there were some things they simply couldn't avoid. On 1 April a single mortar shell had hit a house where the commander of *SS-Aufklärungs-Abteilung 1* and most of his staff had stopped to rest and eat. The well-placed round killed most of them. One month later the same thing happened to the command post of the mixed German and Hungarian *Luftwaffe* unit. A direct hit on the command post severely wounded 13 men, including the commanding officer,

---

8   This is a strange statement, however, given the timeline of the creation of the two divisions. Supposedly the northern division was not renamed until 6 May, but reconciling timelines from this period is problematic.

9   Brettner, *Die Letzten Kämpfe Band I*, p. 118.

and killed one. During the night the wounded were carried to a nearby inn for further treatment. In a unit that started the war with only 116 men this was a crushing blow.

1. Panzer-Division

In the Ebersdorf and Hartberg regions, *1. Panzer-Division* had established strongpoints which the Russians didn't attack. The successful counterattack during April inflicted heavy losses on the Russians who, combined with their paranoia about an Allied-German alliance, convinced them not to waste any more men in the area. The Germans took advantage of the lull to teach basic combat skills to their newest replacements from the *Luftwaffe*, *Nebelwerfer* battalions and Hitler Youth.

It's illustrative of the German ability to repair damaged vehicles that, according to Brettner, the *1. Panzer-Regiment* had 35 panzers of varying types combat ready on 1 May.[10] Under the guidelines of a Type 1945 panzer division, this was nearly full strength. How many may have still had problems isn't known, and it's likely that all were scarred and dented. Nevertheless, the ability of first-line German divisions to regenerate themselves stands out as a remarkable achievement. Of course, all of those panzers were useless without fuel.

Heeresgruppe G

Commanded by *General der Infanterie* Friedrich Schulz, *Heeresgruppe G* had defended the far left flank of the Western Front abutting the border with Switzerland. Its two component armies were *1.* and *19. Armee*'s, both of which were little more than shells that had been bled dry by combat and desertion. In Austria *19. Armee* defended the southern flank, with *1. Armee* to the north.

Arrayed facing north and starting on the left was *AOK 24*, composed of *Kampfgruppe Merker* and the *405. Ausbildungs-und-Ersatz-Division*. Not much is known about Merker's unit, although during combat in Germany it had been composed of trainees, surplus men from wherever they could be found, and even some Russian volunteers who proved unreliable. Likewise, *405. Ausbildungs-und-Ersatz-Division* doesn't even show up in many lists of German training divisions and its composition was haphazard.

The British

Far to the south, along the Adriatic coast, troops of the Slovenian IX Corps entered the city of Trieste. This city was acknowledged by the Western Allies as under their control, but the communists refused to hand over control for nearly 6 weeks. During this time they massacred thousands of anti-communists, fascists and people considered hostile to their cause. The ravines and deep gorges around the city are dotted with mass graves, and the number of those murdered will probably never be known. As the situation developed in Austria the potential for a repeat loomed high, but this time the British were determined to get there first.

---

10   Brettner, *Die Letzten Kämpfe Band I*, p. 57.

32

Wednesday, 2 May

At 2:00 p.m., throughout western Austria and northern Italy the soldiers of *Heeresgruppe C* began laying down their weapons in accordance with the surrender agreement signed on 29 April. Nearly a million German troops became prisoners of war in one fell swoop. Despite ongoing negotiations and misunderstandings, *Heeresgruppe C* ceased to exist, giving the British Eighth Army a clear path into the Austrian state of Carinthia. *Heeresgruppe Ostmark* now had enemies on its southern flank, as well as in the east and west.

The Americans and French

The 56th Armored Engineer Battalion, of 11th Armored Division, pulled up to the Mühl River with the same mission they'd had countless times before; build a bridge to replace one blown up by the Germans. But this time they had a better idea. A dam downstream made the river at the crossing deeper than it should be, so they blew it up. That lowered the water level enough so that a bridge wasn't necessary. Instead they built a ford and the American vehicles drove right through the greatly reduced stream.

* * *

Despite pleas from the Austrian resistance, the commander of the French 5th Armored Division had waited long enough for the die-hard fanatics defending Bregenz to surrender. After a heavy artillery bombardment his men attacked and captured the town. Sixty-two people killed in the fighting were interred in the graveyard of St Gallus Catholic Church.

* * *

Private First Class Frederick Schneikert drew sentry duty for the anti-tank company of the US 324th Infantry Regiment, 44th Infantry Division. When a young German in civilian clothes approached his post riding a bicycle, Schneikert did his duty and stopped the man, who gestured and spoke in snippets of bad English interspersed with German. Unsure what the man said, or what to do with him, the private turned him over to First Lieutenant Charles L. Stewart.

It took a while for Stewart to understand that the man, who gave his name as Magnus von Braun, was the representative for a group of German rocket scientists who wanted to surrender. Once Stewart understood, he issued passes so the Germans could safely enter American lines.

Shortly thereafter three truckloads of Germany's top rocket engineers, including Magnus' older brother Werner von Braun and *Generalmajor* Walter Dornberger, motored into the *lager* of the 44th Infantry Division. It is no exaggeration to say that America's Moon landing program began on 2 May 1945 in the wild uplands of western Austria.

Despite the excitement of capturing the brains trust behind the V-1 and V-2 rockets, 44th Infantry's day also involved heavy fighting at the Fern Pass. Had the National Redoubt actually been a reality, the combat at Fern Pass showed how hard it would have been to dig out motivated and well-supplied troops: 3/71st Infantry had battled the entrenched Germans all day on 1 May, without breaking through. The regiment then committed its 1st Battalion to help dislodge them. Tanks could only engage at long distance and artillery was of limited value among the jumbled boulders.

As 1st Battalion approached the pass, five men suddenly appeared from the surrounding forest and identified themselves as resistance members. In another parallel to Thermopylae they offered to lead the Americans on a little-known footpath over the mountain on the pass's east side, which exited behind the Germans' blocking position. The Americans captured the town of Fernstein and before dark attacked the German position from behind. Caught in a trap, the German resistance ceased.

Near Passau, Germany

The Neuburg Forest was a range of heavily forested hills to the west and north of Passau. For the hiking-obsessed Germans and Austrians it had long been an idyllic retreat, a quiet place to stroll and possibly see a deer scampering through the underbrush, or a golden eagle wheeling overhead.

On 2 May the silence under the broad green canopy echoed from a gunshot. *Generalmajor* Erich Hassenstein had gone there with a purpose. Having been named as defender of Passau, Hassenstein couldn't bear the disgrace when all of the men under his command fled in the face of overwhelming American power.

His headquarters was at a villa and he had been accompanied by a *Major* Bishop. The two men descended into the cellar. With less than a week left in the war, he was so depressed at not being able to achieve the impossible that either he or Bishop put a gun to his temple and pulled the trigger. The bullet reportedly went through both his head and the cellar door.

The Nazis left Passau one final gift; all of the bridges over the Danube, Inn and Ilz Rivers had been destroyed. By this time the Americans had become professionals at river crossing, so while it barely slowed them down, it seriously disrupted the life of Passau's citizens. In addition to the bridges, the water and electric lines had also been disrupted. In fact, however, Passau was not as pacified as Hassenstein thought. An SS unit had decided to fight for the city.

* * *

The US 13th Armored Division closed on the Inn River at Braunau and Obersberg. In the process of cutting through Bavaria they had liberated 11,000 Allied POWs, including many from the camps around Vienna, including *Stalag 17B*, along with all of their guards. Dealing with this sudden influx of needy men put a strain on the division's resources. Then they captured the entire Hungarian General Staff, along with the Secretary of State in Szálasi's government. When they reached Austria they were ordered to hold in place to allow the 71st and 80th US Infantry Divisions to drive east to meet the Russians.

* * *

No American division drove further and faster into Austria than did the 80th Infantry Division. It closed on Braunau am Inn late on 2 May. Orders were to cross and relieve elements of 13th Armored Division across the river, then speed across Austria to meet the Russians at the demarcation line, the Enns River. Near midnight they began the crossing.

* * *

In Braunau am Inn the citizens waited anxiously for the Americans. Rumors spread that the Americans gave the city an ultimatum, to surrender or be destroyed, and by mid-morning it was confirmed. Either Braunau gave up or it would burn.

Parts of the town were already on fire from the previous day, and while snow fell during a relatively quiet night it did nothing to quench the conflagration. Since the Nazis still controlled the means of communication, word spread orally to hang white flags and congregate in front of the local army barracks to demonstrate good faith in surrender.

With no permanent bridges the American passage over the swift Inn River, swollen by the spring thaw, was accomplished over an engineer-built pontoon bridge. Although a marvel of engineering, the strong current of the river threatened to break the bridge apart and sweep it downstream. The quantity of modern equipment available to the Americans astounded the citizens of Braunau, and once inside the city there was no resistance. Indeed, citizens lined fences and fought to get a glimpse of the invaders. For many, relief was palpable.

The *Heer* unit charged with the military defense of the region was *Kampfgruppe Grünwaldt*, commanded by *Major* Wilhelm Grünwaldt, part of *487. Ausbildungs-und-Ersatz-Division*. Resistance could have been fierce, since Braunau had a very high brick retaining wall along the river bank, much like an ancient walled city. But despite the proclamations and exhortations of *Kreisleiter* Fritz Reithofer, *Major* Grünwaldt understood how futile any resistance would prove. His half-trained and under-equipped little *Kampfgruppe* would be wiped out by the battle-hardened Americans in a matter of hours.

The entrance of the Americans was more like a parade than an occupation. The only man killed was a German soldier cavorting in a house with a local girl, who was caught '*in flagrante delicto*' by a G.I. When ordered to put his hands up the man instead turned and ran, and was shot in the back.

Tragically for the town, a number of railroad cars, including two filled with butter, were destroyed. Worse, the last railroad bridge leading into the city was blown up by retreating troops who still had some fight left in them. Braunau would be without a rail service for more than a month.

Among those liberated by the Americans were some 300-400 Rumanian prisoners-of-war, who were marched from Vienna to keep them out of the hands of the Russians. Several hundred from their original number had died along the way and those who remained were in terrible condition.

As for *Kreisleiter* Reithofer, who was charged by *Gauleiter* Eigruber to defend the city to the last man and last bullet, he disappeared without a trace. In 1951 he was declared dead by a German court, but in fact he was very much alive. After hiding out with relatives, he sneaked into the American zone of occupation and petitioned for reversal of his death decree, which was granted. Suspicion of war crimes couldn't be proved and he lived until the age of 99 in Pfarrkirchen, making his living as a pharmacist.

SS-Panzergrenadier-Regiment Deutschland

When most of *Deutschland* pulled back to Eferding, some of it appears to have stayed behind in Passau: perhaps three companies or a battalion. And while two days before a company of captured Americans had been released and allowed to head back to their own lines, on 2 May the 65th Infantry Division encountered heavy resistance at Passau. The defenders appeared to have been about 300 men from *Deutschland,* the *Pionier-Bataillon* from *25. Waffen-Grenadier-Division der SS Hunyadi* and some Hitler Youth. The Hungarians appear to have fought despite their own leaders' decision to only fight against Russians, not Americans. The motivation for this probably came from the skirmishes with the American spearheads, after which some Hungarian SS prisoners were claimed to have been found executed.[1] But in the confusion of the war's last days it's impossible to be certain.

---

1   Landwehr, 'Waffen-SS Miscellany', Siegrunen 55, p. 84.

* * *

Sometimes the flotsam of war could be quite valuable, if not priceless, washed ahead of victorious armies like driftwood on a flood tide. So it was with the Hungarian Crown Jewels and the Crown of Saint Stephen.

One story has it that someone had stolen the crown and jewels from the Palace of Buda in Budapest. Later in 1945, troops of the US Army encountered a group of Hungarian SS men who admitted hiding the treasure in an oil drum sunk in a marsh near the village of Mattsee in Bavaria. Mattsee was the headquarters of Hungarian Arrow Cross leader Ferenc Szálasi. Troops of the US Seventh Army found the jewels and they were taken to the USA. There were Hungarian SS formations camped in the Mattsee area at this time, as well as their higher commands, giving this version of events some credibility.

Another quite different story has it that on 2 May 1945 the Holy Crown and other jewels were handed over by a Hungarian Army general to a US Army colonel near Egglesberg, Austria. The crown had been escorted by the commander of the shattered Hungarian Third Army, Colonel-General Jozsef Heszlenyi, who met and shepherded both the crown and its keeper, the Commander of the Crown Guards, Colonel Erno Pajtas, out of Hungary and across the Austrian frontier to safety. The crown had been packed in a large black satchel. It was initially sheltered in Wiesbaden, in the American Zone, but was later transferred to the United States Gold Reserve at Fort Knox, Kentucky. It was not considered as spoils of war; rather, the US Government stored it in hopes of returning it to the Hungarian people one day. Colonel-General Hezslenyi was urged to flee to the west and safety but refused. On 15 May he committed suicide.

Orphaned Hungarian units crawled all over western Austria and Bavaria. Not far over the border in Germany, near Rosenheim, the Hungarian 9th Border Guard Division surrendered to 121st Cavalry Squadron of the 106th Group, US Army, with little fanfare and no violence. But not all encounters came off as peacefully as Ferenc Szálasi and his commanders had hoped. A *Kampfgruppe* from *Hunyadi* knocked out five American tanks near Timelkan in Upper Austria, three days before the armistice. When, exactly, this took place is harder to say. The armistice took effect on 8 May, so three days previously would be 5 May. Also, a *Kampfgruppe* from *26. Waffen-Grenadier-Division der SS Hungaria* reportedly destroyed a further two American tanks five days before the surrender, near Reid and St Martin. But most of the two Hungarian SS divisions surrendered on 5 May, so was three days prior, then, 2 May? Was five days prior 30 April? Regardless, despite the Hungarian leadership's desire to avoid conflict with the Americans, some of the Hungarian SS men had no intention of surrendering to anybody.

Schwere-Panzerjäger-Abteilung 653

In December 1944 the special-purpose battalion received a full complement of 42 of the formidable *Jagdtigers*. During March and April it had conducted a fighting retreat through southern Germany and inflicted heavy losses on both the pursuing French and Americans. At least as many *Jagdtigers* suffered mechanical breakdowns in combat and wound up destroyed by their own crews as by the enemy, and one was lost when it collapsed the Mangfall Bridge at Kolbermoor, Germany, thereby destroying both bridge and *Jagdtiger*. By the time the remnants of the battalion reached Austria it had two machines left in working order, although crews waited at the *Nibelungenwerke* to pick up some new models that were nearly finished. Assembling near Salzburg, the battalion was officially assigned to *Heeresgruppe Ostmark*.[2]

---

2   Of particular interest is that this was taken from an official order, which referenced *Heeresgruppe Süd* and not *Heeresgruppe Ostmark*.

* * *

On *Heeresgruppe Ostmark*'s far left flank the scramble was on to cross American lines and avoid surrender to the Red Army. For units like *37. SS-Freiwilligen-Kavallerie-Division Lützow* the effort was literally life and death. Although the division had existed for less than three months, was composed of largely ethnic Germans from Hungary and not Germans from Germany, and had never even found its entire complement in the same place at the same time, it was still an SS formation that had fought the Russians, and fought them tenaciously. There were no illusions about what that meant. The roads south and west were clogged with desperate men swept before the flood tide of the Red Army, seeking safety with the Western Allies.

Rolf Michaelis relates the story of *SS-Unterscharführer* Franz Wunsch during this period. Wunsch was in the anti-tank platoon of *SS-Aufklärungs-Abteilung 37*, stationed in the small village of Wostrowitz, south of Prague, as the headquarters of *Lützow* was in the area trying to complete its formation. Sometime around 2 or 3 May they were ordered to head south for Sankt Pölten. Stocking up on gasoline they were astonished to find some *Kriegsmarine Kubelwagens* in a nearby field, although only half of them worked; what navy vehicles were doing in the middle of what would soon become Czechoslovakia was anybody's guess. The SS men hitched up the half that did not work to the half that did, then attached their anti-tank guns to those and drove off headed south.

Along the way Wunsch saw signs of Czech nationalism everywhere, flags especially. Boys jeered at them and the roads were clogged with retreating *Landser*, men on horseback, men walking, men traveling by any and every means possible. Food and fuel were scarce, and once Wunsch had to draw his pistol to obtain gasoline. They eventually reached the area of Zwettl, in Austria, where they learned of the end of the war when the battalion commander assembled them in a field.[3]

* * *

Although all elements of *SS-Brigade Ney* had been summoned to join the headquarters, part of the unit was still fighting in eastern Austria.[4] The remainder was ordered to join *5. SS-Panzer-Division Wiking*, but refused, and instead moved off to join *25. Waffen-Grenadier-Division der SS Hunyadi* in western Austria. One source gives the brigade's casualties during the last weeks of combat as 472 killed and 32 missing, a testament to how vicious the fighting was until the very end.[5]

* * *

The *3. SS-Panzer-Division Totenkopf* was still in the area of Stockerau-Krems, when it was ordered to form blocking positions to the west along the line Danube-Dimbach-Weissenbach-Sankt Oswald-Freistadt. Moving west to face the Americans must have seemed like a dream come true for the men involved, since it was obvious the war would soon be over and surrender to the Americans was much preferred to surrender to the Russians. But much of the division's remaining strength had to stay behind and man the line of the Danube so the Russians could not cross.

3   Michaelis, Rolf, *Cavalry Divisions of the Waffen-SS* (Atglen: Schiffer, 2010), pp. 130-131.
4   Perhaps 2 companies were engaged in combat under *Hauptsturmführer* Edui, according to one source. <http://www.hunyadi.co.uk/>, (Accessed 15 April 2018).
5   <http://www.hunyadi.co.uk/page5.php>, (Accessed 28 August 2018).

6. SS-Panzerarmee
9. SS-Panzer-Division Hohenstaufen

No German general was more hated by the *Waffen-SS* field divisions than *General der Panzertruppe* Hermann Balck. The commander of *6. Armee* had had major run-ins with everyone from Sepp Dietrich to *SS-Obergruppenführer* Herbert Otto Gille of *IV SS-Panzerkorps*, starting the previous year and continuing during *Unternehmen Frühlingserwachen* and the subsequent withdrawal. It had been Balck who sparked the Cuff Band Order by asking how, if the *Leibstandarte* couldn't stop the Russians, he could be expected to. So when *SS-Brigadeführer* Sylvester Stadler discovered that his division, *9. SS-Panzer-Division Hohenstaufen*, would now be directly subordinated to *6. SS-Panzerarmee* and not Balck, he was ecstatic. *Hohenstaufen* was ordered to defend the line of the Enns and Danube Rivers in the area west of Steyr. Aside from the relatively unscathed nature of the land, the SS men would also have only a short drive to surrender to the Americans. Stadler's now over-strength division even received more reinforcements when the orphaned *SS-Panzergrenadier-Regiment Deutschland* was attached to *Hohenstaufen*.

* * *

Armed patrols moved out west of Eferding to find the American spearheads and report their positions, so troops could withdraw without fighting them. Everything now was about holding the Russians so as many people as possible could escape to American lines.

Nobody understood better than Sepp Dietrich and his staff that the end was near. Vital supplies were nearly exhausted and no more were on the way. The southern flank stood wide open, *Heeresgruppe Mitte* was almost surrounded so the northern flank was no longer secured, there was no significant defense line in the west and the Russians were still attacking in the east. Hitler was dead, which theoretically released every member of the armed forces from the oath of allegiance they took to Hitler. The only reason to stand and fight was to shield those fleeing for American lines, so Dietrich kept his corps commanders apprised of all events and also made it known that the time had come to begin planning a withdrawal to the west.

I SS-Panzerkorps

SS-Gruppenführer Hermann Preiss ordered all inoperable heavy weapons, along with the remaining repair stations, vehicles, supply personnel and medical facilities moved either to the Jessnitz River valley, well to the west of Schwarzenbach an der Pielach, or to the area near Türnitz. Many of the weapons required towing, but with prime movers in short supply it would take time. Meanwhile, the corps staff began planning for the move west to the Enns River.

12. SS-Panzer-Division Hitlerjugend

While the rest of the world celebrated the death of Adolf Hitler, the men of the two divisions that bore his name on their cuff-bands spent the day in silent depression. They intended to keep fighting as *Grossadmiral* Dönitz had ordered, to save as many German civilians as possible, but in Austria many people preferred that the Germans go away and let the Russians capture them. It wasn't that they were communists, although some were, but people who lived simple lives didn't want their towns to suffer the same destruction as others to the east had. If the Russians were coming anyway, they wanted to at least have a roof over their heads.

Kampfgruppe 1. SS-Panzer-Division Leibstandarte Adolf Hitler

The Russians spent their time on 2 May digging in behind their own lines and organizing the local populace to construct defenses. That left the SS men to shiver in their foxholes and dream of food. And for some there was also an empty feeling, since their unit had been formed to guard Hitler's life and now he was dead.

6. Armee
1. Volks-Gebirgs-Division

Heavy fighting raged along the division's front line, with gaps being closed by smaller and smaller groups of men. Ammunition was running out, empty bellies rumbled with hunger and nobody knew what might come next. All the troops could do was fight and hope the Americans hurried up and overran Austria from the west.

The steady rain of Russian artillery and mortar fire never let up during this period, with occasional attacks hitting isolated groups of Germans. Quiet periods were infrequent. At Mönichwald, on the southern end of the Wechsel Mountains, the town and the surrounding area were wrecked, with many farms looted and destroyed, and most buildings in the town either totally or partially ruined. The same held true across the entire Wechsel range.

2. Panzerarmee
13. Waffen-Gebirgs-Division der SS Handschar

Earlier in the war men of *13. Waffen-Gebirgs-Division der SS Handschar* had mutinied twice, and killed several of their officers. But now, for more than a month the once-heavily Muslim division had fought the Russians to a standstill before superior firepower forced them back from the Mur River. The *SS-Waffen-Gebirgsjäger-Regiment 27* anchored *Handschar*'s left flank and only retreated when the right flank collapsed. In recognition of his command's stalwart stand, the regimental commander, *SS-Sturmbannführer* Karl Liecke, received the Knight's Cross from *Genderal der Artillerie* de Angelis, the commanding officer of *2. Panzerarmee*.

* * *

Word of *Heeresgruppe C*'s surrender left General de Angelis scrambling to put together a blocking force to protect his rear areas. After sending *Generalmajor* Wilhelm Söth to block the Americans coming from the west, de Angelis ordered *XVII Gebirgskorps* to pull out of the line and head west, along with *16. SS-Panzer-Grenadier-Division Reichsführer-SS* and whatever else could be scraped together.

Heeresgruppe E

Generaloberst Alexander Löhr, commander of *Heeresgruppe E*, realized what the surrender of *Heeresgruppe C* meant to him. A native Austrian, Löhr was under no illusions what would happen to the 400,000 men under his command if they were captured by the Russians or, even worse, the Slovene Partisan Army. Nor did he have to think about the fate of his homeland if communists beat the British into its heartland, knowing it would then forever fall under Bolshevik influence. So on 2 May Löhr contacted *Grossadmiral* Dönitz in faraway Flensburg to request that the government make contact with British Field Marschal Alexander and beg that the Eighth Army hurry up and move into Austria.

33

Thursday, 3 May

SS-Panzergrenadier-Regiment Deutschland

SS-Obersturmbannführer Wisliceny desperately needed to know what his superiors wanted his regiment to do, but when he again tried to call *Gauleiter* Eigruber he discovered the man and his entire staff had donned civilian clothes and melted into the woods. Unaware that his regiment had been attached to Hohenstaufen, he and his men were on their own.

Wisliceny decided to move over the Enns River to the east and headed for Ernsthofen. As they marched, Weidinger reports they became entangled with American columns, apparently with no shooting by either side.[1] The move was mostly accomplished on foot, as both fuel and vehicles were in short supply.

Mauthausen Concentration Camp

After being ordered out of Vienna by *Gauleiter* Baldur von Schirach, the Vienna Fire Department followed a twisting path that finally led them to Mauthausen. They arrived there on 13 April and, since after the *Anschluss* they had technically become part of the police, were forced to take over some of the guard duties the next day. But not only some of the duties, because a number of SS remained there and only on 3 May did the SS evacuate the entire complex, leaving the firemen alone and in charge.

The Americans

As the US 65th Infantry Division moved into Austria and crossed the Inn River, and it captured the German *Donauflotille 2* and the Hungarian Navy. Reportedly this consisted of 50 boats of between 40 and 60 tons each.[2] At 3:15 a.m. that same day, the division's 261st Infantry Regiment obtained the surrender of Passau from the town's mayor and the head of the military medical staff in the city. The bombardment of the city and its defense by an unnamed SS unit had left the ancient *Oberhaus* badly damaged, especially the roof. After the armistice more than 30,000 of the ancient tiles had to be replaced.[3]

Like so many other cultural sites throughout Germany and Austria, the *Oberhaus* dated back more than 700 years to its construction in 1219 as a fortress for the Prince-Bishop of Passau, Ulrich II. Renovations over the centuries made the fortress impregnable to direct attack, until

---

1   Weidinger, *Das Reich*, p. 401.
2   'Oberhaus Now Preparing New Dance Hall', (*Thunderbolt*, Weekly Newspaper of the 83rd Infantry Division, Vol. 5, No. 21, September 22, 1945), <http://www.staatliche-bibliothek-passau.de/staadi/thun/pdf/thun5.21. pdf>, (Accessed 19 June 2018).
3   It's hard to know what SS unit this might have been, unless *Deutschland* had still been there for the first attacks.

20th-Century artillery blasted out its defenders. In the summer of 1940 more than 2,000 Hitler Youth attended a play there. Five years later the Americans would again turn it into a recreation facility for the occupation forces.

* * *

The previous day, men from the US 13th Armored Division happened upon the POWs from *Stalags 17A* and *17B* in their forest encampment near Braunau am Inn. On 3 May, three jeeps with six men officially liberated them, since the guards surrendered immediately. They totaled more than 11,000 men, more than four thousand of whom were Americans. Within a week the first Americans were flown out by C-47s.

SS-Panzerjäger-Regiment Oberdonau

Any hopes the Austrians had that the German troops would lay down their arms to the Americans were dashed on 3 May. In the tiny little town of Eidenberg, five miles northwest of Linz, word came that the Americans were getting close could arrive at any time. Driving on Linz was Combat Command A of the 11th Armored Division, and standing in their way was the SS company that had moved into Eidenberg two days before. As daylight waned, smoke filled the sky in the direction of Grammastetten, less than two miles to the southwest, and the people could hear the distant sounds of battle. They feared the worst for their quaint town. But the SS men did what few Germans were still willing to do, namely, they marched to the sound of the guns and left Eidenberg for Grammastetten. As they left, the night sky glowed red, and the townspeople breathed a sigh of relief.

The defense of that town was in the hands of the *5. Regimentsgruppe* of the *487. Ausbildungs-und-Ersatz-Division*, commanded by *Oberst* Bernhard Engel. It was composed of bits of this and that formation, including the Reich Labor Service, the *Volkssturm*, a special-purpose company from *Ersatz-Bataillon 2, Grenadier-Regiment 642*, some men from *SS-Panzergrenadier-Ersatz-Bataillon Neuzelle* and perhaps even a contingent from *Wiking, SS-Sturmgeschütz-Abteilung 5* assault gun battalion, as well as various stragglers. Engel's command had been subordinated to *SS-Panzerjäger-Regiment Oberdonau.*[4]

When the American 11th Armored Division slammed into the widely scattered regiment at Grammastetten, it held fast amid hard fighting. But only for a while, as cohesion unraveled fast during combat and hastily thrown-together units tended to disintegrate when faced with superior firepower. And the US Army in May 1945 certainly had overwhelming air, artillery and tank support. Even with the reinforcements of the SS men from Eidenberg it wasn't enough to stop the Americans.

The battle lasted long into the night and included an artillery duel. In sustained but confused fighting the Americans penetrated into the heart of the town. As midnight neared the shooting slackened off, and the Americans prepared for another attack at first light. Meanwhile, elsewhere other elements of the 11th Armored Division got across the Danube at Ascach an der Donau.

* * *

4   'Um Jugend und Leben betrogen', <http://www.ooezeitgeschichte.at/Zeitgeschichte/umJugend_u_Leben_betrogen_2.html>, (Accessed 21 July 2018).

Further south, near Salzburg, three American divisions poured across the Inn and Salzbach Rivers, heading east. The US 65th Infantry Division headed toward Linz, the 71st Infantry toward Steyr and the 80th Infantry got the prize target of the Salzkammergut.

The 80th Infantry Division crossed the Inn River in strength and began moving southeast toward the Austrian lake country. Near Vöcklabruck it encountered a blocking force from *26. Waffen-Grenadier-Division der SS Hungaria*. It's unclear whether a battle was fought or the Americans simply bypassed the roadblock.

Another encounter with the Hungarians ended with American blood spilled at Reid im Innkreis, where a second small *Kampfgruppe* from *Hungaria* refused to go down without a fight. Some American Shermans were definitely destroyed, although the number ranges from two to five in the sources. Nor are German losses known, but it's likely the SS men were either killed or dispersed. One thing that is certain is that from now on, the Americans were wary of Hungarians.

* * *

Even three days after Hitler's death, SHAEF couldn't abandon chasing the chimera of the National Redoubt. And so, after meeting the advancing Russians at Steyr on the Enns, the US 80th Infantry Division was redirected 30 miles west to the small town of Vorchdorf, due north of the presumed center of the National Redoubt. Meanwhile, at an estate about 50 miles to the southwest near the small Alpine resort town of Strobl, one of the most powerful Nazis of them all held a meeting to assess the situation and figure out what to do next.

SS-Obergruppenführer und General der Waffen-SS Ernst Kaltenbrunner, one of Hitler's most trusted paladins, chaired the meeting at the villa he shared with his wife and three children. Himmler had appointed Kaltenbrunner as commander in the south should Germany be cut in two. The agenda of the meeting is unknown, but not the guest list. In attendance were the former mayor of Vienna, Hermann Neubacher, now the ambassador to Belgrade; *General* Edmund Glaise-Horstenau, the last Vice-Chancellor of independent Austria and the former German minister to Croatia; *Gauleiter* Friedrich Rainer of Salzburg; *RSHA* foreign intelligence area chiefs *SS-Obersturmbannführer* Wilhelm Waneck and *SS-Sturmbannführer* Wilhelm Höttl; *SS-Oberführer* Katejan Muehlmann, an art historian who helped steal Europe's masterpieces for the Nazis; and finally the most dangerous man in Europe, commando extraordinaire *SS-Obersturmbannführer* Otto Skorzeny.

The Nazi escape route out of Germany, the rat line, led through Alpine Austria south to Italy. Many high-ranking officials and *Waffen-SS* officers made it out that way, including *SS-Obersturmbannführer* Adolf Eichmann. Although none of the attendees escaped Austria, it would not be a leap to assume the meeting touched on how to blend in with the mass of displaced persons without being picked up, but regardless of the agenda there was no hiding the fact that Patton's Third Army was closing in.

6. SS-Panzerarmee

Like an Austrian diaspora, the clearing weather and drying roads filled the countryside with hordes of people flooding west. Near the front, strafing Russian ground-attack aircraft sometimes struck the columns of horse-drawn wagons piled high with household goods, blanket-wrapped mothers shuffling onward with children in tow, cows, goats and sheep, and the occasional car or truck of a Nazi functionary or military formation. But the Red Air Force rarely flew more than 20 miles behind the front lines, so even in the clear weather the bedraggled hordes crawled west unimpeded by the Russians.

The clogged highways and back roads did complicate troop movements, however. And while most of the *Wehrmacht* units maintained discipline, stragglers and deserters were a constant threat to soldier and civilian alike. When a Hungarian battalion crossed Austria to join Ferenc Szálasi at his headquarters, they encountered some Germans on the road. The Germans disarmed them and appeared to have bad intentions, but the Hungarian commander had suspected trouble and hidden his own men in the woods. They surprised the Germans and got all their weapons back, but without his forethought things could have turned ugly.[5]

12. SS-Panzer-Division Hitlerjugend

Just like that the shooting war ended for *Hitlerjugend*. The division was pulled off the front line and moved to army reserve ten miles to the northwest of its position at Eschenau. Training continued, as much for something to occupy time as for necessity, and there was speculation about going into battle against the Americans. It was a time for rumors.

Refugees who slipped through Russian lines from the east told horror stories. The population hung homemade red and white Austrian flags to greet their liberators, and a few even put out the red flag of communism, but it had the opposite to the desired effect. Their conquerors treated houses with a red flag worse than they did others, singling them out for special abuse.[6]

Kampfgruppe 1. SS-Panzer-Division Leibstandarte Adolf Hitler

The technology of German binoculars during the Second World War was second to none. Long before 1939, German manufacturers such as Emil Busch, Ernst Leitz, Hensoldt and Carl Zeiss were seen as worldwide leaders in the design and creation of optical equipment. Throughout the war this had given German troops the inestimable advantage of seeing their enemies before their enemies saw them.

One anecdote which illustrates this advantage stems from an incident on 3 May. An artillery observer left a high peak named the Hochstaff without taking his scissors binoculars with him. Some infantry defending the mountain found them. From atop the 4,000 foot-high mountain, Melk Abbey could be seen in the clear weather, a distance of 40 miles. They could even see troops moving in the region, although whose troops, whether American, German or Russian, wasn't clear.[7]

6. Armee

The survivors of *SS-Polizei-Regiment 13* took over defense of the Vorau. With so many buildings damaged or destroyed, the regiment's headquarters set up in the hospital.

---

5   Detre, Guyla László, *History First Hand* (Lakitelek: Antológia, 2007), p. 34.
6   Meyer, *The 12th SS*, p. 497.
7   Tiemann, *The Leibstandarte IV/2*, p. 318.

34

Friday, 4 May

Berchtesgaden, Germany

Führungsstab Süd had been operating at Berchtesgaden since mid-April, with *Generalleutnant* August Winter running operations. During the afternoon of 4 May, elements of the 7th US Infantry Regiment, 3rd Infantry Division, rolled into the home of Hitler and most of the Nazi Party, captured the High Command and left individual army commanders to go forward on their own. The 2,000 men defending the town surrendered without a fight.

* * *

Most histories of the week after Hitler's death ignore the heavy combat that occurred in *Heeresgruppe Ostmark*'s sector. Indeed, of all the German Army Groups extant on 1 April, only *Heeresgruppen Courland, Süd/Ostmark* and *E* remained intact and fighting until the very end.

General der Infanterie Carl Hilpert's *Heeresgruppe Courland* had been wasted by Hitler's demand that it stay bottled up in northwestern Latvia, despite the *Kriegsmarine*'s assertion that it could evacuate the army through the Baltic. It remained intact because the Russians saw no reason to devote the resources necessary to crush it, since it occupied no strategic ground and could cause no harm where it was.

Generaloberst Gotthard Heinrici's *Heeresgruppe Vistula* disintegrated under the hammer blows of Rokossovsky's Second Belorussian Front, Zhukov's First Belorussian Front and Konev's First Ukrainian Front, after fighting hard to defend Berlin. By 4 May only remnants and refugees were left, all of them fleeing west toward the Americans who had stopped at the Elbe River. The Battle of the Halbe Pocket, with *9. Armee* desperately fighting to join *12. Armee*, was unmatched in its ferocity, but *Heeresgruppe Vistula* had long since disintegrated.

As for *Generalfeldmarschall* Ferdinand Schörner's *Heeresgruppe Mitte*, after smashing the Germans defending Berlin, the left wing of Konev's First Ukrainian Front had turned south and crushed what was left of the *4. Panzerarmee*. Directly to the east, General Andrei Yeremenko's Fourth Ukrainian Front overran *1. Panzerarmee*, while Tolbukhin's Second Ukrainian Front continued shoving *8. Armee* back into Czechoslovakia. With Patton's Third US Army pouring into Czechoslovakia from the west, Schörner's command found itself surrounded on all sides in a pocket east of Prague. The Russians suffered heavy casualties during terrible fighting, but the issue was never really in doubt.

That left only *Heeresgruppe Ostmark* and *Heeresgruppe E* as undefeated German formations still conducting an effective defense, and in places the combat was as intense as any during the entire war.

But that was about to change.

* * *

Near the small Austrian alpine town of Timelkam, northeast of Lake Attersee, units of the *25. Waffen-Grenadier-Division der SS Hunyadi* drove off an American task force attached to the US Third Army, knocking out five Shermans in the fighting. The fight had started on 2 May and lasted three days. The Americans wouldn't forget the bitter encounter with Hungarians wearing SS uniforms.

Salzburg

During the war American bombers had inflicted severe damage on Salzburg. Even so, when the US 3rd Infantry Division rolled into town on 4 May the people lined the roads to see the men they viewed as liberators, after watching Hungarian SS troops parade through the city the day before. Mercifully, Mozart's home town was spared further suffering when the remaining Nazi Party officials left without organizing a futile resistance. The Americans wasted little time doing what Americans always did, namely amusing themselves. In particular they supplemented Army rations with fresh trout caught in the Salzach River, and toured the Hohensalzburg.

American Third Army

The 11th Armored Division neared the outskirts of Zwettl after having been delayed crossing the Muhl River, and once again the biggest issue was dealing with huge numbers of surrendering Germans. Moving onward the division stopped at Galneukirchen because thousands of new prisoners were taken. Late at night on 4 May some of the first SS guards from Mauthausen gave themselves up.

* * *

At Passau, fighting flared as the Americans set off through the newly fallen city. Die-hard SS men refused to surrender and fought them at every step. They were likely members of *SS-Panzerjäger-Regiment Oberdonau*, and former camp guards at Mauthausen. By the time it was over more than 500 SS men lay dead, along with a lot of Americans.

487. Ausbildungs-und-Ersatz-Division

Less than three days before Germany surrendered the struggle for Grammastetten flared up again early on 4 May. Combat Command A of the US 11th Armored Division renewed the attack with a barrage from its tanks and artillery, and rocket, bomb and strafing attacks from low-level ground-attack aircraft. Once again the Germans put up a stiff fight, but with ammunition running low and without heavy weapons it was over quickly. The broken Germans retreated over the mountains and woods. Casualties on both sides had been extremely heavy. They had been some of the last men to die fighting in Europe, for a small town with no strategic value whose capture or loss was completely irrelevant to the war's outcome.

Eidenberg finally met the Americans when US tanks trundled into the little town later that afternoon. The Austrians breathed a collective sigh of relief at having been captured without a fight, except for 40 involuntary occupants who were ecstatic. Those men were French prisoners of war, who'd been working as forced laborers since July 1940, and greeted the Americans with hugs and tears of joy.

But then shots rang out and an American was wounded. Three Hitler Youth had attacked a convoy and been killed. They weren't from Eidenberg and had been overheard to say that if Hitler was dead, they didn't want to live any longer.[1] In a fusillade of return fire, the Americans made their wishes come true.

---

1   'Um Jugend und Leben Betrogen', <http://www.ooezeitgeschichte.at/Zeitgeschichte/umJugend_u_Leben_betrogen_2.html> (Accessed 21 July 2018).

* * *

Despite the sacrifices at Grammastetten, by late afternoon on 4 May the US 65th Infantry Division was within artillery range of Linz on the south side of the Danube, and began shelling the city. It was too late in the day to attack that day, but the specter of house-to-house fighting the next morning drove the German commanders to action. Seeing no point in a useless defense, Rendulic ordered all German forces in and north of the city to move behind the Traun River, on both sides of Ebelsburg.

SS-Panzergrenadier-Regiment Deutschland

The concept of a front line was becoming more and more irrelevant. During the march to Ernsthofens the commander of *I./Deutschland* was in his staff car when it drove into a group of Americans at Bad Schallerbach, a mere seven miles southwest of Eferding. For *SS-Hauptsturmführer* and Knight's Cross winner Franz Grohmann it was quite possibly the reprieve of a death sentence, as he not only survived the war but lived another 55 years.[2]

As for the rest of *Deutschland,* the march took them across Hörsching Airport in Linz, where ME-262s burned in neat rows to keep them from being captured. Large numbers of Hitler's most successful wonder weapon, and the best fighter aircraft in the world, sat unable to defend the country that created them because of lack of pilots and fuel. It was the perfect metaphor for the last days of the Second World War.

6. SS-Panzerarmee
I SS-Panzerkorps

The assembly of weapons, vehicles and specialty shops at Türnitz and in the Jessnitz Valley continued. The strongpoints that comprised the main line of resistance were weaker than ever, but the Russians seemed more content to continue preparing for an attack than in moving forward themselves. Nevertheless, skirmishes between patrols of both sides continued.

* * *

The US 44th Infantry Division's 324th Infantry Regiment set off before dawn to clear Imst, south of Fernstein. They had waited at Fernstein on 3 May while engineers repaired the road through the Fern Pass so tanks and artillery could catch up. By 8:30 a.m. the town was in American hands, and along the way they had met up with the reinforced company that had been sent to flank the Fern Pass.

The division's objective was to pass through the Arlberg Pass and seize Landeck, so the task force built around 1/324th kept moving south. Not far out of Imst, however, they again came to a strong roadblock and faced an enemy who "defended their good positions doggedly with small arms, moderate mortar and 88mm fire, and very heavy 20mm *Flak*. There were an estimated 350 of them and although they were young, former labor troops, they were banded together by vigorous officer and NCO pressure into a good fighting group."[3] Fighting lasted most of the day but eventually the superior American firepower blasted through.

---

2   Weidinger lists Grohmann's date of capture as 1 May, but that seems highly unlikely since the Americans had not yet reached the vicinity of Bad Schallerback on that date.

3   'Combat History of the 324th Infantry Regiment, 44th Infantry Division', (University of Wisconsin, 1975),   <https://archive.org/stream/CombatHistory324thInfReg/CombatHistory324thInfReg_djvu.txt>, (Accessed 24 July 2018). If this German unit had a name it is now lost.

Unaware that the French were racing to beat them to Landeck, Major General Dean didn't push his men to risk their lives by speeding up operations. Then he became distracted by the sudden arrival of *General der Panzertruppe* Erich Brandenberger, commander of the German *19. Armee*, who wanted to arrange the surrender of his army to the Americans. The *19. Armee* spent much of the previous six months fighting the French First Army, which generated hatred on both sides. Now the highly decorated Brandenberger, winner of the Knight's Cross with Oak Leaves, wanted to end the bloodshed. Brandenberger was passed up the line to General Jacob Devers, commander of the US Sixth Army Group.

6. Armee
1. Volks-Gebirgs-Division

Elements of *Gebirgsjäger-Regiment 98* launched attacks northwest of their positions in the Wechsel Mountains, against the Russian columns moving from the northeast into the seam between the division and *9. Gebirgs-Division (Ost)*. For their part the Russians launched simultaneous attacks to drive into the division's rear.

35

Saturday, 5 May

Nazi leaders always talked a good game. Men like Heinrich Himmler, Martin Bormann, Herman Göring and countless others wore carefully tailored uniforms with grandiose titles, and awarded themselves impressive medals and spoke often about sacrifice and duty. They had no problem telling other people to fight and die to protect the Nazi state. That was, after all, the basis for Nazism, subsuming the needs of the individual to protect the *Volk*, the German people. All for one and one for all…and every man for himself.

Because while the German *Landser* died by the hundreds of thousands holding back the enemy, those same leaders used their sacrifice to flee for safety. Instead of picking up a *Mauser K-98* rifle or a *Panzerfaust,* many of them scurried to hide in the wreckage of their country they'd helped create. Some found sanctuary and escaped, such as Adolf Eichmann and Josef Mengele, but the majority did not. Of those who got away, most went through Austria.

8. Armee

Viewed from a strategic standpoint, *8. Armee* was in a desperate situation. To its north *Heeresgruppe Mitte* still held what appeared to be a contiguous front east to Breslau, but major components of that Army Group were echeloned farther east with their northern flank nearly turned. Over the previous weeks *8. Armee* itself had been driven back to the northwest, with its left flank crumpled all the way to Brno. Had the date been 1943 or 1944, Hitler's staff would have been warning of an impending disaster. But it wasn't one or two years before, it was 1945, Hitler was dead, *8. Armee* could count on no more reinforcements or supplies, and the only thing on *General der Gebirgstruppe* Kreysing's mind was how best to keep his army from disintegrating until the time came to surrender, after which reaching the American lines became paramount.

Facing his solitary army were no less than eight Russian armies of Second Ukrainian Front. From north to south they were the Fortieth, Fourth Rumanian, First Rumanian, Sixth Guards Tank Army, Fifty-Third, First Guards Cavalry, Seventh Guards and Forty-Sixth Armies. On Kreysing's far right flank, two armies of Third Ukrainian Front continued trying to ford the Danube, the Fourth and Ninth Guards Armies. There were thus ten armies facing his one; even taking into account that Russian armies equated to German corps, he was still outnumbered by five or six to one and the disparity in heavy weapons probably approached twenty to one.

Everyone knew the war couldn't last much longer, but unfortunately for Kreysing and his men he was about to get a new commanding officer, the odious *Generalfeldmarschall* Ferdinand Schörner. The *8. Armee* was detached from *Heeresgruppe Ostmark* and given to *Heeresgruppe Mitte.* Schörner was an ardent Nazi and favorite of Hitler's who allowed no retreat and reveled in the shooting of Germans for disciplinary purposes. Talk of surrender was usually good for a bullet. For his part, Rendulic agreed with this philosophy but never seemed gleeful about its necessity.

Schörner did make one exception to this draconian rule, though: himself. Schörner talked a tough fight and promised to lead his troops into captivity, but when the time came to give up he abandoned his army group and tried to blend in with the mass of refugees in Austria. It didn't work.

* * *

The town of Traun sits on the north bank of the Traun River about four miles south-southwest of Linz. The earliest settlement of the area dates to Roman times, but it is first mentioned in documents in 790 AD under the name Dru, the Celtic word for river from which Traun drew its name.

When *Luftgaukommando 17* left Vienna during the battle it wound up in Traun, along with numerous other vagabond headquarters. Before long the little town was overrun with military, government and party organizations trying to stay away from the front. At 2:00 p.m. on 5 May the Americans pulled into the little town. The SS pulled out rather than fight, after blowing up the river bridge.

* * *

Three miles northeast of Traun, and about the same distance southeast of Linz, the town of Ebelsberg was jammed with German troops. During the previous night the garrison of Linz and all forces north of the Danube had withdrawn to Ebelsberg, but that only delayed the inevitable confrontation with the American 65th Infantry Division. When morning dawned a one-sided artillery battle broke out. The Germans tried to fight back but it was hopeless, as batteries of the US 11th Armored Division joined the fight by shooting across the Danube from the area of Steyregg, and the entire artillery of the 65th Infantry Division fired from the west.

* * *

The surrender of the *25. Waffen-Grenadier-Division der SS Hunyadi* was arranged and accepted by the US Third Army in the region of Lake Attersee in Upper Austria.[1] Something like a third of the division went into immediate American captivity while officers stalled for time, disbanding their units and letting the men escape if they could. Some sources indicate that the two Hungarian SS divisions were actually somewhat to the east, at Molin. The likelihood is that they were scattered about the area in various encampments, since their number was more than 40,000 at this point. Rather than dissolving the Hungarian headquarters immediately, the Americans let it remain in existence into June to help smooth out the processing of Hungarian troops, many of whom had melted away into the countryside amid the torrent of refugees.

As was often the case with SS troops captured by the Western Allies, though, many of the Hungarian SS officers were handed over to the Soviets and the new pro-Soviet Hungarian government, with the result that most were tried, imprisoned and executed. Count Ferenc Szálasi and the military commanders had hoped for political asylum from the Western Allies but it was not to be. Other officers and men were assured of their safety if they returned to Hungary, but the only Hungarian to voluntarily return home after the war, the former commander of the 61st Regiment, was imprisoned for 15 years and died in poverty. The Inspector General of the Hungarian troops, *SS-Obergruppenführer* Jeno Ruszkay, was later handed over to the Russian-controlled Hungarians, who tried him as a war criminal and executed him on 22 June 1946, five years to the day after the start of *Unternehmen Barbarossa*.[2]

---

1   One source puts these surrenders as taking place on 6 May.
2   Savich, Carl, 'Vojvodina and the Batschka Division', (Serbianna, 2008), <http://www.serbianna.com/columns/savich/070.shtml>, (Accessed 21 February 2012).
      Ruszkay was not the only high-ranking Hungarian later extradited by the victors to Communist Hungary. "Laszlo Deak was sentenced to death by hanging by the Vojvodina Supreme Court on October 31, 1946, for the mass murder of 5,000 Serbs and Jews in Novi Sad in January, 1942, during the Great Raid. He was executed on

* * *

Mauthausen concentration camp was liberated on 5 May by American troops. The 11th Armored and 26th Infantry Divisions liberated the camp, and two plaques now commemorate the event. The guards were a mixture of Viennese firemen and SS, but Mauthausen was not a death camp, although thousands died there. Instead, it was a fairly conventional concentration camp for resistance fighters, mostly from the Catholic countries of the West. Just inside the prisoners' entrance was a brothel for the use of the privileged inmates, who paid for the brothel visit with camp money they earned by working and which could only be spent inside the camp.

This is not to say that prisoners were not executed; they were. Nor that Jews were not sent there to work and die; they were, in large numbers. One of the great ironies of Mauthausen was that while it was one of the worst camps in the Nazi system, it was built with great attention to aesthetic detail, and even to beauty. The doors to the prisoners' gate were heavily carved wooden wonders, and the front entryway was quite handsome.

In March 1946 the United States began a trial of 61 men associated with Mauthausen and the crimes committed there, with most of them ultimately being executed. It seems that an anonymous inmate charged with typing ID cards for camp guards, then destroying them when they were reassigned, had instead kept them buried in a nearby yard until they could be turned over to war crimes investigators. Among those condemned and executed was August Eigruber, the former *Gauleiter* of Upper Austria. Franz Ziereis, *Kommandant* of Mauthausen, was captured on 23 May 1945, but was then shot while 'attempting to escape'.

Linz

American spearheads rolled into the city and captured one of Hitler's 'five great cities of the Reich'. His plans for Linz were to make it a major cultural center and his retirement home. During the war it became a center of the German armaments industry, with the *Hermann Göring Reichwerke*, the *Stickstoffwerke Ostmark* and other factories being built there, at least partially using slave labor. Three concentration camps went up in the vicinity to house the laborers. Money poured in to finance all of this, including the *Nibelungenbrucke*, the Nibelungen Bridge, over the Danube, and new residential buildings.

The US Fifteenth Air Force bombed the city 22 times during the war, killing 1,679 people and causing heavy damage. After the war, the city of Urfahr, directly across the Danube, was in the Russian zone. Guard positions made crossing from one zone to another without the proper paperwork dangerous in the extreme, with the Danube River performing the same function as the Berlin Wall.

* * *

The officers of all German units in the Graz area were called to an afternoon conference and told of the surrender of German forces in Italy, and the consequent general surrender soon to come.

November 4 or 5, 1946 in Vojvodina, along with *Generalfeldmarschall* Ferenc Szombathelyi and Josef Grassy. Grassy had been an *SS-Gruppenführer* and a *Feldmarschalleutnant* of Hungary. He had commanded the 26th SS Grenadier Division 'Ungaria' from March to May, 1945 and the 25th SS Division 'Hunyadi' from October, 1944, to March, 1945. He had earlier commanded the 15th Hungarian Infantry Division from January, 1941 to October, 1943. Grassy was apprehended by US troops and extradited to Hungary in November, 1945. He was tried and convicted of war crimes in a Hungarian court in Budapest on January 8, 1946 and sentenced to death. He was subsequently extradited by Yugoslavia, where he was tried, convicted, and again sentenced to death for war crimes. He was hanged on November 5, 1946 in Vojvodina."

For the men of *Kampfgruppe 5. SS-Panzer-Division Wiking* and other SS units who were non-Germans, or were *Volksdeutsche* whose countries had been overrun, the future was grim indeed. Spirits sank, as few of them had any illusions about their fate, until food stockpiles of the highest quality were suddenly distributed to all of the units in the area.[3] Although the rank and file may have thought the unexpected largesse bore an eerie resemblance to the last meal of the condemned, none shied away from gulping down the luxuries; who could say for certain where their next meal might come from?

* * *

For the first time in the war, troops of *Kampfgruppe 3. SS-Panzer-Division Totenkopf* fought Americans when they encountered a United States armored task force near Königsweisen, east-northeast of Linz. The battle lasted into the next day.

* * *

The human flotsam of Germany was flowing south in the ever-shrinking Reich, seeking a refuge from capture or, if that was not possible, surrender to the Western Allies rather than to the Soviets. At the small Austrian alpine village of St Leonhard, Austria, American troops captured a group of scientists and workers from the Bachem-Werk, the company run by Erich Bachem that was developing the world's first vertical takeoff rocket, the *Natter*. Two weeks after leaving Kirchheim unter Teck in Germany, just ahead of the Americans, they'd finally run out of places to go to keep their invention away from the Allies.

Along with their human booty, the Americans also found four intact versions of the weapon, two of which were shipped back to the United States. German scientists and their creations were highly prized trophies. Thus ended one of the most revolutionary weapons programs of the Third Reich, a true wonder weapon that, if developed and deployed on time, might have altered the course of the strategic air campaign.

* * *

To the French and Americans overrunning Austria from the west there was no telling who they might encounter next. In early May the French encountered another of Germany's strange foreign units who were recruited to fight against the British, originally known as the Free Indian Legion, *Legion Freies Indien*, but after being transferred to the *Waffen-SS* designated as the *Indisches Legion der SS*. This regimental-sized unit contained more than 2,000 well-trained and heavily armed troops who had been scraped together from a variety of sources, including Allied prisoners captured in North Africa. Their purpose in joining the Germans was to free India from British rule, and they'd seen some action during a harrowing retreat across France after D-Day.

But despite the desperate shortage of infantry and their possession of scarce weapons, the Indian Legion was never committed to battle in the east. Instead, it spent months languishing at the Heuberg Training Area at Simaringen less than thirty miles inside Germany, north of Lake Constance. Indeed, it became such a joke that one man designated to command it never even showed up, and Hitler himself joked about it at the same conference when he ordered *Galizen* disarmed.

Now, with the Allies closing in, the Indians marched south to avoid capture and tried to slip through the mountain passes into Switzerland. They were caught marching along the shore of the lake. Rumors circulated that the French shot some of them at Immenstadt, just over the German border from Austria and a few miles east of Lake Constance.

---

3   Strassner, *Das Reich*, pp. 331-332.

As it turned out the Indians' fears were largely unjustified because, while trials were planned for treason, the positive feelings toward them among the Indian populace made this an unpopular and dangerous proposition. They were seen as freedom fighters against the rule of the hated British. In the end only a few of the 3,115 men who made up the Legion were tried and most had the charges dropped because of unrest.

Korps von Bünau

Less than 48 hours before Germany's general surrender *General der Infanterie* von Bünau spent his day readying his command to resist the Americans. On a personal level von Bünau didn't see the point in continuing to fight a lost war, but as a diligent soldier he obeyed orders. To that end, a new divisional command was incorporated into his corps, that of *232. Infanterie-Division*. There were no combat troops associated with this unit, as the division had been shattered and then captured in Italy; only the headquarters elements remained. Von Bünau intended for it to command miscellaneous army and *Waffen-SS* units on his corps' left flank, should it come to a last-stand fight. Fortunately for all involved that never happened. As for the *232. Infanterie-Division* staff, when the corps withdrew west many of them became detached from the body of the corps and were never heard from again.

9. SS-Panzer-Division Hohenstaufen

Having regrouped and absorbed huge number of replacements, *Hohenstaufen* arrived in the area south of the Danube. There was now a large SS army crammed into northwestern Austria, having incorporated replacements and got as combat-ready as they ever would be. Had *Generaloberst* Rendulic been in the mood to go down fighting, the end of the war in Austria could have been very bloody. Fortunately for everyone involved the subject never came up.

SS-Panzergrenadier-Regiment Deutschland

The former commander of *2. SS-Panzer-Division Das Reich*, the charismatic and widely respected *SS-Gruppenführer* Werner Ostendorff, was posthumously awarded the Oak Leaves to his Knight's Cross by *SS-Oberstgruppenführer* Sepp Dietrich. No record has been found authorizing the award[4] from any higher headquarters, although given the state of chaos existing in Germany at the time, lost or incomplete records would be no surprise. The date of the award is known from a broadcast by *6. SS-Panzerarmee* on 5 May.

As for Ostendorff's former command, most of *Das Reich* had long since been detached from *Heeresgruppe Ostmark* and sent north, but on 5 May the orphaned *SS-Panzergrenadier-Regiment Deutschland* was officially attached to *9. SS-Panzer-Division Hohenstaufen*, making that unit probably the largest remaining division in the entire *Wehrmacht*. For the commander of *Deutschland*, *SS-Obersturmbannführer* Wisliceny, it must have come as a great relief to again have a higher headquarters in his chain of command, even if everything around them was disintegrating.

---

4   Bolstering the case that Ostendorff may have died on 5 May instead of 1 or 4 May, it would make sense that Dietrich awarded him the Oak Leaves as he lay on his death bed. Otherwise the award was posthumous.

Having arrived at Ernsthofen the previous day, his regiment skirmished with Americans approaching the Enns River north of that little town and up to the Danube. With Russians at their back and Americans facing them across the Enns River, the SS men knew the end was near. But without a formal surrender and orders to maintain a defense, they fought on.

Besides *Deutschland*, one other element of *2. SS-Panzer-Division Das Reich* that stayed in Austria when the division moved north was the *SS-Panzer-Instandsetzungs-Abteilung 2,* the Panzer Repair Battalion. Most of the division's vehicles had been lost in the recent fighting, but not all of them. Now, on 5 May, the battalion moved north and loaded onto trains at Zwettl, leaving the *Ersatz Kolonne*, Replacement Column, behind to finish its work and then follow the next day.

During this short period the column went to Linz for supplies but returned empty-handed. There was nothing left. But along the way signs of dissolution were everywhere. Uniforms, helmets, weapons and abandoned or broken-down vehicles littered the roads as men streamed west, their only thought to flee the Russians.[5]

* * *

The 41st Cavalry Reconnaissance Squadron, of the US 11th Armored Division, rolled into Sankt Georgen an der Gusen, east of Linz on the north bank of the Danube, and captured the nearby *B-8 Bergkristall* underground aircraft factory. This vast complex was run by the Messerschmidt Company and produced fuselages for the ME-262 *Stürmvogel* jet fighter, as well as V-2 rockets. The scale of the construction was enormous, with tunnel openings twenty feet tall. More than 1,000 fuselages were built there, using slave labor from the two nearby camps, Mauthausen and Gusen. The mortality rate among the men forced to work there was unusually high, even for those caught up in such a deadly enterprise. Estimates of the dead begin at 40,000.

An unfinished maze of tunnels nearby called the *Kellerbau* was used to manufacture machine guns and their parts, and was also built and maintained by slave labor. In late 2014 a new tunnel system was reportedly discovered in the area that might have been connected to *B-8 Bergkristall* and which purportedly could have been used in the German atomic weapons program. At the time of writing this book the site's existence had not been verified by archaeological digs.

I SS-Panzerkorps

The men of the *LAH* could only watch as Russian fighters and ground-attack aircraft buzzed their positions. For several days the fighting had died down, and they only had to worry about fatigue, food and being cold. The planes didn't attack them, but while they flew overhead nobody could relax.

US Seventh Army
French I Corps

On Austria's far northwestern frontier, the French I Corps had crossed the border with three divisions, the 5th Armored, 2nd Moroccan Infantry and 4th Moroccan Mountain Divisions. Following the battle at Bregenz they pushed further east against sporadic but minor resistance until all three divisions moved south into the far western state of Voralberg. It was 5th Armored Division that blasted the fanatical Germans at Bregenz and drove on to Feldkirch before turning east toward Langen.

5   Weidinger, *Das Reich*, p. 402.

US VI, XI and XV Corps'

Pouring into the Tyrol were the American 44th and 103rd Infantry Divisions, and the 10th Armored Division. Speeding through the idyllic Austrian countryside, by the day of surrender the 103rd Infantry Division had passed through Innsbruck and the Brenner Pass to Sterzing, where it met the spearheads of the US 88th Infantry Division, from the US Fifth Army, moving north out of Italy.

To their right were 36th Infantry Division and 2nd French Armored Division of XI Corps, which moved through the heart of the Alpine region against occasional resistance, which was usually formed around mountain passes. None of the defenses were large enough to be significant obstacles, but reminded the Americans what could have happened had the *Alpenfestung* become reality. Salzburg had fallen the previous day to the US 3rd Infantry Division, which sped through to Bad Ischl and then to Bad Aussee.

After leaving Steyr two days before, the 80th Infantry Division reached Vorchdof and found agents of the Counter Intelligence Corps (CIC) waiting on them. After interrogating a local Nazi Party official the agents discovered that two days earlier August Eigruber, the *Gauleiter* of Upper Austria, had passed through on his way to Gmunden on Lake Traunsee. *Gauleiter*s were major figures in the Nazi hierarchy and capturing one of only 42 in all of Germany was quite a prize. Moreover, Eigruber had wanted to destroy all the art that had been looted for the planned Adolf Hitler museum, a total of more than 6,500 of the world's greatest paintings and a large number of sculptures. He'd been talked out of it only with difficulty by the unlikeliest of men, Ernst Kaltenbrunner.

A chic resort town like Gmunden was exactly the sort of place fleeing Nazis might go, so backed by a task force from the 80th Infantry the agents headed south to Gmunden. Once there they discovered that Eigruber wasn't even the biggest fish in the pond they were fishing in. The week before no less impressive personages than *Reichsleiter* Robert Ley and *SS-Obergruppenführer und General der Polizei und der Waffen-SS* Ernst Kaltenbrunner had passed through Gmunden on their way to the Salzkammergut.

Kaltenbrunner had taken over for Reinhard Heydrich after the latter's assassination in Prague in 1942 as head of the RSHA, *Reichssicherheitshauptamt,* or Reich Main Security Office. In such capacity his job was to protect the Reich from all enemies, be they foreign or domestic, and had been instrumental in setting up the concentration camp system, particularly in Austria. Kaltenbrunner was a Hitler favorite, and late in the war he stopped reporting to Himmler and instead met with the *Führer* directly. This was possible because he became friends with Martin Bormann, who controlled those who could see Hitler. Even Himmler feared Kaltenbrunner's ascendancy.

Robert Ley had been an early convert to Nazism. Like Göring, Ley had been a fighter pilot in the First World War and was shot down in 1917. Among his injuries was damage to the frontal lobe of his brain. After the war he went to school, earned a doctorate and worked as a food chemist for I.G. Farben, but Ley was a notorious alcoholic and the job didn't last long. When the French occupied the Ruhr in 1923 it so infuriated Ley that he turned into a rabid nationalist, and in 1925 he joined the Nazi Party.

The incident that cemented Hitler's personal favor toward Ley occurred in 1925, after the *Führer* was released from Landsberg Prison. During a party meeting in Hanover, a furious row erupted between Hitler supporter Gottfried Feder and the Strasser brothers, Otto and Gregor,[6] about whether the property of the former Royal family should be confiscated by the state. Hitler thought this policy to be wrong but found little support. Even the newly joined Joseph Goebbels spoke out

---

6   Among the earliest party members, the Strasser brothers were ideologues to a much greater extent than the more pragmatic Hitler. They were anti-capitalist, anti-Semitic and anti-communist.

against Hitler's position. But the one man other than Feder who supported Hitler was Robert Ley, and the *Führer* never forgot his loyalty. Despite the progression of Ley's Labor Front into nothing more than a way for him to funnel money to himself to pay for luxurious villas and drunken orgies, he retained Hitler's favor until the very end.

Moving south along the Traunsee, the CIC men were now escorted by an armored battalion. The pursuit of Kaltenbrunner and Ley had become a reconnaissance in force into the heart of the feared National Redoubt. On the main highway south of the Trauensee they discovered the Ebensee Concentration Camp and stopped. Horrified at what they found, the task force deployed for the night while the CIC agents waded through the dead and listened to the dying beg for food the Americans didn't have.[7]

US 80th Infantry Division

The division's advance across Austria had been more like a race than a military drive, with the only thing slowing it down being the sheer number of surrendering German soldiers crowding the roads, many of whom had already thrown aside their weapons. Every conceivable type of cast-off military equipment lined the sides of the road, or in places blocked it. Thousands of prisoners of war were taken and most were simply told to keep walking west, since the division had neither time nor resources to escort them. At all costs they had to reach the demarcation line before the Russians crossed it.

Parts of the division encountered no resistance, but as it advanced on multiple routes there were inevitable encounters with armed Germans. Some were bloody, but most weren't. Outside the town of Schwanenstadt on the Ager River, one jeep stumbled upon a *Luftwaffe* airfield and captured it single-handed, including its entire complement of personnel. But elsewhere some elements had run into an SS detachment that had dug-in around a 20mm gun with no intention of surrendering, so the divisional elements simply went around them. It is possible this was the men from *26. SS-Waffen-Grenadier-Division der SS Hungaria*, who were encountered near Reid im Innkreis. There had also been another costly skirmish near Vöcklabruck. Even so, 80th Infantry Division had moved more than eighty miles in three days, and the next day would find them at their ultimate destination, Spital.

Since entering Austria they had sliced through *Kampfgruppe Grünwaldt, 26. Waffen-Grenadier-Division der SS Hungaria*, the remnants of Vienna's military staff *Stetvertretendes-General-Kommando-XVII-Armeekorps* and were entering the defensive zone of *Kampfgruppe Sperrverbande Söth*, who'd been sent by Hermann Balck to stop them.

* * *

At 10:00 p.m. word filtered down to the men of the US 44th Infantry Division that *General der Panzertruppe* Erich Brandenberger had signed the instrument of surrender for the German *19. Armee*. As Brandenberger negotiated the surrender of his army, representatives arrived from *Heeresgruppe G*, of which the *19. Armee* was a part, to arrange for the surrender of the entire army group. It looked like aside from fanatics who refused to follow orders, the shooting would soon be over.

Then the French found out. General de Lattre was furious at being out of the loop of these negotiations and threatened to keep on fighting even though the Germans surrendered. Devers

7   CIA, 'The Last Days', https://www.cia.gov/library/center-for-the-study-of-intelligence/kent-csi/vol4no2/html/v04i2a07p_0001.htm, (Accessed 13 January 2018).

tried to placate his ally but de Lattre was having none of it. Things could have gone very badly, but eventually the French general's fury was overcome by events. Not only did the Germans facing his troops melt away but the general surrender was signed.

* * *

Kesselring wanted to surrender all forces under his command, which included both *Heeresgruppe Ostmark* and *Heeresgruppe E*, in addition to *Heeresgruppe G*, and requested permission from the new *Führer, Grossadmiral* Dönitz, to do so. But Dönitz only granted permission for him to surrender *Heeresgruppe G*, so in most of Austria the shooting continued.

6. Armee
1. Volks-Gebirgs-Division

Tired and hungry to the point of starving, discipline in the ranks of the *Gebirgsjägers* began to become an issue. Several times officers had to stop panicked men from fleeing, and the incessant rain of mortar and artillery shells kept a steady stream of wounded men headed for the aid stations.

The last meal some men in *4./Gebirgsjäger-Regiment 99* ate during their time manning the lines came on 5 May. They shared four loaves of bread, some sardines packed in olive oil, five tubes of cheese, a few cans of beef and a handful of cigarettes. They were also able to fill their canteens with ersatz coffee. But the field post office system no longer worked, and none of the men had bathed for more than a week. Nor was there a chance to wash their uniforms, or replace lost items.[8] They had what they had.

Kampfgruppe 3. Panzer-Division

Generalmajor Söth, commander of the division, had left on orders from *Generaloberst* Balck to block the Americans from overrunning the army's rear areas, but was now instructed to make contact with the Americans in the west and begin surrender negotiations for all of *6. Armee*. Only motorized elements had been sent, so when he'd left he took with him most of the division's remaining combat power; *Panzergrenadier-Regiment 3, Panzer-Regiment 6* and *Panzeraufklärung-Abteilung 3*.

Showing the importance of his mission, the group traveled by train, few of which were still running. During a stop along the way, on May 7, they learned from the crew of a *Flak* position that the war had already ended, but didn't believe them. Arriving in Liesen the *Kampfgruppe* detrained and deployed, while *Generalmajor* Söth attended a conference called by *Generaloberst* Balck at Gleisdorf. There he learned it was all true. Balck laid out the planned withdrawal to all of the army's division commanders, which was made to allow them to disengage from the Russians and cover each other's movements to the west. This operation was estimated to take up to two weeks.

1. Ukrainische Division der Ukrainischen National-Armee

The division formerly known as *14. Waffen-Grenadier-Division der SS Galizen (Ukrainische Nr. 1)* received orders from General Shadruck to distribute all remaining stocks of food, ammunition and other equipment to the troops in preparation for withdrawal to the west. Shadruck was under no

---

8   Brettner, *Die Letzten Kämpfe Band I*, p. 62.

illusions about the fate of he and his men should they fall into Russian hands. All operable vehicles were fueled and made ready to move. Any machines that were inoperable, or for which there was no fuel, were destroyed or disabled. *SS-Brigadeführer und Generalmajor der Waffen-SS* Freitag bombarded the headquarters of *6. Armee* for an exact time of retreat, but none was forthcoming.

US Third Army

Patton's men had fought their way into northwestern Austria and by 5 May stood at the demarcation line along the Enns River south of the Danube, from the town of Enns all the way south to Liezen. North of the Danube the 11th Armored Division had made it to Königwiesen and Grein, where they clashed with elements of *Totenkopf* for the first time in the war. Most of the fighting and dying done by the Americans in Austria was done by Third Army. Light resistance was still encountered here and there, particularly at Grien, but aside from the skirmishes with *Totenkopf* they suffered no casualties and then withdrew.

US Fifth Army and British Eighth Army

The surrender of German *Heeresgruppe C* in Italy sped the advance of Lieutenant General Lucian Truscott's US Fifth Army out of the Po Valley toward Austria. The primary unit moving north was the 88th Infantry Division. With no organized German resistance, it closed in on the Italian-Austrian border by 4 May, and kept going to meet the 411th Infantry Regiment of 103rd Infantry Division at Sterzing, just inside the Italian border. The Americans were driven by a desire to end the war as soon as possible, but to their east the British Eighth Army was in a race of a different kind.

Tito's Yugoslavian Partisan Army was in full-blown land-grab mode, which Winston Churchill adamantly opposed. With the prime minister breathing down his neck, Eighth Army commander Lieutenant Richard McCreery ordered his units to make all possible haste to seize parts of Austria in the British zone of occupation. In some locations they would make it ahead of the communist partisans, and in others they wouldn't.

Heeresgruppe E

Generaloberst Löhr believed that unless the British hurried and took southern and southeastern Austria, it was inevitable that a communist state would be created by whichever eastern army overran the region. But Löhr was as delusional as many German officers when it came to cooperation with the Allies. He wanted to offer Alexander the use of *Heeresgruppe E* to maintain order and keep the communists out of Austria, and Dönitz even gave him permission to contact Alexander and negotiate such an agreement, but it's unknown whether the new *Führer* thought anything would come of it.

It's doubtful that Löhr could have believed Alexander would accept his proposal, either. In reality, he probably saw in the oncoming British Army the last chance to save his Army Group from capture by the communists. In pursuit of this last-ditch hope, *General der Gebirgstruppe* Ringel made contact with the British to put forth Löhr's offer but, predictably, his efforts went nowhere. He was not even allowed to meet Alexander.

* * *

The hastily built defensive position facing south against the British and Yugoslavians sounds more formidable than it really was, since by now the vast majority of the *Landser* wanted nothing more than to surrender to the British at the earliest opportunity. Listed from west to east, *Kampfgruppe Harmel* blocked the main highway used by the British Eighth Army inside Italy, as part of *XXXXVII Armeekorps*. Next came *XXXIV Armeekorps* south of Villach, *LXIX Armeekorps* near Klagenfurt with *Korps Rösener* to their south. *Division-zur-besonderen-Verwendung 487* faced Fourth Yugoslavian Operations Zone on their south. *XXII Armeekorps* was next, with *16. SS-Panzergrenadier-Division Reichsführer-SS* on the far eastern flank linked to *Heeresgruppe E*; *2. Panzerarmee* was to the south of this line.

36

Sunday, 6 May

Heeresgruppe Ostmark

With Hitler's death and the transfer of power to the Dönitz government, and with Zossen no longer available to disseminate information, the German field commanders were out of the loop on the latest events. To *Generaloberst* Lothar Rendulic's mind the extensive Russian defensive preparations in the conquered areas of Austria, including forcing civilians to dig air raid shelters when the *Luftwaffe* was absent from the skies, lent credence to the possibility of a German alliance with the Western Allies. But if that was ever going to happen, the deadline had arrived. Needing information before deciding on what to do next, Rendulic sent the Chief of Staff of *6. Armee, Generalmajor* Heinrich Gaedcke, to make contact with George Patton's US Third Army.

Gaedcke's orders were to ask Patton for two things. First, that medical supplies stored south of Salzburg and now in American hands could be shipped through the lines to *Heeresgruppe Ostmark* headquarters; and second, that German troops be allowed to redeploy through American lines from west to east. Rendulic had been told that a political solution would end the war and this was his way to ascertain whether or not the rumors of an alliance against Russia were real. The answer, an emphatic 'no' to both questions, told him all he needed to make a decision on the army group's fate.

Then, in a reversal of unwritten policy up to that point, a message arrived from *Generalfeldmarschall* Kesselring, the *Oberbefehlshaber Süd*: "It is decisive for the fate of the Reich that the Eastern Front be held. Effective immediately, determined resistance is also to be offered to the Americans along the Enns."[1]

Rendulic was stunned by the message. He had no knowledge of the surrender negotiations going on at SHAEF headquarters. Fighting against the Russians he understood, but shooting at Americans no longer made any sense. After considering this order for a while, the ardent Nazi Rendulic disobeyed a direct order and issued one of his own, that a cessation of hostilities on the army group's western front would take effect at 9:00 a.m. on 7 May. Furthermore, after praising his men for their valor and dedication, all units facing the Russians were ordered to begin a general withdrawal to the west at nightfall on 7 May.

* * *

On direct orders from *XXXXIII Armeekorps*, funeral services were held at all commands for the fallen *Führer*, Adolf Hitler. In truth, most of the men didn't think Hitler was dead. Whether they simply couldn't face the truth or not, the majority thought he had slipped away at the last moment.

* * *

Relaying a dry fact such as the German disengagement and withdrawal from the front simplifies what was a very complicated endeavor. The man responsible for organizing and maintaining discipline during the withdrawal of *8. Armee* was *Generalleutnant* Konrad Offenbaecher, the *Kommandant Rückwartiges*, or Rear Area Commander. To help guide and protect the retreating columns he

---

1   Newton, *German Battle Tactics*, p. 233.

had two formations, the *177. Ersatz-Division* and *Panzer-und-Kradschützen-Ausbildungs-Bataillon Wehrkreis XVII*, Tank and Motorcycle Training Battalion from Vienna.

It was their job to direct traffic, settle disputes, report on problems and guarantee that food and fuel stops were properly shared. Without a strict presence the timetable of retreat would break down. If the columns were then overrun by the Red Army they would be in no position to fight back, and might be massacred. As things turned out the operation was a success.

* * *

With the war rapidly coming to an end, Sepp Dietrich had some unfinished business. None of the normal *Wehrmacht* bureaucracy remained intact and so, on his own initiative, Dietrich intended to award commendations to those he deemed worthy.

SS-Brigadeführer Sylvester Stadler, commander of *9. SS-Panzer-Division Hohenstaufen*, and *SS-Obergruppenführer* Wilhelm Bittrich, commander of *II SS-Panzerkorps*, were awarded the Swords to the Knight's Cross. *SS-Standartenführer* Karl Kreutz was awarded the Oak Leaves to the Knight's Cross for his action on 9 April in moving *Das Reich* artillery into the streets of Vienna to cover the infantry's withdrawal over the Danube Canal. *SS-Sturmmann* Lange, first name probably Günther, received the Knight's Cross for his action during the Battle for Vienna when, after leading his men in wiring a bridge for demolition, he waited to blow it up until 30 or 40 Russians were marching across. This action probably took place on the night of 9-10 April, as the bridge in question spanned the Danube Canal. *SS-Sturmbannführer* Hans Hauser received the Knight's Cross for his *Kampfgruppe*'s stand at Münchdorf in early April, which prevented the Russians from cutting *Das Reich* in half. *SS-Hauptsturmführer* Franz-Josef Dreike was given the Knight's Cross for his actions on 5 April at the Laaer Berg, when he personally took command of an 88mm gun that had been abandoned by the *Luftwaffe* and turned back a massive Russian tank attack. There were many more such awards given out that day.

The awards became controversial in the postwar years. Dietrich supposedly had authorization to hand out awards up to the Swords and Oak Leaves to the Knight's Cross, but there is very little documentation to support this, making the awards themselves somewhat dubious. Of course, Hitler had been dead for almost a week by then, Berlin was in Russian hands and the rump government of Grand Admiral Donitz had other things to worry about.

3. SS-Panzer-Division Totenkopf

For the second consecutive day, men from *Totenkopf* battled American troops, this time elements of *III./SS-Panzergrenadier-Regiment Theodore Eicke*.[2] The clashes took place near Zel and at Köningswiesen. Rumors had it that you would have to surrender to whoever you fought last, but it's unknown if that played a part in *Totenkopf*'s one and only clash with the Americans.

* * *

For more than a month the people of Stockerau had become a society living underground. In the meadows south of the town, along the banks of the Danube, increasingly desperate groups of deserters had to scrounge and steal to survive. Rumors had circulated for weeks that the Reich was dying, that the Nazis were leaving, that the *Wehrmacht* was about to surrender, but even though civil authority had loosened there were still people ready to shoot defeatists, and despite the Russians being at the city limits, they'd been there for most of April and the city hadn't yet fallen.

---

2   Landwehr, *Siegrunen 76*, p. 6.

Early on 6 May the familiar crump of a heavy artillery bombardment rattled dishes in the town, with hundreds of rounds being fired by the Germans over the Danube. If the townsfolk wanted to scream about the pointless nature of the firing, they couldn't. Most huddled in dank, and by now filthy, air raid shelters. And while anti-Nazi activities had already begun, defeatist talk was still punishable by death.

When not in hiding, they were marched out to build defensive positions. It had been nearly a week before when parts of the army had marched out, with refugees following them, and all seemed to be coming to an end. But it didn't end. It was beginning to seem like it might never end.

Nor was the brutal schizophrenia of the Nazi state over yet. A young married couple were denounced and shot, along with their two children, reportedly by members of *Totenkopf*, and yet the seriously wounded townsfolk were treated in the military hospital and the local pastor was allowed to give last rites. As if to punctuate the futility of continuing a fight long since lost, and the murder of people whose only crime might have been wondering what was going to happen, a shell or bomb landed near the White Rose Inn and shattered the beloved bay window.[3]

9. SS-Panzer-Division Hohenstaufen and SS-Panzergrenadier-Regiment Deutschland

Hohenstaufen's commander, *SS-Brigadeführer* Sylvester Stadler, and *SS-Obersturmbannführer* Günther-Eberhard Wisliceny of *Deutschland* both tried to negotiate with the Americans to arrange the surrender of their commands, but the only terms offered were unconditional surrender. The SS men rejected them.

* * *

While the front lines had been starved of infantry for months, and both *Totenkopf* and *Wiking* had abolished their panzer regiments to use the members as *Panzergrenadiers*, the rested and fully replenished (with personnel) *II./Panzer-Regiment Brandenburg* found itself at Hohentauren in Central Austria. While the battalion's parent division, *Panzer-Division Brandenburg*, died defending Berlin, the tankless panzer crews languished in a safe, picturesque backwater, sunning themselves in the warm spring weather not far from the front lines of *Heeresgruppe Ostmark* to the east, north and west. Life was good.

SS-Kampfgruppe Keitel

6. SS-Panzerarmee ordered the *Kampfgruppe* to send representatives to find the Americans and make arrangements for surrender. Acting on these orders, the *Kampfgruppe*'s chief of staff, *SS-Sturmbannführer* Gustav Etzler, who once commanded the artillery regiment of *22. SS Freiwilligen-Kavallerie-Division Maria Theresa*, headed west to find the Americans.

6. Armee
1. Volks-Gebirgs-Division

News that the Americans had reached Gmunden, some 150 miles to the west, made each man wonder if the word would come to head west, or if they should await the Americans' arrival in

---

3   Brettner, *Die Letzten Kämpfe Band II*, p. 171.

their rear areas. In the meantime the division's leadership was determined to hold out against the Russians, despite having nothing to eat and very little ammunition to fight back with.

But desertions increased as empty stomachs drove men to leave their comrades. Only then did the rank and file discover that the supply chief of *Gebirgsjäger-Regiment 99, Oberleutnant* Bröger, had already taken off for the American lines along with all of his men, animals and vehicles. This left half of the division without any supplies, or the ability to distribute what might be found.

For most of the day, however, the defenders were spared more attacks. The Russians appeared to be looking for new gaps in the line. Then after nightfall a strong Russian attack drove men out of the front lines and into the artillery positions, where a terrible firefight cut down many men on both sides.[4]

* * *

In Graz, west of Fürstenfeld, an officers' meeting was held at General Ringel's home at 5:00 p.m., where *Oberbefehlshaber Süd Generalfeldmarschall* Albert Kesselring alerted all units that the capitulation was imminent.[5] Kesselring must have been aware of the extraordinary circumstances. Theoretically nothing had changed: the *Wehrmacht* was still the *Wehrmacht* and he was the supreme commander of all the forces present. Yet the operations he had to come arrange would dissolve that very same *Wehrmacht*. Would the Germans' rigid discipline and adherence to orders hold in place until it was all over? Or would terror break down order as the men fled before the near certain death of Russian captivity? He walked a tightrope in giving orders and wound up allowing a great deal of operational freedom. Some commander used it to pull out early, but the majority did their duty to the last.

Generaloberst Alexander Löhr, the commander of *Heeresgruppe E*, stressed in the strongest terms that if *Heeresgruppe Süd* surrendered early then his men would be trapped in Yugoslavia, where Tito's forces would show them no mercy. This meant that *6. Armee* and *2. Panzerarmee* would have to hold in place long enough for them to get away. *Genderal der Artillerie* Maximilian de Angelis was sympathetic to Löhr's predicament, but *2. Panzerarmee* could only hold on for so long if it too wanted to avoid Soviet captivity.

The most incredible part about all of this was the senior German leadership's multiple requests to Eisenhower to send medical supplies to the Germans at the front lines and even to allow reinforcements to come to them. Emissaries were sent out for those purposes, including *Generaloberst* Rendulic himself. The Germans actually believed that with Hitler dead the Western Allies might join them in fighting the Russians, and Russian preparations for just such an event encouraged their delusions. In every case, however, they were quickly disabused and it was only after being refused that plans were made to abandon the front lines in the east.[6]

When *SS-Oberführer* Karl Ullrich returned to *Wiking* during the night of 7-8 May after the meeting with Kesselring, the division was told that it only had until 12:00 p.m. on 8 May to disengage from the Russians, then to drive 140 miles to enter American lines.[7] The war was over; now began the race to survive.

---

4   Brettner, *Die Letzten Kämpfe Band I*, p. 59.
5   Balck, *Order in Chaos*, p. 437. Balck says he met Kesselring during the night of 6-7 May at Judenberg, just west of Graz, and that he discovered nothing new during the meeting. According to him *6. Armee* received the surrender order by radio. However, Balck was almost assuredly at this meeting, because elements of *6. Armee* were given the unenviable job of being the rearguard. Assigning those duties with Balck not in attendance seems highly unlikely.
6   Lucas, *Last 100 Days*, p. 110.
7   Strassner, *European Volunteers*, p. 332. Strassner says that Ullrich attended a meeting west of Fürstenfeld, which almost surely was the meeting at Ringel's house. Dates and places for the meeting vary among the sources.

* * *

At the Gasthof zur Seewirt, in Mattsee northeast of Salzburg, Ferenc Szálasi calmly awaited arrival of the Americans. Hundreds of Hungarian soldiers milled about the village when the Americans finally rolled in. The Arrow Cross leader and self-proclaimed *Führer* of Hungary had sent his personal bodyguards out to find the Americans. Once the Americans faced him in person he reminded them that he had never declared war on the USA. He told them he only fought on to defeat International Bolshevism. The Americans were having none of it, and their commander refused to shake Szálasi's hand. One Hungarian-born American officer openly accused Szálasi of being a war criminal.

* * *

At Steyr, the US 71st Infantry Division encountered minor resistance in the western half of the city in closing on the Traun River. The exact identity of the unit holding the city remains uncertain, even today. Most sources list it as the remnants of the *153. Grenadier-Division*, which continued to hold out on the eastern bank of the Traun. The 'Grenadier' designation makes this unit sound better than it was. For most of its existence it had been the *153. Ausbildungs-und-Ersatz-Division*, and was commanded by *Generalleutnant* Karl Edelmann. During the crisis in Hungary it had been committed to front-line service and was crushed at Székesfehérvár the previous December. The survivors were returned to Austria in no more than regimental strength. But the *153. Grenadier-Division* was part of *LXXII Armeekorps* at the beginning of April, on *Heeresgruppe Süd*'s extreme left flank. It was no longer listed on the 1 May Order of Battle for *8. Armee*. For it to be defending Steyr means it would have had to march more than 125 miles and change armies. Now, at Steyr, whoever the defenders were, less than 24 hours before the end of the Second World War some of them found a reason to die fighting.

* * *

The US 80th Infantry Division faced no significant opposition as it sped through Bad Ischl and Gunnden to the weakly guarded Pyhrn and Pötesheim Passes. Once there, however, the Americans stopped, unwilling to absorb casualties with the war scheduled to end the next day.

Heeresgruppe E

During the meeting at Graz it became clear that only through strictly coordinated retrograde movements between *Heeresgruppe E* and *2. Panzerarmee* could the right flank of *Heeresgruppe Ostmark* not collapse during the withdrawal west. To ensure perfect cooperation, therefore, *General der Artillerie* de Angelis' *2. Panzerarmee* was detached from *Heeresgruppe Ostmark* and subordinated to *Heeresgruppe E*. But de Angelis realized that time was short, especially for his right wing corps, the *LXVIII Armeekorps*, and had already ordered it to begin the retreat.

37

Monday, 7 May

Reims, France

At 2:41 a.m. Central European Time, at a small red brick schoolhouse, *Generaloberst* Alfred Jodl signed the instrument of unconditional surrender of all German military units, effective at one minute after midnight on 8 May. The war was officially over, but the fighting and dying went on.

Heeresgruppe Ostmark

After five-and-a-half years of triumph and defeat, of suffering and pain both given and received, of watching countless comrades, loved ones and enemies die and of continuing to fight in the face of overwhelming odds and certain defeat, for the men of the army group, the time had come to run for their lives.

Orders filtered down from Rendulic's headquarters for all units to withdraw as quietly as possible from their front-line positions, to leave behind a weak rearguard, and then run like hell for American or British lines. Many in the *Waffen-SS* thought it would be their salvation. It wasn't.

* * *

As for Rendulic, his war ended before that of most of his army group. Early on 7 May, right after issuing the withdrawal order, he phoned *6. SS-Panzerarmee* to say that an American armored reconnaissance group had just captured his headquarters and Sepp Dietrich now commanded *Heeresgruppe Ostmark*. His final order was for Dietrich to carry out the surrender according to the document signed at Reims, a copy of which was teletyped to *6. SS-Panzerarmee* headquarters. Everything was sent to the armies and corps, with instructions to cross the demarcation line for the American forces, the Inns River, no later than 1:00 a.m, German Summer Time, on 9 May.[1]

It's surprising that Rendulic turned over command to Dietrich and not to Hermann Balck. He hated the *Waffen-SS* at least as much as Balck did and had a particularly low opinion of Dietrich, but his decision may have been influenced by the large number of SS formations in *Heeresgruppe Ostmark*, or perhaps, being a die-hard Nazi himself he knew Balck's disdain for the Party. Whatever the reason, Sepp Dietrich was now the acting commander of *Heeresgruppe Ostmark*.

---

1   Maier, *Drama*, p. 371.

North of the Danube

8. Armee

The commander of *96. Infanterie-Division*, *Generalmajor* Harrendorf, spent long hours negotiating the surrender of his men to the US 26th Infantry Division. His persistence was successful and the Germans gladly marched into American captivity.

* * *

The town of Laa an der Thaya had been the objective of Malinovsky's final offensive against *8. Armee*, but had been saved by the stubborn resistance of *Panzerkorps Feldherrnhalle*. Now, on the day of Germany's surrender, the residents learned their protectors were leaving and the Russians would soon be there. The women were warned of what was to come, both the very young and the very old. Laa had been heavily bombed in the previous month but had been spared urban combat. Now it would suffer all the same.

* * *

The *II SS-Panzerkorps* ordered all of its units to move out of their positions that night, cross the Enns River and make for Amstetten, where they were to surrender to the Americans.

The Americans

The 56th Armored Engineer Battalion, part of 11th Armored Division, had performed every imaginable mission during their march across Europe, but on 7 May they got one they would never forget. The battalion was ordered into Mauthausen to bury 3,000 rotting corpses. There was no time for identification, all they could do was dig huge trenches and bulldoze the bodies into them.

6. SS-Panzerarmee

As Patton's Third Army approached the defensive line of *9. SS-Panzer-Division Hohenstaufen*, the Americans noted that instead of active resistance, the greatest deterrent to their progress came from the hordes of German soldiers throwing down their weapons in surrender and then clogging the roads. But if the SS generals wanted to go down fighting, *Hohenstaufen* was in a position to do so. When combined with the attached *SS-Panzergrenadier-Regiment Deutschland*, *SS-Brigadeführer* Stadler had nearly 23,000 men under his command, many of them battle-hardened veterans.

When *I SS-Panzerkorps* joined *II SS-Panzerkorps* in ordering its units to assemble in the Amstetten area, there was therefore "the extraordinary spectacle of four *Waffen-SS* panzer divisions, the 1st, 3rd, 9th and 12th, and a complete regimental KG of another, the 2nd, all concentrated in a part of Lower Austria measuring only 50km by 40km".[2] The concentration of so many *Waffen-SS* divisions constituted an *Alpenfestung* all by itself, since this aggregation probably represented more than 60,000 men, while *Hohenstaufen* alone now had 35 operational panzers, *Jagdpanzers* and *Sturmgeschütze*. Between all four divisions there were probably some 80-100 machines in working order, along with many may more SPWs. Had they followed their *Führer's* example of fighting to

2   Reynolds, *Sons of the Reich*, p. 312.

the last[3] it could have led to one final bloodbath. Fortunately for the Americans, neither Stadler nor Sepp Dietrich had any intention of fighting to the last man. Instead they opened surrender negotiations.

Korps von Bünau

The ad hoc military formation that began life as *Korps Schultz* in the emergency following the Russian capture of Tulln, and later became *Korps von Bünau*, had grown in the past three weeks to a force of more than 20,000 men. This would not have made it the size of a corps during peacetime, but in May 1945 it was a remarkable total. *General der Infanterie* von Bünau was ordered to pull back to a position near Melk, both in anticipation of moving west to meet the Americans, and because it was the narrowest point of the Danube Valley between the river and the Alps.[4]

The main consideration was how to get across river barriers. The corps was so short of basic equipment that fording a significant river without a standing bridge was no longer possible. Crossing the Danube was nearly impossible, since there were no bridges west of Krems left in German hands. Therefore units were attached and detached to whatever headquarters seemed best able to get them across the Enns before it was too late.

After dark the corps withdrew west, unhindered by the Russians. The professionalism of von Bünau and his staff came into play now to prevent a descent into chaos and flight. Everything had been so well planned that routes west were not congested and the men slipped away in the night.

12. SS-Panzer-Division Hitlerjugend

A high-ranking delegation from *Hitlerjugend* sought contact with the US 65th Infantry Division to arrange terms of surrender. On a hill on the east bank of the Enns, overlooking Steyr, they met an American patrol in a jeep who directed them to a marked path through a German minefield. Once through that obstacle they were led to a factory where American officers asked the location and strength of the division. Told its position, and that its ration strength was around 10,000 men, the Americans celebrated such an accomplishment on their division's war record.

The standard conditions were given. All guns and ammunition had to be left a mile from the American lines. Panzers were to haul their ammunition behind them, with guns pointed to the sky. Every vehicle would fly a white flag and anyone still on the east bank after midnight on 8-9 May would go into Russian captivity.

SS-Brigadeführer Kraas ordered two variations when he heard the terms. First, no white flags would be flown. And second, because of the danger of Russian attacks, guns and ammunition would be kept for as long as possible. He complimented his division on its long and hard service and wished his men well in the future.[5]

---

3   This is what Dönitz had told them in his broadcast and nobody at the time knew the truth.
4   Rauchensteiner, *Die Krieg in Österreich*, p. 195.
5   Meyer, *The 12th SS*, p. 498.

Kampfgruppe 1. SS-Panzer-Division Leibstandarte Adolf Hitler

Word of the surrender filtered up to the front lines, along with the deadline to reach the Enns. Most German formations maintained unit cohesion, because while the men knew the war would end less than 48 hours later, there were no guarantees that the Russians would allow them to escape to the American zone. This was especially true of the *Waffen-SS* units. But cohesion between units was a different matter.

Around Lilienfeld some of *SS-Kampfgruppe Peiper*'s artillery men had been working with an Army battalion who pulled out during the night without telling them the war had ended, or that they were on their own. When the SS men woke up the next morning they were alone and, worse, their guns had been blown up.

As cooperation and the chain of command fractured, another of those bizarre anecdotes of war happened to some panzer men from the *LAH*. With the war virtually over and no need for new weapons, panzer crews were ordered to Kirchberg an der Peilach to pick up four factory-fresh Panzer Mark IVs. They had arrived just in time to be driven west to the Enns, where their crews promptly drove them into the river.[6]

SS-Kampfgruppe Keitel

The sleepy spa town of Windischgarsten had so far seen nothing of war, although 122 of its citizens had died in the conflagration on battlefields across Europe. Located in the Traunvertiel[7] and surrounded by mountains, settlement of the area dated to Imperial Roman times. It had once been a waypoint for travelers to the Crusades.

The previous day, the Chief of Staff of *SS-Kampfgruppe Keitel*, *SS-Sturmbannführer* Gustav Etzler, had been ordered by *6. SS-Panzerarmee* to make contact with American forces and begin surrender negotiations. At 10:00 a.m., at Windischgarsten, *SS-Sturmbannführer* Etzler became the first representative of *6. SS-Panzerarmee* to meet with the Americans. As the day wore on three more members of Dietrich's staff joined him.

* * *

Still holding the line in the Krems bridgehead, as it had been since 14 April, *SS-Kampfgruppe Trabandt III* pulled out of the line and crossed the Danube at Krems with all of its equipment and wounded, and headed for the American lines to surrender.

6. Armee

In accord with Army Group Commander *Generaloberst* Rendulic's order of the previous day to begin a westward withdrawal at nightfall, *General der Panzertruppe* Hermann Balck's *6. Armee* pulled up stakes and headed for the demarcation line far to the west. When the Russians figured out what was going on they began a terrible artillery barrage and attacked immediately. The fighting over the next 24 hours would be so vicious that no less than eight Knight's Crosses would be handed out in American prisoner of war camps after the surrender.

* * *

---

6   Tiemann, *The Leibstandarte IV/2*, pp. 319-320.
7   The Traunvertiel is an area of Upper Austria through which the River Traun flows.

The Russians arrived in Vorau just after sunrise. Despite the town lying in ruins, and the overt subservience of the remaining population, the first thing they did was look for women and girls.

9. Volks-Gebirgs-Division (Ost)

Rumors had run rife through the German ranks for weeks, but early in the morning on 7 May a new rumor circulated among the men. There were several variations on the message, but the essential core was that a truce was coming. Everyone wanted to believe it, but they'd heard this type of thing before. Except this time, in the afternoon, *Volkssturm* men serving at the front began marching home.

* * *

The commander of *3./SS-Gebirgsjäger-Ausbildungs-und-Ersatz-Bataillon 13 Leoben* was still with his men defending the Kobermannsberg area, when orders came to report to Breitenstein. Once there he learned all the company commanders had been summoned. Sometime after dark the battalion commander informed them that Germany had surrendered, and laid out plans for the surrender. The men were told that for another four or five hours they should obey orders, because the Russians wanted to bag all of *6. Armee* at one time, including their battalion. This, he went on to say, must be avoided at all costs and through any evasive maneuvers necessary.[8]

The SS men all knew what capture by the Russians meant, but by 7 May the situation of the battalion from Leoben was dire. They were the most easterly unit left on the Austrian front, with German lines to both north and south far to the west. Withdrawal would only be possible via a narrow corridor through steep mountains, and they had very little time to make it to the American lines.

* * *

The platoon leaders of the *5./SS-Gebirgsjäger-Ausbildungs-und-Ersatz-Bataillon 13 Leoben* attended the same conference and received the same order to withdraw. Furthermore, they were ordered to destroy their remaining heavy weapons, meaning in their case, the *Nebelwerfers*. But knowing there would probably not be any more rockets coming to them, the SS men had been very judicious in using the ammunition they had. On the night of 7 May they still had 600 rounds left.

So men who knew the war was about to end and only wanted to survive, fired every last rocket they had at men who also knew the war was about to end and only wanted to survive. At 8:00 a.m. the next morning they joined the exodus west.

1. Volks-Gebirgs-Division

The situation of the desperate, exhausted survivors of *Gebirgsjäger-Regiment 99* seemed like it couldn't get worse, until it did. They'd been fighting more or less continually for going on two months in drenching rains, whipping winds and icy fog, with too little food and rest, watching comrades die on a daily basis. They had endured day after day of saturation shelling from heavy artillery and Katyusha rockets, followed by wave after wave of Russian infantry. Whenever ground was lost they pushed their aching bodies to their feet and immediately counterattacked before their enemy could dig in. And throughout it all they had protected Styria from being overrun.

---

8   Brettner, *Die Letzten Kämpfe Band 1*, p. 108.

They never heard that *Generaloberst* Jodl had signed the instrument of surrender in Reims, France, and were determined to fight as long as they could. Their motivation was the belief that the Americans were coming from the west and they wanted them to capture Styria, thus saving the region from the depravations of the Red Army. But on 7 May continued resistance became impossible when the men of the regiment's pack train deserted, taking all of the mules with them. Now, the only food and ammunition was that on hand. Without resupply, protecting Styria was no longer possible.

Unfortunately for them Hermann Balck had designated their parent division, *1. Volks-Gebirgs-Division*, as the army's rearguard, so they had no choice except to stay put and fight on. To their north the newly formed *9. Gebirgs-Division (Ost)* also had to stand their ground. Meanwhile *6. Armee*'s two mobile formations, *IV SS-Panzerkorps* and *III Panzerkorps*, packed up and motored west.

All over Austria the winding mountain back roads filled up as hundreds of thousands of men all headed west at essentially the same time, screened only by two worn-out mountain divisions. They rode in every conceivable vehicle, from cars and trucks to APCs, *Kübelwagens*, SPWs, Panzers, wagons, carts and on horseback. Most walked. Anything edible they found along the way quickly disappeared, although incidents of looting or the killing of livestock appear to have been rare.

Most Nazi officials fled with them, to havens prepared in advance for the higher-ranking members, or any hideaway they could find for the others. A few stayed in place to keep the civil government functioning and to avoid total chaos. In Graz men from banned political organizations formed a government to meet the Russians with the complete acquiescence of the former Mayor.

On the last day of the war *Gebirgsjäger-Regiment 99* had a combat strength of 1,565 men of all ranks. In addition, 229 Hungarians were attached. A fascinating addendum is that the regiment also listed the Russian *Hiwis* on their roster. *Hiwis* is an abbreviation of the German word *Hilfswilliger*, which means 'willing helper'. They were Russian nationals who joined the *Wehrmacht* either because they opposed Stalin, or to stay out of prisoner of war camp or for other reasons. They wore German uniforms, ate from German field kitchens and sometimes carried a rifle. Typically, however, they helped maintain equipment, worked in the supply companies and generally performed whatever tasks needed doing. *Gebirgsjäger-Regiment 99* listed 1,515 *Hiwis* on their rolls.[9]

Strangely, not all of the *Hiwis* were Russians; there were also a few Italians among them. Unfortunately for them, when the division headed west most of them were left to fend for themselves.

Both of the division's two *Gebirgsjäger* regiments suffered horrific casualties, repudiating the idea that fighting in east-central Austria was minimal. At full strength, either of the regiments should have had about 3,064 men in total. On 7 May *Gebirgsjäger-Regiment 99* had 1 officer, 240 NCOs and 1,324 men of other ranks on its rolls, for a total of 1,565, almost exactly 50 percent of its authorized strength.

The *1. Volks-Gebirgs-Division* spent the last month of the war fighting in the Hartberg-Fürstenfeld district of Styria. Many of the 1,193 German soldiers buried in eight cemeteries around the district came from its ranks. Alongside them are 513 of the Russian soldiers they killed. More are buried outside the district at Sankt Kathrein and at Rettenegg. A further 64 members of the division were buried in Burgenland at Mattersburg.

* * *

9   Brettner, *Die Letzten Kämpfe Band 1*, p. 59.

During the day, *Heeresgruppe Süd* sent out warning orders to make preparations for moving toward the Americans. Such a large and complex operation required tremendous pre-planning even in times of plentiful fuel, clear roads and adequate rail transport, but in the dire logistical circumstances and jammed highways in early May 1945, good staff work became even more important. Only by thinking about every necessity and maintaining discipline could the army group safely pass to the west.

2. Panzerarmee

Late on 7 May the army laid down a massive artillery bombardment, firing off most of its remaining ammunition, and then pulled out for the demarcation line between the American and Russian zones of occupation, the Enns River. The ruse of the barrage worked. A full day passed before the Russians realized they were gone.

Heeresgruppe E

All along the German front, the time had come to run. *Heeresgruppe E* began moving into Austria, while *Generaloberst* Löhr gave his corps commanders permission to open negotiations with the nearest enemy. The commander of *XXXIV Armeekorps, Luftwaffe General der Flieger* Hellmuth Felmy, was told to contact the British at Villach.[10] *General der Artillerie* de Angelis was to contact the Russians, while Löhr saved the worst assignment, opening negotiations with Tito's Yugoslav Army, for himself.

De Angelis ordered *General der Kavallerie* Gustav Harteneck, the commanding officer of *I Kavallerie-Korps*, to begin discussions with the Russians, but it was a bluff. In fact, he wanted to hide their true intentions from both the Russian Fifty-Seventh Army and the First Bulgarian Army. While negotiations were underway the army would pull out.

The Russian refused the German overtures, using the excuse that combat forces still manned the front, but in fact negotiations offered them no advantages. The rebuff left de Angelis' conscience clear and he sped up the retreat, but the problem was that nobody knew the location of the demarcation line between the British and the Russians. Some said it was the Mur, but that turned out to be wrong.

---

10   Rauchensteiner, *Krieg in Österreich*, p. 321.

38

Tuesday, 8 May

Jagdgeschwader 52

Not everyone was finished fighting. The greatest fighter pilot of all time was one of them, and early on the morning of 8 May *Major* Erich Hartmann's ME-109G lifted off for a reconnaissance mission to Brno. His orders were to determine if the city was still in German hands or not, and how far the Russian spearheads had penetrated toward Deutsch Brod. His frame of reference was a road leading east.

Hartmann flew despite the chaos all around him. By this point *Heeresgruppe Mitte* was essentially surrounded, the *Wehrmacht* had surrendered and the roads of Austria and old Czechoslovakia were clogged with fleeing troops and refugees. In the distance he spotted a black mushroom-shaped cloud of smoke rising from Brno. Licking flames were evident all over the city, and columns of Russian vehicles were pouring into its streets. That's when he spotted eight Yak-11 fighters darting in and out of the smoke cloud in strafing runs, presumably on German troops below. The Russians hadn't encountered the *Luftwaffe* for quite some time and didn't expect them to show up over Brno.

Complacency in battle is usually fatal, and so it was on 8 May. One Russian pilot seemed intent on showing off to the troops below, and when his plane appeared almost in front of Hartmann's sights the 'Blond Knight' attacked. His beloved ME-109G, nicknamed *Karaya Ein,* responded to his touch like a well-trained horse. He dove into firing position just as the Russian reached the top of his loop and hung there inverted. The range decreased rapidly until the Yak filled Hartmann's gun-sight. He pressed the trigger and watched as hits sparkled all over the Russian aircraft. Rolling over, the Yak burned and tumbled earthward, a plume of black smoke marking its death plunge. The Yak was Erich Hartmann's 352nd victory.[1]

That wasn't the end of the mission, however. Hartmann was looking for a second victim when he saw above him a dozen silver aircraft flashing in the sun; American P-51 Mustangs. Outnumbered six-to-one, and without the advantage of height, Hartmann and his wingman plunged into the smoke and headed west, fortunate that neither side followed them. Instead, the Americans and Russians mistook each other for the enemy and fought it out in the skies over Brno.

* * *

After he landed, Hartmann and his commander knew they were caught in a vice. With the Russians in nearby Brno and already shelling their makeshift airfield at Deutsch Brod, and the Americans reported to have spearheads on the Moldau River just to the west, there was nowhere left to retreat. The two winners of the Knight's Cross with Diamonds were ordered to fly west to Dortmund, and there to surrender to British forces. Between them they had destroyed almost 550 Russian aircraft and were under no illusions about the treatment they would receive if captured by

---

1   Toliver, Colonel Raymond F. & Constable, Trevor J., *The Blond Knight of Germany* (New York: Ballantine, 1971), p. 176.

the Russians. And yet neither man could fly off and leave his comrades from *JG-52* to their fate at the hands of the Red Army.

Burning their beloved ME-109s and destroying anything of military value, the two *Luftwaffe* heroes stayed with *Jagdstaffel-52* and led a column of trucks and miscellaneous vehicles to Pisek, where they surrendered to the Americans. Unfortunately, they were captured east of Pilsen, and by agreement at the highest levels, Germans captured east of Pilsen were handed over to the Russians.[2] Hartmann wouldn't see Germany again for 10 years.

North of the Danube

Heeresgruppe Ostmark
8. Armee

During the final night of 7-8 May, the Germans at Laa an der Thaya fired off all of their remaining ammunition at the Russian lines. Then they blew up all the bridges and evacuated the town, leaving the citizens to the mercy of the Russians.

* * *

The German front around Hollabrunn had held solid for more than two weeks after the Russian attacks shifted west from the Staatz area. There had been occasional air raids, and a few houses had been damaged, but nothing dire. Cannon fire echoed around the town day and night, but in Hollabrunn life went on much as normal. The more clear-thinking of the townspeople must have realized that it couldn't last forever, but some also probably suffered from the delusion that, since the Russians had been stopped short of the town, they would remain stopped. If so, that hope died on 8 May.

The first Russian patrols moved in around 1:00 p.m. and before long the Russians were shelling the retreating German columns. Air attacks went in to hit them as well, but after a while it died away, and the people of Hollabrunn were left to adjust to their new reality.

25. Panzer-Division

Like all German units facing the Russians, the men of *25. Panzer-Division* wanted to surrender to the Americans. But fighting near Brno meant they had Russians to the west, north and east. The only way out was south, so the division scraped together the last of the fuel and sped for American lines around Linz.

6. Panzer-Division

Further north than *25.Panzer-Division*, *6. Panzer-Division* was still fighting in the Brno sector as part of *Heeresgruppe Mitte*. With most of Schörner's Army Group caught in a pocket east of Prague, *6. Panzer-Division* pulled away from the front and headed for the American lines in western Czechoslovakia. In a race against time the division would make it over the demarcation line in time, and the Americans would accept their surrender.

---

2   Tolliver and Constable, *The Blond Knight*, pp. 177-181.

But only for one day, and then the Germans would find themselves handed over to the Russians after all.

Kampfgruppe 3. SS-Panzer-Division Totenkopf

No division had a bleaker outlook if it fell into Russian hands than did *Totenkopf*. During the long years of war it had only in the past week fought the Americans, while the suffering it inflicted on the Soviet Union was fresh in Russian minds. Moreover, no divisional trappings signified National Socialism more than those of *Totenkopf*. So when surrender negotiations with the Russians turned out less than satisfactorily, approval was given for it to speed west and surrender to the Americans at Gallneukirchen. As the SS men drove into American captivity they were surprised by the heavy guard force watching them. Sherman tanks pulled into the German column at regular intervals, with riflemen perched on the turrets.

The reason soon became obvious; they were to be turned over to the Russians. They'd been tricked. Once in the hands of the NKVD it's not hard to imagine their fate. The vast majority of the men died in the terrible Russian prison system, although some noted that they were treated better than the average free Russian citizen.[3]

* * *

Shielding the Danube crossing on the north, so that *SS-Kampfgruppe Trabandt III* and other formations could pull out toward the Americans in the south, was *SS-Kampfgruppe Neff*, containing the last remnants of *Totenkopf*'s panzer regiment. Formed three weeks before in Vienna, it still had three Tigers and two Panthers under the command of *SS-Obersturmführer* Neff. The *Kampfgruppe* was ordered by *II SS-Panzerkorps* to cover its withdrawal to the west and south until 5:00 p.m. At that time they were to blow up their machines and follow the corps.

All three Tigers headed for Weinzierl am Walde to block any Americans coming down from the northwest, while the Panthers went north of Krems to Stratzing. No sooner had the Tigers made it to Weinzierl before all three broke down. Five weeks earlier *SS-Hauptscharführer* Warnick and his crew had collected one of the six repaired Tiger Is at the Vienna Arsenal. The other five had all since been lost but Warnick's panzer was still battle-worthy. Except now there would be no more battles, so the SS men did the only thing they could do; they blew up their Tiger, while the crews of the two others did the same. Their crews also blew up the two Panthers.[4] None of them encountered the enemy.

Blowing up your own tank wasn't always easy or safe. One of the Tiger crewmen forgot to unscrew the detonating cap of the demolition charge, so to set it off he threw hand grenades into the turret. It did the trick, but the explosion was so powerful he had to be taken to a hospital in Melk. The panzer men rejoined the survivors of their regiment and surrendered to the Americans the next day, only to be turned back over to the Russians a few days later.

South of the Danube

The largest panzer factory of the entire Third Reich was the *Nibelungenwerke* at Sankt Valentin, Austria, just south of Mauthausen across the Danube. During construction it gained the nickname

---

3   Ullrich, Karl; Translated by McMullen, Jeffrey, *Like a Cliff in the Ocean, The History of the 3. SS-Panzer-Division "Totenkopf"* (Winnipeg: J.J. Fedorowicz, 2002), pp. 275-278.
4   Wood, *Tigers of the Death's Head*, pp. 245-246.

of the *OKH Speilzeugfabrik*, the Toy Factory. Of some 3,100 Panzer IVs produced in 1944, more than 2,800 were built there, despite the factory having been heavily damaged by aerial bombardments. The *Nibelungenwerke* also produced the monstrous *Jagdtiger*, with its 128mm main gun. Like most other factories it had a well-equipped repair facility, which *Heeresgruppe Süd* used throughout the battle for Austria to put badly damaged panzers back into operation.

* * *

The following incident illustrates the waste and futility of Hitler's vision for his armaments program. The *Führer* liked big, new and powerful weapons, at the expense of producing multiple good but lesser weapons systems. Eight brand-new *Jagdtigers* awaited delivery to the Army at the *Nibelungenwerke*, which represented nearly ten percent of the total production run. Since this was in the vicinity of where the *LAH* found itself on 8 May, it has sometimes been said the SS division took possession of the mammoth panzers, probably because of the similar acceptance of the four Panzer IVs on 7 May. Instead, the *Jagdtigers* were turned over to crews from *Schwere-Panzerjäger-Abteilung 653*, who were at the factory awaiting delivery. The shining 73-ton behemoths each represented a huge investment in time, manpower and especially precious steel.

Eight such monsters might have had a significant impact on the combat along the Danube, or perhaps in the mountain valleys. But now it was too late. After taking possession of them, the first thing their new crews did was blow them up. Then they headed west to surrender.

* * *

In the final months of the war parts of the *Nibelungenwerke* complex were moved underground. On V.E. Day the 259th US Infantry Regiment, part of 65th (Battle-axe) Infantry Division and commanded by Major General Stanley E. Reinhart, overran Sankt Valentin and captured the factory. Surviving foreign workers and slave laborers from Mauthausen were taken under US Army protection.

6. SS-Panzerarmee

The Enns River was the finish line, the barrier beyond which the Germans thought they would be safe in American hands. The river was a typical wild-water river with origins in the Radstädter Tauern Mountains near Klagenfurt, from where it flowed in a generally northerly direction 157 miles until its junction with the Danube. For most of its length it was not a river that was safe to swim. Swift currents could swirl a man downstream, never to be seen again. This made bridges imperative to cross to the western bank. The main bridges stood at Steyr and Weyer, and that's where the army headed.

As for the mass of *Waffen-SS* jammed into the area bounded by the Enns and Danube Rivers, and Steyr, if the men harbored any hopes of decent treatment by the Americans of XX Corps they were quickly dashed. At the time and after the war the men of the *Waffen-SS* never fully understood that it wasn't them personally who were painted as war criminals, unless they were among the relative handful who actually were so charged, but instead it was the nature of their organization that condemned them. The *Waffen-SS* was the military arm of the Nazi Party itself, and while they saw themselves as being no different than other branches of the *Wehrmacht*, their enemies didn't share that view. "*Anyone* who wore SS runes was seen as part of a diabolical machine that had caused endless misery and countless deaths – as a barbarian who deserved to be treated as such."[5]

---

5   Reynolds, *Sons of the Reich*, p. 313.

The SS formations complied with instructions to unload their weapons before approaching the American lines, and then got the first taste of how they were viewed by the outside world. Hundreds, or perhaps thousands, of freed concentration camp inmates, probably from Mauthausen, had acquired guns and waited for them in fields on either side of the road. While the first of the now-disarmed SS men drove to surrender, they had to run a gauntlet of small-arms fire, and even had people jump onto their vehicles trying to drag them off. The SS officers complained to the Americans, who were more stunned that the Germans didn't understand why they were being shot at than by the actions of the former prisoners.

SS-Panzergrenadier-Regiment Deutschland

After a brief speech by the regiment's commander, and the distribution of the last medals, *Deutschland* made for Enns by way of Amstetten and St Valentin. March discipline was good. At the Enns bridge over the River Enns, "Regiment Deutschland passed in a motorized march, neatly dressed, including field kitchens and supply vehicles, as if on parade".[6] And so into history passed one of the first *Waffen-SS* formations.

Korps von Bünau

By morning the first troops of the corps had made it to the Melk defensive positions and were settling in to fight, if it came to that, when without warning orders came to keep moving and get over the Enns River by 1:00 a.m. the next day, a distance of more than 50 miles. For tens of thousands of men and hundreds of vehicles, most of whom had no idea how to get where they needed to go, on unfamiliar roads, that was a long distance to cover in such a short time. All food stocks were immediately issued to the men, while ammunition and weapons were offloaded so that every vehicle could carry as many men as possible. They clung to every protruding bit of metal on anything that moved, because in the back of every man's mind was the thought that surely the Russians had caught on by now and were giving chase.

Which they were. There was a skirmish near Amstetten as the Russians sped forward to catch the fleeing Germans, but it was too late. *Korps von Bünau* had given them the slip.

Around noon *General der Infanterie* von Bünau himself made contact with elements of the US 65th Infantry Division to arrange the surrender of his corps. Other parts contacted the US 71st Infantry Division to surrender elsewhere, but by day's end it was all over. The hard-bitten soldier who'd sacrificed his family on the altar of Hitler's war went into American captivity. He would live to assist his captors in assembling important biographical works by senior German officers by telling his own story of command in Vienna and later at *Korps von Bünau*, and those documents would live on to help later historians, such as this one, write about this period with greater accuracy and understanding.

Schwere-Panzerjäger-Abteilung 653

When the battalion pulled out of Kirchberg an der Pielach, in addition to the destroyed *Jagdtigers* from the factory, they left behind an assortment of vehicles, both damaged and undamaged, due

---

6 Weidinger, *Das Reich*, p. 410.

to a lack of fuel. Among them were at least half a dozen SPWs and at least one more *Jagdtiger*. All were sabotaged.

Schwere-Panzer-Abteilung 509

Out of an authorized strength of 45 Tiger IIs, nine still remained on 8 May. Whether because fuel was too scarce, or the machines were not operational, or perhaps because they couldn't bear to surrender them in one piece, the crews blew up their panzers in preparation for surrendering to the Americans.

Kampfgruppe 1. SS-Panzer-Division Leibstandarte Adolf Hitler

Straddling the border between Upper and Lower Austria, and bisected by the Enns River, the city of Steyr was the last objective of the *LAH*. When the division pulled out of its final positions it had already destroyed the inoperable heavy weapons, as well as vehicles without fuel. Any equipment that could be used by the Russians was ordered smashed. All they took was food, fuel and personal weapons.

Settlement of the ancient city by the Celts can be dated to at least 600 BC, and it was part of the kingdom of Noricum. It was conquered by the Romans in 15 BC and the area prospered because of the local iron mines. The area had been important for millennia, and therefore the road network leading to and from the valley of the Enns River had also grown to accommodate the commercial traffic. But even when the Roman legions marched through the area, the roads in the Steyr region had never seen traffic on the scale of 8 May 1945.

Traffic jams clogged back roads all across Austria, but the nearer they got to the Enns River bridges the worse it got. The road through the river valley was impassable as thousands of vehicles and at least 100,000 men tried to get across in time.

Some units also made for the bridge at Weyer, but the situation there was no better than at Steyr. The division commander, *SS-Brigadeführer* Otto Kumm, ordered a liaison group forward to make contact with the Americans. They didn't even get across the river before encountering a spearhead patrol from the US 71st Infantry Division, who disarmed them, took their watches and other personal effects. Then they were led across the river to the American division's command post.

Former *Heeresgruppe Ostmark* commander *Generaloberst* Rendulic was already there, along with several American officers. They were told all the right things and the Americans seemed sympathetic to the *LAH* situation. Officially, the Germans were assured that capture by the Russians would not lead to dire consequences. Rendulic agreed with this assessment. Privately, it was made known that another bridge over the Enns, the one south of Steyr at Ternberg, would not be blocked until 12:01 a.m. on 10 May, 24 hours later than announced.

Kumm heard their report and ordered the division to make further preparations for going into captivity. The rest of the heavy weapons were destroyed to save fuel and increase speed. Stragglers joined the column, many of whom had lost their *Soldbuch*, the soldier's handbook that contained every detail of their military service. Without this document a soldier was subject to execution, and the Americans would certainly be suspicious of any man who didn't possess his. So, even as they moved west, the headquarters company created new ones for those that were lost.

On the outskirts of Weyer the Americans had set up a checkpoint. "Every vehicle in the endlessly long line had to stop and we listened to the words of the Yankees: 'watches, pistols, photos…'

and then 'get along!'" German medals were especially popular with the Americans, such as the German Cross in Gold.[7]

The roads became so hopelessly jammed that many men abandoned their vehicles and marched on foot, sometimes overland. Many men used a footbridge south of Steyr, including *SS-Standartenführer* Peiper and his staff. The Americans spread the word that there was no reason to cross the river and the Germans should just stay on the east side, where they would be perfectly safe. But nobody was fooled. Staying meant capture by the Russians, and none of them doubted that meant either execution or exile to slave labor camps.

Some men stayed with their vehicles and eventually made it to safety. For others, however, the risk was too great. Little by little these men broke up into small groups and crossed the Enns by whatever means possible.

* * *

Rumanian *SS-Hauptsturmführer* Emilian and his motley unit were in the vicinity of the *LAH* as the time to surrender drew near. Emilian's troops had no illusions about the fate that awaited them if they surrendered to the Red Army, so they made their way west, looking for an American army to accept their surrender. They were directed by American forces to a POW collection center at Liezen, where they were told they would be treated like a German army unit. Mixed in with troops from the *LAH* they were trucked west until the convoy suddenly stopped near Altheim, in the vicinity of Braunau am Inn, Hitler's hometown. Here, some 27,000 men were dumped into open fields with no shelter. There were also a large number of wounded *Waffen-SS* men there, some of whom were seriously injured or amputees, with no way to care for them. Soon enough they were dying of exposure or starvation, and a large percentage of them, perhaps even a majority, did not know why. Thiele put it this way: "[T]hose *Waffen-SS* officers, NCOs and soldiers who marched into the Allied prisons could not comprehend why the victors expressed such hatred toward them."[8]

At length the non-German SS men were transferred to the former concentration camp at Ebensee. There seem to have been some 3,000 or so Rumanian troops, as well as 5,000 other Europeans, imprisoned at the camp. In July, most of them were moved to another camp near Steyr and to yet another camp near Linz in the autumn. Representatives of the Soviet-puppet regime in Rumania met with the Rumanian SS men and promised good treatment if they returned home; some accepted and found the promises hollow, but Emilian was warned in advance and stayed put. Eventually the remaining Rumanians were given displaced person status as the Western Allies began to see their POWs as a potential bulwark against their former Russian ally. Many of them later emigrated to America.

SS-Brigade Ney

SS-Brigade Ney was officially dissolved on the orders of the by now *SS-Obersturmbannführer* Ney, with all stores and supplies that could not be taken with them being destroyed. Between 1,000 and 2,000 men joined a column from *6. Armee* heading west, looking for safety in numbers. Many other of the SS men made their way back to Hungary, where they were immediately imprisoned by the Soviets and treated as traitors. Others tried their luck with the Western Allies,[9] surrendering to

---

7   Tiemann, *The Leibstandarte IV/2*, p. 347.
8   Thiele, *Beyond "Monsters" and "Clowns"*, p. 125.
9   Some 1,000-1,200 men attached themselves to *6. Armee* columns heading west for the safety of American lines.

the Americans at Steinach in the picturesque Salzkammergut; two of them were reportedly killed by American MPs.[10] During its brief lifespan the brigade had destroyed some 50 Russian tanks.

Kampfgruppe Volkmann

Around noon, under bright and sunny skies, *Generalmajor* Dietrich Volkmann led his remaining men across the line of demarcation at Radstadt, separating the American zone from the Russian. For any German, military or civilian, that was a moment of relief. Volkmann wanted to try and make it back to Germany but was picked up by Americans the next day. Compared to many high-ranking German officers, Volkmann's fate was benign. He was released on 17 February 1947.

* * *

The last guards at *Stalag 17B* fled before the Red Army could arrive. The remaining prisoners, mostly sick British men and their doctors, waited behind for liberation by their Soviet allies. It promised to be a joyful day, until the day arrived and they discovered otherwise.

* * *

At Rohr im Gebirge the last German troops pulled out before dawn, but not before blowing up all of the local bridges. The Russians gave them a final sendoff with a two-hour artillery storm, which ended after noon.

6. SS-Panzerarmee

For the men of *SS-Kampfgruppe Trabandt III* it was high time to evacuate the Krems bridgehead they had been helping hold for the past three weeks, and to head west to surrender to the Americans. The division commander, *SS-Brigadeführer* Wilhelm Trabandt, decided to release all of his Russian prisoners; once this was done, the *Kampfgruppe* crossed the Danube bridges at Krems and headed due west.

12. SS-Panzer-Division Hitlerjugend

No German division suffered worse than *Hitlerjugend*. The division had transferred after the Ardennes Offensive and only arrived in the region on 8 February, exactly three months before, but in those 89 days it had suffered 7,500 men killed, wounded or missing. Like most German units the wonder is that it retained cohesion after such horrific losses. According to Michaelis, on 8 May it had 9,870 men of all ranks, about 52 percent of authorized strength.[11]

The division's former commander, Hubert Meyer, gives a more detailed accounting of the ruinous losses suffered by *Hitlerjugend*. From 8 February until 8 May, Meyer has a lower total of losses than Michaelis, although still terrible, with 4,376 men of all ranks listed as casualties and 1,498 of those men killed. He agreed with Michaelis on the number of men on hand at the surrender.

---

10   Pencz, *Siegrunen 76*, p. 23.
11   Michaelis, *Panzer Divisions*, p. 308.

Armor losses were almost total, including 32 Mark IVs, 35 Panthers, one *Wespe* self-propelled artillery vehicle, 11 light field howitzers, one heavy howitzer, one 100mm cannon and six *Nebelwerfer* rocket-launchers. Nevertheless, the repair companies had pieced together numerous vehicles and put them back in service, so that *Hitlerjugend* ended the war with six Mark IVs, nine Panthers, one *Wespe*, 17 light and four heavy field howitzers, two 100mm cannon, seven 150mm *Nebelwerfers* and even seven captured Russian 76mm guns. The division had lost some of its field howitzers and other guns to other units because it no longer had the transport capacity to move them.

Hitlerjugend's last march began after dawn and proceeded uneventfully until the column was within sight of Enns, the town. That's when several SPWs filled with former Mauthausen inmates sped up to the German vehicles and began rummaging through them, taking whatever they wanted and roughing up the SS men. To solve the problem without violence, a Panther was brought to the front of the column to block the other lane.

The Germans asked the Americans for help in stopping this harassment before it led to fighting and, despite the poetic justice of inmates bullying *Waffen-SS* men, the Americans complied and stopped any further excursions. One friendly-fire incident sent American casualties rushing past the German column to the aid station in Enns. A missing American patrol had made it to Amstetten, where the townsfolk poured into the streets in celebration. Suddenly seven Russian ground-attack aircraft strafed and bombed the gathering.[12] By the midnight deadline all of *Hitlerjugend* had passed into American captivity, and out of existence.

SS-Kampfgruppe Keitel

During the night of 7-8 May the survivors of Keitel's depleted *Kampfgruppe* quietly withdrew from their front-line positions in the mountains between Rohr im Gebirge and Schwarzau am Gebirge. Like all SS men, they knew their lives depended on crossing into American territory. The line of retreat passed through Schwarzau and by dawn they were gone.[13] By 3:00 p.m. that afternoon the Russians had taken the town.

Most of the civilians had long since fled. The retreating SS men confiscated the town's fire trucks and loaded them with *PAK* ammunition they'd found. Left behind, however, were some badly wounded German soldiers who were so filthy and their bandages so crusted with blood, that they were unrecognizable. Many of them couldn't even speak German but were *Volksdeutsch*, ethnic Germans from outside the Reich who spoke dozens of different languages.[14] Keitel took as many of his own wounded as possible, but there was no transport or care available for the rest of them. No one had any illusions about the fate that awaited them.

6. Armee

Unnoticed by the Russians, *6. Armee* began pulling out at 2:00 a.m., as planned. At precisely 4:00 a.m. the sky east of *6. Armee*'s front lines erupted in flashes of yellow and orange light as hundreds of Soviet artillery pieces fired a massive barrage. The *Landser* sank to the bottom of their trenches and covered their heads, expecting yet another avalanche of explosions. Instead, the shells burst high overhead and tens of thousands of leaflets rained down on the German positions announcing

12   Meyer, *The 12th SS*, pp. 500-502.
13   Some sources say this took place on the night of 8-9 May, not the night before, but that seems improbable.
14   Brettner, *Die Letzten Kämpfe Band I*, p. 198.

the end of the war. But many of the leaflets fell on empty foxholes, as the front-line units had already fled west, leaving *1. Volks-Gebirgs-Division* behind as a rearguard. It was only later in the afternoon that they heard the edict that all German units should surrender to units of the nation they had last fought against.

* * *

Later in the morning the *6. Armee* commander, *General der Panzertruppe* Hermann Balck, satisfied that the withdrawal was going smoothly, pulled out himself. He stopped in Graz for one last meeting with *Gauleiter* Ueberreither and found him depressed about the retreat. He'd been dreaming of a glorious last stand in which he defended Styria to the last bullet, but when it became obvious this would never happen he despaired and loaded his revolver, intent on suicide. Balck talked him out of it. Also while there he helped Ueberreither get his wife's father's papers out of Austria to safety in the west. Her father was Alfred Wegener, the father of the theory of continental drift, and his notes and notebooks constituted a treasure trove for science.[15] Ueberreither vanished soon after but wound up as a witness at the Nuremberg Trials.

From Graz, Balck drove to Liezen on the Enns River, where he found the Americans stalling about accepting the Germans into their lines. Knowing the Russians were hot on his trail, Balck personally negotiated with the commander of the US 80th Infantry Division, Major General Horace McBride, to accept the surrender of his army. Balck had taught himself English so the two men got on well, even drinking some coffee together.

Traffic over the Liezen bridge was supposed to be cut off at 1:00 a.m. on 9 May, but McBride said he wouldn't send a force there until 8:00 a.m., giving Balck's men a further seven hours to escape over the Enns to safety. During a wild night men and vehicles raced toward the bridge. Officers from Balck himself all the way down to company commanders shouted orders and cajoled, threatened or pleaded with the men to get across before it was too late. Everyone gave a maximum effort and did everything possible to get the men over the river, but there were just too many of them.

The Americans didn't turn up until 9:00 a.m. Thousands of men from *6. Armee* were still on the eastern side of the river, but instead of blocking the bridge the Americans leaned against the railings, and smoked and joked while letting the Germans stream by all day long. With night closing in the Russians appeared, and the German officers frantically tried to hurry their men across. Most of them made it. Even the trainloads of wounded made it, by having American guards and flags covering the trains as they moved through Russian territory to the railroad bridges. Only a few score *Gebirgsjägers* wound up captured by the Russians.[16] Some stragglers melted into the mountains.

In a humorous postscript, Balck tells the story of 400 men who wanted nothing more than to strip naked, bathe in the river and then lay in the spring sunshine. They'd been freezing in the mountains for weeks, unable to bathe or even wash their uniforms. Unfortunately they chose the east bank of the river to do it, and when the Russians showed up they didn't have time to get dressed or dash across the bridge. The only way to safety was to swim for it, which they did, and went into captivity dripping wet and completely nude.[17]

---

15   Balck, *Order From Chaos*, p. 438.
16   Lucas, *Last 100 Days*, p. 110. This is contradicted by James Lucas, who says requiring the mountain troops to act as the rearguard was "the equivalent of a death sentence".
17   Balck, *Order in Chaos*, pp. 440-441.

9. Gebirgs-Division (Ost)

As most of the division withdrew to the west, the rearguard worried most about a pursuit along the Semmering railway lines. The tunnels cut through some of the roughest territory, and with no shortage of fuel or vehicles they could potentially run the Germans down from behind. On orders from higher command, plans were drawn up to blast all of the tunnels and viaducts in the division's area, but *Oberst* Raithel countermanded them on his own authority. Such damage would have taken months or years to repair and presumably Raithel knew the ill effects that would have on the people of Styria. Instead, in at least one place, they loosened some of the rails and drove locomotives and rolling stock over them, derailing the trains, completely blocking the tunnels.

1. Volks-Gebirgs-Division

Gebirgsjäger-Regiment 98 was part of the rearguard and they were determined to protect their comrades as they withdrew. The best way to do that was to attack, so they did, in company strength. With the war officially over it was the last thing the Russians expected, and the Germans drove them back, but the fascinating part is that one German eyewitness says there were Rumanians among the Russians.[18]

The *Gebirgsjägers* had been the last rearguard, and sped to catch their comrades on the jammed roads leading west. But only at midnight did the last Germans soldiers pull out of Mönichwald, driving west with a *PAK* in tow just in case it was needed. The division's fallen soldiers were buried in cemeteries all over eastern Burgenland and northern Styria, 214 at Mönichwald alone. Eight more were interred at Schwengerer Hof atop the Rieglhof, along with 18 Russians.

Kampfgruppe 3. Panzer-Division

The veteran panzer division was divided in two, with the panzer and reconnaissance battalions at Liesen along with *Panzergrenadier-Regiment 3*, and the rest of the division still at Altenmarkt. The previous night *General der Panzertruppe* Balck had presented a detailed plan for a two-week withdrawal west across Austria, but at 6:30 a.m. the division's commander, *Generalmajor* Söth, was notified that instead *3. Panzer-Division* had until 7:00 a.m. the next morning to cross the demarcation line into the American zone, or become prisoners of the Russians. It should be remembered that Söth took the division's mobile elements with him to block the Americans, necessitating that it flee west in two parts. Thus began their race for salvation.

As desperate as they were, the Germans couldn't simply turn and run. A rearguard had to stay behind and take its chances. *Panzer-Pioneer-Bataillon 39* and *Panzergrenadier-Regiment 394* were picked. They would follow 24 hours later and pray the Americans let them into their lines.

In glorious spring weather the columns set off through a now openly hostile landscape. Behind them townsfolk tore down barriers to let the Russians pass through, and hung red and white flags out of their windows. Open hostility greeted the retreating columns, although nobody was stupid enough to shoot at them. Nevertheless, the glares of armed citizens made them aware of how much the Austrians wanted them gone. In one town they saw not just the red and white Austrian flag, but red ones, too. Those they burned with signal flares. One man became so angry he opened fire

---

18   Brettner, *Die Letzten Kämpfe Band I*, p. 118.

with a 20mm *Flak* cannon at the sight of a red flag. Like a bull in the arena, the red communist flag drove him mad.

Any vehicle that ran out of fuel or broke down was shoved aside, or down the banks into the Mur River, everything from luxurious Mercedes staff cars to the German version of the American jeep, the Volkswagen-built *Kübelwagen*. Weapons and military equipment littered the roadway, everything from rifles, sub-machine guns and anti-tank guns, to helmets, worn-out boots, knives and hand grenades. Some were picked up by the Austrian resistance but that, too, was risky. If the Russians discovered military weaponry in a home they usually became trigger happy. But others could pick up the cast-off weapons too, the gangs of deserters, Nazis in hiding or freed concentration camp inmates and prisoners of war.

The commander of *I./Panzergrenadier-Regiment 3* dissolved his battalion on his own authority and told the men they were free to do as they pleased. Still in possession of a few SPWs with fuel, they sped for the Enns and were fortunate enough to run into American patrols.

Kampfgruppe 1. Panzer-Division

Like everywhere else, the race for the American zone was on. The division's route from the mountains of Styria to Linz would put them on the same narrow, crowded roads as the rest of the troops and civilians desperate to avoid capture by the Red Army.

1. Division der Ukrainische National-Armee

At 6:00 a.m. the phone call that *Brigadeführer und Generalmajor der Waffen-SS* Freitag had been waiting on finally came through from *IV SS-Panzerkorps* headquarters: withdraw! And with the much-anticipated order came the caveat that the division only had 27 hours to cross the line of demarcation into the American zone, by 9:00 a.m. on 9 May.

While the front-line units pulled out of their trenches and bunkers for the mad dash to the west, the artillery batteries fired off all remaining ammunition to cover the retreat. As a rearguard each regiment left a company behind to repel any attacks, and those men didn't have to wait long for the Russians to come. With the war officially over, along the division's entire front they launched attack after attack to break through and disrupt the withdrawal.

Once they ran out of shells, the crews of the artillery disabled their guns by burying the breech blocks and followed the others on the crowded roads. They weren't the only ones. As soon as the rearguards pulled out, the Russians followed. Several times during the division's retreat, elements were attacked by pursuing Russians and fierce firefights erupted.

The countryside swarmed with fleeing men wearing the uniforms of every conceivable branch of the *Wehrmacht*, including the *Kriegsmarine*, and their allies. Beside Hungarians in the dress of both the *Honved* and the *Waffen-SS*, Rumanians, Croatians, Albanians, Yugoslavs and Slovenes all also wearing SS runes, and ethnic Germans from a dozen countries, the Ukrainians were simply one more group caught up in the maelstrom of war. With any luck they would now reach safety behind American lines, but without 729 of their comrades who lay buried in the fertile soil of Austria.[19]

---

19   Melnyk, *To Battle*, p. 273.

Not all of them made it. The Russians were not hampered by fuel shortages or crowded roads. When they showed up, people fled. So in a few cases Ukrainians found themselves surrounded and had no choice except surrender or death. But most got away to the west.

I Kavallerie-Korps
3. and 4. Kavallerie-Divisionen

I Kavallerie-Korps had been ordered to stay put in anticipation of surrender to the Soviets, but its commander, Knight's Cross winner and *General der Kavallerie* Gustav Harteneck, had no intention of obeying such a suicidal order. Starting on 8 May the corps moved out for the Tamsweg area where, on 10 May, advance elements of *4. Kavallerie-Division* ran into British troops moving up from Italy. The corps' cavalry divisions had no reputation for war crimes so the British treated them well. Negotiations followed and the cavalry was allowed to cross the Mur River into the Mur valley. The combined strength of the two cavalry divisions was estimated at the time at 22,000 men and 16,000 horses. It did not take long to strip the area of vegetation from over-grazing. They were then admitted into the American sector to feed their mounts, which must have been just fine with them.

5. SS-Panzer-Division Wiking

According to Strassner, the withdrawal to the west would be made in three stages, each triggered by its own code word, and with the issuing of the third code word "would the command authority of the field army expire…the field army…issued the last code word at 0300 hours, *Funkstill* (radio silence)".[20]

The deadline to enter American lines was 12:00 p.m., but as the night wore on *Wiking* had to launch one last attack to cover its withdrawal westward. Unfortunately for *Wiking*, the unit to its left withdrew too early and the Russians filled the void, outflanking them and forcing *SS-Panzergrenadier-Regiment Westland* to fight its way out. Nevertheless, the division reached Graz in good order, only to find chaos in the streets. People begged to be taken with the retreating SS men to avoid the oncoming Red Army, including not only Austrian men and women, but also Russian prisoners of war who knew their fate when returned to the Soviet Union.[21] Red and white Austrian flags flew here and there; some people cursed the soldiers, while others thanked them. Some soldiers sang as they marched through the streets.

Later components of the division moving through Graz did not have such an easy time of it, however, finding both Russian cavalry and T-34s already in the city. They were fired on and suffered casualties. Strassner says that half of a *Pionier* platoon of *SS-Panzer-Regiment 5* made it through to Tamsweg, where they were taken prisoner by the English, but escaped during the night and eventually wound up in Radstadt.[22]

---

20   Stassner, *European Volunteers*, p. 332.
21   Unlike most other countries, the Soviet Union officially considered their own troops who had become prisoners of war as traitors. To Joseph Stalin, men should fight until death and never be taken prisoner under any circumstances. When his own son was captured Stalin would not ransom him but allowed him to die in German custody. POWs knew this, and knew what fate awaited those whom Stalin considered enemies of the state.
22   Strassner, *European Volunteers*, p. 335.

Throughout the day confusion reigned as orders were countered, reissued and countermanded. Roads into the mountains were jammed. Around 6:00 p.m. the division resumed its march to Mauterndorf.

The Americans

The failure of the American intelligence services in feeding General Eisenhower incorrect information about the National Redoubt is a perfect illustration of the sometimes positive results of the Law of Unintended Consequences. If the American drive had continued on a more northerly route through Central Germany, leaving Austria to the Russians, would Stalin have given it back? The evidence seems to indicate that he would not or, at least, would have wanted a *quid pro quo*.

By 8 May he had already set up a pro-Soviet Austrian government headed by Karl Renner, and tried to get the Allies to recognize it. Moreover, the same things were happening in Hungary, Poland, Czechoslovakia and the Baltic countries. Tensions between Great Britain and Tito's Yugoslav Army boiled over in Trieste, where the communists tried to form a government despite the city being agreed to as in the British sphere with intentions to return it to Italy. As time passed and the Cold War began, it became obvious what a disaster Russian possession of Austria could have been.

The British

With Bulgarians and Slovenes from the Yugoslav Army racing for the capital of Carinthia, the British 6th Armored Division from Lieutenant-General Charles Knightley's British V Corps sped into Klagenfurt less than two hours ahead of the Slovene irregulars who were coming to claim control of the city. The first faint rumblings of the Cold War had begun to shake the foundations of the alliance that defeated the Third Reich, and the British had no intention of allowing communists to have any influence in their agreed-upon zone of occupation. Moving swiftly and with purpose, the British occupied all the important buildings and facilities before the Slovenes got there.

2. Panzerarmee
23. Panzer-Division

After more than a week of small skirmishes and patrols, both *23. Panzer-Division* and *3. Kavallerie-Division* were suddenly hammered by severe Russian attacks. A penetration through *Panzergrenadier-Regiment 128* was sealed off and thrown back by a counterattack, but losses on both sides were heavy. Meanwhile, in yet another twist of irony that might have been funny to the German *Landser* had it not been so tragic, a train arrived with 17 factory-fresh Mark IV tanks earmarked for *Panzer-Regiment 23*. Eight days after Adolf Hitler killed himself, Albert Speer's armaments industry delivered new weapons for a war that was technically over.

There was nothing to do except destroy them, but with explosives in short supply the mechanics climbed onto the rail cars, drained the oil and cranked the engines until the pistons froze. Then they removed the breechblocks from the cannon, and the sighting optics, and threw them into the Mur River.

Despite efforts by *1./Panzer-Aufklärungs-Abteilung 23* to find the British by scouting to the northwest, no contact was made. This left the division to move out in the general direction of where they believed the British to be, and hope for the best. Seeing few choices, the division commander, *Generalleutnant* Joseph von Radowitz, sent an emissary to discuss surrender terms with the Russians. The Germans requested a ten-hour ceasefire and the Russians agreed. Rebentisch tells of a tragic incident during this period, when drunken Russian soldiers approached the German lines bearing schnapps but no weapons. Overjoyed at having survived the war, they grabbed 20 or so Germans and brought them back to their own lines to meet their friends and drink like they were all long-lost friends. But Russian officers immediately made them prisoners and there was nothing the Germans could do to get them back.

But the Germans weren't going to let their emissary become a prisoner. *Major* Lenberger of *Panzergrenadier-Regiment 126* was an original member of the division, and if he didn't come back they were going to launch a full-scale attack in reprisal. Presumably the panzer regiment regretted destroying the 17 Mark IVs at this point, because all remaining panzers, SPWs and men were in position to go. In fact, the first rounds of the preparatory bombardment were fired just as the major returned.

The Russians gave *Major* Lenberger a list of instructions and promised good treatment. Lenberger agreed, and von Radowitz ordered the division on alert to move west. Quiet was essential. If the Russians discovered they'd been duped, and attacked after the front lines had been evacuated, it would be catastrophic for *23. Panzer-Division*. The men could only take personal weapons and enough food for two weeks, with the exception of the reconnaissance battalion, which went fully armed.

But *I Kavallerie-Korps* ordered it to cover the retreat of its neighbors to the left, the remnants of *44. Infanterie-Division Hoch und Deutschmeister* and *4. Kavallerie-Division*. Both of those units had a difficult route out of the mountains.

The plan was for *Panzer-Aufklärung-Abteilung 23* to move into the front line replacing the infantry division, with three remaining *Jagdpanzers* as a reserve. Right before the ceasefire went into effect all ammunition was fired off to cover the noise of this switch. Then, when the Russians stayed silent, the reconnaissance battalion pulled out as quietly as possible.

Fortunately for the Germans, and despite their fierce assaults during the day, neither the Russians nor Bulgarians pursued them. When the time came to blow up the last bridges over the Mur River, however, the local citizens and *Volkssturm* tried to intervene. The combat units would never return, but the residents would have to live without a way to cross the river until the bridges were rebuilt. Their pleas fell on deaf ears and the bridges crashed into the water. Then the columns of *I Kavallerie-Korps* resumed their desperate march to the northwest.[23]

* * *

Heeresgruppe E was like a stag fighting off a pack of snarling hounds as it withdrew to the west. Russians, Bulgarians, Yugoslavs, Slovenes and Croatians nipped at their heels to force them to turn and fight, while others raced westward to cut the Germans off. Screening the army group's withdrawal was *Kampfgruppe Fischer*, commanded by the highly decorated panzer commander *Major* Gerhard Fischer. His *Kampfgruppe* consisted of a battalion of crews and support personnel from *Panzer-Regiment 23*, with no panzers operational; apparently the 17 Mark IVs arrived too late to be incorporated into the *Kampfgruppe*.

His mission was to hold the tiny settlement of Unterdraubing and shield the withdrawal of the *68. Infanterie-Division*, the *71. Infanterie-Division*, the *118. Jäger-Division*, the *13. Waffen-Gebirgs-Division der SS Handschar (Kroatische Nr. 1)* and *Generalleutnant* Helmuth von Pannwitz's *XV SS-Kosaken-Kavallerie-Korps*. And Fischer was exactly the right man for such a job. During

23 Rebentisch, *From the Caucasus*, p. 467.

the war he participated in more than 200 tank battles, one of the few men, if not the only one, to have done so.

The Bulgarians weren't about to let *Heeresgruppe E* get away so easily, though. After being rebuffed about a demand that Fisher surrender his *Kampfgruppe*, throughout the day they launched attack after attack on Fischer's positions, and were repulsed every time with huge losses. Finally, after dark, when all of the units he'd been screening had moved on, Fischer's command slipped away.[24]

24   Kurowski, *Panzer Aces III*, p. 106.

39

Wednesday, 9 May

6. *SS-Panzerarmee*, acting as *Heeresgruppe Ostmark*

Early on 9 May Sepp Dietrich ordered the 1A for *6. SS-Panzerarmee*, Deputy Chief of Staff for Operations *SS-Obersturmbannführer* Georg Maier, to head for the ancient town of Radstadt, where a center had been established to coordinate movements toward the Americans. He went in the company of *SS-Obersturmbannführer* Schrörder-Vontin, the army's Chief of Staff for Transportation. Afterwards the two men were supposed to drive to US Third Army headquarters at Ried im Innkreis. Before getting that far, however, they were taken prisoner by American patrols north of the Attersee. Maier survived rough treatment by the Americans and went on to write *Drama Between Budapest and Vienna, The Last Battles of 6. Panzer Army*, which has been a great help in writing this narrative.[1]

* * *

The most remarkable legacy of *Heeresgruppe Süd/Ostmark* might be that a detailed Order of Battle was drawn up the day after Germany's official surrender. Since the Army Group headquarters had already been taken prisoner that left only the staff of *6. SS-Panzerarmee* to compile the document, while simultaneously arranging for transportation routes, supplies and all of the other necessities to get their troops across the line of demarcation.

As *2. Panzerarmee* had been detached two days before, that left only *8. Armee, 6. SS-Panzerarmee* and *6. Armee* in *Heeresgruppe Ostmark*.[2] Nevertheless, the army lists its ration strength as 450,000 men. This is a drastically lower number than had been estimated in April, but matches the estimate made by *Generalfeldmarschall* Keitel while he was in custody. Keitel almost certainly arrived at his figures independently, as he was no longer in contact with the Army Group by this time. On 8 May he signed a second surrender document in Berlin.

Given the separate estimates from two men whose positions lend credence to their opinions, therefore, the 450,000 is probably the correct one. Nevertheless, even if a lower number is accurate it's easy to understand why Eisenhower feared a National Redoubt so much. Unfortunately, numbers for panzers, artillery tubes, SPWs and the like were not recorded.

General der Gebirgstruppe Kreysing's *8. Armee* commanded *XXXXIII Armeekorps* and *Panzerkorps Feldherrnhalle*, with eight divisions between them. The *6. SS-Panzerarmee* had three corps: *I SS-Panzerkorps, II SS-Panzerkorps* and *Korps von Bünau*. Sepp Dietrich's army also had a long list of depleted divisions, *Kampfgruppen*, shattered units, brigades, alarm battalions and miscellaneous formations. Hermann Balck's *6. Armee* had one corps, *IV SS-Panzerkorps*, and another formation listed as *Armee Unmittelbar*, which best translates as 'direct army', meaning it was under the direct

---

1   Maier, *Drama*, p. 373.
2   The *8. Armee* had supposedly been detached prior to the surrender and sent to *Heeresgruppe Mitte*, but was included in the *Heeresgruppe Ostmark* final Order of Battle.

control of *6. Armee* headquarters. This had whatever remained of *III Panzerkorps* and the newly formed *9. Gebirgs-Division (Ost)*.[3]

25. Panzer-Division

With blessed relief the division surrendered to the Americans between Linz and Passau. The division had been rebuilt multiple times during its career and most of the men had been drafted into it long after the war began. No doubt they felt safe once they passed through American lines. But for some of them that proved an illusion, as they were handed over to the Russians anyway.

SS-Regiment Ney

SS-Regiment Ney, although officially attached to *25. Waffen-Grenadier-Division der SS Hunyadi*, in fact never joined that unit and, on 9 May, some of the brigade's remaining elements surrendered to American forces in the Alpine lake region of Attersee near Salzburg, Austria, most notably the headquarters staff.

6. Panzer-Division

The previous day the division had surrendered to the Americans in western Czechoslovakia. The relief was palpable. But like happened to so many German units, on 9 May they were turned over to the Russians. The only good news was they weren't *Waffen-SS*, they were *Wehrmacht*. Some of them survived captivity. Not many, but some.

2. SS-Panzer-Division Das Reich

A perfect illustration of how difficult it is to nail down figures for the last day of the war is the example given by Karl H. Thiele for the surrender strength of *2. SS-Panzer-Division Das Reich*. According to him, the division had "11 operational panzers, 45 officers, NCOs and 1,330 soldiers, about a battalion and a half of manpower".[4] And yet *Das Reich* was scattered all over Austria, old Czechoslovakia and eastern Germany, so such figures seem more likely for one part of the division instead of the whole thing: for, say, *SS-Panzergrenadier-Regiment Deutschland*, which had an authorized strength of more than 3,000 men. Calculating a total for a division whose component parts surrendered in at least four places seems impossible.

Kampfgruppe 1. SS-Panzer-Division Leibstandarte Adolf Hitler

Much of the division had already passed into captivity. For those still on the east bank of the Enns, desperation set in. Little towns and villages along the river were overwhelmed with men trying

---

3   Maier, *Drama*, p. 476.
4   Thiele, *Beyond "Monsters" and "Clowns"*, p. 272.

to cross lightweight foot bridges, some of which collapsed. Word went round that the bridge at Ternberg was still open, and many others made for it.

Along the way to their crossing points a new sight greeted the men: Austrian Home Guards with white and red armbands. Although armed, these irregulars wanted no part of armed SS soldiers and didn't interfere. Burning and burned-out vehicles belched black smoke for miles along the east bank as men got over the river any way they could. Some tried to swim across in the cold, fast water, and some even made it.

The *7./SS-Panzer-Regiment 1* still had 60 men, so when word came that the Russians were driving on Steyr from the north, they decided to head south for the bridge at Altenmarkt. This was the company that drove the four Panzer IVs into the Enns. They surrendered to an American lieutenant and the officers were allowed to keep their sidearms.[5]

Once on the other side, if they hadn't crossed at a place with an American checkpoint, the German soldiers and SS men had to choose between presenting themselves to the Americans and trying to melt into the countryside.

How many men were in the division when it surrendered? This figure varies wildly, depending on the source, and with the division breaking up and crossing the Enns in multiple positions, it's doubtful that a precise number will ever be agreed on. The total strength of the LAH at the time of surrender is given by Thiele at "57 officers, 229 NCOs and 894 soldiers".[6] On the face of it this seems ridiculously low, since that total is little more than a battalion and would put the division at only five percent of authorized strength. But elsewhere Michael Reynolds notes that between 8 and 10 May the US 71st Infantry Division recorded 3,777 men from the *LAH* as taken prisoner, and that an unknown number more were simply waved on to the west. Added to that number would also have to be members of the division who surrendered to other American units, since those would not be part of the 3,777 recorded by the 71st Infantry Division.

A better idea may be obtained by extrapolating the figures for *12. SS-Panzer-Division Hitlerjugend*. Thiele gives numbers for *Hitlerjugend* so low as to defy belief, being "1 panzer, 48 NCOs and 391 soldiers left".[7] Curiously, his surrender-day strength of *3. SS-Panzer-Division Totenkopf* lists "44 officers, 229 NCOs and 962 men". The odd coincidence of both the *LAH* and *Totenkopf* having 229 NCOs on surrender day seems hard to credit.

Michaelis, on the other hand, has a drastically different total for *Hitlerjugend*, listing strength returns for 8 May as 328 officers, 1,698 non-commissioned officers and 7,844 other ranks, for a total of 9,870 men. This was exactly half of the authorized officers but only about 40 percent of the non-coms and just over 50 percent of the enlisted men,[8] which seems far closer to being a realistic number. Using this as a reference, and while we can never know for certain how many men of the *LAH* survived to surrender, an estimate of *LAH*'s ration strength in the 6,000-8,000 range seems reasonable and perhaps even a bit conservative.

* * *

And so the *1. SS-Panzer-Division Leibstandarte Adolf Hitler* passed into history. By 1945 most of its newer members were drafted into the division, as the volunteers of the first muster had mostly fallen by then. The remaining men of the *LAH*, and all of the other *Waffen-SS* divisions, fought for a cause and a leader so brutal that any empathy, sympathy or understanding of their motives is beyond the ken of most people. Its legacy was marred by a long list of war crimes, both

5   Tiemann, *The Leibstandarte IV/2*, p. 354.
6   Thiele, *Beyond "Monsters" and "Clowns"*, p. 264.
7   Thiele, *Beyond "Monsters" and "Clowns"*, p. 336.
8   Michaelis, *Panzer Divisions*, p. 308.

substantiated and alleged, but it was also a first-rate combat unit that sometimes achieved the seemingly impossible. Arguments will likely rage forever whether it justified its exalted reputation or was a wasteful indulgence of Heinrich Himmler's egotistical ambition.

Kampfgruppe 1. Panzer-Division

The forward elements of the oldest panzer division in the *Wehrmacht* staggered into American lines at Windischgarsten, on the Enns River, and the town of Enns, southeast of Linz on the Danube. The men would continue pouring into those areas well into the next day. In 1938, the same division rolled through Austria heading east during the *Anschluss*. Seven years later its defeated remnants were all too glad to reach the west. Whether any men still filled the division's ranks from that first operation was doubtful.

Kampfgruppe 5. SS-Panzer-Division Wiking

The war had officially ended, but not the movements or the shooting. During the afternoon of 8 May *Wiking* had pulled out of its front-line positions and headed west, using the last drops of its carefully hoarded fuel. They passed through Graz and made a point of singing to illustrate their still high morale. In the vicinity of Leoben, rifle fire stopped them in front of a bridge.[9] Partisans fired from a nearby building, which was quickly demolished by two *Sd.Kfz.*[10] *251/9* half-tracks, SPWs mounting 75mm low-velocity cannon. The anti-Nazi fighters had either been foolish enough to ambush a *Waffen-SS* column, or unlucky enough to mistake it for supply troops or even refugees. Whatever the case, the shooters were wiped out by the veteran *Wiking* men. Later, the SS column was strafed by Russian fighters and incurred losses.[11]

Sometime during the night of 8-9 May, *Wiking*'s lead elements ran into American sentries near Mauterndorf, 110 miles west of Graz. Strassner states that the Americans were less concerned with capturing the Germans than with moving as far east as possible to block the Russians.[12] This left the SS men to wander the back roads headed for home, many still bearing their weapons.

Sankt Valentin

The day before, the American 259th Infantry Regiment had captured the *Nibelungenwerke* at Sankt Valentin. On 9 May they handed it over to the Russians, who immediately restarted production of Panzer Mark IVs. They didn't need the obsolescent panzers for their own army, but Stalin wanted working examples for the Victory Parade in Moscow.

* * *

Setting off from Bad Ischl, an American tank and infantry task force headed for the isolated mountain resort town of Alt Aussee. The idyllic Austrian countryside was in full bloom as the Americans passed rivers cascading over rocks beside the road, and slopes thick with towering trees

---

9   Klapdor puts this as happening on the morning of 9 May, but that seems unlikely. What is probable is that this occurred over the night of 8/9 May.
10   *Sonderkraftfahrzeug*, literally 'special motor vehicle'.
11   Klapdor, *Viking Panzers*, p. 437.
12   Strassner, *European Volunteers*, p. 334.

and meadows of mountain flowers. The arrival of the American war machines must have seemed like both a violation in the placid Austrian countryside, but also a relief. The fate of the locals was in the hands of the Americans, not the Russians.

When the Americans arrived at Alt Aussee they discovered Kaltenbrunner, Ley and a few other Nazi officials had disappeared into the mountains, reportedly with some heavily armed SS troops. With the help of local resistance members and an Austrian-born British agent who parachuted into the region on 20 April, the Americans got a lead on a local radio transmitter being run by Wilhelm Waneck, *RSHA* Intelligence Section Chief for Southeastern Europe and one of those who attended Kaltenbrunner's planning meeting on 3 May. Helping him were Wilhelm Höttl, another attendee, and Werner Göttsch, who once had Waneck's job, along with some lower-ranking officials.

After surrounding the villa where the Germans were holed up, the Americans moved in and captured quite a haul of important Germans, both civilian and military, most of whom had:

> …fled to Alt Aussee, seeking… time to collect their thoughts and prepare their anti-Nazi alibis – Gunther Altenburg, Minister Plenipotentiary to Greece; General Erich Alt of the *Luftwaffe*; Joseph Heider, who had been detailed by Eigruber to blow up the Alt Aussee salt mines wherein was stored a fabulous collection of looted art treasures for the projected Great Hitler Museum in Linz; Dr Hjalmar Mae, head of the puppet state in Esthonia; Walter Riedel, construction chief for the V-2 weapons at Peenemünde; Ernst Szargarus, Foreign Office secretary in Rome; Spiros Hadji Kyriakos, Under Governor of the National Bank of occupied Greece; William Knothe, General Counsel of the Foreign Office; Dr Carlos Wetzell, head of the pharmaceutical industry; and Dr Bailent Homan, minister in the Hungarian puppet government.[13]

But no Kaltenbrunner and no Ley.

6. Armee

Tens of thousands of Germans shuffled along the eastern bank of the Enns River, desperate to get across before the Americans closed their boundary to new surrenders. Most crossed one of the remaining bridges, a few desperate men tried swimming across and some even made it. Among the milling mass of men in German uniforms were thousands of *Hiwis*, Russians who had volunteered to help the Germans destroy communism in their country. They knew that, if the odds were against Germans soldiers captured by the Russians being repatriated home, their odds were 100 percent against their survival. Their fate was to face the executioner, probably after a long period of torture. But the Americans refused to allow the turncoat Russians to enter their lines, and there was nothing their German comrades could do to help them.

Across the eastern border area of Styria graveyards maintain mute witness to the brutality of the fighting. At Münichwald 176 German soldiers are buried. In the area north of Rieglhof lie eight Germans and 18 Russians. Another 38 Germans were interred at Hochwechsel. St Kathrein am Hauenstein is the final resting place of 112 more German soldiers. There are scores more cemeteries like them all over eastern Austria.

---

13   CIA, 'The Last Days of Ernst Kaltenbrunner', <https://www.cia.gov/library/center-for-the-study-of-intelligence /kent-csi/vol4no2/html/v04i2a07p_0001.htm>, (Accessed 22 November 2018).

1. Volks-Gebirgs-Division

The *III./Gebirgsjäger-Regiment 99* were the final rear-guard for the entire division, the last men to pull out, but the division was determined that none of its men would fall into Russian hands. Like everyone else fleeing west they were driven by terror. Leaving in the middle of the night, unhindered by the Russians, they joined hundreds of thousands of German soldiers, *Luftwaffe* ground crewmen, nurses, Nazi officials, Hungarian peasants, Austrian women leading wagons piled high with their possessions and every conceivable farm animal, from horses, cows and goats, to donkeys, chickens and dogs; a diaspora of humanity fleeing the dreaded fate that awaited those who fell into the clutches of the Red Army.

Graz

The new socialist government of Austria's second-largest city coordinated with officials of the Red Army to make their entry into the city smooth and without incidents. Soviet thanks came in the shape of informing them that their government had no authority and the Red Army was in charge now. They weren't physically booted out of the doors of the City Hall, just figuratively. Austria was a conquered country, not a liberated one, despite Allied declarations to the contrary. That had dire connotations for the populace. As with everywhere else the Russians set foot in Europe, rape and plunder were the order of the day.

Heeresgruppe E and *2. Panzerarmee*

At 1:00 a.m. the fighting should have stopped everywhere, as the time limit for crossing into American and British lines had passed. The Germans were required to lay down their arms and give up to the nearest Allied forces. But the men of both *Heersgruppe E* and *2. Panzerarmee* simply refused to believe they would be forced to surrender to the Russians, Yugoslavs or Slovenes. The Croatians and Cossacks, in particular, knew that capture by anyone except the British meant instant death. They intended to capitulate to the British, no matter what happened. Many were able to do just that, only to discover they'd been deceived.

In the meantime, the Russians who'd been tricked into agreeing to the ceasefire so that *I Kavallerie-Korps* could get away were angry in the extreme. They sped to catch up and sent clouds of Ilyushin IL-2 Sturmovik ground-attack aircraft to bomb and strafe the fleeing columns. Armistice or no armistice, the war in the east was far from over.

I Kavallerie-Korps

The bedraggled column of cavalrymen had almost made it to Köflach, due west of Graz, when motorized Russian units heading for that city sent panic through their ranks. Strung out on the roads, hungry and exhausted, they were the last remnants of a defeated army, and few of the men had a stomach for more combat. Regardless of their feelings, combat had found them. Russian ground-attack aircraft dived on the column and were met with *Flak*. Confusion reigned and the column came to a halt as men scattered into the countryside or shot back at the strafing aircraft. Eventually it got moving again, bypassing Köflach into Judenburg.

* * *

The Bulgarian First Army had been tasked with reaching the line Ehrenhausen-Maribor by 8 May, but in reality was a full day slower to get there, having got stuck at the Mur River where the bridges were down. The 12th Bulgarian Infantry Division pushed on with the object of meeting the British at Klagenfurt the next day. For their part, the 14th Yugoslavian Storm Division was already in the area trying to block the retreating Germans who were trying to cross into Austria from Slovenia. When, on 8 May, the spearheads of the British 9th Armored Division moved into Austria, the Yugoslavs also turned for Klagenfurt. Men from at least three Allied armies were on the move to capture the capital of Carinthia. But the British knew what happened in cities where the Slovenes got there first, as that very day so-called Fascist sympathizers were being paraded through the streets of Trieste before being shot. This time they had no intention of being second.

A veteran armored division could move very fast when it needed to, and on 9 May it did. At 10:30 a.m. the British moved into Klagenfurt and spread out to occupy all major buildings, crossroads and bridges. Half an later the Slovenes entered the southern part of the city, only to find that the British had the city under their control.

Having beaten the partisan army into Klagenfurt by scant minutes, acting Lieutenant-General Charles Frederic Keithley, commander of V Corps, of the famed British Eighth Army, agreed upon a demarcation line between his command and that of Lieutenant General Vladimir Stoychev's First Bulgarian Army. A year before, had anyone predicted to Adolf Hitler that a British and a Bulgarian general would meet each other in southern Austria to avoid clashes between their two armies, he would have had them shot. Of course, the *Führer* couldn't do that now because he'd been dead for eight days.

But when the Slovenes showed up as part of the Yugoslavian Army they immediately made territorial claims and demanded zones of occupation. It was now clear that, with the common enemy defeated, the erstwhile allies of the British and Americans were preparing to feast on the carcass of the defeated Reich.

40

Thursday, 10 May

The *I Kavallerie-Korps*, with *Kampfgruppe 3. Panzer-Division* subordinated, surrendered to Major Mountjoy of the British 5th Northampton Regiment at Mautendorf. The *23. Panzer-Division* had a strength at the end of about 2,000 men in its combat formations. It had been one of the best German tank divisions of the war and its record and losses are illustrative of how first-rate German divisions fared during the war. According to Mitcham, *23. Panzer-Division* lost 7,476 men killed, approximately 20,921 wounded and 2,883 captured or missing. Roughly 10 times as many men were casualties as survived to surrender. It was credited with destroying 2,672 Soviet tanks and assault guns.

* * *

By 10 May the surrender of *6. SS-Panzerarmee* and *37. SS Freiwilligen-Kavallerie-Division Lützow* was arranged. First the men of *Lützow* destroyed their heavy weapons and then, accompanied by the last two *Hetzers*, they passed through Schwarzau in the Mariazell Mountains and Wildalpen in Altenmark/Enns on their way to the demarcation line. On 11-12 May a further march was undertaken to Windishgarten, where the Americans took their surrender. They were transported by truck and train to Mauerkirchen-Altheim. At this point *SS-Kampfgruppe Keitel*, which had begun with more than 2,000 men, had been reduced to 180. Going along with it into American captivity were the remnants of *Kampfgruppe 356. Infanterie-Division*.

To the north, *Lützow*'s heavy artillery detachment, fighting in Czechoslovakia, heard rumors that the Russians were shooting every SS man they captured over the rank of NCO. The artillery pieces had already been destroyed and only motorized transport was left. Having no other choice they sped westward to the demarcation line on the Budweis-Linz road north of Freistadt, and reached it on 10 May. To their immense relief many of the men were released, but the officers were held.

* * *

SS-Kampfgruppe Trabandt III had driven some 125 miles west in less than two days after pulling out of the Krems bridgehead. At Gallneukirchen they surrendered to US troops, thinking they were safely in Allied hands. The next day, however, the men were moved a few miles east to Pregarten, where they were handed over to the Russians. *SS-Brigadeführer* Trabandt did not return to Germany for almost ten years; most of his men never returned at all.

* * *

In Alt Aussee the CIC agents began to develop a network of informants in their search for Nazis, with Ernst Kaltenbrunner and Robert Ley topping the most-wanted list. In the meantime they found a smorgasbord of VIPs, and not-so VIPs, all pleading their cases as to how much they despised the Nazis. In most cases the CIC didn't care much about them because they were looking for influential political and military figures that could encourage continued resistance to the Allied occupation.

Among the figures encountered during these warm spring days were various artists, including famous German movie stars Ernst von Klipstein and Lotte Koch and the Austrian actor Hans

Unterkirchner; the creaky old Italian comic opera composer Ermanno Wolf-Ferrari; the flamboyant composer and pianist Peter Kreuder, who both joined and resigned from the Nazi Party because of opposition to the swing and jazz elements of his music from the Nazi censors; and the prolific composer of film scores and comic operettas, Nico Dostal. None of these people suffered unduly after the war because of Nazi sympathies, since working as an artist in the Third Reich meant at least paying lip service to government policies.

The Dutch-born movie star Johannes Heesters was a different story. After moving to Germany in 1935 he actively cultivated the approval of senior Nazis and met Hitler on several occasions. Joseph Goebbels had him added to the list of actors who were crucial to German culture, and Heesters spent the war touring and performing for troops at the front in a German version of the USO (America's United Service Organizations). He got along particularly well with high-ranking SS officials. After the war he fought against this legacy and denied much of it, but despite this he kept working right up until the end of his long life. Heesters died on Christmas Eve 2011 at the age of 108.

Also caught was British turncoat Norman Baillie-Stewart, whom the British public knew as the 'Officer in the Tower'. Baillie-Stewart had been a disillusioned army officer in the 1930s. After falling in love with a German woman he betrayed his homeland and went into German service as a spy, gathering information about an experimental tank, the Vickers A1E1, as well as the organization and order of battle of British tank forces. Tried and convicted under the Official Secrets Act in 1933, he was imprisoned in the Tower of London until his release in 1937. During the war he performed a series of services for the Germans, including reading English-language propaganda broadcasts,[1] but his greatest contribution to the Allied cause was translating the lyrics of the haunting German song *Lili Marlene* into English. Strangely enough, Joseph Goebbels hated the song but it was so popular with German soldiers, and *Generalfeldmarschall* Erwin Rommel, that he grudgingly allowed its broadcast. The intent of the translation had been to demoralize Allied soldiers by making them homesick, but instead it wound up as a reminder of what they were fighting for. In their own unique way, American troops changed the lyrics and it even ended up mentioned in the popular cartoon 'Willie and Joe'. When captured, Baillie-Stewart wore soft leather shorts, decorated suspenders and a fine hunting jacket. Despite his guilt in aiding the Axis, Baillie-Stewart only served five years in jail and died a free man living in Ireland.

But the promising leads to Kaltenbrunner's whereabouts came from the capture of Iris Scheidler, wife of Kaltenbrunner's adjutant *SS-Obersturmbannführer* Arthur Scheidler; Dr Rudolf Praxmarer, Iris' ex-husband and a dear friend of Kaltenbrunner's from their days studying together at the University of Graz; and from Kaltenbrunner's mistress, Gisela von Westarp. Von Westarp met the scarred SS man in 1943 while she was employed at the SS Main Office in Berlin, and in March 1945 bore him twins in a barn in Alt Aussee.

Iris Scheidler was part of a group of younger people who gravitated around Eva Braun and liked to have fun. Eva was a personal friend of hers, as were Heinrich Hoffman, *SS-Gruppenführer* Hermann Fegelein and the *Gauleiter* of Vienna, Baldur von Schirach and his wife, Henriette.

Praxamer, as it turned out, had equipped Kaltenbrunner for his escape into the mountains and even helped load weapons into his car. Informants against Praxamer also told the CIC agents that former Vienna Gestapo Chief *SS-Brigadeführer* Franz Josef Huber had been admitted to the local hospital, where he was arrested.[2]

This was all well and good, but these weren't the quarry the Americans were after. Ley and Kaltenbrunner were still at large.

---

1   It is likely he was the inspiration for the derisive sobriquet 'Lord Haw-Haw'.
2   Although tried for war crimes, Huber never served any time in prison. After this he returned to private life working as a bookkeeper and died peacefully in Munich on 30 January 1975.

SS-Gebirgsjäger-Ausbildungs-Aus-Ersatz-Bataillon 13 Leoben

Starting as far east as German-held territory still extended in Austria, the *SS-Gebirgsjäger* trainees had pulled out and sped to the River Enns by whatever means possible. Despite being nearly surrounded when they headed west, a lot of them made it and surrendered to the Americans. But some didn't.

* * *

Not only had Puchberg am Schneeberg seen weeks of heavy fighting, widespread damage and death, but there was no more food for the locals. The Russians, however, spent most of their time gorging on their own ample food stores and getting drunk on whatever alcohol they could find. Seeing the plight of the starving townsfolk, the Russians shared their food.

I Kavallerie-Korps

After nightfall on 10 May most of the once-proud corps, the only cavalry corps in the entire German Army, dragged into the town of Unzmarkt, northwest of Judenburg. The town is also on the Mur River and the corps would have to re-cross again to get to the west. But this time the bridges remained intact, as waiting for them were the British. They couldn't rest yet, as the last march under British direction was to Tamsweg, another 40 miles west, but presumably they didn't resent every additional mile put between them and the Russians.

Most of the corps had made it to safety, but not all. And even for those who had passed through British lines the shooting wasn't over yet. Russian attacks from the air continued even behind British lines, and only stopped when the Royal Air Force showed up to run them off and provide air cover.

And what of the crews from *Panzer-Regiment 23* who traveled north to pick up the brand-new Panthers at the *Nibelungenwerke* tank factory? They were on their way back to join the division in the front lines when news came of the surrender. It was a complete surprise and the tank column immediately turned around. Then they ran into various other parts of the division that had become separated from the main body, some 2,000 men in all. Marching northwest, they eventually found the American lines at Liezen, south of Linz, where they turned over the Panthers to their captors.

It's interesting to note that one week after Hitler's death, *Panzer-Regiment 23* had been given a total of 27 newly built panzers. This was nearly two full companies, or about half of the panzer allotment of a Type 1945 panzer division. Combined with the still-functioning machines this would have brought *23. Panzer-Division* up to near full strength in panzers, the only such unit left in the German inventory.

Kampfgruppe 3. Panzer-Division

Like many units of *Heeresgruppe-Ostmark*, *3. Panzer-Division* had long-since ceased to be a cohesive whole. Yet the small groups that were still together maintained discipline to the end. Furthermore, the columns were able to help themselves to anything they needed from the cast-off detritus lining every road, including food and drink. Some mounds of discarded equipment were higher than a man's head. Certainly the local population helped themselves.

The weather remained perfect, warm enough to feel good but not so much to be uncomfortable. Skies remained the fresh blue only seen in rural mountain areas, with sunshine that seemed a harbinger of better days to come. For anyone looking for a sign of coming events it could not have been more encouraging.

At no point did the local population attack the retreating column, but there was no mistaking the widespread disdain and outright anger directed toward the men. The division began crossing the Enns River into the American zone around 9:00 a.m., although it was 24 hours later than had been agreed to with the Russians. American guards stood around watching and must have seemed like the embodiment of everything they'd heard about the *Amis*. They leaned back chewing gum and seemed disinterested in the whole process.

Without warning the crossing was closed at noon. *Generalmajor* Söth immediately protested, argued, pleaded and cajoled, until it was agreed that the barriers would be removed for a few more hours. So the remaining men of *Kampfgruppe 3. Panzer-Division*, along with thousands of other German soldiers on the east bank of the Enns, had one last chance to move into what they believed to be the safe zone. The line of vehicles extended nearly 13 miles to the east.

The result was predictable.

It never became a stampede, but it got close. When the crossing reopened the pace wasn't fast enough for some men, and hundreds threw themselves into the cold current of the Enns River to swim across. Most made it, some didn't. Once across to the west bank, the now-disarmed Germans kept moving in their own vehicles to the collection points further west. Eventually, some 180,000 men and 3,000 vehicles would be in the ten camps set up between Mattighofen and Hitler's birthplace of Braunau am Inn. Organization of the camps was left up to the staff of *6. Armee* under the command of *General der Panzertruppe* Hermann Balck.

Panzer-Regiment 3 had been one of the first German armored units formed. It fought from the first day of the war until the last. During five-and-a-half years of war it suffered 92 officers and 581 other ranks killed, and thousands more wounded or missing. As much as could be said of any German regiment that fought in Russia, the Armored Bears, or as they were alternately known, the *Berliner Bärendivision*, the Berlin Bear Division, conducted a 'clean' war. The division itself was never accused of major war crimes.

* * *

Although some did fall into American hands, most of the Ukrainians of *1. Division der Ukrainischen National-Armee* wound up surrendering to the British. The men were herded into a large POW camp for processing, where along with members of *13. Waffen-Gebirgs-Division der SS Handschar* they used hydrogen tablets to obscure the blood group tattoos in their armpits. "When moistened and dabbed on the arm, the resulting skin irritation was sufficient to ensure that the tattoos came off within 2 or 3 days."[3]

One man who didn't need to worry about disguising his *Waffen-SS* membership was *Brigadeführer und Generalmajor der Waffen-SS* Freitag. The man who tried repeatedly to hand over his command to someone else felt no moral compunction to accompany the men he'd led into captivity, as most commanders did. When he suggested a plan for the division staff to melt into the countryside and escape, it was rejected. Knowing the likely fate that awaited him as a high-ranking *Waffen-SS* officer, Freitag walked off into the woods and shot himself.

As for the division itself, the fate that Freitag so feared never came to pass. Had they been turned over to the Russians many would have been executed out of hand, and the rest sent to the Gulags. Most, if not all, would likely have died. But that never happened. Instead they remained in British custody until 1947, when they were released and allowed to emigrate to whatever country they chose. In a bizarre twist of fate, while they had not freed the Ukraine, in the end they had freed themselves.

3   Melnyk, *To Battle*, p. 276.

41

Friday, 11 May

On the shores of Lake Attersee, the largest lake in the Salzkammergut, the alpine resort of Attersee had welcomed water sports enthusiasts for many years. The deep lake's clear, cold waters would have reflected the blue spring sky as peace settled over Europe. On 11 May some 1,500 members of the *1. SS-Ungarische-Schi-Bataillon* surrendered to troops of Patton's Third Army there. Other members of the unit had made their way to Klagenfurt, where they surrendered to British troops. Along with the Ski Battalion other Hungarian formations surrendered simultaneously, including what was left of both Hungarian SS divisions, and the last remnants of *SS-Brigade Ney*.

* * *

On the morning of 11 May the first substantial clue as to Ernst Kaltenbrunner's exact whereabouts came from the Austrian resistance. Along with a few others he was said to be hiding in an isolated cabin high in the mountains about a five-hour hike from Alt Aussee. The snow pack at that altitude averaged between twenty and thirty feet, with a hard crust. The cabin itself was surrounded by open slopes, which made it impossible to approach without being seen. Not knowing what they would find, the CIC agents put together a group of guards and guides and prepared to leave during the night.

Heeresgruppe E and *2. Panzerarmee*

Despite the deadline to enter Allied lines having passed two days before, columns of German soldiers still filled the back roads of Austria, including parts of *I Kavallerie-Corps* that had been held up and diverted by the Russian attack two days before at Köflach. On the morning of 11 May they approached Judenburg, two days behind the rest of the corps, only to find themselves cut off by Russian tanks coming south from Leoben. With no other choice, the Germans turned back to the east.

As had happened on 9 May, Russian ground-attack aircraft showed up to bomb and strafe the German columns, except this time something that must have seemed miraculous happened: the Germans got fighter support from the British. When the RAF appeared overhead, the Russians broke off their attacks to avoid any accidental fights with their erstwhile allies, since it was they, the Red Army, who had violated the Demarcation Line and crossed into the British zone. Nevertheless, until the very last moment the Germans feared they would be turned over to the Russians.

As for the Bulgarians, they headed for Vollermarkt in pursuit of *2. Panzerarmee*, but before catching up to the fleeing Germans they ran into the British 6th Armored Division, which had already been there for two days. Regardless of how badly they wanted to catch the Germans, the Bulgarians had been too slow.

* * *

Heeresgruppe E

Generaloberst Löhr's army group had the furthest to go of all the scattered German units and, as if 400,000 men plodding westward wasn't already enough of a migration, they were joined by the 220,000 men of the Croatian Army under General Djuro Grujić. Their path to freedom took both forces through Slovenian territory, where anyone who fell into partisan hands could expect no mercy. When the shambling mass turned northwest and came to Dravograd, however, they found their worst fears had come true: the Slovenes were on the north bank of the Drava River waiting for them.

The *XV SS-Kosaken-Kavallerie-Korps* was able to cross the river and fight its way to the road leading toward Völkermarkt and the British. But the other half a million men had to try and cross a smaller tributary of the Drava River, the Meža.

* * *

The German force was so huge that the main road was jammed with vehicle after vehicle from Dravograd to Celje, a distance of close to 40 miles. With such gigantic German columns held up by their forces, in their country, the Slovenes increased their demands for Austrian territory. The Chief-of-Staff of *Heeresgruppe E*, *Generalmajor* Erich Schmidt-Richberg, drove to Portschach am Worthersee to negotiate with the staff of the British Eighth Army in an attempt to surrender the entire army group to them.

42

Saturday, 12 May

Kampfgruppe 5. SS-Panzer-Division Wiking was getting close to the point of surrender to American forces. Strassner says that the division commander, *SS-Oberführer* Karl Ullrich, had given his officers and men the option of melting into the mountains and trying to make their way home, or of going into captivity and that uncertain fate that would await them. Everyone stayed; they would live or die as one. During the night of 12-13 May the division entered American lines and became prisoners of war. Himmler's model SS division that embodied a Pan-European war against communism ceased to exist. For many, if not most, of the non-German members of the division, the years following the war would be harder than those during the war. They were branded as traitors and criminals and many were tried as such.

* * *

The day had come when Ernst Kaltenbrunner's luck finally ran out. Accompanied by a squad of infantry and led by four local guides, the American CIC agents found him in an isolated cabin with his adjutant *SS-Obersturmbannführer* Scheidler and two SS guards. For a few moments it appeared the Germans might try to shoot their way out of the trap but then they surrendered, with Kaltenbrunner and Scheidler claiming to be other people. Kaltenbrunner called himself a doctor and was outfitted with everything a medical doctor might need. Anybody else might have got away with it, but the *de facto* final leader of the SS stood 6'4" tall, weighed 220 pounds and had a heavily scarred face.

The final shreds of their disguises were ripped away when the group marched back into Alt Aussee and their wives ran to embrace them. Kaltenbrunner even had his mistress run to him too. In subsequent interrogations he claimed to have been innocent of any crimes and only to have used his intelligence services to offset the evil influences of Foreign Minister Joachim von Ribbentrop, of all people. The Allies bought none of it.

Although at the Nuremberg Trials all eyes focused on the physically reviled and unrepentant Hermann Goring, a case could be made that none of the defendants wielded more real power than Kaltenbrunner. On 16 October 1946 he was hanged along with nine of his fellow defendants in the gymnasium of Nuremberg Prison.

SS-Kampfgruppe Keitel

Freiwilligen-Kavallerie-Regiment 93 and the rest of *SS-Kampfgruppe Keitel* began its service career in late March with more than 2,000 men. On 12 May the 180 remaining members trudged into Windischgarsten and negotiated their surrender. The Americans promised they would receive equal treatment with men of the other services, and the SS men accepted them at their word. They were immediately taken to prisoner of war camps.

The *Kampfgruppe* itself had been subordinated to *Kampfgruppe 1. SS-Panzer-Division Leibstandarte Adolf Hitler*, but *SS-Obersturmbannführer* Keitel wound up in command of the remnants of *356. Infanterie Division*. This included some of the *Fahnenjunkern* from *Kriegsschule Wiener Neustadt* who had survived five weeks of intense combat.

Although thrown together in the last months of the war, Keitel's command had fought with distinction for more than a month and suffered ruinous casualties while inflicting heavy losses on the Russians. The battlefield success of such hurriedly trained and assembled units allowed Hitler's Reich to survive for weeks and months after it should have been overrun.

* * *

At 8:00 a.m. the first Russian soldiers came through the gates of *Stalag 17B*, near Krems. The British POWs and doctors expected better treatment from their allies, and immediate repatriation to their own forces. They were wrong on both counts. The Russians treated them far worse than the Germans ever did. Many said it was the worst period they spent in the camp. They faced physical abuse, robbery and even rape by the Red Army.

Americans, however, reported an entirely different reception. Although the Russians wouldn't give them food or water, they didn't bother them and soon enough transport was arranged to the lines of General Patton's US Third Army.[1]

* * *

Panzer-Aufklärung-Abteilung 23 crossed the Mur bridge at Tamsweg, deep in the British zone, and joined the rest of the division already there. Remarkably, they still had all of their vehicles and *23. Panzer-Division* was still a cohesive military formation. The British treated them as beaten but honorable enemies, a radically different attitude than that they showed toward the *Waffen-SS*. The decision had been made not to send *I Kavallerie-Korps* to the Russians, but instead to demobilize them in Germany. In order to maintain security in their own bivouac area, the officers of the division were allowed to keep their side arms and even rifles were allowed for the sentries. This was mostly to keep other German soldiers who streamed into the area from trying to settle into the division's area. The men of the division were so trusted they were allowed to roam into the nearby mountains on hikes and sightseeing expeditions. In the weeks to come many members of the division would help feed the local civilians, clean up damaged farms and move wrecks off the roadways.

1   'Stalag XVIIB The Final Days', <http://www.stalag17b.com/final_days.html>, (Accessed 27 July 2018).

43

Sunday, 13 May

37. SS-Freiwilligen-Kavallerie-Division Lützow

On the night of 13 May, after learning that *Waffen-SS* men would not be allowed to go back home like *Wehrmacht* troops, some men of *Lützow* carried out a successful mass escape from the Altheim POW camp. Many of the men remained free, although *SS-Sturmbannführer* Etzler eventually gave himself up after a month to be with his men. And so the little-known *37. SS-Freiwilligen-Kavallerie-Division Lützow* passed into history. For a unit that was thrown together from the remnants of at least two German divisions, one Hungarian division, some Army troops and some teenage Hungarian boys who barely spoke German, *Lützow* performed remarkably well on the field of battle.

Alarm Bataillon 2, Luftkriegsschule 7

Having been in existence for five weeks, the tired remnants of the *Luftwaffe* alarm unit surrendered to the Americans north of Linz at Altenberg. Although accused of no war crimes, and not even being Army or *Waffen-SS*, some of the men were nonetheless handed over to the Russians. Years in Soviet prisons followed for those who survived.

Heeresgruppe E, 2. Panzerarmee and the Croatian Army

The little Meža River was a typical fast-flowing Alpine river near its source north of the Austrian border near Mount Olševa, Uschowa in German. For a short period the river left the surface and flowed underground before re-emerging. By the time it began to approach Dravograd, where it emptied into the Drava River, it slowed to a fairly sluggish stream. After the war it gained the reputation as the most polluted river in Europe because of a large mine and steel works that emptied their waste into its waters.

By that point the last German army group still at large more resembled a shambling tribe of dirty, hungry nomads than a military formation. Some of the men had fallen by the wayside, unable to keep up, and some had deserted. But not many; the countryside was hostile, the populace weren't native German-speakers and the partisans were ruthless. Fear kept the Axis soldiers together like a herd of sheep surrounded by a wolf pack. Finally, late on 13 May, the amorphous mass crossed over onto Austrian soil.

They found no salvation there. At Bleiburg, two miles inside Austria, *Generaloberst* Löhr faced the 6th British Armored Division, the 11th Slovene Brigade and the 51st Division of the Third Yugoslavian Army. Theoretically he outnumbered these forces by more than ten to one, but his men were in no condition to fight a pitched battle almost a week after the Germans officially surrendered. Between 150,000 and 160,000 of the men diverted elsewhere.

As Churchill had long suspected, Russia and her communist allies had every intention of grabbing as much Austrian territory as possible. After the First World War, the Slovene people became part of the newly created kingdom of Yugloslavia, but the border with the Republic of Austria had not yet been established. Disputes escalated into full-scale war between the two countries over the border region and only ended with the Treaty of Saint-Germain in September 1919. Neither side got everything it wanted from the treaty, and now, in 1945, the Slovenes intended to take advantage of the military situation to rectify their perceived loss.

On 9 May they had occupied Volkermarkt. Feistritz im Rosental had been attacked by two Slovene partisan battalions, and soon three brigades from the 14th Storm Division showed up. Skirmishes blunted the retreating Germans from crossing the shallow Vellach River at Rechberg and the Drava River at Kuhnsdorf. The Vellach in particular was shallow enough in many places to cross on foot, but the thousands of wagons and vehicles needed roads.

The problem for the partisans was the increasing desperation of an enemy who outnumbered them fifty to one in places. The mass of Germans, Croatians, Chetniks, pro-Axis Slovenians and assorted anti-communists couldn't be stopped by a small force of partisans, no matter how well equipped they were. But regardless of where they were or what they did, until the British accepted their surrender en masse the wandering army group remained in limbo.

44

Monday, 14 May

Three-quarters of the former members of *3. SS-Panzer-Division Totenkopf* were herded together near Gallneukirchen. After nearly a week in American custody many men from the Death's Head Division harbored secret hopes they would stay there. But the Russians were insistent; they wanted those SS men. And so they were then handed over to the Russians, from whom they could expect no mercy. The final casualty count for the division listed about 20,000 men killed, 40,000 wounded and 3,000 missing; more than 300 percent casualties during the war.[1]

---

1   Michaelis, *Panzer Divisions*, pp. 165-166.

45

Wednesday, 16 May

The Americans finally caught up with Robert Ley, who was living as Dr Ernst Distelmeyer at Schleching, a small town near Berchtesgaden. They found him wearing pajamas, and when he tried to swallow poison his captors stopped him. A second cyanide vial was found in his ring. A photograph taken the day of his capture shows the empty face of a beaten man. A thin beard covered his cheeks and upper lip, and deep lines cut through his loose skin, but it's in the dull eyes of a hopeless alcoholic that one sees how sick he truly was. Once dressed in average clothes, he appeared as nothing more than a drunk who might be found lying in the gutter of an alley. After his arrest he became one of the defendants at the Nuremberg Trials, although he never made it to court, committing suicide on 25 October 1945.

Of all the bizarre characters in the leadership of the Third Reich, Ley came closest to being an outright cartoon. Aside from a terrible speech impediment, he had lasting brain damage from the First World War, when he'd been shot down as a fighter pilot. Worsening this was his out-of-control alcoholism. He seems to have had some genuinely progressive ideas on improving the workplace environment, including many which are now considered normal, such as a green space for employees to relax during breaks. But his incoherent babbling and impediment, combined with his usually being drunk, made him a figure of ridicule even to the other high-ranking Nazis.

Unlike Speer's careful admission of partial guilt, in his suicide note Ley took responsibility for his part in the Holocaust, and asked God's forgiveness for his actions. Perhaps because he was sober for the first time in decades, Ley seems to have finally understood the consequences of his actions. He made no effort to justify or mitigate his own culpability, unlike every other Nuremberg defendant, including Speer.

46

Saturday, 19 May

Although *Generalfeldmarschall* Keitel had outlawed award of commendations after the German surrender of 8 May, Hermann Balck ignored that directive and gave *Oberst* Heribert Raithel the Oak Leaves to the Knight's Cross for leading the defense of Semmering Pass during the previous month. Technically speaking the German Army still existed, since the Dönitz government was theoretically still in power on 19 May, but because of Keitel's declaration no physical award could be given.

47

Sunday, 20 May

Otto Skorzeny finally decided the time had come to surrender. Several times he had contacted the Americans and asked for a jeep to drive him and his men into Salzburg. Shockingly, the Americans seemed apathetic about his surrender, and although the jeep was at the designated place on time, the Americans sent only one man to collect the most notorious German commando of them all. And so, with a few heavily armed close friends, he made his way into Salzburg, completely unaware that the Allies had built him into the ultimate Nazi boogeyman.

It took a while to find someone to believe that he not only wanted to surrender himself but also his *Kampfgruppe*. The problem was that nobody believed that he was really Otto Skorzeny. When they finally did take him seriously, and he tried to arrange for the capitulation of his 250 remaining men, the Americans immediately disarmed and handcuffed him. By pre-arranged signal, Skorzeny had told his men that if he wasn't back within three hours for them to melt away and do whatever they felt best.

Skorzeny's career was far from over. After being held prisoner at Nuremberg as a witness, he himself was tried for his part in *Unternehmen Greif*, the operation during the Ardennes Offensive to disguise German commandos in American uniforms. He was acquitted by calling British commandos to testify in his defense they had done the same thing as he had. But he still wasn't released. All Nazis and suspected sympathizers had to go through denazification, which could means years more imprisonment. For Skorzeny three years behind bars without being convicted of a crime was enough, so he did what the 'Most Dangerous Man in Europe', as he had been labeled, should have been expected to do: he escaped.

Making his way to Spain, he opened a small engineering business. And as far as the world knows for certain, that was the end of Otto Skorzeny until he published his memoirs and eventually died of cancer in 1975.

But Skorzeny wasn't the type of man to retire to the quiet life. Aside from allegations that he traveled to Egypt in 1952 to act as military adviser to the new ruler General Mohammed Naguib, at the request of former General Intelligence wizard Reinhard Gehlen and the CIA, in 1989 the Israeli magazine *Matara* claimed the Israelis had paid Skorzeny to spy on the Egyptian rocket program being developed by German scientists. Then, in 2016, *Haaretz*, another Israeli publication, made the astounding claim that Skorzeny hadn't just spied for Israel, he had also been a hitman for Mossad, even killing a fellow German during a trip to Munich. Skorzeny always had a flair for self-promotion and publicity. The irony of Hitler's favorite commando working for the Jewish state notwithstanding, he would undoubtedly have laughed that 41 years after his death, the Most Dangerous Man in Europe still made headlines.

48

Wednesday, 23 May

The horrors of Mauthausen had become known when the US 11th Armored Division first liberated the camp on 5 May. All of the secrets of the Nazi death machine were laid bare. What wasn't known, however, were the whereabouts of Camp Commandant *SS-Standartenführer* Franz Ziereis. By most accounts, on 23 May he was discovered hiding either in or near the town of Spital am Pyrhn, although some sources say the date was different. Ziereis had a hunting lodge near the town and a few reports say he was captured there, but one of the American GIs who rounded him up claimed it was 23 May.

Somehow Ziereis wound up being shot, although whether by prisoners or soldiers is in debate. In the official version of events there is a photo of him purporting to give a death-bed confession about activities at Mauthausen as he lay dying in a US military hospital. The authenticity of the photo in question has since been challenged. In this version of events, eight months later a released prisoner working at the hospital gave a lengthy word-by-word deposition of Ziereis' statement, which had lasted between six and eight hours. He gave this statement strictly from memory. That document was later used as evidence against Ernst Kaltenbrunner during the Nuremberg Trials, although the prisoner was never made available as a witness.

But in another version, a GI named Donald Leake stated that he and some others responded to a disturbance call from Spital. When a man bolted from a house in the village one of them shot him three times in the back. It was Ziereis, and the story about what happened in Spital was related to him by the soldier who'd actually shot Ziereis. Taken back to Mauthausen, he was put in a lounge for the SS guards. Leake helped guard him for three days and heard no confession, and later stated emphatically that Ziereis never regained consciousness while he was on duty. He also said the former commandant was never taken to a hospital after being shot, and died a few days later.[1] Regardless of how and when Ziereis died, there's no real doubt that he met his ultimate fate beginning on 23 May 1945.

* * *

The man who made it possible for Ziereis to become commandant at Mauthausen in the first place, the former *Reichsführer-SS* Heinrich Himmler, spent the previous night hiding in a mill at Bremervörde, in far northwest Germany. In custody of the British, who suspected something but hadn't yet identified him, Himmler confessed his true name. During a strip search, the doctor inspecting him noticed something in his mouth and reached in to get it out, but Himmler bit down on both a glass ampule and the doctor's fingers. Within seconds cyanide sent him into convulsions. The British did everything they could to keep him alive but it was useless. At 11:14 p.m., Himmler expelled one last breath and never inhaled another one.

---

1   Mauthausen History, 'The confession of Franz Ziereis, Commandant of the Mauthausen concentration camp', (2012), <https://www.scrapbookpages.com/Mauthausen/KZMauthausen/ZiereisDeath.html>, (Accessed 30 July 2018).

The man who single-handedly created the *Waffen-SS*, the concentration and death camp systems and spread terror throughout Europe, died quickly, leaving others to face the world's fury at his crimes. It is doubtful that many *Waffen-SS* men cried at hearing the news.

49

Friday, 25 May

"How many men have you hung today?"

The most hated German general officer of the war started every briefing with that question. His notorious brutality elevated him far beyond the levels which his technician's competence warranted. As a Nazi fanatic he slaughtered his own men in huge numbers even a week after Hitler's suicide, handing out death sentences for little or no reason to stiffen resistance at the front. You could die fighting the Russians or you could die hanging from a lamppost, was his message. But above all, you could not retreat regardless of circumstances.

He was *Generalfeldmarschall* Ferdinand Schörner, Hitler's favorite general and the commander of *Heeresgruppe Mitte*. On 9 May Schörner did the very thing he'd killed thousands of his countrymen for doing: he fled to avoid capture. With the last territory under German control about to be overrun by the Red Army, the diehard Nazi boarded his personal *Fiesler Storch* aircraft and flew south to Austria, despite the begging of his staff to stay and share the fate of the men he'd promised to stand by.

Schörner's intent was to hide in the Tyrolean Alps. During the First World War he'd won the Pour L' Merite for bravery, but thirty years later he chose to flee rather than share the fate of his men. Schörner later justified his flight with a series of excuses.

Sixteen days later, on 25 May, east of the small market town of Wagrain in the Salzburg district, elements of the US 42nd Rainbow Division detained someone wearing the clothing of a working man; short pants, dark socks and coat. In the flotsam of war and amid the floods of Germans driven west by the Russian advance, *Generalfeldmarschall* Schörner at first glance appeared to be just another aging man looking for sanctuary. But despite his disguise there was no covering up his impeccable grooming, or the unrepentant jut of his chin. He stood out as a man used to giving orders.

The Americans turned him over to the Russians. Uncharacteristically, the Russians went easy on Schörner. He was imprisoned for ten years but then released. Newsreels outside his home in 1955 show that he'd lost none of his imperious bearing. The West German government then tried him for manslaughter for ordering all of those Germans killed, and jailed him for another four years. Even so, unlike the men he condemned to death, Schörner lived into old age and died in 1973 at 81.

* * *

What was the cost of the Battle for Austria? In material terms, much of Austria was ripped apart and destroyed, and not all of that was bad. The societal costs, for example, replaced the Nazi culture with one that eventually became the democratic society of modern Austria. No total of the fallen can ever be considered 100 percent accurate, but it can be safely said that the price in human lives was staggering.

In Lower Austria the dead totaled 14,968 German soldiers and 25,768 Russians. In the 'quiet' section of the front, where Balck's 6. *Armee* shielded Styria, 10,000 Germans and 16,000 Russians died. And in Burgenland, which only saw fighting for a brief period, another 2,575 Germans fell, compared to 2,212 Russians.[1] Russian statistics agree with these numbers surprisingly well.[2] Vienna cost the Germans 19,000 dead and the Russians 18,000. Combat deaths from *2. Panzerarmee*, and units in the west fighting the Americans and French, aren't known. Nor do they include the wounded men who later died of their wounds, the missing or those who became prisoners of war and never returned home. For the Germans captured in Austria these numbered in the tens of thousands, especially among the *Waffen-SS*. All of *3. SS-Panzer-Division Totenkopf* and much of *1. SS-Panzer-Division Leibstandarte Adolf Hitler* surrendered to the Americans but were turned over to the Russians. The same fate awaited the *Führer-Grenadier-Division*.

Civilian numbers aren't known, but had to have been horrific. Not only those killed outright in the American bombing raids in support of the Russian offensive, or directly in the fighting, but also refugees strafed and bombed by the Red Army, or preyed upon by stragglers and escaped foreign workers; and women raped by Russians, stragglers, criminals and other opportunistic predators, many of whom later committed suicide. There were also those who died of starvation; exposure; untreated illness; people killed in personal vendettas and a thousand other ways to die.

* * *

Wars don't just end all at once. Like earthquakes there are aftershocks, some large, some so small that only a few know about them. Stalin considered any man who encountered Western Civilization to be suspect because of the potential bourgeoisie influence. For example, what effect did it have on a man who'd never seen toilets before when he encountered indoor plumbing? Not merely in the homes of the rich, but also in a working man's home? Did he not then wonder why Russia had no such conveniences?

And while Stalin was paranoid about anything and everything, in this case he had some reason to be. Many Red Army soldiers deserted and fled into the hills, and there are few countries more amenable to deserters than Austria in spring. They didn't want to return to the grinding poverty of the Motherland, precisely as Stalin feared. But they had to eat, and the only way to do that was to steal from the locals.

Other men also took refuge among the high slopes and dense forests of the Austrian mountains: criminals, liberated slave workers, Russian *Hiwis* facing a grim fate in the USSR, Nazis officials and men of the SS for whom surrender meant prison or death. They all preyed on the peasantry too, and sometimes carried on the war against each other in the fight for survival. Every now and then, "the sound of automatic pistol fire…announced that…two opposing groups had clashed".[3]

Echoes of the war continued long after it ended. Even in the 21st Century, parts of Austrian cities continued to be shut down because of unexploded ordnance being discovered during road-works, or when tearing down an old building. Mines continued to be an issue in the high mountains where they once protected German and Russian emplacements. People kept on dying long after the guns fell silent.

Like all wars throughout history, even when the war was over, the killing was not.

1   Brettner, *Die Letzten Kämpfe, Band II* p. 235.
2   Krivosheev, *Soviet Casualties and Combat Losses*, p. 157.
3   Lucas, *Last Days of the Third Reich*, p. 113.

Afterword

It is perhaps fitting that no country during the Second World War saw armies from more countries on its soil than did Austria. After all, Hitler was not German, he was Austrian. By the end of the war men from the French, British, American, Rumanian, Bulgarian, Yugoslavian, Russian, Croatian, Hungarian and German armies were in the country. Of the Allies, only the Canadians weren't represented. It would be stretching a point to say the Ukrainian Army was also there, since just before the war ended the *14. Waffen-Grenadier-Division der SS Galizien* left the *Waffen-SS* to become the first unit of the Ukrainian National Army.

The campaign in April and May 1945 to capture Austria has long been overlooked in the West because for the American divisions of Third and Seventh Armies, it was at the time considered little more than a road march under tactical conditions. This book has hopefully shown there was resistance to the Americans after all. A portrayal of the American advance as being a cakewalk does a terrible disservice to the G.I.s who were wounded or killed liberating the country, and yet overselling it as being more than it was does a disservice to the historical record. Certainly it has to be granted that the Russian experience was vastly different.

This book posed the question of whether Stalin would have given up territory in the American and British zones had his armies pushed that far west, or would he do as he did in other countries and install a pro-Soviet government in Austria? The evidence strongly suggests the latter course.

First, Renner's government was clearly set up as a puppet controlled by Moscow. The fact that Renner himself turned out to be more of an independent leader than the Russians had intended doesn't negate their original purpose, namely, in having a socialist in control in Vienna.

Second, Stalin intended for the Yugoslavians to seize as much of Italy and Austria as possible. This is shown by Britain's near-shooting war with Tito's forces at Trieste, and the demands of the Slovenes in southern Austria.

Third, the strong assaults not only on Vienna, but west along the Danube Valley and into Styria, showed that Stalin didn't mind spending oceans of Russian blood to acquire as much Austrian territory as possible. But why? The zones of occupation were already agreed upon regardless of who captured it. Part of the answer could be Stalin's distrust of his Western Allies, but it could also show his intentions. If he'd conquered British and American territory, would he have given it back? Maybe, maybe not; at the very least possession of those lands would have made for a strong bargaining position.

But Stalin had long-since realized that conflict with the West was inevitable. Including Austria in the pro-Soviet bloc he was already planning, that would become the Warsaw Pact alliance, would leave the West in a strategically unviable position in Germany. Any defense of that country would be outflanked on the south by Russian forces and their allies on the Austrian border. Accepting that Switzerland would remain neutral in any future war, Austria as a pro-Soviet country would also cut the shortest route between Germany and Italy. In turn this would inevitably increase Russian influence in Italy itself.

The greatest *prima facie* evidence of Stalin's mindset is the mass-construction of Russian fortifications behind their front lines beginning in mid-April. The Russians considered it likely that the Western Allies would break their alliance with them, and form a new one with Nazi Germany. Granting such a hare-brained idea validity shows just how warped Russian paranoia could become, and how much it could influence military actions. In such an environment it is not much of a stretch to think that Stalin wanted to overrun all of Austria, and that, having done so, he wouldn't give it back.

It is one of the great historical ironies that Dwight Eisenhower prevented this by falling for the hoax of the National Redoubt. On his own accord he changed the course of history by ceasing the agreed-upon invasion of central Germany, and instead sending his armies southeast into Austria. Once it became obvious that the Americans would grab western Austria, the Russians began moving forces north for the fight against *Heeresgruppe Mitte.* Rarely in the annals of mankind has a general been so thoroughly tricked into doing something so right.

Whether this theory holds up to scrutiny or not, the Battle for Austria was one of the most important campaigns of the Second World War. We will never know exactly why Hitler committed so much of his country's waning military power to defend what most of his advisors considered a secondary theater. Maybe it really was all about the oil; maybe a latent streak of sentimentality for his home country influenced him; or maybe he gave the idea of holding out in the Alps more credit than is currently given. It seems likely that it was a combination of all of these.

In the end it made no difference where he deployed the *Waffen-SS* panzer divisions. Had they gone north, Berlin might have held out another week or two, but it would have fallen regardless. However, doing so would have left Austria far more exposed than it was. Whatever his reasons, for Austria the torment of 1945 eventually gave way to a transformation into a modern democracy.

Bibliography

Ailsby, Christopher, *SS Hell on the Eastern Front: The Waffen-SS War in Russia 1941-1945* (Osceola: MBI, 1998).

Altner, Helmut, *Berlin Dance of Death* (Havertown: Casemate, 2002).

Angolia, J.R., *The HJ Volume 1* (San Jose: R. James Bender, 1991).

Angolia, J.R., *The HJ Volume 2* (San Jose: R. James Bender, 1991).

Axell, Albert, *Stalin's War Through the Eyes of His Commanders* (London: Arms and Armour Press, 1997).

Balck, Hermann, Edited and Translated by Major General David T. Zabecki, USA (Ret.), and Lieutenant Colonel Dieter J. Biedekarken, USA (Ret.), *Order in Chaos, The Memoirs of General of Panzer-Troops Hermann Balck*, (Lexington: The University Press of Kentucky, 2015).

Barea, Ilsa, *Vienna* (New York: Knopf, 1966).

Barnett, Correlli, editor, *Hitler's Generals* (New York: Grove Wiedenfeld, 1989).

Baryatinskiy, Mikhail, *The IS Tanks: IS-1, IS-2, IS-3* (Hersham: Ian Allan Publishing, 2006).

Battistelli, Pier Paolo, *Panzer Divisions 1944-45* (Oxford: Osprey, 2009).

Bender, Roger James & Taylor, Hugh Page, *Uniforms, Organization and History of the Waffen-SS Volume 1* (Mountain View: Bender, 1971).

Bender, Roger James & Taylor, Hugh Page, *Uniforms, Organization and History of the Waffen-SS Volume 2* (Mountain View: Bender, 1971).

Bender, Roger James & Taylor, Hugh Page, *Uniforms, Organization and History of the Waffen-SS Volume 3* (San Jose: R. James Bender Publishing, 1986).

Bender, Roger James & Taylor, Hugh Page, *Uniforms, Organization and History of the Waffen-SS Volume 4* (San Jose: R. James Bender Publishing, 1986).

Bender, Roger James & Taylor, Hugh Page, *Uniforms, Organization and History of the Waffen-SS Volume 5* (San Jose: R. James Bender Publishing, 1986).

Benz-Casson, Lotte, *Wien 1945* (Vienna: Paul Kaltschmid, 1945).

Bessonov, Evgeni, *Tank Rider: Into the Reich With the Red Army* (London: Greenhill Books, 2003).

Bishop, Chris, *Hitler's Foreign Divisions: Foreign Volunteers in the Waffen-SS 1940-1945* (London: Amber Books, 2005).

Bishop, Chris, *Panzergrenadier Divisions 1939-1945* (London: Amber, 2007).

Bishop, Chris, *Waffen-SS Divisions 1939-1945* (London: Amber, 2011).

Bonn, Keith E., editor, *Slaughterhouse: The Handbook of the Eastern Front* (Bedford: Aberjona, 2005).

Bradley, General of the Army Omar N. and Blair, Clay, *A General's Life, An Autobiography* (New York: Simon & Schuster, 1983).

Brettner, Friedrich, *Die Letzten Kämpfe des II. Weltkrieges, Fotoband I* (Berndorf: Kral, 2014).

Brettner, Friedrich, *Die Letzten Kämpfe des II. Weltkrieges, Fotoband II* (Berndorf: Kral, 2014).

Brettner, Friedrich, *Geflüchtet Vertrieben Besetzt, Niederösterreich, Burgenland, Steiermark und Kärnten Kriegsende-Nachkriegzeit* (Kral: Berndorf, 2014).

Brettner, Friedrich, *Die Letzten Kämpfe des II Weltkrieges, Pinka-Lafnitz-Hochwechsel-1743 m: 1 Gebirgsdivision – 1 Panzerdivision – Divisionsgruppe Krause – 117. Jägerdivision – Kampfgruppe Arko 3* (Gloggnitz: Eigenverlag Friedrich Brettner, 1999).

Brettner, Friedrich, *Die Letzten Kämpfe des II. Weltkrieges um das Semmeringgebiet* (Wiener Neustadt: Brettner, 2003).

Brett-Smith, Richard, *Hitler's Generals* (San Rafael: Presidio Press, 1977).

Bukey, Evan Burr, *Hitler's Austria: Popular Sentiment in the Nazi Era 1938-1945* (Chapel Hill: The University of North Carolina Press, 2002).

Chambers, John Whiteclay II & Piehler, G. Kurt, editors, *Major Problems in American Military History* (Knoxville: The University of Tennessee Press, 1999).

Churchill, Winston S., *Triumph and Tragedy* (Boston: Houghton Mifflin, 1953).

Citino, Robert M., *The Werhmacht's Last Stand, The German Campaigns of 1944-1945* (Lawrence: University Press of Kansas, 2017).

Clemens, Diane Shaver, *Yalta* (London: Oxford University Press, 1972).

Cornish, Nik, *Armageddon Ost: The German Defeat on the Eastern Front 1944-45* (Hersham: Ian Allan, 2006).

Davis, Brian L., *Waffen-SS* (London: Blandford Press, 1987).

Degrelle, Leon, *The Waffen SS On the Eastern Front* (Torrance: Institute For Historical Review, 1986).

Detre, Gyula László, *History First Hand* (Lakitelek: Antológia, 2007).

Domanski, Jazek & Ledwoch, Janusz, *Wien, 1945* (Warsaw: Wydawnictwo Militaria, 2006).

Duffy, Christopher, *Red Storm on the Reich* (New York: Atheneum, 1991).

Dulles, Allen, *The Secret Surrender* (New York: Popular Library, 1966).

Dunn, Walter S., Jr., *Hitler's Nemesis: The Red Army, 1940-1945* (Westport: Praeger, 1994).

Eby, Cecil D., *Hungary at War: Civilians and Soldiers in World War II* (University Park: Pennsylvania State University Press, 1998).

Eisenhower, Dwight D., *Crusade in Europe* (New York: Doubleday & Co., 1948).

Ertel, Heinz & Schulze-Kossens, Richard, *Europaische Freiwilligen im Bild* (Coburg: Nation Europa Verlag, 1997).

Fey, Will, translated by Henschler, Henri, *Armor Battles of the Waffen-SS 1943-1945* (Mechanicsburg: Stackpole Books, 2003).

Fischer, Thomas, *The SS Panzer-Artillery-Regiment 1: Leibstandarte Adolf Hitler (LAH) 1940-1945* (Atglen: Schiffer, 2004).

Foedrowitz, Michael, *The Flak Towers in Berlin, Hamburg and Vienna 1940-1950* (Atglen: Schiffer, 1998).

Foley, Charles, *Commando Extraordinary, The Remarkable Exploits of Otto Skorzeny* (New York: Berkley Medallion, 1969).

Fritz, Stephen G., *Frontsoldaten, The German Soldier in World War II* (Lexington: The University Press of Kentucky, 1995).

Galland, Adolf, *The First and the Last* (New York: Ballantine, 1963).

Glantz, David M., *The Role of Intelligence in Soviet Military Strategy in World War II* (Novato: Presidio Press, 1991).

Gilbert, Martin, *Churchill: A Life* (New York: Henry Holt & Co., 1991).

Goldsworthy, Terry, *Valhalla's Warriors: A History of the Waffen-SS on the Eastern Front 1941-1945* (Indianapolis: Dog Ear Publishing, 2007).

Guderian, Heinz, *Panzer Leader* (New York: Ballantine, 1968).

Guillemot, Philippe, *Hungary 1944-45: The Panzers' Last Stand* (Paris: Histoire & Collections, 2011).

Hargreaves, Richard, *The Germans in Normandy* (South Yorkshire: Pen & Sword, 2006).

Heiber, Helmut & Glantz, David M., *Hitler and His Generals: Military Conferences 1942-1945* (New York: Enigma, 2004).

Heike, Wolf-Dietrich, *The Ukrainian Division 'Galicia' 1943-45* (Toronto: Shevchenko Scientific Society, 1988).

Hogg, Ian V., *The Guns 1939-1945* (New York: Ballantine, 1971).

Holzträger, Hans, *In A Raging Inferno, Combat Units of the Hitler Youth 1944-45* (Solihull: Helion, 2008).

Hughes, Dr Matthew & Mann, Dr Chris, *Fighting Techniques of a Panzergrenadier 1941-1945* (Osceola: MBI Books, 2000).

Huxley-Blythe, Peter J., *Under the St Andrew's Cross: Russian & Cossack Volunteers in World War II 1941-1945* (Bayside: Europa Books, 2003).

Infield, Glenn B., *Skorzeny, Hitler's Commando* (New York: St Martin's Press, 1962).

Isaev, Aleksei & Kolomiets, Maksim, translated and edited by Britton, Stuart, *Tomb of the Panzerwaffe, The Defeat of the Sixth SS Panzer Army in Hungary 1945* (Solihull: Helion Books, 2014).

Janjetovic, Zoran, *Between Hitler and Tito: Disappearance of the Ethnic Germans From the Vojvodina, 2nd Revised Edition* (Belgrade: University of Mary, 2005).

Jentz, Thomas L., editor, *Panzer Truppen 2: The Complete Guide to the Creation & Combat Employment of Germany's Tank Force 1943-1945* (Atglen: Schiffer, 1996).

Jordan, Franz, *April 1945 – Die Kämpfe im nordöstlichen Niederösterreich* (Österreichischer Militärverlag: Salzburg, 2003).

Jurado, Carlos Caballero, *Breaking the Chains: 14 Waffen-Grenadier Division der SS and Other Ukrainian Volunteer Formations, Eastern Front, 1942-1945* (Halifax: Shelf Books, 1998).

Keegan, John, *Waffen SS: The Asphalt Soldiers* (New York: Ballantine, 1970).

Kern, Ernst, *War Diary 1941-1945: A Report* (New York: Vantage Press, 1993).

Kershaw, Ian, *The End: the Defiance and Destruction of Hitler's Germany, 1944-1945* (New York: The Penguin Press, 2011).

Kissel, Hans, *Hitler's Last Levy: The Volkssturm 1944-1945* (Solihull: Helion, 2005).

Klapdor, Ewald, *Viking Panzers* (Mechanicsburg: Stackpole, 2011).

Krhesheev, Colonel-General G.F., editor, *Soviet Casualties and Combat Losses in the Twentieth Century* (London: Greenhill Books, 1997).

Kurowski, Franz, *Hitler's Last Bastion: The Final Battles for the Reich 1944-1945* (Atglen: Schiffer, 1998).

Kurowski, Franz, *Infantry Aces* (New York: Ballantine, 2002).

Kurowski, Franz, *Panzer Aces* (New York: Ballantine, 2002).

Kurowski, Franz, *Panzer Aces III* (Mechanicsburg: Stackpole, 2010).

Kursietis, Andris J., with Munoz, Antonio J., *The Hungarian Army and Its Military Leadership in World War II, 3rd Revised Edition* (Bayside: Axis Europa, 1999).

Landwehr, Richard, *Estonian Vikings: Estnisches SS-Freiwillingen Battalion Narwa and Subsequent Units, Eastern Front, 1943-1944* (Halifax: Shelf Books, 2000).

Landwehr, Richard, *Fighting For Freedom: The Ukrainian Volunteer Division of the Waffen SS* (Silver Spring: Bibliophile Legion Books, 1993).

Landwehr, Richard, *Romanian Volunteers of the Waffen-SS, 1944-45* (Brookings: Siegrunen, 1991).

Landwehr, Richard, *Siegrunen Vol. XIV No. 2 – Whole Number 82 – Fall, 2013* (Bennington: Merriam Press, 2014).

Landwehr, Richard, *Steadfast Hussars, The Last Cavalry Divisions of the Waffen-SS* (Bennington: Merriam Press, 2006).

Liddell Hart, B. H., *Strategy, Second Revised Edition* (New York: Meridian, 1991).

Liddell Hart, B. H., *The German Generals Talk* (New York: William Morrow, 1975).

Liddell Hart, B. H., *The Red Army* (New York: Harcourt, Brace & Company, 1956).

Linderman, Gerald F., *Embattled Courage, the experience of combat in the American Civil War* (New York: Free Press, 1989).

Littlejohn, David, *Foreign Legions of the Third Reich Volume 1: Norway, Denmark, France* (San Jose: R. James Bender Publishing, 1979).

Littlejohn, David, *Foreign Legions of the Third Reich Volume 2: Belgium, Great Britain, Holland, Italy and Spain* (San Jose: R. James Bender Publishing, 1979).

Littman, Sol, *Pure Soldiers or Sinister Legion, the Ukrainian 14th Waffen-SS Division* (Montreal: BlackRose Books, 2003).

Lochmann, Dr Franz-Wilhelm, Rosen, Richard Freiherr von & Rubbel, Alfred, *The Combat History of German Tiger Tank Battalion 503 in World War II* (Mechanicsburg: Stackpole, 2000).

Lochner, Louis B., *The Goebbels Diaries* (New York: Popular Library, 1948).

Logusz, Michael O., *Galicia Division, The Waffen-SS 14th Grenadier Division 1943-1945* (Atglen: Schiffer, 1997).

Loewenheim, Francis L., Langley, Harold D. and Jonas, Manfred, editors, *Roosevelt and Churchill: Their Secret Wartime Correspondence* (New York: Saturday Review Press, 1975).

Loza, Dmitriy, translated & edited by Gebhardt, James F., *Commanding the Red Army's Sherman Tanks: The World War II Memoirs of Hero of the Soviet Union Dmitriy Loza* (Lincoln: University of Nebraska Press, 1996).

Lucas, James, *Battle Group: The Story of Germany's Fearsome Shock Troops* (London: Rigel, 2004).

Lucas, James, *Last Days of the Third Reich, The Collapse of Nazi Germany, May, 1945* (New York: William Morrow and Co., 1986).

Lucas, James, *Das Reich, The Military Role of the 2nd SS Division* (London: Arms & Armour Press, 1993).

Maclean, Major French L., *The Unknown Generals – German Corps Commanders of World War II* (West Point: The US Military Academy, 1974).

Maeger, Herbert, *Lost Honour, Betrayed Loyalty, The Memoir of a Waffen-SS Soldier on the Eastern Front* (London: Frontline Books, 2015).

Maier, Goerg, *Drama Between Budapest and Vienna, The Final Battles of the 6. Panzer-Armee in the East – 1945* (Winnipeg: J.J. Fedorowicz, 2004).

Manvell, Roger, *SS and Gestapo* (New York: Ballantine, 1973).

Manvell, Roger and Fraenkel, Heinrich, *Himmler* (New York: Paperback Library, 1968).

Mawdsley, Evan, *Thunder in the East: The Nazi-Soviet War 1941-1945* (London: Hodder Arnold, 2007).

Maslov, Alexander A., *Fallen Soviet Generals: Soviet General Officers Killed in Battle, 1941-1945* (Abingdon: Routledge Press, 1998).

Megargee, Geoffrey P., *Inside Hitler's High Command* (Lawrence: University Press of Kansas, 2000).

Melnyk, Michael James, *To Battle: The Formation and History of the 14th Galician Waffen-SS Division* (Solihull: Helion, 2002).

Merridale, Catherine, *Ivan's War, Life and Death in the Red Army, 1939-1945* (New York: Metropolitan Books, 2006).

Messenger, Charles, *Hitler's Gladiator, The Life and Wars of Panzer Army Commander Sepp Dietrich* (New York: Skyhorse Publishing, 2011).

Meyer, Hubert, *The 12th SS, The History of the Hitler Youth Panzer Division: Volume Two* (Mechanicsburg: Stackpole, 2005).

Michaelis, Rolf, *Cavalry Divisions of the Waffen-SS* (Atglen: Schiffer, 2010).

Michaelis, Rolf, *Panzer Divisions of the Waffen-SS* (Atglen: Schiffer, 2013).

Military Intelligence Division, War Department, *Order of Battle of the German Army March, 1945* (Washington D.C.: US Army, 1945).

Military Intelligence Division, War Department, *The German Replacement Army (Ersatzheer) February, 1945* (Washington D.C.: US Army, 1945).

Mitcham, Samuel R., *Hitler's Legions, German Army Order of Battle World War II* (London: Leo Cooper, 1985).

Mitcham, Samuel W., Jr, *The German Defeat in the East 1944-45* (Mechanicsburg: Stackpole, 2007).

Mitcham, Samuel W., Jr, *The German Order of Battle: 1st-290th Infantry Divisions in World War II* (Mechanisburg: Stackpole, 2007).

Mitcham, Samuel W., Jr, *The Panzer Legions: A Guide to the German Army Tank Divisions of WWII and Their Commanders* (Mechanicsburg: Stackpole Books, 2007).

Mooney, Peter, *Dietrich's Warriors, The History of the 3. Kompanie/1st Panzergrenadier Regiment, 1st SS Panzer Division Leibstandarte Adolf Hitler* (Atglen: Schiffer, 2004).

Mosier, John, *Deathride: Hilter vs. Stalin, The Eastern Front 1941-1945* (New York: Simon & Schuster, 2010).

Mosley, Leonard, *The Reich Marshal: A Biography of Hermann Goering* (New York: Dell, 1974).

Mujzer, Dr Peter, *The Royal Hungarian Army 1920-1945, Volume II, Hungarian Mobile Forces* (Bayside: Axis Europa, 2000).

Munoz, Antonio J., *For Croatia & Christ: The Croatian Army in World War II 1941-1945* (Bayside: Axis Europa Books, 2003).

Munoz, Antonio J., *Göring's Grenadiers, The Luftwaffe Field Divisions 1942-1945* (Bayside: Axis Europa Books, 2002).

Munoz, Antonio J., *Hitler's Eastern Legions: Volume II The Osttruppen, 1941-1945* (Bayside: Axis Europa Books, 2004).

Munoz, Antonio J., editor, *The East Came West: Muslim, Hindu, and Buddhist Volunteers in the German Armed Forces 1941-1945* (Bayside: Axis Europa Books, 2001).

Nafziger, George F., *German Order of Battle World War II, Volume I, Panzer, Panzer Grenadier, Light and Cavalry Divisions* (Nafziger: West Chester, 1994).

Nafziger, George F., *The German Order of Battle Panzers and Artillery in World War II* (London: Greenhill Books, 1999).

Neumann, Peter, *The Black March: The Personal Story of an SS Man* (New York: Bantam, 1967).

Nevenkin, Kamen, *Fire Brigades: The Panzer Divisions 1943-1945* (Winnipeg: J.J. Fedorowicz, 2008).

Newton, Steven H., *German Battle Tactics on the Russian Front 1941-1945* (Atglen: Schiffer, 1994).

Niehorster, Leo W.G., *The Royal Hungarian Army 1920-1945* (Bayside: Axis Europa Books, 1998).

Novak, Josip & Spencer, David, *Hrvatski Orlovi: Paratroopers of the Independent State of Croatia 1942-1945* (Bayside: Axis Europa, 1998).

Orgill, Douglas, *T-34 Russian Armor* (New York: Ballantine, 1971).

Pencz, Rudolf, *For the Homeland: the 31st Waffen-SS Volunteer Grenadier Division in WWII* (Mechanicsburg: Stackpole, 2010).

Perrett, Bryan, *Knights of the Black Cross* (New York: St Martin's Press, 1988).

Piekalkiewicz, Janusz, translated by Heurck, Jan van, *Tank War 1939-1945* (New York: Historical Times, 1986).

Pierik, Perry, *Hungary 1944-1945: The Forgotten Tragedy, 2nd Edition* (Nieuwegein: Aspekt, 1998).

Poirier, Robert G. and Conner, Albert Z., *The Red Army Order of Battle in the Great Patriotic War, including data from 1919 to postwar years* (Novato: Presidio Press, 1985).

Porter, David, *Order of Battle: The Red Army in WWII* (London: Amber Books, 2009).

Rauchenstiener, Manfred, *Schriften des Heeresgeschichtlichen Museums in Wien Band 5 Krieg in Össterreich 1945* (Vienna: Osterreichischer Bundesverlag Fur Unterricht, Wissenschaft und Kunst, 1970).

Ravenscroft, Trevor, *The Spear of Destiny* (York Beach: Samuel Weiser, 1982).

Rebentisch, Dr Ernst, *To the Caucasus and the Austrian Alps: The History of the 23rd Panzer Division in World War II* (Winnipeg: J.J. Fedorowicz, 2009).

Reynolds, Michael, *Men of Steel, I SS Panzer Corps, The Ardennes and Eastern Front 1944-45* (New York: Sarpdeon, 1999).

Reynolds, Michael, *Sons of the Reich, II SS Panzer Corps, Normandy, Arnhem, Ardennes, Eastern Front* (Havertown: Casemate, 2002).

Reynolds, Michael, *The Devil's Adjutant: Jochen Peiper, Panzer Leader* (New York: Sarpedon, 1995).

Richter, Klaus Christian, *Cavalry of the Wehrmacht 1941-1945* (Atglen: Schiffer, 1995).

Riemer, Hans, *This Pearl Vienna* (Vienna: Jugend und Volk, 1946).

Rikmenspoel, Marc, *Soldiers of the Waffen-SS: Many Nations, One Motto* (Winnipeg: J.J. Fedorowicz, 1999).

Ringler, Ralf Roland, *Illusion einer Jugend, Hitler-Jugend in Österrech* (St Pölten: Verlag Niederösterreichisches Pressehaus, 1977).

Ripley, Tim, *The Waffen SS at War: Hitler's Praetorians 1923-1945* (St Paul: Zenith Press, 2004).

Rosado, Jorge & Bishop, Chris, *Wehrmacht Panzer Divsions 1939-1945: The Essential Tank Identification Guide* (London: Amber, 2006).

Rottman, Gordon L., *Soviet Rifleman 1941-1945* (Oxford: Osprey, 2007).

Ryan, Cornelius, *The Last Battle* (New York: Simon & Schuster, 1967).

Sanchez, Alfonso Escuadra, *Feldherrnhalle: Forgotten Elite, The Panzerkorps Feldherrnhalle and Antecedent Formations, Eastern and Other Fronts, 1942-1945* (Bradford: Shelf Books, 1996).

Scheibert, Horst, *Bildband der 6. Panzer Division* (Bad Nauheim: Hans-Henning Podzun, 1958).

Schirach, Henriette von, *Der Preis der Herrlichkeit, Erlebte Zeitgeschichte* (München: Herbig, 1975).

Schmidt, Hans, *SS Panzergrenadier, A true story of World War II, Second Edition* (Pensacola: H. Schmidt Productions, 2002).

Schneider, Wolfgang, *Tigers in Combat II* (Mechanicsburg: Stackpole, 2005).

Schneider, Wolfgang, *Totenkopf Tigers* (Winnipeg: J.J. Fedorowicz, 2001).

Shukman, Harold, editor, *Stalin's Generals* (New York: Grove Press, 1983).

Sklar, D. *The Nazis and the Occult* (New York: Dorset Press, 1989).

Skorzeny, Otto, *My Commando Operations, The Memoirs of Hitler's Most Daring Commando* (Atglen: Schiffer, 1995).

Snyder, Timothy, *Bloodlands: Europe between Hitler and Stalin* (New York: Basic Books, 2010).

Stewart, Emilie Caldwell, *Signatures of the Third Reich* (New Jersey: Private, 1996).

Stone, David R., editor, *The Soviet Union at War 1941-1945* (Barnsley: Pen & Sword Military, 2010).

Strassner, Peter, *European Volunteers: The 5. SS Panzer Division Wiking* (Winnipeg: J.J. Fedorowicz, 2006).

Sundin, Claes & Bergstrom, Christer, *Luftwaffe Fighter Aircraft in Profile* (Atglen: Schiffer, 1997).

Sydnor, Charles W., Jr., *Soldiers of Destruction, The SS Death's Head Division, 1933-1945* (Princeton: Princeton University Press, 1977).

Számvéber, Norbert, *Days of Battle, Armoured operations north of the River Danube, Hungary 1944-45* (Solihull: Helion Books, 2013).

Taylor, Hugh Page & Bender, Roger James, *Uniforms, organization and history of the Waffen-SS, volume 5* (San Jose: R. James Bender Publishing, 1986).

Thiele, Karl H., *Beyond Monsters and Clowns, The Combat SS: De-Mythologizing Five Decades of German Elite Formations* (Lanham: University Press of America, 1997).

Thorwald, Juergen, *Defeat in the East, 1945: The Collapse of Hitler's Germany and the Russian Drive on Berlin* (New York: Ballantine, 1967).

Tieke, Wilhelm, translated by Steinhardt, Frederick, *In The Firestorm Of The Last Years Of The War, II SS-Panzerkorps with the 9. And 10. SS-Divisions "Hohenstaufen" and "Frundsberg"* (Winnipeg: J.J. Fedorowicz, 1999).

Tiemann, Ralf, *Chronicle of the 7. Panzer-Kompanie 1. SS-Panzerdivision "Leibstandarte"* (Atglen: Schiffer, 1998).

Tiemann, Ralf, *The Leibstandarte IV/2* (Winnipeg: J.J. Fedoriwicz, 1998).

Toland, John, *The Last 100 Days* (New York: Bantam, 1967).

Toliver, Colonel Raymond F. & Constable, Trevor J., *The Blond Knight of Germany: The True Story of Erich Hartmann, the Greatest Fighter Pilot of all Time* (New York: Ballantine, 1971).

Tooze, Adam, *The Wages of Destruction: The Making and Breaking of the Nazi Economy* (New York: Viking, 2007).

Trang, Charles, *Totenkopf* (Bayeux: Heimdal, 2006).

Trevor-Roper, Professor Hugh, translator and editor, *Final Entries 1945: The Diaries of Joseph Goebbels* (New York: Avon, 1978).

Tsouras, Peter G., editor, *Panzers on the Eastern Front, General Erhard Raus and his Panzer Divisions in Russia 1941-1945* (London: Greenhill Books, 2002).

Ullrich, Karl, *Like a Cliff in the Ocean: The History of the 3. SS-Panzer-Division Totenkopf* (Altona: J.J. Fedorowicz, 2002).

Vassiltchikov, Marie, *Berlin Diaries, 1940-1945* (New York: Alfred A. Knopf, 1987).

Veterans of the 3rd Panzer Division, *Armored Bears, The German 3rd Panzer Division in World War II* (Mechanicsburg: Stackpole Books, 2013).

Walther, Herbert, *The 12th SS Panzer Division HJ: A Pictorial History* (Atglen: Schiffer, 1989).

Warlimont, Gen. Walter, translated from the German by Barry, R.H., *Inside Hitler's Headquarters 1939-1945* (Novato: Presidio Press, 1990).

Weidinger, Otto, *Comrades to the End, The 4th SS Panzer-Grenadier Regiment "Der Führer" 1938-1945, The History of a German-Austrian Fighting Unit* (Atglen: Schiffer, 1998).

Weidinger, Otto, *Das Reich, Volume V: 1943-1945* (Manitoba: J.J. Fedorowicz, 2012).

Weingartner, James J., *Hitler's Guard, Inside the Führer's Personal SS Force* (New York: Berkley Books, 1990).

Welch, David, *The Third Reich: Politics and Propaganda* (London: Routledge, 1995).

Werth, Alexander *Russia At War 1941-1945* (New York: Avon, 1970).

Weyr, Thomas, *The Setting of the Pearl: Vienna Under Hitler 1938-1945* (Oxford: Oxford University Press, 2005).

Wilbeck, Christopher W., *Sledgehammers: Strengths and Flaws of Tiger Tank Battalions in World War II* (Bedford: Aberjona Press, 2004).

Winninger, Michael, *The OKH Toy Factory – The Nibelungenwerke: Tank Production in St. Valentin* (Havertown: Casemate, 2013).

Wood, Ian Michael, *Tigers of the Death's Head, SS Totenkopf Division's Tiger Company* (Mechanicsburg: Stackpole, 2013).

Wood, Ian Michael, *History of the Totenkopf's Panther-Abteilung* (Bessenyei György: PeKo Books, 2015).

Yeltin, David K., *Hitler's Volkssturm: The Nazi Militia and the Fall of Germany, 1944-1945* (Lawrence: University Press of Kansas, 2002).

Yerger, Mark C., *Knights of Steel: Das Reich Volume 2. The Structure, Development and Personalities of the 2. SS-Panzer-Division* (Lancaster: Yerger, 1994).

Yerger, Mark C., *SS-Sturmbannführer Ernst August Krag* (Atglen: Schiffer, 1996).

Yerger, Mark C., *SS-Obersturmbannführer Otto Weidinger* (Atglen: Schiffer, 2000).

Yerger, Mark C., *Waffen-SS Commanders, The Army, Corps and Divisional Leaders of a Legend, Ausberger to Kreutz (v. 1)*, (Atglen: Schiffer, 1997).

Yerger, Mark C., *Waffen-SS Commanders, The Army, Corps and Divisional Leaders of a Legend, Krüger to Zimmermann (v. 2)*, (Atglen: Schiffer, 1999).

Zaloga, Steven J. and Ness, Leland S., *Red Army Handbook 1939-1945* (Stroud: Sutton Publishing, 1998).

Zaloga, Stephen J. and Grandsen, James, *The Eastern Front Armor Camouflage and Markings, 1941-1945* (Carrollton: Squadron/Signal Publications, 1983).

Zaloga, Steven J. and Volstad, Ron, *The Red Army of the Great Patriotic War 1941-1945*, (Oxford: Osprey, 1984).

Zirk, Georg, *Red Griffins Over Russia* (Mesa: Champlin Museum Press, 1987).

Index

Index of People

Index of Places

Index of Military Formations & Units – Germany and Allies

Divisions

Brigades

Kampfgruppen

Index of Military Formations & Units – Soviets and Allies

Index of Military Formations & Units – Western Allies

Index of General & Miscellaneous Terms